CONTEMPORARY ZOROASTRIANS

An Unstructured Nation

Rashna Writer

D1713544

UNIVERSITY
PRESS OF
AMERICA

Lanham • New York • London

Copyright © 1994 by
University Press of America®, Inc.
4720 Boston Way
Lanham, Maryland 20706

3 Henrietta Street
London WC2E 8LU England

All rights reserved
Printed in the United States of America
British Cataloging in Publication Information Available

Library of Congress Cataloging-in-Publication Data

Writer, Rashna.
Contemporary Zoroastrians : an unstructured nation /
Rashna Writer.
p.   cm.
Includes bibliographical references and index.
1. Zoroastrianism.   I. Title.
BL1571.W75   1993   295—dc20   93–10858 CIP

ISBN 0–8191–9142–6 (cloth : alk. paper)

 The paper used in this publication meets the minimum requirements of
American National Standard for Information Sciences—Permanence
of Paper for Printed Library Materials, ANSI Z39.48–1984.

Dedicated to

My parents Katie and Minoo

and

Jehanjir, Mahrukh and Khosrow.

CONTENTS

PREFACE

As a Parsi Zoroastrian, I have long felt a need to learn more about my heritage: how it was that a once mighty people have come to be so diminished in size as to be virtually on the verge of extinction. As a political scientist, my primary interest lies in the contemporary Zoroastrian community. Issues relating to its minority status in the ancestral land; the impact of migration on the small group which departed north-eastern Iran in the 10th century for India, and have now been domiciled in that country for some thousand years; the concept of national identity of a migrant group; the acceptance or rejection of a foreign language and culture, are some of the central questions I have addressed. The cultural distinctions that have now developed between the two major constituent groups, the Iranian and Parsi Zoroatrians, play a not insignificant role in their self-perceptions of their Zoroastrianness.

Some of the chapters of the present work were researched at Manchester University. Others were undertaken specifically when this book was planned, and a thematic outline for it was in place.

The sections in Chapter 1 on 'Parsi migration and acclimatisation in India', and 'The Zoroastrians of Iran', were written while at Manchester University. So were Chapter 4 on 'Present-day community shibboleths and legal precedents'; Chapter 5 on 'Zoroastrians in the old countries', and Chapter 6 on 'Zoroastrians of the diaspora'.

The research for these chapters was funded by several individuals and institutions, without whose generosity it would not have been possible for me to have undertaken this work. I extend my grateful thanks to the World Zarathushtrian Trust Fund; Mr.Mehraban and Faredoon Zarthosty; Mr.Mehraban Faranghi, and Mr.Tahamtan Aresh, for assisting in the extensive foreign travel, on three continents, for the collection of material relating to chapters 5 and 6. The two academic years (1987-89) I spent at Manchester University were made possible by a Postgraduate Award by the University, and a Fellowship of the British Institute of Persian Studies.

I have also been the fortunate recipient of immense hospitality throughout the course of my field work. In Karachi, I was hosted by the Dastur Dr.Dhalla Memorial Institute; in Bombay, by Mr.and Mrs.Savak Shroff; in Toronto, by Mr.and Mrs. Hozi Patel; in Vancouver, by Mr.and Mrs.Faredoon Amrolia; in Los Angeles, by Dr.and Mrs.Ali Jafarey, Mr.and Mrs.F.Motiwala, and Mr.and Mrs.Tahamtan Aresh. In Chicago, my hosts were Mr.and Mrs.Rohinton

Rivetna; in New Jersey, Dr.and Mrs. Lovji Cama. In my home base of the United Kingdom, I was offered every assistance by the Zoroastrian Trust Funds of Europe. To them, and the several individual Zoroastrians who so kindly allowed me to interview them, I remain most deeply grateful.

The interviews (for chapters 5 and 6), were conducted in English and Gujarati, according to the wishes of the interviewee. In the case of the Farsi-speakers, I had access to interpreters from among the community.

A total of 326 persons, from the ages of 16 to 86 have been canvassed for this work. This material was collected by means of structured, personal, in-depth interviews, with a questionnaire designed exclusively for this purpose. The statistical findings are detailed in the Appendix, and every issue raised by the questionnaire is analysed with reference to the country in which the community resides, and verbatim quotations are used on occasion to assist the reader to'hear' the voice of the interviewee. In addition, great care was taken to balance the sample between Parsi and Iranian Zoroastrians, and the findings are computed by generations.

It was as a result of the extensive field work that I first became aware of a distinctive sense of a Zoroastrian identity: what I have called a nebulous sense of a national identity. Repeatedly, respondents spoke of being 'different' from the majority groups by whom they were surrounded; repeated emphasis was put on their Zoroastrianism as being 'a way of life'. Their intrinsic pride in being Zoroastrian, regardless of whether they understood the theology or practised the religion, were recurring themes. These views are reflected across the age spectrum as well as country of domicile. I thus began to investigate the possibility of a peculiar 'Zoroastrian national identity', and whether the disparate cultural units within the community, without territorial rights, could in fact constitute a national grouping.

To place these issues in context, the first section of Chapter 1 on 'Zoroastrian antecedents'; Chapter 2 on 'Disparate cultures: Parsi and Iranian Zoroastrians', and Chapter 3 on the 'Contemporary Political Milieux in Iran and India', were written. The final chapter places the small, dispersed and disparate contemporary Zoroastrian community in a tentative political context.

Zoroastrian technical terms, and some Islamic terms which recur regularly, are to be found in the glossary. Certain Zoroastrian terms are spelt as per the Parsi pronunciation: thus *anjuman* rather than the more correct Persian *anjoman*, for which I crave the reader's indulgence. Certain Parsi proper names are written with the 'ji' or 'jee' suffix, a common Indian usage connoting respect. This continues to apply to such historic figures as Dadabhai Naoroji, Jamsetji Tata and several others who appear in this work. The maps, it is hoped, will help to clarify the important regions and towns of Iran in the closing days of imperial rule, as well as to indicate the geographical locations of the two major provinces of Fars and Khorasan. The main towns and hamlets in Gujarat, on the west coast of India where Parsi populations were to be found, are also indicated.

A research project such as this cannot be accomplished by an individual without the help and co-operation of several other persons. I acknowledge, with gratitude, Professor John Hinnells of Manchester University, especially his observations pertaining to the 'living community'. My Iranian Zoroastrian friends, particularly Mr.Shahrokh Vafadari, who has been prepared to discuss, clarify, and help me understand the situation of the Zoroastrians of Iran, I most gratefully acknowledge. It is a privilege to learn of one's own lost heritage in the ancestral land from persons who have spent their own formative years in that country. Dr.Silvia Casale, who first read the manuscript and encouraged me to publish; and to Zerine Tata, I extend my deep appreciation. I am most grateful to Farrokh Vajifdar for graciously sparing time to read a set of proofs; and I am indebted to Roger Ryder for his painstaking efforts with the camera-ready preparation of the manuscript. To several other Zoroastrians, some of whom I have encountered only briefly, but whose observations have helped clarify ideas I might have been struggling with, I also extend my thanks. Needless to say, they are not responsible for any errors that may occur.

No work I have ever undertaken could have reached fruition without the support of my family. My parents, Minoo and Katie, instilled in me a quiet awareness of my Zoroastrianness, and raised me in a Parsi environment. I have drawn on my experiences and remembrances of my youth, and consider myself immensely blessed to have such parents.I extend also, my deepest filial affection to my brother Jehangir and his wife, Mahrukh, who have rejoiced in my interest and study of our Zoroastrian heritage. And to my young nephew, Khosrow and his generation of young Zoroastrians, I dedicate this work.

AUTHOR'S NOTE

The reader's indulgence is further requested in the matter of absence of diacritics. Accordingly, scholarly c, s sibilant, the usage of the Greek letters beta, gama, delta, theta and khi are transcribed here respectively as: ch, sh, bh, gh, dh, th and kh.

Eras are conveyed by BCE and CE connoting Before Common Era and Common Era corresponding to the usual BC and AD.

INTRODUCTION

If people do not recognise what you are, how do you identify yourself? The Zoroastrians are, arguably, the world's smallest religio-ethnic minority, some 150,000. The very label 'Zoroastrian' denotes membership of a religious group, and the convention of marriage within the fold helped consolidate their group boundary. Contemporary Zoroastrians have been reduced in numbers so that their very survival is now in question. One feature, however, makes them somewhat unique: the rest of the world appears not to have heard of them.

Zoroastrianism was the first revealed prophetic religion and, as the state religion of three Iranian empires which flourished almost continuously from the sixth century BCE to the seventh century CE, it dominated the lands from the shores of the Black Sea to the River Indus, and from the Caspian Sea to the Nile. Iran's imperial power lent great prestige to the faith and imbued its people with imperial confidence. Then came Islam, and Iran was converted to the new faith which the Arab conquerors brought with them.

The striking feature of Zoroastrian history of the past thousand years is the pertinacious hold on doctrine and tradition by the two major constituent units, the Iranian Zoroastrians and the Parsis of India. In Iran, despite persecution and victimization by the Muslim majority, the small communities in Yazd and Kerman retained their beliefs and practices, often at great personal cost. The more hospitable Hindu environment in which the Parsis found themselves, meant that they kept virtually intact the beliefs and practices they took with them when they departed from Khorasan in the 10th century.

The traditional Zoroastrian identity, prior to the migrations to the two major urban centres of Bombay (18th/19th century) and Tehran (in the 20th century) was distinct: it emphasized the Zoroastrian religion; it was all-embracing: one spent one's life within the group. Thus communal consciousness was continuously reinforced. The migrations of the community from rural to urban centres in the old countries, and from the old countries to the West, has shattered the sense of continuity and introduced a new set of perceptions. The structure of Zoroastrian society has been altered, injecting a new set of values, priorities and beliefs.

The re-definition of modern Zoroastrian identity requires a coming to terms with the past. Is being a Zoroastrian the most important thing about oneself - the dominant aspect of one's consciousness? There is today an internalised, perceptive process among Zoroastrians regarding their Zoroastrianism. It is not an erudite elaboration of theology or remarkable scholarship of ancient

Iran and Parsi contributions to India that they outline. Rather, a sense of conditioning and consequential acceptance of the religio-racial dimensions of their individual and group persona.

The emphasis on the distinctiveness of the Zoroastrians from the majority peoples surrounding them is a legacy of their history. The experiences of persecution and hostility in Iran, and the non-integrationist nature of the Hindu caste structure in India, helped develop the group's consciousness of its boundaries. Thus in both Muslim Iran and Hindu India, the community survived by maintaining a rigid distance between themselves and the 'others'. The initial stimulus was the preservation of their religion. The cumulative result was the development and consolidation of group identity. Zoroastrians have, therefore, become accustomed to seeing themselves as 'different'.

The contemporary community, however, is not a monolith. There is an awareness of internal distinctness: Iranian Zoroastrians and Parsi Zoroastrians. The cultural 'baggage' the different groups have acquired as a result of residence in separate geo-cultural areas, has gradually solidified into distinctive cultural patterns. The historical experiences of the two major groups, as well as communities settled in Pakistan, East Africa and the Far East, have reinforced the divergences of cultural and religious traits. For the first time in over a thousand years, the Iranians and Parsis have come together in the western diaspora. Contemporary Zoroastrians are a people rapidly acquiring the veneer of their age. In the process, they may be called upon to compromise on their most intrinsic inheritance: their Zoroastrianness.

CHAPTER ONE

HISTORICAL BACKGROUND

Zoroastrian antecedents

Throughout its long history Iran has revealed a deep paradox within itself. It is at once the most traditional of nations, while being capable simultaneously of affecting very far reaching permutations of national identity. While retaining significant features of their ancient heritage, Iranians nevertheless accepted Islam which they helped fashion into a universal religion and culture. The coming of Islam was to reshape the history of the entire Near East, while the very course of Iran's history and national ethos was to undergo a profound transformation. The glory of imperial Persia was never forgotten even while the new ideology was being absorbed.

Iran entered recorded history firstly with the creation of the Median empire, in the 7th century BCE, which gave rise to the great Achaemenid world state from 550-330 BCE. The universal laws of the Persians, and their tolerance, established the pattern which was to inspire successive Iranian dynasties. The short interregnum of the conquest of Iran by Alexander of Macedon, and the resurrection once again by the northern Arsacid Parthian dynasty which revived the Iranian national spirit and laid the foundation for the creation of the great Sasanian dynasty, is the record of ancient Iran. Then came the Arabs who were to repeat the conquest of Alexander, except that the new conquerors had come to stay. They brought with them their new religion and ideology which Iran embraced over time, thus substituting its ancient indigenous faith, the religion of the Iranian prophet Zarathushtra, with the new Semitic faith.

The Arabs, having conquered the Sasanian empire in its entirety, were to inherit the imperial model of Sasanian Iran virtually intact. At the apex of the Iranian state was the King of Kings, a title made sacrosanct over millenia. Despite the erosion of prestige of the house of Sasan in the final decades of imperial rule, the throne retained the loyalty of the common folk. The custom of dating documents from the regnal year of the new king continues in use among the Zoroastrians, and their calendar dates from 631 CE, when the last Sasanian King Yazdgard III, ascended the throne. The central and elevated position of the king ruling by divine right and imbued with the *farr* (NP) or royal 'glory', and whose position since antiquity as 'the King of Kings of Iran and non-Iran', had long since established itself as a critical element of Iranian national consciousness.The Shahanshah thus presided over Iranshahr, the sphere over which the religion of Zarathushtra was dominant. By the Sasanian era Iran had come to epitomise a distinctive religion, culture and ethos that was the summation of, and which went beyond, its imperial position. The interdependence of the Zoroastrian religion and the Sasanian state was a central feature of pre-Islamic Iran. The religion of Zarathushtra, which assigns to the Creator Ahura Mazda the divine Wisdom, was not consigned to abstract principles alone. God's word and scheme of things were deemed to operate on earth within a definite social structure, one which would emulate the natural order *(asha)*; this structure was the social hierarchy of the state. With Ardashir, the founder of the Sasanian dynasty, and his heirs, a new national consciousness forged by the close and seemingly irrevocable linkage between the state and the religion of the king came into being. Thus, the overthrow of the one resulted in the demise of the other.

Towards the end of the empire, the Zoroastrian church was on the defensive, weakened both internally and externally. Heretical movements continued, such as Manichaeism, which gained new converts especially in Central Asia. The rise and spread of Christianity was a particularly dangerous development for the state, with the growth of Nestorian bishoprics across the empire and the conversion of prominent Persians as well as the commonalty to the new faith. The decline of the Zoroastrian state church and the parallel rise of the new and vigorous Islamic faith, which in time supplanted the old religion of Iran and spurred the Arabs to unexpected successes in the religious and military sphere, were to usher in a new era in the history of the Iranian peoples.

What then were the reasons for the decline of the Zoroastrian state and church? The internal emasculation of Iran became evident after Khosro I (531-579), with a further fragmentation of the state and reduction of centralised authority.The large class of *dihqans* had arrogated powers unto themselves in their local areas, which led to a systematic weakening of royal authority. The situation was further exacerbated by the growth in power and assertiveness of the bureaucracy and military aristocracy left unchecked by the old balance of power exercised by the royal family and the great families of the land *(vaspuhragan)*. Towards the close of the Sasanian era, the power resided with the generals, the heads of the religious establishment and the bureaucracy, rather than with the King of kings. Indeed, many priests had become bureaucrats, thus strengthening its ranks.

The highly structured nature of Sasanian society meant the prevalence of a rigid class structure sanctioned by the state Zoroastrian church. The hereditary priesthood belonged to one class, with the rest of society divided among warriors, scribes and artisans. During the formative years of the Sasanian dynasty, this rigid system would have helped consolidate the nation, but with the advent of a foreign power bent on conquest, the system did not lend itself to co-operation across class boundaries. This inherent weakness in

Sasanian society greatly assisted the Arabs in the subjugation of Iran. As though to compound the rigidity of the class structure, the corruption of the Zoroastrian *mobeds*, and their interference in matters of state, lowered their respect among the common people already burdened by the demands of what had become a highly ritualised church. Indeed, it is ironic that the cupidity of the religious hierarchy in the closing decades of Sasanian rule contributed indirectly to the ultimate overthrow of the ancient faith of the land.

Religious dogmatism was exacerbated by the perceptible weakness of the government which in the course of four years put no less than eight ineffectual rulers on the throne. The treasury was depleted by recurring wars with Byzantium; the royal family nevertheless maintained its pageantry, while the inexorable rise in taxes fell heaviest on the lower classes of society. The collapse of Sasanian Iran was the result, therefore, of the material and spiritual insolvency of the ruling classes: the very classes which had once contributed so much towards making Iranshahr the greatest power of its day.

Religion and royalty were so intimately connected that the 9th century Zoroastrian text, the *Dinkard*, categorically informs us that 'Religion is royalty, and royalty is the Religion' (*Dinkard*,ed.Madan, 47.6, henceforth *DkM*). Accordingly, a few words on the church and the state are apposite to our discussion.

The rigidity of Sasanian Zoroastrianism, with its structured ritualism and ecclesiastical exactions, meant that Zoroastrianism itself was ripe for reform and a return to earlier pristine usages. The teachings of Zarathushtra are indeed life-affirming, and had in their original form enjoyed the allegiance and deep devotion of all sections of Iranian society. By the 7th century, however, when the Arabs invaded Iran, Zoroastrianism laboured under its immense antiquity which pitted some of its more antiquated doctrines against the new faith of Islam which had yet to establish its dogmatism and was at the time still popular, priestless and simple.

Since the Zoroastrian religion had come to be closely linked with Iranian secular power, it all but vanished with the loss of state support. Indeed, the King of kings ruled by divine right, and it was royalty's primary duty to defend the faith. Royal power based firmly on the Good Religion ensures a just society:

> ...the Empire will prosper, the common people will be freed from fear and enjoy a good life, science will advance, culture will be looked after, good manners will be further refined, and men will be generous, just, and grateful; many a virtue will they practise, and perfect will their goodness be (*DkM*: 335.20-336.2).

The religion of Zarathushtra was seen, therefore, as the cornerstone of kingship in Iran. The overthrow of the Zoroastrian Sasanians by the Arabs, inspired by the spirit of Surah 9.29 of the Quran which enjoined them to 'Fight those who believe not in God and the Last Day and do not forbid what Allah and his Messenger have forbidden...', meant that the conquest of the empire had been undertaken, in the first instance, to expand the realm of Islam. The Arab conquest was thus altogether different in its scope and magnitude than the earlier conquest of Alexander had been.

Despite the Arab victory and the subsequent inducements and compulsions to embrace Islam, the Iranians preserved many beliefs and customs from their pre-Islamic heritage which remains in evidence to the present time, emphasising the great continuity of practices and the conservatism of the people. Thus, the No-Ruz or New Year, which in Zoroastrian Iran was celebrated in devotion to the creation of fire and as foreshadowing the Frasho-kereti (renovation of the world), continues to be celebrated in Islamic Iran as the New Year.

The pre-Islamic customs and usages, as well as the national holidays which were found to be amenable to Islam, were retained. Indeed, the borrowings were legion and would require a separate volume. Specific Zoroastrian religious practices, such as prayer five times a day, resembled Islamic practice in such identical terms that they are now perceived in the general consciousness to have originated in the Semitic faith. The complementarity of certain religious practices was to make conversion to Islam easier in the early stages of the conquest.

The great national epic, the Shah-nameh (Book of Kings), while having been composed by Ferdowsi in the 11th century, is in the main the pre-recorded legendary history of the land, and arguably 'Zoroastrianised' in terms of historical references. It was within the Kayanian milieu, in the reign of Kay Vishtasp, that Zarathushtra lived. Accordingly, for priests and laity alike, this epoch forms an integral part of the group's emotional historiography. The Shah-nameh, therefore, combines both religious and national symbols. While contemporary Zoroastrians regard it as a 'religious history' of Zoroastrianism, the Iranian people as a whole view the epic as their nation's great literary heritage.

As though in keeping with Herodotus' observation that no people are so inclined to accept foreign ideas as the Persians (Herodotus I.135) and then reshape them to their own genius, the Iranians retained links, some tenuous, others close, with their Zoroastrian past, while accepting Islam and proceeding to universalise it. In due course Iran became an integral part of the Islamic world and was to break the continuum of perception that 'Arab equals Islam',[1] in the process expanding the breadth of Islamic culture to embrace the world. Inverse borrowings gradually emerged, such as the impact

of Arabic grammar and vocabulary on the New Persian language, so that
attempts at eradicating the Semitic linguistic input would be akin to removing
Latin contributions to the English language. It could not realistically be done.
And yet, the Iranians retained distinctive elements of their past culture while
simultaneously acquiring Islamic ideology.

Through the many centuries of contacts with foreign people: Assyrians,
Babylonians, Greeks, Egyptians, Hindus, Chinese, Romans, Jews, among
others, the essentially Zoroastrian ethos of the nation had been retained. The
Arab conquest of Iran was to have an altogether different effect on the land
and her peoples.

The edifice of Sasanian Iran, the veritable colossus of its day, was
dismantled by tribes of Arabs who had previously posed no threat to the
empire and would have been considered of no consequence by the Great
Kings. Yet, it fell to them to vanquish the major power of the day.

> Whatever thou hast said regarding the former condition of the
> Arabs is true. Their food was green lizards; they buried their
> infant daughters alive; nay, some of them feasted on dead
> carcasses, and drank blood...Such was our state. But God, in
> His mercy, has sent us, by a holy Prophet, a sacred volume,
> which teaches us the true faith.[2]

It would be instructive to turn to the question of relations between Iran and
the Arabs prior to the latter's conversion to Islam.[3] Not only were the Arabs
neighbours of Iran, but defeats at the hands of successive Sasanian kings
meant that they had been dispatched to various parts of the empire and
re-settled - a common practice of the time. Thus, at-Tha'alibi mentions
Shahpur II's massacre of rebellious Arabs and their deportation to various
parts of Iran, the Bakr b.Wa'il being sent to Kerman, and the Bani Hanzala
to Fars.[4] In due course, such deportees were assimilated into the local
population. This, in addition to trade links between the two nations, meant
that the Arabs were not unfamiliar with Iran and the Iranians. The contacts
between Arabs and Iranians 'were not few and slight but many and profound'
(Frye,*Golden Age of Persia*, 1975,26). The overthrow of the Persian Empire
by the Arabs, newly galvanised by their messianic faith ought, therefore, to be
seen in its geo-political perspective which preceded the later development of
zealous conversion of the conquered nations to the word of the Prophet
Mohammad.

The Arabs were no strangers to Mesopotamia and Egypt centuries before
Mohammad's birth. By the Hellenistic period they dominated trade between
their peninsula and the eastern Mediterranean. Even before the birth of
Christ Arabs were to be found in the Fertile Crescent, and until they were
checked by the imperial power of the Sasanians, they ruled in Hatra, Palmyra

and elsewhere. The Ghassanid Arab kingdom was a vassal of the Byzantine empire; the Lakhmid Arab kingdom had its capital at al-Hira on the Euphrates. They subscribed to Monophysite and Nestorian Christianity respectively, and served as effective buffer states for both the Byzantine and Sasanian empires. When the Sasanian King Khosro II deposed the Lakhmid King Nu'man in 602 and the Ghassanid kingdom was vanquished, the Byzantine and Sasanian empires were in due course to become targets for the bedouin Arabs, for the greater calamity then waiting to be enacted.[5]

The Arab victory over the Iranians at Nihavand 641-2 CE, marks the dawn of a new epoch in Iranian history. The Arabs advanced virtually unrestrained, with the exception of some semi-independent *marzbans* offering resistance to the invading army. Within fifteen years of the Battle of Nihavand, with the exception of Makran and Kabul, the Iranian plateau succumbed to the Muslim Arabs. The rapid decline of the Sasanian realm was the consequence of the lack of a co-ordinated resistance to the victors, even though the conquest of all Iran continued into the Umayyad caliphate, conducted on several fronts, and was, in fact, an 'organised infiltration'.[6]

Tabari outlines the early annexation of the provinces which were left to their own devices without assistance from the Centre.[7] The Caliph Umar instructed the victorious army to consolidate the victory over the Persians at Nihavand by marching to Isfahan, where the aged Persian *marzban* fled the city but returned to surrender on terms of payment of *kharaj* and *jizya*, in 644. The following year the Arab army marched on Kerman. In the wake of their victory in this province, they moved to Jiruft in the south-east, and thence to Kohistan. Another column marched on Seistan. Other major centres were rapidly over-run by the invading Arab army. Hamadan, ancient Ecbatana, was taken soon after Nihavand, as was the sacred city of Rayy, which fell without much resistance, owing to the conversion to Islam of a certain Farrukhan, a local notable. After the fall of Rayy, the governor of Damavand struck an independent deal with the Arabs and agreed to pay two hundred thousand *dinars* as *jizya* annually, which kept Damavand free of Arab attacks for the next hundred years.

Two columns moved on Azerbaijan, which submitted to the Arabs after the fall of the provincial capital Ardabil, which city acquiesced to the imposition of *jizya*. In the reign of the Caliph Uthman (644-56), the province of Gurgan on the Caspian littoral was taken. This caliph attempted the attack on Tabaristan, where its topography of pathless forests and its long line of hereditary princes, the *sipahbad*, courageously defended their province, which did not fall till the mid-8th century. The warriors of the Faith marched on Khuzistan, and the Arabs penetrated as far as Qum. The conquest of Khorasan, in the north-east, was undertaken last.

Several Iranian towns staged uprisings after their capture, which meant that the Arabs were engaged in a continuous series of skirmishes designed to recapture them to consolidate previous gains. Fars, the seat of the great imperial heritage, and heartland of the Sasanian Zoroastrian state, lay on a strategic route. By 644 the *marzban* Shahraj was killed; the governor of the provincial capital Istakhr made peace, and by 648 the *amir* of Basra was in possession of Shiraz, Shulistan, Darabjird, Fasa, Istakhr and Firuzabad (Zarrinkub, 'The Arab Conquest of Iran and its Aftermath', in *CHIr*,vol.IV, 1975, 21-2).

While the Great King Yazdgard III remained alive and in flight from the Arabs, Iranians continued in sporadic fashion to break their terms of surrender. Yazdgard fled from province to province in search of means with which to repel the Arab tide. His journey took him through Rayy, Isfahan, Istakhr, Kerman, Seistan, Khorasan, when finally in 651/2 he was murdered in Marv.

Some provinces and peoples attempted a return to their Zoroastrian religious beliefs and customs by breaking treaty obligations made earlier with the Arabs. Thus, the district of Shapur rose in revolt; Kazerun rebelled; in both Hamadan and Rayy insurrections against the Arabs ensued; Azerbaijan, Fars and Kerman did likewise. Khorasan and Transoxiana, despite Arab attempts at administrative consolidation of their north-eastern outposts, remained in turmoil.

At this point, it is worth stressing the distinctive patterns of Arab settlement and control in the south and west of the country, around the principal province of Fars; and the north-east, around the major province of Khorasan. In due course, in their own particular ways, both Fars and Khorasan were once again to play central roles in the unfolding events, just as they were in the new chapter emerging in the story of the diminishing Zoroastrian community. For the migrants who departed Khorasan in the 10th century were the founding fathers of the Parsi community of India; and the scattered remnants of Zoroastrians in Iran fled to the inhospitable desert city of Yazd in Fars province, and to Kerman. The later developments, however, had their antecedents clearly discernible in the Arab formula of settlement and administration.

The southern and western provinces of the plateau in geographical proximity to the Arab heartland had fewer opportunities for rebellion, especially after the establishment of garrisons at Jibal (Azerbaijan) and Shiraz. Local *marzbans* negotiated peace and the agreement to pay the *jizya*, with the possibility of salvaging some minor privileges for themselves. In the early years such surrender meant that life could continue without major changes, but in time the settlement of Arab tribes and the imposition of *jizya*, with its harsh implications, was to lead to the large-scale conversions from the old religion to Islam as a means of escape from the tax. The Arab settlements in Iran following the conquest is a subject seldom referred to; yet in the first one hundred years after the *Hijra*, various Arab tribes settled in substantial numbers in places like Hamadan, Isfahan, Fars, Qum, Kashan, Rayy, Qazvin, Azerbaijan, Khorasan and Seistan (Zarrinkub,1975,27). Among these settlers there were those bent on *jihad* and an expansion of the frontiers of Islam. In due course, the Iranians were to show their contempt of the immigrants. In Hamadan the Arabs were referred to as devils; in Seistan they were deemed the followers of *ahriman*, arguably the most damning of all Zoroastrian epithets. In Qum, the local Iranians would shout insults and throw refuse into Arab dwellings (Zarrinkub,1975,28). These responses, however, were in themselves the reactions of the defeated. The flood of Arab migrants to Iran was further consolidated once they began to acquire property and contract marriages between themselves and the local people. The children of such unions gradually increased in numbers, and Arab pride in tribal lineage lent this class a new cohesion which was to help enhance its status.

Khorasan became a favoured domicile for several Arab tribes; the sources[8] inform us that in 672/3 as many as 50,000 Arab warriors and their dependants,both Basra and Kufar Arabs, settled in Khorasan. In 683/4, another group of tribes settled in this north-eastern province, the large numbers which settled beyond city limits continued their former Bedouin life-style. In the earliest years of the conquest, in fact with the fall of Ctesiphon, the *marzbans* and local aristocracy of Khorasan had despaired of a return to Zoroastrian dominance and had submitted peacefully to the Arabs. A fixed sum, paid annually to the conquerors, secured them a kind of peace. Thus it was that individual treaties were ratified by cities in Tabaristan, Kohistan, Nishapur, Nasa, Abivard, Tus, Herat and Marv. In Khorasan, revenue collection fell to local *kadkhudas*, or overseers, working in collaboration with local religious heads. The amount stipulated in the treaties at the time of conquest was paid to the Arabs, a portion of what was collected was ascribed as *jizya*. The conversion to Islam of an individual or family implied, as elsewhere, that the individual or family unit was absolved of the tax.

The Arabs, having effected a complete conquest of the Sasanian realm, were bequeathed the sophisticated bureaucracy and legal machinery of imperial rule. While the scribes and bureaucrats of the old regime were kept in place to execute matters of state, in due course the new Islamic faith and its distinctive religious ideology had to be accommodated to Iranian conditions. For our study of the Zoroastrian peoples, no other development was of greater long-term consequence than the intricate problem of taxation.[9]

In the early period of conquest, subject peoples' payment of tribute in kind was referred to as *kharaj* or *jizya*, while later, *kharaj* developed as a land tax, and *jizya* a tax on movable property and persons.Later still, *jizya* evolved into a poll-tax on non-Muslims, and it was this specific mechanism of raising revenue by the exchequer which relates most directly to our theme. The gradual 'de-islamicization' of taxation as Arab conquests increased, meant that by the 4th century of the *Hijra* only the *jizya* remained as a religious institution, with the *zakat*, or alms, developing as a social tax on the balance of productive wealth.

Initially, the Arabs emulated the Sasanian method of tax collection, so that the land tax was the collective responsibility of village or town. Thus, according to this scheme, the conversion of an individual or family to Islam did not reduce the tax payable by the village. At first, this simply meant that the new convert joined the Arab army and gave up his land entitlements. As the ranks of converts swelled, the central government obviously had to devise other methods of earning revenue, while simultaneously drawing the distinction between Muslim and non-Muslim. Thus, the poll-tax evolved as the chief distinguishing feature in terms of social recognition between Muslim and non-Muslim, with the imprimatur of the state.

By 'people of the book' or *dhimmis*, Mohammad is thought to have inferred the Jews, Christians and Sabians. To them the choice given was death, Islam, or payment of tribute. Theoretically, other infidels (those not 'of the book'), had only two choices: Islam or death. The sheer numbers of Zoroastrians conquered by the Arabs with the fall of Iran meant that, once the fighting was over and the bureaucracy had been recouped, local terms were agreed and the Zoroastrians were treated as *dhimmis*, i.e. on payment of *jizya*.

The vast numbers of Zoroastrians led initially to a legal problem, and their admittance to the ranks of the *ahl al-kitab* ('people of the book'), came after lengthy confrontations. It was reluctantly conceded by the authorities that, on payment of *jizya*, the Zoroastrians would receive government protection. The uncertainties regarding the extension of even elementary protection of the subjugated peoples remained contentious for a long time, and was left in the hands of the local *dihqans* who acted as tax collectors. Obviously, it was of some significance to the tax gatherers as to who precisely qualified as a Muslim, since the acquisition of revenue for the state (and the *dihqans'* own commission) depended heavily on this.

In return for payment of the *jizya*, the state afforded a certain level of protection on condition that the *dhimmis* showed respect for Islam and the Quran; refrained from social contact or marriage with Muslim women; did not proselytize among the Muslim community; wore distinctive clothing which set them apart from the Muslim population; erected buildings which were lower than those built by the Muslims. Further, the sounds of their devotions were not to reach Muslim ears; they were to desist from openly consuming wine or from showing signs of their religion; they were admonished to inter their dead secretly and separately; to refrain from constructing new places of worship, and were not permitted to carry weapons or ride horses.[10] As will be shown in subsequent chapters of this work, the Zoroastrians of Iran continued to labour under several of these limitations well into the 20th century. Indeed, the lowly status of this class of persons was enshrined in a guide

... to the duties of a civil servant, the following instructions for the collection of poll-tax are given...The dhimmi...has to stand while paying and the officer who receives it sits. The dhimmi has to be made to feel that he is an inferior person when he pays...He goes on a fixed day in person to the emir appointed to receive the poll-tax. (The emir) sits on a high throne. The dhimmi appears before him, offering the poll-tax on his open palm. The emir takes it so that his hand is on top and the dhimmi's below. Then the emir gives him a blow on the neck, and one who stands before the emir drives him roughly away...The public is admitted to see this show.[11]

By the time of the Umayyads (661-750) Iran had become a part of the caliphate, and the number of Iranians who had comprehensively embraced Islam forestalled a return to 'Zoroastrian rule'. Relations between Arab Muslims and non-Arab Muslims (*mawali*) were regulated by religious decrees, but tensions remained. The latter, treated in the early decades of conquest as second-class citizens, had social grievances, such as the injunction of some Arabs that the *mawali* should not dress as Arabs. Nevertheless, the fact that the conquered Iranians were at a higher level of culture and achievements, dominant in the bureaucracy and with their imperial past still fresh in their collective minds, meant that a form of socio-cultural accommodation between the victor and vanquished would have to be effected. When the line of divide between Arab Muslims and non-Arab Muslims was finally eradicated under the Abbasids, the situation for the Zoroastrians progressively became harsher, for then the test of wills was between the followers of the Prophet and the 'infidel'.

Before we discuss the Abbasid caliphate which brings our survey of the early centuries of Arab rule in Iran to a close, consideration must be given to the strategic province of Khorasan, which played a key role in the Umayyad period, and from where the revolt inaugurating Abbasid rule broke out.[12]

The elite cavalry corps, the *asawira*; the imperial guard, the *jund-i shahanshahi*, and some prominent Persians, converted in the early years to Islam to avoid payment of the *jizya*. In western Iran however, the conversion of the aristocracy did not lead to the large-scale conversions of the common people. This was not the case in Khorasan and Central Asia. In the first instance, the conquests in the north-east were primarily to raise revenue; conversions were therefore a secondary consideration. The local populations suffered severely as a result of this Arab stratagem which helps explain the end of the ancient cultures of Sogdia, Khwarezmia and Bactria. Even by medieval standards, the conquests of this part of the country were exceptionally brutal. It would be inaccurate to suggest that life in western Iran was peaceful, for instance in Qum, following local disturbances the Arabs are reported to have beheaded several prominent Zoroastrians.[13] It was, however, more problematical for the Arabs to consolidate their victories in eastern Iran than had been the case in the west, not least owing to the frequent uprisings in the eastern provinces.

During the Umayyad caliphate, there were great movements of Persians from west to east, attempting to escape the Arabs and their rule. Many people from Fars fled to Transoxiana where they found others from their province who had travelled there following the murder of Yazdgard. There were movements of peoples from Isfahan to the east, from Marv to Bokhara, and from Kabul to Termez in 740. Likewise, some Sogdians migrated to Ferghana rather than submit to heavy taxation.[14]

There were no religious revolts in Khorasan and Transoxiana in Umayyad times, while under Abbasid rule there were several. Frye suggests (1975,100-1) that Islam encountered a plethora of religions in this region, namely Buddhism, Manichaeism, Nestorian Christianity, Judaism, Hinduism and local Zoroastrianism, which aided Islam's progress on the frontiers; while in western Iran the state Zoroastrian church took longer to dislodge. Islam initially was just another religion come to Central Asia, and was in that sense the more easily digestible by the locals.

In due course, the Arabs of the garrison cities of Khorasan contracted marriages with the indigenous peoples and became part of the local population, so that soon Arab armies became Muslim armies. By the time of Abu Muslim, the Arab tribes had become assimilated into eastern Iran and Central Asia. The central stage on which this scene was enacted was Khorasan, and Seistan to a lesser extent. This was to lay the foundation for the creation and nurturing of Islamic culture in the east. The nature of Khorasani society as well as that of the Transoxiana region, which were then primarily trading and commercial areas, assisted this development. Most importantly, however, the fact that more Arabs had settled in the outlying areas rather than the interior of the plateau, meant that it was in the north-east that the greater mix of peoples occurred.

While Iranians generally continued to resent Arab power, a certain level of inter-dependence was inevitable. The talents of the Iranians were obvious in terms of administrative experience and cultural achievements, and the Arabs found these impossible to ignore. The government in Damascus appointed Iranians to the position of governors and other high offices, not only those who had embraced Islam, but Zoroastrians and other non-Muslims as well. However, despite elevation to high office, the non-Muslims were subject to strict Islamic regulations as applied to the 'infidel'.Accordingly, payment of the *jizya* was mandatory, and support for the government and submission to the Islamic law, the *sharia*, were strenuously inculcated. The *dhimmis* thus continued to have no personal rights, only community rights.

Despite the complexities of subjugating a vast land with an ancient heritage, a high level of assimilation between Arabs and Iranians had been achieved by the end of the Umayyad caliphate, which process was completed during the Abbasid period. While Persian *mawali* and Arabs gradually found common ground, the Zoroastrians remained, by definition, beyond the pale. Muslim officials dealt with representatives of the subject communities which, in the case of the Zoroastrians, were the *hudinan peshobay* (leaders of those of the Good Religion). Indeed, this office had been in existence since Sasanian times. The Zoroastrian populace was however, contemptuously styled 'gabr' or 'gaur' meaning infidel, by which pejorative term they continue to be referred to in Iran to the present day.

As shown above, there was a steady stream of converts to Allah, since worldly advancement clearly rested with the new power. Some conversions were voluntary, others were enforced. There were always individual Muslims anxious to proselytise by any means. The towns with Arab garrisons were especially vulnerable and, with great regularity, the urban fire temples were extinguished one by one and given over to mosques. The Zoroastrians were compelled to flee.

Perhaps the greatest long-term blow to Zoroastrianism was the substitution of Middle Persian, written in Pahlavi script, by Arabic, by the Umayyads in about 700 CE. The entrenchment of Arabic as the holy tongue of Islam became gradually widespread, while Pahlavi became the preserve of the Zoroastrian priesthood. Middle Persian works in Pahlavi script were subsequently translated into Arabic, such as the Sasanian chronicle *Khwaday Namag*, which came to be used selectively by Muslim historians. The ancient legends of the *pahlavans* (heroes) of Zoroastrian civilization were shorn of their original religious connotations in order that Iranian aristocrats, newly converted to Islam, could continue to claim descent from historical figures without jeopardising their new allegiance to Islam. Zoroastrianism's unique link with Iran's heritage became thus further eroded.

Iranian Muslims evolved a tradition partly designed to make Islam appear of Iranian pedigree, to help enhance national pride. Thus, the historical figure of Salman al-Farsi *(Dastur* Dinyar), the Persian who abandoned Zoroastrianism and became an early follower of Mohammad, was elevated by Iranian Muslims and decried by the Zoroastrians. More significant, however, was the legend that Husayn, son of Ali (Mohammad's grandson by his daughter Fatima and the fourth caliph), had married the Sasanian Khatun Banu. This fictitious princess was thought to be the mother of the historical fourth Shi'a Imam, and the Shi'a or 'Party' of Ali, held that the caliphate belonged to him and his descendants but had been wrongfully usurped by the Umayyads. Iranian converts swelled the Shi'ite faction against the Arab nationalism of the Umayyads and, by emphasising the role of Khatun Banu of Sasanian royal blood, further weakened the position of the diminishing Zoroastrians, who were then portrayed as not having the sole monopoly of close links with Iran's ancient heritage.

Once the novelty had worn off, however, adoption of the new faith was often regretted; but even the nominal Muslim is proscribed from recanting his faith, for which offence the penalty is death. Such dilemmas must have been plentiful, for a 9th century Zoroastrian text puts the case before the *hudinan peshobay*: 'A man who has put off the *kusti* repents within a year. But he cannot tie the *kusti* again for fear of his life...'.[15] The *kusti*, being the outward badge of membership of the Zoroastrian fraternity, was the obvious target of derision, and as from the 8th century and well beyond, Arab tax collectors would forcibly remove the sacred girdle from the waist of the Zoroastrian, hang it around his neck, and ridicule the individual and his God. Not surprisingly, therefore, even among the contemporary Zoroastrian community in Iran, the *kusti* is worn on religious occasions or to visit a fire temple, rather than its continuous wearing as prescribed in the texts. For the Zoroastrians, Arab rule was to be tolerated as best it could, and as late as 729, when a local noble in Bokhara converted to Islam, he was said to have become an 'Arab'.[16] Although many would have been reluctant converts, or adopted Islam to escape payment of the *jizya*, nevertheless, the offspring of even superficial converts grew up within an Islamic milieu, having substituted prayers in Arabic for the ancient *Avesta*, and with successive generations of Iranians the Islamic faith was the only one they had ever known. The gradual erosion of the memory of the Zoroastrian religion and its accompanying ethos for the majority of the Iranian population was thus achieved.

In 749, Abu al-Abbas made his inaugural address in Kufa for the first Abbasid caliph, outlining the reasons for the overthrow of the Umayyad caliphate and the Abbasids' own proclivity to confine the caliphate of the Islamic community to the members of their family.[17] The Iranians of Khorasan province have often been perceived to have been the prime instigators of the successful Abbasid revolt against Umayyad rule, implying Iranian success at the expense of the Arabs. The Khorasani Abu Muslim, however, had support from the Arabs and the Iranians for a new regime. The Arab tribesmen who had settled in that province and had vested interests in their new homes, were reluctant to give up their newly-acquired sedentary security and continue to serve in the army. Most significantly, the Umayyads had demanded the land-tax from them, thus obliterating the vital distinguishing feature between the Arab and non-Arab population. Therefore, when in 748, Abu Muslim began openly to recruit men for his army, not along tribal lines as had the Umayyads before him, but rather with reference to residence, the new reality of the Iranized Arabs and the Iranian Muslims was acknowledged. In time, this Abbasid army was seen as representative of Khorasan, spoke the *lugha ahl khorasan* (Mottahedeh,'The Abbasid Caliphate in Iran,*CHIr* vol.IV,1975, 62), and the soldiers of this army were designated 'sons of the daula', which distinction was handed down to their offspring. It was this Khorasani army based in Iraq which, arguably, had been instrumental in blurring the line of divide between Arab and Iranian. Henceforth, the distinctions were between the Muslims and non-Muslims, and the Zoroastrians were to experience greater levels of misery as a result.

The establishment and consolidation of Abbasid rule (750-1258) was to witness great changes in Islamic society. Indeed, the 'Islamicization of Iran' was now under way, achieved by means of emphasizing the unity of the Muslim community and the exclusion of the 'infidel' as an outsider. The Abbasid era was to see an increase in Muslim populations in towns such as Marv and Nishapur owing to their strategic positions. Towns such as Isfahan and Kerman, though under Muslim rule, continued to have a substantially mixed population which included Zoroastrians and Jews.

Let us turn to the Zoroastrian population of the day, of which very little is heard, with the exception of the Zoroastrian books written in Pahlavi script in the 9th century. Fars province remained the centre of this diminishing population. Abu Zaid al-Balkhi noted of the Zoroastrians of Fars province that

> ...the Zoroastrians have preserved the books, the fire temples and the customs of the era of their kings, thanks to an uninterrupted succession; they retain their ancient usages and conform to them in their religion. There is no country where the Zoroastrians are more numerous than in Fars, because that country is the centre of their power, rites and religious books.[18]

The 'intellectual renaissance' of the 9th century in Fars has been well documented by Bailey and de Menasce, among others, but our concern here is to determine the condition of the Zoroastrians of the time, and Muslim-Zoroastrian relations.[19]

The problem of studying the conditions of the Zoroastrians with the rapid Islamicization of Iran, is the scant information available on the subject. Occasional references to them in Arab geographies and books on religion, compels one to extrapolate from these in order to piece together a picture of the Zoroastrians and Zoroastrianism in Abbasid times.[20]

Fars and Kerman were the main centres of Zoroastrianism; isolated areas in the Caspian provinces, Azerbaijan, Rayy and Isfahan continued to retain a few fire temples which attracted worshippers. While the early decades of Islam had witnessed Zoroastrian-Muslim conflicts, relations between the two communities gradually became regularised, and the Zoroastrians retreated sullenly into their ghettos. Ibn Balkhi records that the earlier revolts in Fars, especially in the Sasanian city of Istakhr, were suppressed, and with the augmentation in the ranks of the Muslims, the Zoroastrians appear to have become resigned to their position.[21] Shiraz replaced Istakhr as the provincial capital, probably in the 9th century, and a Zoroastrian population was to be found there as in Kazerun.

Kerman was governed independently under the Abbasids, but was seen in fact as a virtual extension of Fars. It would appear that a greater part of the Kerman population embraced Islam earlier than did the inhabitants of Fars, under Saffarid rule (869-903). Nevertheless, the relative isolation of Kerman meant that until the present times it has, together with Fars, remained a centre for Iranian Zoroastrianism.

Media, the ancient centre of Zoroastrianism in western Iran, continued to have small pockets of population in Abbasid times. The plateau with the three main cities of Hamadan, Isfahan and Rayy were referred to as al-Jibal by the Muslims. Few Zoroastrians remained in central Iran, and these mainly in the villages along the desert from Rayy to Qum, Kashan, Nayim and Yazd. The perusal of Arab geographies referring to Zoroastrian pockets in Iran, reveal the paradoxes of the Zoroastrian condition. Thus, despite their diminishing number and gradual impoverishment, they appear not to have been confined to ghettos, at least not universally. Abu Dulaf met a prosperous Zoroastrian in Rayy in 944, who had apparently accrued his wealth by supplying the army of Khorasan with provisions and was well-known for his generosity.[22]

There were villages in Azerbaijan where Zoroastrians were to be found in the Abbasid period (Frye,1975, 114). Indeed, one of the three great fires of Zoroastrianism, the *Adur Gushnasp*, at Shiz, is thought to have continued to function beyond the 10th century. Azerbaijan, like Transoxiana, was a frontier province which attracted persons seeking refuge from the caliphate; whereas the Caspian provinces, through Abbasid, Saffarid, Samanid and the Buyid periods, paid only nominal allegiance to Baghdad. While the Sunni sect had reached Gurgan and parts of Tabaristan, the tenacity of Zoroastrianism in the Caspian area and the continuation of religious practices into late Islamic times appear to be confirmed by the presence of two towers with Arabic and Pahlavi inscriptions at Mil-i Radkan in western Gurgan, and another at Lajim in eastern Tabaristan. To date, these are the latest Pahlavi historical inscriptions to have survived in Iran: the Radkan tower was completed in 1020, and Lajim in 1022, erected by the ruling family in those mountain areas.[23] In this region, at least, these 11th century inscriptions bear witness to the durability of the Pahlavi script, which had long since been replaced by Arabic on the plateau. With the advance of Islam in the Caspian provinces, however, this region too saw a rapid increase in the number of Muslims and the erosion of the close religious and linguistic links with the past.

Finally, Seistan, with its famous Karkoy fire temple, survived until the 13th century, owing in all probability to the isolation of this province.

The Abbasid caliphate was firmly ensconced by the end of the 8th century, and the retreat of the Zoroastrians throughout Iran would have appeared complete. They existed now, not as in previous eras, primary citizens of the land, but rather as a vanquished people whose communal identity was most precariously maintained. In time, Islam came to provide an all-encompassing unity to the various regions of Iran, and the cultural distinctiveness of western and eastern Iran, Fars and Khorasan for example, was unified under the aegis of Islam as it had not since Achaemenid times.

The mid-9th century marked a watershed: the return to a Zoroastrian society was by now irrevocably past. The Umayyads were unenthusiastic missionaries, since the increase in numbers of converts meant a reduction in tax revenues. Under the Abbasid caliphate, however, the numbers of new converts to Islam rose inexorably and led to changes in attitudes. The conversion of all the subjects of the caliphate to Islam was the objective of the increasing band of missionaries. The new faith's incremental growth in dialectical sophistication was to help enhance its theology. This in turn resulted in the rapid increase in numbers converting to the new faith.

The 9th century Pahlavi literature is an invaluable source for the history of the Zoroastrian community of the day. It is both 'explanatory' and 'polemical', and the vehicle through which the Zoroastrian doctrine is set forth, in some instances as a counter to Islamic theology.[24] The *hudinan peshobays* were at the forefront of this creative work, the first known is Adurfarnbag Farrokhzadan who lived around 813-33 and defended his Zoroastrian faith most commendably at the court of Ma'mun.[25] A later *hudinan peshobay*, Manushchihr (fl.c.881), author of the *Dadestan-i dinig* or 'Religious Judgements', dealt with questions by laymen on religious issues. The position of the community can thus be adduced; the issues cited are, for instance, queries as to why the faithful should have to suffer such evil; whether it is a sin to give up the Good Religion for 'foreignness and evil religion'; whether one can conduct business with 'non-Iranian' infidels. Manuschchihr urges the faithful to continue steadfastly to uphold the laws of their faith, since Zoroastrianism could only survive if it did not deviate from the original revelation of Zarathushtra, and adhered to his message without compromise with the new ideological force which now pervaded Iran. Indeed, he rebuked his brother Zadspram's innovative compromises with traditional practices, by maintaining that discussions and concurrence of views between 'the priests who are the leaders and heads of the community...members of the assemblies of the different provinces',[26] must be the method whereby communal matters are appraised. This serves to illustrate the fact that even in reduced circumstances the Zoroastrians managed to retain communal unity.

The surviving Pahlavi literature deals chiefly with everyday aspects of Zoroastrian life such as the correct performance of rituals, purity laws, the symbolism of the *kusti*, and statements of beliefs. The priests exhort the laity to repeat the formula: 'I must be without doubt regarding...', as a mechanism to stiffen their resolve against apostasizing. These are the last extant body of works in Pahlavi without Arabic words, and would have been easily comprehensible to the laity. Indeed, some among them were themselves authors of Pahlavi works, the best known being Mardanfarrokh, whose 9th century text *Shkand-gumanig Vizar* or 'Doubt-dispelling Exposition', is a comparative study of Zoroastrianism and other faiths. The essential axiom of the Zoroastrian message, namely, that Ahura Mazda is the Creator of only that which is good, the seven creations, and as such is not the author of afflictions upon his creations is, reasons Mardanfarrokh, a more rational message than that of the Abrahamic faiths where God bears responsibility for good and evil.

The *Dinkard*, begun by the first *hudinan peshobay* and edited and enlarged by a later descendant, Adurbad-i Emedan, towards the end of the 9th century, while encompassing various matters relating to the 'Acts of the Religion' suggested by its title, includes an invaluable summary of the contents of nineteen books of the *Great Avesta* with a detailed analysis of three. The Sasanian *Avesta* contained twenty-one *nasks* (volumes), and Adurbad informs us that in his time the *Avesta* and its *Zand*, or commentary, had been wholly lost. One could surmise that such grave loss of invaluable scriptural texts must have resulted from the carnage at royal Istakhr, as related by Baladhuri (II,389), where presumably a copy of the *Great Avesta* was held in the royal library. The sacred fire in the city had been carried away, the city lying in ruins, and the loss of the Zoroastrian liturgical texts from what had been the royal city of the Sasanian dynasty was a loss never to be recouped.

By the 9th century Islam had made rapid progress in Iran, and some of the new faith's most creative minds came from among the new Iranian converts. Simultaneously, the numbers of Zoroastrian *mobeds* skilled enough to withstand dialectical debates with Islamic scholars steadily declined. The number of priests qualified to conduct rituals, and who alone could approach the sanctum sanctorum of the consecrated fires, also diminished appreciably. Instruction and guidance of the laity in the essentials of custom and law from a Zoroastrian perspective, being thus irretrievably lost, the resort to writing was a method of application of catechisms as a means of forestalling large-scale conversions to Islam or, perhaps worse still, indifference fuelled by ignorance.[27] These texts are evidence of the life and conditions of the community, and this body of literature produced by priests and laity, particularly in Fars and Kerman, in time became the priceless treasures of the Zoroastrians, a testament to their tenacious survival in the face of relentless opposition. Later, in the 18th and 19th centuries, the Parsis brought these valuable texts: *Dinkard, Dadestan-i dinig*; *Selections of Zadspram*; *Rivayat of Emet-i Ashavahishtan* and the *Shkand-gumanig Vizar*, to India for safe-keeping.

References to Zoroastrians and their fire temples by 10th and 11th century

Muslim geographers, especially in Fars province, testifies to the continuing existence of the community in southern Iran. A useful compendium of classical references to the location of Zoroastrians merits reiteration.[28] Thus, we are told by Yaqut that near the town of Idhaj in Khuzistan, there was a fire temple in the time of Harun al-Rashid. A Turkish governor of Qum destroyed an important fire temple in 895 in the town of Farahan. Ibn al-Athir refers to a riot in 979 in Shiraz when local Muslims attacked the Zoroastrians. A last brief period of respite was afforded to the community when the Buyids established control over much of Iran. This dynasty claimed descent from the Sasanian King Vahram V, and were amenable to appointing Zoroastrians in the governance of Fars. The Buyid 'Abd ad-Dawla, is believed to have had a magus as his secretary and had an Arabic inscription carved on the stones of Persepolis commemorating his visit there in 955. The *mobed* of Kazerun in Fars, the erudite Marasfand, was said to have read and interpreted the Pahlavi inscriptions for him.[29] Despite this short reprieve, their numbers declined steadily in Fars and elsewhere. The problem for the Zoroastrians was exacerbated by the missionary zeal of the Sufi order, whose founder Abu Ishaq al-Kazeruni's (d.1034) relentless activity greatly augmented the ranks of the Muslims and led to a corresponding decline in the numbers of Zoroastrians. Thus it was that towards the end of the 10th century, an increase in emigration of Zoroastrians to western India got under way.

Despite on-going controversies regarding the date of arrival and the numbers of Zoroastrian migrants in India, the small-scale exodus from Iran to India must arguably have continued in staggered fashion over a period of time, particularly as conditions in Iran became more intolerable and those in Gujarat remained a haven of relative security.[30] However, the Zoroastrians also fled further afield, and evidence of a Zoroastrian presence in China was excavated in 1955, when a bilingual Pahlavi and Chinese inscription dated 872 on a tombstone in Shansi province, recorded the death of the daughter of a deceased Persian general in the Chinese army who happened to belong to the Suren feudal family.[31] Contemporary Zoroastrian community folklore maintains that a substantial number of Zoroastrians settled as far west as Germany.

In the following pages we shall examine more closely the conditions of the two branches of the Zoroastrian community as they developed separately in southern Iran and on the west coast of India in Gujarat. By the mid-9th century, the Abbasid caliphate, ruling from Baghdad, was at its prime; antagonism between Arab and Iranian had yielded to antagonism between Muslim and non-Muslim. While the Zoroastrians managed to remain a considerable minority and experienced a brief renaissance in compiling, composing and editing Pahlavi literature, persecution of non-Muslims was intensified from the late 9th century. In 917, the founders of the Parsi community left their native Khorasan, departing from the little town of Sanjan in the south-west of the province, having abandoned hope of ever finding justice and peace under Muslim rule. They sailed from the Persian Gulf and landed, in 936, on the west coast of India to open a new chapter in their story. For those Zoroastrians remaining in Iran, little direct information is available of their plight under the Seljuk Turks who swept through Iran from Central Asia in the early 11th century. The greater calamity of the Mongol invasions 'whereof the sparks flew far and wide, and the hurt was universal'[32], meant that once Ghazan Khan (1295-1304) embraced Islam and the Mongol converts swelled the ranks of the Muslims, the dwindling numbers of Zoroastrians were further reduced in size and their sufferings redoubled. Fars had submitted to the Mongols early in their march across the plateau, and thus avoided large-scale slaughter. And it was here, in Fars, around the oasis city of Yazd and in the more remote province of Kerman that the Zoroastrians came together to seek a final refuge for themselves and their sacred fire Adur Khwarrah, and where they would remain to the present time in poverty and obscurity.

NOTES:

1. Richard N.Frye, *The Golden Age of Persia: Arabs in the East*, (London 1975), p.x.
2. 'The Arab Ambassadors' Address to Yazdegird III', as quoted in Percy Sykes, *A History of Persia*, vol.I, (London 1930), p.488.
3. For a detailed discussion see Richard Frye, 1975, pp.24-26.
4. Tha'alibi: *Histoire de rois des Perses*, ed.H.Zotenberg (Paris 1900), p.529.
5. For a detailed discussion on the Arab buffer states and their strategic roles in Byzantine and Sasanian geo-political calculations, see Richard Frye, *The Heritage of Persia*, (London 1965, repr.), pp.240-1.
6. Abd al-Husain Zarrinkub, 'The Arab Conquest of Iran and Its Aftermath', in *Cambridge History of Iran*, vol.4 (Cambridge University Press, 1975), henceforth *CHIr*, pp.18-27 for a discussion of Arab methods of waging war and a detailed exposition of the early years of conquest.
7. Tabari: *Ta'rikh al-rusul wa'l-muluk*, ed.M.J.de Goeje, 3 sections (Leiden 1879-1901). See also, *CHIr*, vol.4, al-Husain Zarrinkub, *op.cit.*, pp.18-28 for an account of the Arab campaign in Iran; also Percy Sykes, *op.cit.*, vol.I, pp. 500-2.
8. al-Husain Zarrinkub, *CHIr*, vol.4, *op.cit.*, p.28.
9. Cf. D.C.Dennett, *Conversion and the Poll Tax in Early Islam*, Harvard Historical Monographs, XXII, 1950, and F.Lokkegaard,*Islamic Taxation*, (Copenhagen 1950).
10. al-Husain Zarrinkub, *CHIr*, vol.4, *op.cit.*,p.31.
11. A.S.Tritton, *The Caliphs and their Non-Muslim Subjects*, (London 1930, repr.1970), p.227.
12. For a detailed analysis of the role of Khorasan as a major centre for Islamic learning and its contributions to the caliphate, refer R.N.Frye, 1975, pp.74-103.
13. *Ta'rikh-i Qum: Hasan b.M.Qumi*, ed.Jalal ad-din Tehrani, (Tehran 1935), pp.254-6, 262.
14. Cf. R.N.Frye, 1975, p.96.
15. *Rivayat of Adurfarnbag and Farnbag-Srosh*, ed.and transl.in 2 vols, by B.T.Anklesaria, (Bombay 1969), LII.
16. Tabari, series II, p.l508.
17. Roy Mottahedeh, *CHIr*, vol.4, *op.cit.*, 'The Abbasid Caliphate in Iran', pp.57-63.
18. H.S.Nyberg, 'Sasanid Mazdaism according to Muslim sources', *Journal of the K.R.Cama Oriental Institute*, (henceforth,*JCOI*) 39, 1958, p.9.
19. On the philological problems of the 9th century texts, refer H.W.Bailey, *Zoroastrian Problems in the Ninth-Century Books*, (Oxford 1943); de Menasce's chapter on 'Zoroastrian Literature after the Muslim Conquest' in *CHIr*, vol.4, *op.cit.*, pp.543-565, and his analysis of the 'intellectual renaissance' in western Iran and elsewhere, 'Problemes des mazdeens dans l'Iran musulman',*Festschrift fur Wilhelm Eilers*, (Wiesbaden 1967),pp.220-230.

20. For a detailed outline of the Zoroastrian population in Iran during this period, refer R.N.Frye, 1975, pp.110-119.
21. Ibn Balkhi, *Fars name*, ed.G.Le Strange (London 1921), p.117.
22. Cf. R.N.Frye, 1975, p.113. See also the following section on the 'Zoroastrians of Iran' and the interesting similarity in the career of Jamshid Jamshidian, who at the turn of the 20th century made his wealth in Tehran as chief contractor to the Qajar army.
23. Cf.R.N.Frye, 1975, pp.118-9.
24. de Menasce, *CHIr*, vol.4, *op.cit.*,p.543.
25. Mary Boyce, *Zoroastrians: Their Religious Beliefs and Practices*, (London 1979), pp.153-156.
26. *Epistles of Manushchihar*, I.iv, transl. E.W.West, *Sacred Books of the East* XVIII, (Oxford 1882), 12,14.
27. It is instructive to draw attention to a parallel development in the contemporary Zoroastrian community where a level of ignorance among sections of the population relates to an absence of understanding of their religio-cultural heritage. See under Chapters 5 and 6.
28. R.N.Frye, 1975, pp.144-6.
29. M.Boyce, *op.cit.*, p.159.
30. Cf.J.J.Modi, *Dastur Bahman Kaikobad and the Kisseh-i Sanjan*, (Bombay 1917), and S.H.Hodivala, *Studies in Parsi History*, (Bombay 1920), pp.1-36.
31. Cf. as quoted in R.N.Frye, 1975, p.146.
32. E.G.Browne, *apud* Boyce, 1979, p.161.

Parsi migration and acclimatisation in India

The earliest substantial record of the Parsi migration and settlement in India was compiled in 1600, by the Zoroastrian priest Bahman Kaikobad Sanjana, the *Kisseh-i-Sanjan*, a narrative poem which encapsulates the oral traditions of the community. The founding fathers left their native Khorasan in north-eastern Iran in 917 and arrived in Gujarat in the town of Sanjan, in 936.The *Kisseh* tells of the local *rajah* (king), Jadi (Jaydev?) Rana, having granted religious refugee status to the Parsis upon the fulfilment of five conditions:

 * The Parsi priests would have to explain their religion to the king.
 * The Parsis would have to relinquish their native language and adopt the local Gujarati.
 * The Parsi women would have to give up their traditional dress for the Indian saree.
 * The Parsi men would have to lay down their arms.
 * The Parsis would have to conduct their marriage ceremonies after sunset.[1]

Once the migrants felt confidently secure in their new home, they applied to the *rajah* to permit them to build an *Atash Bahram*, and were granted permission to do so. Accordingly, they sent messengers overland to Khorasan to bring back the necessary ritual objects for the consecration of the fire, and ash from an existing *atash bahram* in the mother country, thus retaining a link between the newly consecrated Indian *Atash Bahram* and a sacred fire from Iran. There were several priests among the original group of migrants qualified to perform the consecration ceremonies: the *Kisseh* informs us that 'several parties of priests and laymen of righteous life had also arrived at that spot' (Hodivala,*Studies in Parsi History*,1920,106). The Sanjan settlement must have continued to attract Zoroastrians from Iran as well as individuals who had sought refuge in India.

Arguably therefore, the safeguarding of their Zoroastrian religion had initially motivated them in their flight from Iran. The religious dimension was the chief feature of the group. In the early centuries of their residence in Gujarat the Parsis were in the main agriculturists and artisans, grateful for the refuge granted to them to continue the practice of their faith.

'Three hundred years, more or less' passed, in the *Kisseh's* rapid transit across this period of time. In accepting the protection of the Hindu *rajah*, the Parsis were, by degrees, to acquire a certain level of Indianization. Total assimilation into India has never convincingly been acquired, despite long residence in the country. However, such outward manifestations of Indian influence - those in keeping with the *rajah's* mandatory stipulations - are in evidence to the present day. The Parsis acquired the Gujarati language and in due course relinquished their original native Persian; the Parsi women wore the saree in the particular style of the women of Gujarat, and Parsi marriage ceremonies are conducted in the main after sunset. Other cultural adaptations, such as staining the forehead with vermillion on auspicious occasions, the wearing of red bangles by married women are, without question, their adoption of Hindu customs. The list of borrowings are in fact legion. The congenial environment of Hindu India, as opposed to their collective memory of Islamic persecutions suffered in Iran, doubtless encouraged the Parsis to accommodate themselves to the culture surrounding them. The acceptance, therefore, of social practices in the early centuries of residence, such as child marriage and separate dining of men and women, were among some of the concessions made to the host society.[2] Concessions made by the Parsis, originally to conciliate the prejudices of their Hindu hosts, and gradually as a product of acclimatisation to their adopted country, did not, however, dilute their intrinsic Zoroastrianness in terms of 'national' identity.

The settlement in Sanjan gradually flourished, and small numbers among them moved further afield along the Gujarat coast. Parsi settlements were established at Vankaner, Broach, Variav, Ankleswar, Cambay, and Navsari. As these new communities prospered, they would send for priests from Sanjan to join them. As a result, the priests found themselves fully occupied and, in order to serve the communities adequately, divided themselves into *panthaks* (groups of lay families) to which a priest served as their *panthaki*. In due course, this office came to be hereditary. Indeed, the Parsis had applied Gujarati terminology for the old system as it would have prevailed in Iran. By the 13th century, Gujarat had been divided ecclesiastically into five *panths*, each with its own council to administer its affairs, but all remaining closely linked to the mother-settlement at Sanjan and the venerable presence of its *Atash Bahram*. Sanjan remained a place of pilgrimage for the Parsis from the earliest years of their settlement in India.

In keeping with Jadi Rana's requirement that the Parsi priests explain their religion, once the community had acquired mastery of the Old Gujarati language, learned priests with access to Sanskrit set about explaining the tenets of their Zoroastrian faith to their Hindu hosts. Neryosang Dhaval, a Sanjan priest who lived toward the late 11th/early 12th century, undertook the translation of Zoroastrian religious texts into Sanskrit from the Pahlavi. Neryosang's work displays a remarkable knowledge of both Sanskrit and Pahlavi, and was a high watermark in Parsi scholarship.

Political events were re-shaping India, and this was to affect the Parsis as much as their Hindu compatriots. A Muslim sultanate was established in Delhi in 1206, and in 1297, its army set out to conquer Gujarat. The wealthy port of Cambay was ravaged and its tiny Parsi population suffered severe losses. Indeed, 'the citizens were taken unawares...The Muslims began to kill and slaughter on the right and left unmercifully, and blood flowed in torrents'.[3]

It must have appeared to the Parsis that their tranquil existence had come to an abrupt end and their difficulties, similar to those experienced in the mother country, were once again being visited upon them. Gujarat was henceforth ruled from Delhi, and a period of religious intolerance was inaugurated. The Parsis, together with the Hindus, were subject to payment of the *jizya*, and this tax served the more zealous sultans as an instrument for conversion to Islam.

The primacy of their Zoroastrian faith in the retention of links with Iran, and the maintenance of their distinctive religious identity in India, would appear to have remained in the forefront of the community's thinking. An Iranian Zoroastrian priest, Rustam Mihrban, visited Gujarat in 1269. He was a copyist of renown, and the manuscripts he had copied from the Pahlavi remained in the possession of his family. His great-great-nephew Mihraban Kay Khosrow, the greatest of all the priestly copyists, continued this activity. Mihraban Khosrow was subsequently invited to India and took the manuscripts with him, and the first codex of the *Shah-nameh*, was said to have been written by Mihraban in 1321. He continued his scribal activities in Gujarat for the next thirty years, having received an honorarium from the Parsi merchant Chahil for this purpose.[4]

Muslim incursions into India continued apace, and in 1398 the Tatar Timur-i lang occupied Delhi. The Muslim governor of Gujarat, Muzaffar Shah, declared his independence in 1401, and a period of turmoil in the province ensued. The carnage at Variav, a village where the local Parsis were mercilessly put to death by the Hindu *rajah* for refusing to pay the extortionate taxes, occured during this time. A ceremony commemorating the event continues to be solemnized annually.

The politically unsettled climate which now gripped parts of India had repercussions on the Parsis. In 1465 Sultan Mahmud Begada's (1458-1511) army sacked Sanjan, and the *Kisseh* relates the Sanjan Parsis' valiant stance in the battle, fighting beside their Hindu benefactors against the Muslim army (Hodivala,1920,108-13). It was as a result of this that the Sanjan *Atash Bahram*, rescued by the priests, was removed for safe-keeping to a cave on 'a hill named Bahrot', some distance from Sanjan. For the next twelve years the Fire remained in this isolated spot; later when conditions permitted, it was removed to Bansda, a small town in the Sanjan *panth*. A further two years elapsed and 'from every district in which there were people of that pure creed... just as before men used to go...to far-famed Sanjan, so now the Parsis came to Bansda...' (Hodivala,1920,113). The *Atash Bahram* of the Parsis, the most tangible and sacred link they had with Iran, remained a focal point of the expanding community's devotions and loyalty.

The *Kisseh* then introduces one of the great men of early Parsi history, Changa Asa, a wealthy layman from Navsari. Indeed, he is referred to by the ancient Iranian title *dahyubad* or 'lord of the land', and we are informed that 'he would not suffer the faith to fall into neglect...He gave money from his own wealth to those who had no *sudre* or *kusti*' (Hodivala,1920,114). Changa Asa recommended to the Parsis of Navsari that their town should host the *Atash Bahram*, and accordingly, extended the invitation to the Sanjana priests. The Bhagaria priests of Navsari prepared a 'fine house' for the Fire, and Navsari now came to be the religious centre of the Parsis. On this note ends the *Kisseh*.

With a more permanent abode for their Fire, a relative easing of political tensions, and their own modest prosperity, the Parsis began to turn their attentions to the correct maintenance of religious traditions in India. They turned naturally for guidance to the *mobeds* of Iran, and thus was inaugurated the series of *Rivayats* or treatises on religious questions exchanged between the Zoroastrians of Iran and India. This corpus began in 1478 and continued until 1768.[5] This invaluable collection of missives sheds light on the conditions of both communities in the middle ages, revealing the orthodoxy of both Parsis and Iranian Zoroastrians, and their continuing resolve to maintain, with the utmost constancy, their religious beliefs and practices which they continued to perceive as their greatest asset.

When the Moghals came to India and had consolidated their power over a substantial part of the sub-continent, the Parsis were to gain a modest prosperity, despite Muslim dominance. An important event for the community during this period was the invitation to the Court of the Moghal emperor Akbar, in 1578, of a learned priest from Navsari, Mehrji Rana. Akbar was interested in religions generally, and had invited distinguished theologians of various faiths to debate at his Court. The event, recorded by a Muslim historian, alludes to the presence of the Zoroastrian priest thus:

> Fire-worshippers also have come from Navsari in Gujarat and proved to his Majesty the truth of Zoroaster's doctrines: they called fire-worship the great worship, and impressed the Emperor so favourably that he learned from them the religious terms and rites of the Parsis, and ordered...that the sacred fire should be kept burning at court by day and night, according to the custom of the ancient Persian kings.[6]

Akbar abolished the *jizya* throughout his domain, and Mehrji Rana, on his return to Navsari, was conferred the office of high priest; to this day, a *Dastur*

Mehrji Rana is the religious head of the Parsis of Navsari.

The Parsis remained a marginal group in India and were subject to the vicissitudes which affected the land. A reversal of Akbar's policy of tolerance and the reintroduction of the *jizya* by his successors meant that Muslims were once again given precedence over other Indians. Violence occasionally erupted as a result, and the case of the Parsi weaver from Broach, one Kama Homa, whom a Muslim called a *kafir* (unbeliever), led the Parsi to retort spiritedly that it was the Muslim in fact, who was the *kafir*. The local magistrate when called to rule on the case, declared that no infidel was permitted to so cast aspersions on a worshipper of Allah and, therefore, Kama must embrace Islam or face death. He chose the latter and was beheaded in 1702.[7]

What marked the Parsis as distinct from other Indians was the Zoroastrian religion they had brought with them in their initial migration from Iran. Indeed, this was frequently remarked upon by foreign travellers who encountered this small group. From the 17th century Europeans began to arrive in India for trade, some having previously encountered the Zoroastrians of Iran (pejoratively termed 'gaurs'), and the parallel accounts of the two groups reflects a similarity in beliefs.[8]

Ovington remarks of the Parsis that they live in unostentatious single-storeyed dwellings similar to the 'gaurs' of Isfahan, and unbelievers are not invited in. Those who inhabited these abodes however, were

> very industrious, and diligent, and careful to train up their children to arts and labour. They are principal men at the loom in all the country, and most of the silks and stuffs at Surat are made by their hands.[9]

On the religion, Ovington noted of the Parsis that

> They own and Adore one Supreme Being, to whom as he is the Original of all things, they dedicate the first Day of every Month, in a solemn observance of his Worship. And enjoin, besides these, some others for the Celebration of Publick Prayers...They shew a firm Affection to all of their own Sentiments in Religion, assist the Poor, and are very ready to provide for the Sustenance and Comfort of such as want it. Their universal   kindness, either in employing such as are Needy and able to work, or bestowing a seasonable bounteous Charity to such as are Infirm and Miserable; leave no Man destitute of Relief, nor   suffer a Beggar in all their Tribe (*loc.cit.*218).

Lord learnt much of the beliefs of the Parsis when, in 1620, a Parsi clerk at the English factory in Surat interpreted discussions between a *mobed* and the Englishman. He was told that, at about the age of seven, a child is educated by the priest '...to say some prayers and instructs it in the religion'.Once put on him the *sudre* and *kusti* '..he ever weareth about him, and (which) is woven...by the preacher's own hand'. Furthermore, Lord was informed that '..their law alloweth them great liberty in meats and drinks...', and this obviously struck the Englishman as particularly distinctive in India.[10]

Henry Briggs was perceptive of some prominent aspects of Parsi identity, namely their convivial nature and their high respect for education.

> In disposition the Parsi is inclined to be sprightly - nay, even jocose; he is benevolent...fond of entertaining his friends, however indigent in means, or humble in position; a gourmand in point of living, and an undoubted bon vivant...The Parsis are notoriously given to good living.[11]

On the importance of education, Briggs notes

> However narrow the pecuniary means of a Parsi, he will contrive to obtain for his sons a knowledge of the rudiments of Gujarati, and, if he can endeavour it education in English follows...With respect to the education of their females, it ought to be more generally known that most of them can both read and write the Gujarati...A few families among the wealthy have permitted their daughters to acquire a knowledge of English...Many of the Parsis speak and write English with a facility scarcely credible for foreigners (*loc.cit*.21).

Bombay became a British possession in 1661, administered by the East India Company; in their attempt to make it a thriving port, they declared complete religious freedom for those who chose to live and work there. Hindus and Parsis began to settle in the new port city, initially to escape harassment by the Moghals and Portuguese (who had earlier acquired some possessions in western India). The Company's prime motive was trade, and consequently they did not wish to be encumbered with the task of governing. Accordingly, the different 'nations' were encouraged to manage their internal affairs through their own representatives. Communal assemblies or *panchayats* were created, the Bombay Parsi Panchayat being constituted in 1728. Despite the Indian nomenclature, the newly formed assembly was essentially the traditional Zoroastrian council of elders.[12]

Lay and ecclesiastical affairs of the community were controlled by the trustees, much of whose work was similar to the responsibilities of the elders of earlier times. As Bombay's importance grew under British rule, and the Parsi population of the metropolis increased, the Bombay Parsi Panchayat played a central role in community affairs, its *de facto* remit extending beyond the city's limits. Thus, the Panchayat served as a veritable communal court of justice, where delinquent Parsis could be beaten with shoes by way of punishment, and where excommunication from the communal weal was a very real deterrent. The total exclusion of the individual could extend to his non-acceptability at religious ceremonies: if he died in disgrace his body could not be disposed of by Parsi rites, and priests too would be prohibited from offering him their services.

By the late 18th century, the British authorities recommended that the Panchayat should be more equitably based, and the trustees' powers ought henceforth to be conferred rather than assumed, and defined by government. Accordingly, the authorities advised that the Panchayat should be granted powers to settle petty disputes and matters pertaining to the religion. On 1st January 1787, the re-constituted Bombay Parsi Panchayat was composed of twelve trustees, six lay and six priests. They were to adjudicate on social and religious matters affecting the community. The creation of a body appointed by government carried greater weight with the community and its decisions commanded universal respect. This state of affairs, however, did not continue, and, with the gradual demise of the original trustees, followed a diminution of power and respect for the body. In 1818, leading members of the Parsi community attempted to resurrect the old Panchayat. Eighteen members were elected of whom six were priests and twelve were laymen. The newly-elected trustees convened a public meeting where, by a unanimous vote, certain rules for the conduct of community business were agreed. A significant aim of the Panchayat was to eradicate social and religious accretions which had attached themselves to the Parsi community as a result of their long residence in India.

The 18th century Panchayat interceded in social matters by attempting to uphold the stability of marriage and regulate divorce. In the religious sphere they sought to discourage Parsi attendance at Hindu shrines. The Panchayat resolutely opposed proselytising or acceptance of outsiders into the faith, and were against the investiture (*navjote*) of children of Parsi fathers and Hindu mothers.

In 1823, another and very significant facet of the Panchayat's work was introduced with the appointment of four of their members as trustees to administer their growing charitable funds. These helped maintain the *dakhmas* ('towers of silence'); organised *gahambar* feasts which continued to be attended by rich and poor alike; provided for the sick, destitute, widows and orphans, as well as funding soul-ceremonies for the poor. Thus, even though the Panchayat's real powers diminished over time, this communal body - the closest the Parsi community came to having a self-governing forum - continued to exercise considerable authority throughout the 18th and into the mid-19th century.

Bombay came to play a major role in the evolving story of the Parsis. It was from this port city and their growing contacts with the British that the Parsis were, in due course, to move from their former position of rural artisans and agriculturalists, to become the mercantile elite of India. The seeds of their later prosperity were evident to observers by the 18th century. In 1794 Lieutenant Moore observed

> The Parsees...are the principal native inhabitants of the island of Bombay, in regard to wealth and numbers: not only the most valuable estates, but a very considerable part of the shipping of the port belongs to them...
>
> We have observed them as the favourites of fortune; let us add, they are deservedly so, for we find them doing very extensive acts of charity and benevolence...
>
> Some of them also have poor Europeans on their pension list, to whom are given a weekly allowance, and food and clothing...
>
> A Parsee beggar was never known; and their women, who are fair as Europeans, are proverbially chaste; so that a harlot is as rare as a beggar.[13]

Writers on Parsi history have emphasised the Parsis' high esteem of the British; what is less often stated is the reciprocal high regard of the British for the Parsis. Hinnells observes therefore, 'that the regard was mutual was probably a major factor in the growth of Parsi wealth and power'.[14] Indeed, the elevation in stature of the Parsis by the British was arguably the main causative factor in the small community's growing fortunes. Certainly, the community's ethos assisted this process, their Zoroastrian religion being no impediment, but rather a spur to develop contacts with the new masters of India. Zoroastrianism does not advocate asceticism, and in theological and practical terms is a life affirming religion. As Herodotus (I.135) had observed millenia ago of the Persians that there were no people more amenable to foreign ideas, so the modern Parsis were continuing a long tradition of adaptability.

The advantageous effects of Anglo-Parsi relations soon became clearly discernible. In 1808 Sir James Mackintosh observed:

> The Parsees are a small remnant of one of the mightiest nations of the ancient world, who flying from persecutions into India, were for many ages lost in obscurity and poverty, till at

length they met a just government under which they speedily rose to be one of the most opulent mercantile bodies in Asia. In this point of view I consider their prosperity with some national pride. I view their wealth as a monument of our justice, and I think we may honestly boast that the richest inhabitants of this settlement [Bombay] are not of the governing nation.[15]

By the beginning of the 19th century, the Parsis had become the foremost economic figures in Bombay. At the turn of the 19th century, they owned more companies in that city (18), than the Hindus 15, Europeans 9, in 1805. In 1795-6 they owned more than half the tonnage of European-captained Indian ships putting into Bombay (9,588 of 17,284 tons); while their size remained miniscule, only 10,000 Parsis inhabited the island of Bombay at that time.[16] The significance of the elevation of the Parsi mercantile power was the fact that, while British rule had created the climate in which Parsis flourished, the British had not begun to make their fortunes in Bombay at the end of the 18th century. The Parsis had become the predominant economic power of the island prior to the British. Indeed, it was from their base in Bombay that they went on to increase their wealth.

Parsis became in due course pioneers in the textile trade, and their trade was facilitated by the flotation of banks. Sir Jamsetji Jeejeebhoy (the first Indian baronet, honoured for his vast and general charities), was one of three in a syndicate controlling the lucrative opium trade with the Far East.[17] The Charter Act of 1813 abolished the monopoly of the East India Company, and by the 1830s, Bombay was enjoying boom years with the opening of the Suez Canal, coupled with the opening up of the hinterland through the introduction of the railways to India. By the 1840s almost all the private trade entering Bombay passed through Parsi hands so that when in 1836 the Bombay Chamber of Commerce was started, all ten of the Indian members were Parsis.[18]

Proximity to the English, their language, customs, education, form of government, resulted in the eager acceptance by the Parsis of the opportunity to study the English language, imitate certain English mannerisms, and fully avail themselves of educational opportunities which opened up for them careers in the sciences, law and government amongst others, while imbuing them with a respect for, and oftentimes deep attachment to the British system of governance. In all these areas, the Parsi was often caricatured as a 'brown sahib', someone who imitated the English overlord. Certainly, the description was in the main apt. Like all generalisations, it would require qualification. Just as the Parsi borrowed from his Hindu compatriots without becoming Hindu, so he modelled himself after the English without turning himself into an Englishman. A certain process of assimilation into the 'English' way of life developed, more especially among the urban Parsis.

The question poses itself: why did the Parsis develop a close empathy for the British? Their relative lack of caste restrictions enabled greater flexibility in terms of access to the European, and led to their ready acceptance of Western education. While the Hindus were restricted by such caste injunctions on commensality and intermixing which the Parsis too had earlier acquired, the latter were quick to shed the alien accretions when necessity prevailed. The nature of mercantile endeavours such as shipping and international trade in which the Parsis established an early primacy, led the community towards wealthy international markets.[19] This, together with their traditional values of integrity and hard work, meant that they were uniquely positioned to take advantage of the new horizons British enterprise opened up to India.

The establishment and expansion of British power in western India led a growing number of Parsis to benefit from the new economic power, resulting in the acquisition of political dominance for some. By the first half of the 19th century Parsi economic influence was tangible in two areas: first, almost all trade between Europe and India, insofar as it moved through Bombay, went through Parsi hands.[20] Here they acted as shipping agents, brokers, providing storage and auction facilities. They were thus the chief economic mediators between Europeans and the Indian hinterland. The direct overseas trade to Europe, however, was monopolised by British trading companies. Second, since direct trade with Europe remained inaccessible to them, the Parsis developed a primary position for themselves in trade with the Far East, gaining an early monopoly in opium exports. Indeed, the 'Parsi aristocracy' of prominent families: Jeejeebhoys, Banajis, Readymoneys, Dadisetts, Camas, built their fortunes on the Far Eastern trade. Even the Tata family, pioneer industrialists in India (and on the Asian continent), initially traded with China prior to Jamsetji Tata's establishment of his iron and steel works in India.

The wealth creation of the community, and their willingness to participate in the various commercial endeavours of the British Empire, led to a growing recognition of the value of a 'western' and 'scientific' education. Parsi enthusiasm for western education, from the 19th century onwards, was to contribute to the most fundamental changes within the community while making them the most literate of all Indians.

The first important English school was established in Bombay in 1825, and again it was in Bombay that the first college classes were organised at the Elphinstone College in 1834.[21] The Parsis were quick to make the transition from Gujarati vernacular to the English medium of education. By 1852, they had outnumbered the Hindu students at the Elphinstone Institute by a third. By 1881, they were the most literate group in Bombay.[22] In 1848, the *Students' Literary and Scientific Society* was established. In October 1849, as a result of a lecture by Behramji Khursedji Gandhi on female education, the Society moved into this field and opened four Parsi and three Marathi girls' schools.[23]

In 1857, the Parsi Girls' School Association was founded with a subscription of Rs.15,000 by some leading members of the community.[24] The Society considered the education of women to be of crucial importance, in which regard the Parsis proved themselves far ahead of their time. This was reflected in the attendance figures: in 1855 the Society's nine schools for girls were attended by 740 girls, of whom 475 were Parsis, 178 Maharashtrian Hindus and 87 Gujarati Hindus.[25]

The Parsis of Bombay, having realised the need for formal education, took it upon themselves to extend the same facilities to their kinsmen living in Gujarat. They gradually endowed schools, some of which were only open to community members, throughout the Parsi settlements in the province. With the continual migration of Parsis from Gujarat to Bombay, and with the equalising force of education, the differentials between rural and urban Parsis were becoming considerably blurred. Indeed, the contemporary community is predominantly urban.

The zeal for education, which by the last decades of the 19th century had extended to virtually the entire community, meant that they had acquired the highest literacy rate of all Indian communities. In 1911, 71% of Parsis in Bombay Province were literate. The 1931 Census of India shows Parsis with a 79.1% literacy rate, with 84.5% of the men and 73.4% of the women being literate.[26] The 1961 Census of India attributes illiteracy among Parsi 'workers' at 1.20%, whereas it is 32.55% for Greater Bombay, and 68.65% for the state of Maharashtra.[27] Understandably therefore, the 1961 Census shows Parsis of 'all ages' with a literacy rate of 89.89% for the males, and 90.45% for the females.[28]

While the relative absence of caste restrictions had, in the first instance, allowed the Parsis to accept Western education, their receptiveness to education in the English medium must, partly, be explained by their lack of deep roots in the Gujarati language and culture. Thus, while in Parsi schools, Gujarati was initially the medium of instruction, after the 1870s English was added as the language of instruction. While Parsis continued to speak Gujarati at home, it was no longer their cultural and educational tongue. The complexity of Parsi identity was demonstrated by the remarkable attachment they displayed towards Persian, which some among them saw as a link to their historical past. In 1889, of 401 Parsis admitted to the matriculation examinations, 337 chose Persian as their second language, 25 Latin, 21 Gujarati, 15 French, 1 each Sanskrit, Marathi and Portuguese.[29]

The important role of language in the formation of Parsi group identity is a subject beyond the scope of this work. Nevertheless, so significant has the English language become to the 20th century Parsi, that no analysis of the community would be complete without reference to it. The advent of British India, the educational and commercial successes of the Parsis during the Raj, had as its lynchpin the acquisition of fluency in the English language. In the strictest sense, the Gujarati language is for the Parsis as much a stepmother-tongue as is English. The severance of the umbilical cord of thought and expression in one's native tongue, if by that is meant the language that is transmitted from the ancients to the moderns, has meant that for the 'thinking' Parsi there is not the same deep emotional tie to Gujarati as there is for the Iranian to Farsi. A certain geographical coincidence, namely, Parsi arrival on the Gujarat coast, led to their mandatory acceptance of the Gujarati language. The Gujarati spoken by the Parsis bears a remarkable affinity with the Persian phonology and terminology which they brought with them. The accommodation process[30] must have persisted over a long period of time. Indeed, the Parsis had maintained their speech form over generations. Modi argues that, the community displays a 'tremendous amount of life in their language...Their greetings, leave taking, curses, jokes, condolences, compliments, all are marked by sociopsychological features. Parsis attempted to search for and create dimensions in which they would be sociopsychologically distinct from other groups'. Owing to the operational strictures of caste boundaries, even as late as the 19th century, the Parsis socialised very little indeed with speakers of Standard Gujarati, namely, the Gujaratis.

When the Parsis began to lead the field of educational and professional endeavours in India in the 19th century, they wrote 'in Gujarati on every single subject possible' (Bharati Modi,'Parsi-Gujarati:A Dying Dialect'1989). After the 1860s, when the proliferation of knowledge in virtually every field became available to the Indian intelligentsia and creative literature flourished, the Parsis became the pioneers in printing and publishing. Simultaneously, the Parsis came to dominate in the professions that required English by acquiring proficiency in that language.[31] At this point in the history of Parsi- Gujarati, when the Parsis made written contributions to the various fields of knowledge, they realized their own lexical deficiency in Parsi-Gujarati. Modi suggests that, they 'resourcefully drew upon their Persian scholarship, borrowing more and more Persian vocabulary - shaping a new dialect which would have flowered into a very good full language'. However, the vigour of the dominant language, English, meant that their scholarship in Persian died a premature death. The pervasiveness of Western education meant that by the 1920s Parsi-Gujarati creativity had subsided into writing, and to a large extent thinking, in English. The usage of Parsi-Gujarati suffers a gradual decline.[32]

While their acumen in English permitted Parsis access to the commercial and professional world of British India, it was precisely their acquisition of English as the 'thinking language' of the intelligentsia which was to transform their position and the community itself. Hinnells makes an astute observation[33] of the changes wrought within the Parsi world by the widespread introduction of this vehicle of westernization: the English language. 'There was a danger that the tide of education might tear the ship of Parsi identity from the mooring of its historic character'.

There was a shift in the 'power base' of the community. At the start of the 18th century Parsi dominance was based on wealth, whereas by the end of that century they 'shared in the work of the rulers'(Hinnells,'Parsis and the British',1978,56) as a result of education. Accordingly, Parsis gained access to the legal profession, medicine, journalism, textile and steel industries where 'there was a need for a new class of men, those with a British education'(Hinnells,1978,57). By the close of the 19th century, Parsis held leading positions in these diverse fields.

Indeed, the 19th century bore witness to a significant transformation for urban Parsis. This was caused chiefly as a result of education which led, in its turn, to a greater participation in commerce and industry as well as the impact of Protestant Christian missionary activities in India. Initially, the East India Company had prohibited missionaries, but in 1813 it renewed its charter, having given in to the pressures of new missionary groups in Britain. The first missionaries arrived in Bombay in the 1820s. In 1829, the Scottish missionary John Wilson arrived in Bombay, where he was to play a central role in the Parsis' re-assessment of their Zoroastrian beliefs.

The laity were familiar with the fundamental tenets of their faith and were practitioners of long established rituals, while the study of *Avesta* itself remained a matter for the *dasturs*, much as the Latin Bible was the preserve of the Roman Catholic priesthood. John Wilson appraised himself of the Parsis' 'very influential position' in Bombay, considered them ideal candidates for conversion to Christianity, and set about to accomplish his task.[34] He ridiculed the religion, poured scorn on ancient texts, portrayed Parsis as worshippers of the natural elements of fire, water, etc., and accused them of dualism. The matter came to a head when two young Parsis were converted to Christianity by the Rev.Dr.John Wilson.[35] In vain the Panchayat filed a Suit before the High Court: in its petition even threatened the British Government that,'if government would not help there would be a terrible uprising in the country, and the results would be disastrous'.[36]

This event emphasized for the Parsis the precarious position of their religion and, therefore, their community. Their acceptance of Western education and cultural values had not resulted in a diminution of their religious fervour. The Parsis gave the impression of being 'westernized', but they were not, in fact,'western'. Christianity was perceived as the religion of the English, as Hinduism and Islam were deemed the religions of the Indian masses. Parsis saw their distinctiveness and uniqueness as stemming from their Zoroastrian religion, and when they discerned a threat to it they reacted sharply. They had not thus deviated since the first centuries of domicile in India.

The conversion of the two Parsis by John Wilson served as a watershed in Parsi history. A discernible community awareness developed as a result - the recognition that, if the Parsis were to combat encroaching Christian missionary zeal for converts, the Parsis themselves, and their priests especially, would need to be trained in Zoroastrian theology and literature. To this end, the Mulla Feroze Madressa was founded in Bombay in 1854; followed in 1863 by the Sir Jamsetji Jeejeebhoy Zarthosti Madressa; in 1884 the Nusserwanji Ratanji Tata Madressa followed in the priestly town of Navsari; finally, in 1932 the M.F.Cama Athornan Institute was formed in Bombay. These seminaries became centres for modern Iranistic studies which were becoming popular among sections of the community who wished to re-learn their national glories, and whose enthusiasm for Zoroastrian Iran was re-kindled. In 1864, K.R.Cama, one of the founders of 'Young Bombay' and a Parsi Iranist of immense stature, founded the *Zarthosti Din-ni Khol Karnari Mandli* (The Society for Furthering Intellectual Research on Zoroastrianism), which came to be the leading association of Parsi Iranists for decades.[37] Their prime objective was to bring about a 'purification' of the Zoroastrian religion by ridding it of such non-Iranian accretions as had attached themselves and impeded social and intellectual progress. With the creation of the *Rahnuma-e Mazdayasnan Sabha*, formed to popularise religious reforms, the wide disparity between 'orthodox' and 'progressive' Parsis was emphasized clearly for the first time.

The ferment of ideas unleashed by the 'Parsi Protestants' (as they had been styled by the orthodox), resulted in the secularisation of a broad section of the community. Substantial numbers of Parsis were less influenced by their religion in their daily lives. With the gradual removal of the central pillar on which their communal identity had been constructed - the Zoroastrian religion - the several external factors, at variance with one another, began to compete for a place in the re-shaping of Parsi identity.

The special character of the Parsi community is indeed composed of three essential ingredients: their Iranian Zoroastrian stock; their Hindu-Indian socio-cultural dimension, and their voluntary acceptance of Western (specifically British) educational and secular value systems. These three factors may vary in magnitude among individual Parsis, but its impact upon the group is evident.

The Parsis, who constitute a mere 0.016%[38] of India's massive population, are therefore an immensely complex community. The fact of their historical circumstances: the descendants of a small band of religious refugees, unobtrusively settled in rural Gujarat for the first seven hundred years of their residence in India, visibly distinct from the host community and retaining pride in their 'religion and race', came in time not only to be perceived as different by other Indians, but indeed became accustomed to see themselves as different. The size of the community, the exclusivity it felt it possessed as a result of its unique religious heritage, together with its demonstrable ability to adjust to the dominant cultural values without becoming absorbed, became the dynamic of Parsi group persona. The accumulation of new economic power, and the subsequent political influence wealthy Parsis could wield on behalf of their community, led to the development of a particular set of perceptions: the British saw them as distinct from other Indian communities, and the Parsis held a parallel view of themselves. Initially, the British had perceived them as industrious, honest artisans, which developed into an admiration of their affluent life-styles.[39] Not surprisingly therefore, the Parsis were held in high regard by the European rulers, which was not the case with the remainder of the indigenous population whom the British commonly treated with critical condescension and were often openly racially hostile.

The Parsis had been on the periphery of Indian society prior to the arrival of the British, whence they became significant intermediaries between the Western rulers and the Indians. While the British were prepared to elevate them so far as it served their commercial and political purposes, they did not however, see the Parsis as 'Englishmen'. With the approach of Indian independence the Parsis became disillusioned with Westminster at its seeming disregard of Parsi loyalty. This then further fuelled the community's feelings of isolation in India.[40] On the chessboard of 20th century Independence politics the Parsis' numerical inferiority meant that they were no longer a major determinant in the complex format that modern India and the newly created Pakistan were assuming. The reality of their minority status thus came to be emphasized.

'The root of the identity crisis lies in the consciousness of most of the Parsis of being first of all Parsis and only secondly Indians...'.[41] This inner dynamic of the group has resulted in tensions, below the surface, of Parsi-Indian relations. There was, however, a small vocal number among the intelligentsia who stressed their affinity with the land and ethos of India and the emerging Indian nation. Men such as Dadabhai Naoroji ('The Grand Old Man of India' and the first non-white Member of the British House of Commons), Sir Pherozeshah Mehta, Jamsetji Tata, among others, were the exceptions to the general Parsi rule. J.N.Tata being told by a friend,'You can have no concern with Congress, you are not a native of India', received this reply from the great industrialist,'If I am not a native of India, what am I?'[42] The perennial question vis-a-vis Parsis remained: does a millenial residence qualify one as a 'native' of the land? It is not that the criteria of citizenship is being challenged rather, the self-perception of Parsis and the perception of them by their fellow Indians. By 'selective assimilation' (Kulke,*The Parsis in India*,1974,79) the Parsis had retained their distinctive identity. They had never entirely divorced themselves from Iran. The advent of the Indian independence movement, the reluctance of the English to consider the Parsis as 'Europeans', and the Parsis' own antipathy to identify with fellow Indians 'led to a mental estrangement from India' (Kulke,1974,140).

Perceiving Indian nationalism as Hindu-inspired, the Parsis in the main continued to stress their distinctness and refrained from seeing themselves as 'children of the Indian soil'.[43] Their over-riding fear was that the emerging Indian nation would emphasize its Hindu roots which would compel the Parsis in time, to assimilate and thereby lose their identity. Their fear of the overwhelming numerical preponderance of the Hindus which would result, as they saw it, in the elimination of their community, meant that in the collective imagination the image was that the 'Parsi community stands alone and by itself'.[44]

The dilemma of the Parsi position in India is therefore the result of several inter-related and paradoxical factors. Their studied aloofness from Indian society prior to Indian independence was the result of their own distaste for several elements of Hindu Indian culture, which meant they had at best only limited access to the culture of the nation which was being created, and of which they were citizens.[45] Their own sense of identity was built on several foundation blocks: their Zoroastrian religion, which they perceived as theirs exclusively; their ethnic distinctness which, together with their religion they saw as linking them to another, generally perceived 'superior' civilization - Zoroastrian Iran; their historical experience of persecution in Iran which had compelled them, in the first instance, to flee their land, and their outstanding achievements in and contributions to India, which engendered a self-perception of elitism. One question above all else poses itself in the understanding of the Parsis: does a millenial residence in another land create inalienable ties with the adoptive country?

NOTES:

1. S.H.Hodivala, *Studies in Parsi History*, (Bombay 1920), pp.102-103.
2. J.N.Farquhar, *Modern Religious Movements in India*, (New York 1918), p.83.
3. M.S.Commissariat, *A History of Gujarat*, vol.I, (Bombay 1938), p.3.
4. M.Boyce, *Zoroastrians: Their Religious Beliefs and Practices*, (London 1979), p.170.
5. B.N.Dhabhar, *The Persian Rivayats of Hormazyar Framarz And Others*, (Bombay 1932).
6. M.S.Commissariat, vol.II, *op.cit.*, p.222.
7. Cf. Boyce, 1979, p.186.
8. See Nora Firby, *European Travellers and Their Perceptions of Zoroastrians in the 17th and 18th centuries*, (Berlin 1988).
9. J.Ovington, *A Voyage to Surat in the Year 1689*, ed. H.G.Rawlinson, (Oxford 1929), p.219.
10. Henry Lord, *A Display of Two Forraigne Sects in the East Indies*, (London 1630), pp.40, 46-7.
11. Henry George Briggs, *The Parsis or Modern Zerdushtians*, (Bombay 1852), pp.15-23.
12. For an authoritative history of the Parsi Panchayat see Shapur F.Desai, *History of the Bombay Parsi Panchayat 1860-1960*,(Bombay 1977); see also, D.F.Karaka, *History of the Parsis*, vol.I, (London 1884).
13. *A Narrative of the Operations of Captain Little's Detachment*, pp.379-83 as quoted in J.R.Hinnells, 'Parsis and the British'*,JCOI*, 1978, pp.11-12.
14. Hinnells, *op.cit.*, p.12.
15. *Bombay Courier*, 20th August 1808.
16. Hinnells, *op.cit.*, pp.13-14.
17. *Ibid*, p.14.
18. *Ibid*, p.15. The justly famous Parsi achievements are well documented in D.F.Karaka, vol.I, *op.cit.*, ch.6; see also E.Kulke,*The Parsis in India:A minority as agent of social change* (Delhi, paperback, 1974), 2.1.4 and 2.2.4; also P.Nanavutty, *The Parsis*,(Delhi 1977), ch.7.
19. For a detailed analysis of this phenomenon see Hinnells, *op.cit.*, pp.14-17; see also Ashok V.Desai, 'The

origins of Parsi Enterprise', *Indian Economic and Social History Review*,1968, V, pp.307-17.

20. Karaka, *op.cit.*,vol.II, p.245.

21. Christine Dobbins, *Urban Leadership in Western India*, (OUP 1972), p.27. On Parsis and education see Kulke, *op.cit.*, 2.2; also Hinnells, *op.cit.*, pp.42-64.

22. J.C.Masselos, *Towards Nationalism*, (Bombay 1974), p.25.

23. *Ibid*, pp.29-30.

24. Dobbins, *op.cit.*, p.58.

25. Kulke, *op.cit.*, p.84.

26. Census of India 1931, Vol.I, Part II, p.426.

27. Census of India 1961, Vol.X, Maharashtra: 'Parsis of Greater Bombay', p.15.

28. *Ibid*, p.13.

29. *The Bombay Government Gazette*, November 12, 1889.

30. For a critical assessment of the Parsis' linguistic facility in Gujarati, refer Bharati Modi,'Parsi- Gujarati: A Dying Dialect', paper presented to the *K.R.Cama Oriental Institute International Congress*, (Bombay, January 1989).

31. Hinnells, *op.cit.*, pp.42-64.

32. Modi, *op.cit.*, argues that Parsis below 40 years of age show very little command of Parsi-Gujarati; those up to 25 years of age make use of English as their main language.

33. Hinnells, *op.cit.*, p.58.

34. For a closely argued exposition of Wilson's and other missionary activities among the Parsis, see Boyce, *op.cit.*, pp.196-199,

35. D.Nauroji, *From Zoroaster to Christ, An Autobiographical Sketch of the Rev.Dhanjibhai Nauroji The First Modern Convert to Christianity from the Zoroastrian Religion*, (Edinburgh 1909).

36. *Ibid*, p.59.

37. J.J.Modi, *A Glimpse into the History and Work of the Zarthosti Din-ni Khol Karnari Mandli*, (Bombay 1922), p.15.

38. Shiavax Nargolwala, 'Population of Zoroastrians in the World and in India' (For private circulation through the Bombay Parsi Panchayat).

39. For an analysis of the Parsi work ethic see, Robert E.Kennedy,'The Protestant Ethic and the Parsis' in The *American Journal of Sociology*, vol.68, 1962/63, pp.16-20.

40. *Hindi Punch*, Bombay, January 18, 1931.

41. Kulke, *op.cit.*, p.146.

42. F.R.Harris, *Jamsetji Nusserwanji Tata: A Chronicle of His Life*, (Bombay 1958), p.249.

43. *Rast Goftar*, May 15, 1889.

44. *Rast Goftar*, May 19, 1889.

45. Until the most recent times, it has been more acceptable for young Parsi children to learn the violin or piano rather than the sitar or tabla, and to enjoy Western 'pop' culture rather than Indian clasical art or music. Towards the closing decades of the present century however, this is changing. As Indian cinema and television become more ubiquitous, Parsis, like other Indians, are more exposed to Indian cultural influences, and some have become front-ranking contributors in diverse fields of Indian classical music, art, theatre etc. For a more detailed analysis of this phenomenon, refer Chapter 5 'Zoroastrians of India'.

The Zoroastrians of Iran

The history of the Zoroastrians who remained in Iran following the Islamicization of the country was clearly distinct from their kinsmen who had found refuge in India. Successive waves of invaders of Iran, spurred by religious fervour, led to the systematic decimation of the Zoroastrians. In the 9th century, with the Abbasid caliphs ruling from Baghdad, persecution of non-Muslims intensified. The Mongols who conquered Iran in the 13th century and overthrew the Baghdad caliphate, perpetrated enormous slaughter resulting in increased suffering for the Zoroastrian minority. It was most probably in the late 13th/early 14th century, that the chief *Dastur* withdrew to the inhospitable desert cities of Yazd and Kerman.[1] It is here that the Zoroastrians remained, a small community with minimal contact with the world beyond.

It has been observed above, in connection with the Parsis, that while they are Indians they do not perceive themselves to be of India. The case of the Zoroastrians of Iran is diametrically opposite to this. They see themselves as inherently *of* Iran. They consider themselves 'purer' Iranians than the Muslims, who were not proscribed from marrying invading Arabs, Mongols, Turks and Afghans.[2] It was as a result of the 7th century Arab invasion that the 'feeling of historical oneness of Muslim and Zoroastrian Iranians was marred'.[3] While Muslim and Zoroastrian Iranians share a common language and culture which can help alleviate the memory of the severity of persecutions suffered by the minority, it is the great 'religious differential' which is a barrier of no small magnitude to the unity of the peoples. When such an overwhelming majority of the Iranian people adheres to Shi'a Islam, membership of another and often bitterly hostile system makes identification with the majority difficult.

The 'gaur' or 'gabr', the pejorative terms in continuous use to describe Zoroastrians, came to the attention of foreign travellers in Persia since the 17th century. Striking similarities between the Zoroastrians of Iran and India are revealed in the travellers' reports.

Pedro Teixeira referred to the Zoroastrians of Yazd thus:

> ...They serve the sun, and fire, which they preserve with great care, so that in more than three thousand five hundred years, it has not been extinct for an instant. This is on a mountain one day's march from Yazd, called Albors Kuyh, or Mount Albors, and also Atex quedah or 'the House of Fire'. And there are always many people attending on it.[4]

The Zoroastrian method of disposal of their dead has always excited the imagination of foreigners. Chardin remarked on the *dakhma* of the Isfahani Zoroastrians, the round tower built outside the city, 'from large dressed stones...about 35 feet high and 90 feet in diameter, with no door or entrance', in case someone attempted 'to profane a place for which they have more respect than either the Mahometans or the Christians show for the tombs of their dead'.[5]

Pietro della Valle noticed 'a very great number of Gaurs' whom the Safavid Shah Abbas brought from Yazd to Kerman, where they were settled in homes that were 'low, single-storeyed, without any adornment, suited to the poverty of those who inhabit them'.[6]

Chardin commented that:

> ...these ancient Persians have gentle and simple ways, and live peaceably under the guidance of their elders, from among whom they elect their magistrates, who are confirmed in their office by the Persian government. They drink wine, and eat all kinds of flesh...but otherwise they are very particular, and hardly mix at all with other people, especially not with Mohometans.[7]

Edward Browne, writing in the last decade of the 19th century, noted that 'a Zoroastrian was bastinadoed for accidentally touching with his garment some fruit exposed for sale in the bazaar, and thereby, in the eyes of the Musalmans, rendering it unclean and unfit for consumption by true believers'.[8] During Browne's visit to Persia (1887-88), he was informed that there were between 7,000 to 10,000 Zoroastrians in Yazd and its environs (1984,404). Most of them were engaged in 'mercantile business or agriculture. From what I saw of them both at Yazd and Kerman, I formed a very high idea of their honesty, integrity and industry...' (*loc.cit*.405).

They were deemed thus to be honest, diligent, peace-loving, and keeping to themselves, yet the Zoroastrians could not avoid discrimination. The litany of restrictions upon them merits enumeration. Napier Malcolm writing in 1905 noted:

> A few years ago Yazd had the reputation of being one of the most bigoted of the towns of Persia. The presence of the Zoroastrian remnant, who were subject to the grossest persecution, served only to keep alive the fire of religious hatred...Up until 1895 no Parsi [as the Zoroastrians of Persia were referred to by foreign travellers] was allowed to carry an umbrella...Up to 1895 there was a strong prohibition upon eye-glasses and spectacles; and upto 1885 they were prevented

from wearing rings...There was also a prohibition against white stockings and upto about 1880 the Parsis had to wear a special kind of peculiarly hideous shoe with a broad turned-up toe. Upto 1885 they had to wear a torn cap...Upto 1891 all Zoroastrians had to walk in town, and even in the desert they had to dismount if they met a Musalman of any rank whatsoever...

Then, the houses of both the Parsis and Jews, with the surrounding walls, had to be built so low that the top could be reached by a Musalman with his hand extended; they might however, dig down below the level of the road. The walls had to be splashed with white round the door...

About 1891 a *mujtahid* caught a Zoroastrian merchant wearing white stockings in one of the public squares of the town. He ordered the man to be beaten and the stockings taken off...[9]

The American scholar A.V.W.Jackson was struck by the paucity of scriptural texts available for inspection by visiting travellers. This related, as did so much else, to the historical events following the 7th century conquest of Iran. Jackson himself was shown a copy of the *Vendidad Sadah* and a text of the *Yasna*. A transcript of the *Vishtasp Yasht* too was shown to the visiting academic.[10] The reason for such limited availability of their vital texts was related to him, which Jackson notes

It is worth repeating. About a century and a half after the Arab conquest, or more accurately in the year AD 820 there was a Mohammedan governor of Khorasan, named Tahir, who was the founder of the Taharid dynasty...He was a bigoted tyrant, and his fanaticism against the Zoroastrians and their scriptures knew no bounds. A Musulman who was originally descended from a Zoroastrian family made an attempt to reform him and laid before him a copy of the book of the good counsel, *Andarz-i Buzurg-Mihr*....and he asked the governor for permission to translate it into Arabic for his royal master's edification. Tahir exclaimed:'Do books of the Magians still exist?' On receiving an affirmative answer, he issued an edict that every Zoroastrian should bring to him a *man* [about 14 pounds] of Zoroastrian and Parsi books in order that all these books might be burned, and he concluded his mandate with the order that any one who disobeyed should be put to death. As my informant added, it may well be imagined how many Zoroastrians thus lost their lives, and what a number of valuable works were lost to the world through this catastrophe... The story as it exists today among the Zoroastrians is an illustration of their pertinacity in keeping up the tradition regarding the loss of much of their literature after the Mohammadan conquest as well as during the invasion of 'Alexander the Accursed' (*loc.cit*.359-60).

Despite the severity of the conditions and continued persecution at the start of the 18th century, under Safavid rule, there were estimated to be one million Zoroastrians in Iran.[11] The relentless decimation, however, is well illustrated by an historical event. In 1719 the invading Afghan army which was to overthrow the Safavid dynasty, slaughtered an untold number of Zoroastrians on its march through Kerman. The Kermani Zoroastrians had been compelled by the Safavids to leave the city and live in the outer suburbs, which meant that they suffered the brunt of the Afghan onslaught. Karaka remarks that it was

> ...during this invasion of Ghilji Afghans (that) the Zoroastrians of Kerman drank their full share of the cup of suffering. Indeed, it would almost seem as if they were made the special objects of the vengeance of the Persian troops, at whose hands they suffered heavy losses both by massacre and compulsory conversion.[12]

The onset of Qajar rule in 1796, and its duration until 1925, was a period of grave suffering for the Iranian Zoroastrians. It was with the advent of the Pahlavi dynasty (1925-1979), that the condition of the Zoroastrians improved. Indeed, so precarious had been the position for the followers of the Good Religion in their ancestral land, that it is no exaggeration to state that, from some thirteen hundred years this group of people were treated with human dignity and a semblance of equal rights, for approximately fifty-four years, under the reign of Reza Shah Pahlavi and his son Mohammad Reza Shah. The Islamic Revolution of 1979 was to see Iran return to a fundamentalist, theocratic state, where the non-Muslims were once again perceived to be beyond the pale.

There can be no doubt of the severe hardships suffered by the Zoroastrians of Iran from the inception of Islamic rule in that country. Even though there was only the most limited contact between the Zoroastrians of Iran and India (the exchange of treatises between 1478 and 1768; and *Dastur* Jamasp-i-Vilayati of Kerman's visit to Surat in 1720),[13] once the Parsis began to flourish in British India, they turned their attention to their kinsmen in Iran. One particular event which served as catalyst was the marriage of the beautiful Iranian Zoroastrian lady, Gulistan, to the Parsi, Framji Bhikaji Panday.

Gulistan's reminiscences of the suffering of her people in Iran, inspired her husband Framji to aid 'with body, mind and money' those Zoroastrians who came to Bombay from Iran, and it is said that he earned the title 'the father of the Irani Parsis'.[14] Their eldest son Burjor started a fund to assist Irani Zoroastrian refugees, and in 1854 another son, Mehrwan, started a fund for such assistance which came in turn to be referred to as the *Society for the Amelioration of the Condition of the Zoroastrians in Persia* (henceforth, Amelioration Society). Manekji Limji Hataria was the first and the most outstanding emissary the Amelioration Society sent to Persia in 1854 to assess and report back to Bombay on the condition of the Persian Zoroastrians. This event opened another chapter in Zoroastrian history, one which testifies to the determination of these peoples to overcome odds through mutual assistance, with those better off within the community coming to the help of their less fortunate kinsmen.

Boyce is able to state of Hataria that 'his memory remains green among the Zoroastrians of Iran' (Boyce,'Manekji Limji Hataria in Iran',1969,21), on whose behalf he laboured until his death in 1890. He notified the Amelioration Society in Bombay of the Zoroastrian population of Iran in 1854: Yazd and its surroundings had a total of 6,658; Kerman had 450, and in Tehran there were 50 Zoroastrians.A few families in Shiraz were noted.[15] The severe reduction in numbers of Zoroastrians in Kerman was traced to the Afghan invasion of 1719.

Manekji applied himself to the religious and socio-political needs of his Persian kinsmen. Their conditions of misery and poverty must have astonished him, coming as he did from the affluent Indian stronghold of Zoroastrianism in Bombay. He undertook the repair of the *Atash Bahram* building in Yazd in 1855;[16] in 1857 the *Atash Bahram* at Kerman was rebuilt, through the agency of Hataria and the '...help of the charitable gift of those endowed with liberality, the community of the Zoroastrians of India, who are of the race of the ancient Persians of Iran, by the agency and efforts of the behdin of lauded conduct, Manekji, son of the late blessed Limji Hushang Hataria of India, by race a Persian'.[17] In addition, Hataria had repaired the village *adurans* at Qanat-ghesan near Kerman, and Khorramshah outside Yazd. He also had new *dakhmas* built at Yazd and Kerman and at Sharifabad by 1864, and in 1865 a small *dakhma* at Qanat-ghesan (Boyce,1969,23). The upholding of religious traditions was thereby boosted by these efforts which were funded by the Amelioration Society of Bombay.

Social impediments upon the Zoroastrian community received Maneckji's attentions too. In addition to negotiations with the ambassadors of Britain, France and Russia to bring pressure on the Qajar Court for the improvement of the community's socio-economic conditions, Hataria continued a dialogue with the religious authorities, stressing the Islamic concept of justice in the hope of softening attitudes towards the beleaguered Zoroastrians. How could the Muslims justify their disrespect of Zoroastrian temples and *dakhmas*, their insolent and demeaning behaviour toward the Zoroastrian, which was itself often encouraged by leaders of the Muslim community in the town or village? Maneckji condemned the continuing practice of the abduction of Zoroastrian girls, who were then forcibly converted and married to Muslim men and thus lost forever to their families. Not unexpectedly, there was no reversal of policy on any of the several instances of persecution brought to the attention of the clerics. They held to the position that Islamic laws were not being infringed by the Muslim community.

Manekji Limji Hataria is immortalised in modern Zoroastrian history as the prime instigator for the removal of the hated *jizya* or poll-tax. As we have seen, all 'unbelievers' or non-Muslims were required to pay it. Hataria discerned at an early stage, that it was payment of the *jizya* which was the single most severe restriction put upon the Zoroastrian population of Iran, which had in turn become the instrument of their oppression. The capitation tax on the community, was 667 tomans levied annually, according to imperial orders. The tax collectors would add an amount, arbitrarily, for their commission, and the subsequent final demand placed upon the poverty-stricken Zoroastrians would often be in the region of 2,000 tomans.[18] Karaka informs us that some thousand adult Zoroastrians had been assessed for the payment of the tax. Of these '200 were able to bear the burden without difficulty, 400 paid it with great inconvenience, while the rest were unable to do so at all, even at the point of the sword' (Karaka,*History of the Parsis*,vol.I,1884,62).

> Upon the annual collection of the tax the scenes presented at the homes of those unable to pay it were terrible to witness. Some, to save themselves from torture, and as the last resource, gave up their religion and embraced the faith of Mahommed, when they were relieved from the payment of the tax. Others, who would not violate their conscience, abandoned their homes to escape the exactions of the tax-gatherer. These determined individuals, even when they escaped, had always to leave their wives and children behind them. Ground down by poverty, it is not strange that they were unable to pay the smallest tax. (*loc.cit*.62).

While negotiating for the removal of the *jizya*, over a period of twenty-five years, the managers of the Amelioration Society contributed Rs.109,564 in assistance towards payment of the poll-tax for the poorest of the Persian Zoroastrians (Karaka,1884,81).

It is not surprising therefore that Hataria's main preoccupation in his illustrious career in Iran was to achieve the complete abolition of the *jizya* for the Zoroastrian community. This proved to be no easy undertaking. The negotiations for the lifting of the tax lasted from 1857 to 1882 when, in the autumn of that year, it was finally abolished. Hataria and the influential Parsi backers of the Amelioration Society in Bombay brought their influence to bear on the British who, in turn, were prepared to urge the Shah to review the case for the Zoroastrians in his land. Hataria was duly presented to the ruler of Iran under the auspices of the British Ambassador in Tehran, Major-General Sir Henry Rawlinson, when the subject was introduced. An immediate reduction in amount of tax payable was achieved, namely, the sum of one hundred tomans, for a total claim for that year of 920 tomans, the joint annual contribution of Yazd and Kerman (Karaka,1884,75). When 'His Persian Majesty' visited England in 1873, a deputation of Parsis, led by Dadabhai Naoroji and supported by Sir Henry Rawlinson and Mr. E.B.Eastwick, MP, approached him with a petition to abolish the *jizya* 'by way of a propitiatory offering designed to ward off evil from his most royal person' (Karaka,1884,75-6).

The Parsis continued to press their case to Tehran, through the good offices of the British Government. The grievances brought to the notice of the Shah were:

> ...that the Persian Zoroastrians were liable to   forcible conversion; that property belonging to a   Zoroastrian family was confiscated wholesale for the use and benefit of individual proselytes,   notwithstanding the existence of prior claims of lawful heirs; that property newly purchased was   liable to be taxed for the benefit of the *mullahs* to the extent of a fifth of its value; that new houses were forbidden to be erected and old ones   to be repaired; that persons of the Zoroastrian persuasion were not allowed the use of new or white clothes; that they were prevented from riding on horseback; and that such of them as were   engaged in trade were subjected to extortionate demands under pretence of enforcing government custom dues...(Karaka,1884,78).

Finally, on 27 September 1882, the royal *firman* decreeing the immediate abolition of the *jizya* was received by the Amelioration Society in Bombay. It read:

> ...The Zoroastrians, residing at Yazd and Kerman, who are the descendants of the ancient population and nobles of Persia, and whose peace and comfort it is our Royal desire now to render more complete than heretofore.
> Therefore, by the issue of this Royal firman, we order and command that the same taxes, assessments, revenues, and all

other Government imposts, trading dues etc. which are taken
from our Mahommedan subjects residing in the towns and
villages of Yazd and Kerman, shall be taken in like manner
from the Zoroastrians who also reside there, and nothing more
nor less...

The present and future Governors of these provinces are to
consider the claim for the payment of this tribute as now
surrendered forever....(Karaka,1884,80)

This then was Manekji Limji Hataria's single greatest achievement.
Following on thirteen centuries of payment of the *jizya* levied on them as
'infidels', the removal of this unequal tax on the Zoroastrians meant that they
could now, theoretically, join in the wealth creation of their land for the first
time since the 7th century.

Although it had made abolition of the *jizya* a prime objective, the
Amelioration Society had worked simultaneously on other fronts to improve
the lot of their co-religionists in Persia. From 1857, schools began to be
established for the education of Zoroastrian children. An annual contribution
of Rs.600 went towards maintaining schools in eleven villages in the Yazd and
Kerman provinces. Further funds from individual Parsis (Rs.500 per annum
from the trustees of the Nasarvanji Mancherji Cama fund, an undisclosed
amount from Palanji Patel, etc.), resulted in the opening of a boarding school
in 1866 (Karaka,1884,83).

The reason for opening a Zoroastrian boarding-school in Tehran was that
'the fierce bigotry of the *Mullahs*' prevented similar institutions being opened
in Yazd and Kerman.[19] It was thought that the population of Tehran was
more tolerant of the Zoroastrians, and the city *mullahs* less powerful than
those in the provinces. While the initial student intake was small, 'every one
of the boys educated there has contributed largely to the welfare of the
community in later years'.[20] The education received by the youth was to help
their economic advancement in the years to come. Indeed, in those early
decades of Zoroastrian education, sons of poor parents, having acquired a
basic knowledge of 'reading, writing and arithmetic', were able to help change
the living conditions of their families.

It was the emphasis on education with which the Society, under Hataria's
stewardship, was to 'ameliorate', in the true sense of the term, the condition
of Persian Zoroastrians. Education had been forbidden them and the vast
majority were consequently illiterate. Hataria's accomplishment therefore, in
establishing boys' schools in both Yazd and Kerman by 1857 (only three years
after his arrival in Iran), was no mean achievement, in the face of
considerable resentment among local Muslims who considered it an
irrelevance to educate the 'gabr'. By 1882, there were twelve Zoroastrian
schools in Persia: in Tehran, Kerman, Yazd and its villages. Two of the first

teachers in Tehran were Parsis, who had come at Hataria's behest to assist their Persian co-religionists. The education was a modern secular one, and some of the pupils taught by Parsi teachers in the Tehran school returned to Yazd and Kerman to teach there in their turn. Schools continued to be set up in the Zoroastrian villages so that, by the first decade of the present century, universal literacy among Zoroastrian men had been achieved.[21]

Arbab Kaikhosrow Jehanyan started a school for one hundred girls in Yazd, having set aside a substantial amount in trust for its maintenance.[22] Thereafter, a school was opened in Kerman, and yet another in Tehran. Indeed, the Muslims of Tehran appeared impressed by the education provided for Zoroastrian girls in the capital: and among the higher echelons of their society there was an eagerness to allow their daughters to attend the Zoroastrian girls' school.[23] In fact, by 1930, the Tehran girls' school had an intake of 152 girls, of whom 101 were Zoroastrians. The Zoroastrian students received a free education, while the Muslim girls were required to pay fees ranging from Rs.3 to Rs.12 per month. It was the Zoroastrians of Tehran who contributed a 'voluntary tax' which went towards the maintenance of their school.[24]

The Amelioration Society was equally aware of the danger of abduction of young Zoroastrian women by Muslims, and therefore set aside an amount of money whereby orphan girls of marriageable age were 'settled in life'.[25] In this manner, upwards of one hundred girls were given in marriage to Zoroastrian men, with the Society bearing the expenditure for the marriages.

Yet another of Hataria's achievements was the 'opening-up' of Tehran to Zoroastrians. When he arrived in Persia in 1854, the number of Zoroastrians in the capital was 50 souls. Others came for seasonal work. In addition to building the school, Manekji also built a *dakhma* in Tehran, and established a guest-house or *mehman-khaneh* so that 'behdins who come there in flight from other places may stay there to work'.[26] The gradual change in attitudes of the Muslims of Tehran towards the Zoroastrians meant that, over time, larger numbers moved from the provinces to the main city. This was to have as profound an effect upon the Iranian community as the migration from Gujarat to Bombay had in the previous century on their Indian kinsmen. Paradoxically, while the relative freedom of work, worship, education and commercial advancement became available to the Zoroastrians in Tehran in the closing years of the 19th century, it meant that urban life was to erode the close community ties which had kept them together through the centuries of harassment and persecution. With further migrations to Tehran (markedly so under the Pahlavi regime), the urban influences of Bombay and Tehran slowly weakened religious observances, old community ties slackened, and new ambitions helped create discontent. Having arrived at material prosperity through a more circuitous route than the Parsis, the Iranian Zoroastrians nevertheless also underwent the radical changes which inevitably accompany the urbanisation of a community.

Manekji Limji Hataria's mission in Iran had been a remarkable achievement by any standard. To a casual observer it would appear as though this great and tireless man had single-handedly achieved the removal of obstacles from the life of Persian Zoroastrians. In large measure this is in fact true. Nevertheless, influential Parsis in India and Britain had persisted in pressurizing the Iranian authorities on behalf of their co-religionists, and individual Parsis too had continued to contribute to the Amelioration Society in assisting its work among Persian Zoroastrians. The close co-operation between the more affluent Indian Zoroastrians and their depressed Iranian brethren is a remarkable chapter in the immensely long history of the Zoroastrians, where a faithfulness to the memory of their collective ancestry had been kept alive, and the striving for a better life for those less fortunate than themselves had continued until it was achieved. Hataria's endeavours in Persia marks the high-water mark in Parsi-Iranian relations.

A gradual improvement in the overall conditions of life, liberty and property of the Zoroastrians was discernible. A 'Fatwa On The Rights Of Zoroastrians', signed by the *Mujtahid* of Karballa, dated 21 February 1910, reads:

> To vex and humiliate the Zoroastrian community or other non-Muslims, who are under the protection of Islam is unlawful, and it is obligatory on all Muslims duly to observe the injunctions of His Holiness the seal of the Prophets, respecting their good treatment, the winning of their affections, and the guarding of their lives, honour and possessions, nor should they swerve by so much as a hair's breadth from this, please God Almighty.[27]

Regardless of Manekji's achievements and the above-mentioned *fatwa*, there was no guarantee of security for Zoroastrians in Iran until the advent of the Pahlavi dynasty, and even then individual cases of harassment are recorded. An interesting case in point is Ardashir Bonshahi Khaze, whose memoirs record the living conditions of a Yazdi Zoroastrian.[28] Ardashir was born in 1911 in Allahabad, in the province of Yazd. At the time, Zoroastrians in the villages worked chiefly in agriculture. He came from a poor family who did not own the land they tilled.

Ardashir attended the School established by the Amelioration Society at Allahabad. He was educated till the third grade, and informs us of the five disciplines emphasized at the School: cleanliness; nails were to be well cut; respect for one's elders; respect for one's parents and an emphasis on telling the truth. Every day at school, the students were to recite aloud the *kusti-bastan*, *sarosh baj* and passages from the *Avesta*. A thoroughly

Zoroastrian grounding was central to the school curriculum.

Ardashir refers to the fanaticism of the Muslims in the city of Yazd, and relatively less so in the surrounding villages. Nevertheless, brigands frequently attacked the rural areas, which exacerbated the problems already suffered by local Zoroastrians. Local village hooligans too would attack Zoroastrian homes and shops on the smallest pretext.

Ironically, however, the Zoroastrian is esteemed in Iran for his honesty: Ardashir relates how certain tribes, such as the Bakhtiari, would leave their sheep for sale with a Zoroastrian and return the following year to collect their money. On one such occasion, a tribesman who had left some sheep for sale with a Zoroastrian did not return to the village for two years. The Zoroastrian had sold the Bakhtiari's sheep, then given the proceeds for a *gahambar* in honour of this tribesman, setting aside a piece of land for the *gahambar* to be held annually in the Muslim's name. The tribesman returned in the third year to claim his money. The Zoroastrian then explained how the money had been used, taking the Muslim to the *gahambar* to witness his name mentioned in the prayers. He informed the tribesman that once he saw the ceremony, he could decide on what course he wished to take and, if it met with his disapproval, the Zoroastrian would return the money from the sale of his sheep to him.The Muslim tribesman observed the *gahambar* prayers, partook of the *chasni* of fruits and nuts, and instructed the Zoroastrian to continue with the annual prayers in his name.[29]

Most public contacts between Zoroastrian and Muslim were prescribed by rigid codes. Ardashir relates how on one occasion he took his donkey to market with goods saddled onto the beast. As a Zoroastrian, he walked barefoot alongside the animal. Upon reaching the bazaar, he noticed the Muslim stall-holders had sprayed the floor with water. Ardashir, the *bacche gabr* (child of an infidel), would not be permitted to walk across the bazaar precinct. His donkey was led through it, and Ardashir retrieved his animal at the other end of the market place on a dry patch of land. This is in keeping with the Shi'ite dictum that anything wet is easily polluted, and physical contact of a Zoroastrian on wet ground would pollute the ground, given that a Zoroastrian is deemed *najes* (polluted) in his person.

Ardashir, however, gives an even-handed account of the Muslims around him. He relates another incident when, riding his donkey to Yazd, he saw in the distance a Muslim approach towards him. Ardashir dismounted. This particular gentleman was better informed than most, for he chided Ardashir's action and told him to mount his donkey: 'you are the gentlest and authentic people of this country. It is we [Muslims] who have to respect you'.

Even though the *jizya* had been abolished in 1882 and there was a relative improvement in the living conditions of the Zoroastrians, Muslim prejudices against this minority did not disappear simultaneously with the poll-tax. Dr.Rostam Sarfeh came to Yazd in 1910 at the age of two, having been born of Zoroastrian parents in Kerman.[30] At the time there were three main Zoroastrian quarters in Yazd: *Mahalle Dasturan, Mahalle Bozi* and *Mahalle Postekhane Ali*. Near the Zoroastrian school was the *Dar-i Mehr*, and Rostam Sarfeh himself attended the 'Khosrovi' School until the age of twelve.

The significance of the reminiscences of persons like Dr.Sarfeh and Ardashir, among others, is that they bear testimony to the continuing discrimination against Zoroastrians in the early decades of the 20th century in Yazd and Kerman. Thus, Sarfeh recalled wearing 'special' Zoroastrian clothes: 'turban, no shoes, only slippers'. He spoke of

> ....carrying a shawl, and if you have to go into a Muslim home, you must place this shawl on the floor and sit on it because we Zoroastrians are *najes*. We Zoroastrians had to carry a special shawl and wear turban and slippers and wide trousers. We could not wear anything black which was a colour only for the Muslims, because they had to know you were Zoroastrian, not Muslim.
>
> ...In 1926, Kaikhosrow Shahrokh (see below) through his contacts with Reza Shah, said Zoroastrians must be allowed to wear normal clothes. The Muslims said, 'No, we have to recognise them'. So we in Yazd held a strike. Ultimately, Zoroastrians were allowed to wear normal clothes.

In 1927, Rostam Sarfeh went to Tehran, where

> ...life was a little better for Zoroastrians. But still, Zoroastrians only allowed to sell clothes, and [engage] in agriculture. Zoroastrians were not allowed to own shops throughout Tehran, only in special caravansaris. But gradually, the general Iranian populace under the Pahlavi dynasty studied ancient Iranian history. Then a little better treatment of Zoroastrians by Muslims.

Two Zoroastrians - Arbab Jamshid Jamshidian and Arbab Kaikhosrow Shahrokh - were instrumental in improving the conditions of Zoroastrians in 20th century Iran. Each man, in his turn, established for himself a position of trust amongst the Iranian ruling elite, and used their position of influence to induce in the rulers a revaluation of the traditional denigration of the Zoroastrians.

At the turn of the century, under Qajar rule, the Zoroastrian merchant Jamshid Jamshidian - a man highly regarded for his honesty - established close contacts with the Qajar Court.[31] Jamshidian, being Tehran-based, did not have to learn the ways of the city. He obtained the main contract to supply the Qajar army with provisions[32]: a monopoly which led to Jamshidian's financial prosperity. Commencing his career as a contractor, he became the most prominent banker in Iran. The Government would pay for the provisions in instalments, through the collection of taxes. These promissory notes were lodged with Jamshid who thereby came to be the banker to the Government of Iran. (At the time, the main banks in Iran were under foreign control, namely, Russian and British). In his vast commercial enterprises, Jamshid employed between 150-200 Zoroastrians.[33]

One of Jamshidian's employees was Kaikhosrow Shahrokh, who served as his secretary. This man came to play a leading role in Pahlavi Iran, and simultaneously helped improve the lot of his fellow Zoroastrians. Shahrokh was born in Kerman in 1874.[34] He went to Bombay to study to be a teacher. On his return he was sent to Kerman in 1894 as a teacher employed by the Amelioration Society. When he arrived back in his native town, the local school consisted of one room without chairs, the students sitting cross-legged on the floor. Soon thereafter, the Zoroastrians themselves built three schools for girls and one for boys. Harassment of Zoroastrians had not abated, and the general Muslim hostility towards Zoroastrian education led, in one instance, to a school being destroyed as it was adjacent to the home of an influential Muslim's sister, and supposedly the Zoroastrian youth would look into her home. Qajar Iran lacked a constitution, and authority resided with the *mullahs*, who decreed the particular school should be razed. However, Kaikhosrow Shahrokh was tutor to the governor's children at the time, to whom he taught English. He petitioned his employer who granted a reprieve to the school.

Another incident related to the author by Arbab Shahrokh's daughter was of her father's decision, in contravention of established custom, to ride on horseback to the governor's mansion to teach his charges. The Muslims sent a message to the governor that if this Zoroastrian was to continue thus, he would be killed. The governor, however, instructed Shahrokh to continue to ride his horse, and when the *bazaar sayeds* followed him to the governor's mansion, the latter gave instructions that they were to be whipped. Thus it was in Kerman that Zoroastrians were first allowed to ride on horseback, and in due course, no longer required to wear Zoroastrian attire. The Zoroastrians of Yazd were worried by the Kermani innovations, but Shahrokh maintained that the time had arrived to challenge the dated perceptions of Zoroastrians, and if they missed the opportunity they would never succeed in changing attitudes.

In time, Shahrokh went to Tehran where he was employed as Jamshidian's secretary. It was in the course of his duties that he came into contact with the Qajar Court. Following the 1906 Constitutional Revolution and the resultant *majlis*, Arbab Kaikhosrow Shahrokh became the officially nominated Parliamentary representative of the Zoroastrians.[35]

Shahrokh's career was remarkable by any yardstick, and more especially for the revolutionary impact it was to have on the resurgence of the Zoroastrians of Iran. He developed a reputation as an effective mediator in disputes.[36] When Reza Khan, under his dynastic title of 'Pahlavi', came to the throne of Iran in 1925, Shahrokh acted as his unofficial advisor. Several incidents enhanced his national reputation. By chance, a group of Americans on a visit to Iran were onlookers at a Passion Play - the matrydom of Hussein - which they were photographing. The crowd attacked and killed the visiting tourists. This resulted in a break in diplomatic relations between Iran and the United States. Reza Shah sent Shahrokh to Washington to negotiate with the American Government. His mission was successful, and he returned to his country having helped re-establish diplomatic ties with the United States.

On another occasion, during the famine of 1916, the *majlis* appointed Arbab Shahrokh to advise on remedial measures whereby food shortages could be alleviated. Upon investigation he discovered that movement of grain from different regions was slack. There were transportation problems for which he then advised corrective measures. Yet again, the creation of printing facilities of *majlis* proceedings were overseen by a committee headed by Shahrokh. A Zoroastrian was put in charge of the printing of *majlis* debates, and to this day this office is nominally held by a Zoroastrian.

Arbab Shahrokh's access to Reza Shah, and the latter's respect for him, led in time to this gifted man's talents being applied for the upliftment of the country. Shahrokh advised the Shah on the creation of the ancient historical museum of Iran; establishment of the Reserve Bank of Iran; the introduction of the ancient Zoroastrian calendar names of days and months for national use. Some of the innovations inspired by this Kermani are in evidence in Iran to this day.

Kaikhosrow Shahrokh did not, however, distance himself from his Zoroastrian roots. When Reza Shah's coronation was held in December 1925, the Arbab invited several Zoroastrians from Kerman and Yazd to Tehran. They were presented at Court to the new Shah. Shahrokh then took the newcomers to the outskirts of the town and explained his belief that there would be growth and development in the capital city, advising the Zoroastrians from the provinces to invest such monies as they could in buying property in Tehran. It was through property speculation that the growth in Zoroastrian prosperity, for the first time since the 7th century, got under way. It was through the channel of vast ownership of property that the community in Iran came to acquire wealth and an improved standard of living.

Equally, Arbab Shahrokh used his influence with wealthy Parsis to assist financially poorer Iranian Zoroastrians to purchase land in Yazd and Kerman. Correspondence between the Iran League (Bombay) and the Arbab in Tehran reveals that, for the sum of 100,000 tomans (or Rs.150,000), cultivable land for unemployed Zoroastrians could be purchased.[37]

Arbab Kaikhosrow Shahrokh died in 1940. His had been an outstanding career. His active participation in the creation of a newly emergent Iran under a dynasty of secular outlook meant that it attempted to make good the losses earlier sustained. The Arbab was in every sense a true patriot, a great Iranian and a revered Zoroastrian. Regardless of how future historians may assess the Pahlavi regime, the years 1925-1979 were to greatly benefit the small Zoroastrian community of Iran. Central to this was a more secular approach to Iranian affairs, and a re-appraisal of the country's historical antecedents. This was to highlight the contribution of the Zoroastrian religion and its ethos to the glories of ancient Persia. Interest therefore was engendered in Zoroastrian culture to the extent that the dynasty founded by Reza Khan styled itself 'Pahlavi', after the language and culture of the Sasanians.

Indeed, an earlier movement to purge the Persian language of foreign, especially Arabic words had been started in 1869, when Prince Jalaluddin Mirza wrote a brief history of Iran in pure Persian, the *Nameh-Khosrowan*. This movement reached greater heights under Reza Shah Pahlavi, when scholars at the Iranian Academy were devotedly replacing Arabic, Turkish and French words with 'pure Persian'. A revival of interest in Ferdowsi's *Shah-nameh* (whose millenary was celebrated in 1934), resulted in some Muslim Iranians naming their offspring after leading figures from the national epic, such as Rostam, Hoshang, Shahpour, Ardeshir, Manizeh, Faranghis etc.[38] These names, commonplace among the Zoroastrians of Iran and India, was to enhance respect for an ancient civilization which had been inspired in large measure by the Zoroastrian faith.

Greater attention was paid to securing equal rights for Zoroastrian farmers and traders who were now granted all the rights and concessions enjoyed by the Muslims.[39] Zoroastrian youth were permitted to join the national armed forces, and General Nowzari was the first Zoroastrian general of the Iranian army in modern times.[40] Indeed, the overall improvement in conditions for Zoroastrians in Pahlavi Iran was so remarkable that

> ...even the masters of the Islamic Jurisprudence and the Ulema who at one time feared the popular uproar to take any interest in the well-being of the Zoroastrians, have now declared by fatwa that they are under the protection of Islam and, as such, due respect should be paid to their acquired rights, lives and properties.[41]

Almost miraculously, living conditions for the community had perceptibly improved in Pahlavi Iran. After long, harsh centuries of persecution and suppression, the Iranian intelligentsia wished to recoup the lost glories of their land, and the more they investigated, the nearer they came to the realization of the tangible links between ancient Iran's brilliant past and her Zoroastrian heritage. As sections of the larger society came to perceive this, the Zoroastrians themselves had less reason to repress their Zoroastrian credentials. The Pahlavi regime was prepared to acknowledge that it was the Zoroastrians who were intrinsically Iranian. While it lasted, this new and regenerative climate of tolerance allowed the Zoroastrians to recover, in a very short space of time, from the thirteen centuries of injustices inflicted upon them. It was by no means a complete reversal to equal status under Iranian law; for example, no non-Muslim may be appointed a high court judge, nor can a non-Muslim become Prime Minister of the land, to name but a few of the civic restrictions on 'minorities'. Yet, the preceding decades gave the lie to the perception of the Zoroastrians as a backward and illiterate minority, stuck in a superstitious, religious groove. The importance of the reign of Reza Shah and his son Mohammad Reza Shah for their Zoroastrian subjects was the fact that it was in the fifty-four years of their dynastic rule of Iran that these rural peasants and artisans were finally permitted to take their rightful place in Iranian society and contribute to its development. The Islamic Revolution of 1979 was to reverse many of these achievements.

NOTES:

1. Mary Boyce, (London 1979), p.163. See also, Boyce, *A Persian Stronghold of Zoroastrianism*, (Oxford 1977).
2. This has been mentioned to the author on several occasions by older Iranian Zoroastrians interviewed in the United Kingdom and on the North American continent. Indeed, the 'purity' of their Iranian lineage is a theme used in order to decry what are perceived as 'Muslim' traits and draw distinctions between them and the Zoroastrians.
3. Richard W.Cottam, *Nationalism in Iran*, (University of Pittsburg Press, 1964), p.85.
4. Pedro Teixeira, 1902, pp.196-7 as quoted in Nora Firby, 1988, p. 24.
5. J. Chardin, *Voyages en Perse et autres lieux de'Orient*, (Amsterdam 1735), vol.II, p.186.
6. Pietro della Valle, *Fameux voyages de Pietro della Valle gentilhomme romain*, transl. by E.Carneau and F.le Comte, (Paris 1661-63), p.104.
7. Chardin, *op.cit.*, p.128.
8. Edward Browne, *A Year Amongst The Persians*, (London,Century Publishing Paperback, 1984), p.406.
9. Napier Malcolm, *Five Years in a Persian Town*, (London 1905), pp.45-8.
10. A.V.W.Jackson, *Persia Past and Present, A Book of Travel and Research*, (New York 1906), p.358.
11. Rashid Shamardan, *Tarik-i Zarthustian Pas-as Sasanian*, (Tehran, 1982) p.177. I am indebted to Mrs.Farhangis Yeganegi for having translated passages of this work for me.
12. D.F.Karaka, (London,1884), vol.I, *op.cit.*, p.57. The present author was informed by Kermanis now resident in North America that as late as the 1920s, the Zoroastrians of Kerman lived within the strictly defined 'ghettos' of the town, where the gates contined to be closed each evening as a preventive measure against Muslim incursions.
13. Rashid Shamardan, *op.cit.*, p.177.
14. Mary Boyce, 'Manekji Limji Hataria in Iran' in *K.R.Cama Oriental Institute Golden Jubilee Volume*, (Bombay,69), p.20. See also, M.L.Hataria, *Ishar-i siyahat-i Iran* (Bombay 1865) in Gujarati.
15. Karaka, vol.I, *op.cit.*, p.55.
16. Mary Boyce, 'The Fire-Temples of Kerman', *Acta Orientalia* XXX (1966), p.57.
17. *Ibid*, pp.67-8, which is a translation of the text of the inscription of the 'Dar-i Mihr-i Mahalle-yi Sahr'.
18. For a detailed analysis of the Amelioration Society's role in the abolition of the *jizya*, see Karaka, vol.I, *op.cit.*, pp. 62-83.
19. 'The Educational Movement Among The Zoroastrians of Iran', a lecture delivered by Mr.Ardeshir Reporter, re-printed in the *Iran League Quarterly*, April-July 1930, vol.I, Nos.1-2, p.75.
20. *Ibid*, p.75.

54   CONTEMPORARY ZOROASTRIANS

21.   Boyce, 1969, p.29.
22.   Ardeshir Reporter, 1930, p.77.
23.   *Ibid*, p.77.
24.   *Ibid*, p.78.
25.   Karaka, vol.I, *op.cit.*, p.84. The abduction of young Zoroastrian girls, especially the more comely among them, has been a continuing fear of the community and was pointed out to the present author as late as 1989 by a Zoroastrian mother of two girls who had fled Iran.
26.   As quoted in Boyce, 1969, p.29.
27.   'Parsis of Iran, Their Past and Present', talk given by Dr.Ali Asghar Hekmat, Iranian Ambassador and Plenipotentiary in India, re-printed in the *Iran League Quarterly*, Bombay, 1956, p.20.
28.   Rashid Shamardan (ed), *Khaterat-i Khaze*, (Bombay 1984). I am grateful to Mrs.Farhangis Yeganegi for having brought this most interesting volume to my notice, and for having translated relevant passages for my use.
29.   Mrs.Farhangis Yeganegi, now resident in the USA, related how Kurdish tribesmen would migrate with their flock between Hamadan and Tehran. They would give their earnings to her father-in-law, a local Zoroastrian highly respected in the area, for safe-keeping, rather than entrusting it to a bank. The Kurds maintained that 'you are a Zoroastrian, we can trust you with our money'. This practice would have occured between 1935-1945.
30.   I acknowledge with gratitude, Dr.Rostam Sarfeh's kind co-operation in speaking to me at great length of his childhood in Yazd. He has been quoted verbatim in order to convey his personal impressions of living conditions for the Zoroastrian community in the early decades of the 20th century in Iran.
31.   I acknowledge with gratitude, Mr.Shahrokh Vafadari for his painstaking and detailed explanations of the rise, at the turn of the century, of Zoroastrian fortunes in Iran. The following is an evaluation of Jamshid Jamshidian's career by Mr.Vafadari. "The Muslims in Iran may hate you [as a Zoroastrian], but they say,'he is an honest fellow'. They can trust a Zoroastrian more than a fellow Muslim".
32.   This Contract is still in the Jamshidian family, currently in the custody of his grandson, now resident in the United States.
33.   Ardeshir Reporter, 1930, p.76.
34.   Jehangiri Oshidari, *Yadashthaey Kaikhosrow Shahrokh*, (Tehran 1977). I am indebted to Mrs.Farhangis Yeganegi, daughter of Arbab Kaikhosrow, for detailed discussions on her father's career, and references to passages of the Arbab's biography. An English version of the *Memoirs of Kaikhosrow Shahrokh*, edited by S.Shahrokh and the present author, is in preparation.
35.   Prior to that, in the earlier short-lived parliaments, Jamshid Jamshidian had sat as the Zoroastrian representative. However, the first parliament had not achieved any measure of success and this led to its closure for four years. More relevant to our discussions, this is why Jamshidian is best remembered by his community as a wealthy banker and the first Zoroastrian to have gained a lucrative commercial contract from a Muslim ruler.
36.   For the following evaluation of Kaikhosrow Shahrokh's career, I am indebted to Mr.Shahrokh Vafadari.
37.   *Iran League Quarterly*, January 1937, vol.VII, No.2, 'Acquisition of Land in Iran for the Unemployed Zoroastrians of Tehran', pp.93-5.
38.   Dr. Ali Asghar Hekmat, 1956, pp.16-17.
39.   *Ibid*, p.15.
40.   I am indebted to Dr.Rostam Sarfeh for having brought this to my attention.
41.   Ali Asghar Hekmat, 1956, p.16.

CHAPTER TWO

DISPARATE CULTURES: PARSI AND IRANIAN ZOROASTRIANS

From the late 19th century, Zoroastrians from Yazd and Kerman began to migrate to India to escape harassment, poverty and suffering. The Parsis of India became acquainted with the 'Irani', seemingly different from himself, in that the new immigrant retained his rural background, spoke Dari (the Irani Zardushti dialect) at home, a quaintly accented Gujarati in public, and was less educated than the Parsis. Throughout its history, India has accommodated a variety of immigrant groups, who retained their separate identities and became subsequently absorbed into the Indian caste system. The Iranis have been integrated into the Parsi community (while not being fully assimilated); the Zoroastrians in India have maintained a unity despite potentially divisive circumstances. How the community was able to resist the pressures of absorption into the pervasive caste system, with its longer-term implications for community identity, will be considered below.

Iranis are not categorised as such in the census, and it is estimated that they number some 5,000 in India, settled primarily in Bombay, Poona, Nasik and other smaller towns in Maharashtra and Gujarat States.[1]While Irani migrations to western India reached their peak in the 19th century, in the absence of records it would be impossible to state with any authority whether previous epochs saw a comparable influx from Iran to India. Nevertheless, migration to Bombay and the hinterland of Gujarat has been, for several generations of Zoroastrians in Iran, a final resort. India never replaced the home country in their affections. What it offered was a safe refuge and the possibility of a good living. Insofar as these universal requirements are concerned, India has played a generous role in Zoroastrian history throughout the past millennium.

Parsi-Irani relations are complex: many Iranis perceive themselves as Iranians as well as Parsi. The Parsis caricature the Irani as their 'poor cousins'. Certain demographic differentials are noticed. While late marriages and the unmarried status among Parsis is increasing,[2] this is yet not the case among the Iranis. Indeed, the mean age at which Parsi women marry is 26.5, which in the case of Irani women is as low as 20.0 (Axelrod,'Myth and

Identity in the Indian Zoroastrians',1980,159). Genetic studies of the groups show that Parsis and Iranis have different serological characteristics.[3]

These distinctions are, however, more of degree than character. The Iranis are more akin to the Parsis than any other Indian community: both groups marry their first cousins at approximately the same rate; rates of birth and use of contraceptives are comparable in both; Iranis invariably live in Parsi neighbourhoods; indeed, the very classification 'Irani' does not lead automatically to a distinctive behaviour pattern by the Parsi. The Iranis have been received into the Parsi fold through a deliberate effort to establish contact with Zoroastrians in Iran. What Axelrod calls 'caste consolidation' (*loc.cit.*160), as a result of the increased number of marriages between Parsis and Iranis, emphasizes the unique character of Parsi social relationships, in a country where caste boundaries remain impregnable. The Parsis are, arguably, the only group in India to have remained outside the caste system in a way that the other groups - indigenous and non-Hindu groups - have not. The resultant sense of distinctness has been critical in the development of Parsi identity, and as such, a few words on caste would be useful at this juncture.[4]

'Caste - the distinctive moral system of India which defines the population in birth ascribed, hierarchically ranked corporate units'.[5] Indian civilization from earliest times had a sophisticated system of social stratification and occupational demarcation coinciding with the concept of *varna*: brahmanical division of society into four unequal, stratified parts; and *jati*: connoting 'birth' and 'kind', applicable to the multitudinous sections of society. This latter term is coterminous with the concept of caste.

Most of all, *jati* (caste) is birth ascribed and consolidated by strict adherance to endogamy. The adherence to endogamous unions thus raises caste barriers which clearly demarcate one social group from another, creating a sense of exclusivity through descent. The status of the group is reinforced by endogamy, and being self-perpetuating, they strengthen the hierarchical aspect of society which arranges them in order of birth. Hierarchy begets caste.[6] Endogamy thus becomes an adjunct of hierarchy.

The overriding principle and rationale behind the Hindu caste system are its religious precepts. The Hindu concept of *karma*, which determines whether a soul is born in human or other guise, determines the status of this being by his placement within a specific caste, which then ascribes status to the individual throughout this life. Central to this philosophy is the theory of reincarnation, or the deeds of a past life reaping dividends for betterment or the penalties for the worsening in a future incarnation.

The hierarchical structure of Indian society, with the *brahmins* (priests) occupying the supreme position, and the *sudras*, who comprise of groups such as *chamar* (cobbler), *dhobi* (washerman) etc., deemed extremely impure servants, consolidates the unbridgeable divisions in society based on the principles of purity. Since Hindu caste differentials are based fundamentally on religious principles, a high caste Hindu contracts temporary impurity in relation to organic life by coming into contact with a person of lower caste.[7] Theoretically, the lower castes were ascribed with 'impure' tasks leading to a generational acquisition of group impurity. 'Pure' and 'impure' were thus legacies acquired at birth by virtue of having been born into a particular *jati*. Following on from this, is the theoretical fixity of occupations. Caste members traditionally followed caste professions, e.g.*lohar*, blacksmith; *nai*, barber, etc. Occupational hierarchy thus reinforced the hierarchical division of society in its totality.

Having outlined the salient features of the Hindu caste structure, it remains to critically analyse whether the Parsis are, *ipso facto*, a part of the Indian caste system.

Zoroastrianism doctrinally operates on a set of axioms which are distinct from those espoused by Hinduism. Thus there is but one life given to individuals who must, consistently using their Good Mind (*vohu manah*), weigh good and bad, and take full responsibility for their thoughts, words and deeds, for which they will be judged after their death. The souls are then assigned accordingly to heaven or hell, and there they must remain until the final cleansing of the world of *ahrimanic* or evil influences. Upon the world having been regenerated (*frasho-kereti*), all human souls return to the world, which is deemed to have returned to its original pristine state, where goodness is thenceforth deemed to exist in perpetuity. Thus, while Hinduism perceives the human condition as following a cyclical pattern, in Zoroastrianism this is seen as an explicitly linear development.

The premises upon which the two religious systems are based being distinct, how then are the Parsis perceived as an Indian caste? A 19th century juridical definition of caste may be useful at this juncture: 'Caste comprised of any self-defined native community governed for certain internal purposes by its own rules and regulations....'[8]Parsis, as indeed all other groupings in India, would then fit into this system of caste. However, the Parsis acquired an empathy for caste structures insofar as it complemented their particular religious and social conventions, and refrained from accepting such caste strictures as were antithetical to their group persona and interests. Social customs such as commensality and endogamous marriages are the most striking illustrations. They came, therefore, to be perceived as another Indian caste, but because they were theologically alien to the notion of caste, their adjustment to this Indian social mechanism was peculiar to themselves.

The early Iranians did indeed divide themselves according to their professions. Initially, there were three classes: *athravan* (priest); *rathaeshtar* (warrior); *vastrya* (agriculturist), to which was later added *huiti* (artisan). We learn from the *Letter of Tansar*,[9] that under Ardashir I of the Sasanian dynasty, original strictures forbidding movement by persons from one profession to another, without prior permission of the state, had been reintroduced. Indeed, this was one of the several protestations addressed in the *Letter* by the King of Tabaristan to the *dastur*, Tansar, which the latter justified on the grounds that such social divisions were designed to preserve order among the people.

While society in ancient Iran was divided into four groups, as in India, the Iranian migrants to India did not bring with them a socially stratified system. The only groups which were thenceforth distinguishable among the Parsis were priests and laymen. The hereditary Zoroastrian priesthood is not based on a theological assumption of superiority of this 'caste'; hence a Zoroastrian *mobed* is not set apart from his society in the strict manner that is the *brahmin*.

Zoroastrianism has, like Hinduism, strict definitions of pure and impure. In Zoroastrianism, however, any aspect of life which is seen as having fallen under *ahrimanic* influence is considered impure. For example, the occurrence of death, the ultimate triumph of *ahriman*, is accordingly the ultimate contamination whereby the dead body is *nasa* (polluted). Thus the *nasa-salars* or pall-bearers, because of their professional association with dead bodies, are deemed impure. This impurity may be cleansed by a ritual bath implying, therefore, that one is not born into a caste or systemic grouping which is impure; rather, one acquired it, and can correspondingly lose it. This is a fundamental distinction between the Zoroastrian and Hindu systems.

Hindu caste maintains hierarchical divisions as an essential feature of the system. Lacking as it does prescribed divisional boundaries between groups which constitute the societal whole, Indian Zoroastrians have not adhered to the strict occupational hierarchy as tend their Hindu compatriots.Thus, even the son of a *mobed* may not necessarily exercise the priestly vocation, but may, and now increasingly does, specialise in some secular profession. (This is the case also in several contemporary *brahmin* families). In the strictest sociological sense therefore, Parsis do not exhibit any substantive assimilation into their group persona of the ideology of caste. This is so with one exception: endogamy.

The endogamy which the Iranian migrants practised in India might conceivably have started out as a defence mechanism which prevented their tiny numbers from being assimilated into the vastness of Hindu India. It thus marked them as a distinct and particular clan, identifiable by their particular physiognomy which was retained, through generations, by marrying within the group. This particular feature of the Hindu caste system worked to Parsi advantage and was therefore readily accepted by them. Equally, the injunctions of Hindu caste would have prohibited unions between caste members and an alien. The host society, through operation of its own social maxims, imposed upon the Parsis the practice of endogamy. The parameters of Parsi 'caste' were thus decreed by the institution of marriage within the Parsi community.

While Parsis have held positions of power in towns and villages, the ideas of purity and pollution being not absent in Zoroastrian theology, together these aspects of group life have lent an aura of high caste attributes. A relative absence of internal stratification, being an essential ingredient of Hindu and non-Hindu society in India, has meant that where caste boundaries would expectedly have developed, they have not, e.g.: priests and laymen, Parsi and Irani can and do intermarry, where in fact no meaningful caste mechanism is in operation.

The distinctive feature of the Parsi community in India over centuries has been its demonstrable ability to maintain its coherence. This has been achieved through some important adjustments in its practices by borrowing from the majority peoples around them, but without relinquishing the essential features of their particular Zoroastrian civilization. The size of the community may have helped: it was small enough to adjust to the values and practices of the dominant culture. They adjusted themselves to the caste structure and used this complex social mechanism to work for them by erecting insuperable boundaries around themselves as a safeguard against absorption. Within the confines of their caste edifice, they continued in the religious practices of their forbears and, over time, acquiesced to certain Hindu social mores, just as in later centuries they were to assume specific English customs, habits and values, without becoming 'Englishmen'. The caste structure had thus far served the Parsi power base well.

In contrast to the Hindu stratification of society, Islam espouses a universal brotherhood for its followers. Once the new faith had succeeded in establishing temporal and spiritual authority in Iran, the small and steadily diminishing Zoroastrian population were deemed beyond the pale, to be brought into the Islamic fold or marginalised as 'gabrs' or unbelievers. While the Parsis in India retained their distinctive communal features assisted by the mechanism of caste, the Zoroastrians in Iran initially began by being effectively debarred from the social system as infidels, thereafter progressively choosing to remain distant from the Muslim majority, since there was more that divided than united them in religious, social and economic terms. The net result for both Parsis and Iranians was the maintenance of a studied aloofness from the majority: the former, however, was assisted by the social institutions of his adoptive land; the latter, as a means of protective segregation through persecution and mockery.

The Arab conquest of Iran in the 7th century took more than a generation to accomplish (as shown in Chapter 1), and for Islam to be established as the state religion. By the 9th century, the Zoroastrians were distinctly disadvantaged, and those who valiantly remained in the old faith became a progressively diminished and despised minority. However, once the excesses of conquest were over and return to the *status quo ante* made impossible, the Zoroastrians attempted to continue in the old ways. While their intentions may have been laudable, the political reality was a severe impediment. Power now resided with the followers of Allah, and although the maintenance of a contemptuous aloofness from the 'gabr' was advocated, zealous missionary activities progressively swelled the numbers of converts to Islam, which correspondingly depleted the Zoroastrian community. The inducements to conversion were several, not least of which was to grant freedom to a slave who embraced Islam, the automatic right to inheritance of all property by an individual who converted, at the expense of those in the family who adhered to the old faith. Whether conversions were undertaken reluctantly or impelled by self-interest, successive generations were nurtured within Islam, and became generally intolerant of the Zoroastrians.

It was to prevent further desecrations of religious institutions, and with the loyal support of the Zoroastrian villagers of Sharifabad in Yazd province, that the *Dastur dasturan* took refuge in Turkabad, not later than the 11th century. He brought with him the two great sacred fires: Adur Farrbay (Khoreh), one of the three great fires of ancient Iran; and the Anahid Fire, the ancient sacred fire of Istakhr, the 'family' fire of the Sasanian dynasty. Henceforth, the two small villages of Sharifabad and Turkabad, at a prudent distance from the provincial centre of government in Yazd city, evolved in time into the ecclesiastical centres of Zoroastrianism in Iran.[10]

The last compulsory mass conversion in Iran took place in Turkabad in the mid-19th century (Boyce, *A Persian Stronghold of Zoroastrianism*, 1977,7). The oral tradition holds that one autumn day when the men were working in the fields, a group of Muslims seized them and with threats of death to themselves and their womenfolk and children similarly held captive in their homes, forced the conversion of virtually the entire village. Since apostasy resulted in death, Turkabad remained predominantly Muslim, and its fire temple was destroyed. Similar instances of Zoroastrian villages being lost to Islam through compulsory conversions must have occurred, and the inexorable advance of Islam across the Yazdi plain, whether by force or gradual attrition, was inevitable. Boyce notes that as late as the 1960s, a few Muslims would occupy the outskirts of a Zoroastrian village, and one or two Zoroastrian families adopt Islam. 'Once the dominant faith had made a breach, it pressed remorselessly, like a rising tide' (*loc.cit.*7). A pattern would develop: more Muslims would arrive, a mosque would be built and, with an increase in their numbers, harassment of the Zoroastrians would ensue.

The tools of vilification were twofold: the Zoroastrian was denigrated as a 'fire-worshipper' (*atash-parast*); and as being polluted (*najes*) by the very fact of having been born a Zoroastrian.[11] The former pejorative (which in itself is a fundamental misrepresentation of Zoroastrian belief and worship, and as such deeply resented by Zoroastrians who worship the one uncreated God, Ahura Mazda), rationalised their defamation as 'unbelievers' and 'infidels' unworthy of religious tolerance and undeserving of adequate protection of the state legal apparatus; while the latter term of abuse helped reinforce the impression of the untouchability of the Zoroastrians who were consequently debarred from participating fully in the socio-economic spheres of national life. An important point concerning the purity laws of the Muslims, especially in the context of non-Muslims, who for example are not permitted to touch fruits in the bazaar because the Muslim shopkeeper would consider his stock to have become *najes*; or not being permitted to walk along a stretch of earth newly sprinkled with water since water is a conductor of impurity, and so on, emphasizes the precept that the touch of a non-Muslim is *najes*, and this makes him impure for prayers. However, the Muslim can cleanse himself in preparation for prayer through purification with water; an unbeliever can only be cleansed by conversion to Islam. This code therefore, transformed into a formula of social exclusion extending to rules of dress, housing, occupation, etc. was established to demarcate the Muslims as superior to the Zoroastrians, Armenians, Jews and Christians. The persecutions of the Zoroastrian minority seemingly grounded in theological precepts, was therefore to institutionalise their marginalization until the advent of the Pahlavi dynasty, when the rule of law was extended to include the Zoroastrians of Iran.[12]

The instruments of bedevilment of the Zoroastrian community were essentially three: the deriding of the *kusti*, or badge of the Good Religion; pollution of fire, a prime symbol of the faith; and maltreatment of dogs, which the Zoroastrians have traditionally treated with an immense respect.

We have seen how (Chapter 1) Arab tax collectors in the 8th century would tear the sacred girdle from the waist of the Zoroastrian, hang it around their necks, and ridicule the individual and his faith. As a result, the practise of wearing the *kusti*, indeed the very initiation ceremonial of *sedre-pushin*, became less frequent in Islamic Iran for fear of the repercussions on the individuals. Contemporary Iranian Zoroastrians therefore do not consider the continuous wearing of the *kusti* as an essential element of their religious duties, so thorough-going has been Muslim mockery of this ancient custom.

Extinguishing Zoroastrian sacred fires and denigrating the believers as infidels, resulted in the diminishing number of consecrated fires burning in Iran, as well as the resultant practice of concealing the sacred fire in a small, hidden chamber in unobtrusive mud-brick temples. Tavernier sought in vain to enter the Zoroastrian fire temple in Kerman and, by way of explanation, was informed of the case of a Muslim governor who had demanded entry into the fire temple: 'he, it seems, expected some extraordinary brightness; but when he saw no more than what he might have seen in a kitchen or a chamber fire, fell a-swearing and spitting upon it as if he had been mad'.[13]

A further vexation was the ill-treatment of dogs, an animal treated in traditional Zoroastrianism with near-religious respect, but considered unclean by Muslims. To fully comprehend the role of the dog in Zoroastrian life, one needs to understand the dependence on the animal that the nomadic forbears of the Iranians on the Asian steppes would have had.[14] While the sedentary Zoroastrians, once established on the Iranian plateau, would have had less need of the dog, as late as the 1960s every Zoroastrian village maintained a number of dogs. Zoroastrian orthodoxy requires that not only should one feed hungry dogs, but that every household should feed a dog once a day at least. The family pet dog was to receive the first mouthful of food consumed in the home, a custom maintained in Iran as the *chom-e swa* or 'meal for the dog', and in India by the Parsis, the *kutra-no buk*, 'the morsel for the dog'.Additionally, the Zoroastrian *Vendidad* enjoins that a 'four-eyed dog' (i.e. with two flecks over the eyes), is required to be brought along to witness a dead body, and by his sense of smell, verify that death has in fact occurred. This practice, too, continues to be followed by the Zoroastrian communities in Iran and India. Muslim maltreatment of dogs - kicking and beating of the innocent animals - would be in some instances simply to vex the Zoroastrians.Thus, as with discarding the *kusti*, spitting on fire, and abuse of dogs, undertaken initially to distress the Zoroastrian population, was used equally as proven signs of true conversion to Islam by a Zoroastrian.

The Zoroastrians were segregated from the rest of the community by further strictures which were rigorously enforced by the authorities.[15] Thus, the injunction against the *najes* 'gabrs' meant that they were prohibited from engaging in professions or crafts which might bring them into direct contact with Muslims.[16] Zoroastrians continued to wear distinctive clothing until the early decades of the present century - Zoroastrian men were permitted to wear only garments of undyed cotton or wool, to set them apart from the Muslim community. Several stories, written and orally transmitted, are told of abductions and rape of Zoroastrian girls, the prettiest among them voluntarily blackened their teeth and smeared their faces with dirt when stepping outdoors, since Zoroastrian women resolutely refused to veil their faces. The litany of harassments and restrictions, some merely vexatious, others calculated to make their living conditions intolerable, remains in the communal consciousness, and as the rule of law was extended to Zoroastrians only sporadically, security of life and property were never completely guaranteed.

> Again, may the bright minds of the *Dasturs*, *Herbads*, and *Mobeds* of the country of Hindustan be enlightened that the millenium of *Ahriman* is ended and the millenium of *Ormazd* has approached, and we hope to see the face of the victorious

king Varjavand, and Hoshedar and Peshotan will come without
any doubt or suspicion, and there is not the slightest doubt
that the glory of Varjavand will be seen (by us).[17]

It is not surprising that the Zoroastrians of Iran continued to entertain
millenial hopes for the coming of the *Saoshyant* (saviour), as demonstrated in
their letter to their Parsi kinsmen. While the Iranian community suffered
enormously in an oppressive environment, the Parsis had found a safe refuge
in India.

The Parsis of Navsari, under the direction of Changa Asa, sent a courageous
emissary, Nariman Hoshang, to Iran. Hoshang sailed from Broach in Gujarat
to the Persian Gulf, from whence he made his way to Yazd, where he was
warmly received by the chief *dastur* of Turkabad. He had perforce to study
Persian, so necessary to breach the language barrier, before he was ready to
receive instruction (Dhabhar,*The Persian Rivayats of Hormazyar Framarz and
Others*,1932,593).Thus, the *Persian Rivayats* or treatises on socio-religious
instruction, were inaugurated in the 15th century, whereby the Zoroastrians
of India sought advice and learned priestly opinions on the technicalities of
rituals, observances, doctrinal matters, and was the first recorded instance of
the resumption of the tenuous links between the two groups of Zoroastrians
following their separation in the 9th/10th century. On his return to Gujarat in
1478, Hoshang brought back two *Pazand* manuscripts which had been copied
by two Sharifabadi priests for 'the priests, leaders and chief men of
Hindustan'. The letters and missives thus exchanged between Iran and India
until 1768, bear eloquent testimony to the conditions of the Parsi and Iranian
Zoroastrians of the mid-Islamic period. Both communities remained stoutly
orthodox, and adhered steadfastly to their ancestral faith, for which both had
suffered so much. Indeed, no doctrinal differences are perceptible, and the
tenacious attachment to their religious legacy under the repressive conditions
endured by the Iranians, and the marginal status of the Parsis, could not have
been achieved without iron in their souls.

The period spanning the 15th to 18th centuries which comprised the exchange
of the *Rivayats* between the two communities, witnessed intermittent contact
and acknowledgement of the living conditions of the groups in their respective
countries; the later migration and integration of the Iranis into the Parsi
community during the 19th and 20th centuries helped create mythologies of
their mutual idiosyncrasies. These are being overtaken by events in the
Zoroastrian diaspora in the West. Parsi migrations to Europe, North America
and Australia have in the main been inspired by the quest for a better life.
The Iranian Zoroastrians migrated West in the aftermath of the Iranian
Revolution of 1979.[18] The reasons for movement Westwards may have

differed but, once the re-settlement process has been established, there is a fairly unanimous commitment to their lives in the New World. A return to the old countries does not seem a feasible or desirable option for the forseeable future. The dispersion therefore represents the evolution of a new dimension in Zoroastrian history. It is in this setting that Parsis and Iranian Zoroastrians, in their attempts at preserving their traditions and religious beliefs in a Judaeo-Christian environment, have begun to discern internal differences. These stem from the distinctive religio-cultural environments they absorbed over a millennium and which now re-shape their understanding, emphasis and practices pertaining to their Zoroastrian religion. (Refer Table 6).

The encounter of Parsi and Iranian Zoroastrians in the diaspora reveals several differences. They speak different languages: the Iranians 'think' in Farsi, the Parsis are essentially bi-lingual in English and Gujarati, while young Parsis are fluent in English only. Given that there are several languages in modern Zoroastrianism, the thought processes of the two groups are distinctive. The separate religious ideologies - Islam and Hinduism - under which they have lived has affected the emphasis on, and practice of, specific Zoroastrian rituals. At its most fundamental is the wearing of the *sudre* and *kusti*, emphasized by, and seen as inalienable badges of Zoroastrianism by the Parsis, and worn by Iranian Zoroastrians in the main when visiting a fire temple, or attending religious ceremonials. So fundamental is the difference of opinion on the *sudre-kusti*, that grave divisions in the community are being engendered. An average Parsi assessment is 'the Iranian does not wear *sudre-kusti*, he is not a real Zoroastrian'. The Iranian response is 'the Parsis are like Hindus, they are full of symbols and rituals'. The contrasting perceptions of Zoroastrianism now converging in the diaspora has resulted in a confusion of religious and social identity.

The differences between Parsis and Iranians which have developed over time in the diverse areas of language, food, dress, music and rituals connected with their religion, gives the impression of their being two completely different peoples with no tangential meeting point.[19] And nowhere is this notion of the seeming irreconcilability of the Zoroastrians better reflected than in the communities now domiciled in the USA and Canada.

The perceptions of divergence between Parsis and Iranians relate to various community issues. In terms of the practice and expressions pertaining to their religion, a 16 year old Iranian girl explained:'They are two very different people. When I hear my uncle [who is a priest] recite the *Avesta*, and a Parsi priest, I don't recognise it. Everything has been diluted. First they [Parsis] move to India, then out of India. So they have culture mixed with everything'. Her father then illustrated the 'corrupting' influence of Parsi-Gujarati pronunciation of liturgy. Thus, while reciting the *tandorosti* (thanksgiving) prayer, for example, a Parsi priest is inclined to say, *tandarosti jindegani*, which in modern Persian, would translate as 'Tandarosti prostitution'. The correct pronunciation is *tandorosti zhendegani*, which means 'to live'. In fact, this Iranian gentleman had taken the extreme step of keeping his children away from ceremonials where Parsi priests officiated. In the light of this, the creation of the Council of Iranian *Mobeds* of North America on 15 March 1989, and its express purpose to 'serve the North American and Canadian Iranian Zoroastrian community',[20] is more readily comprehensible.

Another young Iranian girl could not contemplate marriage to a Parsi because: 'I find the Parsis so different. To marry a Parsi would be yet another bridge for me to cross'. She elaborated the several differences between the groups: 'Parsis are more free, they "date". With Iranians, its not acceptable. If you do go out, you keep it secret, but you go out with a view to marriage'. Several significant social issues arise here. The differing tastes in food, music, literature, are clearly evident. The inability of the two groups, especially the older generation, to discuss contentious issues in a common language, exacerbates underlying tensions. Thus, while the Iranian clings to the Farsi language, innuendos such as it being problematic to be a 'good' Zoroastrian when one speaks a 'Hindi' language, viz. Gujarati, leads to the Parsi response that English is the language of the adopted country and all communications should be conducted in it. Since no real dialogue between Parsis and Iranians takes place, misunderstandings are compounded at all levels. Thus, one Parsi said, 'Iranians consider us Parsis as second class Zoroastrians. I don't think they have any right to do so. Just because they come from Iran doesn't mean they have a monopoly on the religion or understand more about it'. An Iranian retorted, 'Parsis are influenced by the Hindus. The Muslims could not influence the Iranians, nothing [of the religion] has been changed.[21] Unquestionably, the overt cultural differences cannot be overlooked.

The will and ability to adjust to the new environment also differ greatly. A Parsi lady, one of many, referred to the contentious issue of the annual children's Christmas party. The Iranians did not consider it a Zoroastrian festival and kept their children away. The Parsis maintained that there was no harm in giving the children presents. Accordingly, the Parsi children attended the Christmas parties, while very few Iranian children participated. The areas of cultural divergence are indeed so numerous, and the mechanisms for dialogue and discussion so limited, that any analysis of the contemporary Zoroastrian community has to acknowledge a 'Parsi identity' and an 'Iranian Zoroastrian identity'. While the North American community has deliberately chosen to refer to itself as Zoroastrian, it has not resulted in an automatic convergence of values, perceptions, habits, tastes, or even a mutual rapprochment.

There are, nevertheless, some community members who do not take the extreme positions cited above. A young Iranian lady said,'I love the Parsis. It is strange, I don't have any Parsi background but I feel more comfortable with the Parsis. I like the Parsi people'. Similarly, this author can testify to the initiatives for open discussions between the two groups. As a Parsi, she has almost invariably been treated with the utmost candour and courtesy by Iranian Zoroastrians, and on one particular occasion, following a long and very detailed interview session with an Iranian Zoroastrian family, the head of the household commented:'I don't know you at all, and had never met you before this evening. But I have been able to talk so freely to you because you are a Zardushti. I would never have spoken like this to someone else'.

While the perceptions of differences between the two groups are now well established in the North American community, the responses made by the different local associations to community questions varies. In Toronto, for example, the two groups maintain their different approaches to religious classes for the young. Accordingly, there are education classes for Parsi children, and others for Iranian children. The Parsis continue to celebrate festivals according to the *Shahanshahi* reckoning; the Iranians subscribe to the *Fasli* calendar.[22]

In the spring of 1988, while travelling across the North American continent to collect material for the present work, the Zoroastrian communities of Toronto, Vancouver, Chicago, Los Angeles and New York were studied. There was an element of differing celebrations and religious educational approaches in most of these cities. The case of Vancouver, however, is striking. In relative terms, the community there was attempting to reconcile differences and pay closer attention to the endemic problems of language, food and varying cultural tastes. The fact that the five hundred strong Zoroastrians of Vancouver are almost equally divided in terms of Parsis and Iranians, is an advantage: they do not outweigh one another. In order to achieve a certain harmony between the two, unwritten codes of procedure for community occasions have come to be practised. Since language is a major issue in inter-community relations, public talks held at the *Dar-i Mehr* are loosely translated from English into Farsi. The Farsi translators are not professional interpreters but rather volunteers who take an active part in community affairs. Another contentious issue is food. This has been resolved by catering at *Dar-i Mehr* functions where menus are comprised of Parsi and Iranian cuisine. The 'problem' of food was therefore no major obstacle in Vancouver.Religious celebrations, according to the *Fasli* and *Shahanshahi* calendars, has been resolved through the *Dar-i Mehr* facilities being used on a regular basis by each group subscribing to these respective calendars.

The one area where the Vancouver community is unique is that the religious education classes, held on two Sundays each month, are attended by young Zoroastrians, both Parsis and Iranians. Vancouver evidently appeared to be working towards unity of the two groups. Their annually elected 'Slate of Directors', had a fairly even distribution of seats amongst local Parsi and Iranian Zoroastrians. The overall picture of Vancouver was of the Zoroastrian community striving successfully to co-exist. Tensions remain under the surface as a result of cultural differences. The older generation appears dedicated to the community's group survival. The younger people, especially of college age and above, tend to move away from the Zoroastrian mainstream and adopt a more pronounced Canadian identity. A 29 year old lady said, 'I come here [*Dar-i Mehr*] a few times a year to get a dose of my culture. Once I have a small shot in the arm, its enough to last me for a while. I only return when I need to'.

The British Zoroastrian community is preponderantly Parsi. A palpable remoteness between the two groups mirrors the North American experience. Since 1988, Iranian Zoroastrians have organised separate monthly meetings at the Association headquarters in London. These'Persian evenings'gives them the opportunity to renew acquaintances with other Persians, and encourages the young to intra-socialise and to seek marriage partners from within. Equally, they have the opportunity to converse in Farsi, eat Persian food and reminisce about Iran without inhibitions. Indeed, so distinct are the two groups of Zoroastrians today that the younger generation reflects the prejudices of their parents. The youth groups therefore do not mingle: both Parsis and Iranians retain their separate groupings. As currently constituted, the young Iranians are enthusiastically sports-minded and arrange their weekend group activities around their primary interest. The Parsi youth likewise socialise among themselves, but being more numerous than their Iranian counterparts, pursue varying recreational activities within their group boundaries.

The fact that the British, American and Canadian Zoroastrian youth, Iranian and Parsi, find it virtually impossible to come together to socialise but choose instead to remain within their groups, reflects an imponderable. Why is it that these young persons, who could use the neutral Judaeo-Christian environments to effect a re-acquaintance and communal reconciliation, do not avail themselves of the opportunity? Two reasons are suggested: the first is a genuine lack of understanding of the other's historical and cultural experiences which have resulted in the different perceptions and practices of their particular 'brand' of Zoroastrianism; the second, and equally significant, reason is the lack of will to come together as a people. The fragmentary nature of the community which has developed along national lines makes the prognosis for the future of the diaspora unencouraging.

What in theory ought to have been an opportunity with great potential for the renewal of ties between the two groups in the diaspora, remains hitherto unrealised. Their respective historic experiences have been so distinct, the evolution of separate identities so pronounced, and have been exacerbated by the lack of communal mechanisms for dialogue and discussion to overcome these differences. The Iranians cling to their sense of history: having been condemned to a frightened silence, this was to help see them through the difficult centuries. The Parsis practised their religious rituals in an environment which did not curtail such expressions of identity, and their sense of cohesiveness and community was in turn enhanced. An on-going debate within the Zoroastrian world - one which pits Iranian against Parsi, develops from this. Iranians emphasize the 'philosophy' of Zarathushtra; Parsis show a greater propensity for the rituals of Zoroastrianism. This has evolved into a major religio-cultural differentiation between the two groups. The interpretation and re-examination of the religion is thus a central issue for the contemporary community. The ramifications of this immensely complex question, will doubtless affect several generations to come.

The above discussion has shown the seemingly entrenched differences which have developed between the two main groups of Zoroastrians. For a community of such miniscule size, these distinctive features having evolved along national lines is itself the product of an earlier time when pride in local identity would have conditioned the ancestors of the contemporary Parsi and Iranian Zoroastrians. Two provinces in Iran were at the heart of this development: Khorasan - ancient Parthia - the seat of the Arsacid Parthian dynasty in north-eastern Iran from whence the founding fathers of the Parsi community set sail for Gujarat in the 10th century; and Fars in southern Iran, the seat of the Sasanian dynasty and the region of Yazd especially, where the diminishing number of Zoroastrians fled and remained (along with neighbouring Kerman) to the present day. The differing perceptions of Zoroastrianism in the contemporary world, and the cultural contrasts exhibited by the two groups, are important for our understanding. The key roles played by Hindu India and Muslim Iran are essential to our evaluation; the distinctive features of Khorasan and Fars, in their contributions to early Iranian society, are equally apposite to our theme.

The *Kisseh-i Sanjan* speaks solely of the ancestors of the Parsis having fled from Khorasan for 'Hind'. They consecrated their *Atash Bahram* in India 'with all these resources derived from Khurasan...'[23] The local customs of Khorasan would accordingly have travelled with the early migrants to Gujarat, and subsequent Zoroastrian immigrants from Iran, having joined the Parsis, would arguably have become absorbed into the group dynamic created from the fusion of Zoroastrians from Khorasan domiciled in Gujarat. In Iran, there were two areas where the Zoroastrians managed to maintain themselves in and around the oasis cities of Yazd and Kerman, the enclosed plain upon which the former is situated lying on the northern edge of the ancient kingdom of Persia proper, the homeland of the Sasanians. As and when small groups of Zoroastrians joined the parent groups in Yazd or Kerman, fleeing repressive conditions in other parts of the country, they too would have absorbed the customs and mores of the 'Persian' Zoroastrians. Indeed, the regional differences between eastern and western Iran having become unified as never before 'under the oecumene of Islam',[24] the remaining Zoroastrian constituent groups would have subsumed elements of the particularities of their regional cultures.

First, perhaps, was the retention of local pride which laid the foundation-stone of the two emerging communities, and was later to fuse into characteristic Parsi and Iranian identities. The feudal, heroic culture of the Parthians was the heritage of Khorasan. Indeed, the legendary ancient history of Iran surrounding the Kayanian dynasty, including the epoch of Zarathushtra himself, would not have become universal in Iran until the time of the Parthians themselves.[25] It is now generally agreed[26] that the eastern Iranian Kayanian 'heroic cycle' was in fact one of the primary sources for the later national epic, the *Shah-nameh*, itself a 'Zoroastrianised' form of the narrative. The heroic traditions central to the theme of the *Shah-nameh* would have stemmed from the eastern Iranian tribal society of the earlier Aryan invaders and persisted into Achaemenid times, whereas a more sedentary community was to develop in the west of the country (Frye, *The Heritage of Persia*, 1965, 55). Even so, the Sasanian king Narseh had to acknowledge the importance of Parthia in the Paikuli inscriptions thus: 'the Persian and Parthian royal princes, grandees and lesser nobility', giving the lie to the sustained Sasanian propaganda which had systematically attempted to obliterate the importance of the northern dynasty, while exclusively elevating Sasanian princes and their fictitious direct descent from the earlier Achaemenids.[27]

While official royal biographers had attempted to distort historical facts and exalt the dignity of the dynasty they served, the common folk would have continued to take pride in their local identities and fashion their lives in conformity with local conditions. Thus, by the time of the Arab conquest of the country, Khorasan and Transoxiana were well-established as trading and commercial regions; while major towns in Fars province, such as Shiraz and Isfahan, were better known as agricultural centres, in keeping with Sasanian Zoroastrianism, which deemed the cultivation of the land as the most suitable occupation for adherents of the Good Religion. It is interesting to observe how, centuries later, the Parsis in 18th and 19th century British India, were to amass their wealth primarily through trade. The Persian Zoroastrians were to remain agriculturists well into the 20th century, in Yazd and Kerman. Indeed their skill and care in tilling the land was acknowledged by observers such as A.V. Jackson, Edward Browne and Napier Malcolm.

The several contradictions we have encountered in modern-day Zoroastrians, relates equally to their Zoroastrianism. Both groups fervently maintain they possess the 'correct' understanding of their inherited religion. Yet, once foreign accretions - whether Hindu, Muslim, Christian or others - have been accounted for, regional practices of earlier times could help explain the divergent approaches.

A major source of the separate stance on particular religious practices discernible among contemporary Parsis and Iranians, is the generally preferred usage of the *dakhma* or exposure of the dead among the former; whereas burial is the preferred option among Iranians. While the environmental influences of the Hindu and Muslim societies respectively must be taken into account, earlier precedents applicable to northern and southern Iran, i.e. Parthia and Fars, deserve to be mentioned. Procopius (Wars, I.11.35), writing towards the close of the Sasanian era, mentions that while in earlier times the Persians had various burial customs, once state Sasanian Zoroastrianism was instituted, exposure of the corpse and collection of the bones in *astodans* or ossuaries, which were then buried, became the norm. Indeed, the question relating to the mode of burial among Zoroastrians is more vexed than is generally acknowledged. Frye's hypothesis[28] deserves serious consideration. Prior to the Sasanian epoch, the Persians in western Iran, in regions bordering on Mesopotamia, were in all probability influenced by the practice of entombing. Exposure too would have been practised in these regions (and especially in Media where the 'magi' prescribed it as a religious duty). The custom of exposure of the corpse to birds of prey, and the interment of bones in ossuaries, was in earlier times a common usage in Central Asia. From there it penetrated into Iran and became a religious injunction advocated by the priesthood. (Given that non-pollution of the elements is a central Zoroastrian religious principle, the prescription to feed the mortal remains to wild animals fits admirably into the essentials of Zoroastrian theology. The putrefying corpse is deemed *nasa*, and it is contrary to the religious ordinances to contaminate earth with polluted matter). Increasing archaelogical evidence from several Central Asian ossuaries found, pre-dating the Sasanian era, strengthens Frye's hypothesis.

Regional burial practices in Iran might conceivably have differed. Since Achaemenid times, the western Iranians, more especially the aristocracy, would entomb their dead (albeit in raised graves within lined coffins so as to avoid polluting the earth), given the cultural impact of the older civilizations of Mesopotamia and Egypt. In north-east Iran, the Central Asian mode of exposure may have been imported, obtaining the religious imprimatur of the priesthood, and came to be piously adopted. If our historical conjectures are partially accurate, we could extend this line of reasoning to suggest that the custom of *dakhmas* would have come, in time, to have been seen as an inalienable religious duty among the Parthians just as it is by a large number of contemporary Parsis. Burial, which became the usage of Islamic Iran, while reluctantly accepted by the ancestors of the modern Iranian Zoroastrians, could be rationalised and seen to be in keeping with religious beliefs.[29] While Muslim desecration of Persian 'towers of silence', and their scorn of this method of disposal of the dead would account for the gradual abandoning of this method by contemporary Iranian Zoroastrians, it is possible to speculate that in the south of the country burial might have been a major alternative method of disposal as against exposure. If these conjectures are sustainable in the light of future researches on this subject, then arguably, contemporary Parsis and Iranians demonstrate a tenacity towards their respective earlier customs.

Frye postulates the existence of a northern or Parthian and a southern or Sasanian school of Zoroastrianism.[30] Yet, it was the practices of a ritualised Zoroastrian state church with its various rituals and admonitions, which one learns from the Pahlavi texts, were carried by the ancestors of the Parsis in their migration to India. By the Abbasid period, Zoroastrian Persian culture had retreated into the ghetto, where it remained until the early decades of the 20th century.

A significant achievement of the Sasanian rulers, the ramifications of which would extend for several generations, was the successful impugning of the northern Arsacid Parthian dynasty as an aberration in Iranian history, and the corresponding elevation in stature of the House of Sasan as the true inheritors of the Achaemenid legacy. So pervasive was this myth that even contemporary Zoroastrians (as well as Iranian Muslims) subscribe to this deliberate re-interpretation of history. It is an irony of no small magnitude when Parsis unwittingly minimize the role of their ancestral province and the royal house which helped revive Iranian fortunes following the conquest of Alexander of Macedon. The Arsacid Parthians, contrary to the received wisdom, were in fact devout Zoroastrians. Thus, King

> Valakhsh the Arsacid, commanded that a memorandum be sent to the provinces to preserve, in the state in which they had been found in (each) province, whatever of the *Avesta* and *Zand*, had come to light and was genuine and also any teaching deriving from it which, although now scattered owing to the chaos and disruption which Alexander had brought in his wake, and the pillage and looting of the Macedonians in the kingdom of Iran, either survived in writing or was preserved in an authoritative oral translation.[31]

This attention to the consolidation of religious texts on a national scale suggests a dynasty eager to uphold their ancestral faith.

Furthermore, the three greatest sacred fires of Zoroastrianism, namely *Adur Burzen-Mihr*, *Adur Farrbay* and *Adur Gushnasp*, if they had not already been enthroned in the Achaemenid era, must have been established in the Parthian period. By Sasanian times, these fires were already accorded an hoary antiquity.[32]

Indeed, the judgement concerning the Parthians as perpetuated by the Sasanians and then accepted in the lay and scholarly community generally, meant that the poet Ferdowsi could later say only, 'I have heard nothing but their names, and I have not seen them in the chronicle of kings'. A cursory glance at their record proves otherwise. There is evidence of the existence of fire temples from that era; they were believers in Ahura Mazda; the transmission of the Kayanian epic enshrining the sacred history of Zarathustra's mission and later included in the national epic, the *Shah-nameh*, are but a few illustrations of the fidelity to the Zoroastrian tradition demonstrated by the northern dynasty.

More apposite to our discussion, however, was the damning indictment of the Sasanians that the Parthians displayed an excessively hellenistic zeal in religious and cultural matters, and as such were scarcely Iranian. The House of Arsaces, having regained independence from the Seleucids in 141 BCE, and set about re-establishing Iranian suzerainty from the frontiers of India to the western border of Mesopotamia, were to make Zoroastrianism once more the faith of a great Iranian empire.

Greek craftsmen working in the country would have contributed to the iconography on Parthian coinage; for example, their depiction of Zeus and Apollo would have represented in Zoroastrian terms, Ahura Mazda and Mithra. In all likelihood, Parthian princes and nobles, having the greatest scope for social intercourse with the Greeks, would have led the way in adopting Greek iconography and art. A blending of cultures is thus attested by several surviving archaeological finds. Boyce[33] cites the example of a wayside shrine to Herakles Kallinikos in the Behistun mountain, with a Greek inscription dating from 147 BCE, and an unfinished one in Aramaic. Its position suggests that it was for Greek and Iranian devotees, for Herakles the Victorious was identified with Verethraghna the Zoroastrian *yazata* of Victory, who also cares for travellers. Iranian as well as Greek travellers passing along the highway that runs beside the rock, could both offer their devotions and ask for protection from the deity. The Parthians, therefore, were tolerant of foreign customs (as indeed, the Achaemenids had been before them).

Present-day Parsis are frequently perceived as the most 'westernized' of all Indian communities in that they are deemed to have emulated British customs and conventions more thoroughly than did any other Indian peoples. Their forbears were castigated for an excessive hellenism; just as the 'anglicization' of the Parsis is often berated. It is possible to speculate that there is a thread running through the historical development of the Parsis whose ancestors, after all, could have been inhabitants of ancient Parthia. At the very least, it must be admitted that the Parsis appear, in the main, to be open to foreign influences in secular affairs. This gives the impression to outside observers that Parsi culture is syncretist, overly influenced by the Hindus of India and the later British colonialists. However, a seeming catholicity in secular matters does not extend to the religious sphere where they have demonstrated a remarkably dogged attachment to their traditions. The Scottish missionary

John Wilson's earnest efforts to convert Parsis to Christianity in the 19th century met with universal resistance, and he gained very few converts. Certain parallels in perception of the Parthians and Parsis are not entirely far-fetched: both sets of Zoroastrians have demonstrated an openness to foreign cultures, but remained steadfast to their ancient faith. This dichotomy remains a continuing enigma among the contemporary Parsis and complicates Parso-Iranian relations.

Several issues which will be considered later in this volume, where there is a palpable divergence of views between the Parsis and Iranian Zoroastrians, stem primarily from their millenial separation. This historical fact is exacerbated by the very distinctive religio-cultural milieux in which they found themselves: Hindu India and Islamic Iran. However, as though by means of an over-arching canopy, the earlier regionalisms from ancient Iran, the distinctive developmental patterns in religious, social, cultural and economic terms of the north (as exemplified by Parthia), and the south (as represented by Fars), are to be discerned in the present-day constituent groups of the Zoroastrian community. Whilst a great deal binds them, most specifically the religion of Zarathushtra, echoes of an earlier distinctive approach to the faith are equally clearly evident in the modern Zoroastrian.

NOTES:

1.   For this brief survey of the Iranis of India, see Paul Axelrod, 'Myth and Identity in the Indian Zoroastrian Community', *Journal of Mithraic Studies*, Vol.III, Nos.1&2, 1980, pp.150-165.

2.   See Malini Karkal, 'Marriages among Parsis' *Demographic India*, Vol.IV, No.1, June 1975.

3.   The pioneering work in this field has been undertaken by J.V.Undevia, *Population Genetics of the Parsis*, (Miami 1973).

4.   While the sociological study of caste is a subject beyond the scope of this work, and which is indeed an immensely complex phenomenon, I have limited my comments to those areas of direct concern to the Parsi community.

5.   Frank F.Conlon, *A Caste in a Changing World: The Chitrapur Saraswat Brahmans 1700-1935*, (Berkeley 1977), p.4.

6.   Louis Dumont, *Homo Hierarchicus: An Essay on the Caste System*, (Chicago University Press, 1970), p.113.

7.   *Ibid*, p.47.

8.   D.F.Mulla, *Jurisdiction of Courts in Matters Relating to the Rights and Powers of Castes*, (Bombay, 1901), pp.2-3.

9.   *Letter of Tansar* (transl) Mary Boyce, (Rome 1968), p.38.

10.   Mary Boyce, *A Persian Stronghold of Zoroastrianism*, (OUP, 1977), p.7.

11.   This has been dealt with in some detail in Chapter 5, 'Iranian Zoroastrian Refugees'.

12.   Kaikhosrow Shahrokh, special advisor to Reza Shah Pahlavi, was a central figure in the removal of legal restrictions on the Zoroastrians. See, Jehangiri Oshidari, *Yazdashtaey Kaikhosrow Shahrokh*, (Tehran 1977).

13.   J.B.Tavernier, *Six Voyages en Turquie, en Perse et aux Indes*, (Paris 1676), anon. Eng. transl. (London 1684), p.167.

14.   M.Boyce, 1977, p.139 ff.

15.   See Napier Malcolm, *Five Years in a Persian Town* (London 1905), p.44 ff. which gives a graphic account of the isolation of the Zoroastrians of Yazd at the turn of the 20th century. See also, Rashid Shahmardan (ed) *Khaterat-i Khaze* (Bombay 1984), and Jehangiri Oshidari, *op.cit.* which give vivid descriptions from a Zoroastrian viewpoint, of the conditions of the community in Yazd and Kerman at the turn of the century.

16.   I have often been told by older Iranian Zoroastrians originally from Yazd and Kerman, now settled in the West, of their experiences when visiting a bazaar and being prohibited from touching or picking up

fruits and vegetables by the Muslim stall-holder because it would become polluted by their touch. Indeed, the catalogue of restrictions and petty vexations would require a separate volume to enumerate in its entirety.

17. B.N.Dhabhar (transl) *The Persian Rivayats of Hormazyar Framarz and Others*, (Bombay 1932), pp. 593-4.
18. For a detailed discussion on the diaspora, see Chapter 6.
19. This is not necessarily a view to which the author subscribes. In both Iran and India, the Zoroastrian minority clung with demonstrable determination to their religion and traditions as they came to interpret and modify these according to the environments in which they found themselves.
20. Notice printed in the *Newsletter* of the Zoroastrian Association of Metropolitan Chicago, June 1989.
21. This latter sentiment, often expressed by Zoroastrians from Iran, is a debatable point. They nevertheless hold to the belief with deep conviction.
22. This refers to the *Shahanshai* calendar in use by the majority of the Parsi community where, owing to a lapse in the leap year intercalation after their arrival in India, the calendar 'slipped' back so that while the *No-ruz* (New Year) ought to fall on the fixed date of 21 March, the spring equinox, the Parsis in fact now celebrate their 'Navroz' in late August. The subject of the Zoroastrian calendar is dealt with by Mary Boyce, *Zoroastrians,Their Religious Beliefs and Practices*,(London 1979) through the various epochs of Iranian history. I am grateful to Mr.Shahrokh Vafadari for discussing in great depth, this subject with me.
23. S.H.Hodivala, *Studies in Parsi History*, (Bombay 1920), p.106.
24. Cf. R.N.Frye, *The Golden Age of Persia: Arabs in the East*, (London 1975), p.52, for an elaboration of this theme.
25. Mary Boyce, 'Zariadres and Zarer', in *BSOAS*, 17/3, (London 1955), p.474.
26. Cf. R.N.Frye, *The Heritage of Persia*, (London 1965), re-print, p.36.
27. Mas'udi's *Kitab al-tanbih* outlines how Sasanian religious and political leaders artificially reduced Parthian chronology from a period of 510 years to one of half that duration.
28. Cf. R.N.Frye, 1965, p.236.
29. See Manekji Limji Hataria's *Ishari-i siyahat-i iran* (Bombay 1865) being his report on his first decade's work in Iran and his references to what he held to be the inadequacy of *dakhmas* in Persia. Kaikhosrow Shahrokh, in his Memoirs, speaks of his aversion to *dakhmas* and his commitment to reforming the system in favour of burial, refer Jehangiri Oshidari, *op.cit.*, p.61.
30. R.N. Frye, 1965, p.237. This matter is, however, disputed. Cf. M.Mole, 'Le probleme Zurvanite', *JA* (1959), p.467.
31. *DkM*, 412.5 - 11, R.C.Zaehner, *Zurvan, A Zoroastrian Dilemma*, (Oxford 1955), p.8.
32. Cf. M.Boyce, 1979, p. 87. See also, James Russell, *Zoroastrianism in Armenia*, (Harvard Iranian Series), vol 5, 1987.
33. M.Boyce, 1979, pp.80-92 where relevant examples are cited.

CHAPTER THREE

THE CONTEMPORARY POLITICAL MILIEUX: IRAN AND INDIA

To further complicate the analysis of contemporary Zoroastrians, the distinctive political entities of Iran and India with which they came to be inextricably linked, were to have other and far-reaching effects upon the groups. While the full political history of the two nations will not be considered here because it is beyond the scope of this work, important political landmarks in Iran and India of the late 19th and 20th centuries relating to the Parsis and Iranian Zoroastrians, will be considered in this chapter.

It is now generally acceptable to argue that there exists a plurality of political cultures in society.[1] No society appears to have a uniform political culture; there is a difference between the elite who control the reigns of power and the masses. There is a relative uniformity of the elite culture in India, whereas the masses are fragmented in terms of caste, religion and languages. (This does not imply that the latter distinctions are not identifiable in the former group). In Iran, two broad types of political culture predominate: authoritarian and antiauthoritarian,[2] which have co-existed in Iranian history, often in conflict.

Indian society is so complex and variegated that it makes highly questionable the assertion that there exists something akin to a pan-Indian society in any meaningful sense. India is nevertheless a reality. There is a certain fractured coherence to this political entity stemming, arguably, from the umbrella of Hinduism which can accommodate every conceivable ritual, custom and philosophy under it. For most of its history, Hinduism has not demonstrated the capacity to produce and sustain a pan-Indian order.

> ...the feeling of Indianness is substantially the product of an alien arrangement (the Raj) and language (English) and to admit that its survival continues to depend to a large extent on those factors, though inevitably modified in an independent and democratic India, is however, to acknowledge that our Indianness is rather insecure.[3]

Within this socio-political entity, the modern Parsi attempts to outline his particular sense of rootedness.

Parsis bring their own particular historical experience to this undertaking: that of a religious refugee group whose domicile in Gujarat acclimatised them to the land, and where they were permitted to retain their religio-ethnic discreteness. In a country where caste laws prevail and the village is the nucleus of the political structure, the very concept of nation-building is an immensely complex phenomenon. The regional-linguistic groups of the country have, however, been accommodated in a federal structure in independent India. The Parsis remain in small groups, spread thin in this vast land, with the largest concentration in Bombay, the capital of the state of Maharashtra. While modern Indians are developing their own brand of Indianness, the Parsis perennially retain their peculiar position in the land of their birth.

Parsis are, nevertheless, becoming more emphatically Indian today. They appear to stress their Indian identity. Despite this pragmatic approach, they do not demonstrate to any great extent an intrinsic sense of belonging to the soil of India. Nationalism, after all, is

> ...a state of mind, permeating the large majority of a people and claiming to permeate all its members; it recognises the nation-state as the ideal form of political organisation and nationality as the source of all creative cultural life and economic well-being. The supreme loyalty of man is therefore due to his nationality, as his own life is supposedly rooted in and made possible by its welfare.[4]

But does the Parsi owe his 'supreme loyalty' to India? Despite his incremental Indianness and a perceptible decline in 'Parsipanu' (Parsi-ness), there is a continuing ambivalence. Parsis have become, quite simply, a peculiar people. They are a religious group, yet they are more than a religious aggregation.[5] They possess a culture, albeit syncretist. They are a recognisable group, but lack what all other people possess: a country they can, without reservations, call their own. As a result they are no longer self-assured, and uncertain of what precisely makes them into a 'people'.

On the other hand, the Iranian Zoroastrian continues to sustain the scars of centuries of persecution. In one respect, however, he is supremely confident: he owes allegiance to the very soil of Iran, and considers himself, in the first instance, an Iranian. Having remained in the ancestral land, Iranian Zoroastrians continue to see themselves as true heirs of the ancient Persians and the upholders of an ancient and immensely glorious heritage. It is no exaggeration to argue that this particular mind-set helped them endure the severe deprivations which accompanied the establishment of Islam in Iran.

It is useful to discuss briefly the distinctive political environments in which the constituent groups of Zoroastrians found themselves. The end of the British Raj and the creation of an independent India were to have far-reaching implications for the sub-continent's Parsis. The close of the Qajar dynasty and the fifty-four years of Pahlavi rule in Iran was to profoundly affect the position of its Zoroastrians. They now ceased being rural agriculturists who were permitted to migrate to the capital, Tehran, and participate in the wealth creation of their country - with certain restrictions. The contemporary Iranian Zoroastrian community is the product of the diverse political-economic influences which have been brought to bear upon them, as much as they are, and remain, a religious minority. A brief outline of the political imperatives which shaped modern Iran and India is germane to our understanding of the Zoroastrians, for whom these two countries represent their land of origin.

IRAN. 'Amongst the great Asiatic nations overthrown by the Arabs, Iran was the first and worst of sufferers, its day having been practically transformed into night.[6] Approximately midway through its recorded history, between Cyrus the Great and the present time, Iran adopted a new Supreme Deity whose prophet and his Book substituted the older, indigenous theology of its own native prophet. This resulted in a peculiarly Iranian dilemma creating a 'double identity'.[7]

Arguably, there are two historical determinants which have fashioned Iran and the Iranians: first, the endeavour to keep intact its distinctive identity in the face of foreign invasions ranging from Alexander of Macedon to the Arabs; and second, the resulting 'schizophrenia' of adopting thereby a religion that perceives Persia's ancient heritage as pagan, and therefore, unacceptable.

Forbis contends that these 'historic tensions' are observable in every Iranian, affecting his life and behaviour. Indeed, the fundamental conflict of the Iranian heritage between Zoroastrian Iran and Islamic Iran, between Ahura Mazda and Allah, between Persepolis and Mecca, heightens the national 'split personality'. The dichotomony of allegiances results in part from the elevation in stature, by some Iranians, of pre-Islamic Iran, the great Achaemenid, Parthian and Sasanian dynasties; and the other dimension - that of the devout Muslims - subscribing to Shi'ite Islam.

The Zoroastrian religion prospered concurrently with the state, and all three dynasties, Achaemenid, Parthian and Sasanian, were intimately linked with the religion's history,[8] while the Safavid dynasty (1500-1700 CE) elevated Shi'ite Islam as Iran's national religion. Thus, there is an intrinsic relationship between the Iranian state and its religious character. The sovereignty of the monarch became a central political feature of Zoroastrianism.[9] These notions of monarchical supremacy and divine right remained in modified form in

Iranian Shi'ism. Thus, Iranian perceptions of monarchy stem from two quite distinct ideologies: the one, bearing upon Zoroastrian Iran, the other on Shi'ite Islam.

When Iran imported Islam, it did not relinquish the earlier interdependency between king and church. Indeed, this was absorbed into the country's socio-political ethos. The central position of a charismatic leader demonstrates that, as Watts observes, '...Shi'ism shows the deep desire and indeed yearning of many Muslims for a divinely guided leader'.[10] The close affiliation of religion and politics in Iranian Shi'ism furnished political leaders with a congenial environment in which to associate themselves with divine authority. Shi'ite Muslims evolved therefore as a distinct political-religious community in Iran: a bond nurtured since the 16th century Safavid epoch. The state bestowed political credibility on the Imamate and in return the Shah was granted a religious legitimacy. The Imam nevertheless retained his temporal authority.[11] Iran's monarchy survived for 2,500 years, in no small measure as a result of the long-standing affiliation between the religious and secular order. 'Shi'a not only is a national religious expression,...(but) it may also be regarded as the religious identity of the Iranian nation'.[12]

The uniqueness of Iran is that, of all Middle Eastern countries, it alone maintained its national identity. While history is inaugurated with Mohammad for Arab Muslims, this is not the case in Iran.[13] Here the glories of the Great Kings, from Cyrus to Khosro, are kept alive in the collective memory, helping create a distinctive national pride. Indeed, Iran was to play a decisive role in the universalization of Islam. It would appear that Islam had to be modified before the Persians found it acceptable, and Iranian civilization itself served as a vehicle for the new religion.[14]

The authoritarian features of Iranian political culture stems from the hierarchical system of monarchy through the centuries, and equally, the hierarchical and dominant role of clergy in society and politics.[15] Until and including the proliferation of revolutionary political cultures in the 20th century, monarchical rule was the norm. Iran resisted being subjugated by foreign powers which was indeed a pre-occupation of Iranian monarchs; and even Arab rule in the 7th and 8th centuries was rationalised by the creation of 'an unorthodox brand of Islam' and Shi'ism's subsequent elevation as the national religion.

Religion contributed to Iran's authoritarian political culture, enhanced by elements of Twelver Shi'ism, such as absolutism, hereditary leadership, elitism and obedience (Behnam, *Cultural Foundations of Iranian Politics*,1989,11). The Imamate, moreover, is central to the control structure of Shi'ite Islam, since its theology asserts the deficiency of secular power and the Imamate's stature as the model of perfection, leading to the *ulema's* position as guardians of the community of the faithful against the power of the secular authority.'These ideas inherent in Shi'ite Islam have been a factor in shaping and motivating political action in Iran, and antiauthoritarianism has found expression in its ideals and religious leadership' (Behnam,1989,12).

Shi'ite Islam has accordingly evolved as a focal point of Iranian national identity. The majority of Iranians are Jafari or Twelver Shi'ites, which Shah Ismail Safavi made the state religion in 1501 as an instrument both of nation-building and anti-Ottoman sentiment.[16] The Safavid dynasty laid claim to religious and political leadership in which the *ulema* held official positions, and promoted an authoritative state religion. Intolerance of non-Shi'as was an inevitable consequence. There were attempts to forcibly convert Zoroastrians in Isfahan and Jews in Kashan, Nain and Isfahan. The office of Sadr was empowered to propagate Shi'ism, supervise judges and administer religious endowments. Although a later monarch, Nadir Shah (1736-47), endeavoured to reduce the influence of the Shi'a, it was by then too firmly entrenched to be dismantled. The Qajar dynasty (1785-1926) would once again solicit the *ulema* and Shi'ism to help rebuild the state. The *ulemas* came to be seen therefore, as the defenders of Persian Islamic identity: the ramifications of such a development for the Zoroastrian community are manifest to the present day.

In the 19th century the *ulemas* were in the vanguard of the Constitutional Movement seeking to remove the monarchy which had mortgaged Iran to foreign financiers. This nationalism, culminating in the Constitutional Revolution of 1905-6, and the revolutionary movement led by Dr.Mohammad Mossadegh in the late 1940s and early 1950s, were events which were to shape the later and more radical Revolution which was to overturn the *status quo* by ousting the monarchy and establishing an Islamic Republic. The latter part of the 19th century saw an increase in foreign encroachment in Iran's affairs, and as such, the Iranians' xenophobia, never far from the surface, was renewed. In the 20th century, popular support and political power were meshed together to confront monarchical power.

Iran escaped colonial status by resisting Western political and economic imperialism during the Qajar dynasty, playing off Russia against Britain in the 19th century. As such, the Constitutional Movement was in response to British and Russian interference in the country, and as much an attempt to temper the arbitrary use of power by the monarch. It was the result of discontent with inefficient government, opposition to outside interference, and a desire for independence from imperial power-brokers.[17] The Qajar monarchs granted major concessions of Iranian territory, natural and economic resources, and eventually central elements of national sovereignty to the rival colonial powers of Great Britain and Russia.[18] While nominally independent, Iran under the Qajars, was an eastern outpost of Russian and British imperialism.

The infamous tobacco concession of 1890, and the oil concessions of 1901, precipitated the Constitutional Revolution, and was the first instance of the Iranian peoples uniting against the autocratic policies of their monarch.[19]

Foreign dominance of the tobacco industry, one of the few luxuries enjoyed by all sections of the Iranian community, resulted in a *fatwa* by a leading ayatollah for a boycott of the substance until the government repealed the concession. By popular pressure the concession was abolished in 1892. Similarly, in 1901, Muzaffar-ed-Din Shah granted a concession to a British consortium headed by William Knox D'Arcy to prospect for petroleum; when in 1908 oil was discovered in south-western Iran, the Anglo-Iranian Oil Company was created to benefit from this concession. The British Government, prior to the outbreak of World War I, procured a controlling interest in the Company whereby the Royal Navy had access to a vital resource through both world wars.[20]

Not surprisingly, Iranians were outraged by the squandering of the nation's resources by the Qajar shahs who had played into the hands of the rivalry between Britain and Russia for hegemony of a strategic area. The monarch, Muzaffar-ed-Din Shah, impotent in the face of foreign intervention, had virtually abrogated his traditional position as ruler by divine right; the Constitutional Movement that resulted was to receive support from the vast majority of Iranians, spearheaded by the clerics, merchants, and intellectuals. The Shah was compelled to accede to the demands of the people, and the *majlis* drafted a Constitution (on the Belgian model), which was ratified by the Shah on 30 December 1906, with Supplementary Fundamental Laws to the Constitution ratified on 8 October 1907.[21]

Some observations on this Constitution[22] and the principles it enshrined are apposite to our theme, insofar as they relate to the legalised discrimination against the Zoroastrian community and other minorities not practising the Shi'ite faith. Thus, Article I proclaims Islam in accordance with Shi'ism, which it is encumbent on the Shah to practise as Iran's official religion. Article II states that the 'Holy Islamic prescriptions' and the laws explicitly promulgated by the Prophet may not be overturned by the *majlis*. Indeed, the very existence of the parliament is predicated on the twelfth Imam, the Shah being under the *ulema's* supervision. This is overseen by the establishment of a committee of five of the most erudite *ulema*, whose task it is to ensure that all legislation is in keeping with Islamic law. When in 1949 an amendment to the Articles of the Constitution was mooted, Article II was made expressly exempt from any revision. Article LVIII states that government ministers must be Muslims of Iranian descent and nationality. Furthermore, the influence of the *ulema* is discernible in the Constitution, so that five *mujtaheds* are empowered to veto legislation which contradicts *sharia*; constraints on the freedom of the media and education where they are deemed to dissent from the Shi'ite philosophy; the king, judges and cabinet ministers must profess the Jafari Shi'ite faith, and only four religions, Islam, Christianity, Judaism, Zoroastrianism,[23] are recognised. The Zoroastrians were institutionally disbarred from holding high offices of state as were the other 'minorities', and the elevation of *sharia* was a severe impediment to their freedom of worship, with no guarantees of personal or communal safety in law.

While Zoroastrian oral tradition could recount several instances of discrimination in law, just one illustration must suffice for now, as noted by Napier Malcolm.

> When Manekji (the Parsi agent) was at Yazd about 1870, two Parsis [as the Zoroastrians of Iran are sometimes referred to] were attacked by two Muslims outside the town, and one was killed, the other being terribly wounded, as they had tried to cut off his head. The Governor brought the criminals to Yazd, but did nothing to them. Manekji then got leave to take them to Tehran. The Prime Minister however, told him that no Muslim would be killed for a Zardushti, and that they would only be bastinadoed. About this time Manekji enquired whether it was true that the blood-price of a Zardushti was to be seven tomans. He got back the official reply that it was to be a little over.[24]

Napier Malcolm points to the distinctive position of 'minorities' in Islamic Iran:

> The religion of the Jews is, of course, held in much greater respect than that of the Parsis, for they are people of the Book, and although Persian Shi'as granted the Zoroastrians a certain share in this status, when they allowed them to continue in the country on the same terms as Jews and Christians, the ordinary Yazdi of today hesitates considerably before he allows that Zoroaster was in any sense a prophet. (*loc.cit*.53).

The institutional intolerance of the Zoroastrian in Iran, therefore, is of long standing.

When the rival major powers realized that Iran would not acquiesce to satellite status, Britain attempted to control events in the country by their tacit support of Reza Khan and his Cossack brigades, which marched into Tehran in 1921 and arrested the government.[25] Iran had thereupon reverted from limited constitutional government to monarchical absolutism under Reza Shah.

The new Shah disregarded the Constitution and dominated the political process, building a highly centralised government; in the 1920s and 1930s, by linking himself with Iranian nationalism and defying Western hegemony in the region, galvanised Iran's xenophobic tendencies. Reza Shah kept order in Iran for twenty years. With the outbreak of World War II in 1939, Iran declared its neutrality. Iranian oil, however, was far too important to the Allied cause, and British and Russian troops jointly occupied Iran in 1941. Reza Shah abdicated, and his son, Mohammad Reza Pahlavi, ascended the throne in 1941 being no more than a figurehead in Tehran in the early years of his reign.

A major political figure, Mohammad Mossadegh, appeared on the national scene to make a significant impact on events in postwar Iran. Disparate groups rallied under the banner of the National Front and focused their attentions on the task of ridding the nation of the Anglo-Iranian oligarchy. Dr.Mossadegh led the National Front when, in 1949, it commenced campaigning for free elections and the imperative of nationalisation of the Anglo-Iranian Oil Company. Reluctantly, the Shah appointed him Prime Minister in 1951, which post he held until 1953.[26] The dominant theme of Mossadegh's premiership - nationalisation of Iran's oil - was to fuel tensions between the ruler and the National Front. By 1953, the Prime Minister had gained a measure of control over the army in his capacity as minister of war; in August 1953, he announced his intention to dissolve the *majlis*, whereupon the Shah dismissed Mossadegh and appointed General Zahedi in his place.[27] Subsequently the army, assisted by a non-partisan mob financed by the Central Intelligence Agency, deposed Mossadegh, returning the Shah, who had earlier fled the country, on 22 August 1953, and in his 'second term' of rulership was to become a strong and somewhat ruthless monarch in his effort to consolidate his power over the entire nation.

Contemporary Iranian nationalism was thus, unquestionably, a reactive phenomenon to a government which had permitted itself to be manipulated by foreign powers. Mohammad Reza Shah, who had been reinstated on his throne with CIA assistance, and under whose aegis American economic assistance and finances dominated the nation's wealth creation, was a ruler who from the very outset had seriously undermined the monarchy which now appeared beholden to a new and perceptibly more threatening foreign power, the USA. Some two decades later, the next and more cataclysmic Iranian Revolution would galvanise support by raising the spectre of the American *shaitan* (satan), urging a return to true Iranian values as upheld in the Shi'ite tradition.

The Pahlavi dynasty attempted the separation of state and religion. Reza Shah had secularised education and the legal system, and endeavoured a modernisation of such practices as were associated with Islam, as for example, the unveiling of women, prohibiting flagellation during Muharram, etc. By way of distancing religion from politics, the Pahlavi Dynasty emphasized Iran's proud pre-Islamic heritage, so that in 1971, when Mohammad Reza Shah held a celebration of the 2500th anniversary of Iranian monarchy, he elevated the memory of Cyrus the Great as a symbol of Persian power and glory as well as his stature as a Great King universally recognised for his religious tolerance. The later Shah, re-working the Cyrus imagery, was attempting to legitimise his position as a strong king as well as establishing the position of his dynasty in a modern nation state. The Pahlavi regime attempted to play down the linguistic, tribal, ethnic and religious differences of Iranian society. Some remaining disabilities for non-Muslims however remained, although essentially all citizens were seen as equal before the law. New laws may be passed but old prejudices stubbornly remain, so that during the 2500th anniversary celebrations, the *ulema* in some Yazdi villages warned against the Shah's extolling of Cyrus' historical stature and reiterated their official position that civilization came to Iran with Islam, and that modern Iranians had nothing in common with the 'pagan' fire worship of Cyrus and Khosro.[28] While this theological position was assumed in opposition to the Shah and his regime, the *ulema's* perception of their rightful role as interpreters of the correct Islamic posture and the continual denigration of Zoroastrian Iran, which had evolved virtually as an article of faith, continued alongside the Pahlavi propensity for exalting an earlier era.

The curious bifurcation of the Iranian national character was most clearly discernible in Pahlavi times. The Zoroastrian representative in the *majlis*, Dr.E.Ycgancgi, could therefore propose a constitutional amendment advocating the removal of the remaining discriminations of second-class citizenship, without incurring the accusation of divided loyalties, which would have attached itself to a similar amendment introduced by the Jewish and Armenian representatives (Fischer,'Persian Society:Transformation and Strain',1977,188). The Shi'ite dogma on being perceived as the original Iranians nevertheless fails to account for the several paradoxes of the watershed event of the 7th century Arab conquest of Iran and the country's earlier international stature. The religious imperative to view man-made law as imperfect and divine law as alone capable of organising a just state, with the *ulema's* consequential right to advise Islamic rulers to abide by the Quran and *hadith*, reflect the underlying tensions that existed throughout Pahlavi times. No matter how rigorously the dynasty espoused the establishment of a modern Iran where religion was divorced from matters of state, Shi'ite Islam was too deeply entrenched in the country and any nostalgia for the earlier Zoroastrian model of state remained impossible of achievement.

In an attempt at stabilizing his regime and to gain ascendancy over influential groups in Iranian society including the clergy, Mohammad Reza Shah's 1963 White Revolution was aimed at domestic politics and emphasized land reform, electoral reform, economic development and increased literacy.[29] Implicit in the Shah's programme, however, was an attempt at diminishing what he perceived as the disruptive influence of the religious leadership by incorporating them into a secularly motivated government. Thus, the Shah's programme to establish government-maintained religious schools was redundant in a country like Iran with its long religious tradition.

Once again, the central tenets of the White Revolution were rejected by the *ulema* which found '...the proposal to grant capitulatory rights to American advisors and military personnel in Iran and their dependents; the contracting of a $200 million loan from the United States for the purchase of military equipment; and the maintenance of diplomatic, commercial and other relations with Israel, a state hostile to the Muslims and Islam'[30] as unacceptable.

Ayatollah Khomeini denounced the White Revolution and delivered a sermon denouncing the Shah's rule from his pulpit at the Faiziyeh Madrasa in Qum; on 22 March 1963 the Shah dispatched paratroopers and security police to the seminary. Even though several students were killed, the Ayatollah's denunciations continued and spread to Mashad. Unwilling to tolerate this, the Shah had the religious leader arrested on 5 June 1963.[31] Khomeini's arrest had coincided with the Muharram, and no longer was opposition confined to the clerics, but gained vociferous support from the masses in Tehran and throughout the country. Khomeini was released in April 1964 and continued his denunciation of the Pahlavi regime. Consequently his popularity increased and spread among the middle ranks of the *ulema* and younger clergy. He was once again arrested in November 1964, exiled to Turkey, and later granted permission to move to the sacred Shi'a city of Najaf in Iraq, in 1965, from where he led the opposition against the Shah. Disturbances within Iran continued throughout the 1960s and 1970s, with a historic rapprochement between students in the Nationalist Movement and the anti-Shah clergy. This was to become a central feature in the Revolution of 1979.

> There exists, then, a remarkable continuity in the political role of the *ulema* in Iran, a tradition of opposition to autocratic power that links the 19th century with the present...Despite all the inroads of the modern age, the Iranian national consciousness still remains wedded to Shi'a Islam, and when the integrity of the nation is held to be threatened by internal autocracy and foreign hegemony, protests in religious terms will continue to be voiced, and the appeals of men such as Ayatullah Khumayni to be widely heeded.[32]

On February 1 1979 Ayatollah Ruhollah Musavi Khomeini returned to Iran after more than fourteen years in exile to proclaim the Islamic Republic of Iran and the overthrow of the Pahlavi Dynasty. Dr. Ali Shariati, a major influence in shaping the intellectual rationale behind the movement, emphasized that Muslims ought to 'rediscover true Islam' for themselves.[33] Ironically, it had been Mohammad Reza Shah's neo-patrimonial form of monarchy which, by attempting to neutralise religion and suppressing political opposition, had made religion the principal currency of political protest. 'The voice of the opposition became that of Islam' (Fischer,*Iran,From Religious Disputes to Revolution*,1980,190). The Islamic Revolution reaffirmed Shi'ism as a powerful 'social force' in Iran.

Shaykh Fazlollah Nuri[34] argued that for Iran to follow the 'European model' would be in contravention of the essentials of Islam. Thus, European taxation was in contra-distinction to the Islamic *zakat* and other taxes; European concepts of equality before the law of all citizens was unacceptable in Islamic terms of reference where the Jews, Zoroastrians, Christians and *kafirs* (unbelievers) were deemed unequal in law, a central tenet enshrined in Article VIII of the 1905 Constitution.

By 1971 Khomeini had already advocated non-cooperation with the political order, and enunciated a theory of Islamic government.[35] His concept of Islamic government was 'neither authoritarian' nor constitutional in the modern sense, but rather, it is conditioned by the Quran and *sunnat* (or customs associated with the Prophet and Imams). Further, since all Muslims aspire to follow God's law, government is not dependent on force but merely charts agenda and procedures. Khomeini's antagonism of the Pahlavis was reflected in the position he took that there ought to be no castles or stipends for the royal family 'which eat up half the budget of the state'.[36]

Faith and the morality it generates is, therefore, the kernel of Islamic political and economic theory. Without the acquiescence of the Muslims, the structure of justice would founder. To keep the Islamic concept of faith in the forefront of the communal mind, *rowzas* (sermons), especially in the month of Ramadan, are given.[37] Fischer quotes a *rowza* given by Hashem-Iraqi on 8 Ramadan 1975, in the Husaynabad Masjid at Qum:

...A Muslim who fasts but after breaking his fast speaks ill of his fellow Muslim does as if he were eating the corpse of his fellow Muslim. *Ghaybat* is the food of the dogs ...*ghaybat-i kafir* (speaking ill of an unbeliever) is unimportant, and even, *ghaybat-i Musalman ghayr-i mu'min* (speaking ill of Muslims who are not believers), who are not Shi'a, is unimportant. If you slander them it is too bad, but no matter. God does not accord them honour...

An ethos of harassing minorities has long been a part of Shi'ite Iranian practice. Fischer observes that public water fountains in Yazd were reserved exclusively for Muslims as late as 1970 (Fischer,1980,186); glasses in which non-Muslims were served tea were 'washed with special thoroughness', and indeed, many Muslims would refuse to accept tea from non-Muslims.[38] The rationale for such behaviour is the concept of *najes*, stemming from the Shi'ite *risalas* (explanatory texts on problems of religion), which takes the position that the touch of a non-Muslim is impure.[39] Not surprisingly, non-Muslim Iranians have for the most part remained outside the political protests of the 1970s, which were themselves couched in Islamic idiom. (However, some non-Muslim radicals, including Zoroastrians, took part in the anti-Shah uprisings, as did some officers in the armed forces, some of whom were executed for treason).

The 1905 Constitution had institutionalised the second-class status of non-Jafari Shi'ites by proscribing them from holding positions as judges or cabinet ministers. The minorities had participated in the National Front activities of the 1940s which had emphasized Iranian national identity and independence from foreign interventions in the country. The goals of the 1979 Revolution, however, were overtly Islamic as opposed to secular, and meant that minority groups were fearful for their longer-term future. In the winter of 1978, handbills and graffiti calling for the death of Zoroastrians, Jews, Assyrians and Armenians evoked memories of religious riots that had occurred at the turn of the century (Fischer,1980, 227). In the case of the Zoroastrian community particularly, an event which caused considerable anxiety was the appearance of some 'guerrillas' who, after the installation of the Bazargan government, entered the main fire temple in Tehran, removed the portrait of the Prophet Zarathushtra, and replaced it with one of Khomeini. An old Zoroastrian lady was heard to comment at the time that indeed, that was going too far (Fischer,1980,227).

'The potency of the Islamic Revolution evolved from its Islamic character...Within the last century in Iran, religion expanded further as a forum of opinion-making and political articulation incapable of being throttled by the Iranian state'.[40] Behnam shrewdly observes that, even though leadership has been transferred from the monarch to the clergy, inherent in Shi'ite doctrine is a fundamental mistrust of all government.[41] While content in former times to guide political events (even when actively opposing regimes), the 1979 Revolution, by concentrating political power in the clergy, had catapulted it into becoming the 'political authority' and operating from within the political system. Post-revolutionary Iran, therefore, has effectively denuded itself of the traditional levers of opposition.Since the *mullahs* themselves have been enfolded within government, any political opposition is deemed automatically to be anti-Islamic. 'The Islamic Republican party and Ayatollah Khumayni have arisen from the ashes of the Islamic Revolution as the new political elite, a religious elite' (Behnam,1989,152).

The source of Iranian national identity has been religion. The laws of Islam have greater potency than the laws of the state,[42] and despite the Pahlavis' attempts at the secularization of society, the fact that an overwhelming majority of the population subscribes to the theology of Ithna Ashari Shi'ism helps define the parameters of contemporary Iran. In their daily lives, for several centuries now, Iranians have been steered by the Shi'ite religious order which encompassed the spiritual, secular and economic institutions of the land. It bears reiteration that religion is an ingrained cultural norm in Iran, and those Iranian nationals who do not subscribe to Shi'ite theology remain by definition beyond the social, economic, political, legal and religious parameters of the state.

INDIA. Ever since they settled in India, the survival of the Parsis as a minority could only be assured by their being punctiliously loyal to every ruling authority. They distanced themselves from conflicts between India's diverse groups, and tensions between the centre and provinces. From the earliest years of domicile, the Parsi community in India was aware of its inability to enforce its own interests against the will of the rulers. In due course they came to realize that a tradition of loyalty to the ruling authority would engender a political climate which alone could guarantee their security. The only condition for their fealty to the state was that they could continue to observe their religion unhindered.

The Parsi conception of the good ruler, one included in the *Afringan* prayer,[43] emphasized justice and tolerance.

> Good government is that which maintains and orders (undisturbed) the law and custom of the city people and (the) poor, and thrusts out improper law and custom...and keeps in progress the worship of God, and duties, and good works, and causes friendship and intercession for the poor.[44]

The Parsis traced their security - their economic and social prosperity - to the 'blessing' of British rule, which they identified with 'good government'. Loyalty to the British was thus for them a self-evident maxim. Parsi perception of their status in India was that upon British departure, they would become politically unimportant as a minority. An independent India was seen as being inimical to Parsi interests; continuing British suzerainty as beneficial to the community. They seized every opportunity to demonstrate their loyalty to the British rulers. On royal birthdays, coronations, the arrival of a new viceroy as examples, traditional *jashans* were held at public meetings of the Parsi community in various Indian towns. The religious character of the thanksgiving ceremony, while emphasizing group solidarity, served equally to emphasize allegiance to the ruler. Parsi aristocrats and high priests would preside over these *jashans*, their presence lending them a semi-official status.

Nevertheless, the Parsis were not a homogeneous social group with uniform political attitudes. They had no body or institution authorized to represent the community politically, or make politically binding decisions on its behalf. Since the priesthood had become ineffective in the 18th century, the Panchayat, which had evolved into the chief charitable institution of the community, claimed a certain degree of authority for its representation. There were unofficial leaders, however: specifically the Parsi aristocracy consisting of those families whose members had been raised to the Baronetcy. Among these, the Jeejeebhoy family were the most prominent since the middle of the 19th century.[45] In reality, though, neither the Panchayat nor the aristocrats had a mandate for leadership, and with the changing political climate in India, and impending independence, a void in terms of community representation would make itself noticed.

Indeed, the formation of a homogeneous political attitude presupposes a monolithic community awareness which was absent among the Parsis from approximately the mid-19th century. Tensions having arisen as a result of the divergent degrees of westernization and social mobilization, caused an identity crisis within the whole community,[46] evident to the present time.

The majority of the community members remained aloof from Indian society, some even regarding themselves as a 'purely white race'.[47] Some from among this group aimed at as close a connection with the British as possible; the British on their part reacted sympathetically, directing them into avenues which helped strengthen their colonial system. Thus, by ennobling, some Parsis acquired a rather exalted position within the community, while being simultaneously indebted to the crown, engendering a fairly universal community loyalty to the ruler. By 1946, 63 Parsis had been knighted; of the four Indians who had been made hereditary baronets up till 1908, three were Parsis.[48] Furthermore, many British considered the Parsis like themselves to be foreigners in India, occasionally perceiving of them as an elite:'Then, gentlemen, Parsis, I would ask you to remember that you have what is called the very bluest blood in Asia'.[49] The mutual admiration of the great imperial power and a dependent minority nonetheless had its limitations. The English hesitated at considering the Parsis as one of their own, despite sections of the latter community being on a par with them in terms of education and manners. The Parsis' own disinclination for identifying themselves with other 'natives' resulted in an 'intellectual alienation' from India without, however, their finding an independent identity of their own, or reference to either the British or the Indians.[50]   Despite their attitude of detachment from the emerging Indian nation, the Parsis were accepted as members of this polity,[51] no doubt owing to their leading role in the early phase of the nationalist movement. Parsi contributions to social reform, education and economic development in India, and their well-known generosity which often benefited non-Parsis in India and abroad[52], reinforced their acceptability by fellow Indians. Not surprisingly, therefore, the Hindu patriot, Sir Narayanrao Chandavarkar, at Dadabhai Naoroji's funeral, spoke of him as a '...second Zoroaster sent to India to make the sun of righteousness and of India's future progress shine more and more...'[53]

Dadabhai Naoroji, Sir Pherozeshah Mehta and Dinshaw Wacha played a leading role at the turn of the 20th century in Indian politics. They spoke on behalf of all Indians in seeking independence from the imperial power, and proclaimed themselves Indians first and foremost, and Parsis second. Mehta's famous utterance confirms this position:

> ...To my mind, a Parsi is a better and truer Parsi, as a Mohammedan or Hindu is a better and truer Mohammedan or Hindu, the more he is attached to the land which gave him birth, the more he is bound in brotherly relations and affections to all the children of the soil...[54]

Initially, the concept of an 'autonomous Indian identity' was instigated by socio-cultural as opposed to a pan-Indian national consciousness. The shift in status from an inactive British subject to participant within the political system was available, within limitations, to the metropolitan elites of Calcutta, Bombay and Madras.

> Those Indians coming into contact with European ideas and values went through an extensive process of acculturation that led, in an osmotic permeation of two cultural systems, to a reformulation, both of the individual as well as the collective identity, a process that aimed, in its political dimension, at a gradual participation in various socio-political spheres.[55]

By the mid-19th century, Western education in India had resulted in the establishment of political associations in those three major cities. The regional limitations of their activities meant that a pan-Indian national consciousness was lacking. In due course, with the infiltration of European ideas throughout the land, a reactionary neo-Hindu renaissance was created. It challenged the European political and socio-cultural ideolgy and helped fashion a distinct 'Indian' identity.[56] The developing national consciousness inspired the various politically active groups across the country to band together, resulting in the founding in Bombay in December 1885 of the Indian National Congress.

The founder members of the Congress were in fact a product of British-Indian education; they were Indians who had enthusiastically embraced European political philosophy and subscribed to western concepts of democracy and the nation-state. The principal aim of the architects of the national party was the reformation of British rule in India. Their basic attitude remained one of loyalty to the Crown, and through active participation in the Government's decision-making, aspired to achieve its declared goal. This remained the dominant theme of Congress politics upto the first decade of the 20th century, when its strategy and prime cause were modified with the rise to prominence of Tilak, the extremists (as opposed to the earlier moderates), of Bengal and Punjab especially, and finally, Gandhi. With Gandhi's policy of non-cooperation and civil disobedience directed towards achieving political independence, the Congress became a mass movement on a national scale. Some Parsis had been instrumental in the earliest phase of the Congress: Dadabhai Naoroji was a founder member of the nationalist movement and its first president, and while it remained in its moderate phase, supported by westernized intellectuals, there was an influential group of Parsis who were closely involved with it. It was the ascendancy of Tilak and Gandhi, and the transformation of the philosophical core of the movement, which led to the alienation of the Parsi community from Congress' expressed goals and its methods of achievement.

The chief endeavour of the bulk of the Parsi community was to fix an identity outside the emerging Indian nation, but for a small group who were active in Congress and indeed referred to as 'Congress Parsis'. For the latter, the only rational way forward was for the community to progress in harmony with the other Indian groups participating in Congress to gain Indian independence.

For Dadabhai Naoroji, his citizenship of the Indian nation was indeed of greater significance to him than being a Parsi.

> Whether I am a Hindu, a Mohammedan, a Parsi, a Christian, or any other creed, I am above all an Indian. Our country is India; our nationality is Indian.[57]

While 'Congress Parsis' such as Naoroji, Mehta and Wacha were applauded by the Indian nationalists, their activities were regarded with some mistrust by the majority of the Parsis. Expressing his frustration, Naoroji sets out his position in a letter (in 1888) to Wacha:

> I have been much distressed about the view some Parsis are taking that we should dissociate ourselves from the Hindus and Mohammedans. Nothing could be more suicidal. We are India's and India is our mother country, and we can only sink or swim with, and as, Indians. If we break with the Indians, our fate will be that of a crow in peacock's feathers. The English will in no time pluck out our feathers.[58]

The perennial question of Parsi identity vis-a-vis Indian identity therefore, assumed critical proportions in the community's assessment of its position in an independent India. If the country opted for a secular nationalism, minorities such as the Parsis (and others, such as the Muslims of India), might participate in the movement and embrace the exercise with uneasy confidence; were Hindu renaissance to become the fulcrum of the freedom movement, the Parsis, habitually aliens in Hindu and Muslim socio-cultural and religious environments, could be expected to continue to maintain their distance from the political scenario. The fact that the 'Congress Parsis' continued strenuously to proclaim their 'Indian identity', as much for the benefit of their Indian audience as well as to clarify their position for their co-religionists, emphasizes the Parsi quandary: their millenial domicile in India had not automatically resulted in their acquisition of a socio-emotive bond with the country. Since the invention of a turn-of-century pan-Indian political philosophy in reaction to the foreign ruler, the Parsi community's position on the margins of the nationalist movement was not as isolated as has often been portrayed.

The multi-ethnic, multi-religious conglomerate of India indicated that, were the nationalist movement to emphasize the Hindu dimension of the country's religious and philosophical base and apply it in fashioning the independent state, the longer-term future for the country would be bleak indeed. Perceiving such danger, Dadabhai Naoroji advocated a secular nationalism for shaping an all-Indian nationalism by ignoring the several diverse religious traditions of the sub-continent. This concept of secular nationalism was a central tenet of Congress in its earliest phase; later, the national movement was radicalised by the neo-Hindu revanchism of persons such as Tilak, Lajpat Rai, Vivekananda and Sri Aurobindo. Parsis, being external to the Hindu tradition, thus had, at best, very limited access to the 'socio-religious nationalism' of the Congress under Tilak and Gandhi.

While 'Congress Parsis' reflected sincerely patriotic Indian sentiments, their roles in the Indian National Congress concentrated on creating a genuinely secular democracy once the British departed from India. Some Parsis participated in the Congress meetings of 1885-1909. By 1906 the political agenda in India was being perceptibly altered. In that year the Muslim League was established - an event coinciding with Tilak's policy of combining religious symbolism with political ideology. Parsis began to fear that the Congress could turn into a Hindu religious movement. For the community therefore, uncertain of their future security in an independent India, was their perception of the twin pronged negative developments they had always feared: the introduction of religion into the political arena, and the development of communalism with the creation of the Muslim League. The British Government's introduction of the Morley-Minto Act in 1909, establishing the principle of separate electorates, was later to influence Parsi political demands.

The accelerating political developments compelled the community to reassess its position. Their historical memory made them apprehensive of militant Hinduism which might conceivably inflict similar suffering upon the Parsis as had been visited upon their ancestors by the Arab conquerors of

Iran. An overwhelming majority therefore felt that their own interests would best be served by a continuing British presence in India

> ...The union of the Mohammedans and the Hindus, and with them the union of the Parsis, no doubt looks very well on paper, but alas! how ghastly and impracticable is such a scheme...Instead of working for the cause of the Home Rule and the so-called union between Indian communities, let us concentrate all our attention on keeping our homes, our religion, and our society safe.[59]

With political power in the independence movement being transferred from western educated moderate politicians to the extremists, by 1931 the British Government was preparing to exit from India's political stage. From then on, the Parsis' role in shaping India's future had become inconsequential. Gandhi's rise in national politics and the central role of the non-cooperation movement resulted in violent reactions against British hegemony in India.

The Parsi called for a Panchayat meeting to discuss the issue of the community's loyalty to the government.[60] The *Hindi Punch*[61], however, cautioned against it for fear that by singling out the Parsis, it might conceivably weaken their future position in the country.

Not only were large sections of the community fearful of being engulfed by a religious revival of Hinduism as a backlash to British rule, but the provisions for what appeared to them as over-representation of the Muslims on the Viceroy's Executive Council led to the reflection that:

> ...the Parsis, too proud to beg, are nowhere in the scheme, except in as much as a minority may hope to break through the serried ranks of an overwhelming majority. But it must be remembered that they are only 'refugees' and runaways from their native land and ought to be thankful even for small mercies.[62]

The *Hindi Punch* was reflecting a growing unease in the community, an increasing perception of themselves as aliens in the land of their birth. Their unease regarding their future in an independent India had been compounded by having been so obviously ignored by the British Government, in terms of separate representation as outlined by the Reform Bill introduced in Parliament on 16 February 1909.[63]

Thus, even before the outbreak of World War I, the Parsis were beginning to revaluate their notion of their relationship to India, which they saw as the 'motherland', and to Iran, their 'fatherland'. The general feeling of the community was that, following the close of Raj, India would be dominated by its two major constituent factions, Hindus and Muslims. They began to question where precisely they would fit in. The dilemma was heightened, through the community's failure to produce other charismatic personalities on the communal and national stage who could replace Dadabhai Naoroji and Sir Pherozeshah Mehta - by 1911, they were no longer protagonists on the Indian political stage. With their departure the Indian independence movement was advancing inexorably towards a non-radical political stance.

The majority of Parsis had desisted from endorsing Gandhi's activities in removing the British from India, and this was bound to result in some derision being poured on them, as was the case when the veteran Hindu politician, V.J.Patel asked rhetorically, 'did the Parsis think that if Hindus and Mohammedans ruled them they would be hanged?'[64]

In 1921 Gandhi had successfully mobilized Indian opinion against the visit of the Prince of Wales. The majority of Indians boycotted the celebrations; those who did not, were victims of a violent riot. The Parsis were indeed the major target, with fifty-three killed in four days of rioting.[65] Parsis had

> ...never dreamt in their wildest dreams that they would suddenly be pounced upon by Hindu and Muslim hooligans, their leaders subjected to insults and assaults, their heads broken, their properties destroyed and their places of religious worship threatened with desecration...[66]

Gandhi suspended the boycott, took the blame for the violence upon himself, and called a meeting of Hindus, Muslims and Parsis. The event nevertheless reinforced Parsi fears for their longer-term safety under Hindu and Muslim rule, this having been the first recorded incident of Hindus and Muslims joining forces against them. There is an inversely proportional 'distinct relationship'[67] between the fortunes of Gandhi and the Parsis in Indian politics: as the former's influence in national politics waxed, the latter's waned.

Parsi authority on the national stage had been based on their educational superiority, through which they had prospered during the late 19th and early 20th century when politics was firmly in the hands of the intelligentsia. With the transference of political power from the preserve of the western educated to the grasp of the masses, the Parsis began to absent themselves from the events shaping the nation. There were of course some exceptions, notably Khurshed Nariman and Minoo Masani, who were affiliated to the so-called extremist wing of the Congress Party. In the main, the Parsi politicians such as Naoroji, Mehta, Wacha and Malabari, had risen from the liberal ranks. With the *swarajists'* (independence) success in both council and Legislative Assembly elections in 1923, the fate of the moderates had doubtless been sealed. Only one moderate Parsi was elected to the Bombay Legislative

Council, Dr.Dadachanji,[68] emphasizing the fact that the Parsis were indeed, '...numerically small, a microscopic minority, a negligible quantity'.[69] In October 1929, the Labour Government of Ramsey MacDonald announced the first Round Table Conference to be held in London to discuss India's political future. It was meant to prepare the country for dominion status.[70] Gandhi made unrealistic demands, one being that Conference should be preceded by an amnesty for all political prisoners; another that the Congress Party should have majority representatives at the talks, and again, that the talks should result in the declaration of dominion status for India.[71] The then Viceroy, Irwin, not surprisingly, would not concede to Gandhi's demands, whereupon the latter boycotted the Conference and resumed civil disobedience. The National Liberal Federation, presided over by the Parsi, Sir Pheroze Sethna, took a more positive attitude to the talks.[72] The famous Salt March, led by Gandhi, then commenced on 6 April 1930 when he made salt at Dandhi. The Parsi politician Khurshed Nariman, who was president of the Bombay Provincial Congress Committee, had masterminded the mass meeting in Bombay when salt was made at Worli[73] and, like Gandhi, he was arrested and sentenced to four years' imprisonment.[74]

According to *Hindi Punch*, Nariman's arrest had steered the Parsis towards the nationalist movement. Even though the majority of the Parsis had refrained from joining the nationalist movement, the 'residue is large enough to cause surprise to the community itself and to outsiders'.[75] The Parsis' renewed interest in Indian nationalism was reflected in the increased popularity of the Parsi Rajkiya Sabha, started a decade earlier,[76] and made noticeable at a particular meeting in July 1930 where the Parsi women were all wearing nationalist sarees. This was the first public indication of the Parsis having joined the nationalist movement in sizeable numbers.

In January 1931, despite Tory opposition, particularly from Winston Churchill, the Round Table Conference was a success. The Parsi delegates, Sethna, Mody and Jehangir were among those who had signed an appeal to both government and the Congress to arrive at an accord which would enable the Conference to be more representative.[77] India was now firmly on the road to independence, and the Parsis were preparing to counter the difficulties experienced in adapting to their position in an India without the protective umbrella of the British.

Kulke argues convincingly[78] that since Hinduism was the cultural heritage of India, it could manifestly become the ideological basis of an Indian nationalism and contribute towards a novel Indian 'historical consciousness', whereas the Parsis, who 'lacked a corresponding access and attachment to Indian history', were outside the unfolding independence movement. As nationalistic tendencies in India escalated, a corresponding religious renaissance, dormant since the mid-19th century, came to prominence in the Parsi community - the rediscovery of their Iranian heritage. The Parsis' high degree of westernization was juxtaposed alongside the more traditionally perceived historical determinates such as the Persian language;[79] the renewed enthusiasm to review the national epic, the *Shah-nameh*; and the glorying in the achievements of the ancient Achaemenid, Parthian and Sasanian dynasties. The quasi-historical past of Iran, the Pishdadian and Kayanian dynasties, the latter epoch being the period of Zarathushtra's birth itself, was most especially invoked by the community at large. The Parsis came to emphasize their historical and religious roots in psychological terms which, for them, were still those of Zoroastrian Iran.

They were stimulated in their nostalgia for Iran through two developments: the steadily improving conditions in Iran for the Zoroastrians following the efforts of the Amelioration Society to remove the *jizya*;[80] and the Pahlavi dynasty's proclivity in viewing the Parsis as relatives of 'modern' Iranians, and to consider Iranian national identity as an additional dimension of their own group consciousness. The Iran League was founded in 1922, and among its several goals were that Parsis ought to continue to maintain their links with Iran; to regard Iran with patriotic fervour as in the past; to better the conditions of Zoroastrians in Iran, etc.[81]

The rise of modern Iranian nationalism under Reza Shah Pahlavi led to the Zoroastrian religion being elevated as the authentic Iranian religion and an integral part of the national heritage.[82] The Iranian government was well disposed to Parsi overtures and, from 1923, semi-official authorities in Iran invited Parsis to return to their home country.[83] The *Parsi Prakash* recorded an appeal to the Parsis by Mirza Ali Khan Hekmat Shirazi at the Court of Reza Shah:

> ...I am happy that since the last two years the Parsis of India have turned their thoughts towards Iran and are coming to their beloved country. In earlier times they had to go away compulsorily from the country...It is necessary for this country that it gathers its children around it, and strives for greatness and prosperity, and at the same time, its lawful children have the right to benefit from its soil and waters...There is no doubt that Zoroastrians are Iranians...[84]

Similarly, Reza Shah, welcoming a Parsi delegation in 1932 stated:

> You Parsis are as much the children of this soil as any other Iranians, and so you are as much entitled to have your proper share in its development as any other nationals...We suggest that the Parsis who are still the sons of Iran though separated from her, should look upon this country today as their own, and differentiate it from its immediate past, and strive to benefit

from her developments...[85]

Within the Parsi community, too, several articles and speeches by individuals appeared urging re-establishment of ties with the *madar vatan*. A good illustration of how some Parsis felt alienated from India and inspired by patriotic fervour for Iran, was an article by a Mr.Mehrjee:

> For a Parsi to forget Iran is to forget the best part of him - his individuality...The modern Parsi, claim he ever so stressfully his Indian citizenship, is, and must ultimately be, Iranian...That the Parsis of the 20th century will be severely handicapped in the competitive struggles of the future is an assured truth...For the Parsi way of life is not the way of life of the Indian, and the Parsi way of thinking is not the Indian way of thinking.[86]

Other writers emphasized their belief that Parsis were indeed Iranian nationals;[87] some journals reported that the Parsi Association was investigating possible Parsi investment in Iranian commerce and industry.[88] Mr.J.P.Mistry, Secretary of the Association, had in fact made applications on behalf of Parsis to the Persian government for posts in revenue, customs, the municipality, police and telegraph departments.[89]

The Parsis had thereby begun to seek refuge in their Iranian identity. They suffered misgivings concerning their future in India, curiously at a time when they still retained their position of superiority in political, commercial and social spheres.[90] The community appeared to have been at a turning point in its relationship to India. By asserting the Iranian dimension of their group identity, they were reinforcing the point that they saw themselves as racially (and religiously) distinct from other Indians; they retreated into their Iranian 'self' as a reflexive response to their fears concerning India's unknown future, when Hindus and Muslims in the country were rapidly beginning to usurp the positions of economic and social superiority formerly occupied by the Parsis. In a very real sense, therefore, the Parsis had begun to absent themselves from Indian society and the emerging polity.

It would be inaccurate to suggest, however, a complete unanimity of pro-Iranian sentiment in the community, as reflected by the observation that the Parsis had originally fled from an 'intolerant fatherland to seek the willing hospitality of alien shores'.[91] The uncertainty regarding their place in an independent India led some sections to call alternatively for a 'mini' Parsi state, or a 'Parsi Colony' of, for instance, 6,000 acres outside Sukkur in Gujarat, where they could return to the ancestral vocation as agriculturists.[92] Yet others recommended that the entire community should emigrate and found a separate 'Colony' beyond India. The call for a distinct Parsi Colony was made as early as 1905, by Khan Bahadur Patel of Quetta:

...Even previous to the advent of the British, they (the Parsis) were not considered natives of India, and if the British were to leave India, should this ever come to pass, they will still be looked upon as aliens. It is therefore, wise and politic for the Parsis to prepare for themselves a haven of refuge by founding a colony...[93]

Even though the community failed to realize either a return to Iran or the establishment of a 'Colony' or independent country, it was quite clearly a manifestation of their acute sense of insecurity concerning their future in a country from which, despite their millenial residence, they were considerably distanced.

There were well-defined responses from within the Parsi community to India's independence. The 'Congress Parsis' had achieved the aim for which they had long struggled; but the majority of the community which had in fact resisted the national movement and been reluctant to see the British depart, were compelled to reinterpret their position in Indian society. The instinctive pragmatism of the community, well-honed over the centuries, was to assist them to arrive at a workable formula for the new political realities. In fact, the transition process was relatively painless for the Parsis. Kulke argues that the new rulers of India accepted them as Indians without the need for the latter to justify themselves as such, and in this the community was aided by having 'a nationalistic alibi', namely, the three great Parsi politicians, Naoroji, Mehta and Wacha. This Parsi 'heritage' which had lain dormant for some decades was revitalised now that the occasion demanded it.[94]

A certain urgency became noticeable in the adjustment process to the new India. A.D.Shroff suggested at the Parsi Nationalist Conference that, 'instead of claiming all sorts of concessions as a minority, we should identify ourselves with Indians and make ourselves indispensable to the country'.[95] On 10 August 1947, five days prior to Independence, Parsis marched in procession to the statues of Naoroji, Mehta and Wacha, led by the Parsi mayor of Bombay, Ardeshir Sabawala,[96] culminating in a meeting where the President of the Parsi Panchayat, Sir Shapur Billimoria stated, '...we will continue to give our best to the country and the Government'.[97] Official pronouncements made on behalf of the community now testified to a positive attitude towards independent India.

For the vast majority of Parsis, nevertheless, Indian independence had never been a desirable aim, and their apprehensions were to remain. Even while individual Parsis began participating in Indian politics (Sir Homi Mody was appointed Governor of Uttar Pradesh in 1949; later his son, Piloo, entered Parliament; Homi Taleyarkhan held several portfolios such as Minister of Education for Maharashtra 1962-67, Governor of Sikkim in 1981, and latterly with responsibilities on the 'Minorities Commission', to name a few prominent

Parsi politicians), the community retained a healthy mistrust of the success of the newly independent nation. The persistent Parsi restraint in relation to the new political authority in the country is a novel feature of their history in India. They appear, however, to make a clear distinction between the system in general (secular democracy) of which they approve, and the political parties vying for power, which they find in the main objectionable. They retain their self-conscious awareness as an elite, based on their past achievements, which privileged position they have lost after 1947. However, while they have been diminished politically and economically, the Parsis have not been endangered to date, either by Indian society, or the government.

Unlike Iran where the Zoroastrians and other minorities were proscribed from participating in business and secular activities, there were never any such prohibitions upon the Parsi community, since the Constitution of India is emphatically secular. To the contrary, they have shared in the wealth creation of India without restrictions having been placed upon them either by the British rulers or, latterly, by the Indian government. Once the country had achieved independence and the British had departed, the Parsis, by and large, having absented themselves from political activity, continued to participate in spheres as diverse as: economic, military, educational, legal, medical and cultural. Parsi contributions to India through the generations came to be out of all proportion to their miniscule size, and while these have been thoroughly documented,[98] some contemporary Parsis who have made outstanding contributions to the country, deserve to be mentioned.

Jamsetjee Tata's establishment of an iron and steel industry on a national scale, when on December 2, 1911 the first iron ore was mass-smelted in India, was to help the country move into the industrial age. The House of Tata was to develop and expand into several areas, from hydro-electric works to engineering and locomotives, civil aviation, the establishment of the first (Tata) Institute of Social Sciences in the country, a research centre for cancer, patronage of the arts and the establishment of a scholarship foundation for higher education.[99]

After the House of Tata, another industrial giant in India is Godrej Ltd., founded by Ardeshir Godrej, best-known for manufacturing locks and safes, and having expanded since 1958 to manufacturing the first Indian refrigerators, forklift trucks, and oil-based chemicals for industry.

Another major contribution to India's industrial development has been made by Minoo Dastur, founder of M.N.Dastur, Calcutta, and Dastur Engineering International GmbH, Dusseldorf, the first Indian firm to be established as international consulting engineers.

The Parsis have also been well-represented in the professions: Homi Seervai, a former Advocate General of Bombay; Nani Palkhiwalla, a former Indian Ambassador to Washington and an expert on Indian Constitutional Law; the former nuclear physicist, Dr.Homi Bhabha; former Air Marshal Aspi

Engineer; Field Marshal Sam Manekshaw; Dr. Rustom Vakil referred to as 'the father of Indian cardiology'.Equally, Parsis were pioneers in several other fields, such as ship-building (the Wadia family); banking (the person responsible for revolutionising Indian banking was Sir Sorabji Pochkhanawala); opthalmology (Dinshaw M. Dastur & Co. of Bombay is over a hundred years old); dairy products (the Polson family). In the arts, among the well-established names of recent years are Jehangir Sabhavala, Pinaz Masani the internationally renown *ghazal* singer; Zubin Mehta retiring conductor of the New York Philharmonic Orchestra, and several others.

In independent India, the Parsis have kept alive their wealth-creating activities, since the state itself has not circumscribed such enterprise. Their earlier fears of living in a country without a protective outside power have so far been unfounded. This does not, however, signify any increased level of confidence in the new political environment; rather, Parsi ambiguity towards their country remains in evidence.[100] So long as a secular democracy continues to underpin the political philosophy of this disparate land, the Parsis will continue to retain some degree of guarded confidence. The secular nature of Indian democracy, and the democratic structure of the government remain fragile in the Indian environment. The reality of their numerical paucity among India's masses implies that the Parsis' singular position in the country: perennially on the margins of Indian society, a community the nature of whose economic stature has not led to persecutions or pogroms by the majority, has unexplicably resulted in undermining Parsi self-confidence. The community's westernization in secular matters combined with pride in their religion, has hindered access to Indian society and its value system. This delineates the marginality of the community's existence, which persists through to the present time.

This brief overview of the political environments of Iran and India - in the former, where Zoroastrians are noticeable by their absence from the national stage, in the latter, where the Parsis played leading roles in British India and the early years of the Indian independence struggle - points to the distinctive historical experiences of the two communities. Nevertheless, two features of the Zoroastrian position are clearly in evidence: their marginality in both Iran and India, and the role of religion in shaping national identity. In the case of India, as discussed in Chapter 2, the Hindu caste structure based on Hindu religious principles, by compartmentalising society, permits the constituent elements of that society to evolve their distinctive identities; in Iran, Jafari Shi'ism is the proclaimed national religion. Within these two enforcing parameters, the Zoroastrians of Iran and India have been compelled to operate.

The major impedimental characteristics of minority peoples are, (a) powerlessness: a belief that they cannot corporately alter the existing system; (b) meaninglessness: an individual's belief that his work and position in society are worthless; (c) isolation: which results from the distinctive beliefs and customs of the majority peoples and the consequential social segregation which culminates in alienation from their societies. All these indicatives of minority status are conspicuous in the Iranian Zoroastrian community where the monolithic Muslim majority perceives them as insignificant, at best, and at worst, as an unclean (*najes*) people. Hence their absence from the decision-making process has been a central feature of the community in Iran. The Parsis, on the other hand, fit more readily into what Robert Park[101] referred to as 'marginal man' status. His definition of the term is applicable to the Parsi condition:

> ...a cultural hybrid, a man living and sharing intimately in the cultural life and traditions of two distinct peoples...which never completely interpenetrated and fused (*loc.cit.*892).

Parsi familiarity with Hindu (especially Gujarati) culture, their later acquaintance with the English, their language, customs and manners, meant that they could move comfortably into the role of mediator between the two major actors on India's stage, the indigenous population and the foreign ruler. Since they were neither persecuted nor apprehensive of the dominant groups, they retained, as a minority, their mediating role in the country. The Parsis do not evince feelings of being branded by their status.

The contemporary Zoroastrian community does not expend much intellectual energy on analysis of their marginal status; rather, they appear to rejoice in it, emphasizing the 'exclusiveness' of the 'club' to which they belong. Indeed, their 'clubbability' is articulated in terms of their Zoroastrian religion, and it is no exaggeration to state that religion is as much a part of Zoroastrian identity as their particularity of customs, race, gender and nationality. Perhaps because of the palpable insignificance of their numbers, their religion has become a defensive identity shield: in Iran, where legalised discrimination has been operational for centuries it has served to emphasize group boundaries; in India where the traumas of enforced migration to a foreign religious environment with its caste regulations, necessitated emphasis on religious uniqueness.

While Hinduism in India did not spawn a pan-Indian polity, Shi'ite Islam became the kernel of Iran's national identity and consciousness. The Zoroastrians, by historical definition outside this religious system were suspect in every area of life. With their self-imposed silence, they sought refuge in their distinctive religious identity which was elevated, in due course, to equal their national identity since Iran, from its inception, had been a Zoroastrian land. As the Iranian Zoroastrians could not participate in their nation's affairs, and because they continued to maintain the closest allegiance to the soil of Iran, it was the Zoroastrian religion alone which was important enough to fill the void. For entirely different reasons, their Parsi kinsmen in India too would elevate their Zoroastrian faith, so that in time it became tantamount to their particular 'national identity', one exclusively their own.

NOTES:

1.   The expression 'political culture' originated in the sociological and anthropological works of Ruth Benedict, Margaret Mead, Clyde Kluckhohn, Abram Kardiner, Ralph Linton and others. Gabriel Almond first used the term in stating that, 'every political system is embedded in a particular pattern of orientations to political action. I have found it useful to refer to this as the political culture', in 'Comparative Political Systems', *Journal of Politics* 18 (1956), p.396.

2.   Cf. M.Reza Behnam, *Cultural Foundations of Iranian Politics*, (University of Utah Press, 1989), p.9.

3.   *The Times of India* (Magazine), Nov/Dec 1988: Girilal Jain, 'The Moral Vacuum'.

4.   Hans Kohn, *The Idea of Nationalism*, (New York, 1944), p.16.

5.   See Chapter 3 'Parsis of India'.

6.   Firoze Davar, *Iran and India Through the Ages*, (London,1962).

7.   William H.Forbis, *Fall of the Peacock Throne: The Story of Iran*, (New York, 1981), p.30 for an elaboration of this theme.

8.   See Chapter 1.

9.   Kermal H.Karpat (ed), *Political and Social Thought In the Contemporary Middle East*, (New York, 1968), p.377.

10. W. Montgomery Watt, *Islamic Political Thought: The Basic Concepts*, (Edinburgh University Press, 1968), p.115.

11. See Hamid Algar, *Religion and State in Iran, 1785-1906*, (University of California Press, Berkeley, 1969); Shahrough Akhavi, *Religion and Politics in Contemporary Iran: Clergy-State Relations in the Pahlavi Period*,(State University of New York Press, Albany, 1980), pp. 10-15.

12. Edward A.Bayne, *Persian Kingship in Transition*, (New York, 1968), p.44.

13. For example, the paradox that, despite Egypt's ancient heritage, the pharaohs fail to elicit a similar degree of emotion and veneration, as do the Great Kings of ancient Persia. On this see Richard N.Frye, 'Iran and the Unity of the Muslim World', *Islam and the West*, R.N.Frye (ed.), (The Hague, 1956), p.187.

14. Cf. R.N.Frye, *The Heritage of Persia*, 1965, p.254.

15. M.Reza Behnam, *op.cit.*, pp.10-12.

16. Cf. Michael Fischer, 'Persian Society: Transformation and Strain', in Hossein Amirsadeghi (ed), *Twentieth Century Iran*, (London, 1977), pp.186-7.

17. M.Reza Behnam, *op.cit.*, p.19.

18. Charles Issawi (ed), *The Economic History of Iran, 1800-1914*, (University of Chicago Press, 1971), pp. 358-61 where some of the concessions granted by the Qajar monarchs are listed: 1864 - telegraph concession, Britain; 1874 - right to build railroad from frontier to Tabriz, Russia; 1889 - Imperial Bank of Persia (with right to issue notes, mining privileges), Britain; 1893, 1898, 1899 - highways and mining, Russia; 1901 - oil concessions throughout Iran, except five northern provinces, reserved for Russia and Britain.

19. For a detailed account of this concession and the period, see Nikki R.Keddie, *Religion and Rebellion in Iran: The Tobacco Protest of 1891-1892*, (London, 1966); also, Edward G.Browne, *The Persian Constitutional Movement*,from the Proceedings of the British Academy, Vol.12, (London, Oxford University Press, 1918).

20. For a discussion of the strategic significance of the Persian Gulf and Indian Ocean to the British in safeguarding their Indian colony, see Rashna Writer, *The Identification of Developing Soviet Strategic Interests in the Indian Ocean, 1968-1974*, (unpublished Ph.D. thesis, University of London, 1979).

21. M.Reza Behnam, *op.cit.*, p.24.

22. Erwin I.J.Rosenthal, *Islam in the Modern National State*, (Cambridge University Press, 1965), pp. 307-8; see also Amos J.Peaslee, *Constitutions of Nations*, 2nd ed. vol.2, (The Hague, 1956), 2:396-411.

23. Michael Fischer, 1977, p.187.

24. Napier Malcolm, *Five Years in a Persian town*, (London, 1905), p.50.

25. For further reading see, Richard H.Ullman, *Anglo-Soviet Relations, 1917-1921*, vol.3, (Princeton University Press, 1972), pp.383-89; N.R.Keddie, 'The Iranian Power Structure and Social Change, 1800-1969: An

Overview', *International Journal of Middle East Studies*, 2 (January 1971), 2:10.
26. M.Reza Behnam, *op.cit.*, p.35.
27. *Ibid*, p.40.
28. Cf. Michael Fischer, 1977, p.188.
29. M.Reza Behnam, *op.cit.*, pp.74-77.
30. Hamid Algar, 'The Oppositional Role of the Ulama in Twentieth-Century Iran' p.246, in Nikki Keddie (ed), *Scholars, Saints and Sufis*, (University of California Press, Berkeley, 1972).
31. For a detailed examination of the events, see M.Reza Behnam, *op.cit.*, pp.75-77.
32. Hamid Algar, *op.cit.*, p.255.
33. For a detailed analysis of the Iranian revolution, see Michael Fischer, *Iran, From Religious Disputes to Revolution*, (Harvard University Press, 1980), pp.181-244.
34. Cf. Michael Fischer, 1980, p.149 where this thesis has been analysed in some depth.
35. Cf. Michael Fischer, 1980, pp.153-4 for an analysis of Khomeini's work on the state, *Hukumat-i Islami* (1971), pp.52-53, 205.
36. These ideas were restated in 1971 by the Ayatollah Khomeini in a series of lectures published as *Islamic Government: Guidance by Religious Experts*, ff Michael Fischer, 1980, p.153.
37. Michael Fischer, 1980, from where the following quotation is taken, p.159.
38. This corroborates the evidence of the Zoroastrian refugees, see Chapter 5; similarly, it puts one in mind of the Hindu caste strictures, where those of 'higher' caste shall refrain from social intercourse with those of 'lower' caste, and where strict rules of commensality are observed.
39. See Chapters 2 and 5.
40. M.Reza Behnam, *op.cit.*, p.143.
41. *Ibid*, p.151.
42. Richard W.Gable,'Culture and Administration in Iran', *Middle East Journal* 13 (Autumn 1959):412.
43. See J.J.Modi, 'The Khutba of the Mahomedans and the Dasturi of the Parsis', *Journal of the Anthropological Society of Bombay*, vol.XII, Part 5, p.629.
44. E.W.West, *The Book of the Mainyo-i-Khard*, (Amsterdam repr.,1979), Ch.XV, 16-20, p.148.
45. E.Kulke, *The Parsees in India: a minority as agent of social change*, (Delhi, paperback, 1974), p.137.
46. *Ibid*, pp.137-38.
47. *The Parsi*, vol.I, No.11, p.533.
48. S.K.H.Katrak, *Who are the Parsis?* (Karachi, 1965), pp.288-93.
49. The English Governor of Bombay, Sir J.R.Carnac on August 11, 1877, in *Journal of the National Indian Association*, No.82 (October, 1877), p.260.
50. E.Kulke, *op.cit.*, p.140.
51. Even V.Savarkar, chairman of the communalistic Hindu Mahasabha, in 1939, promised the Parsis equal rights in an independent India, *The Iran League Quarterly*, vol.IX, No.2, (January 1939), p.89.
52. Among the well-known Parsi philanthropists one could list most of the 'Parsi aristocracy' and their charitable donations to schools, libraries, colleges, hospitals, flood and famine victim relief assistance etc. The following families, Jeejeebhoy, Tata, Cama, Masena, Jehangir, Petit, to name but a few, have all funded various charitable institutions. What is less well known are acts of generosity across the Indian spectrum: for example, Parsi donations to the Muslim Khilafat movement of the early 1920s was proportionally higher than from the Muslims themselves, *The Pioneer* (Allahabad, November 21,1921). For a detailed exposition of Parsi charities in India see, J.R.Hinnells, 'The Flowering of Zoroastrian Benevolence: Parsi Charities in the 19th and 20th Centuries', in *Papers in Honour of Professor Mary Boyce*, *Acta Iranica*, vol.X, 1985, pp.261-326.
53. Maneck Pithawalla, *The Light of Ancient Persia*, (Madras,1923), p.230.
54. Pherozeshah Mehta's speech before Congress in Calcutta, December 26,1890, reproduced in J.R.B.Jeejeebhoy, *Some unpublished and later speeches and writings of the Hon.Sir Pherozeshah Mehta*, (Bombay, 1918), p.292.
55. E.Kulke, *op.cit.*, p.159.
56. For a further elaboration of this thesis, see E.Kulke, *op.cit.*, pp.164-7.
57. Dadabhai Naoroji as President of the Indian National Congress in his Presidential Address, 1893, reproduced in G.A.Natesan, *Speeches and Writings of Dadabhai Naoroji*, (Madras, 1910), p.61.
58. D.Naoroji to Wacha, (December 20, 1888), Naoroji Papers.
59. *Kaiser-e Hind*, 15 July, 1917.
60. David C.Mellor, *The Parsis and the Press: An In-Depth Study of The Hindi Punch - 1906-1931*, (unpublished M.Phil. thesis, Victoria University of Manchester, 1985), p.44.
61. *Hindi Punch*, 30 August, 1908.
62. *Hindi Punch*, 21 November, 1909. I can recall an interesting episode while a student at Calcutta University, in the late 1960s, a Professor of International Politics, addressing a seminar on Indian Foreign Policy, the better to emphasize India's 'Open Door' policy through the ages, pointed to me saying, 'you

people came here as refugees, and we gave you sanctuary'. *Hindi Punch's* reference to Parsis as 'refugees' in India, is merely a refrain, which on occasion is even used by other Indians to remind Parsis of their origins in India.

63. David Mellor, *op.cit.*, p.47.
64. *Hindi Punch*, 12 December, 1920.
65. E.Kulke, *op.cit.*, p.141.
66. *Hindi Punch*, 27 November, 1921.
67. David Mellor, *op.cit.*, p. 135 for an elaboration on this theme.
68. *Hindi Punch*, 11 November, 1923.
69. *Hindi Punch*, 10 September, 1922.
70. B.N.Pandey (ed), *The Indian Nationalist Movement, 1885-1947, Select Documents*, (London, 1979), p.110.
71. S.A.Wolpert, *Jinnah of Pakistan*, (Oxford University Press, New York, 1984), p.110; H.Alexander, *Gandhi Through Western Eyes*, (London, 1969), p.60; M.Bence-Jones, *The Viceroys of India*, (London, 1982), p.256.
72. David Mellor, *op.cit.*, p.176.
73. *Hindi Punch*, 6 April, 1930.
74. *Hindi Punch*, 25 May, 1930.
75. *Hindi Punch*, 8 June, 1930.
76. E.Kulke, *op.cit.*, p.212.
77. D.R.Mankekar, *Homi Mody, A Many Splendored Life*, (Bombay,1968), p.106.
78. E.Kulke, *op.cit.*, pp.142-6.
79. In 1889, of 401 Parsis admitted to the matriculation examinations, 337 chose Persian as their second language, *The Bombay Government Gazette*, (November 12,1889).
80. See Chapter 1.
81. A.N.Joshi, *Life and Times of Sir H.C.Dinshaw*, (Bombay,1939), p.112.
82. R.W.Cottam, *Nationalism in Iran*, (Pittsburg, 1964), pp.86-7.
83. *The Zoroastrian*, vol.I, No.2 (July 1923), p.29
84. *Parsi Prakash*, vol.VI, 1 November 1925, p.235.
85. A.A.Hekmet, *Parsis of Iran*, published by the Iran League, (Bombay, 1956).
86. P.P.Meherjee, in *Journal of the Iranian Association*, (March, 1919), p.433.
87. M.B.Pithawala, *The Light of Ancient Persia*, (Bombay,1923); I.J.S.Taraporewala, 'Some Aspects of the History of Zoroastrians', *JCOI*, (Bombay, 1928); R.F.Rustamji, *India and the Parsis*,(Nagpur, 1944).
88. *Hindi Punch*, 11 September 1910.
89. *Loc.cit.*
90. E.Kulke, *op.cit.*, p.169.
91. *Hindi Punch*, 10 September, 1922.
92. *Hindi Punch*, 21 March, 1926.
93. *The Parsi*, June 1905, p.209.
94. E.Kulke, *op.cit.*, p.263.
95. *Times of India*, 9 August, 1947.
96. *Iran League Quarterly*, October 1947 - January 1948, p.162.
97. *Ibid*, p.161.
98. See E.Kulke, *op.cit.*, also J.R.Hinnells, 'Parsis and the British', *JCOI*, 1978; *Ratanbai Katrak Lectures*,Oxford,1986; 'The Parsis: A Bibliographical Survey' in *Journal of Mithraic Studies*, vol.III, Nos.1&2, 1980, pp.100-150; Piloo Nanavutty, *The Parsis*, (New Delhi, 1977), among the considerable body of literature on this subject.
99. The diversity of activities on a national scale, and the House of Tata's several overseas involvements are too numerous to mention. For a biography of Jamsetjee, see, F.R.Harris, *Jamsetji Nusserwanji Tata: A Chronicle of His Life*, (Bombay, 1952), 2nd ed.
100. See Chapter 5.
101. Robert E.Park, 'Human Migration and the Marginal Man', *American Journal of Sociology*, 33 (1928), pp.881-93.

CHAPTER FOUR

PRESENT-DAY COMMUNITY SHIBBOLETHS AND LEGAL PRECEDENTS

There are two issues, intermarriage and conversion, which have evolved as *the* shibboleths of contemporary Zoroastrianism. By threatening to re-draw the ethnic boundary of the group, and seemingly impinging on theological axioms, the debates activated by these two issues, often seen as inter-related, arc themselves the cause of communal disharmony. A High Court judgement which came to be seen as a legal benchmark by the Parsi community - the Parsi Panchayat Case of 1906, dealing with both questions, appeared to have been the final word on these vexatious matters.

Intermarriage and conversion, the former essentially a sociological phenomenon, the latter a question of religious principles, have bedevilled the Zoroastrian world since the early part of the present century. Brief historical analyses of these phenomena and an exposition of a crucial legal judgement are set out in this section. It will be seen in the discussions following, where the communities in India, Pakistan, North America and Britain are considered, that these two issues are not merely of theoretical significance, but continue to exercise the intellects of a cross-section of the Zoroastrian community. A brief over-view of intermarriage and conversion from an essentially Zoroastrian perspective would be useful at this point.

Intermarriage

Over the millenia Zoroastrians lived within closed societies, whether in the villages of Yazd and Kerman in Iran, or the hamlets and towns of Gujarat in India. Urbanization, with resultant increase in education, acquiring of professions, and the opportunities to socialise with people other than Zoroastrians, have led to an increase in intermarriages. No precise and accurate data of the rate of Zoroastrian intermarriages are available. A statistical data-base is lacking quite simply because such analytical work has not been undertaken to date. However, it is generally correct to state that in almost every modern Zoroastrian family, whether from Iran, the Indian sub-continent, eastern Africa, lands of the western diaspora, one member at least will have, or have had, a non-Zoroastrian spouse. It is a trend which, having been established, can be expected to continue and increase, given the inherent adaptability of the Zoroastrian in new surroundings, with his continued emphasis on higher education and high achievement in secular spheres.[1]

In Zoroastrian and Islamic Iran, marriage within the community was the norm. Marriages outside the fold were not encouraged: it was deemed a religious duty to marry within the faith. Thus, the *Dinkard* inculcates that

> Men who are bound by the precepts of the religion ought, with the object of avoiding sin and strife, to tie the knot of marriage with such believers in the religion, as that strength might accrue to them and the people of their race for deliverance from hell by means of prayers and devotions to God. The prosperity of the progeny of men is (secured) by marriages entered into with this object of receiving mutual assistance.[2]

This convention, deeply ingrained over centuries in the communal mind of the Zoroastrians of Iran and India, persists to this day. The relatively recent practice of an increase in the incidence of exogamous marriages is seen as a threat to communal solidarity. It diminishes numbers, where the non-Zoroastrian spouse is considered ineligible to participate in religious and community affairs, and the subsequent loss to the fold of the offspring of such unions are seen as an inevitable drain on the human resources of the society.

The deep-seated suspicion of intermarriage persists among the more traditional, older Zoroastrians, and sections of Zoroastrian youth who are witness to the steady increase of what they consider the undoing of their race and religion. The younger Zoroastrians, who are acculturated in a predominantly non-Zoroastrian society, have increased opportunities to meet and marry persons outside their restricted religio-ethnic group. They often find such a pairing to be personally suitable.

Since exogamous marriage would not have been a matter of great concern in Zoroastrian Iran where the commonality of religion, town or village resulted in marriages within the fold, there are only occasional textual references to 'cohabitation' with persons of another faith, and the sinfulness of such acts. Legal texts such as the Pahlavi *Madiyan-i Hazar Dadistan*, elaborates upon the five modes of marriage among the ancient Iranians. The *padikhshay* mode, when a young maiden marries with full parental consent; the *khwad-sray*, when she does not receive parental consent; the *chagar* form of marriage which involves the union of a widow to a widower, a widower to a spinster or a widow to a bachelor; the *ewagen* mode when the daughter, being an only child, pledges her first-born son's adoption by her father, whence the grandson inherits his grandfather's 'residuary fortune'; and lastly, the *stur* marriage, upon the death of an unmarried male or one having died childless, her relatives financially assist a maiden to contract a marriage and pledge a child of theirs for adoption by the deceased.[3]

Traditional wisdom - that indefinable quality which grips the imagination of a peoples and often carries the weight of legal precedents - would seem to indicate that in ancient Iran, while the men in the course of their national duty (royal princes, soldiers stationed overseas, etc.) did take non-Iranian brides, Persian women would not have been encouraged to do likewise. It is said that when Khosro I made peace with the Arabs of Yemen, a special clause was inserted in the peace treaty prohibiting any Arab from marrying a Persian woman.[4]

Exceptions to the rule must have been made, though documentation is sparse, of marriages between Persian and non-Persian. Alexander of Macedon encouraged his men to take Persian brides, and himself set an example by marrying Statira, the daughter of his defeated rival Darius III, as well as the daughter of a Bactrian chieftain, Roxanne, who bore him a son posthumously. Persian monarchs too, married foreign princesses, well-known among them being Bahram V, Khosro I and Khosro II, and Yazdgard. The relevance of such unions would fall more often into the realm of politico-military considerations, these lying outside our present analysis. Suffice it to say that, while a general convention existed in Zoroastrian Iran for unions within the Iranian Mazdayasnian fold, exceptions to the rule occurred. Endogamous marriages among the common people of Iran would have been the norm, quite simply because unions were arranged more by way of emphasis on regional and class awareness, and that the overwhelming population of the land was Zoroastrian.

A determinant factor in the elevation of the issue to community consciousness today is the socio-cultural environment in which the group now finds itself. In Zoroastrian Iran an imperial people would have faced scant external pressure upon the regulation of their socio-religious practices. This was reversed with the Arab conquest of Iran in 641 CE. While the Zoroastrians of the day feared the extinction of their religion as a result of enforced or voluntary conversion, and consequently made the rejection of one's ancestral faith a sin of the highest order, *margarzan*,[5] the extant Pahlavi literature does not explicitly deal with the subject of exogamous marriages. One can only deduce therefrom that the institution of endogamous marriages was deeply entrenched among Iranians as they strove to cling to their Zoroastrian religion. The abhorred Arabs would not at all have been perceived as suitable partners; the later conquerors, the Turks, Mongols and Afghans, were similarly categorised by the adherents of the Good Religion.

The *Rivayat-i Hemit-i Ashawahistan*, compiled in 955 CE, deals here with the religious consequences for a Zoroastrian man who consorts with a Muslim woman:

> (Question 42) 1: He who commits the sin of consortium with a Moslem woman and due to that consortium a child is conceived in the womb, then what is the (degree of that) sin? If she gets married and that child is born and is brought up as a Muslim (what would be the degree of the sin), and if that child is killed either in the womb or outside (what would be the degree of the sin) or, if that woman had been a virgin, or if she had been a Zoroastrian, what would be the prescription for each case?

> Answer 42 2: If there is nothing else implied in this (question), a Zoroastrian who copulates with a Moslem woman and owing to this copulation she becomes pregnant, (the fact of) giving a child to a Moslem is immediately (considered) a *tanapuhl* sin [A sin which disables the sinner from traversing the Bridge of the Separator after death].

> If that child reaches the age of 15 and remains a Moslem, on the account of this (child) remaining a Moslem, the conceiver is a *margarzan* [A sin for which there is no atonement and death is the punishment].

> If the woman is married, he (the violator) has to atone to her husband for this fornication...[6]

The emphasis in the above excerpt from a Zoroastrian legal precedent, as with other Pahlavi writings, is on the preoccupation of the Zoroastrian community striving to withstand the onslaught of Muslims around them. The need to regulate social behaviour under changing circumstances received utmost priority.

This theme is reiterated in the *Vaetha Nask*, in a 'Supplementary Note on Atonement and Repentance' thus: '#40-41: Nobody who is of the Mazdayasnian Religion, man or woman (shall) cohabit with a person in the religion or of alien faith'.[7] The paucity of written evidence on the subject of union between a Zoroastrian and non-Zoroastrian would indicate that in general such unions were discouraged, not least because they were deemed to encourage infiltration of the religious stock by the much hated Muslims.

Any analysis of contemporary Zoroastrian responses to intermarriage would be inaccurate were it to convey a suggestion of community-wide unanimity of approach. There are differences in attitude to intermarriage between the Parsi and Iranian Zoroastrian. Whereas they are both part of the long tradition of antipathy towards mixed marriages, the Parsi, having lived in the more cordial environment of Hindu India where they were permitted to practice their faith and develop societal norms unhindered by the host community, deemed intermarriages to be the coupling of Mazdayasnian with 'daeva' worshippers. There was thus a religious overlay on conjugality, and kinship with the exogamous was removed in one fell swoop. Furthermore, the Hindu caste system which by definition restricts the inter-caste movement encourages a closed, inward-looking development of the group within the confines of his caste. This particular Hindu social mechanism benefitted the Parsis inasmuch as they were viewed as a distinct caste expected to keep their distance from other castes. The Parsi perception of marriage within their 'caste' grouping was reinforced by the Hindu practice around them, and was in harmony with their own custom of endogamy which they had brought with them in their early migration from Iran.

The Iranian Zoroastrians, by contrast, lived in the suppressive and often-times dangerous confines of Islamic Iran, where they practised their faith with restrictions that could be imposed upon them randomly by the authorities. The act of marrying out was deeply regretted and seen as an inevitable loss to the community: marriage to a Muslim was seen as inflicting grave damage on the individual contracting such a union through the loss of the person to their family and village. Nevertheless, those Iranian Zoroastrians having moved to the West have shown remarkable pragmatism in dealing with the problem. They are prepared to accept the non-Zoroastrian partner, if non-Muslim, into the Zoroastrian fold. This author has been informed on numerous occasions that, with the advent of the Pahlavi dynasty and the lifting of restrictions on Zoroastrians, there were no serious impediments to the acceptance of the non-Zoroastrian spouse and children into the Zoroastrian fold, provided they were non-Muslim. There are instances of Zoroastrians settled in the West who marry Muslims by Zoroastrian religious rites.[8] Cases where Iranian Zoroastrians wishing to marry non-Zoroastrians were not permitted to have the Zoroastrian religious ceremony performed because of local priestly disapproval, have been reported with equal authority. There is no set pattern acceptable to Zoroastrians of varying persuasions on the methodology of conduct in instances of exogamous unions. In this there exist similarities of attitudes in the Parsi and Iranian communities. The institution of intermarriage continues to be disliked, and where it is presented as a *fait accompli* to a family, some accept it more easily than do others. While some priests are prepared to officiate at such ceremonies, others are not. A uniform approach on a community-wide basis is lacking at the present time.

However, there is a problematic inner dynamic at work among both the Parsis and Iranian Zoroastrians. While certain sections of the Parsi community are highly vocal in their disapproval of intermarriage, it is the others with their greater levels of adaptability to the external environment (perfected during the millennial residence in India), among whom the rate of increase of intermarriage is seen to be increasing dramatically.[9] Among Iranian Zoroastrians there are strong internal regulatory features operating, which make exogamous unions a less frequent occurrence. Young Iranian Zoroastrians 'date' less than Parsis do; and when they do 'go out on a regular basis' with another Iranian Zoroastrian, it is with the intent of marriage.[10] So rigidly conformist does the Iranian Zoroastrian group appear to an outsider, that this author has been informed by interviewees not infrequently that they would not marry Parsis because that too would be 'like intermarrying, the language, food and culture are so different'. There is therefore the reluctance to adjust to an inferred 'foreignness' which, for the present, has meant a lower rate of exogamous marriages among Iranian Zoroastrians than among Parsis.

There is another factor which distinguishes the Iranian Zoroastrian attitude from the Parsi's. The Iranian people take great pride in their Farsi language. Their attachment to their literature, poetry and indeed, the particular thought process engendered by the language, is a striking feature of Iranian national identity. Therefore, it is not uncommon to hear Iranian Zoroastrians lament their non-Iranian spouses' inability to communicate in Farsi

...how can I explain to her my deepest feelings in English? She cannot share with me my love of poetry. How do you translate Ferdowsi?

in the words of a young Zoroastrian, when asked to discuss his views on intermarriage with particular reference to his American wife.

Similarly, a mother of a thirteen-year old boy was asked why she and her husband frequented the Zoroastrian Centre in London.

...we hope he will find an Iranian wife, then they will come to

Zoroastrian House too. I don't mind intermarriage, but if the wife can't speak Persian, she then stops the husband from attending Iranian functions because she feels left out.

Clearly, the importance of self-expression in the Persian language is a powerful inducement to the young and old to stay within the group. A likely consequence is the fear of older Zorostrians that their children might marry Iranian Muslims, since nothing other than religion separates them. The modern Parsi does not place a similar emphasis on Parsi-Gujarati.

Exogamous unions, while regarded with deep opprobrium in the Zoroastrian world, resulted in a flurry of debate within the Parsi community at the turn of the century as a result of the marriage of R.D.Tata, scion of the great industrialist family, to the French lady Suzanne Briere. Lesser known Parsis too were forming mixed unions, to which the responses of the Parsi Panchayat Trustees and the majority priesthood would seem to indicate their efforts at preventing this phenomenon from becoming unmanageable.

While the community lived in a majority Zoroastrian society, the imperative to restrain exogamy was less needed than it became once they were relegated to minority status. The codification, therefore, of marriage laws, with the primary intention of unions from within the Zoroastrian fold, was undertaken as and when necessitated. Long centuries after their migration to India, *The Parsi Marriage and Divorce Act*, India Act No.III of 1936 was codified.

> 2. In this Act, unless there is anything repugnant in the subject or context: 'husband' means a Parsi husband; 'marriage' means a marriage between Parsi whether contracted before or after the commencement of this Act; a 'Parsi' means a Parsi Zoroastrian; 'wife' means a Parsi wife.[11]

The 1936 Act was introduced to amend the *Parsi Marriage and Divorce Act* of 1865, where the definition of 'Parsi' was not given, but was specified in the new Act. Here the word 'Parsi' was defined as being a Parsi Zoroastrian, i.e. a Parsi by race and Zoroastrian by religion.[12] The restrictions on marrying outside the fold were thereby couched in legal form by the Parsis in the foregoing Act. Several references therefore, are made in the *Parsi Prakash* and other Parsi journals which chronicle Parsi activity in diverse fields. In 1918, a body of the clergy (*athornans*) passed a resolution boycotting all Parsi women with non-Parsi husbands. In an endeavour to further prevent community losses, the *athornans* subsequently extended the boycott to Parsi males with non-Parsi wives.[13]

The position of Parsi women married to non-Parsis remained undecided. Mr.Poonawala, Advocate of Poona, in a letter dated 30 November 1936 to the Bombay Parsi Panchayat sought guidance in the matter of Parsi women marrying non-Parsi men, about the rights of such women, and whether they could attend Parsi Zoroastrian ceremonies such as the *paydast* (funeral) and *uthamna* (third day rites following death).

In reply it was stated that a Parsi woman could marry an alien in one of three ways: (a) the *Special Marriage Act III* of 1872 (where she has to declare that she is not professing the Zoroastrian faith); (b) the *Christian Marriage Act XV* of 1872 (where she has not to so declare), and (c) converting to other religions like the Hindu, Muslim, Christian etc. and marrying according to the rites of that religion. The Panchayat noted in its reply that to date no question had arisen of women marrying under categories (a) and (c). It had on record one case of category (b) when the opinion of the then Advocate General, Mr. Strengman, was taken stating that although the woman was professing the Zoroastrian faith, as she had married a husband of a different community she should be considered as having gone 'out of the community'. The Trustees indicated acceptance of the Advocate General's assessment. As for categories (a) and (c), it was clear that such Parsi women were considered excommunicate and as such, without rights to the Funds and Properties of the Bombay Parsi Panchayat. They advised other *anjumans* to follow their procedures.

One question, however, remained unresolved. In the eventuality of her 'foreign' husband's death, or a divorce, could the Parsi woman revert to the Zoroastrian religion? The Trustees acknowledged their awareness of the reversion of Parsi men, i.e. their re-admission into the fold. They had no knowledge of Parsi women having done likewise, and therefore, did not advance an opinion. 'All the above pertained to women only. Men do not go out of the community if they marry *juddin* (alien) women. But, if they married according to the Special Marriage Act, they are deemed to go out of the religion'.[14] Clearly, therefore, while the Parsi community has traditionally frowned on intermarriage, the fate of Parsi women choosing exogamous unions is virtually that of institutionalised ostracism. This entrenched viewpoint informs sections of the community to the present day.

It would appear that suspicion of intermarriage was not peculiar to the Parsis, but could perhaps be attributed to one aspect of their common early Iranian heritage. Thus, the *Parsi Prakash* records that the Iranian government passed a rule in 1940 that no Iranian woman would be allowed to marry a non-Iranian national, except if she had received permission from an authorised official of the Iranian government. Those Iranian women wishing to marry British nationals under the *3rd Indian Special Marriage Act* of 1872, the *Indian Christian Marriage Act* of 1872, and the *Third Parsi Marriage and Divorce Act* of 1936, were informed that, although such marriages were valid in British India, the Iranian government would not consider them to be so in Iran.[15] There are distant echoes of Khosro's treaty stipulation with the subject Yemeni Arabs in this modern Iranian governmental decree!

Within the Zoroastrian world generally, and the Parsi community in particular, the general unease over exogamous marriages was amplified in time into a community convention decreeing outright ostracization of the female, and only the most grudging tolerance for the out-married male. Some Parsis are apprehensive that an increase in intermarriage will lead to the decline of their race, and consequently of the Zoroastrian religion as practised by them. Some Iranian Zoroastrians fear that intermarriage will mean a loss of their children to foreign cultures and, through non-practice of the religion and its accompanying ethos by their grandchildren, an inevitable erosion of their Zoroastrian heritage. The crux of the present community debate on exogamous unions is the perception of an inseparability of race and religion.

Given that the issue of intermarriage is a highly sensitive one divisive of the community, the observably accelerated rate is compelling individuals and some Zoroastrian associations to address themselves to it. Their responses hitherto are on an *ad hoc* basis, and improvisatory. The North American diaspora community feel an urgency to re-examine their traditional antipathy towards exogamy, sections of this community and their co-religionists in other Western nations sensing a certain inevitability that their offspring will choose non-Zoroastrian partners.[16] A young mother in Canada expressed a balancing opinion: 'I have two children. I think one will marry a Parsi and one will intermarry'. The precise rate of intermarriages in the diaspora nevertheless remains unknown.

What is certain is that in a socio-cultural environment far removed from their 'roots', the thinly-spread Zoroastrian peoples fear an escalation of exogamous unions among their children, those who have known no other country and social environment than the Judeo-Christian ones of the United Kingdom, the United States, Canada and Australia. Their parents make efforts to accommodate this developing dynamic. The results are reflected in the Membership Charters of several North American Zoroastrian associations, where the realization that 'overseas, every third marriage is a mixed marriage',[17] has led to membership of Zoroastrian Associations being consequently defined by commitment and participation, rather than an inherited identity, thereby acknowledging and accommodating non-Zoroastrian spouses within the social network of the various communities of North America. On the issue of the admission and initiation of children of mixed marriages, the Zoroastrian Association of British Columbia, for example, approves 'performing the *navjote* of a child irrespective of whether the parents are non-Parsis or Zoroastrians...it is immaterial'.[18]

This is not, however, a universal principle, and the responses of the various diaspora communities demonstrate their differing approaches. The British Zoroastrians have yet to achieve a workable formula for the acceptance of the offspring of a Zoroastrian woman and a non-Zoroastrian man. In the United Kingdom there is no common principle amongst the voluntary officiating priests with regard to the initiation of a child of a Zoroastrian father and alien mother. Some UK-based priests perform such *navjotes*, others have declined.

The problem of intermarriage is, therefore, the single social issue in need of urgent appraisal within the Zoroastrian world. The trend towards exogamy within the diaspora community can be expected to increase. Altered patterns of customs, beliefs, practices, and perhaps the very overview of the community may develop as a result.

In the old countries of Iran and India, the dynamics of national regeneration will partly lead to a growing propensity for the young, urbanised Zoroastrians of Tehran, Bombay, Delhi, Bangalore, to socialise with greater frequency at school, college and work place with non-Zoroastrians. In India, especially, there is an awareness of a growing 'Indianization' across society, implying that the Parsis, if they are to continue to live in that land, must single-mindedly adopt the Indian national identity. Independent India is witness to an incremental growth in Parsi secularity; its corollary is a rapid increase in the levels of intermarriage. The social taboos earlier associated with intermarriage have not been lifted, despite which young Parsis demonstrate a greater willingness to choose partners from the diverse regions and cultures of the Indian sub-continent. Among Iranian Zoroastrians, the 1979 Islamic Revolution is thought by some to have halted the level of mixed marriages (which were never proportionately high), owing to an openly fundamentalist attitude by the government of the day. This socio-political condition need not be permanent. Indeed, the trend towards increasing exogamy in the Zoroastrian community is a universal phenomenon, based largely on socio-cultural imperatives: a miniscule group, some of whose members choose to marry out into the surrounding larger groups, instigated in part by the perception of a relative lack of choice from within their own group.

In 1981, the Bombay Parsi Panchayat decided to deny Parsi women married to non-Zoroastrians the right to vote in the forthcoming Panchayat elections. Six Parsi ladies, thus disenfranchised, took their case against the Panchayat to court. They held the view that, in spite of having married outside the community, they retained their right to vote. Furthermore, they claimed that by being debarred from exercising their franchise they had been discriminated against - tantamount to a denial of their status as Parsis.[19] A Judgement in the City Civil Court on February 12, 1981 ruled that the women were not permitted to vote.[20] That same afternoon an appeal was lodged in the Bombay High Court which ruled that, although the women had married outside the community, nevertheless continuing to profess the Zoroastrian religion, they were entitled to be registered as voters by the Bombay Parsi Panchayat. The Judge instructed the appellant's attorneys to inform the Panchayat, in writing, that their clients continued to profess the Zoroastrian faith and thereby retained their right to vote. Their names were accordingly to be included on the 'D' Register of voters.

The significance of this case, in the penultimate decade of the present century is that in Bombay, deemed by several sections of the community to be the centre of Zoroastrian 'orthodoxy', a High Court has decreed that Zoroastrian women who have married exogamously and continue to profess their faith, may no longer be excommunicated by the Panchayat. This opinion legally overturns the *de facto* excommunication of the Parsi women with non-Zoroastrian partners.

The dilemma of exogamous unions remains unresolved by the Zoroastrians. An institutionalised approach to a central social phenomenon is exigent, as a reliance on current *ad hoc* responses to individual instances shows signs of weakening the community by creating irreconcilable factions within it. The universality of the institution of mixed unions, where arguably every extended Zoroastrian family is demonstrably touched by it, and the extraordinary *de facto* position of Zoroastrian women who choose alien partners, might lead to the women themselves challenging entrenched community mores in national courts, and in time compelling an historic revaluation of the community's views to intermarriage.

NOTES:

1. John R.Hinnells, 1986 *Ratanbai Katrak Lectures* (Oxford University Press, forthcoming), henceforth *Katraks*.
2. Dastur Peshotan's *Dinkard*, vol.II, p.91, Book III, 80.
3. Sohrab J.Bulsara, transl. *Matikan E Hazar Datastan*, (Bombay 1937), ch.XXIII, pp.244-307.
4. R.E.Enthoven, *The Tribes and Castes of Bombay*, vol.III,1922 (Bombay), p.204.
5. See following section on 'Conversion'.
6. Nezhat Safa-Isfehani, *Rivayat-i Hemit-i Ashawahistan*, Harvard Iranian Series, vol.2, pp.282-284.
7. Helmut Humbach & K.M.JamaspAsa, transl.and annotated, *Vaetha Nask: An Apocryphal Text on Zoroastrian Problems*, (Wiesbaden 1969), p.31.
8. I have been told of such instances during the course of field work in North America, and similar instances occurring in Europe have also been brought to my notice.
9. See following Chapter on India and Pakistan. I gratefully acknowledge Mr.Homi Ranina, Bombay Parsi Panchayat Trustee, for having granted me an interview. He maintained that '...the Parsis marry people of other religions at the drop of a hat. There is absolutely no compunction when it comes to marrying someone from other communities. This is how I see the complete loss of identity we are suffering today.'
10. I am grateful to the Iranian Zoroastrian ladies in North America for having elaborated on the social mores observed within their group.
11. C.N.Wadia & S.B.Katpitia, *The Parsi Marriage and Divorce Act*, (Surat 1939), pp.10-11.
12. *Ibid*, p.15, drawing heavily on the Judgement of Justices Davar and Beaman in the 1906 Parsi Panchayat Case; see following section for an evaluation of the Judgement.
13. *Kaiser e Hind*, 2 June 1918, and 16 August 1918 respectively.
14. *Parsi Prakash*, vol.VII, 30 January 1937, p.347.
15. *Parsi Prakash*, vol.VII, 21 March 1940, p.578.
16. J.R.Hinnells & R. Writer, *Living Flame: Zoroastrianism in Britain* (forthcoming); see also the discussions in Chapter 6 on the North American and British communities.
17. Jamshed Pavri of Vancouver, quoted in *Parsiana*, August-November, 1977.
18. *Ibid*.
19. *Bombay Samachar*, 18 February 1981; *Indian Express*, January 17 and February 13, 1981.
20. *Times of India*, February 13, 1981.

Conversion

On January 8, 1903, R.D.Tata married a Frenchwoman, had her *navjote* performed, and declared to the Parsi community that his wife was now a Parsi Zoroastrian.[1] This was the first recorded instance of the initiation of an outsider into the Parsi community, and the repercussions of that action were to emphasize the deep divisions within Parsi society on the issue of conversion. Ideological positions were assumed, and the individual's response to the intake of the *juddin* or one of different religion, coupled with the issue of marriage outside the fold, was the litmus test of the 'orthodox' and 'liberal' persuasions of individual community members. The conversion debate has been a festering sore within the Zoroastrian community from the early decades of the 20th century, and continues to be the focal point of community debate among the diaspora, particularly on the North American continent.

The debate on conversion commences with the poser: if Zarathushtra did not convert, how would there have been any Zoroastrians? The Prophet's wish to seek the spread of Mazda- worship as the proper path in life, is the undeniable message proclaimed in his *Gathas*:

> (45.5) Now, I shall speak of what the most virtuous one told
> me, that word which is to be heard as the best for men: 'Those
> of you who shall give obedience and regard to this (Lord) of
> mine, they shall reach completeness and immortality...'[2]

Zarathushtra's teachings were a socio-ethical code for universal application. Perceiving the animosities and fears surrounding him, he stressed in his revelations the fundamental distinction between good and evil and the innate justice of God. Zarathushtra attributed all that is good as emanating from Ahura Mazda. Two original principles co-existent from the beginning were twinned as the two *Mainyus* - motivating forces confronting humankind on earth. One is *Spenta*, which adheres to Ahura Mazda; the other is evil, further explained as *Angra*, which is hostile and inimical. They are diametrically opposed in Thought, Word and Action, the pivotal ethical triad of Zarathushtra's teachings. There is therefore, no compromise with *Angra Mainyu* in the Zoroastrian tradition. Man is given choice and free will to choose between good and evil, becoming thereby for the first time in human thinking, responsible for his own destiny. The heaven or hell he went to after this life was deemed to be the direct result of his thoughts, words and actions.

Since, however, the Iranians did not record their history at the time of Zarathushtra, and indeed, beginning to do so only some centuries later, it is not possible to determine the early practices relating to the spread of the message of Zarathushtra and his followers.

Through extrapolation from Gathic references and the Yasht indications, some broad outlines may be presented. Thus we are informed of the 'conversion' of the court of King Vishtasp and his Queen Hutaosa, who 'came forward as the arm and help of the religion, the Ahuric Zoroastrian' (Yt.13.99). The tradition appears to suggest that the Mazda-worshipping religion taught by Zarathushtra spread gradually to the various Iranian peoples in the north and east of the country before it was carried, primarily through trade, to the western Iranian peoples, the Medes and Persians.[3]

The creation of the first Persian world empire by Cyrus II (the Great), was to establish a precedent of respect for the religions of the conquered peoples. In the 'Cyrus Cylinder' the King declares himself to his Babylonian subjects as chosen by their gods to rule over them peaceably. Cyrus informs us that he became 'the king of Babylon...whose rule [the gods] Bel and Nabu love, whom they want as King...My numerous troops walked around in Babylon in peace. I did not allow anyone to terrorize any place...I strove for peace in Babylon, and in all other sacred cities'.[4] His religious tolerance extended equally to the Jewish exiles who were permitted to return to Jerusalem and rebuild their temple with financial assistance from the Persian exchequer. Not surprisingly therefore, Cyrus is the only gentile referred to as 'the anointed', or the long-awaited messiah (Isaiah, 45.1) of the Hebrew Old Testament.

The dynamics of Cyrus' policy which was emulated by later Achaemenid kings would seem to indicate that political realism, rather than any tendency for religious proselytism, was among the monarchs' primary concerns. It was politically expedient to follow a policy permitting the conquered peoples to continue worship of their gods. Two reasons suggest themselves. The Persians had conquered civilizations which pre-dated their own (Egypt, Mesopotamia, Assyria, Greece, India), and which had established cultures. Further, the empire was too vast to permit a military and religious domination. Considerations such as these might have led to the overall state policy, ensuring religious freedoms to the subjugated peoples. It is possible to argue the point further that, mindful of *realpolitik*, the early Iranians came to develop the view that as conquerors they could reawaken religious commitment among people, perhaps because they felt that each group of peoples followed their particular religions. The Babylonians would continue in their worship of Bel and Nabu; the Iranians in their worship of Ahura Mazda. Zoroastrianism, it would appear, spread and was consolidated primarily within Iran.

The later development of the empire, and the establishment, over centuries of an imperial people who came to regard their Zoroastrian faith as the imperial religion, led to occasional reversals of the earlier policy of tolerance towards the subject peoples. In Sasanian Iran, with the growth of internal religious heresies such as the Zurvanite doctrine, Manichaeism and Mazdakism; and the foreign religious systems of the Buddhists, Hindus, Jews and Christians, necessitated the establishment of a state Zoroastrian church. The Sasanian monarchs' objective of the maintenance of national security implied that social upheavals, resulting from diverse religious movements, would best be dealt with by the promulgation of an official orthodoxy. During the reign of Shapur II (309-379 CE), the priest Adarbadh, having successfully disputed before the convocation of leaders of all the religions in Iran to vindicate the irrefutable 'truths' set forth in the Zoroastrian religion, impelled Shapur to proclaim:

> Now that we have seen the Religion upon earth, we shall not tolerate false religions and we shall be exceeding zealous'.[5]

A uniform practice was thus developed in Zoroastrian Iran for the eradication of perceived heresy. Since the king had rendered support of the doctrine as confirmed by Adarbadh, the idea of its reformation, or any challenge thereto, was tantmount to treason. The 'traitor', having offended the national interest as enshrined in the state religion, could expect scant mercy. The notion of the 'exclusive truth' was thus reinforced.

The justification of the policy of Zoroastrian Iran's monarchs would appear less through an evangelical zeal to convert the 'non-Iranian' or *anarya*, than to achieve balance and harmony within Iran. The social structure of the country was pyramidal, with the king at the apex, followed by the nobility headed by the seven great families, and then the common folk. Since the king ruled by divine right, it was incumbent on him to enforce the cosmic order on society through the mechanism of religion. Indeed, at that time, the distinction between religion and politics was made inviolable.

The loosening of church-state bonds following the Battle of Nihavand (641 CE), overturned the Zoroastrians' former historical position of superiority. The proselytizing fervour of Islamic Iran which continued down the centuries, compelled the small number of Zoroastrians in that country to somehow maintain their religious practices under extremely difficult circumstances. There was no opportunity in Islamic Iran for the 'gabrs' to proselytise, making the missionary activities of the Zoroastrian faith henceforth impossible.

The migrant Zoroastrians in India being subject to its caste laws were seen as a religious and racially distinct 'caste' by the Gujaratis among whom they lived. It may be argued, however, that the institutional structures of Indian society were put to admirable use by the Parsis whereby they retained their distinctive religio-ethnic dimension, the very purpose of their initial migration to India. The question of spreading the message of the *Gathas* among the Hindus was never a necessary option, for their Indian hosts also saw religion as being closely interwoven with race.

For varying reasons, therefore, both Iranian Zoroastrians and Parsi

Zoroastrians were to keep their religion to themselves. The discussion among Zoroastrians about the issue of conversion stems partly since the early decades of the 20th century, from the perceptible decline in numbers, leading to real fears of the extinction of the Zoroastrians and Zoroastrianism. (The observed increase in intermarriages has exacerbated this fear). Since the race and religion have come to be closely, even inextricably linked, the authority for conversion of outsiders is sought from religious texts. Indeed, the present debate is couched in terms unsuited to an early Zoroastrian history, invoked repeatedly by the protagonists. Both sides of the divide quote ostensibly from the *Gathas* of Zarathushtra for justification of their particular stance. There are, however, several translations of the *Gathas*, and contemporary Zoroastrians fail to examine modern-day requirements with a *mutatis mutandis* understanding of the different conditions and imperatives under which their ancestors laboured.

Zarathushtra as the Prophet who, through his revelation had come to teach the truth of his credo, was occupied in the first instance with the eradication of irreligion and the *druj* (lie). Achaemenid, Parthian and Sasanian Iran demonstrated their adherence to their Zoroastrian faith as part of the common religious heritage of the Iranian peoples. The timbre of Iranian life was irrevocably altered with the coming of the Arabs. The relentless onslaught of proselytizing Islam which, within a short period of time, had substituted Mohammad for Zarathushtra as the Prophet of the revealed truth, meant that the dwindling Zoroastrian population now came to view apostasy, perhaps more than ever before, as the most heinous of crimes. Throughout the past millenium, the preoccupation of the Zoroastrian priesthood was to discourage apostasy and prevent further in-roads into their community's diminishing numbers. For some of their 20th century descendants, the response to the deep-seated fear (diminishing numbers), is to convert outsiders to Zoroastrianism. The 'problem' has remained unchanging over a thousand years: the decreasing size of the community. Solutions to deal with the situation have differed. While earlier generations decried apostasy, some among the present generations advocate conversion.

At this point, references made to some significant Pahlavi and Persian writings on this perplexing issue, are instructive. The emphasis is to be found on steadfastness to the ancestral faith and rejection of the apostate. Reflecting the worsening conditions of a beleagured minority over-run by an alien religion, the 9th century Pahlavi text, the *Zand-i-Vohuman Yasn*, decries the 'irreligous' acts practised in Iran and the implications for those 'who shall wear the sacred thread-girdle'.[6] Having outlined the conditions in the land, once the 'div-worshippers' had established suzerainty, the *Vohuman Yasn* proceeds (Chapter V) to enquire of Ahura Mazda, whether 'in that perverse period, will there be holy persons and will there be religious persons who will wear the sacred thread-girdle on their waist?'.[7]

(2) He, Auhrmazd, replied to Spitaman Zaratuhst: 'The best of men will be that one, who in that perverse period, will wear the sacred thread-girdle on the waist...'
(5)The best of holy men will be that one, who will remain in the Good Religion of Mazda-worship, the Religion of self-sacrifice will continue in his family.[8]

The position of the apostate, the severity of his actions, the relinquishing of the religion of his ancestors and its damaging effects upon the Good Religion, are recounted in a passage from another Pahlavi text, *Dinkard VI*:

(216) They held this too: There is no one who is a greater enemy to religion than heretics. For apart from heretics there is no enemy who can thus come from without through the wall into religion's outermost (region). The heretic enters across the outermost wall in the guise of one who carries the sacred word: some come even up to the selfness and nearness of the religion.[9]

Not only the post-Sasanian Pahlavi literature, but also the later treatises, provide evidence of the community's concern with safeguarding their religion while surrounded by majority peoples with an alien worship; the correct observation of religious rituals, and a preoccupation with a fidelity to their Zoroastrian religious tradition. These are to be found in that body of works which came to be known as the Persian *Rivayats*. The modestly prosperous Parsis, having felt the need for authentication of their practice of Zoroastrianism on Hindu territory, commenced sending emissaries for further understanding and confirmation of theology and ritual. Iran remained for them the ancestral land, and they looked to the *dasturs* there for instruction on specific matters. The ensuing *Rivayats* offer us many an informative insight into liturgical and social issues concerning the Zoroastrian communities from the 15th through to the 18th centuries.

It is in the *Rivayat* of Kaus Kama, that the specific terms of *juddin* or *darvand*, i.e. non-Zoroastrians, are explained. He states that 'those who obey the commands of God are *behdins*, but those who do not are *darvands*'.[10] It is from the *Rivayats* that we learn of early Parsi concern regarding conversion. In the *Rivayat* of Kaus Mahyar, on the issue of 'Peaceful and Forcible Conversion', the question is asked: 'Can a grave-digger, a corpse-bearer and a *darvand* become *behdins*'?, to which the answer given is: 'If they observe the rules of religion steadfastly and (keep) connection with the religion, and if no harm comes to the *behdins* (thereby), it is proper and allowable'.[11]

Shapur Bharuchi learnt from the *dasturs* of Iran, that

> if a person (of foreign faith) exercises tyranny over a man of
> the good religion and tells him to turn Musalman with his
> family, then out of helplessness he should commit suicide but
> he should not turn Musalman,[12]

which serves to emphasize how extreme a point was being made with regard to apostasy. It further shows the severe pressures under which Zoroastrians lived under the Timurid and Safavid Muslim dynasties. The perennial loss of *behdins* from the community would have been the primary social concern for the elders of the Zoroastrian congregations.

With reference to the historical situation prevalent in Iran from the 15th to 18th centuries when the *Rivayats* came to be written, on the question of conversion, only two direct statements to the bestowal of *kusti* upon *juddins* - in the *Rivayats* of Kaus Mahyar (MU.I.p.281 II) and Nariman Hoshang (MU.I.p.282 II 11-18) - arc made. The bulk of the chapters on 'Juddins' and 'conversion' contained in the treatises, deal with the distance that *behdins* must keep from aliens in all spheres of activity, and with the penalties for apostasy. Indeed, it was the abnegation of the Good Religion for Islam, which was a real and continuing threat to the ever diminishing numbers of Zoroastrians in Iran, indicating that it was apostasy which was the socio-religious concern of the day. Where a religious tenet is interpreted in essentially social terms, it is the contemporaneous social climate that determines the crux of the debate. Medieval Iranian *dasturs* saw encroaching proselytism endangering their peoples, and prudently formulated rules to combat it. Modern Zoroastrians similarly see a community diminishing in numbers, and some among them advocate conversion as a method of rejuvenating their religion and reflating their numbers.

The issue of conversion as debated by the Parsis in the 20th century, hinged clearly on the significance of retaining a racial distinctness within India, which had been maintained through the two-fold process of endogamy and religious exclusivity. The gradual erosion of the strongly enforced social convention of intra-marriages, is seen to be a threat of encroaching conversion of aliens, where the non-Zoroastrian spouse and offspring would ultimately become eligible for entry into the racial/religious group. The accumulated treasury of vast funds which had been established by wealthy community elders as a socio-economic bulwark for their peoples, would also be available to persons of non-Parsi stock. (These charitable endowments were in addition to the great number of universal charities which had been established by wealthy Parsis). It was a pressing need to preserve racial and religious identity, and to safeguard a social welfare system unmatched on the Indian sub-continent, which made the conversion issue the highly emotive community question that it was to become.

The divisions within the Parsi community on the issue of conversion (and its concomitant, intermarriage), formed along 'orthodox' and 'reformist' factions. For the former, the retention of community exclusiveness would alone lead to the preservation of identity; for the latter, religion could not be seen in terms of race.

The great exponent of the 'orthodox' school of thought in the early decades of this century was J.J.Vimadalal. He contributed several articles to the monthly *Oriental Review* in 1910, his main thesis being the preservation of the community's distinctiveness which ought to be retained, since Parsis had evolved certain 'national' characteristic traits.[13] The preservation of identity as against dilution of the Parsis' hereditary traits, was re-emphasized by him in his 1922 publication *Racial Intermarriage, Their Scientific Aspect*. He spoke perhaps for a large lobby in wishing to retain the 'racial' characteristics of the community. In Vimadalal's view, a non-Zoroastrian spouse in a mixed marriage had insufficient justification to convert to Zoroastrianism.[14]

The eminent scholar-priest, Dastur Dr.M.N.Dhalla, wrote prolifically in favour of conversion. He perceived Zoroastrianism as a proselytizing faith with a message of universal application.'The prophet is convinced that the religion which His Heavenly Father has commissioned him to preach is the best for all mankind'.[15] He recounts in his *Autobiography* his desire intellectually to perform *navjotes* of children of one Parsi parent, but fears communal ostracism.[16] Dhalla maintained that the consequences for the Parsi community in banning the admission of outsiders was that 'if Zoroastrianism is to live in this world as a living faith, it must have sufficient numbers in their fold to keep up its validity'.[17]

The positions on both sides of the dialectic had become clearly entrenched by the second decade of our century. The 'orthodox' wished to preserve the identity and exclusiveness of the community; the 'reformers' argued that religion could not be confused with the issue of race. The 'orthodox' rejoice in the caste exclusiveness of the Parsi community; the 'reformers' emphasize the universal applicability of the message of Zarathushtra. At a fundamental level the world-view of the two groups are diametrically opposed.

Although the Zoroastrians of Iran did not have a 'conversion debate' as vigorous and divisive of community solidarity as the Parsis of India, a division of opinion among this group, on this most contentious issue, nevertheless becomes evident upon prolonged discussion.

A deep-seated fear prevails among them that, were Zoroastrians to attempt proselytizing amidst Muslims there would be a most violent back-lash against this small minority. Several older Zoroastrians argue convincingly that they survived despite their diminished numbers not least because the community had never encouraged Muslims to apostatize (as opposed to the Bahai's inducements in Iran). The more persistent feature of the discussions with older Zoroastrians is the extent of acrimony for Islam and those who abandoned the old faith to embrace this alien religion. It is not uncommon for persons expressing this viewpoint to embellish their discussion with reference to a Persian proverb: *siah sefid nemishe* (black cannot become white). They maintain that since Iran was a Zoroastrian land originally, the Iranian Muslim is merely a turncoat who, fearing persecution, had abandoned his religious heritage. To convert such persons back to Zoroastrianism (in the hope that it will augment community numbers, and by introducing fresh blood perhaps generate a Zoroastrian renaissance), is countered by the argument that cowards and opportunists ought not to be so readmitted. The underlying fear and scepticism felt by some sections of the Iranian Zoroastrian community against the Muslim oppressors is seldom publicly voiced, but is clearly discernible upon cautious enquiry. This section of the community emphasizes the purity of their racial descent from the 'ancient Persians' who, despite the harshness of their sufferings through the centuries, never abandoned their religious heritage, and by marrying within the fold, retained their racial exclusiveness. This concept of belonging to an exclusive 'club', resembles the views expressed by those Parsis who similarly reject the advisability of conversion of aliens to Zoroastrianism.

There is, however, a growing demand among another group of Iranian Zoroastrians for allowing conversion. Cautious steps in this direction have recently been taken in Iran in Pahlavi times, but halted after the Revolution of 1979. This has not been emulated by their Parsi counterparts. Iranian Zoroastrians have already begun to admit foreign wives; children of mixed unions (even where the father is non-Zoroastrian); new converts to Islam have been re-admitted into the fold, as well as those Zoroastrians who embraced Bahai'ism and wished later to revert to the old faith. Since Muslim decrees concerning apostasy, rather than Zoroastrian willingness or reluctance to accept aliens, govern conduct in this delicate area, the Zoroastrian *anjumans* and *mobeds* have remained cautious in any overt actions. The general willingness of the Iranian Zoroastrians, especially those from Tehran, to accommodate outsiders has resulted in the Zoroastrian Anjuman of Iran passing a resolution,

> Subject to the laws of Iran (i.e. a Muslim man may marry a non-Muslim woman since by Islamic law the children belong to the father), the marriage of a Zoroastrian and a non-Zoroastrian shall be performed in accordance with Zoroastrian rituals and shall accordingly be registered with the Registrar of Zoroastrian marriages provided an application is made to the Tehran Zoroastrian Anjuman together with the following documents: (1) an affidavit signed by the non-Zoroastrian party to the effect that the said person believes in the Zoroastrian faith and sincerely wishes to be accepted in the Zoroastrian community; (2) a certificate issued

by an authorised *mobed* testifying that the person in question has learnt the basic prayers and the essential principles of the Zoroastrian faith; and (3) a certificate by seven Zoroastrians that that person is of good character and integrity.[18]

In the closing decades of the 20th century, the epicentre of the conversion debate has shifted from the old Zoroastrian homelands to the North American continent. The controversy was fuelled anew by the *navjote* performed in New York in 1983 of the American, Joseph Peterson. While this event might indeed have been the spark which ignited the conflict, the groundwork for the North American polemic had been laid prior to this event.

The discussions on conversion being revived in the 1970s and 1980s by the Zoroastrians of North America, were undertaken at two levels, both of which became enmeshed in their final analyses: reference to the *Gathas*, with a corresponding devaluation of the Pahlavi literature, and a critique of Parsi traditions that had developed in India. The North American community has employed a pruning process and accepts such parts of the Zoroastrian heritage which appear amenable to their particular requirement, rejecting such segments that seem irrelevant or unworthy of the whole. An enduring characteristic of the conversion debate has been the ability of the debaters to tailor the data to suit specific needs. In this the North American Zoroastrian is no different from his Indian or Iranian counterpart.

In the USA and Canada, through the medium of conferences and newsletters (chief among which are *The Zoroastrian* and *Gavashni*), the relevance of conversion and the correctness of the reversal of the non-proselytization policy is being argued. While pockets of resistance remain, the American and Canadian settings themselves are a spur, which expedites the reappraisal of conversion and the intake of aliens. The hidden fear of the conversion lobby revolves on the question of their minority status. Equally, the older first generation immigrants fear the loss of their children from the fold as a result of intermarriages, or quite simply by being drawn inexorably into the magnetic host society. The encouragement to 'outsiders' to embrace Zoroastrianism is seen therefore, as a positive step towards halting a deteriorating situation.

The Zoroastrian, the bulletin published by the California Zoroastrian Centre, Los Angeles, responded to a reader's query by stating its position on conversion,

> ...California Zoroastrian Centre...favours the acceptance of qualified persons who, after studying and fully comprehending the Message of Asho Zarathushtra, exercise their free will and choose the Good Religion...The spread of the Zoroastrian religion in the civilized world was but through propagation,

first by Asho Zarathushtra, then by his succeeding teachers, and thereafter by the upholders of the faith down to the downfall of the Sasanian empire. History shows that the Zoroastrian religion had the largest number of adherents in the world only 1500 years ago - from the Nile to the Indus and the Jaxartes to the Indian Ocean - as many as 30 million souls. This was not achieved by birth alone. The multiplication had many other factors, and preaching was the major one.[19]

An important contributor to the North American discussion on the acceptance of aliens is Dr.Kersey Antia who, as one of the four officiating priests at Joseph Peterson's conversion, has drawn severe reproof upon himself by some members of the priesthood in India and beyond. Speaking on the occasion of Peterson's *navjote*, Dr.Antia expressed his view that

> ...those from the old world that want to enforce their mandate against conversion do not seem to have the good of our progeny or religion in their heart or mind, and would care less if our entire offspring ceased to be Zoroastrian, as per their rule, because it was forced to marry outside the community for no fault of theirs. To align with them is to align with those that will destroy any chances of our children and grand-children remaining Zoroastrian, even though our children will have practically nothing to do with them.[20]

As the gap between the old and new worlds of Zoroastrianism widened, individual Zoroastrian associations in the USA and Canada were establishing guidelines in order to meet the needs of an escalating situation. In January 1983, a Report was placed before the Zoroastrian Association of Greater New York's General Meeting on 'Acceptance/Non-Acceptance To Zoroastrianism And The Future'. The 'compelling factor' of having settled in a 'totally different social environment than one's country of origin', had meant that ZAGNY members wished to revaluate their positions. Attempting to answer the question, 'who is a Zoroastrian?', the response arrived at was: 'Any person who has been confirmed into the religion by the performance of the *navjote* ceremony, and/or the offspring of any person who is Zoroastrian by *navjote*, as long as the offspring has not adopted another religion'.[21] The emphasis was thus placed on the acceptance into the religious fold of the non-Zoroastrian spouse and children of mixed unions.

Some North American Zoroastrians however, took a different stand. In a letter addressed to the trustees of the Guiv Foundation and signed by eleven 'concerned members of the Zoroastrian Association of Chicago', they made clear their point of view that, '...the universal brotherhood with non-Zoroastrians would not be desirable if that brotherhood is brought about by sacrificing the existing brotherhood within our community'.[22]

With the growing tide of support for the acceptance of aliens into the Zoroastrian faith, the Fourth North American Zoroastrian Congress held in Montreal in April 1983 delegated to the Zoroastrian Association of Quebec the task of compiling the 'views of knowledgeable people' on 'acceptance'. Some nineteen persons were asked to comment on questions related to conversion - they ranged from scholars in the field to eminent lay Zoroastrians.[23] The survey demonstrated in stark terms the widely divergent views of Zoroastrian priests and scholars alike. Once the exercise of compilation of opinions had taken place and made available to a global audience of Zoroastrians through the columns of *Parsiana*, the Montreal Survey was laid to rest, except perhaps in serving as a spur to urge on the rate of 'acceptance' of aliens in the USA and Canada.

Being denizens of the technological age, the contemporary Zoroastrians, while establishing new ground-rules for their communities in the New World, were not immune from critical assessments of their position by fellow Zoroastrians in the Old World (especially India). Some within the Indian community strenuously objected to the developing 'American' position on conversion. A prominent spokesman in this connection was Mr.Khojeste Mistree, Director, Zoroastrian Studies, Bombay. In his pamphlet, 'Conversion - A Mandate For Disunity', he attempts to state his position:

> The main argument in favour of conversion seems to be one founded upon a fear of the rapid diminution of our numbers and therefore, the dwindling of our race...However, many of the pro-conversion lobbyists seem to argue this issue in a rather inconsistent way. They want conversion to be permitted in order to stem the decline of a dying race and therefore the religion, yet they claim that the race should not determine the criteria for entry into the religion which they believe is universal. Why, then, has the religion remained inseparable and in fact confined to a single ethnic family for thousands of years?[24]

Three prominent *dasturs* of India, Dastur Dr. Hormazdyar Mirza, Dastur Kaikhushroo JamaspAsa and Dastur Dr.Firoze Kotwal, published articles rebutting the stance of their Iranian colleagues, the *Council of Mobeds* in Tehran, who favoured the 'acceptance' of aliens into the religious fold. The latter, who had been asked to give their considered opinion on the conversion of Joseph Peterson, responding after having quoted scriptural references, concluded:

If we Zoroastrians believe that our religion is one of the great living religions of the world and that it is beneficial to all the peoples of our world, we must persevere to propagate it. We must accept persons who want to embrace the Zoroastrian religion. In fact, we should follow those who set us an example.[25]

The chief *dasturs* of Iran and India appeared to hold diametrically opposed views on a crucial community dilemma.

The issue of conversion quite clearly raises more questions than it can provide answers. In a very real sense there are areas of deep confusion among the lobbies now established within the community, and the lay Zoroastrian, with no specialist knowledge of the subject, but guided by emotions or preference for one individual or another, is unable to make educated choices.

The conversion controversy has gained such momentum that the polemics are now highly-charged and hinge primarily on religious texts. The current debate is polarised between the Gathicists and the Vendidadists, the latter text itself a compilation on rituals, purity and contractual matters composed hundreds of years after the Prophet, by priests. Historical and theological data are given novel interpretations, dependent on the particular party's stance in the debate. The opposing factions tend to introduce further lines of division within the community, so that confusion is compounded and tensions aggravated. The dilemma facing the contemporary Zoroastrians is quite simply presented as a choice: were 'acceptance' of aliens to become widespread, it would eradicate the ethnic boundaries within which the Zoroastrian religion has been practised over some thirteen hundred years; if 'conversion' is not extended, even in limited cases such as the non-Zoroastrian spouses and children of mixed marriages, the arithmetical improbability of survival of a mere 150,000 souls, scattered thinly over five continents, would become a real issue of an impending extinction. While no universally acceptable method of circumventing the problems have been worked out by the community, the gravamen of the conversion debate remains: race vs.religion.

NOTES:

1. See the following section on the Parsi Panchayat Case, Suit 689 of 1906.
2. *The Gathas of Zarathustra*, transl. S.Insler, *Acta Iranica*, 8, Leiden, 1975, p.75. Refer also, Maria Wilkins Smith, *Studies in the Syntax of the Gathas of Zarathustra Together with text, Translation and Notes*, Linguistic Society of America, Philadelphia, 1929; James Hope Moulton, *Early Zoroastrianism*, The Hibbert Lectures, Second Series, 1912, (London 1913); J.Duchesne-Guillemin, translated by Maria Henning as, *The Hymns of Zarathustra*, Wisdom of The East Series, (London 1952); Irach Taraporewala, *The Gathas of Zarathushtra*, (Bombay 1962).
3. Mary Boyce, *A History of Zoroastrianism*, Vol.2, (Leiden 1982), pp.1-13; 40-46.

4.   J.B.Pritchard, *Ancient Near Eastern Texts*, (Princeton 1969), p.315.

5.   *DkM*, 1911, p.412. Also, R.C.Zaehner's translation in, *Zurvan: A Zoroastrian Dilemma*, (Oxford 1955), p.8.

6.   Behramgore Tehmuras Anklesaria, *Zand-i Vohuman Yasn and Two Pahlavi Fragments*, (Bombay 1957), p.109 (27).

7.   *Ibid*, chapter V, p.114.

8.   *Ibid*.

9.   Shaul Shaked, *The Wisdom of the Sasanian Sages, (Denkard VI)*,(Westview Press, Colorado, 1979), p.85.

10.   Bamanji N.Dhabhar, *The Persian Rivayats of Hormazyar Framarz and Others*, (Bombay 1932), (as per MU I.p.283 II 5-9, Kaus Kama) p.277.

11.   *Ibid*, p.275, (MU.I.p.281 II.1-2 = H.F. f.441); p.454.

12.   *Ibid*, p.275, (MU.I.p.281 1.6).

13.   *Oriental Review*, June 29, 1910.

14.   J.J.Vimadalal, P.D. and C.D.Mahaluxmivala, *Racial Intermarriage, Their Scientific Aspect*, (Bombay 1922), pp. 5-6, 26,41.

15.   M.N.Dhalla, *Zoroastrian Theology: From the Earliest Times to the Present Day*, (New York 1914), pp.11-13.

16.   Dastur Dhalla, *An Autobiography* (transl) Gool and Behram H.J.Rustomjee, (Karachi 1975), p.385.

17.   Dastur Dhalla, 1914, p.368.

18.   S.D.Nargolvala, 'Zoroastrians of Iran', *The Realist* 3(4): 16-20.

19.   *The Zoroastrian*, California Zoroastrian Centre, Los Angeles, No.5-2, April and May 1987, p.5. The extreme of hyperbole 'from the Nile to the Indus' is not at all substantiated by historical evidence.

20.   Dr.Kersey Antia, Speech delivered on the occasion of Joseph Peterson's *navjote*, New York, March 5, 1983.

21.   'Acceptance/Non-Acceptance to Zoroastrianism and the Future', January-February 1983 Circular, Zoroastrian Association of Greater New York. This Report was placed before an inquorate General Meeting of ZAGNY. However, a vote taken on the guidelines showed 80% of those attending in favour of the Report.

22.   Letter dated February 20, 1983 from 'Concerned Members of the Zoroastrian Association of Chicago' to the trustees of the Guiv Foundation.

23.   *Parsiana*, May 1984.

24.   Khojeste Mistree, 'Conversion - A Mandate For Disunity', Zoroastrian Studies, Bombay, 1983.

25.   Letter dated May 24, 1983, No.466 from the *Council of Mobeds*, Tehran, to Ervad Bahram Shahzadi. English translation by Dr. Ali Jafarey.

The Parsi Panchayat Case Suit No.689 of 1906 in the High Court of Bombay

As has been shown in the preceding sections, since the turn of the century the question of the admission or otherwise of proselytes into the faith has vexed the Parsi Zoroastrians. There is, in the collective consciousness of these peoples, an ingrained awareness of having landed on India's shores as religious refugees some thousand years ago, surviving with their religion and identity intact because of the tolerance of their Hindu hosts, and because as a migrant group, they did not impose their religion and culture upon their neighbours. The Parsis came to India to live in peace, and India in turn treated them hospitably. Within the corpus of Parsi mythology there developed a persuasive legend that the original founding fathers 'had to keep the promises made to King Jadi Rana of Sanjan (that) they had to keep aloof lest they should incur the wrath of the people and their king'.[1] Thenceforth, they nurtured the belief that their Zoroastrian religion and Parsi identity were preserved in India because they had not abused the terms of hospitality set forth by the King, and had refrained from proselytising among local Hindus. Non-conversion came to be viewed as a fundamental Zoroastrian religious tenet, the corollary being that one had to be born to Zoroastrian parents and acquire the appellation by hereditary means alone. As a result of their particular historical experience, Parsis came to imbue conversion into the Zoroastrian faith with irreligion, as something impermissible in religious terms.

At the turn of the present century, two events took place which were to focus the community mind on the question of conversion and bring the matter to the Bombay High Court, where the Judgement handed down came, in due course, to carry the weight of law among the Parsis. On January 8, 1903, Mr.Ratan Dadabhoy Tata married Suzanne Briere, a Frenchwoman, in Paris. On the couple's arrival in Bombay, Mr.Tata had Dastur K.J.JamaspAsa perform his wife's *navjote*, and subsequently the *ashirvad* marriage rites of the Parsis, were conducted. Mrs.Tata was deemed to have been duly initiated into the Zoroastrian religion and thereby to have become a Parsi. This conversion of his wife led Mr.Tata to claim that she was eligible to participate in the religious institutions of the Parsis. Thus, Suzanne Tata was to have access to all fire temples and the privilege of having her body consigned to the *dakhma* upon her death, if she so desired.

The *navjote* ceremony performed on Mrs.Tata was the first recorded instance amongst the Indian Zoroastrians of initiation of an alien into the Zoroastrian faith. As such it was a milestone in Parsi history, and it brought into sharp focus the admissability or otherwise of the *juddin* into the religious fold. This unprecedented occurrence in the community led to deep divisions and resulted in several public meetings with the appointment of a committee on 2nd August 1903 to determine whether *juddins* should be initiated into the Zoroastrian religion. The Committee appointed a sub-committee to investigate the matter.[2] The sub-committee's Report took the position that Zoroastrianism, following the end of Empire, had ceased to be a missionary religion. It held that upon arrival in India the Parsis had accepted into the fold those desirous of embracing the faith. Given the stance of this particular Report which was to have been put before a public meeting, a powerful lobby group prevented its publication. The Committee disowned ever having received a Report from the sub-committee, and maintained there were therefore no recommendations upon which they could act.[3]

Such peremptory handling of sensitive material by the Committee resulted in protests from some community members who held that the Panchayat had no right to establish such a committee. The lack of suitable institutional mechanisms for 'determining grave religious and social questions affecting Parsis', implied that 'any number of Parsis would require or restrain a single individual of the Community from practising a tenet of his religion on the score of social or other considerations.[4]

While these events were being enacted, instigated as they had been by the *navjote* of Suzanne Tata, another incident occurred. A Rajput lady, 'presumably married to a Parsi or living with him and having three living children had her *navjote* performed on 18.3.1904'.[5] She was said to be in poor health and wished, upon her death, to have her body disposed according to Zoroastrian rites, which had been the motivating force behind her decision to adopt the Zoroastrian faith.

The then Secretary of the Bombay Parsi Panchayat, Dr.Jivanji Modi, notified his fellow Trustees, and it was decided to take counsel's opinion as to whether the Rajput lady's body could, in the event of her death, be consigned to the Towers of Silence. Opinions of Advocate General Basil Scott, and Sir Dinshaw Davar were taken, which was further vetted by Senior Counsel Inverarity.[6] They were asked to opine on twenty-six Questions relating to the issue. Its full enumeration is not practicable here; nevertheless, it reflects the mood of the times and presages the great court battle to follow, and in this context merits attention:

> Question 1: Having regard to the terms of the trusts declared by the General Trust Deed of the Parsee Panchayat with respect to the Tower of Silence...are the French lady and the Rajput lady or is any person in a similar position i.e. a non-Parsee by birth converted subsequently to the Zoroastrian religion and invested with the sacred thread and shirt entitled to claim or are their relations or friends after their death

entitled to claim for them that their remains shall be exposed on one of the Towers of Silence vested in the Querists?

Opinion of the Advocate General

1. In my opinion these ladies and any others similarly circumstanced are members of the Parsee Community professing the Zoroastrian religion and their friends are after their death entitled to claim for them that their remains shall be exposed on the Tower of Silence in the same manner as the remains of other Parsees. I think that the term 'Parsee' where it is used in the Trust Deeds can generally be said from the context to be used in the sense of a person professing the Parsee or Zoroastrian religion...

Opinion of Sir Dinshaw Davar

1. My answer to this query is in the negative...

Opinion of Mr.Inverarity

1. I am of the opinion that these ladies are not Parsees, they are not members of the Parsee Community although they are converts to the Zoroastrian religion. I don't think a person who follows the Zoroastrian religion thereby becomes a Parsee. To be a Parsee, I think, it is necessary that the person should be a descendant of the ancient pilgrims or emigrants from Persia, in the male line. I think no others can be members of the Parsee Community. In my opinion, a member of the Parsee Community must satisfy two conditions (1) he must be a Parsee by birth; (2) he must follow the Zoroastrian religion. If he only fulfils the first condition I think he ceases to be a member of the Parsee Community entitled to the benefit of the Trust Deeds. If he only fulfils the second condition, I think he is not a Parsee at all and is not a member of the Community. (Shapur Desai,*History of the Bombay Parsi Panchayet*,1977, 237-8).

Events moved at a rapid pace. A Zoroastrian Anjuman meeting at Albless Baugh, Bombay, under Sir Jamsetji Jeejeebhoy, was called to pass Resolutions on the Report submitted to the Trustees of the Bombay Parsi Panchayat on 2 March 1905 by the Committee appointed on 2 August 1903, on the question: 'whether non-Zoroastrians should be converted to the Zoroastrian faith'.[7]

The 1905 public meeting decreed that the Anjuman meeting ruled against conversion of aliens to the Zoroastrian religion, that only Parsi Zoroastrians, and not converts, could benefit from the trusts and institutions under their control.

Resolution 1:
This Anjuman meeting resolves that in the interest of the community, and looking to the religious and social conditions of the Parsi community, it will be incorrect to convert people from other religions, as such a move would be damaging to the community, and shatter its ancestry and unity.

Resolution 2:
(a) This Anjuman meeting resolves that such non-Zoroastrians who profess themselves as Zoroastrians, and have entered the Parsi Zoroastrian community by any means, that they enjoy no rights and privileges over the funds and institutions of the Parsi Zoroastrian community in Bombay or in any other place, such as   Atash   Behrams,   Adarians,   Daremihrs,   dakhmas, Dharamsalas etc.
(b) This meeting dislikes the act of any Parsi   priest who performs the initiation of a   non-Zoroastrian for converting such an individual   to the Zoroastrian religion. It further resolves that Trustees of all Parsi Zoroastrian charities and Institutions should boycott such priests, and to make public the names and addresses of such   priests and to show their total disregard for such priests. It also requests the Trustees of Parsi Zoroastrian Institutions not to allow such priests to perform religious ceremonies in places under   their jurisdiction and requesting further the entire community not to get religious ceremonies of their household to be performed through such priests, and also to boycott such places of worship or trusts which would allow the initiation of non-Zoroastrians.

Resolution 3:
This Anjuman meeting resolves that the above 2 Resolutions are also applicable to children of Parsi fathers and non-Parsi mothers or mistresses, that they have no rights or privileges over the Parsi Zoroastrian funds, charities and institutions, as they would be prejudicial to the community. However, children by such marriages who have already been initiated into the Zoroastrian religion are not to be affected by this Resolution as a special case.[8]

The stage was thus set for what came to be known as the historic 'Parsi

Panchayat Case' (henceforth PPC), Suit No.689 of 1906, wherein Sir Cowasji Jehangir, Sir Dinshaw Petit, Sir Ratan Tata, Mr.Ratan Dadabhoy Tata [the husband of the French lady], were the Plaintiffs. The Defendants were Sir Jamsetji Jeejeebhoy IV Bart; Mr.H.E.Albless, Mr.J.C.Jamsetjee, Mr.M.M.Cama and Mr.B.D.Petit. Indeed, the cream of the 'Parsi aristocracy' were central participants for and against the proposition. The two presiding judges of the High Court were Justice Davar, an orthodox Parsi, and Justice Beaman, an Englishman and a leading Theosophist.

The Suit dealt with two issues: (1) Whether the Defendants are validly appointed Trustees of the Properties and Funds of the Parsi Panchayat, and whether, in the event of death or resignation of one or more of them, they have the right of filling such vacancy or vacancies as they occur; and (2) Whether a person born in another faith and subsequently converted to Zoroastrianism and admitted into that Religion is entitled to the benefit of the religious Institutions and Funds mentioned in the plaint and now in the possession and under the management of the Defendants (PPC, 5).

While it is beyond the scope of this work to conclusively analyse in-depth the first issue, suffice it to say that the Plaintiffs argued that the Defendants were not validly appointed trustees, nor were their immediate predecessors in that office. The right to appoint trustees of the Bombay Parsi Panchayat, they argued, was vested in the general body of Bombay Zoroastrians - which right, they maintained, had been usurped and exercised by the Panchayat's incumbent trustees. They therefore, asked for a Scheme for appointment of trustees and for the proper management of Trust funds and properties (PPC, 2). The Court ruled that the trustees were indeed not validly appointed and a new election scheme should be drawn: one in use to this day. Until a proper election procedure could be established, the existing trustees were re-appointed by the Court (PPC, 8-44).

Sir Jamsetji Jeejeebhoy IV Bart died on 17 June 1906, while the case was in progress, and his colleagues (the remaining Defendants in the Suit), appointed his son Kavasji, now the Vth Baronet, to fill the vacancy. Thereafter, Hormusji Albless resigned owing to ill-health, and Justice Davar, upon the matter being brought before him, asked for names to be submitted so that elections could be held. Thereupon, the first ever elections of the Parsi Panchayat were held, and Muncherjee Kharegat, Hormusji Wadia, Naoroji Gamadia and Sir Pherozeshah Mehta were elected.[9]

It was the Plaintiffs'contention that the Zoroastrian religion not only permitted, but enjoined, the conversion of aliens (PPC, 3). Once they had been invested with *sudre* and *kusti*, having undergone the *navjote* ceremony, all the rights and privileges of a born Parsi Zoroastrian were then to be made available to the convert. Included was access to the charitable and religious institutions of the Parsi community. The Plaintiffs submitted that it was customary among Parsis to admit *juddins* to the faith (PPC, 53). Mr. R.D.Tata maintained that, having undergone religious initiation, his wife had thereby become Parsi (PPC, 54).

The Defendants, however, while conceding that the Zoroastrian religion permitted conversion into the faith, held that since their arrival in India the Parsis had not admitted a *juddin* into their fold. As a result of this usage, the religious tenet favouring conversion had thereby fallen into disuse (PPC, 3-4).

In accordance with the terms of the High Court Charter, in the event of the two judges differing in their judgement, the opinion of the senior judge would prevail. The two justices - Davar J. and Beaman J. - did differ on a material question involved in the case, but in keeping with the Charter, the case was finally resolved in terms of the opinion of Sir Dinshaw Davar as seniormost, Justice Beaman having eventually concurred with Justice Davar. The Plaintiffs did not include in their number any alien converts to Zoroastrianism, although one of their contentions was to obtain an adjudication on, and a construction and interpretation of, the rights of alien converts under the Deeds of Trust of the Parsi Panchayat charities. Justice Davar was of the opinion that the interested party being absent from Court, the Plaintiffs were not entitled to maintain their action on this part of the case, and he therefore was of the opinion that the Suit should be dismissed inasmuch as it sought an interpretation of the Trust Deeds in the matter of the rights of alien converts. Justice Beaman differed from his learned colleague and expressed an opinion that the Plaintiffs were entitled to maintain their action but that they had failed on its merits.

Since a substantial part of the Case dealt with the rights and privileges of natural born members of the Parsi community, and the Defendants' contention that the same was beyond the reach of *juddins* converted to Zoroastrianism, in a written statement to the Court, the Defendants stated who precisely they regarded as members of the Parsi community.

> ...in the first instance, the descendants of the original Persian Emigrants who came to India in consequence of Mahomedan persecution and who profess the Zoroastrian faith, and secondly, the descendants of Zoroastrians who remained in Persia but who come and settle in India either temporarily or permanently to profess the Zoroastrian faith...In addition to these two classes they say an exception has been made in favour of a third class of persons and these are the children of Parsi fathers by alien mothers (PPC, 4).

Justice Davar, when dealing with the Suit under the heading 'Conversion to Zoroastrianism', states plainly that while all the Plaintiffs are born Zoroastrians, their 'fight is not on their own behalf but on behalf of the 6th Plaintiff's wife' [Mrs.Suzanne Tata] (PPC, p.47), and the conversion to

Zoroastrianism of a Rajput lady. Since Mrs.Tata had not presented herself in Court to seek redress,

> she is an entire stranger to this action. She has abstained from seeking the assistance of the Court and the abstention appears to me to be intentional and deliberate (PPC, 48).

> ...'*Actio non datur non damnificato*' is a maxim of law which governs that branch of the law which deals with the rights of subjects to maintain actions at law. 'An action is not given to him who is not injured' (PPC, 48).

Justice Davar continues:

> It is quite clear that the rights and remedies of these two ladies would not, in the least, be affected by our judgement in this suit...The parties supposed to be injured by the action of the Defendants have not invoked the assistance of this Court, and I am of opinion that the Court ought not to go out of its way and pronounce its judgement on the rights of people who are not before the Court, at the bidding of people who must be regarded as mere strangers (PPC, 49).

The absence from Court of the two ladies converted to Zoroastrianism on whose behalf the Plaintiffs had brought the action, with special reference to Mrs. Suzanne Tata, entailed legal implications which the Judge could not ignore.

> I feel that it would be most unfair to the parties, whose fight the third parties carried on before us, to express my findings on the merits in the absence of the parties whose rights are affected...However adverse my findings may be to the Converts, I feel that they will do no injustice to anybody, as our judgement in this case cannot possibly bind those who now claim to be Converts or those who may make a similar claim hereafter (PPC, 53).

This Judgement in the considered opinion of the presiding Judges was not, therefore, binding on the principal actor - Mrs.Suzanne Tata - and the equally significant participant in the wings, the Rajput lady, owing to their absence from Court throughout the proceedings. It thus questions the value as a precedent for subsequent cases - a fact almost universally ignored by the Parsi community.

The entire part of his Lordship's judgement which deals with the merits of the case at this point, is *obiter* and has no binding force or validity. Factually, there has been no pronouncement on the merits of the 'conversion' question, the Court having decided that the Suit as framed in respect of that question must fail as it could not be maintained by parties who had no personal interest involved in prosecuting such an action. In the judgement of Justice Beaman, that learned jurist noted,

> After spending months of time and thousands of rupees, after inflaming the passions of the whole Community and flooding the Court with unsavoury evidence; after squandering the moneys of the Trust as well as those of private individuals who believed and had every reason to believe that the Court was enquiring into this question of the Converts, we are told, that we really have no power to deal with that at all, and we are very likely told so quite rightly...As it is, the whole of my brother Davar's otherwise valuable and instructive judgement on this part of the case is merely *obiter*; and, of course, if he is right, anything which I may have to add is *obiter* too (PPC, 133).

In legal terms, a vital issue is at stake here. Justice Davar appeared to be saying that his ensuing Judgement cannot be seen as setting a legal precedent. Nevertheless, the Parsi Panchayat Case of 1906 has acquired, over time, the weight of law in the collective understanding of the Parsi community. It is technically incompatible with the reservations expressed by the learned jurists upon those who are 'entire stranger(s) to this action'. The premise on which the Parsi community has continued to argue on the substance and content of the conversion of aliens, and the community's convention of admission to the fold children of Zoroastrian fathers and alien mothers (as per the Judgement of Davar and Beaman discussed below), cannot in fact carry the weight of law, since the chief presiding Judge himself appeared to suggest that his legal opinion is not binding on those who 'make a similar claim hereafter', namely, converts.

The learned Parsi Judge summarised the pivotal issue raised by the Plaintiffs:

> It is both usual and customary for Parsis to admit Juddins into their religon, and give them all the benefits of all religious Funds and Institutions endowed or dedicated for the benefit of their own people (PPC, 54).

The Defendants challenged this assumption:

They say that, although the Zoroastrian religion permits of conversion into the faith, the Parsis, ever since their advent into India, have not admitted a Juddin into their fold; that an entire alien, that is, a person born of non-Zoroastrian parents, has ever been admitted into the faith (PPC, 54).

In order to substantiate their point, Plaintiff's Counsel brought to Court several witnesses whose testimony Justice Davar dealt with at some length. The first witness, Mr.Pestanji Framji Bhownagree, originally from Surat, said 'he thought it was customary amongst his community to convert aliens into the Zoroastrian faith' (PPC, 55), and claimed to have four such *juddin* converts in his family. Upon cross-examination he proclaimed,'I personally know nothing about conversion' (PPC, 55).

What this witness and others in fact brought to the attention of the Court was the practice by certain male Parsis, more especially in the *mofussil* or hinterland, to have *dubra* mistresses, i.e. Hindu women of a lower caste, and have children by them. Some of these illegitimate children - on the Parsi male side - were then initiated into the Zoroastrian religion. Justice Davar elaborated at length on the practice which he considered to have been in decline with the rising prosperity of the Parsi community. Thus, 'this class of people, descended from Dubra mothers, is extremely limited' (PPC, 58).

One of the most important witnesses was Soonabai, a girl allegedly born of Hindu parents, adopted by Dhunjishaw Motabhai Vakil who subsequently 'converted' her to Zoroastrianism and arranged her marriage to a certain Byramji. Justice Davar, extrapolating from the mass of statements made by these various witnesses, came to the conclusion that

> Dhunjishaw alone knows the truth, and the truth it seems to me is that during his residence in the Native States he formed a liaison with some woman who gave birth to this child. He brought Soonabai up as his own daughter, because I believe Soonabai was, as a matter of fact, his daughter (PPC, 62).

Soonabai, when giving testimony claimed to have visited (as a converted Zoroastrian), several *Atash Bahrams* during her visit to Bombay. The Judge reserved scathing remarks for the actions of the Plaintiffs, according to whom Soonabai

> is wholly a Juddin...Each one of the Plaintiffs must have known perfectly well that such visit would be regarded by the great bulk of the Parsi community as a sacrilege, if she was an entire alien as they say...I cannot sufficiently express my sense of disapprobation of tactics such as these (PPC, 63).

As an orthodox Parsi himself, Davar dealt with the flaunting of Parsi custom, viz. the non-entry of *juddins* to religious institutions in order to make a point in Court with the severity that someone of his beliefs, and of his time, might have been expected. Indeed, underlying his entire judgement is the innate sense of his being himself a member of the Parsi Community, and his understanding of the seriousness of the case being tried in his Court.

Sorabji Bomanji Panthaky, a priest from Surat, spoke of a Parsi who wanted the *navjote* performed of his children by his Mohammedan mistress. Panthaky declined, as the Parsi's father pressed against the investiture. The witness nevertheless said,'If he had come to me and asked me again and made proper arrangement for payment to me, I would have done it. The work of he who pays is always done...So far as I was concerned, it was a matter of money - of fees' (PPC, 66). Justice Davar made the point that, 'if the Plaintiffs' contentions were to prevail, the Parsi community would be entirely at the mercy of such men as this one; for it would be open to him to inundate the community with thousands of undesirable aliens' (PPC, 64). This observation of the jurist accentuates the 'low estimate of this man's morality and honesty' (PPC, 65), and the worthless evidence he gave in Court, as much as it gives an inkling of Justice Davar's own specifically orthodox stance in the matter which would bring into question his own impartiality in judging the case before him.

In order to further substantiate the averment of conversion to Zoroastrianism by Indian Zoroastrians, Plaintiff's Counsel put forward three historical precedents:

(a) the conversion of the three learned Hindu Pandits whose names are mentioned in the *Dhup Nirang*;
(b) the conversion of Emperor Akbar;
(c) the conversion of certain men, women and children of Mazagon, who were admitted into the religion by the late Dastur Jamaspji in the year 1882 (PPC, 69).

A prominent witness, the Parsi scholar Dr.Jivanji Modi, stated that in the first case of the Hindu Pandits, their names were not known to Sanskrit scholars, and suggested that they were learned Parsis who were called Pandits. Justice Davar took the view that, 'these three men were good men, who had rendered great services to the Zoroastrians in the early days of their settlement in India...In grateful remembrance of these kindly services, their names were most probably inserted in the *Dhup Nirang* by the Dastoor who composed these prayers' (PPC, 71). Dealing with the same issue, Justice Beaman said that the evidence presented of the conversion of the three said Hindu Pandits 'did not show that these Pandits became Zoroastrians. But the time is so remote that the point has little practical importance' (PPC, 147).

The second historical instance, the conversion of the Moghal Emperor Akbar to Zoroastrianism by the Dastur Mehrji Rana, has entered Parsi mythology as much as having exercised the minds of scholars. Since the Emperor was not known to have consecrated any *Atash Bahrams* and *dakhmas*, and was in fact buried according to Islamic rites, Justice Davar finds it difficult to agree with the Plaintiffs that the Muslim Akbar was a convert to Zoroastrianism (PPC, 72-3). Justice Beaman for his part, made a scathing indictment of Dr.Modi's vacillating scholarship on the question of Akbar's conversion. The scholar-priest had published a brochure 'proving that certain godly priests of Navsari converted Akbar' (PPC, 148), and having 'committed himself to opinions which, when brought to the test of a shattering case, he could no longer maintain' (PPC, 148). What was of significance in Beaman's view, was not whether the Emperor Akbar had in fact

> ...been converted to Zoroastrianism, but rather that right up to the present time one of the leading scholars and ecclesiastical lawyers of the Parsi community of Bombay, so far from saying that such a conversion was contrary to the tenets...set himself elaborately to appropriate the merit of, let us say, the attempt to convert Akbar to his co-religionists. Two important facts emerge: (1) that the idea of converting aliens had not become extinct; and (2) that some, at least, of the religious leaders of the community regarded it favourably within a very short time of this controversy breaking out (PPC, 149).

The third historical instance put forward was of the Mazagon Navjotes of 1882. This event was conducted by Dastur Jamaspji, who initiated nine persons into the Zoroastrian faith. The Dastur published a pamphlet which elaborated the facts of the case as he understood them: there were in Mazagon, eleven persons quietly observing the Zoroastrian religion, dressing as Parsis, but whose *navjotes* had not been performed. Their existence was known to the Bombay Parsi community. Being of humble stock - dockworkers - they feared the wrath of the orthodox sections of the community. These Mazagon persons subsequently petitioned the Trustees that, being 'of true Parsi olad' (PPC, 74), of Parsi fathers, they wished to be invested with *sudre* and *kusti*. A fund was raised for this purpose by 200 leading Parsis. Dastur Jamaspji satisfied himself of their Parsi origin, and publicly performed their *navjotes*.

Justice Davar maintained that 'the details given by Dastur Jamaspji in his pamphlet with reference to each one of the nine persons whom he admitted proves beyond all doubt that they were every one of them, the offspring of Parsi fathers' (PPC, 75). He therefore did not consider this an instance of *juddins* having converted to Zoroastrianism. The position of Justice Beaman was not whether or not the Mazagon *navjotes* sanctioned conversion, but rather that 'it is idle for the Defendants to contend today that the idea of conversion, although an integral part of their revealed and accepted religion, had fallen so completely into disuse' (PPC, 150), that Parsis were now unwilling to acknowledge it.

Nevertheless, the Court was not presented with any incontrovertible evidence that the Parsis in India had practised proselytism. Justice Davar accordingly states:

> Old men...have all been examined in the case. Not one has ever heard of a single Juddin being admitted into the Parsi community of Bombay...The *navjote* ceremony of the French lady, the 6th Plaintiff's wife, was the first instance of such a ceremony being performed in connection with a Juddin (PPC, 77).

The learned jurist offers an explanation for this:

> The fact of the matter is that for years and years after they [the Parsis] obtained a foothold in India, their position in the country was most precarious. They were allowed to land and settle in the country on sufferance. They had no claims on the Gujarat Chief who allowed them to settle in the country...The observance of their own religious rites and the performance of the ceremonies enjoined by their religion must for years have been matters of the greatest difficulty. Who were they to convert: their then enemies the Mahomedans - the people whose persecution had driven them out of their fatherland - or the Hindus, the subjects of the Ruler who had given them refuge?

> ...they made no attempts because they knew not only the utter hopelessness of such attempts, but they knew further that any such attempt would have been so seriously resented that it would have resulted in ruin of the Community, living in the country on sufferance, and whose further countenance in the country depended on the goodwill of the ruling classes, the Hindus (PPC, 80).

> Under these circumstances, while I find that although the conversion of Juddins is permissible amongst Zoroastrians, I also find that such conversions are entirely unknown to the Zoroastrian communities of India; and far from it being

customary or usual for them to convert a   Juddin, the
Zoroastrian communities of India have   never attempted,
encouraged, or permitted the   conversion of Juddins to
Zoroastrianism (PPC, 81).

...The usage of twelve centuries [in India] however, proves that,
under their altered circumstances - away from their fatherland,
amidst surroundings never within the   contemplation of the
Prophet when he promulgated his religion - the enjoyment to
propagate the Zoroastrian religion amongst aliens has fallen
into complete disuse (PPC, 86).

Thus, while the Court had not been presented in the three historical cases
with any irrefutable evidence that conversions were the norm amongst Parsis,
the crux of the matter being discussed, it seemed to both Jurists, was
articulated around the connotation of the words 'Parsi' and 'Zoroastrian'.

The Plaintiffs argued that the term 'Parsi' had a fundamentally religious
connotation, while the Defendants maintained that the term has racial or
tribal connotations. Justice Davar declared, 'The word Parsi has only a racial
significance and has nothing whatever to do with his religious professions'
(PPC, 93). Furthermore, he elaborated, 'The word Parsi, when used in India,
could only mean the people from Pars...The word Zoroastrian simply denotes
the religion of the individual: the word Parsi denotes his nationality or
community, and has no religious significance whatever attached to it' (PPC,
94).

The deliberations in Court as to the exact meaning and significance of the
words 'Parsi' and 'Zoroastrian' were undertaken in order to interpret whether
the Trusts declared in the Deed of 1884 were correctly interpreted by the
Defendants in excluding converts, and to establish whether this was at
variance with the intentions of the donors. It was clarified by both Justices
that the English solicitor employed to draft the Deed of 25 September 1884,
had at the time no idea of the future possibility of an alien convert to
Zoroastrianism. 'Till 1903, the two expressions, Parsi and Zoroastrians, were
used most promiscuously to mean one and the same thing' (PPC, 95).

It was Justice Beaman who analysed the issue of terminology at great length:

The Indian Parsis, as everyone admits, come to India from
Persia. They were soon locally designated Parsis, because they
came from Fars, or Pars, or Persia. Applied to them by the
peoples of India, this term simply denoted place of origin
(PPC, 141).

He continued,

Had this body of exiles any common distinguishing bond, marking them off from others and constituting them a peculiar people, except the bond of religion?...We are concerned now rather with the way in which they regarded themselves. They owed no allegiance to any Persian King; they had no special civic or religious rights as Persians - less still, of course, merely as men from Fars. What they did have was a very special, elevated, and ennobling religion - their own exclusive religion as far as India was concerned, in the practice and profession of which they stood apart from all the alien races by whom they were surrounded...A peculiar people, with no country of their own, no separate national life of their own, owing allegiance to no Parsi or Zoroastrian temporal sovereign, guests on sufferance of races, peoples, who had nothing whatever in common with their religious organisation. They did not know themselves, I have no doubt, as Parsis in any national sense, if in any sense at all, but as members of the Zoroastrian community in India. And if that is correct, does it not follow that the original bond of union between these settlers was the bond of religion, not of nation? (PPC, 142-3).

During the early centuries of settlement in India, the common religious bond was highlighted:

...as the community prospered and acquired wealth and importance, it accepted the popular name of Parsis, as though it really were a national or tribal distinction. And along with this secularising process went a corresponding weakening of the original religious tie, so that, I dare say, it is more accurate to describe the Indian Zoroastrians as Parsis - thereby implying a caste, or communal, or tribal organisation - than it would be to define them as men and women professing the Holy Zoroastrian faith (PPC, 144-5).

This, then, introduces the pivotal issue of Justice Beaman's judgement: Parsis as an Indian caste. The English Judge attempts a brief analysis of Parsi history: the particular conditions prevalent at the time in their fatherland which compelled them to choose exile; the influence in their land of adoption which moulded and then created a new group identity; and the finished product of these historical experiences, which culminated in presenting the face of a distinct and distinguishable Indian Zoroastrian community as presented in Court.

Thus Beaman J. begins his crucial assessment of Parsi history, agreeing with the Plaintiffs that, in fleeing Muslim Iran, they brought with them their one common bond - their ancient religion. Furthermore, in those early, relatively unsettled years in India, these Zoroastrian migrants might conceivably have welcomed the idea of converting to the Good Religion, such converts who 'would do no harm to the Good Religion' (PPC, 151). The logical explanation for this probably was that the allies best disposed to these religious refugees might, in fact, be such persons as had been converted to the faith.

This may be assumed to be the prevalent logic of the early years of settlement in India, indeed, might even explain the entrenched story of Akbar's 'conversion' in Parsi lore. With the progression of time, Justice Beaman perceives two significant factors working to re-mould Parsi sentiments towards proselytism. 'The first, and no doubt the most powerful of these, was the immemorial caste sentiment, with which the whole atmosphere in which they lived was charged. The second was their own growing prosperity' (PPC, 151). Indeed, the latter reinforced the former.

Justice Beaman's analysis of the institution of 'caste' commenced with the telling observation that, it is 'more acceptable to a high than to a low order in its organisation' (PPC, 151). The Indian Zoroastrians, while continuing in their strict adherence to their ancestral faith, were simultaneously erecting around themselves caste barriers which became deeply infused by their specific self-perceptions. Its result was that 'in modern popular language, it has found current expression in the term Parsi, which now seems to me to have as distinctly a caste meaning as essentially a caste connotation as that used to denominate any other great Indian caste' (PPC, 152).

Proceeding to the issues before the Court, Beaman stated, 'The first glance at the Defendant's definition of members of the Parsi community professing the Zoroastrian faith, satisfied me, once for all, that the basis of the controversy had shifted, and that we were not really concerned with a religious, but with a caste question' (PPC, 152). Clearly implying a revaluation of criteria, further analysis of the material presented to the Court revealed irrefutably that 'The Defendants, expressing as we now know the orthodox Parsi view, are prepared to overlook immorality, bastardy - anything but lineage' (PPC, 152). This then would appear to be the central issue of who precisely may be called a Parsi. The Defendants would readily admit any Irani Zoroastrian into their fold, regardless of his pedigree, but the doors would remain shut to the 'most blameless foreigner' (PPC, 152). The Justice's own rhetorical question is answered: 'Why? Because a foreigner is outside the caste, and caste is an institution into which you must be born' (PPC, 152). Extrapolating therefrom, the Judge sees no feature of religious dogma attached to it, rather 'pure, unadulterated Oriental caste' (PPC, 153).

This assessment, which Beaman J. maintained would be irrefutable to any unbiased person, leads to clear-cut consequences. The Zoroastrian community in India were a religious grouping to start with, but became over time a caste,

...singularly powerful, influential, and in every sense, a superior caste...The Indian Zoroastrians had been settled in their adopted country roughly for a thousand years before the period with which we are directly concerned. During the whole of that time, they had been exposed to the powerful impact of all sorts of social and religious conceptions, yet they were not absorbed...It is also to be noted that, however liberal they might have been when first they came to India, the Indian Zoroastrians were precluded - by the very means which they, growing in numbers and influence, adopted for the preservation of their own caste purity - from dissipating and losing themselves, in the vast ocean of Hinduism about them. Caste again. Just as now that they have assimilated in every sense the caste idea, and made it the bulwark of their tribal or caste unity, so they were themselves hemmed in by it (PPC, 153).

The acceptance of caste features and mechanisms might not have developed straightforwardly. After all, it was a foreign institution into which the Parsis had to accommodate themselves. The tensions implicit in the contradictory pulls of Zoroastrian doctrine and Hindu socio-religious structure have persisted to the present times when within the Indian Zoroastrian community the central controversy remains: whether it is permissible and commendable to convert aliens to the Zoroastrian faith. It was because the barriers of caste had been firmly erected around themselves - tight demarcation lines drawn between Parsis and non-Parsis - that 'as a matter of fact, few if any genuine conversions have ever been made; and, so far as our information goes, the conversion of Mrs.Tata is the very first instance of a genuine open conversion of a person' (PPC, 154).

Justice Beaman placed on record his conclusions:

The real, the plain point was simply this, that notwithstanding anything in their sacred writings, notwithstanding their own published utterances to the contrary, notwithstanding the *Rivayats*, notwithstanding everything, they took their stand not on religion but on Caste...That in a nutshell was the whole case for the Defendants...and in the end, I think, that it is a good case and must prevail (PPC, 155).

Detailed examination of the above point by the learned jurist was undertaken to determine, in his mind, the main issue of the case: whether Parsi charitable trusts and funds were available to non-Parsis. Having established that it was via the mechanism of caste, in its strict Hindu sense, that the terms Parsi and Zoroastrian had come to be coterminous within the Indian context, Beaman resolved that,'it was not the intention of the Founders of these Trusts to extend their benefits to anyone who was not in the most rigid caste sense a Parsi' (PPC, 155).

In summing up, Beaman J. glanced in passing at the major Parsi socio-religious-economic institutions assembled over their long centuries' residence in India, viz. their charitable trust funds, *anjuman* properties, religious institutions such as *atash bahrams*, *dakhmas* etc. Documents relating to the immovable properties set apart by the donors of trusts for the Indian Zoroastrians' use reveal the following terminological clauses: 'the entire Zoroastrian Anjuman' is mentioned; 'For the use of the Zoroastrians', 'Anjuman of the Zoroastrian Community', etc. (PPC, 156). Repeated references to the Zoroastrian community are indicative of the caste sentiment in the minds of the founders of these religious institutions. The Judge surmises thus,'It is evident that several of these are couched in the most general terms...certain expressions indicating that the caste spirit was active, such as the Zoroastrian Community, and the constant references to the Anjuman. But in not one do we find the word Parsi' (PPC, 156). It was the progression from 'Anjuman', giving way for the creation of the 'Parsi Panchayat...being essentially a caste institution and working the development of the caste sentiment' (PPC, 157), which reinforces the conceptual notion of caste as entrenched in the communal consciousness of the Indian Zoroastrians. Observing the Parsi community through the sifting of evidence presented in Court, Beaman concludes,

> The furthest that the most liberal of them [Bombay Zoroastrians] seem disposed to go is that, if undesirable converts of that kind must be made, they must be segregated, for purposes of worship and burial, from those who are born into the faith. In other words, while conversion, as a religious dogma is not denied, it, as every other social and religious observance, must fall under the rigid regulation of caste (PPC, 159).

The rationale of caste - exclusivity reinforced by endogamous marriages - became a doctrinaire feature of Parsi social custom, in the opinion of Beaman J. The keeping of '*dubri* mistresses' was tolerated. Since the operational structure of Hindu society is such that the probability of Parsi intermarrying with a Hindu of superior caste remained remote, owing to the proscription of such exogamous unions by the Hindus themselves - the fear of Parsi intermarriage with inferior castes must have caused an incessant anguish among community elders. Since intermarriage and conversion may be deemed two sides of the same coin, and to admit one would logically demand admittance to all, it may plausibly be suggested - as Justice Beaman does - that the Founders of the Trusts opted for a simpler formula: 'No Converts, then, on any terms' (PPC, 160). This Community *idee fixe* has meant therefore, that 'for many hundreds of years the Zoroastrian Community in India has meant one thing - and one thing only to them - their own select people' (PPC, 161).

Arriving by different means at the same conclusion, i.e. that conversion was not a part of Parsi usage, both Justices, Davar and Beaman thus upheld the Defendants' plea. Justice Beaman said,

> In the Zoroastrian Community...while the religion and its ritual purity are still the mainspring of the communal life, they are so intimately bound up with the exclusiveness and purity of the tribe or caste, that they have become practically identical (PPC, 162).

For the English Judge, it was unquestionably the apparatus of caste, in the strict Hindu sense, which had meant they emphasized birth as the determinant of religio-communal membership.

Justice Davar emphasized Parsi usage: non-proselytism, and the reluctant admittance to the fold of offspring of Parsi males and non-Parsi mothers, to rule in favour of the Defendants. Davar's strenuous emphasis on lineage as the criterion of community membership was reiterated:

> It appears that the main reasons which actuated those who advocated the admission of these children born of Parsi fathers was that persons in whose veins Zoroastrian blood flowed should not be allowed to live and die without having the benefits of the religion of their fathers, and that a Zoroastrian's offspring should not be allowed to be buried or burnt after death as a Durvand (PPC, 77).

The basis of this particular Parsi convention - non-admission of aliens into their fold - received differing interpretations by the two Justices. While Beaman saw Indian [Hindu] caste as the chief instrument of distinctivenss of community identity, Justice Davar emphasized Parsi history.

> ...in the early part of the last century, Parsi children by alien mothers were allowed to be invested with *Sudra* and *kusti* without much difficulty, but when the evil grew, there was opposition to this practice, and at first such practices were sought to be restricted by making the previous permission of

the Panchayet necessary, but later on the feeling against such admissions grew stronger and it was resolved not to admit such children at all, and various pains and penalties were prescribed for those who transgressed the Resolutions passed by the Anjuman (PPC, 112-3).

I find that all the indications most unmistakably point out that the idea of admitting a Durvand to their religion must at all times have been repugnant to the Parsis of the olden times (PPC, 113).

Justice Davar, viewing the facts presented before him, came to the conclusion that

...even if an entire alien - a Juddin - is duly admitted into the Zoroastrian religion after satisfying all conditions and undergoing all necessary ceremonies, he or she would not, as a matter of right, be entitled to the use and benefits of the Funds and Institutions now under the Defendants' management and control; that these were founded and endowed only for the members of the Parsi Community, and that the Parsi Community consists of Parsis who are descended from the original Persian emigrants, and who are born of both Zoroastrian parents, and who profess the Zoroastrian religion, who come to India, either temporarily or permanently, and the children of Parsi fathers by alien mothers who have been duly and properly admitted into the religion (PPC, 116-7).

It is this last definition of Davar's which is cited by the Parsi community as 'law'. viz. that it is 'legally' permissible for the offspring of a Parsi father and alien mother to be initiated into the faith, but not for the child descended from the female line. The Parsi Panchayat Case 1906 Judgement, cannot in strict legal terms be deemed to be a law enacted by a legislative body. The present Parsi practice hinges solely on the legal opinion of Justice Davar.
Justice Beaman concluded that

...whether the Zoroastrian religion recommends making Converts or not, the circumstances in which the Zoroastrian refugees found themselves on reaching India put all idea of giving practical effect to any such recommendation out of their heads, so that as time went on, except as a theological dogma, and in a few cases, like those of the Pandits (cited in the *Dhup Nirang*) and Akbar, genuine conversion, as a religious duty, had fallen into such complete desuetude...[that] for many hundreds of years the Zoroastrian Community in India had meant one thing - and one thing only to them - their own select people (PPC, 160-1).

The Parsi Panchayat Case is a legal judgement of considerable significance for the Parsi community. Although very few Parsis have perused the 164 page document, in the community's collective mind it has nevertheless come to be equated with an Ordinance. A custom has developed, believed to be codified in this Judgement, that offspring of Zoroastrian fathers and alien mothers may be initiated into the faith and thereafter participate as members of the Parsi community.[10] Conversely, children of Zoroastrian mothers and alien fathers are not deemed eligible for initiation into the Zoroastrian faith because in the general communal awareness this is seen as being 'against the religion' or 'it is against our laws'.[11] A High Court Judgement has come, in the course of time, to assume the weight of law and, as such, has become a significant legal document wielding immense influence in matters spiritual and temporal pertaining to the Parsi community.

The Parsi Panchayat Case of 1906 was indeed a momentous event in modern Parsi history. It came to be seen as 'community law', and duly treated as sacrosanct. Equally, it passed into community mythology, since few modern Parsis have studied the Judgement, the perceptions of individuals on vital community issues are beliefs and dogma, deemed to be related to their 'community law' which are handed down by successive generations. Whatever the merits of a legal document, on a vital issue such as 'acceptance' into the socio-religious fold of aliens who then acquire the rights and privileges of natural-born community members, it has meant that a Court in British India, presided over by an orthodox Parsi Judge and an English jurist, handed down an opinion on several important issues affecting the Parsi community of India. In the absence of communal structures - legislative, executive and juridical - the Parsi community, at the height of its prosperity under British dominion, was compelled to subject critical issues relating to its religion and community practices to Courts convened by the foreign rulers. A close scrutiny of the Judgement makes one indelible impression upon the reader's mind: that, here are a minority peoples, in a land in which, over centuries of adoption, they have become acclimatised, but from which they feel nevertheless distanced. It is their attempt to retain the two essential ingredients of their identity - religion and race - leading to their exile in India in the first instance, which after a millenium continued to exercise their minds. Given the extraordinary nature of the case, the Judgement handed down was bound to enter into the community annals as an important chapter in the tale of the Zoroastrians of India.

NOTES:

1. Shapur F.Desai, *History of the Bombay Parsi Panchayet,1860-1960*, (Bombay 1977), p.12.
2. *Report of the Sub-Committee Presented to the Anjuman on 2 August 1903*, 'In the Light of the Present State of the Religious Community, Would it be Proper to Take Outsiders into our Religion?'
3. *The Parsi*, February 1905, 'Parsi Proselytism: A Protest and the Committee's Reply'.
4. Protest forwarded to the trustees of the Parsi Panchayat Funds by Sir Pherozeshah M.Mehta and many other leading members of the Parsi Community, Bombay, 28 October, 1904.
5. Shapur Desai, *op.cit.*, p.15.
6. For a record of Counsel's Opinions, refer Shapur Desai, *op.cit.*, Appendix 'A', pp.237-250.
7. *Parsi Prakash*, vol.IV, 16 April 1905, p.14.
8. *Ibid.*
9. Shapur Desai, *op.cit.*, p.30.
10. This custom can vary in several parts of India and overseas where there is a Parsi community. The acceptance or otherwise of such children depends, in the last resort upon the local *mobed* and his willingness or otherwise to perform such *navjotes*.
11. Zoroastrian diaspora communities, especially those in North America, have begun to reverse this negative custom by including into their various Association Charters a proviso of their willingness to accept into the faith children descended on the Zoroastrian female side.

CHAPTER FIVE

ZOROASTRIANS IN THE OLD COUNTRIES

Introductory Remarks on Chapters 5 and 6

Chapters 5 and 6 deal with the results of the field studies conducted in spring 1988 in the USA and Canada; in the winter of 1988/89 in India and Pakistan, and in spring 1989 in the UK.

The persons interviewed are grouped into: youth (aged 16 - 30), and elders (31 years and over). At all times, every possible effort has been made to see that as wide a cross-section of the community is represented in the samples.

The total figures interviewed for this study are as follows:

North America (USA and Canada)	105
India	102
Pakistan	37
United Kingdom	50*
Iranian Zoroastrian refugees	21

* The British sample of 50 Zoroastrians here is additional to the earlier field work conducted in the UK, when in 1986/87, 204 British Zoroastrians were interviewed by me for the joint publication, *Living Flame, Zoroastrianism in Britain*, a comprehensive study of the community domiciled in the United Kingdom.

Additionally, eleven tape-recorded interviews with some leading members of the Parsi community in India and Pakistan were made.

In all, 326 persons aged 16 and over, have been canvassed in a structured, detailed analysis for this section of the work. The statistical schedule is included in the Appendix, where figures for individual countries, and the themes analysed, are to be found in its tables.

The Parsis of India and Pakistan: An Introduction

Prior to Indian independence in 1947, the Parsis were citizens of the political entity that was British India. Subsequent to the Partition of the country, the sub-continental community became either Indian Parsis or Pakistani Parsis. Over four decades in a predominantly Hindu India and an Islamic Pakistan, the Parsis have begun to demonstrate, in varying degrees, their acclimatisation to these newly-created political entities to which they now owed their national allegiance. The effects of the dominant environment within which a minority peoples have to survive, is clearly evidenced by these two groups. The process of 'Indianization' with its preponderant emphasis on the Hindu ethos of the land, and Islam as the *raison d'etre* of Pakistan, are the external variables within which the Parsis must function.

The Parsi population of India is numerically declining: the 1981 census put the figure at 71,630.[1] The Pakistani Parsi population has an approximate total of 3,700 souls.[2] The meagre numbers of the community plays an important part in their overall sense of identity: for some Parsis, a deeply-ingrained sense of belonging to a group with a long, proud historical and religious tradition heightens their sense of pride; for others, declining numbers is evidence of the impending extinction of their race. The polarity of these positions significantly influences its role in determining the numerical viability of the Parsi 'nation'.

Both Indian and Pakistani Parsis are a people with a shared heritage. The novel feature of distinctive political allegiances operates at a level that is far removed from the inner dynamics of community life. Thus, for both groups, the essential features which define them vis-a-vis the majority populations remain the same: they practise Parsi Zoroastrianism; they speak Parsi-Gujarati; they eat 'Parsi food', and their values and mores are those which, over the course of time, the Parsi people have made their own, viz. an admixture of their Zoroastrian ethos and sub-continental influences. It is therefore possible in socio-religious terms for a Parsi from India or Pakistan to see himself as part of the same group. This does not imply that the Parsis of the sub-continent are a monolithic community. Perceptible differences between the inhabitants of Karachi and Bombay, between rural and urban dwellers in particular, persists. Given their small size, the Zoroastrians of the Indian sub-continent display an immense group complexity .

NOTES:

1. 1981 Indian Census, 'Household Population By Religion of Head of Household'.
2. I am grateful to Ervad Dinshaw Sorab Charna of Karachi for having given me access to his records, which he has kept since 1950. The figures quoted were applicable for November 1988: 3,568 in Karachi; 8 in Lahore; 13 in Multan; 15 in Rawalpindi and 25 in Quetta.

The Parsis of India

The Parsis of India display substantially different patterns of adjustment to the majority culture and religions surrounding them. There are historical reasons for this. One thousand years in a predominantly Hindu India has resulted in the community's having arrived at a *modus vivendi* with their fellow Indians. The mandatory conditions putatively set forth by Jadav Rana[1] have been absorbed into the community's culture. In addition to their sense of familiarity with India and Indian conditions, the Parsis of that country are aware that they are the most numerous of the Zoroastrian population.[2] In the metropolis of Bombay where the single largest concentration of Zoroastrians worldwide is to be found - currently estimated at 50,050 souls - there is a sense of regarding their city as the 'capital' of the Parsis.[3]

Indeed, the community is predominantly urban (the rural population in 1981 was 2,954; the urban population count was 68,676),[4] and displays traits characteristic of the urban dweller, viz. that of a literate and professional people. These are admittedly generalisations, and it is not possible to delineate the 'typical' Indian Parsi with any degree of accuracy. There are wide differences in their self-perception and their major preoccupations, dependent on where precisely they live in the enormous diversity of India.

Their shared religious and cultural heritage has meant that, while they attempted to adjust to independent India in various ways, certain intrinsic community issues, a community ethos and the fact that by name and appearance often they can be signalized as Parsis, makes it possible, with reservations, to outline a profile of the Indian Parsi. They are by far the most urbanised community on the Indian sub-continent. It is an ageing population with diminishing fertility (in the decade 1961-71 there was a decrease of 9.86% in numbers);[5] and a growing propensity for late marriages and postponement of marriages altogether.[6] Thus, the 'never-married' in the age groups above 15 years was higher among the Parsis than in the general population, and the proportion of the 'marrieds' was lower than in most age groups, the incidence of non-marriages increasing the higher the level of education.[7] Accordingly, Visaria remarks, 'The Parsi population has been a remarkable exception in the general Indian demographic scene...their fertility is so low that despite a high life expectancy, the number of Parsis has been declining for more than two decades'.[8]

The changing composition of the community in India is based on the ageing process as a result of late marriages and no marriages, combined with low fertility and small families, and a trend towards low mortality. The ethnographic boundary of the community too is being altered by an evidential increase in inter-community marriages (discussed below), and a probable increase in emigration, which must remain conjectural in the absence of available substantive data.

Compounding these variables is the decline in the economic prosperity of the community. After reaching the high watermark of economic achievement during the British period of Indian history, some commentators maintain that its economic decline is the result of a perceptible change in the community's attitude towards work and enterprise. '...An increasing fraction of the community is sliding towards the lower end of the national economic scale: from upper-middle income to middle income, from middle income to lower-middle, and from lower-middle to various grades of poverty'.[9]

To grasp the fundamental alterations in the community's relationship to its environment as a result of a diminishing ability to grasp economic opportunities, or to create them as did their forbears in the 18th and 19th centuries, is to overlook the significant contributions being made by Parsis in diverse creative spheres. The better known illustrations would include Astad Deboo, Dr.Aban Mistry, Pinaz Masani in the various aspects of Indian classical art, Dina Mehta in creative writing, and numerous others of national and international stature.

In order to understand and evaluate the Parsi community of India today, it is essential to assess their earlier history on the sub-continent as a determinedly Zoroastrian migrant group, eager to enhance their individual and communal prosperity through adjustment to the environment and by setting the pace of their enterprise culture. The gradual loosening of socio-cultural bonds as a result of the erosion of community structures, brought about a different world-view. Exposure to other prevailing cultures, chief among which were the Hindu (other than Gujarat Hindus), and British influences, the incorporation of customs and values borrowed from those alien folk-ways, and a corresponding decline in their understanding of their Zoroastrian faith [as opposed to the continued practice of its rituals], served to weaken their original religious allegiance which had been the cohesive element holding them together as a people distinct among India's multitudes. The erosion of their uniquely Zoroastrian traditions has resulted in a decline in community consciousness and their sense of Parsi identity.

Owing to a noticeable decline in 'Parsipanu' (Parsi-ness), a blurring of the awareness of identity and the diminution of their particular culture was under way, compounded by the various socio-economic ills which began to beset a once proud and prosperous people. Several attempts have been made within the past decade to ameliorate, or even postpone, a communal disintegration. In this spirit, the Federation of Parsi Zoroastrian Anjumans of India aims at promoting collaboration between the various *anjumans*, and attempts to achieve solutions to specific local issues as well as safeguard the vast assets of the Indian Parsi community. In this community-wide venture, the *anjumans* representing the small towns and hamlets work alongside representatives of the bigger conurbations. A national perspective of the Parsis of India is beginning to emerge, with specialised studies commissioned by the Federation on the demographic and socio-economic issues affecting it. Since some 70% of the Parsi population is to be found in Bombay, the activities of the community there often have effects which reach far beyond it. The Committee for Electoral Reform (C.E.R.) was set up to investigate the election of members of the *Anjuman Committee* (the electoral college which elects the trustees of the Bombay Parsi Panchayat). As a result, an increased accountability from the trustees towards their public, and their undertaking of important activities such as the much-needed housing programme in Bombay and the suburbs, and efforts at alleviating the imbalance between supply and demand for housing in this congested metropolis is under way.

> Parsis today, have a lack of knowledge of self and a lack of confidence of their various achievements and contributions...I see a disintegration phenomenon [overtaking the community]...There are deeper causes for this. Parsis have not been persecuted by the Hindus...The reverse is happening: the modernization of the Hindu community.[10]

The quintessence of the modern Parsis in India lies in their ability to adjust to the realities of an independent India, and their aptitude as a tiny minority to respond to a diminished economic position in a country where they no longer retain a monopoly on educational and professional excellence, in a country with which they have always assumed an ambivalent relationship, and surrounded by a majority culture which the young within the community are emulating and becoming absorbed into at a noticeable rate. The outward attributes of Parsi recognizability are undergoing change.

Their unchanging minority status contributed to their complex labyrinth of self-perceptions. The interactions between the Parsis and the Hindu majority was, and continues to be, a synthesis of various positive and negative dispositions maintained on both sides. In earlier times the Parsis saw themselves as Indians, but not *of* India. Nevertheless, influential Parsis of the stature of Dadabhai Naoroji, Sir Pherozeshah Mehta, D.E.Wacha, Jamshedji Tata and others, espoused a conscious policy of primary and unswerving allegiance to the country. A short extract from a speech by Sir Pherozeshah Mehta must suffice in illustrating this contention:

> To ask the Parsees to isolate themselves and their interests from those of the other natives of his country is to preach something not equally selfish, but a great deal more short-sighted and unwise. In our case, it would be almost a

suicidal policy. Its ultimate effect would be to reduce us to insignificance...Isolated as Parsees, pure and simple, holding ourselves aloof from the other natives of the country, without common interests, common sympathies and common co-operation, we might still remain an interesting community, but of no account whatsoever in the great march of events moulding the lofty destinies of this magnificient land.[11]

These eminent Parsis who were fervent Indian nationalists remained, however, as a minority within the community; today an increasing number among them stress their Indian nationality.

The dynamic of Parsi community life, forged by its Zoroastrian religion and attendant beliefs, values and customs, has interacted with the Hindu environment. There is a growing body of Parsi opinion today which affirms its patriotic pride of belonging to India. However, the echoes are often those of the zealous convert. The underlying tensions between 'Parsipanu' and the Indian patriot continue to sound a discordant note. In the closing decade of the present century, the Parsis of India are attempting to resolve the dilemma of their religio-ethnic communal pride, with the larger national identity of a country which is emerging as a major actor on the Asian political stage.

Homeland: Understandably, therefore, for the Indian Parsi, his perception of his homeland remains a complex issue. The conflicting emotional imperatives of ancestry, religion, social conditioning and aspirations for oneself and one's family were expressed by various respondents, even though most of the youth and their elders, considered India to be their country (Refer Table 1). Thus, a 24 year old in Bombay said, 'This is my homeland. I was born here, my father was born here, and before that we were born in India. The customs of India that have gone into my system will remain'. A 39 year old gentleman however said, 'No. There is something missing. We are Indians, but Zoroastrians belong somewhere else'. This was a recurring view, of being Indian but somehow less Indian than their compatriots. A 40 year old, originally from the priestly town of Navsari, said, 'I feel rootless in India. There is very little by way of feeling the way a Hindu feels'.

The perceptions of a minority peoples differ substantially from those belonging to large national entities where, precisely because of their size and fact of being, their sense of identity is re-emphasized. The Zoroastrians, on the other hand, have long memories of being a minority people in their ancestral land and the adopted land of Zoroastrianism, India. While the question of patriotism may be a straightforward conviction of loyalty to country for a Dane or a Frenchman, for example, it is plainly not so for the Parsi.

How one wishes to see oneself is to some degree contingent upon how others see one.'Basically, being a Parsi, a small community, we have the greater need to belong. I need a nationality. Being an Indian, the country has given me recognition'. One youth spoke for many, 'I do think I am Indian. But I think Indianness is hard to define'.[12]

The Editor of *Parsiana* (a monthly magazine for the Zoroastrian community with a global circulation), Jehangir Patel, maintained that the dichotomy between being Parsi or Indian first was evident from an earlier time.'This was very strong in the 1950s/60s. But what the community is facing today is a question of survival, and the issues that occupy the mind are survival, existence and competition.' There is grave disquiet among the Parsis and the Zoroastrian community at large, of their rapidly declining numbers. Where two or more Zoroastrians gather, this matter is endlessly debated. The awareness of the paucity of their numbers, and that they must necessarily constitute only a fraction of any national population, has led them to adopt an eminently pragmatic approach to their adaptation to the governing ethos of their countries.

The complexity of the Parsi position is not resolved, however, by comparisons of India with other nation-states, nor is the dilemma decided by equating the Parsi experience with that of the Hindus of India. There are discrete patterns of development for different peoples, and its acknowledgement must be the *terminus a quo* for an analysis and subsequent understanding of the issue.

Language: The distinctive linguistic development of the Parsis is reflected in the findings. Very few of the youth and their elders now 'thought' in Gujarati. (Refer Table 2).

It would appear that the Parsis, newly arrived, made strenuous efforts to acquire the local Gujarati vernacular. A minority from the outset, they saw their advancement in the land of their adoption expedited through a facility with the native tongue. The Parsis however, show an 'exceptionally peculiar position compared to other ethnic groups of India'.[13] Having brought their Persian phonology with them to India, they then proceeded to transfer it to the local Gujarati. This linguistic assimilation must have developed over a long period of time. However, owing to inter-caste constraints, even as late as the 19th century, the Parsis socialised scarcely with speakers of Standard Gujarati. The chief priority of these Parsis was to preserve their ethnic identity, rather than imitate Standard Gujarati.

In the 19th century, as they took the lead in the professions, Parsi creativity in Gujarati in every single subject was clearly evident. Simultaneously, the Parsis came to dominate in the professions requiring functional English by acquiring a proficiency in that language.[14] The pervasiveness of Western education meant that, by the 1920s, writing, and to a large extent, thinking in English, had supervened Parsi-Gujarati creativity. The exceptions to this general rule were the dramatist and writer Adi Marzban, and the pre-eminent Gujarati poet, Ardeshir Khabardar; their creativity in the language was not, however, a community-wide phenomenon, and the steady demise of Parsi-Gujarati was to continue apace.

Bharati Modi indicates that Parsis below 40 years of age show scant command of Parsi-Gujarati. Those upto 25 years of age make use of English as their main language.[15] Not surprisingly, therefore, a 63 year old grandmother lamented, 'Formerly we thought in Gujarati. Now English is thrust upon us because Parsis don't speak proper Gujarati'.

Thus we come to an appraisal of the Parsis' relationship to Gujarati, their adoptive 'mother tongue'. It was the Parsis' overriding sense of ethnic identity which inhibited them from becoming totally enveloped by, and an indistinguishable part of, the Gujarati Hindu cultural ethos. The elevation of Bombay to state capital of Maharashtra wherein Maharashtrians comprise the majority, and the gradual rise of Hindi as the *lingua franca* of North India, in addition to English, has further resulted in the eclipse of Parsi-Gujarati, especially among those under 25. The passing away of Parsi-Gujarati is a cultural loss. More importantly, its effects on the identity of the Parsi community were to be far reaching.

Knowledge of Zoroastrian History: The contemporary community has only limited knowledge of the history of Zoroastrian Iran and Parsi settlement in India: the overwhelming majority of the youth and their elders admitted to having no knowledge. (Refer Table 3).

The only extant record of the early centuries of residence in India, the *Kisseh-i Sanjan*, is no longer read by the Parsis. Precisely because of the absence of familiarity with the document, substantive myths have developed which have a powerful hold on community consciousness. This author was consistently told that, 'we gave the Raja a promise not to convert'; repeated references were made to the *dastur's* blending of 'sugar and milk' so that the Parsis would accordingly blend with, and sweeten the land in which they had sought refuge; and having brought the *Iranshah* fire (the first *Atash Bahram* consecrated in Sanjan), from Iran in the initial migration. Equally, while older Parsis, especially those who spent their youth in Parsi strongholds such as Navsari, Surat, Bombay, attest to their knowledge of the *Shah-nameh*, which gave them a perspective of Zoroastrian Iran, the youth canvassed were oblivious of the Epic, which therefore did not play a part in their cultural formation. Quite simply, the *Shah-nameh* is not the role model for young Parsis that it continues to be for many Iranians, or some older Parsis.[16]

A 29 year old company executive spoke of his own position:

> I have no knowledge of Zoroastrian history. Invariably, somewhere along the line we lose sight of our history and

culture because of two	extremes, Western and Indian
influences. So I can	quote Ghalib [an Urdu poet], but not
anything from Zoroastrian literature. I had never heard of the
Shah-nameh before you mentioned it. Growing up in North
India we had no access to the Zoroastrian religion. I grew up
in the Hindustani heartland, so my cultural in-put is thoroughly
Indian.

The supersedure of the dominant culture must to some extent be held
responsible for the loss of knowledge of Zoroastrian history, but it cannot be
held to be totally responsible therefor. Had the Parsi community in India
wished to cling to their knowledge of their 'glorious past', they had the
resources to do so. As matters now stand, Parsi youth '...have no knowledge.
I learnt history at school, from the Indus Valley to Indira Gandhi'. The
forfeiture of cognizance of their ancestral past must mean the decomposition,
in due course, of their group persona, for a people who do not know their
history are unable to chart their future. The question thereupon poses itself:
can a people survive without memory?

Zoroastrian Identity: The most striking paradox in the study of the
contemporary Zoroastrian community is that despite the internal
contradictions such as issues of rituals and religion, Parsi and Iranian
Zoroastrian cultural differences, the ethnocentric stance against proselytism,
the one universal feature exhibited by this small but immensely complex group
is an innate, almost inexplicable pride in being Zoroastrian. The respondents
in the field studies made no distinction between Parsi and Zoroastrian, and
used the terms interchangeably. They take great pride in being 'born
Zoroastrian': all of the youth identified themselves as Zoroastrians, and
almost all their elders did likewise. (Refer Table 4).

There are prosaic reasons for not denying one's identity: 'I never deny I am
a Zoroastrian. From our looks one can tell that we are Parsis'; to the more
romantic, 'I am proud to be a Zoroastrian; it is an ancestral pride'. There are
equally, constraints on declaring one's Zoroastrian identity. A Parsi lady
married to a Hindu said, 'I do identify, but I can't loudly proclaim it now
because it would not be acceptable to my in-laws'.

While the Zoroastrians emphasize their religion, they are in fact more than
merely a religious group. Their ethnicity, distinctive culture and value system
encompass a wider span. Their self-identification as Zoroastrians is 'more'
than a religious identity for the majority of the youth and their elders (Refer
Table 4(a)). This pattern is repeated within Zoroastrian groups in Pakistan,
North America, and the United Kingdom. The expression most widely used
to describe what being a Zoroastrian meant was that it was 'a way of life'.
One lady spoke for many, '...in the end it is everthing. One is brought up with

the values. I am a Parsi. It means I am something special. That's enough'. A middle-aged professional gentleman maintained that 'It is more the fact of all the qualities of what we learn from our history of ancient Persia. I see myself more in terms of ancient, historical, cultural values'. Here clearly, the Zoroastrian identity closely approximates a national identity. While Zoroastrians themselves, and the world at large perceives them as a 'religious' group, the dynamic of the Zoroastrian community has been in the process of developing an unarticulated, and at this stage, an unsophisticated sense of a'national'identity, to be discussed in Chapter 7. This issue relates equally to the recurring dilemma of whether one is first a Parsi or an Indian. A community elder placed it in context:

> In the last forty years this nebulous word 'secularism' has come in [to the Indian political vocabulary]. Although it is proclaimed, everybody knows that it takes second place to community, caste, region etc. To that extent, you have to read the thinking of the Parsis in the context of the India of today, in the context of all the other communities of India. So if today someone says that he sees himself as Parsi first, let me say that most other Indians see themselves in terms of their own community. As the saying goes, 'the smallest minority in India are the Indians'.

The development, over time, whereby the community has begun to be more self-conscious about itself as something more than just a religious aggregation, has been nurtured in a political environment which itself is prone to segmentation, given the pervasiveness of caste, languages, religions and regional differences. It could be argued that the development of a peculiar type of national identity of the Parsis of India (and the Zoroastrians in other parts of the world), symbolised by their membership in a religious group and subliminally aware of a 'glorious heritage', is equally the product of an environment where the other groups around them see themselves similarly as Punjabis or Bengalis first.

Chief External Influences: The outer parameters of identity of the Zoroastrians, surrounded as they are definitionally by non-Zoroastrians, assuredly take in elements from these diverse cultures. Yet over half the number of the youth and a sizeable number of the elders maintained that the most profound influences upon them were in fact 'Zoroastrian'(Refer Table 5). Some additional explanations are called for (which apply equally to the field work conducted in Pakistan, North America and the UK). The original questionnaire did not contain a sub-section on 'Zoroastrian influences', given that it does not constitute external influences. However, the respondents repeatedly spoke of their 'Parsi home influences', 'Zoroastrian religious influences', 'Parsi family and friends', 'socialise with Parsis only', etc. Thus, the findings had to incorporate this in its calculations with the interchangeable reference to the 'Zoroastrian influences' upon the respondents.

'Parsis adapt the best of everything. On New Year's Eve we go to a dance; on Diwali we burst crackers'. The two-fold influences - Western and Eastern - upon the community, young and old, emphasize the Parsis' own propensities for adaptation, adjustment and blending of the varied external influences upon his community persona. Yet, Zoroastrianism had made a major discrete impact upon some respondents - as a 19 year old Bombay student was prepared to admit, 'Parsi influences...I wouldn't know anything about the [Parsi] customs. I might not even follow them. But my basic values are Zoroastrian. That's important'. This underpinning of the group persona and the implication for each individual by the term 'Parsi' or 'Zoroastrian', was at the nucleus of these discussions. Their being Parsi was intrinsic to their perception of self.'Customs, values, beliefs are Parsi. We are Indians, but we are Parsis. Something very different from other Indians'. A young mother held firmly to her view that, 'Parsis are brought up with the concept of good thoughts, words and deeds. We take these through our lives. We can never fully become a part of Indian society and move beyond our Parsi background and entrenched Parsi views. There is a definite difference between a Parsi and others'.

References have been made to the developing idiom of Indianization through a growing sense of nationhood in a country of diversity which has but recently become independent from foreign rule. One method of achieving this is the compulsory study of the Hindi language at school level in addition to the regional language and English. The eclipse of Parsi-Gujarati for the young Parsi, and his mandatory acquisition of Hindi-speaking skills (more especially in North India), has made it feasible to print the *Khordeh Avesta* (book of daily prayers), in the Devanagari script. Copies of this are in demand by the northern Indian *anjumans* of Allahabad, Delhi, Kanpur, Lucknow and Ajmer, where the youth have a fluent command of the Hindi language.[17] This then is the evolving trend in India today: the attempt at retention of the accustomed *Avestan* and *Pazand* prayers made legible in a language - Hindi - which is becoming a second language of the Parsis of India. Insofar as the Hindi language continues to make inroads through all the states of the realm as the vehicle for the expression of a national consciousness, the Parsis of India will to that extent become increasingly Indianized, and their particular religious invocations may come to be through yet another language than the original *Avestan*.

The Indianization of the Parsis is perhaps the most striking feature for those whose knowledge of the sub-continent and the community is renewed through frequent contact with both. It is what strikes this author most forcefully. There has been a qualitative shift in emphasis on identity now under way. As with all periods of transition, the final results are not clearly discernible yet, but the visible outlines of the future are taking shape. This is a period of greater Parsi ambiguity: their past legacy of aloofness from India is giving way to their recognition of the fact that this is the country in which they must live and come to terms with. If they are to build for themselves and their progeny a worthwhile life, they must do so meaningfully within an Indian context. The experiment is embraced with great enthusiasm by some who speak of themselves unreservedly as Indians; it is a novel and daring adjustment being made by others who find it difficult to jettison their deepest Parsi convictions. A discernible Indianization of the Parsis, now more widespread than at any other time, is a new phenomenon. Often, however, the respondent's reactions reflect his particular experiences and anxieties among the majority peoples. Asked whether they felt that Parsis were rejected, respected or ignored in India, over half the number of the youth and the elders felt that the community was treated with respect in India (Refer Table 1(a)).

A young student in Bombay explained that there were indeed 'various types of Indians, and it depends on their experiences. For the outstanding Parsi they have regard. In our peer group, they ridicule us for wearing *sudre-kusti*'.[18] A middle-aged lady spoke of her experiences: 'I came across a great deal of prejudice and antagonism from the Gujaratis of India. They think of us as a people without a country'. A 37 year old gentleman referred to the diversity of India: 'Regionalism is very strong in India. Thus essentially, we [Parsis] are accepted because we cannot do very much harm. Their attitude is "we will accept you because you are there". It is difficult to tell how much hypocrisy there is when they say, "you Parsis are nice"'.

Indeed the Parsis, like any other group of people, cannot escape the dynamics of their socio-cultural surroundings. In a country of India's diversity, they must inevitably take their share of the prejudices of the land.

Conversion: On the Indian sub-continent, religious and community identity are closely interwoven. Sub-continental Parsis, in the main, find the decoupling of the social and religious an alien concept. It applies to the old as well as the young. When respondents were asked their views on conversion of aliens, over half of the youth as well as their elders were against it (Refer Table 7). There were those who advocated 'selective conversion', but were unable to establish guidelines as to who could be admitted and who should be left out. There were those who were confused on what precisely constitutes a 'convert', i.e. the acceptance into the religious fold of someone of alien faith. There were those who maintained the position held among a substantial number of Parsis that one ought not to change one's allegiance from religion to religion and thereby from one community to another. To advocate conversion therefore was to imply that there were superior and inferior religions.

The question of conversion - precisely because of its emotive content - had left some Parsis perplexed. They did not understand this complex subject. One young gentleman admitted,

> I don't understand the subject of conversion very well. If a person converts in adulthood, his social and cultural background is different. Can we really relate to him as a true Zoroastrian? On the other hand, my sense of equality and fairness tells me that if a person wants to convert, the principle of Hindu tolerance which gave us sanctuary should not be forgotten [by us]. I feel we should also tolerate someone who wants to come in.

There were those who felt that the only way to solve the 'community's myriad problems was to accept converts'. For those who advocated the induction of aliens into the fold, there were often historical precedents to be considered. 'I am totally in favour of conversion. I feel that non-conversion developed as a custom. How did Zoroaster make the first Parsi?' Equally, the perceived religious imperative was invoked: 'No conversion. The religion does not talk about conversion. That's what I have been told'.

The discussion on the question of conversion remains, however, at a theoretical level in India. It is not a predominant community issue, the more urgent concern being intermarriage. It is whether the children of mixed marriages should or should not be taken into the fold, which is often linked with the issue of conversion. This is in contradistinction to the position espoused, for instance, by the community in North America, where the intake of children of mixed unions is not confused with the conversion of aliens to the Zoroatrian religion. Nevertheless, in the common perception, a close connection between conversion and intermarriage has been fostered.

Mr. Aspi Moddie put it in an Indian context:[19]

> In India, I think conversion is not a real problem, because we haven't had cases of conversion. It is a theoretical problem. In other words, people will be 'for' or 'against' it...In India I haven't heard of a non-Zoroastrian who wishes to convert...The really big problem in India is not just intermarriage but the conversion of children of mixed marriages...As I see it, there is a distinction between the Indian and American situations. In America, Christian evangelism is very strong. There you have non-Zoroastrians dedicated to conversion. In India you don't have that phenomenon. Therefore, it is not a social threat to the Parsis here to the extent that it might be to the Zoroastrians in America...There

is another difference. The Parsi Zoroastrian, and maybe the Iranian Zoroastrian too, finds a greater challenge to his identity in the West than he does in India. To that extent, he has to react more strongly on both fronts: intermarriage and conversion.

Intermarriage: If conversion is a theoretical issue for the Indian community, intermarriage has become a very real predicament (Refer Tables 8 & 8(a)). Being a relatively recent phenomenon, it is one that is inadequately researched. Parsis, like their fellow Zoroastrians in Iran, have historically encouraged marriage within the fold. This was the norm in the early centuries of social isolation, when the barriers of caste operated and social mobility was minimal. An ostensibly secular India is attempting to eliminate old barriers. For an urban people like the Parsis, the feasibility of professional and social intercourse with non-Parsis, has become a fact of their lives. It is in the work-place and at social gatherings that they meet and choose to marry persons of other faiths. There is a growing perception among the Parsis of India that intermarriage has increased at a rapid and, some would say, an alarming rate.

The Parsi communities of India are to be found in virtually all parts of the country. There are, consequently, slight but discernible differences among them which must be attributed to the size of the community; its urban or rural setting; the regional influences that are brought to bear upon it, and the composition of the group. While this author was frequently assured that 'every family will have someone who has intermarried', it is useful to draw attention, on this subject, to the differences between the community in Bombay for example, and that in Delhi.

A pioneering work on the Delhi community, prepared in 1978, throws light on the Parsis in the capital city of India.[20] Comparative analyses of the most populous Zoroastrian stronghold, Bombay (population 50,050) and Delhi (population 600 approximately), highlight some interesting features. The age structures of the two communities are roughly similar, with some divergence in the over-50s age group. The higher percentage of older Parsis reflects the longer life expectancy of the community and the declining fertility now attributed to the group. The educational profile of the two groups show significant departures, however, in the higher educational category: 43% of Delhi Parsis have university degrees as opposed to 10.5% of those in greater Bombay.[21] Not surprisingly therefore, there is a fairly even percentage distribution between 'administration', professional and white-collar jobs among the men and women of the Delhi community, whereas in Bombay the majority (19%) claimed to be in white-collar jobs; the professions came next, and administrative employment last of all (Bose & Khullar,1978, 56).

Perhaps the most instructive finding of the Bose-Khullar study of the Delhi community is their observation that,

> ...judging by the evidence that came our way, we cannot say that the Delhi Parsis have a strong cultural identity. This may be attributed to their assimilation in metropolitan/cosmopolitan culture which transcends the community-specific culture. The values they seem to cherish are not insular; they are transcultural values, such as entrepreneurial and vocational mobility, zeal for education, and active involvement in business, commerce, industry, professions and other sections of national life (*loc.cit.*63).

This 'trans-cultural' affinity being a pronounced feature of the Delhi community must in part account for the increasing rate of intermarriages taking place there.[22]

The brief outline of the Delhi community and the growing rate of intermarriages evidenced there, ought not to give the impression that the proportion of intermarriages in Bombay is lower. In the absence of similar demographic work on the Bombay Parsi community, it is difficult to state with any authority the rate of intermarriages occurring in that metropolis. Nevertheless, a widely-held view by the Bombay Parsis themselves is that their young are marrying exogamously at a rapidly rising rate. The distinctiveness of the two groups lies perhaps in the degree and manner of assimilation into the larger group: the Delhi community appears to be aggressively assimilationist; the Bombay community still has access to Parsi religious infrastructures which permeate the city, housing colonies (or *baughs*), *agiaries*, *atash bahrams*, and *dakhmas*, and an old established communal network which acts as a brake on total mergers. To the outsider, Bombay gives the impression, in part, of being a 'Parsi city'. This is why perhaps the perception of the 'alarming rate of increase' of intermarriages among the Parsis of Bombay, as of Parsis elsewhere, presents itself as a major concern. The identity of the community is in fact being reconsidered through the phenomenon of mixed marriages. How the community will deal with it, indeed, whether if at all it will be able to deal with it, will be indicative of the community's future direction. At this stage one can only assess current opinions.

The Parsis of Bombay offer a novel rationale as to why intermarriages have increased so dramatically in their city. They blame it squarely on the appalling housing shortage, where a couple must wait years before finding even a small apartment, which leads to postponed marriages and smaller families. According to this school of thought, if a Parsi lady meets a non-Parsi who offers her marriage and an apartment, she accepts both with alacrity. There has to be some element of truth in this theory, if only because it was so often mentioned as the 'reason' for the increase in intermarriages. However, the theory seems flawed in several aspects, not the least of which is that all Bombay residents are equally affected by the acute housing shortage and congested urban living conditions. Comparative analysis of the rate of intermarriages among the various groups of Bombay citizens is not available, and as such the general theory remains to be accredited.

The reactions to intermarriage are instinctive. Often one's opinions are influenced by a family member having intermarried and the repercussions of it upon the family as a whole. A gentleman whose son had an American wife, put it thus: 'Times are changing. The community is modernizing. No objection to intermarriage should be taken as long as the religion is preserved. The modern generation will not listen to what parents say, anyway'. A poignant response came from a Parsi lady,'I have intermarried. There are different reasons for different people. But speaking for myself, I am against intermarriage. Given the same opportunities, I would go for a Parsi man. I am still a Parsi'.

Whatever the reasons for the many problematical issues facing the Parsi community of India and the Zoroastrian community beyond, the dynamics which cause them are a mix of internal and external factors. The inner mechanisms of the community which have sustained it over a long period of time, viz. the application of the Zoroastrian religion as corner-stone of communal life, the consequential development of their culture - distinct and distinguishable from the rest of India, and the separateness from the other Indian peoples in all but the spheres of professional and business life, have begun to gradually unwind over the past four decades. The India it today inhabits is vastly different from the India of yester-year.

The fear among certain sections of the community in India and beyond is that the newly emergent community bugbears of intermarriage and conversion, were they to gain greater currency, could in due course change the face of the Zoroastrian community. Thus, marriage, which is more a social phenomenon, is overlaid with religion, culture, mores and an inculcated sense of duty, in a peculiarly Parsi idiom.

Long-term future: What then, is seen as the long-term future of the Parsis of India? Half the number of the youth and a sizeable number of their elders consider it as being 'negative' (Refer Tables 9 & 9(a)).

While discussions with a sample cross-section reflected the depth of anxieties felt by some Parsis for the future, there is a pressing need for scientific evaluation of the situation. In the words of one respondent,

> I cannot give an opinion. What will have to be identified is the trend in the attrition rate in terms of intermarriage, conversion,

children's *navjotes* etc. These trends must be looked at in terms of growth or decline of the community.

It is precisely the lack of substantive data on these pivotal community issues, which makes any prognosis difficult.

The issue at the core of the Zoroastrian dilemma over their identity and uncertainty over their future must rest on the fact of their minority status. When a people are reduced to a minority in their ancestral land, and strive to attain a certain level of accomplishment in the adoptive land, an evolving minority psychology must be given due consideration. An understanding of the contemporary community, the preponderant part in India, and those in other countries, needs to acknowledge the interaction with the majority peoples, as forming a crucial part of the overall equation. The intra-communal dynamics are the obverse of that coin.

The Parsi community of India publicly admits there are areas of socio-religious concern. The question then arises: why have no corrective measures been taken to deal with it? It is conceded that the Parsis of India are among the most developed ethnic communities in Asia, excluding Japan. Yet these highly-developed and articulate people have allowed the erosion of their community structures, which would otherwise have helped channel debate and execute policy in national and trans-national terms.

Asked to explain this absence of infrastructure, some eminent Parsis baldly stated that they perceived no need for it, and in any event, considered it inoperable. Panchayat Trustee, Homi Ranina maintained, 'We've never had a centralness. To have a centralness you need a certain discipline'. This author was struck by the lowest priority given to the imperative for communal infrastructures. The absence of mechanisms for full discussion and open debate, followed by legislation on internal domestic community matters, which could then be administered by a qualified representative body, must be a *primum mobile* for the present malaise besetting the group. The will to create a purpose-made organisational framework appears to be lacking since few, if any, Parsis intellectually grasp the dire consequences of the perpetuation of the present unregulated, *ad hoc* system of conducting community affairs.[23]

India's axiality in the history of the Zoroastrian peoples spanning the past millenium, is centripetal. It gave shelter to the Parsis when they needed it. It permitted them to live free from fear, and practice their faith without significant strictures. Zoroastrians the world over are morally obliged to acknowledge and affirm their indebtedness to the Indian system, which allowed them to flourish while Zoroastrians in the ancestral land were being oppressed. Unquestionably, India has developed as the second land of Zoroastrianism.

While the Parsis reached supreme heights of achievement during the 18th and 19th centuries, and developed a self-confidence inspired by their attainments as individuals, they had ignored the dissolution of the internal community structures. Their success in the diverse fields of commerce, science, technology, law, medicine and education, had supplanted their long-held and deeply cherished religious traditions, historical awareness and cultural cohesiveness.

The lack of a sound textual knowledge of the religion, their historical antecedents, the myths and legends of their civilization, together with an appreciation of the beliefs, values and traditions of daily life, issuing from their religio-historical past, is chiefly responsible for the incremental loss of modern ethno-religious identity among the urbanized Parsis of India today.

NOTES:

1. Refer Chapter 1 'Historical Background'.
2. There are no accurate figures available for the current Zoroastrian population of Iran, and the government figure of 90,861 as per the 1986 Iranian Census is suspect.
3. 1981 Census Figures. The Bombay Parsi population has rapidly diminished: it is an ageing population with a declining birth rate. In this connection, refer to a paper by Shiavax Nargolwala,'Population of Zoroastrians in the World and in India', distributed by the Bombay Parsi Panchayat. Further reading on the demographic variables is, Kingsley Davis, *The Population of India and Pakistan*, (Princeton, 1951), p.185. The *Statistical Abstract of British India*, LVII (1912/13-1921/22), 16-17, Tables 8 and 9, shows the Parsi population of British India to have been 102,000 in 1921.
4. Shiavax Nargolwala, *ibid.*
5. Census of India, 1971.
6. Malini Karkal, 'Marriage among Parsis', *Demographic India*, Vol.IV, No.1, June 1975.
7. Parsis of Greater Bombay Part X (I-D), *Census of India*, Vol.X, Maharashtra Census Office, Bombay, 1971.
8. Leela Visaria, 'Demographic Transition Among Parsis: 1881-1981 I'; 'Size of Parsi Population', Vol.IX, No.41; II 'Level and Trends in Mortality', Vol.IX, No.42; and III 'Fertility Trends', October 1974, as quoted in Shankar Bose and Ava Khullar, *A Socio-Economic Survey of The Parsis of Delhi*, Centre for the Study of Developing societies, (Delhi, 1978), p.28.
9. Jamshed Modi, 'Fighting Fire with Fire', Bombay, 1976.
10. I am indebted to Dr.Freddi Mehta, a Director of Tatas, for his viewpoints expressed in his interview.
11. As quoted in G.A.Natesan (ed), *Famous Parsis: Biographical and Critical Sketches*, (Madras,1930), p.332.
12. The author grew up in the city of Calcutta and attended a predominantly Bengali college where she was the only Parsi student. The University lecturers, after endless debates among themselves failed to identify which 'country' she hailed from. The question was ultimately put to her, and upon receiving the reply that she was in fact from Calcutta, she was told it was 'quite extraordinary'. The majority of the academic staff had never before met a Parsi!
13. Bharati Modi, 'Parsi Gujarati: A Dying Dialect', a paper presented at the K.R.Cama Oriental Institute's International Congress, Bombay, January 1989. See also Chapter 1 'Parsi migration and acclimatisation in India'.
14. Refer Chapter 1 'Parsi migration and acclimatisation in India'; see J.R.Hinnells, 'Parsis and the British', *JCOI*, Bombay, 1978.
15. Bharati Modi, *op.cit.*
16. This position however, might be remedied. Dr.Surti of Secunderabad has painstakingly translated the *Shah-nameh* into simple English, the seven volumes of which are widely sold in India and abroad and could rekindle an interest among the youth. Further, *Shah-nameh* elocution contests are held in Bombay, and are a popular event. However, these do not constitute an organised educational system on a community-wide basis.
17. I am indebted to Piloo Nanavutty for this information.
18. This is seen as a repitition of the Iranian Zoroastrians being ridiculed and despised for their *sudre-kusti*, resulting in a decline in numbers of those who would don them.
19. I am grateful to Mr.Aspi Moddie for detailed discussions on various matters relating to the Zoroastrians. He was among the first entrants in the Indian Administrative Service, now retired and still active in

Bombay Parsi community activities.

20. Shankar Bose & Ava Khullar, *op.cit.*
21. *Ibid*, p.55.
22. The cultural commingling depicted by the Delhi community may serve as an indicator for the assimilative tendencies being engendered among the Parsi settlements of North America, and may even help explain the growing incidence of intermarriages among those groups. Refer Chapter 6.
23. The Federation of Parsi Anjumans of India are now attempting to address specific issues at its quarterly meetings. To date, it has not developed a structural pattern for dealing with the social, religious, cultural, economic and juridical issues which affect the community in India. Furthermore, not all the Indian *anjumans* are members of the Federation, a notable absentee being the Bangalore Anjuman.

The Parsis of Pakistan

The creation of Pakistan in 1947 was essentially to give the vast concentration of Indian Muslims a religio-political state where they could live in accordance with the tenets of their faith. Islam has since been the corner-stone of this nation; Pakistani Parsis show a deep awareness of the fact. As a minority, the Parsis are culturally alienated from, and not assimilated into, the larger Muslim society. Since Pakistan itself does not separate religious from national identity, the Parsis too, tend to associate Pakistan solely with Islam and remain remote from the country.

Parsis are, and mean to continue to be, differentiated as a distinct religious minority. Though granted autonomy in social and community matters, in the pursuit of their economic interests they give unconditional civic allegiance to the government of the day. Seal's assessment of the Parsis that, '...with their commercial links and their educational interests...(they) were the only approximation to a bourgeoisie in India...',[1] demonstrates that, unlike the present middle classes of the sub-continent, they resembled the Western middle class, inasmuch as products primarily of economic development and mobility.

The Parsis' traditional political adaptability and pragmatism has meant that they can demonstrate their loyalty to rulers under varying situations. In the newly evolving political systems of the sub-continent, these were signalled by their display of loyalty to the government of what was to become Pakistan. Rustomjee cites eyewitness accounts of the convening of the Karachi *anjuman*, where community leaders reassured them of Jinnah's even-handed treatment of minorities.[2] Indeed, Parsi contributions to Karachi, whether in the establishment of the industrial infrastructure, civic works or architectural monuments, dates from the mid-19th century and the founding of this port city by the British.

The close of the First World War led to the Parsi settlement in the Sind and western Punjab (later to become incorporated into the state of Pakistan) to 'take stock of their position'.[3] The Karachi Parsi Anjuman Trust Fund was formed in 1918 to oversee the Parsi Trust properties and the upkeep of its two *dakhmas*. The Young Men's Zoroastrian Association was founded, and a library, catering for some of the social and religious needs of the community, followed by local Gujarati weekly, *Parsi Sansar and Lok Sevak*. Seth Edulji Dinshaw and H.J.Rustomji began the work of charitable housing construction for the poorer sections of the community. Sir Kavasji Katrak similarly participated in community housing developments, in addition to donating the Katrak Hall, still in use today, for the Karachi Parsis' entertainment and social activities. Parsi charity in Pakistan, as in neighbouring India, was not confined to their co-religionists. In Karachi, Edulji Dinshaw, Sir Jehangir Kothari, Sir Kavasji Katrak, Khan Bahadur Ardeshir Mama and Khan Bahadur Nusserwanji Mehta, gave generously to various charitable causes. In Quetta, Khan Bahadur Ardeshir Marker, and in Lahore the Bhandara family, were generously active in the establishment of schools, colleges, hospitals and other public facilities. Mr.Jamshed Nusserwanji was elected the first Mayor of Karachi and is affectionately known to this day by the deserved title bestowed on him, 'maker of modern Karachi'.[4] The present-day self-sufficiency and sense of community belonging which the author witnessed among the Karachi Parsis, stems unquestionably from the early establishment of a wide-ranging network of communal infrastructure wisely installed by the founding fathers of the Pakistani community.

The Parsi agenda vis-a-vis the Pakistani authorities gives prominence to the upholding of their religio-cultural autonomy, their economic independence in terms of wealth creation, and a stable political environment for a peaceable coexistence: all of which have been granted by the various rulers of Pakistan.

The community infrastructure, most noticeable in Karachi where the bulk of the community are to be found (3,568 in 1988), is maintained on a voluntary basis. The considerable wealth is used as the means by which the extensive network for the dispensing of social welfare to the less privileged within the group operates. The proud boast of the older Parsis that the needs of the less fortunate are met 'from the cradle to the grave', is not an idle one. They can expect their economic needs, whether for education, housing, medical attention and other standard-of-living expenditure, to be met from the community's financial provisions established expressly for these purposes. This redistribution of wealth, while it does not purport to eradicate the distinctions between the wealthy and less wealthy members of the group, does in fact help draw the Parsis together into a close cultural unit which, by emphasizing their religious distinctness from the majority around them, makes the Karachi community in modern times arguably one of the closest-knit communal structures among the Zoroastrians world-wide.

The extensive institutional structures in place and utilised by the bulk of the community, help insulate them from the surrounding society. These date, in fact, from the British administration of port cities. The Parsis, having prospered under British auspices, urged their co-religionists to join them in the Sind. Extensive welfare funds set up by wealthier members of the community were used to establish Parsi housing 'colonies' which, in turn, served as incentives for urban migration. The early self-sufficiency of the Parsi community in the development of the port city of Karachi was thus clearly evident from its inception. Not surprisingly, the Parsis of Karachi were deemed to be the builders of the city, its trade and industry, paralleling the developments in Bombay among their co-religionists there. It can safely be asserted that tasks which ordinarily would fall within the ambit of a government's responsibilities, are in fact provided by this community.

Its Panchayat, the equivalent of a public body, is responsible for the disbursement of monies earmarked for specific purposes. Even though the modern Panchayat's powers are more notional than real, the Karachi body is identified as the authority within the community. As with the larger Bombay Parsi Panchayat, its income derives from the vast sums of private trust funds left for community use by wealthy deceased Parsis, and the shrewd investment of capital enables the Trustees to sustain the existing admirable levels of self-sufficiency for the Karachi community.

The chief priority is housing for the needy, to which the Trustees of the Karachi Parsi Anjuman are attentive.[5] The integral housing system centres round several housing complexes, *baughs* or *chawls*, with several self-contained units for family accommodation, sports and playground facilities for the benefit of the young. This author, in the course of field work was taken to the 'Parsi Colony', 'Jamshed Baugh', 'Panchayat Wadi' and the 'Cyrus Minwalla Colony' to conduct interviews. For families who spend their formative years in the *baughs*, a very noticeable sense of community solidarity emerges. It is estimated that 600 Parsi families, approximately two-thirds of the Karachi Parsi familial units, reside on Parsi Trust properties.[6]

Second only to housing are the community health facilities which are heavily subsidised. Two major hospitals, the B.M.H.Parsi General Hospital (est.1936), and the G.M.Mehta Maternity Home (est.1917), have facilities for the exclusive use of Parsis. Indeed, no Parsi is ever refused medical aid. The community's mechanism for dispensing charity and for social work is within the orbit of the Karachi Zarthosti Banu Mandal, their Parsi women's social work group. Its work in diverse areas with the less privileged, widows and orphans, continues on a regular basis.

Arguably, two of Pakistan's finest high schools, the Mama Parsi Girls' Secondary High School (est.1918), and the B.V.S.Parsi Boy's School (est.1859), provide educational facilities for all Parsis who might wish to avail of them. No Parsi applicant would be turned away. To date, the Principal and entire Board of Directors remain Parsi, although fewer Parsi parents now opt to send their children to the Parsi schools. Indeed, an interviewee took the position that the 'downfall of the Parsis' related to what he considered 'their inward-looking attitude, sending their children only to Parsi schools'.

The community has its own press, now run voluntarily - at a loss - by M.Dastoor, whose father first decided upon providing this subsidised service to his people. The paper, *The Parsi Sansar and Lok Sevak*, printed in Gujarati, is screened by the Ministry of Information. It serves, therefore, as a tool for appraising government of Parsi concerns, as much as publicizing the community's contribution to Pakistani society.

The Parsis' choice of remaining alienated from the Muslim population around it, means that their own socio-cultural activities gain in significance. The community has accordingly many private clubs, organisations and celebration planning committees. Subsumed under this category is the *Agiary Committee* which plans communal congregations and manages general religious matters.

Indicative of the State's tolerance of Parsi semi-autonomy is its willingness to allow the community to continue with the legal concessions granted to them by the British. Thus, Parsis are governed by Parsi laws in specific communal matters covering marriage, divorce, inheritance, acceptance (or otherwise) of children of mixed marriages, and settlement of disputes.[7]

Some critics of the community feel that the system has worked too well, creating a dependency rate of 30%, and consequently diluting work incentive.[8] It is nevertheless remarkable that the various institutional and cultural mechanisms outlined above accomplishes their ends without coercive redistribution of wealth. Not surprisingly, Parsis of all ages see their community in very positive terms, giving the overall impression of a closely-knit group. They refer to themselves as being 'clannish', which is as much the product of their intrinsic pride in being Parsi, as it is the defence mechanism of a very small group surrounded by a monolithic religious majority, a majority seen as historically and now potentially hostile.

Community mores, unwritten, but instinctively adhered to by the majority, are clearly in evidence. The most outstanding feature of a group which has acquired such a high degree of economic success, is that it does not socialise with its Muslim compatriots.[9] This in fact follows the course of 'damage limitation': if one does not have a Muslim friend, the chances of one marrying a Muslim are lessened. The social opprobrium attaching to Parsi-Muslim union was a repeated theme, which was universally disliked across the spectrum of the generations.

The community cohesion necessitates exclusiveness: there are, therefore, in-built levers of a 'conservative' approach to community life, where the term refers to 'one averse to change'.[10] The reluctance to change, and the suspicion of 'outsiders' is reinforced by the sense of pride in Parsi achievements in the spheres of charitable works; politics and diplomacy (represented by men such as Jamshed Mehta, Byram Avary and Jamsheed Marker); the legal field (retired Supreme Court Justice, Dorab Patel); and medicine. Pride in achievement, in turn, here preserves the Parsi sense of distinctiveness.

For these Parsis, therefore, anything beyond the parameters of their community is 'the outside', which includes society at large and the state. They refer frequently to 'them' and 'us', thereby reinforcing the uniform disapproval of extra-community socialising. The resistance to integration goes beyond the implicit taboos on social intercourse with the 'outsider' and extends to a more generalised alienation from Pakistani culture in terms of its symbols (dress) and outlets (language, literature, music).

Indeed, within the Pakistani Parsi community, a certain feudal approach to power operates. Those wealthy Parsis with influence at high governmental levels, act as intermediaries for their kinsmen where access to bureaucratic/governmental departments is required. With few exceptions such as the election of Byram Avary as a 'Minority' Representative in the Parliamentary elections of November 1988, the former ambassadorship to Washington of Jamsheed Marker, who at present is both Pakistan's Ambassador to the UN and Chairman, Group of 77 Developing Countries, the eminent retired Supreme Court Justice Dorab Patel, the Parsis continue to keep themselves aloof from the mainstream of national life, concentrating on their economic activities and intra-community socialising. They deem this to be the circumspect solution to living within a Muslim society.

The resistance to assimilation into Muslim society stems from psychological dislike of becoming absorbed into a 'foreign' cultural milieu. In no other sphere is this more pronounced than that of dress and language. To a limited extent younger Parsis have, with regard to expediency, acquired the local dress (salwaar-kameez), and a proficiency in the Urdu language. In the case of linguistic exigencies, the imperatives of the system demand that they reconcile themselves to acquiring fluency in the national language. School matriculation examinations set Urdu papers, resulted in a fully Urdu-literate Parsi younger generation. Paradoxically their native language proficiency makes them more resilient to assimilation.

In keeping with their reluctance to 'think' in Urdu, this group are least literate in Gujarati, only 14% of the respondents can 'think' in this Indian language, with a minimal facility in its reading or writing. Those young persons interviewed who had a certain facility in Urdu were at pains to inform the author that when they spoke it, their Muslim compatriots detected their accent and thus could instantly identify them as Parsis. There was no emotional tie with Urdu. It was a compulsory educational requirement, and the younger Parsis who had no choice but to continue their education in that country, as well as pursue careers there, acknowledged its usefulness in functional terms. Such use of the Urdu language in no way suggested their national identity.

The attitude to the national language extends as well to the national dress code. Indeed, the question of dress as related to identity, was introduced at an early stage in discussions with the Parsis of Pakistan. The impression gained was that Parsis are deemed 'nationalistic' or 'patriotic' by the clothes they wear. To don Western apparel might be taken as an indicator of being part of the 'inward-looking' Parsi who does not see himself as belonging to Pakistan. Those who wore the salwaar-kameez were in fact making an overt patriotic statement, namely, that Pakistan was their country and they wished visibly to express this fact. Until a decade ago the community would have disapproved of any Parsi daring enough to wear 'Pakistani dress'. Indeed, a disapproval evinced towards those who do, persists.

Homji's charge that the Parsis were '...half educated foreigners in their own country',[11] is a reference to the Pakistani Parsi psyche. Their lives and their interests are quite separate from the majority Muslim population. Islam and its way of life are unacceptable to most Parsis, and for those who show a concessionary attitude to the rules and ethos of Islam, it was done with a studied determination in order to become 'better' Pakistanis.

The eleven-year rule of Zia ul-Haqq which saw the introduction of the 'Hadoot' Ordinance, the institutionalisation of Islam and the entrenchment of theocracy in Pakistan were further spurs to distance the community from the politics of the country. Zia's rule was beneficial to the Parsis insofar as it encouraged 'patron/client contacting'. Parsi interests in the state machinery were represented by Byram Avary in the *Majlis-i-Shoora* or Parliament; Minocher Bhandara's appointment as Minorities Advisor to the President, and Mrs.Gool Minwalla serving as a minority representative in the Sind Assembly.[12] While not powerful in themselves and maintained through governmental patronage, the access to the official levels of the authorities served to mitigate the Parsis' legal inequality.

The author was reminded, however, of the psychological distance between the Parsis and the Pakistani state, which was the result of the introduction of Zia's Hadoot Ordinance. Justice Dorab Patel elaborated on its implications.[13]

...I do think that the fundamentalism of Zia ul-Haqq has adversely affected the position of non-Muslims. The Hadoot Ordinances discriminate expressly against non-Muslims. When you introduce discrimination in the laws, the average, commonly uneducated person in the majority community will begin to think that the non-Muslim is the lesser breed without the law.

The Hadoot Ordinance was promulgated in 1979, a few days after the Supreme Court had, by a majority, and I was in a minority, dismissed Bhutto's [former Prime Minister] appeal against his conviction for murder...A Hadoot is a punishment prescribed in the Quran. Hadoot Ordinances are principally for certain forms of theft, adultery and some other offences which are not likely to affect Parsis. The penalty for adultery for Muslims is stoning to death; penalty for non-Muslims is 100 lashes of the whip. I doubt if any human being can survive 50 or 60 lashes. My objection to Hadoot is, proof of the crime is either to be on a confession which is not retractable, or in the case of theft, on evidence of two male witnesses who are reliable. So, non-Muslims can be flogged on evidence of Muslims. But, evidence of non-Muslims is simply not evidence under these laws. The only proviso is: if the accused is non-Muslim, the testimony of a non-Muslim is evidence.

So now, if a Parsi woman is raped in her house by her Muslim servant, he cannot be punished under the Hadoot law on the evidence of her husband or her children. But who else would be able to give evidence of this offence? That is why I have been openly fighting the Ordinance since 1984.[14]

Homeland: It cannot be repeated too often that for Parsis the concept of a 'homeland' is an immensely complex issue. For those who live in a theocratic Islamic state, the problem is far more complex. However, changing patterns of adjustment to a Muslim state and an evolving sense of patriotism are discernible. 80% of the youth and every one of the elders, consider Pakistan to be their homeland (Refer Table 1).

This allegiance reflects the layered complexities inherent in such an evaluation. One youth spoke for most when he reflected that he did not feel '100% that this is my homeland, only about 70%. But we owe a lot to this country. Yet, I think we have a bond with Iran'. A 27 year old lady said, 'I don't feel settled in this country. I was brought up in a very Parsi home...when I was studying in the USA, I wasn't Western by their standards, equally, here in Pakistan I am not Eastern either'.

In an attempt to understand the several layers of conflicting attitudes to the concept of the 'homeland' and their sense of belonging to it, the respondents were asked to comment on how attached they felt to the country and whether they would wish to spend the rest of their lives there. A 23 year old displayed the strains on her loyalty, 'I think of this as my home. I like it here. But its just that at times you don't feel you belong, because of the laws and social structures'. For yet another young person, the dilemma was that 'I am not very comfortable calling myself a Pakistani woman'. This view, however, was flatly contradicted by an older person who asserted that, 'I am really proud of being a Parsi in Pakistan'.

Justice Dorab Patel was asked for an assessment of the Parsi community in Pakistan:

> Parsis are very much an inward-looking minority. About twenty years ago the orthodox, wealthy section really did not look upon themselves as Pakistanis. They were here only to make money. Then things began to change. The growing patriotism of the younger generation has, however, been deeply shaken by the Hadoot Ordinance. I think the Parsis were developing some sort of loyalty to Pakistan, then came this terrible shock; it put the clock back.

There is, understandably, a certain ambivalence in the loyalty to the State among the young and the old.

Since patriotism is often reflected best in subjective terms, the Pakistani Parsis were asked their opinions and sentiments about India and the Parsis of India. While they may yet be in the process of resolving their own degree of patriotism, it would be wrong to infer that they felt any ties to India. Their perceptions of their Indian co-religionists was, however, a separate issue. One youth said,'I see Parsis all over the world as part of my community'. Another maintained that he felt an emotional bond to Zoroastrians world-wide, but could feel no attachment to India. A young mother of two held strong views on India, acknowledging her anti-Indian sentiments were the result of the wars between these neighbouring states. She refused to visit India, even though her mother's family lived there.

It may perhaps become possible over the following decades, to talk of an increasing fragmentation of the Zoroastrian community along nationalistic lines. The Pakistani Parsi, while expressing reservations vis-a-vis the state, sees himself differently to an Indian Parsi.

Language: Given that modern Parsis demonstrate the propensity for using two languages, and are rapidly becoming an English-speaking people, frequently lapsing into a simultaneous bilingualism, respondents were asked what language they 'thought' in. Roughly half of the junior and senior groups considered English to be their first language, and none could acknowledge a facility in Urdu (Refer Table 2).

A 28 year old lady said that since no one in her household could read Gujarati, they were dependent on older friends to decipher Gujarati letters from relatives. Similarly, a father of three explained that since they only spoke English at home, the children had fallen behind in Urdu at school, and had no Gujarati.

While this indicates the trend for the future, it cannot be assumed to be the norm. For those Parsis who had attended the Parsi schools in Karachi and who lived in the *baughs*, their proficiency in spoken Parsi-Gujarati remains. Most Parsi students now frequent the Christian schools where the medium of instruction is in English: for a 28 year old man therefore, who spoke for others like himself, the assertion was that his age group in Karachi would rather speak Gujarati than English, whereas in Bombay, Parsis are more prone to use English. He suggested that this was because Indian Parsis socialised more freely with non-Parsis. It is significant that the majority of the interviews were conducted in English, with the exception of those held with the older members of the community, when discussions were conducted in Parsi-Gujarati. Indeed, so pervasive are the inroads the English language has made in the Parsi world that the few overtly patriotic Pakistani Parsi respondents all considered English to be their 'thinking language' as opposed to Urdu. Pakistani Parsis, like their Indian congeners, demonstrate the compounding of their identity crisis as related to their loss of proficiency in their 'mother tongue': Parsi-Gujarati.

Knowledge of Zoroastrian History: Perhaps the single most striking feature of the contemporary community is their collective amnesia of Zoroastrian history. In terms of the acquisition of, and transmission of such knowledge to successive generations, Pakistani Parsis demonstrate a similar lack of past awareness as do their kinsmen over the border. Thus, some 3 out of 4 youth, and barely half of the elders, admitted to having no knowledge of Zoroastrian history (Refer Table 3).

In their relative absence of knowledge of Zoroastrian history, the Pakistani Parsis do not emulate the Indian Parsi model. The smaller Pakistani community has studiously kept aloof from the mainstream of the dominant Muslim society around it, retaining its own socio-religious priorities. The dominant culture cannot be held responsible for removal of the tools and mechanisms for the transmission of this knowledge. Rather, in Pakistan as in India, the Parsis, having subsumed the gamut of Zoroastrian heritage within the embrace of 'religion', have dispensed with the need for evaluating their historical antecedents. Quite simply, they see no need for it. Having relinquished the intellectual grasp on the formative events of their past, there does not at present seem to be the will or the inclination within the community to re-educate themselves on their historical roots.

Zoroastrian Identity: Surrounded as they are by a majority at whom they look askance, and wishing to proclaim their distinctness, it was not surprising that both the youth and their elders equally identified as Zoroastrians (Refer Table 4).

It has to be acknowledged that, as with other Zoroastrians, for the Pakistani community, too, being Zoroastrian is more than just a religious label. The phrase most widely used to describe what to them being a Zoroastrian meant, was that it was 'a way of life'. Indeed, their Zoroastrianism encompassed the entire gamut of their lives (Refer Table 4(a)).

A 24 year old lawyer explained that while she was not a religious person, she identified with the community. It related to the habits she had imbibed and the customs she was familiar with. Above all else, her 'pride in being Zoroastrian' stemmed from the fact that for her 'it is almost a nationality'. This, then, recapitulates the point that Zoroastrians everywhere, whilst emphasizing their religion, are much more than just a religious group. The label in fact encompasses their ethnicity, distinctive culture and value system.

Not surprisingly, therefore, it was in response to the supplementary question on whether they would identify as Zoroastrians under all circumstances, which demonstrated their steadfast attachment to their Zoroastrian roots. An 18 year old student said she would 'never disown being Zoroastrian'. Some Muslim colleagues had told her to leave the Zoroastrian religion since it consigned its dead to the *dakhma* where the flesh was devoured by vultures. She continued to ignored them.

Perception of Parsis by fellow Pakistanis: Some Parsis feel compelled to conceal part of their Zoroastrian persona under certain social and political circumstances, which must inevitably reflect upon their group identity and is dependent on how these are viewed by the majority. Most maintained that Parsis were treated with respect in Pakistan (Refer Table 1(a)).

One young man had noticed the socio-cultural differences between Parsis and Pakistanis and did not think that the latter were very comfortable with the minority group. Another young respondent was more analytical. He maintained that the Parsis were generally respected in the country, but conceded that there were two types of Parsis: one group which socialised exclusively among themselves; and another which had both Parsi and Muslim friends. The Muslims' reactions to these two groups of Parsis was noticeably distinct. They were amused by the clannishness of the former, and prepared to befriend the latter. There was a third group, numerically insignificant, which socialised exclusively with Muslims.

Chief External Influences: It follows therefore that the diverse influences on this minority reinforces their sense of self-identity. Surrounded as they are by non-Zoroastrians, the impact of the predominant Pakistani culture merits attention insofar as it helps shed light on the progressive development of the Pakistani Parsi self-perception. Not surprisingly, in the light of the above, only a scant handful of the youth and elders were prepared to concede that 'Pakistani influences' had shaped their sensibilities. (Refer Table 5).

The low percentages recorded for this type of influence relate directly to the community's aloof stance from the majority culture. There is a greater emphasis on the combined influences of 'Western and Parsi' inputs into the individual's frames of reference, re-emphasizing the Parsis' own preference for Western cultural mores, which are blended within the Parsi cultural stock values. In all of these respects, there is no substantive difference between the Indian and Pakistani Parsis.

The younger Parsis, in schools, universities and the work-place, are being increasingly exposed to Pakistani culture. While there is a general reticence in accepting it unreservedly, there are signs of accommodation to the majority culture. One young lady had studied in a Christian convent, and had not socialised with non-Parsis. When she became acquainted with Muslims at college, she developed an understanding of their language and customs. As a result, she had begun to converse in Urdu to a large extent. Indeed, the pervasiveness of the Urdu language, and its statutory proficiency requirements, is compelling the younger generation to enculturate at a level which would have been unthinkable for their parents. A resistance has developed to the notion of being Pakistani, where that implies religious uniformity; but also a willingness to acquire the cultural tools enabling one to participate in the larger society. Pakistani Parsis, like their co-religionists in other countries, show indications of the competing pulls on their loyalties and the consequent paradoxes.

This dysfunctional sense of their national identity was elaborated upon by Mr.Byram Avary, Member of Parliament,

> ...I am a Parsi first...I represented Pakistan at the UN when General Zia ul-Haqq specifically asked me to wear *salwaar-kameez*. I refused and told Zia,'if you wish I won't go, but if I do, I will wear my *duglee* because this is my dress'. *Salwaar-kameez* is a Muslim dress...I believe we must show our identity. We must be proud to say,'I am a Pakistani Parsi'. I believe we must assimilate with them but not lose our identity.

Intermarriage: This sociological phenomenon has arisen phoenix-like into modern Zoroastrian consciousness as the single determinative factor upon which the future viability of the community will depend. In the author's experience, and at the time of writing, Karachi was the only city where discussion of intermarriage did not present the grave threat to communal solidarity as it did in other places of Zoroastrian settlement (Refer Table 8). Unquestionably, the studied distance maintained by the Parsis from the majority Muslim population accounts for this anomaly, as does the novel occurrence of a certain symmetry of viewpoint amongst young and old. There is an innate dislike of the institution of intermarriage.

Societal conditions in a religious state such as Pakistan differ widely from secular societies such as India, the USA or Canada. As such, it is an unfair parallel to compare the responses of the Pakistani Parsis to intermarriage and those of the Zoroastrians of other countries.[15] Suffice it to say that intermarriages are curtailed in Pakistan owing to external factors (Islamic religious laws which demand conversion to Islam prior to marriage), and internal pressures (the ostracizing from the community of the exogamously married Zoroastrian). In the course of field work in the winter of 1988, the author was informed that there had been five cases of exogamous marriages in Karachi within the past two years: these five cases were deemed excessive, and it was widely felt that such marriages ought never to have taken place at all. The general opprobrium attached to intermarriage by Pakistani Parsis, and their assessment that intermarriages were increasing and becoming inevitable in their society, even though their rate of increase, relative to other

Zoroastrian centres is exceptionally low, reinforces the impression of an universal undesirability of this social phenomenon (Refer Table 8(a)).

Exogamous unions seem to be viewed with disfavour by the Parsis of Pakistan, because of the construction of Pakistani society upon Islamic values and laws. Justice Dorab Patel explained the legal imperatives involved in a mixed union with a Muslim, more so in the case of a Parsi woman's choice of such marriage partner:

> *Nikka* (conversion to Islam) is in the interest of the girl herself. She can remain a Zoroastrian if she marries a Shi'a Muslim, because Shi'as can marry Zoroastrians. A Muslim male can only marry a *kitabia* (of the Book). If not, it is not a valid marriage. Any marriage by a Sunni to a Zoroastrian girl would not be a valid marriage if she remains a Zoroastrian. Even though a Shi'a marriage is valid, a non-Muslim cannot inherit from a Muslim. That is why I recommend a Zoroastrian woman having a *nikka*. If the mother is a non-Muslim, in a divorce case the courts may not give custody of the child to a non-Muslim mother. So it is for these practical reasons that a *nikka* would be safer for the girl.

In Pakistan, Parsis can only envisage intermarriage with a Muslim. This point was forcefully made. As such, it is anathema to the community. One young person in Karachi could thus state that 'by intermarriage you betray your religion'. Given the virtual compulsion of *nikka*, this statement does not appear hyperbolic in view of Zoroastrianism's traditional scorn for the apostate. Yet another young lady said,'I don't like it [intermarriage] at all. I wouldn't even think of going around with a Muslim boy, because I know it would not be accepted. You are brought up so'. The expression of communal taboo against active socialising with the majority group, and the virtual excommunication, even of Parsi males with Muslim wives, appears to have the desired result in keeping the numbers of exogamous unions to a minimum.

Two factors operating in tandem have resulted in the Pakistani Parsis desisting from what, in other Zoroastrian settlements, has developed into a major communal problem. The monolithic Muslim society of Pakistan (from which, by definition, they are 'outsiders'), has helped reinforce Parsi pride in their distinctive religio-cultural heritage. It places a premium on remaining within the fold, which to date has been achieved by the community to a remarkable extent. One proviso, however, must be added. Younger Parsis will continue, in the course of their educational and professional lives, to encounter Muslims. The trend established uptil now need not be a static one. The possibility of its being overturned at a future date cannot be overlooked: were that to occur, it would imply that the imperatives of nation-building in

Pakistan, with emphasis on its Islamic heritage, had induced some Parsis to abandon their traditional suspicions of the 'outsider' and participate more completely with the peoples and ethos of the country.

Conversion: Given the general reluctance to choose non-Zoroastrian partners, it is not surprising that the sample canvassed displayed a distaste for the induction of aliens into the Zoroastrian faith. Well over half of the youth and elders were against conversion (Refer Table 7).

A young professional person said that if outsiders were admitted into the religious fold they would bring with them their ideas, culture and previous religion. This would result in a loss of Parsi identity. More significantly, he believed that 'converts come in for charity'. This young man referred to the fundamental issues that were raised from several directions by the respondents. 'Parsi charity', available to Zoroastrians only, had repeatedly been cited by them as a powerful incentive to conversion in a poverty-stricken land. Yet another implication was the 'clannishness' of the Parsis referred to above, where 'being Parsi is a large part of being Zoroastrian', which *ipso facto* sets limits on the acceptance of alien socio-cultural influences upon the Parsi community. The convert, it was argued, would find it difficult to adapt, since he was not born and raised as a Zoroastrian. Owing to a near unanimity of sentiments, the issue of conversion - the initiation of an alien into the Zoroastrian fold - remained at best an academic discussion. A senior member of the community suggested that, this was indeed a futile question on the author's agenda, 'Pakistan is an Islamic country. By law you cannot convert a Muslim. So there is nothing to discuss'.

The Future: The Parsis of Pakistan, as the discussion above has shown, are distinctive in that they have retained, with a high level of pride, their Parsi identity separate from their Muslim compatriots, and underpinned it by the effective functioning of a communal infrastructure. Asked for their assessment of the future of their community in Pakistan, some one-third of the youth and around half of the elders viewed it in a positive light (Refer Tables 9 & 9(a)).

One person fairly typified the opinion of many. 'I am, in the ultimate analysis, proud of being a Parsi. I would like my children to identify as Parsis. Our position, straddling East and West, gives us the best of both worlds. For example, the care of our families. We don't easily jettison such values. This helps us retain our identity'. The future survivability of the Pakistani community, however, could depend ultimately on the Pakistan government's provisions for minorities. A professional person maintained that the next five to ten years would be crucial in determining whether the community had a bright future in the country.

The Parsis have evolved a unique relationship with the State of Pakistan, which has allowed them to co-exist with various regimes. This has enabled them to survive as a discrete minority group retaining its special character and pursuing its own interests. The younger generation, however, appears to be culturally and socially alienated from the mainstream, and are not unaware of the limited political opportunities as non-Muslims. As future leaders, their resentment of the system could have an adverse impact on the community's longer-term relationship with the Pakistani authorities. One method of its circumvention is through migration, which occurs with regularity; alternatively, for those who remain behind, closer participation in the political system may be attempted. Whether the Pakistani state would tolerate such manoeuvres, remains to be seen. While a marginal increase in Parsi participation in national political life would enhance their sense of belonging to Pakistan, as did their economic contributions to the country, it could serve to consolidate their future well-being. At present it remains mere conjecture. The history of the community in Pakistan has been one of studied aloofness and non-participation on religio-cultural grounds. To date, this has served their interests adequately. Future generations too might feel that communal security comes best by faithful adherence to the well-trodden path.

NOTES:

1. Anil Seal, *The Emergence of Indian Nationalism: Competition and Collaboration in the Later Nineteenth Century*, (Cambridge University Press, 1971), p.110.
2. Naomi N.Rustomjee, *Minorities Under Developmental, Populist and Islamic Regimes: Parsis and the Pakistani State*, unpublished B.A. dissertation, Harvard College, March 1985, p.52.
3. D.B.Ghadialy, 'Parsis of Pakistan'. (Privately circulated).
4. *Ibid.*
5. The author was repeatedly told that no Zoroastrian in Karachi need 'go without a roof above his head'. This is truly a remarkable achievement, given the lamentable housing shortage in Bombay, where it is becoming a root cause of serious community problems.
6. D.B.Ghadialy, 'Parsis of Karachi: Facts and Figures', Informal Religious Meetings, April 20 - May 19, 1984.
7. N.N.Rustomjee, *op.cit.*, pp.97-102.
8. H.B.M.Homji, *O Whither Parsi?*, (Karachi, 1978), p.158.
9. From the cross-section interviewed, there were only two families with high national profiles who spoke of close ties with Muslims.
10. *Chambers Everyday Dictionary*, (Edinburgh, 1975), p.146.
11. H.B.M.Homji, *op.cit.*, p.260.
12. N.N.Rustomjee, *op.cit.*, p.93.
13. I am indebted to Justice Patel for having granted me an interview. He was the only Parsi Judge on the Bench of the Supreme Court, and the one dissenting vote against the death sentence on the former Prime Minister, Zulfikar Ali Bhutto. Patel J. resigned from the Bench following the verdict on Bhutto, remaining a well-respected jurist in Pakistan as well as a noted international campaigner for Human Rights.
14. This interview was held on 17 November 1988, the day after the General Elections which led to Benazir Bhutto's Premiership. Bhutto was removed from office in 1990. At the time of writing, the Hadoot Ordinance stands on the statute books.
15. In this connection, there may be interesting similarities between the Zoroastrians of Iran and Pakistan, the two groups continuing domicile in Islamic states. Further research on this would be of great value.

Iranian Zoroastrian Refugees

While the Parsis on the Indian sub-continent and those settled overseas have become accustomed to the physical safety of friendly environments where the practise of their faith and their Zoroastrian way of life can co-exist with the majority non-Zoroastrian populations around them, these have not been afforded the Zoroastrians of Iran. The *raison d'etre* of the present Iranian state is fundamentalist Shi'ite Islamic philosophy, and the Zoroastrian population who by definition are not an Islamic people, are subject to social and economic pressures. These are at times subtle, and on occasion, overt: they are meant to induce them to change their allegiance and substitute Mohammad for Zarathushtra. The net result of the Islamic Republic's policies have led some Zoroastrians to seek refuge overseas, there to await a hoped-for modification of the *status quo* in their homeland. Those among the Zoroastrian community of Iran most affected by the current political climate are the young Zoroastrians: men and women who see no future for themselves as Zoroastrians in an Islamic state, or at best see only limited possibilities for building a life for themselves and their progeny. The internal domestic politics of Iran since the Revolution of 1979 therefore has become a chief causative factor for some Zoroastrian youth who have elected to live overseas as refugees. Their first port of call is quite often the Indian sub-continent where there is an established community of their Parsi co-religionists.

While the author was engaged on field work on the Indian sub-continent in the winter of 1988, she was able to investigate at first hand the question of the Zoroastrian refugee: the mechanics of his short-term sojourn there, his aims for the future, and the rationale which brought him there in the first place.

The refugees had left the Iran of Ayatollah Khomeini who, at the time of their departure, was the spiritual and temporal leader, and had inspired the Islamic Revolution of 1979 which deposed the Pahlavi dynasty. It was the prospect of a bleak and uncertain future that had led some young Zoroastrians to seek to distance themselves from their country. With the death of the Ayatollah in the spring of 1989 and the transfer of power to men who have to be seen to continue the religio-political ideology of their former leader, Iran has entered a period of political unpredictability. The respondents in the sample spoke only of the regime which they had fled, and which had been headed by the Ayatollah Khomeini. Indeed, the forseeable future of Iran was deemed too uncertain to merit meaningful discussion. From the Zoroastrian viewpoint, a fundamentalist Islamic state is antithetical to their interests. Under the present leadership of President Rafsanjani, the political climate has improved considerably, and doubtless the change will have a more favourable impact on religious minorities.

In the town where this research was conducted, there were at the time twenty-one Iranian Zoroastrian youth. They were awaiting permission to migrate to a Western nation which would accept them. The countries they most frequently aspired to were the United States, Canada and Australia, where a relative perhaps or even friends from their home town may have preceded them. The choice of final destination is not entirely their own - rather, it depends on various external variables, such as government policy of the day, or whether they have a relative in the West who could 'sponsor' them. These are, however, seen as their final hurdles; their first considerations are the essentials of the current period of adjustment in the relatively safe haven of their immediate foreign environment.

Individual wealthy Parsis of the town had worked out a method of accommodating the youth. The first step was the verification of the refugee as a *bona fide* Zoroastrian. This was achieved by a rough and ready method: the person was to show proof of his identity by displaying on his person the two symbols of the Zoroastrian faith: the badges of membership of the Zoroastrian fraternity, the *sudre* and *kusti*. He was then asked to recite some of the elementary Zoroastrian prayers, the *Ashem Vohu* and the *Yatha Ahu Vairyo*. The youth will often carry with them an 'identity card' issued by the Tehran Anjuman, verifying that the person is indeed a Zoroastrian. Once the verification process was complete, the Zoroastrian refugee was automatically given accommodation, in groups of three or more, dependent on the availability of space and the current number of refugees at any given time.

Individual Parsis undertake to provide a stipend of Rs.800 per month per person. The refugees are encouraged to study English and are registered for such courses. Without the acquisition of a working knowledge of the English language, their prospects for settlement in any Western nation would be severely limited. Indeed, all the Zoroastrians from Iran were essentially unilingual - the only language in which they have facility is Farsi; some of them could speak Dari, a Farsi dialect spoken by Zoroastrians. Fees for the English language course are paid by individual Parsis.

In theory, there is an undertaking by the local Parsi community to assist the youth with employment, to provide such employment in their own private business enterprises as they can; alternatively, to use their good offices and help secure work for the duration of the refugees' stay. The success of this undertaking, however, is minimal. Of the twenty-one youth interviewed, perhaps at best six were employed.

The years immediately following the Islamic Revolution saw only a small number of refugees crossing the border, upto a half-dozen a year. This number has since increased. In the main, they comprise young men from the ages of 16 to 30; some being of school and college age, their academic studies had been disrupted. Yet others were young professionals who had fled because it had become virtually impossible to continue work in Iran in their particular fields. The professions were widely represented among this small group - from a professional photographer to a biochemist. One obtained the distinct impression that the academically successful young Zoroastrians faced pressures in Iran to renounce their religion and embrace Islam. The refugees came not so much from any particular social stratum, but rather because they were young, aspiring professionals for whom the political climate in a fundamentalist Iran made exile the most prudent option. Many professionals of other creeds face a similar dilemma.

The striking feature of the group was the fact that it was comprised of young males. There were in that town young Iranian Zoroastrian females, but they were not technically refugees, rather, they had succeeded in travelling abroad as holders of Iranian psssports. Nevertheless, their psychological 'condition' was similar to their compatriots. They demonstrated equally the severe sense of grief and alienation at having been compelled to abandon their beloved Iran and their families.

The youth had all left behind them parents, brothers, sisters and other kinfolk. Their conditions of escape were physically perilous and therefore unsuited to female members of the family. The parents would not have been given permission to travel abroad by the government, and when they are permitted foreign travel, they are compelled to leave behind in Iran their property, money and family members as surety. In terms of contemplating settlement overseas, it is the young males who take the first step in re-settlement. Furthermore, the young men who come to the sub-continent as refugees without travel documents, money and often with a scarce change of clothing, have the additional burden of trying to build a life overseas, where they hope their faith will not be an impediment to acquiring an education, professional qualifications and employment.

This small group of refugees therefore may perhaps not fully typify the Iranian Zoroastrian community as a whole. All of them displayed deeply patriotic Iranian sentiments, and yet were anxious to move as rapidly as possible to the West to start their new lives. Given the profile of the small sample of refugees, the discussion below does not attempt to present them as representative of the typical Iranian Zoroastrian, but rather, by reflecting versions of their conditions in Iran at the time of their departure, assesses the living conditions of this minority.

The Parsi response is to improvise methods of dealing with a situation over which they have no control, viz. the improvement of conditions for Zoroastrians in Iran. Their reactions to the Iranian Zoroastrians in their midst points clearly to areas of cultural and socio-religious differences that have developed over the thousand-years' separation of the two groups of

Zoroastrians.

When, for instance, an Iranian Zoroastrian is asked by a Parsi to give proof of his Zoroastrianness by displaying his *sudre* and *kusti* on his person, and reciting from his *Avesta*, there is every possibility that the applicant for assistance might not be in possession of these religious accoutrements, quite simply because the *sudre-kusti* does not have the same distinguishing role in Iranian Zoroastrianism as it does in Parsi Zoroastrianism. Serious doubts about the applicant's genuineness often thereby arise.

A Zoroastrian youth having arrived on the sub-continent, was advised by his fellow Iranians to present himself before the Parsi who would authenticate his identity, after which material assistance would be forthcoming. The youth had undergone a harrowing border crossing. A Baluchi smuggler had been engaged for the purpose. Upon reaching the Iranian border town of Zahedan, he was instructed to remove all visible signs of belonging to a religious minority. Accordingly, the youth removed the *kusti* he had on his person, and sewed a 'pocket' onto the front of his *sudre*, in the shape of a substantial pouch so that it passed for a pocket in which to carry his money. This complied with the Baluchi's instructions for his safety. On reaching the sub-continent, he took off the *sudre*, which with its 'pocket' was unsuitable for wear.

When the youth presented himself to the Parsi, he was asked to show his *sudre*. His explanation as to why he did not have it on his person, and his recitation of the *Ashem Vohu* prayer, failed to convince the Parsi who then proceeded to brand him a Muslim. As a result, this now angered young man received no financial assistance from the community and resided with a friend of his father. This, despite the fact that he had on him the Tehran Anjuman's identity card, which in recent years had been tightened for security purposes and required verification signatures from eight local Zoroastrians.[1]

Whereas over the centuries the Parsis have seen their *sudre* and *kusti* as inseparable badges of their Zoroastrian faith, their co-religionists in Iran have been deprived freedom of practice of their faith, as has been emphasized in earlier chapters. When the tempo of religious persecution quickened and any outward manifestation of Zoroastrianism could mean increased harassment or even loss of life, Iranian Zoroastrians relaxed the practice of universal initiation into the faith, and would only don the *sudre-kusti* when visiting the fire temple or for religious ceremonials. The Parsis, far removed from this environment of fear, have shown an inability to realize the gravity of the Iranian situation and have arrived at a simplistic definition of who is a Zoroastrian: no *sudre-kusti* implies one is a non-Zoroastrian. In this general atmosphere of cultural unawareness, a genuine Zoroastrian refugee seeking assistance from the Parsis may occasionally suffer.[2]

Once the verification process - membership of the Zoroastrian community - is completed, and the refugee is given accommodation and a monthly stipend, his task begins in earnest. His goal during his stay on the sub-continent is to secure from the United Nations authorities the 'Blue Card' establishing his official position as a refugee, and without which he would not be accepted for permanent settlement in any of the Western countries. In the absence of an Iranian passport, this Card then becomes his travel document.

This is the greatest challenge faced by every individual refugee. Each has a different background, and each case history is treated individually by the authorities. Most of the youth are young enough to work and build a new life for themselves in their adopted lands. Some have left without full schooling, having been expelled for some indiscretion in the name of religion as was a young boy who, while playing football during the lunch recess at school, accidentally kicked the ball so that it struck against a portrait of the Ayatollah Khomeini. Yet others have left with their university education incomplete. The length of time they spend on the sub-continent varies from one and a half weeks to over two years. The obstacles in the way of migration to the West frequently appear vexatious, so that the youth interviewed therefor showed high levels of stress and despondency. Some hurdles assume alarming proportions, so that one youth committed suicide in 1987 after repeated efforts at securing the 'Blue Card' had failed. In the words of the interpreter, 'They say, "our work will not be done. We will not be able to go to the West. It is hopeless"'. For these youth to re-cross the border into Iran where they have been officially classified as 'cowards', could mean at worst, loss of life, or at best, a life lived surreptitiously.

The fact that the refugees are almost all young men, points to another growing predicament. They leave behind homes and families and cross the border illegally in order to secure some kind of future for themselves. 'They are 100% sure that if they were to live in Iran their lives would be in danger', the interpreter explained. Their parents and siblings remain in the old country. There is a growing fear, cautiously expressed, that the young Zoroastrian girls in Iran may be abducted for marriage by Muslims: a method of conversion to Islam for the female section of the population. The uncertainties faced by these divided families is compounded by the unestablished final destination of the refugees. The possibility of their return to Iran remains remote, and the reunions with parents and siblings, imponderables for the forseeable future.

There was an impression conveyed by the refugees that conditions for the Zoroastrians in the Islamic Republic of Iran was precarious at best. The monthly *Parsiana*, in its July 1988 issue, had printed a notice stating that there were believed to be 90,891 Zoroastrians in Iran, according to the government census for 1986. This was put to the youth for comment. They did not accept the validity of such statistics, and in the words of one young man, 'we are very few in numbers'. Another concurred, since he held the view that 'Zoroastrians are coming out [of Iran]. Some Zoroastrians become Baha'is.' (Some Baha'is have at present chosen to opt for the seemingly lesser of the two evils and refer to themselves as Zoroastrians rather than Baha'is. This partly helps explain the high number of Zoroastrians recorded in the government figures). In fact, there are no accurate figures for the Zoroastrian population of Iran, and the estimates vary between 30-45,000 souls.

According to several refugees, following the Revolution, Zoroastrians were pressured to convert to Islam. They face prejudice in the field of education, whether at school or university, and in their attempts at securing emloyment commensurate with their qualifications. For participation in religious ceremonials too, they must ask for, and receive, permission from the authorities prior to the observance of a particular ceremony. Indeed, the insidious theme of the fundamentalist position on the Zoroastrians as *atash-parasts* (fire-worshippers) who are, by definition *najes*, was alluded to by every interviewee, and became the official explanation for excluding minorities from various employment opportunities, educational facilities and, finally, curtailing their future security in the Islamic Republic. It is this perception of a hardening sectarian prejudice which has been instrumental in increasing the sense of awareness of identity among the Iranian community, as well as inciting the younger males to flee their ancestral land for a more secure future overseas.

A respondent explained that it was the deeply-entrenched conviction of the *maulvis* (clergy) that the Zoroastrians were untouchable fire-worshippers. This continues to underpin the theological perspective from which a fundamentalist Muslim views a Zoroastrian.[3] In the main the refugees were from Tehran; one, however, came from Yazd where the position was said to be even more fraught. In this rural community, most people refrained from contact with Zoroastrians whom they continued to denigrate as *najes*. This resulted in severe restrictions for job opportunities: if a Zoroastrian wished to open a restaurant he would not be given permission to do so.

This attitude is not confined to the work-place. A youth explained that at school most people continued to view them with suspicion, and tried to compel them to visit the mosque for *namaz* [prayers]. Another youth recounted the experience of a Zoroastrian student at university who was approached by a faculty member and assured of every facility to further his education if he converted to Islam. The Zoroastrian refused this inducement, and when conditions deteriorated, he felt compelled to leave his studies incomplete, moved to the sub-continent as a refugee, and later proceeded to the United States.

At one interview session of youth who had left their school and university studies in Iran unfinished, they were asked to list their personal experiences. Some maintained that they saw no future for themselves and believed it would be impossible to get commensurate employment. Yet others held the view that the Muslims persisted in seeing the Zoroastrians as 'different people'. If the Muslims saw Zoroastrians as different, what was the Zoroastrian perception of the Iranian Muslim? Most of the respondents conceded that the Muslim Iranians were different from their Zoroastrian compatriots.[4]

One youth explained through an interpreter why he had sought refuge on the sub-continent.

> At school his teacher castigated him as a fire-worshipper and admonished him for his Zoroastrian faith. The young man felt compelled to retort that this was an out-dated view and the educationist ought to revise his opinions of the Zoroastrians. He was reminded that he could not address him thus, 'because I am a Muslim teacher'. At the end of the academic year, the principal notified the student that owing to his unacceptable altercation with a faculty member, the matter would be placed on his file. The young Zoroastrian felt that his prospects for completing his education and establishing a career were severely blighted following this incident.

Yet another case history related to a youth who was employed in a large commercial organisation, but lost his post when his employers learnt that he was a Zoroatrian. He was forced to join the army and fought in the Iran-Iraq war for a year and a half. The restrictions on employment opportunities extended to the proscription of Zoroastrians from government departments; some respondents felt constrained to observe that it was best to limit oneself to manual work, since the authorities were inclined to 'take the boys and put them into the army... the war between Iran and Iraq is a war between Muslims, and the Zoroastrians do not want to take sides. Yet, all of us would have had to join the army'.

The general impression that young Zoroastrian men fled Iran to escape being drafted for military service during the Iran-Iraq war (1980-1988), was not borne out by the refugees encountered by the author. The instances cited above were the only direct references to having been called to the war-front, alluded to by the refugees. In the main, their reasons for leaving Iran were primarily that as Zoroastrians they were discriminated against in the various spheres of life: education, employment and religion. Their future prospects therefore appeared bleak.

Another youth referred to the severe restrictions on his father's employment under the fundamentalist regime. As a university professor who refused to renounce his faith, he was encouraged to 'retire'. He gave up his teaching post and continued to earn a living by privately tutoring students from home.

Given the various incidences of discrimination, they were asked whether they were on the sub-continent seeking refuge because they were

Zoroastrians. 'This is an important reason.' The restrictions on employment were numerous. Zoroastrians were not eligible to join the military as members of the officer corps; they were not permitted to work in a government department, and especially not in the ministry of education. For those Zoroastrians who had their own business establishments, they 'cannot be the boss' under present circumstances.

To the obvious question, then, of how Zoroastrians earned a living in Iran, the responses gave significant insights into prevalent conditions. Some people worked in restaurants; some others owned shops. Even so they encountered difficulties. One refugee spoke of his father who owned a restaurant. The authorities notified him that as a Zoroastrian he was not to touch food since he was *najes* and would pollute the food consumed by Muslims who ate at his establishment. It was reported that some Zoroastrians worked in television repairs, one of the safest employments, as there was no *najes* associated with this.

Restrictions on employment prospects may be placed prior to the completion of one's technical education.

> They don't permit Zoroastrian students to continue studies at higher levels. Once you complete the B.Sc. [degree] and want to continue to the M.Sc. and pass the exams with good grades, you still cannot continue. They fault you on ideology: Islamic ideology.

In the mid-19th century the Zoroastrian minority had been permitted to establish Zoroastrian schools, first in Yazd and Kerman, and then in Tehran.[5] Their primary purpose was to give the Zoroastrian youth, both boys and girls, an education which would include study of the Zoroastrian religion and history. The four Zoroastrian schools in Tehran today are permitted by the Islamic authorities to remain open. The best known, *Firuz-e Bahram*, was spoken of affectionately by members of its alumni among the refugees. The *Rostam Abadian, Jamshid Jam Primary School* and the *Anoshirvan High School for Girls*, continues to attract Zoroastrian students. (The name of the *Anoshirvan High School* was changed soon after the Revolution, owing to the revised perception that King Khosro I (Anoshirvan) had persecuted the Mazdakites. He was thus considered an evil king by the post-revolutionary authorities. The school is now known as the *Pendar-e-Nik*, meaning good thoughts.)

The schools are currently permitted to teach the Zoroastrian religion, with Islamic studies also on the curriculum. Approximately one hour of Zoroastrian religious instruction is permitted; followed by Islamic theology. The refugees maintained that, even in the Zoroastrian schools attempts were being made to convert the students to Islam. While the majority of teachers are

Zoroastrians, Muslim teachers are employed as well. The entire student body, however, are Zoroastrians. Prior to the Revolution, Muslims too attended the schools - especially the prestigious *Firuz-e Bahram*. The Tehran Anjuman continues delicate negotiations with the government authorities to keep it exclusively Zoroastrian on the grounds that it enjoys Zoroastrian endowments. The Zoroastrian students are taught the *Avesta*, and the Anjuman, where necessary, finances the performance of *sedre-pushin* of groups of children. As a result, these ceremonies were being regularly performed in Tehran especially, where children from the Zoroastrian schools were being invested with *sudre-kusti*. Indeed, the emphasis on Zoroastrian education and religious practices is a reactive response on the part of the community to the Islamic indoctrination which surrounds them. During the relaxation of tensions under the Pahlavi regime, the community was permitted religious and economic freedom for the first time in some 1300 years. They were enticed by their new-found liberty to relegate their religio-cultural identity in the relaxed atmosphere of Pahlavi Iran. The fundamentalist regime which had replaced the earlier dynasty, however, had inflicted severe restrictions on its Zoroastrian minority. The community was making an effort to revaluate its heritage, and had begun by re-educating themselves on the fundamentals: they had begun by studying Zarathushtra's *Gathas*, and by attempting to understand what precisely it meant to be a Zoroastrian. These observations and many others made by the youth, confirms the consolidation of Iranian Zoroastrian identity in the face of cumulative discrimination.

The precariousness of the current situation was repeatedly invoked. The youth were prepared to concede that some Zoroastrians might have contemplated embracing Islam in order to enjoy the facilities which they had under the Shah. Despite the inducements to convert, they remained in the old faith. Taking the longer view, one respondent was sombre: 'If they continue this pressure for the next fifteen to twenty years, our people [Zoroastrians], those who want to work and get an education, may feel compelled to convert'. In order to retain the uneasy *status quo*, the Zoroastrians conducted their ceremonials 'very quietly', and were held in private without ostentation and with subdued rejoicing.

There is a significant ingredient in Zoroastrian religious ceremonials - those not connected with death - which are joyous by nature, where the assembly rejoice following the solemnization by prayers; where men and women, young and old, come together to participate in thanksgiving for Ahura Mazda's blessings. Festive occasions such as the *sedre-pushin*, the marriage ceremony, the important *gahambars* and *jashns*, were drastically curtailed in the first years after the Revolution. All the respondents wished to add their personal grievances on the substantial reduction of ceremonials. Being Zoroastrians, they found it difficult to come to terms with the enforced solemnity of Shi'ite Islam, but at odds with the essentials of Zarathushtra's teachings which are to enhance life and combat the life-negating forces. The Government of Iran permitted restricted celebration of the *mehrgan* and *sadeh* festivals, although Zoroastrians were not allowed time off by their employers to attend the religious ceremonials. '...We have to take their permission to celebrate *mehrgan* and *sadeh*, and no music is allowed because the orthodox *mullahs* don't like it'.

The restrictions on Zoroastrian observances relate to the fear of some *mullahs* of apostasy on the part of Muslims who might find Zoroastrianism more appealing. Given that apostasy by a Muslim is a fearful capital offence, the Zoroastrian Anjuman of Tehran adopts a circumspect policy. The Zoroastrian elders fear that if the government sees them assisting Zoroastrian youth, they might be deemed to extend this 'help' to poor Muslims, and then 'convert' them to Zoroastrianism. In fact, the *dastur* had been instructed by some Muslims not to convert Muslims, since he, as a Zoroastrian, did not have this right.

One youth, whose journey across national frontiers was heroic by any standards, and daring in its hair-raising details, was asked of his contact with the family he had left behind in Iran. 'It is very difficult for our parents to part from us. I spent six days on the road and my parents believed I was dead. The telephone lines were not working, and it was several weeks before I could reassure them'. While they spoke of the painful separation from their kinfolk, there were no references made to the religiosity, or otherwise, of their parents. They were Zoroastrians who held to their ancient faith, and that sufficed by way of explanation - with the exception of this youth, who volunteered that he had undertaken the dangerous journey into exile because 'if in any situation I must choose between my nationality and my religion, I will choose my religion'. Thereupon he was asked whether he came from a particularly religious background. While his mother was very religious, his father was not. She prayed from the *Avesta* three or four times a day for all her children. This young man movingly spoke of being sustained by his mother's prayers.

It is for these manifold reasons that the youth have risked their lives to seek refuge overseas.

> We come here as refugees and wait for the Blue Card from the United Nations. We have come to secure a better future for ourselves, but we feel that all doors are closed to us.

The pride these youngsters displayed centred primarily on their ancient religion. The conflicting rationale between Islam and Zoroastrianism was a thread running through several respondents' thinking. Since they had been exposed to fundamentalist Islam and been compelled to endure its restrictions, they were unanimous in proclaiming their pride in their

Zoroastrian religion. Others reflected on the religio-political dimensions, which they considered significant. They were cognizant of Islam as a powerful world religion; having themselves been subjected to inducements to embrace that faith, these young persons demonstrated a remarkable resilience. In the words of one of their group, '...just because force is used, why should we give up our Zoroastrian religion?'

Indeed, the linkage between politics and religion had come to acquire special meaning for several youth.

> Zoroastrians feel proud that despite many difficulties we have not left our religion. We still believe in good thoughts, good words and good deeds (the Zoroastrian credo)... Zoroastrians want to help build Iran. When Iran was a Zoroastrian land, we had a great empire.. we were respected in the world.

He defined his religion as, 'all of the things I do. It is a way of life'.[6]

If their Zoroastrian religion was an inalienable part of their identity, was it at odds with their Iranian nationality? Did they at all see themselves as Iranians first and Zoroastrians second, or vice versa? The individual perceptions of this differed, but the unmistakable impression conveyed was that the youth saw Iran as a Zoroastrian country for it had been a Zoroastrian land prior to its conversion to Islam. Since they were Zoroastrians, they saw themselves as the 'original' Iranians whose ancestors had shaped and built the land. Their religion - Zoroastrianism - was seen as being bound inextricably with the idea of Iran. Events in modern Iranian history were thus perversions of the original *ideal type*. A school-age youngster put it succinctly, 'I am first Iranian and then Zoroastrian, because Spitama Zarathushtra was first of all Iranian and then he became a Zardushti. I am first an Iranian because Iran is the land of the Zardushtis'.

It was not uncommon for the refugees to feel an immense gratitude to their Parsi hosts, even though cultural differences made communication between the two groups difficult. The Iranians were asked whether they felt that they were as one people with the Parsis or whether two separate ethnic groups. 'I think both of us are one people. I think they [the Parsis] came originally from Iran. Their fathers are Iranian. Our religion is one, our Prophet is the same. So we belong to one group.'

Relations between Parsi and Iranian Zoroastrians are on a complex footing, as has been outlined in Chapter 2. Some of the intricacies of dealing with persons who have adapted a language, culture, mannerisms, humour, cuisine and much more than what is deemed authentically Zoroastrian, were indicated by some of the respondents.

Nominal differences between the two groups were remarked: most notably, Parsi emphasis on the *sudre-kusti* and recitation of prayers. The influence of 'foreign' culture on the Parsis had not escaped the refugees' attention: such as *tili* (red vermillion dot on the forehead); wearing the saree; putting *chalk* patterns on their door-steps. All these were understood in their context as borrowings from the Hindus. Furthermore, it had been noticed that the 'Parsis like food', but beyond and above all these, what made the Parsis different was their preoccupation with the minutiae of religious ritual, and a corresponding absence of understanding of the philosophical message of Zarathushtra. These were fundamental differences between the Iranians and Parsis, and remarked upon by all the respondents.

> The Parsis of India and Pakistan don't think about the philosophy of Zoroastrianism. In Iran, Muslims and Zoroastrians think deeply of the metaphysics of [their respective] religious philosophies.[7]

The understanding of different cultures and historical development however, did not extend to the youth perceiving the Parsis as 'foreign'. This indeed seemed paradoxical. They insisted that in spite of the differences, they saw the Parsis as being one with themselves. One youth referred directly to this Parsi author, saying simply, 'I think both of us are one'.

It is instructive to bear in mind that these Zoroastrian refugees constitute a group who have, for personal reasons, felt compelled to flee post-Revolutionary Iran. Their censure of the Iranian Muslims is therefore understandable. Among the Zoroastrians from Iran who have already settled in the West, the indications are that the cultural differences between themselves and the Parsis are seen as such insurmountable barriers that, some among them find it easier to socialise with Iranian Muslims in preference to Parsis.

The refugees saw their sojourn on the Indian sub-continent as temporary, *en route* to a hospitable Western nation. Nevertheless, having displayed their innate attachment to Iran, which they felt was intrinsically Zoroastrian, and the Islamic regimes an aberration, the final questions put to them were, whether they hoped to return to Iran, and if they cherished a dream that some day their country would return to being a Zoroastrian land? One young man stated categorically, 'The Zoroastrian religion is going to disappear.' There were those who took a pragmatic approach, and felt they were not in a position to answer, but would contemplate returning when the fundamentalist regime was no longer in power; yet another said,'I dream that maybe some day Iran will be a Zoroastrian country as it was 2,500 years ago'.

This exposition necessarily presents the opinions of a group of Iranian refugees. Earlier in the same year, in the course of field work in North America, the author had the opportunity to enquire of a visiting Zoroastrian the conditions prevalent in Iran for the community. His assessment corroborates the opinions of the young refugees. Indeed, his opinion was that 'present-day Iran has returned almost to *jizya* days'. He listed the drastic changes which had been introduced following the 1979 Revolution:

* Zoroastrian principals at Zoroastrian schools had been replaced by Muslims.
* Names of Zoroastrian schools - those receiving government subsidy - had been changed.
* Restrictions on Zoroastrian businesses: Zoroastrians were not permitted to run grocery stores; or to own hairdressing establishments nor laundries.
* Although there were Zoroastrians serving in the Iranian Army, there was no induction of Zoroastrians at officer level.
* Prior to admission to a university, neighbours were asked for their assessment as to whether an individual was a 'good Muslim'. In the event that he failed to get such positive endorsements, the candidate was denied admission.
* In earlier centuries, Zoroastrians who worked in Muslim homes carried a shawl over their shoulders, which they placed on the floor before sitting, so they would not pollute the ground. This requirement had been re-imposed in a few villages in the Yazd area.[8]

The predicament of the Zoroastrians in the Islamic Republic of Iran evidentially appears to be precarious. They are a tolerated minority who have historically been viewed as *atash parast* and *najes*. This has proscribed their full participation in Iranian national life since the Arab invasion. The short respite the Zoroastrians had enjoyed in the early decades of the present century has been curtailed by the Revolution of 1979. Where the State's very being rests on the belief in, and practice of, a religion which by definition excludes those not professing the same faith, then these non-conformists become marginal to its society. Alternatively, they are encouraged to change their religious affiliation and profess the state approved doctrine. Iranian Zoroastrians have historically endured their excluded-class status but have stoutly adhered to their ancestral faith.

Iranian Muslim antipathy to the Zoroastrians is not, therefore, a novel phenomenon. Its antecedents are rooted in the history of a land which rose to the zenith of its temporal power as a Zoroastrian nation, when the religion and ethos of its civilization was over-run by an alien power which then forced its own doctrinal beliefs and values upon the conquered peoples. The old order was eradicated and the new took its place. Over the 1300 years since elapsed, the Islamic faith in Iran has firmly rooted itself and attempted to remove all trace of the earlier Zoroastrianism of the land and the people. The small populations of Zoroastrians now serve as a poignant reminder of a time long past. Some intellectual Iranians continue to see the Zoroastrians as the 'true Iranians'. For the more extreme among the Shi'ite clergy, however, they are a small group who ought to embrace Islam, thereby entering into the mainstream of Iranian life. Among the Zoroastrians themselves, it appears to have become a matter of honour to retain their hereditary link with their Zoroastrian religion because they have 'Zoroastrian blood', and because they believe that to be Iranian is to be Zoroastrian. This author was told by an Iranian Zoroastrian in North America, that his mother refused to leave Iran and seek sanctuary with her son in the West. Her argument was, 'the Arabs could not drive me out in the 7th century, the *mullahs* won't make me leave my father's land. I am a Zoroastrian'.

NOTES:

1. This additional safeguard has been introduced by the Tehran Anjuman owing to the infiltration of some Baha'is and Muslims who have attempted to obtain 'Zoroastrian Identity Cards' to assist them in travelling abroad.

2. Other contrasting 'identity markers' between the two groups which the refugees stressed were the differences in the recitation and pronunciation of *Avestan* prayers. The Parsis are seen as 'praying with Hindi accents'. Similarly, the rituals cause confusion, such as the Parsi emphasis on *dakhmas* and the Tehrani Zoroastrians' preference for burial. However, seemingly the most wayward Parsi custom to Iranian minds, is the celebration of the 'Parsi New Year' in August, rather than on 21 March.

3. Owing to their deficiencies in the English language, the statements by some refugees have been transposed into indirect speech.

4. There are several layers of thought behind this simple assertion. In the larger cities like Tehran, during the relaxation of restrictions on the Zoroastrians under Pahlavi rule, there was a growth in social and economic contacts between Zoroastrians and Muslims. Unquestionably, some personal friendships were thus consolidated during that time and marriage between Zoroastrians and Muslims were also solemnized. However, in the general perception, the fundamental differences of religious values and customs would have remained. Similarities between the Parsi experience can equally be drawn.

5. Refer Chapter 1 'Zoroastrians of Iran'. See also Mary Boyce,'Manekji Limji Hataria in Iran', *K.R.Cama Oriental Institute, Golden Jubilee Volume*, Bombay, 1969; see also, D.F.Karaka, *History of the Parsis*, vol.I, (London 1884), pp 55-85.

6. This takes a similar point of view as the Parsis of the Indian sub-continent, where they see their religion as 'much more, a way of life'.

7. It is interesting to read Edward Browne's assessment of the Persians of some hundred years before in this connection: 'The most striking feature of the Persians as a nation is their passion for metaphysical speculation', in Edward Browne, *A Year Amongst the Persians*, (London 1893 and 1984, paperback), p.133.

8. I am grateful to this gentleman for having brought these matters to my attention. The above conditions were prevalent at the time of the government headed by the late Ayatollah Ruhollah Khomeini.

CHAPTER SIX

THE ZOROASTRIANS OF THE DIASPORA

The Zoroastrians of North America: The USA and Canada

The Zoroastrian community of North America - the United States of America and Canada - is a dynamic section of the Zoroastrian community world-wide. It is a relatively recent settlement since the mid-1960s, comprising a highly professional cadre of men and women[1] who have chosen to make their home on the continent because it offers financial, educational and career opportunities, and is deemed a safe haven. There are no accurately verifiable figures of the exact numbers who have migrated, because the US and Canadian census figures do not specify the number of Zoroastrians categorised in religious and ethnic terms. Estimates vary from 5,000 to 7,000, with some maintaining that the Zoroastrian population is some 10,000 souls.[2]

The striking feature of the North American community is that it is not monolithic. It comprises Parsis from India, Pakistan and other parts of the world. Iranian Zoroastrians began arriving in North America, in the main following the Iranian Revolution of 1979. Both Parsis and Iranian Zoroastrians are represented by a small number who have migrated to North America after having spent some years in the United Kingdom. The Parsi migrations have been inspired chiefly by a search for economic advancement. The Iranian Zoroastrians have felt compelled to emigrate because of the growing pressures of living as a religious minority in a fundamentalist Islamic country. The reasons for movement West may have differed, but once the re-settlement process has been established, a return to the old countries does not seem feasible for the forseeable future. Some Parsis are said to have expressed the hope of retiring in India,[3] but the author, in the course of field work, did not encounter any such. The Iranian Zoroastrian, on the other hand, clings steadfastly to the 'dream' of returning to his country, yet acknowledges that such possibility becomes remote upon viewing the political realities of modern Iran.[4] Zoroastrians in the USA and Canada are therefore permanent residents.

A profile of the North American Zoroastrians can only be usefully drawn once two key issues have been delineated. The variant migrant 'psychology' of the Iranian Zoroastrian and Parsi migrants needs clarification. It relates to the particular concept of an American or Canadian identity and the New World Zoroastrian community's reconciliation with their historical conditioning in the old countries of Iran and India. Further, the 'traditionalist' vs.'liberal' schools of Zoroastrianism are evolving within a North American context. It can be seen that the common strand of these discussions are the differing perspectives of the Iranian Zoroastrians and the Parsis. It is only after an understanding has been effected of the quintessential role of the adoptive lands - the United States and Canada - in fashioning the North American Zoroastrian, that the fundamental issues emerging from the questionnaire may be analysed.

The historical conditioning of the Iranians and Parsis has been distinct. Americans and Canadians, being largely unaware of the Zoroastrians, perceive of this religious-ethnic group as 'Indians' or 'Iranians' without distinguishing them from the majority religious groups of those countries. Indeed, the fact of Parsi and Iranian Zoroastrians as cognate constituents of the community, their distinctive religious, traditional, cultural appreciation of their Zoroastrian heritage, can be seen most clearly on the North American continent. Any study of this community has to take account of the distinct Iranian and Parsi perspectives over every issue pertaining to it.

The impact of environment on religious observance is often subtle and, over time, inevitable. Iran and India are fundamentally very distinct cultures. In consequence the two groups of Zoroastrians have developed in disparate ways. These are exemplified by Iranian assertions that Parsis 'still believe in *dakhmas*', and 'they think you are a Zoroastrian only if you wear *sudre-kusti*'. On the other hand, there are Iranian Zoroastrians who wish to see Zoroastrianism purely as a philosophy and wish to have no connection with the long tradition inspired by Zoroastrian perspectives, and developed in keeping with the tenets of the religion. Older Iranians rationalise that their modern-thinking offspring cannot relate to such traditional Zoroastrian practices as *dakhmas*. An Iranian Zoroastrian domiciled in North America saw a very bright future for the religion if the young were taught the philosophy underpinning the faith, without stressing the traditions and customs of Zoroastrianism. He recalled older kinfolk in Iran emphasizing the importance of having the *sedre-pushin* and regular prayers which, for him did not constitute the essence of Zoroastrianism. 'To me it is good thoughts, words and deeds'. An equally emphatic Parsi youth reaffirmed his Zoroastrian identity, which had been shaped from childhood by the simple aspects of morning prayers, and the donning of *sudre-kusti*. He maintained that these practices helped create 'a special type of identity'. Clearly, therefore, the very concepts of what makes one a Zoroastrian differ widely for the Parsi and the

Iranian.

These distinctive attitudes in religion, culture and historical experiences are manifested most forcefully in North America, where the two groups have again met up after a separation which spanned a millenium. The Iranian Zoroastrians are concentrated in Los Angeles, Vancouver and, to a lesser extent, New York and are not as dispersed throughout the continent as are the Parsis. It is the realignment of the Parsi and Iranian conceptualizations of Zoroastrianism, interacting with an American and Canadian environment, which will determine the future outline of the North American Zoroastrian identity.

Given that the two branches of the Zoroastrians are the products of such widely differing experiences, it becomes necessary to analyse their particular attitudes to the phenomenon of migration. The processes and perceptions of adjustment to a foreign environment diverge. The Parsis have known migration once before, in the 10th century, when they left Iran and settled in India. The trauma of re-settlement, the adjustments that had necessarily to be made, the acceptance of the finality of separation from the ancestral land - Iran - has somehow been assimilated into the Parsi psychology. Furthermore, with the advent of the British in India, and the high level of westernisation of the Parsi community there, has meant that the settlement pattern in the West was one that they could adjust to with relatively greater ease than the Iranians.

The case of the Iranian Zoroastrian migrant is very different. Their long centuries of residence in Yazd and Kerman was interrupted only recently with the ascension of the Pahlavi dynasty in Iran, when Zoroastrians were permitted to live and work in Tehran. The enforced migration to the Western nations sequent upon the Iranian Revolution, is keenly felt by the Zoroastrians who have made the USA and Canada their country of residence. Indeed, most Iranian Zoroastrians persist in their view that their sojourn in these lands is at best an extended stay. They do not, or cannot, accept the finality of their severance from Iran. It is only after much agonising that some amongst them acknowledge the obstacles to an impending return to Iran. They are acutely aware of the distance separating them from their homeland and have not yet recovered from the grieving process of estrangement from the old country.

Thus, Parsi and Iranian present two different aspects of migrant psychology. It is within the ambit of the variant re-settlement process, where each maintains his particular religious stance to be the 'correct' one (the Parsi emphasis, for example, on rituals; Iranian emphasis on the philosophy of Zarathushtra), that questions of intra-community relations will be resolved. In terms of their capacity for adjusting to a foreign environment, the Parsis demonstrate a greater aptitude, as compared with their Iranian co-religionists. Proximity to the English when they ruled India, their language, customs, education, form of government, resulted in the eager grasp by the Parsis of the opportunity to study the English language, fully availing themselves of educational opportunities which opened up careers in the sciences, law, and government.[5] The determinative factor in the divergent attitudes of Parsis and Iranian Zoroastrians is their respective historical experiences in India and Iran.

If the Parsis are deemed adept at adjustment, and the Iranian Zoroastrian apparently less so, they operate within the specificity of the North American environment. From the American perspective, the issue of a Zoroastrian identity is itself a misnomer, where the religion of the person is not considered important, rather his country of origin.[6] The average American has never heard of a Zoroastrian. His perception of this immigrant in his midst is of an Iranian, an Indian, or a Pakistani. The Iranian Zoroastrian emphasizes with pride his country of origin. The situation is more complex in the case of the Parsis.

'Parsipanu' (Parsi-ness) is a commingling, in terms of self-perception, of the Zoroastrian religion and the ethnic distinctness of Persian immigrants in India. In the true sense, Parsi is the ethnicity and Zoroastrianism the religion professed by this group of Indians.[7] The general discernment is such that, at the subconscious level of Parsi and Indian perceptions, race and religion have come to be both interchangeable and complementary.[8] What some Parsi Zoroastrians in North America regard as the community's 'muddled thinking' on the equivalence of religion with race as applicable to the Parsis abroad, is seen to be incompatible with the situation prevalent in the United States. In order to circumvent this confusion, there is a conscious effort to cease using the term 'Parsi' because it is seen as an ethnic label, and instead use the term 'Zoroastrian', which is seen as the religious denomination of this group from the Indian sub-continent, as well as of their exiled Iranian compatriots.[9]

The enigma of Parsi identity was clearly enunciated by several respondents in answer to the question: 'As a Parsi, describing yourself to a Western person, would you use the term Iranian or Persian?' One said,'I use the term Persian. When they ask whether I am Indian I say, "well, we are Indians, but our ancestors came from Persia"'. It is not just the younger Parsi whose exposition of identity is labyrinthine; their elders present a similar confusion. A middle-aged man, originally from Bombay, said: 'Although I am happy to say I am Indian, I definitely don't want to be classified a Hindu. I am a different Indian'.

While the attempt at accommodation to the requirements of American government and societal norms is being made by the Parsi Zoroastrians, there are legacies they have inherited from their Indian environment which will take longer to reconcile with the standards of American society. The concept of Indian nationalism is a phenomenon of recent vintage, at best a development dating from the mid-19th century.[10] It does not yet display the substratum of matured nationalisms such as the French or the Danes. On the canvas of Indian nationalism comprising disparate 'nationalities', many Parsis have seen themselves as distinct and different from other Indians. The question arises whether the terms 'Parsi' and 'Zoroastrian' have meanings that are wider in scope than simply being religio-ethnic labels? If in India, the Parsi had not easily reconciled himself to his Indian nationality, is it realistic to expect that in his country of adoption he will, in the process of Americanization, successfully reconcile the various competing demands on his loyalty: his Iranian stock, his Hindu Indian conditioning, his recently acquired veneer of Westernization?

It must therefore be conceded that what appears initially as a simple adjustment by the Parsi to American and Canadian norms is not the case upon closer examination. Ironically, such considerations do not apply to the Iranian Zoroastrians, who in fact are the reluctant immigrants. When the next generation of Iranian Zoroastrians is 'Americanized' they will continue to be proud and comfortable to say they came from Persia, the land of their Prophet and their Kings. The Parsi Zoroastrian youth has yet to redefine himself before he can definitively indicate to his American hosts the land from whence he springs.

The nature and composition of American and Canadian society, the creation of modern nation states by earlier immigrants from the five continents, enhances the new immigrant's ability to consider it his 'homeland', the country to which he is going to henceforth belong.[11] Yet, the official governmental policies on the enculturation of the migrant population are different in the USA and Canada. Upto the present time, the Canadian government has espoused a policy of developing a multi-cultural and multi-ethnic nation where the very diversity of its peoples is now celebrated, and are encouraged to become Canadians through their distinctive cultural traditions. This is a conciliatory response to the earlier problems of racism within Canada with the arrival of different immigrant groups. The United States, as a global power, espouses a policy of the homogenous American identity. The 'Americanization' of the new immigrant is a conscious programme of an accelerated release of ties with the old countries, and acquisition of American nationality, with its corresponding ethos.[12] The process of becoming American or Canadian, irrespective of the country and ethnic group from which the migrant originates, is peculiar to these two North American countries. The creation of an 'American Zoroastrian' and a 'Canadian Zoroastrian', as distinct and specific types of Zoroastrians, is in the process of being created. This is quite different for example, to being a 'British Zoroastrian', who does not belong to the Anglo-Saxon or Celtic races and is seen as quite another type of British citizen.

In the discussion on the Zoroastrian immigrant,[13] it was pointed out that the first generation of Parsi immigrants (mainly from the Indian sub-continent) who came some twenty or thirty years ago to the USA and Canada, establishing careers and families in their new homes, had a substantial difference from the first American-born generation. While the immigrant generation was conditioned to face the difficulties of life, the minor, routine discomforts of everyday living in India and Pakistan, this had in fact, put 'some iron in their backs'. This, however, was not the case with the new American and Canadian generations. They had become accustomed to the comforts of North America, and were consequently unable to face upto hardships. This, then, was a major generational difference: the former could, and did, endeavour to achieve goals, the latter expect success and an ease of life-style as of right. It was further argued that if in future, the Zoroastrians collectively were to encounter some handicap in the North American setting, they would in all probability be unable to cope with the strain, not having had any previous experience in dealing with it. If this prognosis of Mr.Rohinton Rivetna contains even a germ of accuracy, it strengthens the argument that the western Zoroastrians are moving further away from their eastern roots. There is one historically attested feature of the Zoroastrian community which is their tenacity in the face of adversity. The view outlined above may contain substantive elements of truth, with caveats. The experiences and methodology of an older generation in another place and time, need not necessarily be of use in a future which the young cannot envisage or grasp. Equally, the "sterner stuff" alluded to by older generations in reference to their experiences of the migration process, may lie dormant until activated for specific purposes by the next generations as and when required.

While some sections of the community have adapted to their new countries with enthusiasm, the conflicts over their loyalty to their Zoroastrian traditions and values has been responsible for creating strains in intra-community relations. Among the North American Zoroastrians a new lexicon has evolved. The 'traditional' and 'liberal' allegiances of the community receive novel interpretations. The polemics centre not on America and Canada: the systems, societies and life-styles they have come to adopt. These in fact, are relegated to a secondary position in the debate. The thrust of the 'traditional' and 'liberal' argument is to ensure that, in the shaping of the North American Zoroastrian identity, *the* socio-religious dilemma of conversion should be viewed from a North American perspective. The discussions on conversion being waged by the community is central to their self-perception as an eastern peoples wishing to make an adjustment in a technological society of the West. The North American polity is a determinant, but it is the interpretation of the 'authentic' precepts of Zarathushtra's *Gathas* by two widely divergent groups within the community which will, in large measure, account for the formation of Zoroastrian identity in North America. The pivotal issue is conversion: the position adopted on the subject classifies an individual as a 'traditionalist' or 'liberal'.[14]

Within but not exclusively the North American context, the determining feature of the 'liberal' Zoroastrian would be the fundamental, and oftentimes exclusive pre-eminence he would attach to the *Gathas*. Given that the essentials of the prophet's teachings are contained in his five groups of hymns, this then should be the highest referral on matters pertaining to the religion acceptable from the 'liberal' perspective. Conversely - and inaccurately - the 'traditionalist' Zoroastrian is perceived as placing inordinate emphasis on the indiscriminate mix of the Later Avesta, and the obscure Middle Persian or Pahlavi texts. The Parsi priests are regarded as steeped in a 'corrupted Hinduised' and 'ritualistic' Zoroastrianism, far removed from the spirit of the *Gathas*. Within this line of reasoning, the Parsi predilection for the *Vendidad*, with its emphasis on purity laws, are emphasized by orthodoxist practitioners, whereas the 'liberal' Zoroastrians of North America would wish to consciously remove such perceived accretions to the faith, thereby making it more amenable to his adoptive environment.

The establishment of the Zoroastrian faith, first in eastern Iran, and its subsequent spread to the western Iranian peoples, did not lead to a widespread export of the teachings of Zarathushtra to the non-Iranian [*anarya*]. The Iranians came to view Zarathushtra's message as 'part of their own racial heritage'.[15] This mind-set developed into custom, and with exceptions (as during the Sasanian High Priest Kirder's long term of office under the early Sasanian kings, when his inscriptions refer to 'many people who were unbelievers became believers'),[16] it generally served to confirm the rule. It is this specific aspect of Zoroastrian history, the delimiting of the religion to a specific people, the making of 'Ahura Mazda into a tribal god', which is seen as anachronistic by the liberals, and through an earlier historical imperative as an inalienable religious heritage by the traditionalists. The central question of the North American search for their identity is: who is a Zoroastrian? The impetus behind the movement to' re-assess the Gathic message has a secondary actor in the piece, North American society itself, where the egalitarian concept is enshrined in the national constitution. A specifically Zoroastrian issue, the role of the *anarya* in Zoroastrian society, is being revalued in the socio-political environment of North America, which hitherto had played no part in Zoroastrian civilization. However, the emigres to this continent, from the old lands of Zoroastrianism - Iran and India - wish to revive a particular part of their legacy which they deem unsuited to their adoptive environment. In the process of the creation of a North American Zoroastrian identity, the outcome of the current debate on conversion will play a fundamental role, for the quintessence of the dialectic is: who is a Zoroastrian?

The conceptual framework within which the conversion issue is pursued by this community is couched in terms distinct and irreconcilable: 'Zoroastrian traditions' vs.'Zoroastrian philosophy'. The deliberations further place subjective labels, so that the 'rituals' and 'traditions' are deemed a negative manifestation of the pristine aspect of the teachings of Zarathushtra, viz. its theology. The inherent intellectual anachronisms, which by logical extension wishes to abrogate the corpus of the traditions and ethos which developed in the Zoroastrian world and took as their *raison d'etre* the teachings of Zarathushtra, is not yet adequately addressed in the North American debate.

The loose theoretical parameters of the debate are further reduced to the apportioning of labels whereby the Parsis are deemed the 'traditionalists' and the Iranians, the 'liberals'. This is necessarily a simplification of a complex cultural preconception, where the Parsis' proclivity for the 'traditions' of *dakhmas*, *sudre-kusti*, the admittance of Zoroastrians only to the fire temples, for example, are seen as the negative manifestation of a tradition they acquired for themselves during their long residence in Hindu India. The Iranian Zoroastrian prides himself in his attachment to the great metaphysical message relayed in the *Gathas*, and having had no cultural interference from the Muslims in his Zoroastrian practices. While sections of the community might earnestly subscribe to the above stereotypes, the author finds such a demarcation of the community inaccurate.

What in fact underlines the issue is the exacerbation of tensions in the perceptions of Zoroastrianism to which the Parsis and Iranian Zoroastrians subscribe. The community divide is being built upon a philosophical infrastructure to delineate cultural differences between the two groups, compounded by the historical and geographical separation of the past millenium. A simplistic schema then shows: Parsi equals Indian ('Hindi') equals traditions; Iranians equal Zoroastrian equals Zarathushtrian philosophy. Were this elementary equation to serve as an actual model, one would accept it, albeit with reservations. The truth, however, is contrastive. The author encountered Parsis who wish to abandon 'traditions' and 'accept' converts - indeed, some of the most enthusiastic partisans of the conversion lobby at the time of writing are Parsis; Iranian Zoroastrians who wish to retain 'traditions' and 'accept converts selectively, no Arabs'.

The equation is compounded by the fact that the Iranian Zoroastrians in North America are, in the main, affluent, professional people, and not orthodox members of the community from the Zoroastrian villages of Yazd and Kerman. The pivotal outcome is therefore not what appears at first glance as Parsi vs.Iranian, but in essence an urban vs. rural perspective of religious texts, philosophy, traditions at the very nub of Zoroastrianism. Quite understandably, the confusions of the old countries have been imported into the New World, and with the urgency and rapidity of decisions necessitated by their adoptive environment, the North American Zoroastrians are attempting to re-define themselves and their group persona within mere decades, and thereby overturning long centuries of their historico-religious legacies.

Homeland: Prior to the acceptance of a foreign land as one's new domicile, the question arises as to whether the migrant perceives his newly adopted country as his 'homeland'. Roughly half the youth and the elders in the USA and Canada considered these to be their 'homelands' (Refer Table 1).

The sense of belonging to the new country was felt more strongly by the Parsis and less so by the Iranian Zoroastrians. For a 22 year old Parsi it was '...deductive reasoning. I have no other homeland. I consider India and Pakistan my transitory homelands. No matter how long I lived in Pakistan, I could never consider myself "Pakistani"'. The differences in perceptions were demonstrated by a 26 year old Iranian lady who said, 'I was born and rooted in Iran. Iran is my only home'. The strength of one's familial bonds can militate against the acceptance of the new country, as in the case of a young Iranian who did not consider the USA his home and still felt he owed his parents an apology for marrying an American. Indeed, the author did not encounter a single Iranian Zoroastrian, young or old, who maintained that America or Canada was their home.

The ability to adjust to a new environment, to sever the links with the old country, assuredly differs from one individual to another. The propensity to judge the Parsis as content and well-adjusted, and the Iranians as dissatisfied and unhappy in their new homes, is ill-founded. A Parsi gentleman said that on occasion the Canadians accepted him, and 'rejected' him when it suited them. Another older person asserted that he felt a stranger in the United States since his formative experiences had been elsewhere. A young Parsi mother acknowledged that while she considered Canada home, she did not consider herself a patriot. 'I don't think I have a homeland'.

The question of degrees of acceptance of the new country becomes a complex issue for the immigrant. In order to measure the levels of attachment therefore, respondents were asked how attached they felt to their adopted country, and whether they contemplated spending the rest of their lives there. Once again, there were widely varying attitudes. A young Parsi bride said she felt amazement when her American husband unfurled the American flag on the 4th of July. A young Iranian conceded that her values were formed in Iran and it remained her country, but in the United States she was independent and had the potential for growth.

There was a certain degree of ambivalence among Zoroastrians settled in North America, rather than its straightforward acceptance or rejection. A 61 year old gentleman spoke for many when he referred to 'some sort of duality among us who are not born here'. Outward appearances to the contrary, the Zoroastrian immigrants show the various strains on their loyalty, and in this are not unlike other groups of migrants. The adjustment process will take generations, rather than a few short years to accomplish. There are no clear lines of separation in their levels of attachment to their new homes. There are Parsis who demonstrated their pain at the severance of their roots from the

Indian sub-continent, just as Iranians do. There were Iranians who had adjusted because they were married to Americans and established a family which helped see the new country in a positive light. As with all major issues confronting the Zoroastrian community, there is no consensus of opinion where the subject matter itself is deeply personal.

Language: The issue of languages - Farsi for the Iranians, and Gujarati in the case of Parsis, shows clearly different attitudes. Over half the youth and the elders tend to 'think' in English, and registered it as their primary conduit of expression (Refer Table 2).

The extent to which English has become the *lingua franca* of the younger Zoroastrians was outlined by a 21 year old Bombay-born Parsi ordained for the priesthood [*navar*]. He had never learnt to read or write Gujarati, and the prayers for the *navar* ceremony were written in Roman script. A 16 year old Iranian born in the USA said, 'English was the first language I learnt'.

While it is not possible to accurately gauge the vital role played by the Farsi language in reinforcing ties with Iran, so significant is the part played by the language in the creation of national pride, that all Iranians cling tenaciously to it, while some respondents even suggested that since the Parsis do not speak Farsi, they may not be 'good Zoroastrians'.

The inroads made by the English language into the western communities must in due course be seen as an important causative factor in the re-shaping of their identity. A 36 year old Iranian said that in the company of Americans he thought and spoke in English; while amongst Persians, he reverted to thinking and speaking in Farsi. He felt that this gave him a 'double personality... you don't know which direction to take'. The loosening of bonds with the old languages of the Zoroastrian peoples - Farsi and Gujarati - can happen in other ways. A Parsi whose deep patriotism for America was evident throughout the discussions, said he was 'not emotionally attached to the Gujarati language' and spoke English which, after all, was the language of his adopted country.

Knowledge of Zoroastrian History: In order to assess the issue of the specific identity of the Zoroastrians in the Old and New worlds, a crucial question which needs to be raised is the awareness of their particular historical antecedents: whether or not they have a knowledge of the history of pre-Islamic Iran and Parsi domicile in India. The reasoning behind this enquiry is, as research indicates[17], that for the Zoroastrians, their religion covers the gamut of their individual and collective personas. To what extent the history of ancient Persia has been subsumed under the category of religion was borne out by the sample: barely a fifth of the youth and around half of their elders claimed to have an adequate knowledge of their history. (Refer Table 3).

Statistics, however, tell only a part of the story. The general impression made on the author was that while the older Iranian Zoroastrians had a clear idea of historical developments in Iran, the Parsis were, at best, unsure of their facts, and at worst, had no knowledge whatever of Zoroastrian history. Those who claimed little knowledge, vaguely recounted what they knew, often mentioning 'Cyrus and Darius' by way of an assumed knowledge of the kings. It is doubtful if they could effectively list the dynasties and better-known kings of a particular era. There is a tendency among the Parsis of North America, as there is among those of the Indian sub-continent, and the UK, to erase from their collective minds their awareness of their historical roots.[18]

The virtual loss of this phenomenon among the contemporary Parsis has not been emulated by the older Iranian Zoroastrians, while the Iranian youth appear to have eschewed historical awareness. It may be argued that one not entirely insignificant reason as to why the Iranian Zoroastrians survived centuries of persecution was because they determinedly clung to their collective memories of the glories of their ancestors. To obliterate the past from the communal consciousness, is to reject the compass which can guide future generations. Modern Zoroastrians are in danger of forgetting their communal awareness of their shared historical antecedents.

Identity: It has been stated that, despite their small numbers, the Zoroastrians present an immensely complex face to the world. Despite the enthusiastic acceptance of their new countries, most of the youth as well as the elders were prepared to identify themselves as Zoroastrians (Refer Table 4).

It would appear that North American Zoroastrians see their Zoroastrianism as a primary and fundamental ingredient of their individual and group persona. A young lady explained that she could identify only as a Parsi. A young Iranian felt he was 'unique being Zoroastrian'. Another maintained that he had imbibed his Zoroastrianness with mother's milk, and despite discrimination in Iran had never denied his identity.

While most respondents, both young and old, showed their deep attachment to being Zoroastrian, the few who wished either to be distanced from it, or even disowned it, did so for their own compelling reasons. A 17 year old student explained:

> When I first meet someone, I am hesitant to reveal my identity as a Zoroastrian. In America you don't want to be seen as eccentric. If I am asked where I spend my weekends, I generally reply that I go to my church. I don't say *Dar-i Mehr* until I know them well, and they understand my religion'.[19]

While adolescents display a certain confusion of loyalty, some older Zoroastrians too gave evidence of the uneasy compromises forced upon the immigrant. A young mother exemplified this dilemma. She had herself been educated in the West and had known discrimination, which she maintained attached to her foreign name. As a consequence, she had given both her daughters Christian names to 'protect them'. The surname remained Parsi. It becomes questionable whether this lady has in fact helped, rather than hindered, her children's ability to see themselves as Canadians and be accepted as such among their peers. The given name of an individual is his outward badge of identity. When this is compounded - a Western forename and an Eastern surname - it is likely that the individual could develop an ambivalence towards both cultures.[20]

What precisely their Zoroastrian identity represented, varied with each individual. It was not simply a religious identity: it appeared to encompass sizeable composites (Refer Table 4(a)). For a 28 year old it was '...my cultural identity, my colour and my religon'. For yet another,'it is my tribe and my culture'. For one youth, it was his way of life. An older Iranian elaborated: he identified primarily as a Persian and then as a Zoroastrian. Since Muslims, Armenians, Jews and Christians were also Iranians, it was his identification as a Persian which distinguished him from fellow-Iranians in terms of culture, religion and heritage.

It was generally acknowledged that the majority peoples had no idea of who in fact the Zoroastrians were. It is this fact of non-recognition as a people which compounds the perplexed identity of the Western Zoroastrian. The host society merely labels them as Indians or Iranians, extending the majority's perceptions and prejudices concerning these foreign nationalities. The prevailing American antagonism towards Iran and the over-all anti-Middle Eastern sentiment, while it did not injure the Iranian Zoroastrian's pride, has not left him unaffected.

The issue becomes acute in the case of the young Zoroastrians born and reared in the new countries, when the parental imperative is to retain their religion and culture in the home, and the peer group's virtual non-comprehension of the Zoroastrian in their midst. He must begin, therefore, by explaining 'who' he is, and his distinctive beliefs and cultural patterns. It is the resolution of this central issue of what a Zoroastrian is supposed to mean, that will point to the future of the community in North America, and in other lands of the diaspora.

Chief External Influences: Given that Zoroastrians are surrounded by majority peoples who are non-Zoroastrians, and whose religio-cultural imperatives are different from this small minority's, respondents were asked to elaborate on the chief external influences upon them.[21] Less than half the youth and the elders claimed to have been most heavily influenced by their Zoroastrian environment of family and friends, while Western influences had made an impact on a sizeable part of the youth and a small proportion of the elders

(Refer Table 5).

It bears reiteration that for differing reasons both Parsis and Iranian Zoroastrians have over long centuries maintained an aloofness from the majority peoples surrounding them. A middle-aged Parsi, originally from India, said that

> ...as Parsis, we kept very much within the Parsi community. At college and at work, we had non-Parsi friends. But we were never encouraged to mix with them on a social level. In fact, we were actively discouraged from having non-Parsi friends.

Equally emphatically, a middle-aged Iranian stated:

> We were always discriminated against by the Muslims and so we lived in the Zardushti *mahalle* (locality), and never spent time with Muslims. We mixed only with Zoroastrian boys and girls.

A pattern distinct from the above is emerging among the younger Zoroastrians. A young mother who completed her schooling in North America, spoke of peer pressures at school which had induced her to emulate Western icons. Motherhood had led to an emphasis on her Zoroastrian identity. The influences on a 16 year old Iranian girl were, 'Western values with obvious hints of Persian'. While some young persons attempt a compromise of divergent values and cultures, there are those who do not. A Parsi youngster said that American society had been a primary influence on him, since he was the only Parsi at his school. An Iranian youth spoke of similar strains, 'the coping with Western culture with an Iranian background is very difficult'.

The parameters of Parsi and Iranian Zoroastrian identity have been shaped, in large measure, by the socio-religious distance they have kept from the majority Hindus and Muslims around them in the old countries. For a Zoroastrian, therefore, there are distinctive aspects of his identity which the internal community dynamic regularly reaffirmed. Identity is, however, not a static phenomenon, and as such there occurs in the diaspora a re-shaping of this Zoroastrian persona. The memories of the old countries, which the older generation have brought with them to the New World, may serve as a navigational aid to the younger Zoroastrians in the process of re-charting their respective American and Canadian Zoroastrian identities, although it is difficult to make such assertions at the present stage in their development.

Prejudice: It was repeatedly stated by respondents that the average American and Canadian had never heard of a Zoroastrian and did not possess the least notion as to who these people were. Given that Zoroastrians demonstrate an intrinsic pride in their Zoroastrian heritage, the logical extension would be to examine whether or not they had felt their high personal regard of self was in fact reciprocated by their fellow Americans and Canadians. Any suggestion that they had suffered prejudice in North America was overwhelmingly rejected by well over half of the youth and the elders. (Refer Table 1(a)). An important caveat attaches to the question of prejudice, implicit or otherwise, related to race.[22]

A sample of the reactions of some of the youth canvassed is an indication of the varied reactions. 'They say you don't look Indian and don't speak like an Indian. I don't have Indian friends at school because I don't like being associated with the negative connotations attached to India'. For an Iranian youth, as indeed for the majority of Iranian Zoroastrians who acknowledged the existence of prejudice, it was the current nadir of political relations between Iran and the outside world which affected them. Once the classification 'Iranian' was appended, it made it difficult to be accepted. Other Iranians referred to themselves as Persians, since this term had positive connotations.

Older Parsi Zoroastrians rejected their 'Indian' label. A university professor maintained that his contributions in his specialist field had been overlooked, and occasionally a 'white man' had received credit for his work. Yet another put it in equally strong terms: 'To an American there is no difference between an Indian and a Parsi. But we are culturally very different from Hindus. I do suffer from this stereotyping, and have to prove myself constantly'.

There were very few who were prepared to say, as did one professional lady that, '...my ancestors and religion originated in Iran, but I identify myself very much as an Indian.' The impression generated is that, in spite of their outward ability to adjust to their new environment, the prejudices and preconceptions brought with them to their new homelands have not been erased. Parsis in the main show a dislike of being labelled 'Hindi'. Iranian Zoroastrians wished to clarify their ancient historical links with the soil of Iran before the Arab conquest. The fact that their hosts have no comprehension of the complex bias imported by these immigrants into their adoptive surroundings, suggests that the settlement process is more involved than is sometimes supposed by community members themselves.

Indeed, while discussing the subject of prejudice, no respondent alluded to the vexed issue of 'acceptance' of converts,[23] and its relationship to their own preferences for some races more than others. Some North American Zoroastrians wish to institute the 'acceptance' of aliens into the Zoroastrian fold. On legal (American and Canadian constitutional provisos) and theological grounds, 'acceptance' must imply a complete open door. If Parsi Zoroastrians find the label 'Hindi' offensive, and the Iranian Zoroastrian retains his apprehension of the Arabs, how then is the intellectual concept of open 'acceptance' of all to be introduced? Prejudice, like all human sentiments, frequently boomerangs. While some North American Zoroastrians were prepared to concede their own partialities vis-a-vis other races, no attempt appears hitherto to have been made to deal with the reverse situation: 'acceptance' within the fold of races historically less favoured by Zoroastrians. The longer-term ramifications of the hidden face of prejudice, i.e. the Zoroastrian bias against others, will assuredly create a fresh set of problems for the North American community once the communal doors are opened to all aliens.

Conversion: The question which most exercises the mind of the American and Canadian Zoroastrians is the issue of conversion. It is through this mode of 'acceptance' of aliens into the fold, that one faction hopes to reverse the demographic trend, revive the Zoroastrian religion and ensure the continuity of the community. Well over half the youth and the elders favour the intake of aliens within the Zoroastrian religious fold (Refer Table 7).

An event which galvanised the North American community was the performance of Joseph Peterson's *navjote* ceremony on March 5, 1983 at the New Rochelle (New Jersey) *Dar-i Mehr*. Four priests officiated at that ceremony: two Parsis and two Iranian Zoroastrians. Peterson is an American of Christian parentage. A milestone in modern Zoroastrian history was thus reached, when a determined non-Zoroastrian who had embraced Zoroastrianism through study and with deep conviction, approached members of the American Zoroastrian community with the express desire to be officially initiated into the Zoroastrian fold. This was active conversion into the Zoroastrian religion, the infrequently recorded instances over the past millenium of the faith's history having thus been reversed.

The North American Zoroastrian community persistently refers to the issue of the intake of aliens into the fold as 'acceptance', not 'conversion', of non-Zoroastrians. Some indicators suggest themselves. The first is semantically devised. 'Acceptance' implies the act of accepting an outsider into the fold, while 'conversion' is a "change" from one's religion into another religion - here Zoroastrianism - implying coercion, whether overt or otherwise. As this proposition is anathema to the majority of Zoroastrians who have refrained, over a substantial part of their history, from forcible conversions of aliens, the North American Zoroastrians stress their antipathy towards 'proselytisation'. Secondly, those within the community amenable to the intake of aliens, emphasize the American and Canadian legal and constitutional guarantees on the equality of all. How, therefore, could they reject anyone who wished to practice their Zoroastrian faith, and yet remain law-abiding American and Canadian citizens? Thirdly, is the community's move toward 'accepting' the offspring of a Zoroastrian and non-Zoroastrian union, irrespective of whether the mother or father is a Zoroastrian. The non-Zoroastrian partner too, if he or she requests it, is thus 'accepted' rather than 'converted.' Using a semantic device, the North American Zoroastrians could demonstrate their abhorrence of coercion in religious affiliation, and yet welcome through acceptance into the fold the devoted alien (juddin).

The debate on the conversion question continues both in the USA and Canada, but it seems to be more widespread in the greater Los Angeles area. Three Associations coexist there: the Zoroastrian Centre with an overwhelming Iranian membership; Zoroastrian Association of California with a largely Parsi membership, and the Traditional Mazdayasnan Zoroastrian Association formed in March 1988, representing a small group of families who consider themselves orthodox. Until 1991, Dr.Ali Jafarey was the resident Scholar at the Zoroastrian Centre and a pivotal figure in the conversion debate.[24]

Dr.Jafarey is an Iranian Muslim by birth who has converted to Zoroastrianism. He sees Southern California as the chosen area for his 'mission' of promulgating the Gathic teachings of Zarathushtra as expounded by Dr.Jafarey. He believes there are sizeable sections of exiled Iranian Muslims and 'intellectual' Americans who would wish to embrace the faith. He 'chooses only intellectuals' as the 'New Zoroastrians', and sees his work as eliminating the distractions of race and religion which have developed in the Zoroastrian world over the centuries and, in his opinion, more especially among the Parsis. Thus, Dr.Jafarey would opt for the safeguarding of the religion and not of those professing the Zoroastrian faith. Insofar as the question of the diminution of the number of natural-born Zoroastrians is concerned, Dr.Jafarey sees his work as being the only feasible answer to the disappearance of the Zoroastrian religion. To put conversions in the West in the context of his former domicile in Iran, and the safety of Iranian Zoroastrians in light of such actions, Dr.Jafarey considers this 'a price that has to be paid'.

His emphasis on the Gathas mostly excludes the traditions that have developed over centuries in the corpus of Zoroastrian practices. The Parsis are deemed the arch traditionalists in that they are seen as practising a Hinduised version of Zoroastrianism and excluding non-Parsis from the fold.[25]

Dr.Jafarey outlined the core issues in his proselytizing 'mission' to the author in 1988, since when he has further elaborated on them with the creation of the Zarathushtrian Assembly. This is outlined in the internationally circulated Zoroastrian monthly, Parsiana (June 1991), thus: The preamble of the Assembly's constitution 'proclaim(s) the message of Zarathushtra to a world in need of its enlightening wisdom'. Membership is open to anyone who considers him/herself Zoroastrian by birth or choice and has 'knowledgeably performed his or her initiation (navjote/sedre-pushin)'. It is a non-political, non-profit, religious organisation, which has been accorded tax exempt status in the United States; its intentions are to open other branches in North

American cities, in London and Paris. It is not explained by the founders of the Zoroastrian Assembly why no branch offices are planned in Asia, Africa or Latin America.

The Assembly commits itself to the upholding of a set of six 'Paramount Principles', among which, 'we recognise that the *Gathas* are the only source of Zarathushtra's teachings, and takes precedence over all later inconsistent teachings, customs, rituals and traditions', and as such appears to be a deliberate rejection of the corpus of the Zoroastrian religious heritage.

Since the debate on conversion is most vociferous in the North American context, and was expounded initially as a Parsi versus Iranian religious argument, it becomes necessary to analyse the demarcation made between Parsi and Iranian attitudes to this question. Thus, Iranian Muslims who wish to accept the Zoroastrian religion are considered by some within the community to be returning to their original faith. The Iranian culture - language, food, habits, thinking processes - are deemed similar for Muslim and Zoroastrian Iranian alike. Therefore, to change allegiance from Mohammad to Zarathushtra means, in this sense, an addition of numbers for the Zoroastrians, with no change in cultural requirements for the proselyte. This is one part of the argument presented. Some older Iranian Zoroastrians - those who have spent their formative years in Yazd and Kerman - put forward a different view. They insist that there are real differences in the mentality, attitudes, values and even personal hygiene habits of the Muslim and Zoroastrian. Some among them take the point further, in that they consider themselves the 'true Persians' and the Muslims as having mixed blood, that of the various invaders of Iran: Arabs, Turks, Mongols and Afghans.

Dr.Jafarey took this writer to meet two Iranian proselytes, Muslims whom he had converted to Zoroastrianism, in Southern California. Having elaborated on their fervent attachment to the Zoroastrian creed and reiterated their own commitment to continue the mission of converting persons to the Zoroastrian faith, they were asked: 'what do you consider your position vis-a-vis those born of Zoroastrian parents?' One convert responded that, on festivals, she had attended functions at the Zoroastrian Centre in greater Los Angeles. Her fellow Iranian Zoroastrians had treated her most coldly and made no attempt to socialise with her, as a consequence of which she had stopped attending the Centre. Arguably, therefore, while Iranian Zoroastrians are perceived as applauding the conversion of persons into the Zoroastrian faith, the removal of centuries of prejudice - a social rather than a religious issue - will take longer to accomplish. In this respect, the Iranian Zoroastrian is very similar to the Parsi Zoroastrian.

It may be argued that Parsis who oppose the intake of converts see the world from their particular perspective. While Parsis have acquired a certain veneer of Indianization, it has been adopted in a selective manner. Their idiosyncratic use of the Gujarati language; their ability to grant a degree of educational, social and economic independence to their women earlier than did other Indian communities; their emphasis on family life with a corresponding emphasis on Western usage such as the nucleus family, are just some of a wide range of admixture of Indian with a non-Indian perception of society. A curious blending of the Zoroastrian heritage (such as independence of thought) has taken place with Hindu culture (arranged marriages, for instance, in earlier times). For Parsis, therefore, the introduction of 'foreigners' into the community's religious base would imply a reorganisation of the community's ingrained usages and mannerisms peculiar to Parsis alone, and passed on in a characteristic hereditary way. A certain reservation against the idea of intake of converts, is largely discernible amongst Zoroastrians who come from the ancient strongholds of Zoroastrianism in Iran and India.

In view of the author's detailed discussions with Dr.Jafarey, there has now emerged another dimension to the conversion issue, viz. the question of proselytisation (given Dr.Jafarey's 'mission' to 'convert only intellectuals'). The Zoroastrians of North America who were interviewed, and whose opinions are reflected in the statistics, favour 'acceptance', i.e. the inclusion into the Zoroastrian fold of an individual who chooses to enter. There was a marked unease with the notion of proselytisation, i.e. an action to seek to change. Those who wanted the community to open its doors to outsiders repeatedly stated that 'I believe in acceptance totally, but not in the use of propaganda'. The mental reservation of the Zoroastrian majority to active proselytisation is understandable, in view of its historic development, since the Zoroastrian religion has not been actively propagated. At certain historically attested moments, e.g. under the kingships of Bahram II, Shahpur II, Bahram V, Yazdgard II, their evangelizing religious prelates Kirdir, Adharbadh, Mihr-Narseh actively attempted to proselytize among the *arya* of alien faiths and the *anarya*. Even so, the chief emphasis of state policy was to stem the conversion of Zoroastrians in Iran to Christianity, Buddhism, Hinduism and Manichaeism.

On this vital subject of conversion, it is instructive to summarize the respondents' views. A 22 year old Parsi admitted that he would find it difficult to accept an outsider within the communal fold. Another youth reflected that, although he had been impressed by Joseph Peterson's Zoroastrian convictions, it was doubtful that having failed to find fulfilment in the religion of one's birth, the convert would find satisfaction in another faith. Some young folk saw the conversion controversy affecting them personally in future. Those who contemplated marrying exogamously wished to be allowed to bring their future spouses into the religious fold, even though they were aware of the obstacles they might encounter. This was bound to cause conflicts with community traditions.

The perspective of a middle-aged Iranian father of three, contained several contradictory attitudes, not the least of which was the concept of 'selective conversion'. In fact, several respondents who agreed to conversion did not want 'any and every one to be brought in'. Some Iranian Zoroastrians favoured conversion but said, 'I don't want any Arabs to be allowed'. Whether there is not a contradiction in terms between 'conversion' and 'selective conversion' was never elaborated upon by the respondents. Nor was the methodology of conversion discussed. The communal infrastructure, which must be a prerequisite to the intake of a large or small body of persons into the religous fold, inextricably tied to the communal group, were never analysed. Selective conversion, by an exclusion process therefore, must be seen as a safe middle course, one which would ensure the survival of the religion and would not be seen to violate too many historical interdicts, i.e. non-conversion of Arabs.

The statistical data notwithstanding, there is a prevalent confusion among the ordinary Zoroastrians who wish to be seen to bring their religion 'up-to-date' by converting aliens, but have not been able to grasp the dynamics of such a revolutionary move. The parameters of the discussion as it prevails are: the Gathic message is interpreted and analysed; the Parsis are perceived as the prime felons who have made Zoroastrianism into a 'tribal' preserve. The responses to the original question whether Zoroastrianism is a religious label any individual can assume upon initiation into the faith, must therefore, be placed within the confines of the above-stated hypothesis. The veracity or otherwise of the Parsis' alleged responsibility for degeneration of the creed was not analysed by any person interviewed. Nor was there any corresponding intellectual curiosity demonstrated in an analysis of the causative factors influencing Iranian Zoroastrian non-conversion of the outsider (general religious persecution of Zoroastrians, and the penalty of death for the Muslim apostate and his instigator). The result was that, from widely divergent positions and with different historical impetus, both Parsi and Iranian Zoroastrians refrained from converting aliens in India and Iran. Precisely because there evolved a negative custom, i.e. non-acceptance of an outsider into the fold, there were no institutional structures in the eventuality that such a convention may be overturned. As the one was deemed unlikely, the other was regarded as unnecessary; consequently the most vital aspect of the conversion debate currently being conducted in North America is not addressed. North American community publications such as *Gavashni* (Montreal), *The Zoroastrian* (Los Angeles), quote the *Gathas* at length. Individual Zoroastrians in America and Canada too, demonstrate familiarity with Gathic texts and quote references to validate their case for acceptance of the alien. In emotive terms, individual Zoroastrians will admonish Parsi perceptions of their religion and race. These, then, are the parameters of the debate.

When fundamental questions of the precise manner in which such conversions will be successfully tackled, the mechanisms installed to facilitate 'selective conversions' and the criteria of acceptability were met, respondents maintained that these would be effected. If acceptance of *juddins* into the religion, and thereby into the community, is to become a workable choice for the Zoroastrian community of North America, the construction of communal infrastructures: religious educational facilities, requisite study and examination of the candidate, social conditioning of the community to accept the convert, and the feasibility of the 'natural' Zoroastrian to instruct the 'new Zoroastrians' into the precepts and rituals of the faith, need to be in place. There was no evidence of these core issues relating to conversion having been addressed by the North American community at the time the field work was conducted. Their overwhelming will to adapt their religious structures and accept aliens is not in doubt. Their grasp of the enormity of the venture, is.

Intermarriage: The attempt at self-preservation under historically adverse conditions has resulted in the traditional discouragement of marriages outside the fold. With the rising number of professional persons in the community,[26] their mobility, and the acknowledgement that their new home is in North America, the likelihood for exogamous marriages is on the increase (Refer Tables 8 & 8(a)).

The question of intermarriage, while it is perceived to be increasing throughout the Zoroastrian world, presents such a mosaic of contradictions that, in the course of extensive field work on three continents, this writer has yet to encounter an exogamous Zoroastrian who does not take a diffident stance, or its reverse, a highly aggressive posture in relation to the Zoroastrian community itself, or a combination of these conflicting emotions. Intermarriage has come to acquire a two-fold perspective: the immediate familial one, and the other, whereby the Zoroastrian community is affected by its occurrence.

At the most fundamental level is the collective Zoroastrian perception, induced through centuries of conditioning, that he who marries outside the fold has 'betrayed his religion'. This was brought most tellingly to the author's attention when an Iranian Zoroastrian whom she encountered socially in the USA, was prepared to volunteer the information that, in spite of having reached his middle years, he still felt he had been 'disloyal' to his parents and to his religion, since he had married an European. He spoke at great length of the guilt he carried within him for having so betrayed his 'people', by having chosen a foreign wife. He was ready to admit that in most respects his had been a successful marriage, with offspring who had gone on to achieve distinction in their respective professional fields. He could not, however, shake off the years of conditioning in Yazd, where a strong sense of duty to the religion, the family and the community, had been instilled in him. The ingrained distaste for exogamous marriages was emphasized further by a 37 year old Iranian who said he 'remembered when my mother's brother married a Muslim, how she wept. She aged suddenly in a week'.

While Zoroastrians lived as a tightly-knit group in the rural and urban centres in the old countries, the possibility of the survival of the tradition of endogamy was high. The question of the paucity of numbers of Zoroastrians thinly spread over a vast continent, has meant that there has developed the problem of finding suitable Zoroastrian partners. A young Zoroastrian girl who was 'dating' an American with her parents' knowledge, admitted that intermarriage was 'dangerous for the community' as it might expedite the extinction of the religion. However, for someone like herself there was no possibility of finding a Zoroastrian partner locally, and it was unrealistic to expect her to agree to an arranged marriage with someone from India. The issue which exercised her mind most was, whether she 'was allowed by the religion' to bring up her children of mixed parentage as Zoroastrians.

Several Iranian girls' had a preference for an Iranian Zoroastrian partner. This was another, and not insignificant, feature of the issue of exogamous marriage. Given the substantial cultural differences between Parsi and Iranians, the youth interviewed displayed little enthusiasm to marry someone from the other Zoroastrian group. Iranian Zoroastrians in particular spoke of the differences among themselves and the Parsis, and maintained that the problems were seemingly insurmountable. To date, marriages between Parsis and Iranian Zoroastrians do not take place with any appreciable frequency: only two such unions were brought to the author's notice during the spring of 1988.

The issue of intermarriage is addressed with a greater degree of vehemence by young Zoroastrian women. It is this group who have the greatest pressure put upon them to marry a fellow Zoroastrian since, by convention, were they to marry exogamously, neither they nor their children are acceptable within the community. In North America however, this ban is being reversed, and Zoroastrian Associations make provision in their charters of membership for such persons to become fully-fledged members. Nevertheless, while there remains an *ad hoc* approach by the community, and the priests more especially, towards the religious initiation of the children of a Zoroastrian woman and a non-Zoroastrian man, young women demonstrated a high degree of animation over this question. A Parsi girl approved of intermarriage and asserted that she herself would marry exogamously. If her non-Zoroastrian husband wished to embrace the faith and was refused entry, she too would sever all connections with the Zoroastrians.

The prejudices accompanying a Zoroastrian woman's decision to marry out are in the process of being dismantled, but even in the USA and Canada there are those who are strongly opposed to it. Some Zoroastrian women themselves do not wish to see a change in the *status quo*. A 30 year old Parsi lady said that 'only children of both Zoroastrian parents should be allowed to be Zoroastrian, even if we are to become extinct as a race'.

A Parsi gentleman who advocated conversion maintained that Zoroastrian women with foreign spouses ought to be welcomed, the non-Zoroastrian spouse ought to 'promise the children would be Zoroastrian.. It should be a pre-condition'. The survival of the Zoroastrian religion has become, for some members of the community, a matter of such overwhelming importance that, all other socio-religious issues are seen as subservient. The inverse proposition that the non-Zoroastrian partner may have no inclination to adopt Zoroastrianism, nor permit the children to adopt the faith, is seldom seriously contemplated. It appears to be the projection of a religious viewpoint into marriage, which needlessly exacerbates the socio-cultural tensions in mixed unions and contributes to the lack of understanding of the issues of intermarriage among the Zoroastrians.[27]

Nor is there awareness of contradictions displayed by the same individual on the apparently inseparable issues of conversion and intermarriage. A 62 year old Iranian Zoroastrian who spoke at length of his conviction that aliens ought to be admitted into the fold, continued: 'If my daughter were to marry an American, I would find it very hard to accept him as a Zoroastrian. It would be difficult for me to believe that he respects the Zoroastrian religion just because he says so.' When questioned on the intake of aliens he had this to say: 'I give priority to acceptance of outsiders, and fortunately we have many people who want to be admitted into our fold'. It bears reiteration that the bonds of race and religion, whether acknowledged by the interviewee or not, often underlined their responses to questions. There were several instances of contradictions on interrelated issues: conversion and intermarriage have, owing to their mistaken inseparability in the communal mind, developed into issues on which emotional responses rather than cold logic is applied. The virtual inability to distinguish the religious from the socio-cultural continues to confound the debate.

The likelihood of an increase in intermarriages becomes understandable when one investigates the position of the American- and Canadian-born Zoroastrians. A 17 year old stated categorically: 'I see the idea of marrying a Parsi as limiting my freedom'. The argument used by older Zoroastrians that mixed marriage is a clash of cultures and hence unworkable, will be overturned by the first generation born on the continent. Their culture will be predominantly American and Canadian, however these may evolve, and their ability to meet and marry their Indian and Iranian peers will severely put to the test earlier community assumptions of continuity only through in-marriages.

Zoroastrian Future in North America: In the final analysis, the community's perception of the long-term development of Zoroastrian identity in the United States and Canada is central to the understanding of this group. A sizeable number of the youth and some of the elders saw it as being positive (Refer Tables 9 & 9(a)).

Some older Zoroastrians displayed their own considerable ambivalence:

> Our community suffers from an inferiority complex. I think that the Zoroastrian religion will definitely continue, but not as a religion that was practised by our ancestors in the old countries. It will continue in utterly diluted form because of the changed circumstances.

Some among the youth were equally pessimistic: 'Right now there is no hope. We need to create a system'.

While some observations indicate a diminishing expectancy of the continuity of Zoroastrians on the continent, other interviewees saw signs for optimism: 'The rift between Iranians and Parsi will heal over the next generation. A new term will be used, which is "American Zoroastrian"'. One youth, who was an active participant in community affairs, observed that, 'there is a bright future. We will become like the Parsi community in India if we don't return to Iran. We will change but remain Zoroastrian'.

The Parsi community in India was seen by many as a community which, over a long period of time, came to terms with their situation as a minority community and played a significant marginal role in British Indian society. Parsis such as J.N.Tata were pivotal in transforming the Indian nation from a primarily agricultural society to one entering upon the technological age. Individual Parsi achievements had a ripple effect, which permeated through to the outer reaches of the small community and gave a sense initially of achievement and pride, but even more compellingly, a certain bargaining power that was out of all proportion to their miniscule numbers. Significantly, from the perspective of Zoroastrian identity, this adaptation to the Indian environment was achieved without an abnegation of their Zoroastrian beliefs and value system. This then appears to be the model to which some among the North American community hope to attain.

In the case of the North American Zoroastrians it is not possible, at this early stage in their acculturation to determine with any accuracy whether or not they will successfully emulate the Parsi model, or indeed even remain recognisably Zoroastrian in the future. The American and Canadian environments will be prime factors in the shape the group finally assumes. The variations in customs, practices and ideologies of the Iranian Zoroastrians and Parsis, adds an interesting dimension to the question.

What cannot be stated with any precision at this point in time is whether the next generation of American and Canadian Zoroastrians, with the assumption of their newly-acquired national labels, will not result in a corresponding diminution of their Zoroastrian identity. One might put forward the hypothesis that the British Zoroastrian, because he must contend with remaining marginal within his adoptive society, will vigorously strive to retain his Zoroastrianism, making it his sheet-anchor in his adoptive country.[28] To take the theory a stage further would imply that the longer-term future might bear witness to the British Zoroastrians evolving on the 'Parsi model', marginally integrated to their society. The emphasis of the American system on the homogeneity of its citizenry would suggest that the Americanization of the Zoroastrians would remove their particularisms. The Canadian official government policy of evolving a multi-cultural and multi-ethnic society could result in Canadian Zoroastrians being placed amidships of the British and American Zoroastrians, encouraged to become fully-fledged Canadians without abandoning their intrinsic heritage. It is unquestioned that the Western Zoroastrians will in due course come to be recognisably different from their co-religionists in the old homelands of Iran and India.

NOTES:

1. *Proceedings of the 6th North American Zoroastrian Congress*, Toronto, April 1988, J.R.Hinnells, 'Zoroastrian Migration to the American Continent', p.25. See also, J.R.Hinnells, *Katrak Lectures* (henceforth, *Katraks*), OUP, (forthcoming).

2. Talk given by Mr.Khojeste Mistree, Director, Zoroastrian Studies, Bombay, before an invited audience in London, 4 June 1988.

3. J.R.Hinnells, *Katraks, op.cit.*

4. In this connection see Muhammad Anwar, *The Myth of Return: Pakistanis in Britain*, (London 1979).

5. J.R.Hinnells, 'Parsis and the British', *JCOI*, (Bombay 1978), pp.42-64.

6. I am indebted to Mr.Rohinton Rivetna of Chicago, current president of the Federation of Zoroastrians of North America (FEZANA), for discussions with me during the course of my field work in the USA, April/May, 1988.

7. Refer, 'Parsi Panchayet Case, Suit No.689 of 1906' in the Bombay High Court, Justice Davar's Judgement, p.94, as elaborated upon in Chapter 4.

8. Cf.'Parsi Panchayet Case'.

9. This raises problems for atheists who may still want to assert community identity.

10. This discussion is elaborated on in Chapter 3.

11. The considerable research on the migration process and its effects on the migrant, demonstrates the subtle distinctions in the social adjustment processes involved: assimilation, acculturation, integration, adaptation. Refer Muhammad Anwar, *op.cit.* See also, Stephen Cohen, *American Modernity and Jewish Identity*, (Tavistock Publications, New York, 1983).

12. It is worth pointing out that there are hyphenated Americans, e.g. Polish-Americans, Italian-Americans, Jewish-Americans etc.

13. The following views were outlined in discussions with Mr.Rohinton Rivetna of Chicago.

14. Refer Chapter 4 discussion on 'Conversion'.

15. Mary Boyce, *Zoroastrians, Their Religious Beliefs and Practices*, (London 1979), p.47.

16. *op.cit.*, p. 114.

17. J.R.Hinnells and R.Writer, *Living Flame: Zoroastrianism in Britain*, (forthcoming). See also the preceding Chapeter 5 on the Parsis of India and Pakistan.

18. It could be asserted by North American Zoroastrians that in the 'Sunday Classes' on the Zoroastrian religion,taught voluntarily to the young, Zoroastrian history is included. The persons interviewed from the age of 16 upwards for this study, however, did not show any appreciable grasp of Zoroatrian history. In the 'Sunday Class' there is a greater emphasis on Zoroastrian religion than there is on the teaching of pre-Islamic history as witnessed in Toronto, Vancouver, Los Angeles and Chicago.

19. The young man persisted throughout the course of the interview to refer to his 'church' and never once used the appropriate term *dar-i mehr*, where in fact, the interview was being conducted. There is a frequent tendency to substitute American English terminology for the Zoroastrian word.

20. Hinnells & Writer, *Living Flame*, *op.cit.* for a discussion on name and identity.

21. As with the samples on the Indian sub-continent (refer Chapter 5), the questionnaire did not include 'Zoroastrian influences', given that these do not constitute external influences. However, the Zoroastrian influences of home, family, friends and the general environment played a significant role, and as such, is included in the summing-up.

22. While I was conducting interviews in the United Kingdom for the forthcoming joint publication, *Living Flame*, it became evident that Zoroastrians do not, in the main, appreciate discussing racial prejudice. There is a marked reluctance to admit that the 'white man' may not wish to acknowledge the Zoroastrian as a fellow 'white'. Therefore,the findings in North America ought to be treated with circumspection. Rather, the opinions expressed should be analysed closely for signs of where precisely individual's perceptions enter.

23. See detailed discussion, under.

24. I am indebted to Dr.Jafarey for explaining his views on the conversion question while I was in Los Angeles in May 1988. Dr.Jafarey is no longer the resident Scholar at the Zoroastrian Centre, having vacated the post in 1991. His proselytizing 'mission' is now conducted independently without the status as the Centre's representative. He is now Chief Organiser of the Zarathushtrian Assembly, Los Angeles. See *Parsiana*, June 1991.

25. It needs to be stated that, from Dr.Jafarey's particular viewpoint, the position he takes is understandable. As a proselyte, he has acquainted himself with, and gained expertise in, the philosophical core of the religious texts, the practices of the community being more readily available to one who is born into it.

26. J.R.Hinnells, *Katraks*, *op.cit.*

27. Hinnells & Writer, *Living Flame*, *op.cit.* chapter on 'Intermarriage', where the results of the detailed findings indicate cultural clashes at several levels within a mixed union, rather than a religious dysfunctioning, among partners.

28. Hinnells & Writer, *Living Flame*, *op.cit.*

The Zoroastrians of Great Britain

The Zoroastrians of the Indian sub-continent have had a long historical connection with Britain. Indeed, contact with the British dating back to the Raj prior to their migrations, was a significant contributory feature of Parsi perceptions of the 'English' [*velatis*]. Iranian Zoroastrians, on the other hand, have not had a similar experience. Parsi and Iranian Zoroastrians in Britain therefore present differing facades of a migrant community's acclimatisation in, and evaluation of, their new country.

In the absence of census figures, the current estimate of the Zoroastrian population in Britain is put at between 5,000 - 7,000 souls. Parsis were the first Indians to travel to England in 1742, and from the mid-19th century they came to the UK in increasing numbers for education and commercial purposes.[1] In 1861 the Religious Society of Zoroastrians was founded. In 1909 its name was changed to the Incorporated Parsee Association of Europe. As the Association grew with the increase of Zoroastrians in the country, larger premises were purchased and its name was further altered to read The Zoroastrian Trust Funds of Europe, in 1978, thereby incorporating into its nomenclature the Parsi and Iranian Zoroastrian constituent elements of membership.[2]

Twentieth century Zoroastrian migrations to Britain fall into four main periods,[3] the first having occurred between the two World Wars; the second following Indian partition, which brought Parsis from the sub-continent to the UK; the third from Kenya in the late 1960s, followed by the expulsion of 'Asians' from Uganda by Idi Amin in 1972, which saw a fairly substantial increase in (unspecified) numbers of East African Parsis who came to Britain in their capacity as British passport-holders; the main Iranian wave came after the 1979 Islamic Revolution. Throughout this period, Zoroastrian youth - both Parsis and Iranians - had been arriving in Britain for higher education. Some remained, others returned to their country of origin, and yet others, having completed their studies, moved on to countries such as the USA in pursuit of professional goals. The British Zoroastrians therefore are a fairly representative cross-section of the community.

The composition of the community reflects this. The initial group of Parsis who came between the wars were approximately 120 in number,[4] a majority of whom were involved in professional occupations and tended to be 'liberal' with regard to their Zoroastrian religious beliefs and practices. They lived at scattered distances, and hence no cohesive community spirit was engendered. They met socially on the 'Zoroastrian New Year' and for religious occasions at the London-based Association, but remained in the main preoccupied with establishing a successful life for themselves in Britain. Not surprisingly, the children and grandchildren of the first wave of Parsi migrants became absorbed into the mainstream of British society and for the most part, ceased to be recognisable Zoroastrians.[5]

Between the 1950s and 1970s a real growth in numbers of Parsis migrating to Britain was discernible. Parsis from India and Pakistan came because they felt they had the chance of a better life in England rather than in Hindu-dominated India and Muslim Pakistan. The political refugees from East Africa came because of the compulsory expulsion orders on 'Asians' in Uganda, which was the culmination of a growing perception of socio-political insecurity felt by fellow Parsis in Kenya, Tanzania, Malawi, Aden, Zanzibar and South Africa.

The Iranian Zoroastrians who left for the United Kingdom to escape the political convulsions overwhelming their country after 1979, are indeed very few in numbers. The current estimated figure is put at approximately 120 persons.[6] The Iranians' perception of Britain is historically distinct from that of the Parsis. Furthermore, their response to doctrines and ritual of the Zoroastrian religion differs considerably from their co-religionists.

The experience of the Parsis in Britain is different from the Iranians. The former are categorised as 'Asians', an idiosyncratic British nomenclature for persons originating in India, Pakistan and Bangladesh. The Parsis, as a rule, resent this reductionism and stereotyping. Since the British population cannot generally distinguish Parsis from among the multitudinous diversity of the sub-continent and resorts to a label which has acquired pejorative connotations, a substantial number of Parsis do not approve of being so labelled and are alienated as a result. Indeed, Parsis in Britain are hesitant to consider themselves 'Indians' or 'Pakistanis', and emphasize their Iranian descent which is seen as elevating them above the masses of the Indian sub-continent. In Britain there is, of course, little or no understanding of this peculiar Parsi attitude, and scant awareness of the Zoroastrian religion.[7] The resultant dilemma for the Parsis in Britain can be acute. They crave acceptance from the host society which has no understanding of their religio-cultural origins, and they distance themselves from other Indians. They would wish to retain their heritage without being considered as Indians.

The sample interviewed in the United Kingdom reflects the distinctive features of this community as its residence in Britain becomes more permanent. While the sample base is small, and the precise percentages are uncertain, general trends nevertheless have appeared to corroborate the earlier research undertaken by this writer when, in preparation for the forthcoming co-authored publication, *Living Flame: Zoroastrianism in Britain*, she interviewed 204 Zoroastrians resident in the United Kingdom. As will be shown in *Living Flame*, there are unique features developing among British Zoroastrians. They are reacting to the host community's reluctance to accept the 'foreigner', by emphasizing their Zoroastrianness or Persian ancestry. They pride themselves on the antiquity of their heritage. They do not wish to become English, yet they are clearly acculturating to English educational standards and secular values. The British Zoroastrian (like other migrant groups in the UK) is British by definition, insofar as he qualifies to carry a British passport, but is not 'English', inasmuch as he is distinctly non Anglo-Celtic. The several paradoxes of their position in the adopted country are becoming clearly evident.

Homeland: The vexed question of belonging to the new homeland reflects the distinctive British Zoroastrian attitude from that demonstrated by the North American community. Over half the youth and the elders do not see the United Kingdom as their home (Refer Table 1).

The findings corroborate earlier evidence gathered for the *Living Flame*. Paradoxically, while historically the Parsis had seen themselves as 'westernised' and 'anglicised', those Parsis now settled in the UK are admitting the differences between themselves and the indigenous population. The Iranian Zoroastrians, on the other hand, had never thought of themselves as English and, accordingly, there does not appear to be any perceptible change in their attitudes.

There is a developing trend in the Zoroastrian diaspora of the demonstrable attachment to their original roots. By this is meant Zoroastrian Iran. Indeed, the complexity of the Parsi Zoroastrian's perception of 'homeland' is clearly noticeable among the British community. Few among them hanker for the Indian sub-continent. A typical response came therefore, from a 36 year old Parsi lady, originally from Bombay, who maintained that her roots were in ancient Persia, indeed, it was 'where logically the ties are... and it leads to the fact that one does feel a bit homeless as a result'. This is the central theme in the analysis of Parsi perceptions of their homeland.

A further illustration of the problem of establishing a country of origin for Parsis, was the response of a middle-aged lady born in the Far East, who has lived in the UK since the age of twelve, and has visited India twice: 'I feel Indian, but does it mean I belong to India?' Indeed, it becomes immensely problematical to assess the 'Indianness' of persons such as these, given that she had never lived in India, nor had her parents before her; has no facility in the Gujarati language (nor any other Indian language); feels most comfortable in Britain, and has a cultural network of English friends. The logical question therefore asks: what does it mean when a Parsi who has lived in a Western country, maintains that he 'feels Indian'? In connection with Parsi perceptions of a homeland, several such imponderables repeatedly present themselves, attesting to the innate sense of displacement of these peoples.

A different dilemma exists for younger Parsis. A 23 year old, born in Britain, spoke for most:

> I feel Britain is my home. When I was younger I felt torn between the two cultures. Not any longer. I have visited India six times, and I know I could never live there. I now know my identity is more British.

The issue, in fact, is which of the two countries affords better living conditions, rather than the emotional attachment and sense of patriotism which is generally taken to indicate one's feeling for the homeland.

Iranian Zoroastrians, on the other hand, do not face the dilemma of the Parsis. For a 20 year old, there was no issue which merited discussion. 'Not at all. I was born in Iran'. Another maintained that, 'if the situation improves in Iran, I would like to return.'

The dilemma of Parsi sense of belonging to a particular country is the legacy of their history. While British Zoroastrians demonstrate an appreciation of the United Kingdom as a 'safe' country to live in, the bonds of patriotism have yet to be developed. For the Iranian Zoroastrian, a deep affinity with Iran remains unquestionably a prominent feature of his evaluation of Britain. The Parsis see Britain as a preferable option to living in India, Pakistan or an East African country.

A Parsi lady acknowledged only that it was 'by the accident of birth', that she had any tangible connections with India. She felt an affinity for 'Zoroastrian Iran' while she was most comfortable being domiciled in Britain, yet felt constrained to admit that she felt no sense of patriotism for any of these three countries. This viewpoint demonstrates unequivocally that neither the UK nor the countries of origin have established an unshakeable hold on her loyalty. Quite simply, a Parsi is someone whose country of residence does not imply it is the country to which he sees himself as belonging. A constant refrain heard in the course of the field work was, 'we are a people without a country'.

Language: The extent to which the English language has become the stepmother-tongue of the Parsis is reflected in the British sample: around half the youth and their elders consider English their 'thinking' language (Refer Table 2).

Young British Parsis do not think in Gujarati, and it is the exceptional youth who has any facility in the language: to all intents and purposes, the language of young Zoroastrians in the UK is English. Even Iranian Zoroastrian youth, especially British-born, or who came to the country at a tender age, admitted to having equal facility in English and Farsi, while some regretted that they could not 'make jokes in Farsi', the ability to do so being seen as the ultimate test of an individual's level of confidence in a language. Among the youth, therefore, a noticeable disappearance of Gujarati and Farsi is under way; the older Parsis are largely bi-lingual, whereas the Iranian adult, despite a long residence in the country, shows no appreciable mastery over the English language, but continues to 'think' in Farsi.

An Iranian, exceptionally, said 'I speak Zoroastrian', referring to the Dari dialect which was his family's domestic tongue. More forthright was a young Parsi lady's response: 'English. I regret very much that I am not bi-lingual...I think I am not a good Zoroastrian because I can't speak Gujarati. I understand every word of it, but it isn't the same'. Having been born in the United Kingdom where English was the dominant language, she maintained that her parents ought to have made the effort to teach her Gujarati and to have 'compelled' her to have spoken it at home. This is an area of great confusion among the Parsis settled abroad. Not having an appreciable degree of affinity to the Gujarati language in India or Pakistan, and having settled overseas specifically for material improvement in their living conditions, it is not uncommon to meet parents who would wish their children to speak Gjuarati but make no specific efforts to teach it. This is partly related to their being unqualified to teach the language to their children, and the various Zoroastrian associations in the UK have no educational facility for the study of Parsi-Gujarati. Consequently, a virtual erosion of the language among the first generation born British Zoroastrians has occurred.

The loss of Parsi-Gujarati by the younger generation in the UK, is however, the cumulative result of trends that set in among the Parsi community in India. The alacrity with which they embraced the English language in the early 19th century; the gradual replacement of the vernacular by English at Parsi schools; and the initially bi-lingual approach in Parsi homes (replaced in urban communities by almost exclusive use of English at home, socially and in the work-place), has resulted in the Parsi youth in the West, more especially, having been denied the opportunity of learning Gujarati. As such, the disappearance of this language among this age group is not surprising. It is curious that Gujarati-speaking parents, while conversing among themselves in their vernacular, make no demands on their children to do likewise. It must be concluded that Parsis consider fluency in English and its supersedure of the vernacular as prime requisites for their childrens' secular advance. Iranian adults decry the fact that their children do not have a similar facility in Farsi as themselves, but the loss of the Farsi language by the young Iranians is not as acute as it is for the Parsis. Yet, one Iranian mother lamented, '... both my daughter and her husband can speak Farsi, yet they speak English at home'.

Knowledge of Zoroastrian History: The analysis of this data is important since the findings in the British community resemble those of the North American, with the difference that the latter comprises a higher percentage of Iranians. Older Iranian Zoroastrians have an awareness of the history of pre-Islamic

Iran; Parsis, quite simply, do not. In the UK, only a minority of the youth and the elders claimed a sound knowledge of their history (Refer Table 3).

A 39 year old Parsi lady encapsulated Zoroastrian history thus, 'I am aware that when the Muslims came to Iran, the Parsis came to India'. It is not, however, the case that since their arrival in India the Parsis suffered collective amnesia in terms of their historical memory. Rather, the reverse was the case. They have kept alive the memory of their ancestral land. Over time, they were perceived as a religious minority and stressed their distinctiveness in India primarily in terms of their religious identity. Their link with Iranian history extended to their familiarity with the legends of the *Shah-nameh*, which again were seen in a religious context. A particular mental attitude among Parsis is thus discernable. Parsis do not perceive history to be of any importance, hence they do not emphasize it. A middle-aged Parsi had studied the *Shah-nameh* during her youth in Bombay, but had failed to pass on this knowledge to her children.

A further question presents itself: whether the conflict of identity which confronts the contemporary Zoroastrian world is related, in part, to the fact that Zoroastrians have permitted themselves to efface from their memory their collective past. Insofar as this trend has been identified among the Parsis, the British community confirms it. Given the existing lack of educational structures within the community in the UK, it does not appear feasible that this situation will be rectified for the forseeable future.[8]

Prejudice: British Zoroastrians appear reluctant to acknowledge that they may be the targets of racial discrimination. The issue of racial prejudice was included in the questionnaire prepared for this study in which Zoroastrians, other than those canvassed for the *Living Flame*, were individually interviewed. The earlier findings were confirmed. Well over half the youth and elders claimed they had never experienced racial discrimination in Britain (Refer Table 1(b)).

Some Parsis go to great lengths to dissociate themselves from the Indian sub-continent; the Iranian Zoroastrians attempt to distance themselves from any perception of being mistaken for an Arab, in order to adjust to the negative preconceptions of the foreigner in British minds. For one Parsi lady, 'they [the British] can't tell I am Indian...I don't look Indian. I've never suffered from being an Indian in Britain, perhaps because I have never seen myself as such.' For an Iranian gentleman, 'they [the British] get my race confused and call me an "Arab". I definitely find that derogatory and get around to explaining the distinctions. Once they understand who we are, they praise us'.

Some of the British Zoroastrians canvassed found it offensive to be labelled 'Asian' or 'Arab' by their British hosts. Both Parsi and Iranian Zoroastrians are generally inclined to emphasize their Persian heritage. One Parsi lady appeared to have arrived at a workable formula, 'I have not experienced any prejudice. They are very interested when I tell them my ancestors were from Persia. I don't feel Indian'. Equally, an Iranian youth emphasized the point: 'I define myself as Persian not Iranian. Even in Iran, I was a Persian. Persian implies Zoroastrian'.

The British Zoroastrians appear to be making an idiosyncratic adjustment to their country of adoption. While the British attitude to migrant communities is a subject beyond the scope of this work, the generalised perception among the ethnic groupings in the country that they are discriminated against covertly on grounds of race, will elicit different responses from the various ethnic groups now domiciled in the United Kingdom. In the case of the British Zoroastrians the pejorative labels 'Asian' and 'Arab' are countered by attempted historical justifications. By emphasis on a Persian ancestry which was the repository of a great religious and cultural tradition, the modern British Zoroastrian distances himself from the allegedly less acceptable 'Hindus and Muslims' of the Indian sub-continent, or the 'Arabs'. By this act of abnegation, a significant number within the group feel a positive sense of acceptableness by the host society which enormously enhances their particular sense of identity. Whether the Anglo-Saxon and Celtic groups have any real appreciation of these complex nuances of their Zoroastrian compatriots of whom they are largely unaware, remains a moot point.

Chief External Influences: The encroachment of external influences upon Parsi Zoroastrians was an intrinsic aspect of their domicile in India.[9] Its accelerated form in Britain would be a continuation of the same process. The tensions evident among British Zoroastrians - Parsis and Iranians - are occasioned by the inability to successfully juxtapose their Zoroastrian religio-cultural heritage with the subsuming forces of the Judaeo-Christian based society in which they find themselves, and in which their children are being reared. An increasing minority of the youth and their elders maintained that the chief influence upon them was Western (Refer Table 5).

A 23 year old British-born lady, whose parents were 'staunch' Zoroastrians, spoke of Zoroastrian culture, traditions and the civilization as being alien to her. She nevertheless continued to feel an overwhelming pride in belonging to this 'elite group'. The youth among the British Zoroastrians, those born in the United Kingdom and those who have lived in this country from a young age, face the dilemma of belonging to two cultural worlds. Whilst they are unable to grasp the minutiae of beliefs and traditions practised by their parents in the old countries, they are also aware of not being accepted as fully English.

The 'Young Zoroastrians', a loose network of the youth have, since the mid-1980s, begun to socialise among themselves as a result. Using the

Association headquarters in London for informal meetings, parties, social activities, sponsored walks, theatre visits and even planned summer vacations in the country, reflect the need felt by some of these young persons to 'mix with our own kind'. Not all young British Zoroastrians, however, subscribe to these community-based activities, but the creation of such a group, and its continuation, suggests that they feel more comfortable with fellow Zoroastrians. One young person volunteered the opinion that she had a large circle of English friends with whom she socialised, but this did not imply that she was prepared to absent herself from her network of Parsi friends. There was, she felt, a 'definite bond with other Parsis'. Similarly, a young Iranian said that until the age of twelve her circle of friends was limited to her English school-mates. Later, when she began to meet Zoroastrians at Iranian functions, she was surprised to discover how much she had in common with them, especially their shared sense of fun.

Indeed, what appears to be developing is a British Zoroastrian identity which draws on specific Zoroastrian value systems, such as close family ties, the ethos of hard work, the predilection for the 'good life', and to utilise the opportunities available in Britain for bringing these aspirations to fruition. A lingering attachment to their Zoroastrian roots, however, remains in a society which will not unreservedly accept persons of a foreign heritage. The resultant group identity contains the dynamic of tensions between two very distinct social cultures and values, and rather than a fusion of the Zoroastrian with the British, one might expect the creation of an ethnic identity responding to indigenous influences, but operating on the margins of British society.

Intermarriage: The distinctive ethnic identity of the British Zoroastrian, however, might be completely altered if community members were to marry exogamously on an unforeseen scale. Most of the youth and their elders perceive intermarriage increasing in the UK; while an extremely high proportion of the youth and elders consider the increase as inevitable (Refer Tables 8 & 8(a)). Indeed, the issue of the future of the community in Britain as a recognisable religio-ethnic group must take into account the increasing out-marriages, which are re-drawing the ethnic boundaries of the Zoroastrian community.[10]

A divorced Parsi lady explained that it was the lack of opportunity of meeting Parsis when she first arrived in the country some twenty-five year ago, which resulted in her marrying an Englishman. While she was not a religious person, she was disappointed that her daughter was not a Zoroastrian, and on reflection she would now opt to marry a Parsi.

The younger Zoroastrians too appear to face a similar quandary, especially the women. Educated, professional, better integrated with a circle of friends and colleagues drawn from a wide spectrum of society, how do the youth resolve the issue? A young lady spoke of her particular position:

> Five years ago I never had any thoughts of marrying a non-Parsi. At work now, I meet and go out with English boys, because I want to. If I met a Parsi I would not reject him, but I feel very confused.

A young Iranian lady maintained that if she chose a foreign partner it would bring disgrace on the family, since the imperative was to stay within the community. She was keenly aware of the potential for scandal if she married exogamously.

The incremental increase in intermarriages were conceded by all, and some younger Zoroastrians appeared intimidated by the social pressures to marry within the fold. Whether the deterrent of ostracism or lack of acceptance by family and friends succeeds in limiting such unions, however, remains highly questionable. There is a further aspect which is even more crucial in evaluating the future of the group. This writer has encountered several young Zoroastrians in Britain who, as in other countries, admit openly to a complete lack of knowledge of Zoroastrian religion, history and traditions.[11] While some among them demonstrate their willingness to choose a Zoroastrian partner, despite their own lack of grounding in Zoroastrian culture, and their insistence on the desirability of bringing up their children as Zoroastrians, the question put to them was: 'what will you pass on to your children of your Zoroastrian heritage?' The answers received were invariably, 'I will teach them universal values'; or 'I will tell them about good thoughts, good words and good deeds', a reference to the Zoroastrian credo of *humata, hukhta, huvarashta*. This then is the other aspect of the dilemma of the consolidation of Zoroastrian identity among future generations. Given the nature of the community's vague sense of self-perception, and the absence of a blueprint for the future, the prognosis for the coming generations of British Zoroastrians, whether born to both Zoroastrian partners or of mixed unions, is one of uncertainty.

Conversion: The British Zoroastrians, unlike the North American community, have failed to initiate any proper debate on the controversial issue of conversion. They are either vociferously in favour of, or against, the initiation of aliens into the Zoroastrian fold. However, this problem in the British context is reserved for discussion relating to the non-Zoroastrian spouse in a mixed marriage, and whether he or she can be permitted to participate in religious ceremonials. Well over half the youth and a sizeable minority of the elders in the sample, were against the initiation of outsiders (Refer Table 7).

A 40 year old Parsi was amenable to the idea.

> I can accept the outsider after he has undergone a strict test. In my view, a Parsi is recognisable by his behaviour and

attitudes. So the convert may become a Zoroastrian, but not a Parsi. I certainly cannot object to the acceptance of someone who finds Zoroastrianism good for him.

A 21 year old Iranian, however, had reservations, 'No person of another religion can assume or practice our religion'. The fact that the youth sampled presented a relatively more 'traditional' view of a controversial community issue, may be attributed to their desire to consolidate their 'exclusive' Zoroastrian heritage which distinguishes them from their peer groups within the several migrant groups now domiciled in the country, as well as the indigenous British population.

Indeed, it is not the intake of aliens that has exercised the communal mind in Britain, as much as the regulation of the position of non-Zoroastrian spouses. In 1985, the European wife of a former President of the Association, was disbarred from entering the soul prayers for her deceased husband. These communal prayers, held annually to commemorate the souls of the departed, are an important part of the Zoroastrian calendar. The ejection of this lady, who had herself played an important role in community affairs during the life-time of her husband, exacerbated the divisions within the British Zoroastrians. The issue which currently occupies the British Zoroastrians does not extend to the initiation of aliens, but rather to the position of non-Zoroastrian spouses in Zoroastrian religious ceremonial.

At the time of writing, the current policy of the Managing Committee of the Zoroastrian Trust Funds of Europe, is that during the soul prayers (*muktad*) held at 'Zoroastrian House', non-Zoroastrians are requested to absent themselves. However, Zoroastrians who resent this exclusion have initiated a novel method of having a separate *Farvardigan jashan* commemorated at the Brookwood Cemetery, where non-Zoroastrians are welcome to attend. This is countenanced by the London-based World Zoroastrian Organisation. The 'conversion' issue in Britain thus pertains to a specific local issue, but the controversy which has been generated by it emphasizes the demarcation lines which have evolved within the community. The central question: the position of the non-Zoroastrian in Zoroastrian religious practices, remains as vexed in Britain as elsewhere.

Future trends: According to a 30 year old Iranian Zoroastrian, the future was bleak since the communal dimension remained undeveloped. The Zoroastrian community's future in the country must take into account two contributory elements, viz. their minority status in the UK (in fact, they are a minority within a minority); and the resilience of the community itself (Refer Tables 9 and 9(a)). There was a general pessimism in the assessment of the longer-term future in Britain.

> We are going to be a minority in perpetuity. Will we survive
> at all? Will anyone be able to identify us as a distinct
> community? We don't have many chances unless there is a
> radical change in the way the community regulates itself.

The lack of an empowering infrastructure was referred to by some community members, and was considered a major factor in the decline of Zoroastrian self-confidence as a group. The community is perceived as having failed to project a group identity, which is then seen as compounding the problem of adjusting to British society as a Zoroastrian. For an older person, the problem was the inability of the host society to distinguish the group from others: 'I am not happy forever being called a Hindu or Muslim and brushed aside'. A middle-aged Iranian Zoroastrian held the view that,

> As a perpetual minority we will disappear... culturally and
> spiritually we feel deprived. We are in danger of remaining an
> insignificant minority and it makes us feel as though we are
> second-class citizens.

There was, however, one redeeming feature in the opinion of an older Parsi: 'We have learnt how to operate as a minority. We have long experience of it. Other minority groups could learn from us; we have a thousand years' experience of it.'

Indeed, the continuous minority status of the Zoroastrian community over the past millenium ought to work to their advantage in the period of adjustment and acclimatisation in their adoptive country. Two features should be addressed. First, the social, political and legal structures of the host society, and its acceptance or rejection of the foreign migrant; second, the British Zoroastrian community's ability in the ensuing decades to establish workable communal infrastructures which will give cohesiveness and direction to the community. While Britain has evolved a legal system which theoretically provides equal opportunities to the naturalised citizen as it does to any person of Anglo-Saxon or Celtic descent, it is less certain whether the conflicts within the British Zoroastrian community will enable it to evolve unified internal communal structures. At the time of writing, the gulf between the Iranian Zoroastrian and Parsi Zoroastrian remains in evidence. There are differing perceptions of the Zoroastrian religion among the 'liberal' and 'orthodox' Zoroastrians. There is a divergent sense of group identity among those who frequent the Zoroastrian Centre ['Zoroastrian House' in North-West London], and those who studiously keep away from it.

There is a steady 'anglicization' of the British Zoroastrian community, leading to noticeable changes within the practice of their Zoroastrian religion in a British environment. In the absence of places of worship, a reduction in

Zoroastrian practices is noticeable. The gradual diminution in the observation of the faith ensures that future generations of British Zoroastrians will have never witnessed various Zoroastrian ceremonials and thus feel no affinity with them. Additionally, a general lack of knowledge of their religio-historical antecedents will hasten the dilution of their Zoroastrian identity. The vacuum left will, inevitably, be filled by the indigenous culture. The 'Britishness' of the Zoroastrians of these islands could conceivably replace their former identity. The parents of today's young Zoroastrians may appear reluctant to admit such developments, but their disinclination to confront the issues indicates their anguish of an uncertain future.

The 'protestantisation' of their Asian religion in the Western context is seen as inevitable by some members of the community, seeking to interpret their religion in terms that are meaningful in an environment wholly different from that in which they grew up. The adjustment of traditions in new settings leads inevitably to debates on issues of change and continuity. (In Britain, the best illustration of this was the controversy generated over the expulsion of a non-Zoroastrian wife at her husband's soul prayers). The underlying tensions encourage fissiparous tendencies within the group. In the absence of a properly constituted authority to settle community discussions on the divide between tradition and modernity, disintegration becomes a very real possibility. In the new Zoroastrian settlements, such as the United Kingdom, in the absence of religious and communal infrastructures which, however ineptly, exist in the old countries, the dissolution and ultimate assimilation into the larger society remains a distinct possibility. These tendencies are exacerbated by the lack of familial and communal educational facilities, whereby the young could be inculcated with knowledge of their Zoroastrian religious and cultural heritage. Lacking as they do an intrinsic understanding of their unique Zoroastrian culture, a gradual disappearance of the youth identity as Zoroastrians must ensue. This then would be a challenge for which the community is unprepared and to which it may not be adequately able to respond.

*

Conclusions

Reflecting on the findings of the field research focuses attention on the absence of one critical element in the contemporary Zoroastrian world: the singular lack of community-wide infrastructures which encompass a representative body empowered to deliberate and legislate on matters pertaining to the Zoroastrians, and an executive council with the authority to oversee these. The failure to create such mechanisms will mean that the Zoroastrians, in their present disparate state, are in danger of fragmentation without a centre to hold them together.

Issues pertaining specifically to the contemporary community are highlighted: (1) The perennial fear of the paucity of their numbers which is reflected in the current debates on increased exogamy and conversion of outsiders to the Zoroastrian fold. (2) The rapid enculturation in the North American and British environments of the young especially, and the novel phenomenon of an increase in the Indianization of the Parsis through the medium of the ubiquitous Indian television and cinema, regional affinity in dress and cuisine. (3) Iranian Zoroastrian and Parsi cultural distinctions which relate in part, and lead to (4) the lack of knowledge of the historical developments in Zoroastrian Iran and Parsi domicile in India.

For some hundred years now, the Zoroastrians have sought to educate their young in secular educational establishments where, understandably, there is no inclusion of Zoroastrian history and religion in the standard curriculum. As a result, some three generations of Parsis, unversed in their religio-historical antecedents, have depleted the intellectual resources of the community while, paradoxically, individual Zoroastrians have continued to excel in diverse secular fields.

The interchangeable use of the terms 'Parsi' and 'Zoroastrian' by a cross-section of the respondents indicates that within the community itself, no distinction is made between religious and secular matters. As a consequence, various issues ranging from intermarriage to linguistic preferences are reduced to community polemics. Since there are no mechanisms in place for constructive deliberations on issues which affect the Zoroastrians, while the inexorable socio-cultural realities of the outside world continues to impinge on them, the community will be further weakened: by external pressures to enculturate, and the fissiparous dynamics within. In the continuing absence of structural mechanisms to deliberate upon and execute policies pertaining to the needs of the contemporary Zoroastrians, the prognosis for their survivability must remain pessimistic.

NOTES:

1. For detailed evaluation of early Parsi travellers to Britain see, J.R.Hinnells & R.Writer, *Living Flame: Zoroastrianism in Britain, op.cit.* See also, J.R.Hinnells, 'Parsis and the British', *JCOI*, Bombay 1978.

2. J.R.Hinnells, 1978, p.74. See also 'Minutebook of the Religious Fund of the Zoroastrians of Europe', for further details on the establishment of the Fund. On October 8, 1890, a conflation of the charitable funds led to the body being called the 'Charitable Fund of the Zoroastrians of Europe'. In 1909, a new constitution was drawn up under the Company's Act, when it was referred to as the 'Incorporated Parsee Association of Europe'.

3. J.R.Hinnells, *Katrak Lectures*, (OUP), forthcoming.

4.   J.R.Hinnells, 1978, p.73.
5.   While conducting intensive field work for *Living Flame*, I found it difficult to locate a Zoroastrian from this group to interview as they retain only the most minimal contacts with the community in the UK. Reported cases of an individual who might have a Zoroastrian parent but did not consider himself a member of the group were brought to my notice, but there was no opportunity to discuss these issues with such persons.
6.   I am indebted to Mr.Shahrokh Shahrokh for having given me this figure. As a senior member of the Iranian community in Britain, of some 30 years' residence, he is acquainted with virtually every Iranian Zoroastrian family.
7.   For a detailed discussion, see Hinnells & Writer *Living Flame, op.cit.*
8.   In 1985, the author instigated a juvenile education scheme; at the 1987 World Zoroastrian Organisation Youth Conference similarly suggested an advanced educational programme, see R.Writer, 'Re-Birth of the Zoroastrian Heritage: The Role of Education', *World Zoroastrian Youth Conference on Zoroastrian Religion, Culture & History*, London, September 1987, pp.7-12; and in 1989 formulated a structured syllabus on Zoroastrian civilization. Thereafter educational sessions continue with varying attendance figures.
9.   Refer Chapter 1 'Historical Background'.
10.   For a detailed analysis of intermarriages in the British Zoroastrian community, refer Hinnells & Writer, *Living Flame, op.cit.* the chapters on 'Intermarriage' and the 'Case Study'.
11.   Hinnells & Writer, *Living Flame, op.cit.*

CHAPTER SEVEN

CONTEMPORARY ZOROASTRIANS: AN UNSTRUCTURED NATION?

The contemporary Zoroastrian community, as the preceding pages have shown, presents an immensely complex face to a world barely aware of its presence. Their present peculiar position stems from the seminal event of the 7th century Arab destruction of the Persian Empire. The faith of the imperial Persians, Zoroastrianism, which lacked a St.Paul and was never effectively exported en masse beyond Iranian frontiers, remained the religion of one people, thus becoming vulnerable to the onslaughts of political conquests linked with a forceful proselytising faith such as Islam. Following the loss of their political empire, the small bands of the faithful strove to safeguard their religion, and came in time to stress the religious dimension of their group identity as a counter-point to the major religious groups among whom they subsequently lived, the Hindus and Muslims. There came into existence therefore, two distinguishable branches of the Zoroastrian community, the Zoroastrians of Iran and the Parsis of India.

If the Islamicization of modern Iran and the consequential diminution of Zoroastrian religious and temporal vigour are the central historical factors in the decline of the contemporary Zoroastrians, these have instigated communal complexities, not the least of which are the cultural differences between Iranian Zoroastrians and Parsis; and the second major Zoroastrian migration and creation of a Western diaspora in the 20th century. Each country of settlement, aware of its distinctive destiny, will inevitably have to confront the imperative of its specific blueprint to give shape and direction to the future. Here are microcosms of society which exhibit various behavioural and accultured patterns of considerable significance to the present times. A religio-ethnic grouping reduced to minority status over a period of 1300 years and domiciled in two vastly different religio-cultural milieux, it has emerged as two distinctive groups. Their dispersion effects are adding another and novel dimension to their group persona. This has introduced new demands for reassessments, the results of which might significantly determine the survivability of their community.

No matter how distinct the two major groups of Zoroastrians are, and the historical vicissitudes that have brought them to their present state, the Zoroastrian religion has come to shape their 'national' identity and consciousness as a people. It is generally accepted that the religious beliefs and values of members of a society are essential in determining their attitudes vis-a-vis its political system.[1] Even though the position of the Zoroastrians in the old countries is that of being a minority on the margins of society which renders their relationship to the political systems of Iran and India more complex, their very responses to Shi'ite Islamic Iranian nationalism, and the neo-Hindu renaissance movement, have been defined in terms of their Zoroastrian identity. For a sizeable number of Zoroastrians, their membership of the group is virtually a badge of congruity. It matters little whether they practise their faith, subscribe to the essentials of the theology, or are even cognizant of its metaphysical intricacies. What matters is that they identify as Zoroastrians, members of a particular group. The very particularity of their history following the Arab conquest, and their relegation to minority status, as well as their numerical paucity which made highly questionable their survivability, has resulted in a heightened sense of self.

This self-perception of the group as descendants of a civilization which propounded a 'superior' religious message, and as inheritors of a magnificient historical legacy, their 'glorious Persian heritage', has engendered in contemporary Zoroastrians a nebulous sense of a national spirit. Like all inchoate nationalisms, it is as much a product of its specific historic antecedents as a reaction to the world around it. It contains within it the explicit germs of intra-group tensions (Parsi-Iranian relations), and significantly, the lack of specificity of any national boundaries. Historically, Iran is the *madar vatan*. Since the 10th century, India has developed as the second land of Zoroastrianism. From the 20th century, the Western Judaeo-Christian lands of Europe, North America and Australia have been included among the territorial spread of the Zoroastrians.

When the contemporary Zoroastrian refers to himself or his community, it is commonly through the use of the term 'religion' as a tool of self-description. While the Zoroastrian religion has come to serve as an umbrella sheltering group identity, there are secular issues pertaining to the community: such as the assistance given in the last century by the Parsis to their Iranian kinfolk under the auspices of *Society for the Amelioration of the Condition of the Zoroastrians in Persia* ; in recent years, to Iranian Zoroastrian refugees fleeing Islamic Iran and the rehabilitation programme in South Gujarat, all of which in fact, show distinct signs of a 'national' response. Community solidarity across the oceans clearly shows a one-nation attitude to all Zoroastrians.

The historical development of Zoroastrianism has been such that qualification for membership of the group has been through birth, specifically on the male side. This ethnic overlay on the religion, strengthened by centuries of persecution (as in Iran), and marginality (as in India), has emphasized within the group, a palpable awareness of their distinctness from the majority peoples. They have never strayed from perceiving of themselves as a religious group, because it was to keep alive that religion and their fidelity to their ancestral heritage, that both Parsis and Iranians tenaciously persevered in their reduced state. The Zoroastrian religion came to be seen as a lode-star, a talisman with apotropaic powers! Therefore it became a powerfully sustaining force through centuries of persecution and isolation, reinforced and consolidated to become something more: an emblem of their nationalistic aspirations.

Their religious fidelity reinforced the allegiance to the state of Iran conspicuously displayed by the Zoroastrians of that land; furthermore, it impelled the sense of gratitude and in several instances, a deep sense of loyalty to India evinced by generations of Parsis. It is, however, crucial to realize that beneath the surface of Zoroastrian self-perception as a religio-ethnic group, there has developed a particular type of 'national' identity. This idiosyncratic sense of nationality, remains unspoken by Zoroastrians themselves, who sense it but are unable, or unwilling, to articulate it. It contains some of the necessary ingredients for a sense of nationality: a unifying historical legacy; unique linguistic development of their religious and secular literature prior to the Arab conquest; a unifying religion, and a perception of belonging to a body of people marked by common descent. Equally, there are ingredients of nationality that are conspiciously absent, chief among these being territoriality.

Iranian Zoroastrians could never contemplate a 'Zoroastrian land' anywhere other than Iran. Yet, 1300 years of Islamicization of that country, and the renewed entrenchment of fundamentalist Shi'ite philosophy following the Iranian Revolution of 1979, has led Iranian Zoroastrians to inform this writer that they do not realistically envisage the country ever returning to its Zoroastrian foundations. Parsi Zoroastrians, on the other hand, have an ambivalent attitude to India. Paradoxically, the millenial separation from the *madar vatan* has reduced Iran, in Parsi terms of reference, to a foreign land. The dilemma of contemporary Zoroastrianism, the polemics which centre on religious issues, contains a sub-text: the different political perspectives are expressed as religious argument. The lack of territoriality and self-government for a people whose minority status cannot overlook the reality of their past stature as an imperial people - whose ancestors ruled from the Black Sea to the Indus, and from the Caspian to the Nile - has resulted in a feeling of having been checkmated by history. What several commentators from within and without the community see as a preoccupation with the minutiae of religious arguments ought rather to be interpreted as the group's hesitant endeavours to locate itself in the world in which it finds itself.

Throughout history, social conditions have led minority peoples to seek security through various means, among which is religious expression. Although a religious system may undergo transformation and appear to play a less prominent role in a specific society, its tenets, which shape the belief and value systems, continue to influence social behaviour.

Arguably, the social and political changes now confronting the Zoroastrian world are being buttressed by emphasis on the Zoroastrian dimension of the group. Here, the Parsi and Iranian responses are in similar vein. In Iran and India, both still in a politically fluid state, a continuous erosion of the sense of belonging to the majority Muslim and Hindu cultures by the constituent Zoroastrian groups remains a constant feature. Were the politically unsettled state to continue in these two major Asian countries, further weakening the sense of Zoroastrian security within these states; or if further deliberate legal discriminatory measures were at some future date to be instigated in Iran against the 'minorities' (other than those already prescribed in the Iranian constitution), it is possible to envision a more vocal and overt emergent 'Zoroastrian nationalism'. The rejection by the majority of the minority may lead to a novel phenomenon, one yet unheard of: a 'Zoroastrian nationalist'.

This, of course, would lead to the most vexing question of all: a homeland. This then divides the Iranian and Parsi. The former sees Iran as the ancestral land, and the land *par excellence* of the Zoroastrian civilization. The Parsis continue to display an ambivalence towards India, and a significant number among them appear content in the Western diaspora. 'Parsis are traitors to Iran. You went to India and did not return to Iran. Didn't you give a promise to return to Iran?' This observation by a young Iranian Zoroastrian in the course of discussions with the author, signals the fundamental cause of the Iranian Zoroastrian's reluctance to acknowledge the Zoroastrian credentials of his Parsi compatriots. Underlying all the communal polemics on religion, it is the ineluctable perception of the indissoluble links between Zoroastrianism and the sacred soil of Iran, to which the Parsis of India are seen to have been 'traitors', by not returning to the *madar vatan*, that is the ultimate reference point in the issue of a Zoroastrian identity couched in terms of religious argument. Ever since Cyrus the Persian conceived of Iran as a state, and Darius I translated that concept into a reality, the idea of Iran being the birth-place of the Zoroastrian religion and the nation state as underpinned by the Zoroastrian religious and secular ethos, has remained the essential element in Iranian Zoroastrian consciousness. By extension therefore, the Parsis' migration to India, their permanent settlement and Indianization, has resulted in a genuine estrangement of the Parsi from the Iranian Zoroastrian who regards the former as having 'sold out'.

Yet, this peremptory assessment of the national identity of the Parsi Zoroastrians leaves unasked the question: how should one explain the persecution of the Zoroastrians in the *madar vatan*, and the relative safety from physical or religious persecution afforded to the Parsis by the Hindus in India? How do Iranian Muslims who are mainly descended from Zoroastrians, reconcile the pride they take in their historical past, 'the glory of Persia', with the re-working of Iranian history according to an Iranized Islamic specification so that 'history' commences with the coming of Islam to Iran? These questions remain taboo in the Zoroastrian world.

Iran was among the earliest nation states; a far-reaching and deep-rooted patriotism among its people is not surprising. The schizophrenia of contemporary Iran, which cannot reconcile its Zoroastrian past with its Islamic reality, yet proclaims its national antiquity through that past, remains not merely a national paradox, but accentuates the complexity of the Iranian Zoroastrian position. The latter cannot ask the central question: why was the genocide of the Zoroastrians perpetrated in the ancestral land, abetted by persons whose ancestors were, after all, from the same tradition? The Zoroastrian in Iran remains aware of his inalienable links with the land and its history, but is not empowered to demand an explanation of his disenfranchised position. The contemporary Iranian Zoroastrian therefore, reasserting his national identity, couches his arguments in terms of Iranian religion, culture and history, which he sees as remaining steadfast to the Zoroastrian idiom. These automatically eliminate the Parsi from the cultural ambit, since the level of 'Indianization', it is argued, has vitiated his Zoroastrian identity. The perennial dilemma of the Parsi position: his ambivalence towards India, and his selective assimilation into Indian culture, is the result of the continuous theme in Parsi history of being of Iranian stock, and retaining a semblance of patriotism towards the *madar vatan* (more noticeable among the older Parsi). The millenial separation from Iran could never completely diminish their sense of awareness of 'belonging' to the ancestral land; as such, the loss and separation from the ancestral land has never fully been assuaged in the Parsi subconscious. But the paradox remains. In the Western diaspora, the re-acquaintance of the Iranian and Parsi Zoroastrian has served to highlight their cultural differences, so exacerbated by spatio-temporal divides, that they are for all practical purposes foreign to one another.

It is not easy to describe the developments in Zoroastrian society. A plurality of discourses is a central feature of the community; indeed, it is not a monolith. At its most fundamental, there is a quest for identity, a re-defining of the parameters of the group which must take into account the demands of the national environments in which it finds itself. It is now the external variables which are major determinants in the re-evaluation of the contemporary Zoroastrian world.

The re-drawing of community boundaries will determine its own momentum as a result of political developments following the collapse of the Soviet Union. Two former Soviet republics, Tajikistan and Azerbaijan, the former

CONTEMPORARY ZOROASTRIANS

being co-terminous with ancient northern Bactria and Sogdia, the latter with ancient Media, not surprisingly, have small population pockets of persons claiming a Zoroastrian identity. There are no accurate estimates of the number of such Azerbaijani or Tajik Zoroastrians. A few individuals, from Tajiskistan especially, have made hesitant contacts with Zoroastrians in the diaspora. They have long had to suppress their Zoroastrian identity, both religious and cultural, owing to the double constraints of being an 'infidel' minority amidst Muslim majorities, exacerbated furthermore by belonging, in recent years, to the Soviet empire. With the revival of national identities in former European and Asiatic Soviet Union, the Zoroastrians of these countries display a great keenness to assert their Iranian cultural roots and admit to being Zoroastrian. Within their newly emerging nation-states, these Zoroastrians now wish to assert their 'national' identity which they express as Zoroastrian. Indeed, as visitors to Tajikistan attest, the Tajik Zoroastrian's assertion of his pre-Islamic identity is reinforced through language (Tajik is, in fact, archaic Persian with even fewer Arabic words than New Persian itself). They have reintroduced such specifically Zoroastrian religious celebrations as the *Mehrgan*, and now inaugurate the new year on 21 March, *No-Ruz*. There are individuals in the Badakhshan area of the Pamir mountains, who can today give evidence of their Zoroastrian grandparents having been forcibly converted to Islam and denigrated as *gabr* and *atash-parasts*.[2] This outline of the contemporary Zoroastrians of ancient Sogdia contains startling parallels to the experiences of the Zoroastrians of Yazd and Kerman. The position of the community in Azerbaijan, and details emerging of small pockets in the Caucasus regions including Georgia, repeat the story of the millenial suppression of Zoroastrian identity through fear of persecution; and the cautious reassertion of this specific national identity in a world which is rapidly succumbing to revisions of national borders and sentiments.

The Tajik and Azerbaijani Zoroastrians are among a list of Zoroastrians being, quite literally, re-discovered. Among the Kurdish community (the Kurds themselves being descended from an ancient Median tribe), some three million Yezidis claim a Zoroastrian identity. The Yezidi leader, resident in Europe, has made contact with British Zoroastrians, with the hope of gaining recognition as Zoroastrians by the established Zoroastrian community: i.e. the Iranians and Parsis.

It cannot be a matter of incredulity that Zoroastrians, other than those belonging to the dominant groups are emerging, even hesitantly, to re-assert their identity. Zoroastrianism and the culture and ethos that took root from it, would have been well entrenched in these regions which in earlier centuries were intrinsically Iranian. It is indeed astonishing that the tenacity of the Zoroastrians, well documented in the histories of the Iranian and Parsi communities, is now being shown to have been replicated by other groups of

Zoroastrians in various parts of the Zoroastrian *oikoumene*. Their wish to re-claim their Zoroastrian identity is a historical sentiment whose political manifestation is the perception and consolidation of a national identity that is distinct and distinguishable from the dominant society.

The evolution of a neo-Zoroastrian nationalism, so fragmented by historical events, is by no means a straightforward political development. There are substantial issues to be resolved within what could be a hitherto unprecedented Zoroastrian world. The addition of bonafide Zoroastrians, if this term is to include individuals whose grandparent/s were Zoroastrians, from Azerbaijan, the Caucasus, Tajikistan, the Yezidi Kurds, to the established communities of Iranian and Parsi Zoroastrians, will imply heightened cultural tensions. The central Iranian/Indian axis could arguably be extended to include a formerly 'Russified' peoples. The religious and secular tensions within a dispersed Zoroastrian context are certain to evolve in the early decades of the next century. As the Islamic national identities of the Azeris, Tajiks and Iranians intensify, so the Zoroastrian national identity, insofar as it asserts its right to its pre-Islamic heritage, would be a part of the contemporary Zoroastrian equation. Having maintained their Zoroastrian heritage in total isolation; being unaware of the developments that have shaped the Iranian and Parsi communities, as well as having practised a Zoroastrianism which must unquestionably reflect their regional, linguistic and political experiences, suggest that initially, the feasibility of dialogue between the various Zoroastrian groups will itself be difficult to achieve. Yet, the evidence now coming to light as the Russian authorities relinquish their power over their Asiatic subjects, suggests that the Zoroastrians of these lands, with roots as deep in the Zoroastrian experience as those of the Persian Zoroastrians and Parsi Zoroastrians, wish to reclaim their heritage. Zoroastrianness is an identity now seen by some as a value in itself. It is possible to argue that the contemporary Zoroastrians might well evolve a 'nation' quite unlike any other. Their historical development since the 7th century has been so full of reverses that the sudden re-discovery of a few million Zoroastrians could avert the feared extinction of a community presently estimated to be a mere 150,000 at most.

The issue of regulating communal affairs across international borders is confounded by the recent discovery of renascent Zoroastrians in newly independent countries, as well as the continuing inability of the established community to create and sustain any form of organisational infrastructures that would be acceptable to the disparate regional, cultural and ideological components within the group. In July 1980, the World Zoroastrian Organisation was formed. Located in London, the impetus behind its establishment is proclaimed in its logo: 'Zoroastrian Unity World-wide'. It remains, however, a controversial organisation, and the aspirations towards global unification of the Zoroastrians remains unfulfilled. There is no world body acceptable to the majority, empowered to regulate communal affairs. There can be no unified religious authority, given the widely divergent theological positions of the *dasturs* of Iran and India; and no secular authority to oversee such socio-cultural issues which have a direct impact on the Zoroastrians. What is in place, in lieu of unified organisational structures, are local *anjumans* and associations. The responses to diverse issues are necessarily on an *ad hoc* basis. The contemporary Zoroastrian world, therefore, operates as a fractured entity with a minimal degree of unity.

Zoroastrians observably demonstrate little or no interest in the creation of communal infrastructures to deal with the challenges confronting them. The creation of the Federation of Zoroastrian Associations of North America (FEZANA), and its attempts at formulating a federated structure among the North American Zoroastrian Associations; as also the Federation of Parsi Zoroastrian Anjumans of India, which continues in its attempts to secure an 'all-India' membership of the Indian *anjumans*, testifies to the difficulties which these federal experiments in national Zoroastrian administrative structures continue to encounter. The Zoroastrian Trust Funds of Europe is an inappropriate nomenclature for an organisation that serves the Zoroastrians of the United Kingdom. The small numbers scattered through continental Europe have yet to group together in a pan-European association. Most vexing of all is the absence of Iran as a major force in any discussion of a Zoroastrian federation. Indeed, the Indian and Iranian positions on theology, cultural emphasis and a world-view remain so far apart at the time of writing, that no constructive attempt at dialogue has been made. The Zoroastrian national identity, therefore, remains a sentiment and an emotive vision; it continues to lack the vital ingredients necessary to activate it: land and government structures.

It may be suggested that over the past 1300 years the Zoroastrians, once a proud, imperial people, now relegated to minority status, have forgotten how to govern themselves. Some 1300 years, and more, they had sustained a workable ruler-subject relationship through a religio-political conditioning. Today's infrastructures would require at least an appreciation and subsequent re-appraisal of the ancient Church-State symbiosis, with emphasis now instead on guidance by a regionalized educated hieratic leadership. The social upheavals which have disrupted the group have appeared irreconcilable, owing to a conspicuous absence of informed strong leaders. Paradoxically, there is great intellectual vigour among individual Zoroastrians, both in the Old and New worlds, in their respective secular fields. 20th century Zoroastrians, however, have failed to produce men of the stature of Kaikhosrow Shahrokh of Iran, or Dadabhai Naoroji of India. While there continues to be a lack of comprehension of the socio-political dimensions of contemporary Zoroastrianism, there can be no realistic expectation of the creation of a Zoroastrian world body with the charter and the competence to address the broad spectrum of issues: religious, social, cultural, economic and political, which impinge on the Zoroastrians in their various countries. Few societies can survive long without internal structural cohesion. The Zoroastrian community of the present has even less such scope. Its meagre, dwindling numbers (through increased exogamy); the reality of compromises minority groups must continually make in the society in which they find themselves - which applies equally to the Indian Parsis or Iranian Zoroastrians as it does to the American or British Zoroastrians - are accelerated phenomena. The infrastructure of the Zoroastrian consciousness, the religion as taught by Zarathushtra, the ethnic awareness, and the demonstrable pride in their antiquity, would be the abundant reserves the Zoroastrian peoples have to draw upon. Yet, the contemporary Zoroastrians remain enmeshed in the tensions of the composite of cultural polarities, attempting to achieve a semblance of uniformity. The attrition of their intrinsic Zoroastrianism is thus taking place, and their self-assurance, in competition with larger groups, becomes somewhat uncertain. As a result, contemporary Zoroastrianism needs an urgent and substantial re-evaluation of its communal structures which alone would be capable of reflecting and fulfilling the requirements of a culturally diverse peoples who are, fortuitously, held together as members of a distinctive religious fraternity.

NOTES:

1.   Cf. Max Weber, *The Protestant Ethic And The Spirit of Capitalism*, transl.Talcott Parsons, (New York, 1958).
2.   With grateful thanks to Mr.Parvan Khan Jamshidi, a Tajik Zoroastrian, for conveying these matters to a wider Zoroastrian audience.

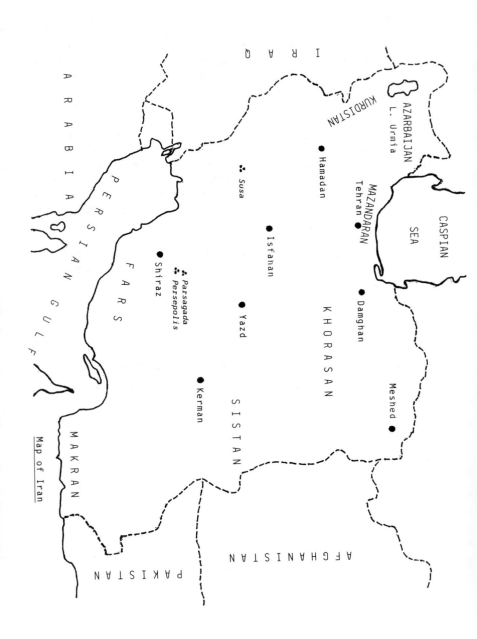

Map of Iran

SIND

PAKISTAN

INDIA

● Karachi

CUTCH

● Bhuj

● Ahmedabad

SAURASHTRA

Cambay ● Baroda

Bhavnagar ●

Broach

Variav

● Surat

Navsari

Diu

Udvada

Sanjan

● Nasik

ARABIAN

Bombay

SEA

Poona ●

Map of Western India

250

APPENDIX

Figures in Percentages

YOUTH - aged 16 years to 30 years

ELDERS - aged 30 years and over

	YOUTH			ELDERS		
	Yes	No	Don't Know	Yes	No	Don't Know
INDIA	96	3	1	87	13	1
PAKISTAN	80	19	-	100	-	-
NORTH AMERICA	67	33	-	57	43	-
UNITED KINGDOM	38	62	-	30	67	3

Table 1   Do you consider this your homeland ?

	YOUTH			ELDERS		
	Reject	Respect	Ignore	Reject	Respect	Ignore
INDIA	23	60	17	25	58	17
PAKISTAN	-	86	14	6	81	12

Table 1(a)   In India/Pakistan, are the Parsis rejected, respected, ignored ?

	YOUTH			ELDERS		
	Yes	No	Don't Know	Yes	No	Don't Know
NORTH AMERICA	21	79	-	30	65	5
UNITED KINGDOM	31	62	6	26	70	4

Table 1(b)   Do you experience prejudice ?

	YOUTH				ELDERS			
	English	Gujarati	Farsi	Combined	English	Gujarati	Farsi	Combined
INDIA	52	8	-	40	44	11	-	45
PAKISTAN	48	14	-	33	50	20	-	30
NORTH AMERICA	64	-	5	31	51	6	13	30
UNITED KINGDOM	44	-	6	50	44	15	11	30

Table 2   What Language do you think in ?

	YOUTH			ELDERS		
	Yes	No	A Little	Yes	No	A Little
INDIA	-	80	20	15	74	11
PAKISTAN	9	76	14	25	40	31
NORTH AMERICA	19	33	48	49	17	33
UNITED KINGDOM	19	31	50	22	48	38

Table 3   Do you have a knowledge of Zoroastrian history ?

	YOUTH		ELDERS	
	Yes	No	Yes	No
INDIA	100	-	95	5
PAKISTAN	100	-	100	-
NORTH AMERICA	90	10	90	10
UNITED KINGDOM	88	12	85	15

Table 4   Do you identify as a Zoroastrian ?

	YOUTH			ELDERS		
	Religious	Much More	Don't Know	Religious	Much More	Don't Know
INDIA	10	90	-	13	83	4
PAKISTAN	14	86	-	12	88	-
NORTH AMERICA	24	71	5	38	62	-
UNITED KINGDOM	50	31	19	33	52	15

Table 4(a)   If you identify as a Zoroastrian, is this only a religious identity or is it something more ?

255

	YOUTH					ELDERS				
	Zor	Indian/ Pakistani	Iranian (Muslim)	Western	Com- bined	Zor	Indian/ Pakistani	Iranian (Muslim)	Western	Com- bined
INDIA	57	10	-	7	30	37	1	-	22	40
PAKISTAN	52	5	-	19	33	25	6	-	12	56
NORTH AMERICA	38	5	5	29	24	44	8	10	13	25
UNITED KINDOM	31	-	-	31	38	56	4	7	22	33

Table 5   What were the chief external influences on you ?

	YOUTH				ELDERS			
	Yes	No	A Little	Don't Know	Yes	No	A Little	Don't Know
INDIA	16	13	-	73	24	2	1	73
PAKISTAN	62	5	9	24	69	6	12	12
NORTH AMERICA	69	14	14	2	81	5	13	1
UNITED KINGDOM	62	-	19	19	52	7	15	26

Table 6   Do you think that the thousand years of separation, in India and Iran, has changed Parsis and Iranian Zoroastrians significantly ?

	YOUTH			ELDERS		
	Yes	No	Don't Know	Yes	No	Don't Know
INDIA	40	57	3	33	64	4
PAKISTAN	24	67	9	37	62	-
NORTH AMERICA	64	33	3	68	30	2
UNITED KINGDOM	31	62	7	55	37	8

Table 7   Do you envisage Zoroastrianism as a religious label that any individual can assume once initiated into the religion ?

	YOUTH		ELDERS	
	Good	Bad	Good	Bad
INDIA	50	50	28	72
PAKISTAN	24	75	12	81
NORTH AMERICA	50	50	40	60
UNITED KINGDOM	37	63	40	60

Table 8   What are your views on intermarriage in general ?

	YOUTH				ELDERS			
	Increasing	Not Increasing	Inevitable	Not Inevitable	Increasing	Not Increasing	Inevitable	Not Inevitable
INDIA	100	-	90	10	97	3	91	9
PAKISTAN	95	5	71	28	94	6	63	37
NORTH AMERICA	81	12	81	14	79	13	76	16
UNITED KINGDOM	87	13	94	6	85	15	89	11

Table 8(a)   In the Zoroastrian community is intermarriage increasing, and is it inevitable ?

	YOUTH				ELDERS			
	Concerned	Confident	Indifferent	Don't Know	Concerned	Confident	Indifferent	Don't Know
INDIA	23	37	40	-	47	27	25	1
PAKISTAN	38	38	24	-	50	31	19	-
NORTH AMERICA	17	24	55	4	25	44	31	-
UNITED KINGDOM	31	6	56	7	41	11	44	4

Table 9   What does it mean to you to be a member of a group which is a minority in perpetuity ?

	YOUTH				ELDERS			
	Positive	Negative	Mediocre	Don't Know	Positive	Negative	Mediocre	Don't Know
INDIA	40	50	10	-	28	46	20	6
PAKISTAN	9	67	24	-	25	44	31	-
NORTH AMERICA	33	40	24	3	27	38	33	2
UNITED KINGDOM	-	81	12	7	18	41	33	8

Table 9(a)   How do you see the long-term future of the Zoroastrian community ?

GLOSSARY

agiary	Parsi (Gujarati) term for a Zoroastrian place of worship, a fire temple
Ahura Mazda	Creator - Wise Lord
anjuman	congregation of Zoroastrians, generally refers to town or village
arbab	Iranian title of respect. When used with a Zoroastrian name, implies 'Sir'
atash	fire
atash aduran	sacred fire of the second grade, housed in an *agiary*
atash bahram	sacred fire of the highest grade
Avesta	sacred book of the Zoroastrians
behdin	'(of the) good religion', i.e. a Zoroastrian
dakhma	place of exposure for the dead, a 'tower of silence'
dar-i mehr	'House of Mihr', term for a place of worship
dastur	Zoroastrian high priest
dihqan	landlords who were almost local potentates
gahambar	one of six holy days of obligation
Gathas	hymns composed by Zarathushtra
jashn/jashan	thanksgiving ceremony
jizya	head tax on non-Muslims
juddin	one professing different religion; a non-Zoroastrian
kharaj	first, simply tax, later a land tax
kusti	sacred cord worn around the waist by Zoroastrians
madar vatan	mother country
marzban	governor, literally, one who protects the borders
mazdayasnian	worshipper of Mazda [Ahura Mazda], i.e. a Zoroastrian
mobed	Zoroastrian priest
mujtahid	one who exercises interpretive reasoning
navjote (Gujarati)	investiture of the young into the Zoroastrian religion
sharia	Islamic law
sudre/sedre	sacred undershirt on which the *kusti* is worn
sedre-pushin (Farsi)	investiture of the young into the Zoroastrian religion
yazata	'worthy of worship', one of the Zoroastrian terms for a divine being
ulema	religious leaders in Islam

BIBLIOGRAPHY

I. BOOKS AND ARTICLES

AKHAVI, SHAHROUGH, *Religion and Politics in Contemporary Iran: Clergy-State Relations in The Pahlavi Period*, State University of New York Press, Albany, 1980.

ALEXANDER,H. *Gandhi Through Western Eyes*, London, 1969

ALGAR, HAMID, *Religion and State in Iran, 1785-1906*, University of California Press, Berkeley, 1969.

-- 'The Oppositional Role of the Ulama in Twentieth-Century Iran', in Nikki Keddie (ed), *Scholars, Saints and Sufis*, pp.231-55, University of California Press, Berkeley,1972.

ALMOND, GABRIEL, 'Comparative Political Systems', *Journal of Politics*, 18 (1956): 391-409.

AMIRSADEGHI, HOSSEIN (ed.), *Twentieth Century Iran*, London, 1977.

ANKLESARIA, B.T., *Zand-i Vohuman Yasn and Two Pahlavi Fragments*, Bombay, 1957.

-- *Rivayat of Aturfarnbag and Farnbag-Srosh*, 2 vols.,Bombay, 1969.

ANWAR, MUHAMMED, *The Myth of Return: Pakistanis in Britain*, Heinemann, London, 1979.

AXELROD, PAUL, 'Myth and Identity in the Indian Zoroastrian Community', *Journal of Mithraic Studies*, Vol.III, (Numbers)1&2, (1980):150-165.

BAILEY, H.W., *Zoroastrian Problems in the Ninth-Century Books*, Oxford, 1943.

BALADHURI, *Futuh al-Buldan*, transl. P.K.Hitti and F.C.Murgotten, *The Origins of the Islamic State*, vol.1, New York, 1916.

BAYNE, EDWARD A., *Persian Kingship in Transition*, New York, 1968.

BEHNAM, M.REZA, *Cultural Foundations of Iranian Politics*, University of Utah Press, Salt Lake City, 1986.

BOSE,S. & KHULLAR,A., *A Socio-Economic Survey of the Parsis of Delhi*, Centre for the Study of Developing Societies,Delhi, 1978.

BOYCE, MARY, 'Zariades and Zarer', in *Bulletin of the School of Oriental and African Studies*, 17, London,1955.

--'The Fire-Temples of Kerman', *Acta Orientalia*, XXX, 1966.

-- transl. 'The Letter of Tansar', *Istituto Italiano per il Medio ed Estremo Oriente*, Rome, 1968.

--'Manekji Limji Hataria in Iran', *K.R.Cama Oriental Institute Golden Jubilee Volume,* Bombay, 1969.

-- *A Persian Stronghold of Zoroastrianism,* Oxford University Press , Oxford, 1977.

-- *Zoroastrians: Their Religious Beliefs and Practices,* Routledge and Kegan Paul, London, 1979.

BRIGGS, HENRY GEORGE, *The Parsis or Modern Zerdushtians,* Bombay, 1852.

BROWNE, EDWARD, *A Year Amongst The Persians,* Century Publishing Paperback, London, 1984.

-- *The Persian Constitutional Movement,*Oxford University Press, London, 1918.

BULSARA, SOHRAB J., (transl.) *Matikan e Hazar Datastan,* Bombay, 1937.

Cambridge History of Iran, (eds.) R.N.Frye; J.A.Boyle; Peter Jackson and Laurence Lockhart; Peter Avery, Gavin R.G.Hambly and Charles Melville, vols.4-7, Cambridge University Press, 1975.

CHARDIN, J., *Voyages en Perse et autres lieux de l'Orient,*Amsterdam, 1735.

CHRISTENSEN, A., *L'Iran sous les Sassanides,* Copenhagen, Second edn., 1944.

COHEN, STEVEN, *American Modernity and Jewish Identity,* Tavistock Publications, New York, 1983.

CONLON, FRANK F., *A Caste in a Changing World: The Chitrapur Saraswat Brahmans, 1700-1935,* University of California Press,Berkeley, 1977.

COMMISSARIAT, M.S., *A History of Gujarat,* vols.1&2, Bombay,1938.

COTTAM, RICHARD W., *Nationalism in Iran,* University of Pittsburg Press, 1964.

Dadistan i-Dinik, transl E.W. West,('Pahlavi Texts',Part 2), *Sacred Books of the East,* XVIII, Oxford, 1882.

DAVIS, KINGSLEY, *The Population of India and Pakistan,* Princeton University Press, 1951.

DAVAR, FIROZE, *Iran and India Through the Ages,* London,1962.

DENNETT, D.C., *Conversion and the Poll-Tax in Early Islam,* Cambridge, Mass., 1950.

DESAI, ASHOK V., 'The Origins of Parsi Enterprise', in *Indian Economic and Social History Review,* vol.V, 1968.

DESAI, SHAPUR F., *History of the Bombay Parsi Panchayat 1860-1960,* Bombay, 1977.

DHABHAR, B.N., *The Persian Rivayats of Hormazyar Framarz and Others,* Bombay, 1932.

DHALLA, M.N., *Zoroastrian Theology From the Earliest Times to the Present Day,* New York, 1914.

-- *An Autobiography,* transl. by Gool and Behram H.J.Rustomjee, Karachi, 1975.

Dinkard, ed.with English transl. by P.B. and D.P. Sanjana, 19 volumes,

264

Bombay,completed in 1928.

DOBBINS, CHRISTINE, *Urban Leadership in Western India*, Oxford University Press, Oxford, 1972.

DUCHESNE-GUILLEMIN, J., *The Hymns of Zarathustra*, Eng.transl.by Maria Henning in 'Wisdom of the East Series', London,1952.

DUMONT, LOUIS, *Homo Hierarchicus: An Essay on the Caste System*, transl. Mark Sainsbury, University of Chicago Press,1970.

ENTHOVEN, R.E., *The Tribes and Castes of Bombay*, vol.III,Bombay, 1922.

Epistles of Manuschchihar, transl. E.W.West, ('Pahlavi Texts', Part 2), *Sacred Books of the East*, XVIII, Oxford,1882.

FARQUHAR, J.N., *Modern Religious Movements in India*, New York, 1918.

FIRBY, NORA, *European travellers and their Perceptions of Zoroastrians in the 17th and 18th Centuries*, Berlin, 1988.

FISCHER, MICHAEL, *Iran, From Religious Disputes to Revolution*, Harvard University Press, 1980.

-- 'Persian Society: Transformation and Strain', in *Twentieth Century Iran*, H.Amirsadeghi (ed), London, 1977.

FORBIS, WILLIAM H., *Fall of the Peacock Throne: The Story of Iran*, New York, 1981.

FRYE, RICHARD N., *The Golden Age of Persia: Arabs in the East*, London, 1988, (paperback edition).

-- *The Heritage of Persia*, London, 1965, (reprint).

--'Iran and the Unity of the Muslim World', in *Islam and the West* (ed.), R.N.Frye, The Hague, 1956.

GABLE, RICHARD W., 'Culture and Administration in Iran',in *Middle East Journal*, 13 (Autumn 1959): 407-21.

GHADIALY, D.B., 'Parsis of Karachi: Facts and Figures',Informal Religious Meetings, April 20-May 19, 1984, for private circulation.

--'Parsis of Pakistan', for private circulation.

GIBB, H.A.R., *The Arab Conquests in Central Asia*, London,1923.

HARRIS, F.R., *Jamsetji Nusserwanji Tata: A Chronicle of His Life*, Bombay, 1958.

HATARIA, M.L., *Ishar-i Siyahat-i Iran*, Bombay, 1865.

HERODOTUS, *History*, transl. Henry Cary, Loeb Classical Library, 1849.

HINNELLS, J.R., 'Parsis and the British', *Journal of the K.R.Cama Oriental Institute*, Bombay, 1978.

-- *Ratanbai Katrak Lectures*, Oxford, forthcoming.

-- 'The Parsis: A Biographical Survey', in *Journal of Mithraic Studies*, vol.III, Nos.1&2, 1980: 100-150.

-- 'The Flowering of Zoroastrian Benevolence: Parsi Charities in the 19th and 20th Centuries, in *Papers in Honour of Professor Mary Boyce, Acta Iranica*, 24, 1985, 261-326.

HINNELLS, J.R. & R.WRITER, *Living Flame: Zoroastrianism in Britain*,

forthcoming.
HODIVALA, S.H., *Studies in Parsi History,* Bombay, 1920.
HOMJI, H.B.M., *O Whither Parsi?,* Karachi, 1978.
HUMBACH H., & K.M.JAMASPASA, *Vaetha Nask: An Apocryphal Text on Zoroastrian Problems,* Wiesbaden, 1969.
IBN BALKHI, *Fars name,* (ed.) G.L.Strange, London, 1921.
INSLER, S., 'The Gathas of Zarathustra', *Acta Iranica 8,* Leiden, 1975.
ISSAWI, CHARLES (ed.), *The Economic History of Iran,1800-1914,* University of Chicago Press, 1971.
JACKSON, A.V.W., *Persia Past and Present, A Book of Travel and Research,* New York, 1906.
JEEJEEBHOY, J.R.B., *Some Unpublished and Later Speeches and Writings of the Hon.Sir Pherozeshah Mehta,* Bombay, 1918.
JOSHI, A.N., *Life and Times of Sir H.C.Dinshaw,* Bombay, 1939.
KARAKA, D.F., *History of the Parsis,* 2 vols.,Macmllan & Co., London, 1884.
KARKAL, MALINI, 'Marriage among Parsis' in *Demographic India,* vol.IV, No.1, June 1975.
KARPAT, KEMAL H. (ed.), *Political and Social Thought in the Contemporary Middle East,* New York, 1968.
KATRAK, S.K.H., *Who are the Parsis?* Karachi, 1965.
KEDDIE, NIKKI, *Religion and Rebellion in Iran: The Tobacco Protest of 1891-1892,* London, 1966.
-- 'The Iranian Power Structure and Social Change,1800-1969: An Overview', in *International Journal of Middle East Studies,* 2 (January 1971): 3-20.
KENNEDY, ROBERT E., 'The Protestant Ethic and the Parsis', in *The American Journal of Sociology,* vol.68, 1962-63: 16-20.
KOHN, HANS, *The Idea of Nationalism,* New York, 1944.
KULKE, ECKEHARD, *The Parsis in India: A Minority as Agent of Social Change,* Vikas Publications, Delhi, 1974, (paperback edition).
LOKKEGAARD, F., *Islamic Taxation,* Copenhagen, 1950.
LORD, HENRY, *A Display of Two Forraigne Sects in the East Indies,* London, 1630.
MALCOLM, NAPIER, *Five Years in a Persian Town,* London, 1905.
MANKEKAR, D.R., *Homi Mody, A Many Splendored Life,* Bombay, 1968.
MASSELOS, J.C., *Towards Nationalism,* Bombay, 1974.
MELLOR, DAVID C., *The Parsis and the Press: An In-depth Study of the Hindi Punch: 1906-1931,* (unpublished M.Phil.thesis, Victoria University of Manchester) 1985.
de MENASCE, J., 'Problemes des mazdeens dans l'Iran musulman' in *Festschrift fur Wilhelm Eilers,* Wiesbaden, 1967.
MISTREE, KHOJESTE, 'Conversion - A Mandate For Disunity?'Zoroastrian Studies, Bombay, 1983.
MODI, BHARATI, 'Parsi-Gujarati: A Dying Dialect', paper presented at the

K.R.Cama Oriental Institute International Congress, Bombay, January, 1989.

MODI, J.J., *Moral Extracts from Zoroastrian Books,* Bombay,1925.

-- *Dastur Bahman Kaikobad and the Kisseh-i Sanjan,* Bombay, 1917.

-- 'The Khutba of the Mahomedans and the Dasturi of the Parsis', in *Journal of the Anthropological Society of Bombay,* Vol.XII, Part 5.

MODI, JAMSHED, 'Fighting Fire with Fire', Bombay, 1976, for private circulation.

MOULTON, J.H., *Early Zoroastrianism,* London, 1913.

MULLAH, D.F., *Jurisdiction of Courts in Matters Relating to the Rights and Powers of Caste,* Bombay, 1901.

NANAVUTTY, P., *The Parsis,* National Book Trust India, Delhi, 1977.

NARGOLWALA, SHIAVAX, 'Population of Zoroastrians in the World and in India', (paper for private circulation through the Bombay Parsi Panchayat).

NARGOLVALA, S.D., 'Zoroastrians of Iran', in *The Realist* 3(4): 16-20.

NATESAN, G.A., *Famous Parsis: Biographical and Critical Sketches,* Madras, 1910.

-- *Speeches and Writings of Dadabhai Naoroji,* Madras, 1910.

NAUROJI, D., *From Zoroaster to Christ: An Autobiographical Sketch of the Rev. Dhanjibhai Nauroji the First Modern Convert to Christianity from the Zoroastrian Religion,* Edinburgh, 1909.

NYBERG, H.S., 'Sassanid Mazdaism according to Muslim sources', in *Journal of the K.R.Cama Oriental Institute,* 39,Bombay, 1958.

OSHIDARI, JEHANGIR, *Yadashthaey Kaikhosrow Shahrokh,* Tehran,1977.

OVINGTON, J., *A Voyage to Surat in the Year 1689,* (ed.) H.G.Rawlinson, Oxford, 1929.

PANDEY, B.N. (ed.), *The Indian Nationalist Movement,1885-1947, Select Documents,* London, 1979.

PARK, ROBERT E., 'Human Migration and the Marginal Man' in *American Journal of Sociology,* 33 (1928).

Parsi Panchayat Case, Suit No.689 of 1906, 'Judgement of Justice Davar and the Hon'ble Justice Beaman Delivered Friday 27th November 1908',Bombay.

PEASLEE, AMOS J., *Constitutions of Nations,* 2nd ed. vol.2, The Hague, 1956.

PITHAWALA, M.B., *The Light of Ancient Persia,* Bombay, 1923.

PRITCHARD, J.B., *Ancient Near Eastern Texts relating to the Old Testament,* Princeton, 1969.

ROSENTHAL, ERWIN I.J., *Islam in the Modern National State,* Cambridge University Press, 1965.

RUSSELL, JAMES R., *Zoroastrianism in Armenia,* ('Harvard Iranian Series', 5), Harvard, 1987.

RUSTOMJEE, N.M., *Minorities Under Developmental, Populist and Islamic*

Regimes: Parsis and the Pakistani State, (unpublished B.A. dissertation), Harvard College, 1985.

RUSTAMJI, R.F., *India and the Parsis,* Nagpur, 1944.

SAFA-ISFEHANI, NEZHAT, *Rivayat-i Hemit-i Ashawahistan,* Harvard Iranian Series, Vol.2., Harvard, 1980.

SEAL, ANIL, *The Emergence of Indian Nationalism,* Cambridge University Press, 1971.

SHAKED, SHAUL, *The Wisdom of the Sasanian Sages (Denkard VI) by Aturpat-i Emetan,* Westview Press, Boulder, Colorado, 1979.

Sikand-gumanik vijar, transl. E.W.West, *Sacred Books of the East,* vol.XXIV, Oxford 1882.

SHAHMARDAN, RASHID, *Tarik-i Zarthustian Pas-as Sasanian,* Tehran, 1982.

--(ed.) *Khaterat-i Khaze,* Bombay, 1984.

-- *Farzahne Gan i Zarthusti,* Tehran, 1984, reprint.

SMITH, MARIA W., *Studies in the Syntax of the Gathas ofZarathustra Together with Text, Translation and Notes,*Philadelphia, 1929.

SYKES, P., *A History of Persia,* vol.I, London, 1930.

TABARI, *Ta'rikh al-rusul wa'l-muluk,* (ed.) M.N.de Goeje, 3 sections, Leiden, 1879-1901.

Ta'rikh-i Qum: Hasan b.M.Qumi, (ed.) Jalal ad-din Tehrani,Tehran, 1935.

TARAPOREWALA, IRACH, *The Gathas of Zarathustra,* Bombay, 1962.

--'Some Aspects of the History of Zoroastrians', *Journal of the K.R.Cama Oriental Institute,* Bombay, 1928.

TAVERNIER, J.B., *Six Voyages en Turquie, en Perse et aux Indes,* Paris 1676, anon.Eng.transl. London, 1684.

TH'ALIBI, *Histoire de rois des Perse,* (ed.) H.Zoltenberg,Paris, 1900.

TRITTON, A.S., *The Caliphs and their Non-Muslim Subjects,* London, 1930, reprint 1970.

ULLMAN, RICHARD H.,*Anglo-Soviet Relations, 1917-1921,* Vol.3, Princeton University Press, 1972.

UNDEVIA, J.V., *Population Genetics of the Parsis,* Miami,1973.

della VALLE, PIETRO, *Fameux voyages de Pietro della Valle gentil homme romain,* transl. E.Carneau and F.le Comte, Paris,1661-63.

VIMADALAL, J.J.; MAHALUXMIVALA, P.D. & C.D., *Racial Intermarriages: Their Scientific Aspect,* Bombay, 1922.

WADIA, C.N. & KATPITIA, S.B., *The Parsi Marriage and Divorce Act,* Surat, 1939.

WATT, W.MONTGOMERY, *Islamic Political Thought: The Basic Concepts,* Edinburgh University Press, 1968.

WEBER, MAX, *The Protestant Ethic and the Spirit of Capitalism,* (Tranls. Talcott Parsons), New York, 1958.

WEST, E.W., *The Book of the Mainyo-i-Khard,* Amsterdam, 1979, reprint.

WOLPERT, S.A., *Jinnah of Pakistan*, Oxford University Press, New York, 1984.

WRITER, R., *The Identification of Developing Soviet Strategic Interests in the Indian Ocean: 1968-1974*,(unpublished Ph.D. thesis, University of London), 1979.

--'Re-Birth of the Zoroastrian Heritage: The Role of Education', in *World Zoroastrian Conference on Zoroastrian Religion, Culture and History*, London, 1987.

ZAEHNER, R.C., *Zurvan, A Zoroastrian Dilemma*, Oxford, 1955.

2. JOURNALS, NEWSPAPERS, NEWSLETTERS

Bombay Samachar
The Bombay Government Gazette
Bombay Courier
Gavashni
Hindi Punch
Indian Express
Iran League Quarterly
Journal of the Iranian Association
Journal of the National Indian Association
Kaiser-e Hind
Newsletter of the Zoroastrian Association of Metropolitan Chicago
Oriental Review
Parsi Prakash
Parsiana
The Parsi
The Pioneer
Rast Goftar
Times of India
The Zoroastrian (Bombay)
The Zoroastrian (Los Angeles)

3. MISCELLANEOUS

COUNCIL OF MOBEDS, TEHRAN, Letter dated 24 May, 1983, No.466 to Ervard Bahram Shahzadi, U.S.A., transl. into Eng. Dr.Ali Jafarey.

Naoroji Papers (Nehru Museum, New Delhi).

Census of India 1931,1961,1981.

Statistical Abstract of British India.

Vth North American Congress, Toronto, 1988.

Zoroastrian Association of Greater New York, *Special Bulletin,* (January 23, 1983).

INDEX

272

POPE PIUS XII LIB., ST. JOSEPH COLLEGE

3 2528 01320 3643

Sovereign
By Raya Morris Edwards
Copyright © 2024 Morris Edwards Publishing

All rights reserved. No part of this publication may be reproduced, stored, or transmitted without prior permission of the publisher of this book.
This is a work of fiction. Names, characters, places, and incidents either are the product of the author's imagination or are used fictitiously. Any resemblance to actual persons, living or dead, events, or locales is entirely coincidental.
FIRST EDITION

This book is for anyone who ever wanted spanked and called a good girl by a hot cowboy. That's not too much to ask, right?

Author's Note: While this is a BDSM romance, for the purposes of storyline and character development, there are instances where BDSM is not practiced properly or safely. As with all fiction, especially dark, please do not look to it for true and accurate information regarding BDSM.

TRIGGER WARNINGS & TAGS

Parental death—in the past
Discussion/flashback of the aftermath of past rape—not MCs
Discussion/depictions of past abusive relationship
References to DV and grooming
Grief
Discussions & depictions of shooting & murder
Discussion of the past death of a pregnant woman via vehicular homicide
Use of gun during sex
Scratching/hitting during sexual situations
Emotionally charged sexual situations
Stalking
Discussion of alcohol abuse/sobriety
Vasectomy/reversal
Arson
Discussion of animal abuse—brief and non explicit
Discussion of a minor being hit—brief and non explicit
Discussions of cheating—not between MCs
Pregnancy & TTC discussions/depictions at very end

SEXUAL CONTENT TAGS/WARNINGS

CNC/Dubcon—*Important note: This book contains a strong overall theme of dubious consent that may range into noncon due to instances of improper BDSM practices, improper safeword practices, a large power/age imbalance, and a forced contract.*
Explicit oral, anal & vaginal sex acts
BDSM—*this is a fictionalized depiction for a dark work of fiction and should not be taken as educational*
Dom/sub based punishment/play

1

Heavy praise and degradation
Size difference (we're gonna make it fit trope)
Restraints—belt, cuffs
Collaring
Gun/fear play
Clit/nipple clamps
Impact play – spanking with hand, switch, belt
Slapping, hitting, scratching in sexual situations
Choking/gagging
Breath play
Light spitting
Brief somnophilia
Blood from sex/period

CHAPTER ONE

KEIRA

"Keira!"

I jump and the coffee cups rattle against the counter. It's late and I'm exhausted after preparing and serving a full meal for everyone at Garrison Ranch. It took me the usual two hours after dinner to clean the kitchen and load all the dishes into the dishwasher. I was about to head upstairs to bed when I heard truck tires come up the drive.

My husband, Clint, told me to go back into the kitchen. Unsurprised, I obeyed, but I lingered just behind the doorway. Listening to the unfamiliar voice of our late night visitor.

It's deep and smooth with a thick undercurrent of gravel. The hairs on the back of my neck stand up although I'm not sure why. I lift my arm and goosebumps are popping up across my skin.

I lean my head against the wall and close my eyes. Their footsteps fade out as they head upstairs to Clint's office on the second floor. It doesn't bother me anymore that my husband shuts me out of everything, including who comes and goes in my own home. I know exactly what I'm good for in his mind and it's not being his equal.

Clint's footfalls ring out again and I make a mad dash for the island countertop. It's empty so I pretend I'm taking forks and knives from the drawer. His boots pause in the doorway and I look up, brushing back my hair.

My husband is a tall man with dusky blonde hair and steel gray eyes. He's handsome, but I stopped feeling anything when I looked at him a long time ago. Maybe less than a year after our wedding.

"Make up some coffee for our guest," he says.

I nod and slide the silverware back into the drawer. "Decaf?"

He glances up at the clock over the stove. It was his grandmother's and then his mother's. I fucking hate it. I wish I could open the back door and pitch it so hard I never have to look at it again. It's yellowed and the wooden frame has cracked from hanging above the stove. But the reason I hate it so much has more to do with how badly his late mother treated me after the wedding.

Before the wedding, she'd been nothing but sweet. But as soon as the ring was firmly on my finger, she stopped speaking to me except to hurl insults. It was a relief when she died.

I used to wonder what I did to make his family hate me. But after a while, I came to accept that nothing made sense anymore. Clint had once loved me too. Now he's disgusted every time I open my mouth.

"Of course," he says.

"How many cups?"

He shrugs. "Make up a tray. And put something to eat on there as well."

He leaves before I can ask him what. I wipe my hands on my apron and unwrap the leftover biscuits. Even Clint doesn't have a bad word to say about my biscuits. They're fluffy, layered perfectly so they can be split open hot and soaked with butter and raspberry jam. I pop them in the oven for a few minutes as I make coffee.

Then I load everything up and slip my house shoes off to carry them upstairs in my socks. I don't want to risk falling and spilling everything.

Clint would lose his shit.

I'm wearing a modest, long-sleeved dress that goes to my knees. At least I don't have to worry about Clint calling me a slut. He likes to do that when I wear anything that shows an inch of skin.

Outside the oak door, I balance the tray in one hand and knock once with the other.

There's a short silence. Then:

"Come in."

I enter, allowing myself one glance over the room. I see a pair of steel-toe boots by the chair in the corner. Clint sits at his desk between the two windows on the far wall. There's a short pile of folders before him, one of them open. I can tell it's paperwork for cattle.

"Set it down on the desk," Clint says, without looking up.

Uncomfortable, I cross the room and put the tray down. My eyes flick to the side, locking on the stranger's boots. They're bigger than normal and the leather is worn. Whoever he is, he's a broad man, I can tell from his feet.

Gathering my courage, I let my eyes run higher.

My heart stops.

He has a pair of pale blue eyes beneath dark, lowered brows. His face is broad and masculine, his jawline defined and covered in a short beard. His nose is heavy with a bump on the bridge, like maybe he broke it once. There's a firmness to his expression and face, but no emotion.

He glances at me and glances away. Then he does a double take.

Our eyes lock and I can barely breathe.

Heat curls in my lower belly. We stare at each other for a second that feels like an eternity. My eyes take in every detail of his face hungrily. The dark, wavy hair, a bit falling over his forehead. The button up that leaves a V of bare skin at his throat exposed. The smattering of hair rising above it that sparks my curiosity.

My gaze flicks down.

He's got a thick, muscled body that fills out his work pants and shirt perfectly. But it's not the physical that stops me in my tracks.

He feels like when the winds change to bring in a storm. Maybe it's because his aura is dark like the cool shadows in the pines. Or clouds rolling over the mountains, soft at first, and then bringing swift destruction.

7

I shudder. He hasn't said anything to me, I have no reason to be intimidated. But I am. There's an edge of darkness to him, like a gravitational pull. It's overwhelming.

"Can you pour the coffee?" Clint says.

I glance up and he's scowling the way he does before he pulls me aside to chew me out. Except he won't do that here because we're being watched. Obediently, I pour two cups and pass one to my husband and one to the newcomer. He reaches out to take it and my eyes fall on a ring on his smallest finger.

There's a silver symbol on it. I tilt my head and make out three letters. SMR.

My brows shoot up to my hairline. I know who this man is. No one else would wear that insignia on a ring like that. He's Gerard Sovereign, the owner of the wealthiest cattle and horse ranch in the state. Sovereign Mountain Ranch borders our land, but I know better than to go there.

I'm not sure why, but we're not friendly with them. I know that much from Clint.

They say he has everyone in his grip. That all roads lead to Sovereign Mountain at some point.

Clint talks about Gerard Sovereign like he's the devil. I half expected him to have horns. But he's handsome, heavily muscled like one of the draft horses we use to pull hay in the winter. His eyes are on me and I get the impression he doesn't lose control easily. His lack of expression is a testament to his restraint.

Especially because I saw his body tense when he looked me in the eyes.

"Do you want cream?" I whisper.

He shakes his head, once.

Clint doesn't take cream in his coffee either, so I turn to leave. My husband clears his throat and I freeze, turning.

"Stay," he says. "We've got someone else coming in a few minutes."

Heat creeps up the back of my neck. He does this to me occasionally and I fucking hate it. It's humiliating having to stand there like I'm on his payroll and wait for one of them to have some need that needs fulfilling. My lashes feel wet as I back up and sink down in the chair in the corner.

Gerard follows me with his eyes.

"Is that your wife?" he asks, his voice soft and deep.

Clint nods, glancing up. Something sparks between them that puts me on high alert. Their gazes lock, like two wolves squaring off. Then Clint turns his eyes back to the desk like it never happened. He passes Gerard a pen and paper without raising his head. I study Gerard's impassive face and I think I see a flicker of amusement.

"Why do you want to know?" Clint says, his tone forced. He's trying to be casual.

"She doesn't need to stay," Gerard says.

Clint glances at me and I swallow hard. "She's fine. It's not like she has anything better to do."

My chest aches. Before our wedding, he never spoke to me like this. Now it's the only way he talks to me and what scares me is that I'm used to it. I get up in the morning with an empty brain and put my hands to work because it's what he wants. It's not like I can leave, I have nowhere to go and no money to my name.

So I cook for the entire ranch, I clean the house spotless, and I fuck him when he wants it.

When he's finally asleep at night, I roll onto my side and take the painted wooden mare from my bedside table. My mother was from Sweden and when she came to America, she brought one of her childhood toys. A red and white wooden mare, beautifully carved. It's running hard, three feet off the ground.

I never met my mother. She died not long after I was born.

At night, I trace the bridle painted to look like a string of stars. The paint is still crisp. Before my father passed when I was seventeen, he had it repainted and sealed with varnish. It was his farewell gift.

After losing my farm and my freedom to Clint, all I have left is the painted mare.

I look up from my corner and he's watching me again. Clint is by the file cabinet in the corner with his back to us. Gerard leans back in his chair, spreading his legs. My fingers clench in my lap.

What is he looking at?

"I have the paperwork here," Clint says, turning and crossing back to the desk.

Gerard drags his cold eyes back to my husband as he holds out his hand and accepts the file folder. Something crackles between them, like they'd much rather be anywhere but in this room together. A tiny shiver moves up my spine. I'm fine-tuned to read my husband's emotions and it's very obvious he's uncomfortable with Gerard.

Downstairs, a car door slams. Clint leans back and glances out the window.

"There's Jay," he says. "Keira, go down and bring him up."

A muscle twitches in Gerard's jaw. He snaps the folder shut with one hand and sets it down.

"I'll go," he says.

Clint frowns. "No, Keira's fine."

Gerard clears his throat. "I mistook her for your paid help with the way you treat her, Garrison."

The room goes deadly silent again. Clint's steel gaze snaps to me like I had something to do with Gerard's words. Heart pounding, I curl back into the chair. Am I going to pay for this later when we're alone?

Clint rises abruptly and crosses the room, yanking open the door.

"I'll get him myself," he snaps.

His footfalls echo down the hall and the room goes deadly quiet. Gerard's lips part and his eyes drag over me. Starting at my feet tucked under the chair. Traveling up my thighs. Lingering on my breasts, throat, and mouth. Then our gazes clash.

The air crackles.

Beneath my dress, my nipples tighten. Heat stirs in my lower belly and curls down until I feel it between my thighs.

It's quickly followed by shame. I'm married, I shouldn't be looking at other men this way. And yet...I can't stop looking at Gerard like I'm starving.

I *am* starving. Clint gives me crumbs of attention. He fucks me, but he doesn't bother going down on me. Or even staying up while I use my vibrator. He says it's not his problem that I can't come while he's fucking me. That's not even the worst thing though. It's the lack of emotional intimacy that really hurts. No hugs, no late night talks, no comforting me when I cry.

All that neglect means I'm left empty.

And Gerard Sovereign looks like an entire meal and then some.

"You're going to get me in trouble," I say, my voice cracking.

"I'm not afraid of your husband," he says quietly.

Before I can stop myself, my mouth opens and I say the one thing I never admit to anyone else.

"No, but I am."

His face goes hard. "Is your husband a mad dog?"

Confused, I glanced back at the door. Listening for footsteps. When I drag my attention back, he's got me in his crosshairs. His eyes aren't just blue as I previously thought. He's got a darker ring edging his irises that makes his stare even more piercing.

"What?" I whisper.

"Mad dogs bite," he says. "There's no cure for it but a shotgun."

My jaw goes slack.

"Are you...threatening Clint?" I whisper.

"Does he need to be threatened?"

I'm struggling to find words. No one has ever spoken to me like this while they unabashedly eye-fuck me.

Oh God, I'm blushing.

Flustered, I brush my hair from my face and straighten my shoulders.

"You should stop," I say firmly.

He cocks his head. "Stop what? You're the one who has bedroom eyes."

I tear my gaze away and fix it at the ground. My complexion is too fair to conceal the heat in my face. It's making pink splotches down my neck and chest.

"You need to stop it," I say, more sharply this time. "My husband gets jealous."

"Again. I'm not afraid of him."

I study him warily. His face is hard to read, but I can feel that he's got a vendetta against my husband. Maybe they had a soured business deal once upon a time. But whatever it is, I hear the subtle distaste in his words when he talks about Clint. Like he's something disgusting that needs to be scraped from his shoe.

"Maybe you should be," I say.

He leans forward and I peek at him through my lashes. "Mrs. Garrison, I could bend you over this desk and fuck you with your husband watching and he wouldn't say a goddamn word."

My jaw drops. The silence rings in my ears. He leans back in his chair like he didn't just say something shocking. Before I can answer, we both hear footsteps in the hall. I scramble to fold my hands and tuck my feet back under the chair.

The door opens and Clint enters with a wiry, graying man in dress pants and a shirt. I recognize him as Jay Reeds, his lawyer. Automatically, I rise to let him have my chair and go to stand by the door. Hands folded and eyes on the ground.

This time, to conceal my bright red face.

CHAPTER TWO

GERARD

I've never hated anyone the way I hate Garrisons, especially Clint. But the moment I lay eyes on his redheaded wife, I'm glad I agreed to meet with him.

Tonight was supposed to be a quick transaction. We're the two biggest ranchers in the state and having to do business together is inevitable. I anticipated a brief meeting where I scrawled my name on paper and walked out without speaking more than I needed to.

But then she walked in.

Nervous, tired, trying to make herself as small as possible so he doesn't look her way. I know exactly what kind of man he is, so it doesn't surprise me that his wife acts like a scared rabbit. But it does surprise me that the moment I lay eyes on her, my body reacts like a live wire.

She's got an hourglass figure with curvy hips and breasts. When she turns, I get a good look at her round ass, big enough I could get a handful and still have plenty leftover, and my mind goes into overdrive. Imagining what it would be like to sink my teeth into her bare ass hard enough to make her scream.

I thought I felt desire before now, but the way my body burns when I look at her face is something new. She is, without a doubt, the most beautiful woman I've ever seen. On screen, on page, in real life.

Until this moment, I didn't know what it felt like to experience chemistry. But I feel it now, and it makes the hair rise on the back of my neck.

The way I need her doesn't care about decorum. It's pure, it's primal.

The unevolved part of my brain is telling me to put a bullet in Clint and drag his wife back to Sovereign Mountain.

It's tempting, but not exactly socially acceptable.

I steal a glance at her. Taking in her oval face, full mouth, and wide blue eyes. Her brilliant red hair is braided loosely and secured with a bit of string. Freckles dust over her cheeks, nose, and down her chest. I wonder if she has them on her breasts.

Fuck, she's exquisite.

My pulse races and sweat trickles down my spine. I force any expression from my face and lean back like I'm unbothered by her presence. We're on either side of the room with Clint and his lawyer talking between us and the tension is so thick I can almost see it.

I stay silent as they go over the contract of sale. I wrote it and I know what I want from it. They have to come up with a counteroffer while I'm waiting.

"Keira," Clint says, glancing up. "Get Jay whatever he needs."

Jay waves a hand. "I'm good, too late for coffee, too early for whiskey."

Clint nods and goes back to the paperwork while his wife stands awkwardly by the door. He's an evil cunt—he always has been—but I didn't realize how good he is at subtle humiliation until now. His intention is clear.

She's his property. If he wants her to stand there all night, she will.

I stand abruptly. "I'm going to use the restroom. Could you show me where it is?"

I'm looking at Clint. He glances up, beckoning to Keira.

"Take Mr. Sovereign downstairs," he says.

She gives me a look. It's subtle, but it lets me know she's onto me. Amused, I follow her out the door and down the hall. My eyes fall as she descends the stairs. Watching her ass jiggle beneath her tight skirt.

"It's down the hall," she says.

We're in the doorway to the kitchen. I glance down the dim hall, to the open door of the bathroom at the end.

"I'm not sure I can find it," I say.

Her brows crease. "It's right there."

"Where?"

She walks halfway down the hall and points. Before she can turn back around, I plant my hand against the wall to block her path back. Her entire body freezes and her tongue darts out to wet her mouth. From this angle, I can see the faint suggestion of her cleavage.

Her breath hitches. Her lips part.

"You weren't looking for the bathroom," she whispers.

I shake my head. My hand comes up and tucks one strand of hair behind her ear. She smells like a woman, like shampoo and perfume and lotion. I'll bet her skin is so fucking soft.

I'll bet it marks easily.

"You need to leave," she says, her voice catching.

I pull back. She darts into the kitchen, putting the island counter between us like a blockade. Her body is drawn up tight and she's got her hands tucked behind her back. I can tell she's used to being submissive.

That's interesting.

But not altogether surprising. Clint is a bully, among other things, so it doesn't surprise me that his wife shrinks at the sight of men. I study her face, wondering if he hits her.

It's not really the Garrison's style. They're better at emotional torture.

I would fucking know after what they did to me.

"Do you drink, Mrs. Garrison?"

She licks her lips, catching the bottom one on her teeth. "I do a shot of whiskey now and then."

15

"Pour me a shot," I tell her.

She obeys at once. For all the wrong reasons, she's well trained. But she has what it takes to be obedient and that interests me. I keep silent as she pours a shot of whiskey and brings it to me. I take it, ignoring the sharp scent.

"Come here," I say.

She shifts closer, glancing at the stairs through the doorway.

"Open your mouth," I murmur.

Her eyes widen. "What are you doing, sir?"

The way she calls me sir solidifies the question I've had in my mind. Do I want her enough to wreak havoc? Or do I just hate Clint Garrison so much that his pretty wife is a temptation?

"Trust me," I say. "I won't hurt you."

She doesn't seem to be afraid, but it's hard to tell. She shifts closer and I reach out and bury my hands in her soft curtain of hair. Right at the nape of her neck. My fingers fist and I gently pull her head back. Her breasts heave and—lucky for me—the top button of her dress unfastens under the strain. I get a glimpse of the prettiest cleavage I've ever seen.

Soft, full. Freckled and perfect.

I'm fully hard, but she can't look down, so who the fuck cares. Slowly, I bend her head back until she's looking up into my face. She's breathing hard and both her hands are wrapped around my wrist. Holding on for dear life.

"Open your mouth, sweetheart," I tell her.

She hesitates, but then she does as she's told. Her lips part and reveal a pink tongue and white teeth. My cock is so fucking hard it's going to have a zipper print on it.

Slowly, I drizzle the shot into her mouth. Her throat bobs until it's gone. We both freeze, the glass still tilted over her face. Her eyes dart to mine, so wide the whites flash. Before she can fight me, I release her and take a step back to give her space.

She claps her hands over her mouth, like we've done something terrible. I turn the shot glass upside down and set it on the counter.

"I'd better get upstairs," I say.

I leave her there, standing in the kitchen as dazed as if I spun her around and let her go. My boots carry me up the stairs and back into Clint's office, but my mind couldn't be further from the dim room where he sits at his desk. He's so smug that I agreed to discuss a deal with him because we both know ten years ago, I wouldn't have given him the time of day.

I lean back in my chair, crossing an ankle over my knee. Clint and Jay are both still reading over the contract. I know he's expecting me to rip him off, I see his eyes move over the words again and again.

The contract doesn't matter to me anymore.

Not after meeting Keira Garrison.

I came here tonight in what I thought was a lapse of judgment. Westin, my right hand, said I was hurting the business by refusing to work with the Garrisons. He understood why, but facts were facts. So I agreed to sell cattle directly to them for a higher cut per head than what I'd get ordinarily. Westin wrote up the contract and I brought it here under a brief white flag.

I hadn't expected her.

Vaguely, I knew Clint was married to the daughter of a local rancher who passed away a few years back. But my path never crossed with the Garrisons by design—the Garrison family and mine are our own brand of Hatfield and McCoy—so I never laid eyes on her before tonight.

Fuck me, she's everything I've ever wanted.

Those bright blue eyes are enough to make me forget I have any morals left. It's the leftover bits of my conscience that stop me from just taking her. I'm an ice cold motherfucker, but I'm not the kind who fucks another man's wife while he still has a heartbeat. As I watch Clint, it dawns on me where I know that scared look on her face.

A long time ago, a different Garrison man broke someone I loved. And I saw the pain on her face then, just as I saw it on Keira's face tonight.

She looks like a bird in a cage. A redbird with clipped wings.

17

I can feel how tight my jaw is as Clint hands back the signed papers. He's gloating, but I ignore the glitter in his eye. Pocketing the contract, I shake Jay's hand and we walk outside to my truck. Clint hangs back for a second, as if he doesn't know how to send me off.

I put my hat on and give him a quick nod. "I'll see you tomorrow for the sale."

I leave him standing on the porch and drive out into the night. My knuckles are white on the wheel as I head home. All I can think about is the redhead back in that house and what she's doing right now. Maybe she's curling up to sleep, her hair loose over her pillow. Or maybe that son of a bitch is fucking her right now.

My fists tighten. The leather steering wheel is going to have indents.

I have my doubts that she's being satisfied. I've never met a Garrison who gave a fuck about anyone but themselves.

There's a place just before I turn into the long drive that leads to my ranch where I can see for miles. I turn the bend and pull off at the overlook. Silence falls. I rummage in the glove box and come up with a stale cigarette.

I don't smoke, but I need a cigarette after meeting Keira Garrison.

I step out onto the gravel and light it, inhaling deeply. The tingling calm seeps through my veins and my eyes roam the dark horizon. The stars hang heavy, there's no light pollution to fade them. I can't make out the ground, but far away I see the opening between the cliffs.

Tomorrow, Clint, myself, and our men will go up to the cliffs and bring the cattle down. I'll sell, he'll deposit the money into my account, we'll shake hands without meeting eyes, and I'll never see Keira again.

That thought makes me fucking sick.

I've heard people talk about soulmates, about the one person out there made just for you. But I never believed it. And I still don't. But I do believe in chemistry, and I felt that electricity spark in my veins as we sat in that office together. I've never had my body respond to anyone that quickly before. And now I have to live with that.

I have to know everything about her or I won't be able to rest.

The cliffs keep my eyes occupied as I finish my cigarette. They're a dangerous area, especially at this time of year when the weather can turn easily. Where all it takes to send a herd of cattle stampeding through the narrow opening is a storm rolling over the hills without warning.

It would be a fucking pity if something were to happen tomorrow.

I stab out my cigarette and get back into the truck. Once I'm home, I go to bed, but I don't sleep. All I can think about is the way she called me sir. Lids lowered, husky voice going right to my groin.

I lie awake until dawn.

CHAPTER THREE

KEIRA

After Gerard Sovereign leaves, I rush upstairs and shut the bedroom door.

My heart pounds. My mouth tastes like whiskey. I rarely drink so it hits my brain right away and warmth creeps over my nerves.

Never, not once, has Clint made me feel like this. Teased, desired, and thoroughly seen. He dragged those pale blue eyes over every inch of my body. If I wasn't married, I know he'd have done the same with his hands.

God, he has big hands. Thick, square at the tips. Neatly trimmed nails, scars on his knuckles, and calloused palms.

My back arcs, pushing my ass against the door. I'm acutely aware the space between my thighs is empty. All I can think of is how good his fingers would feel pushed inside me.

My fist clenches, bunching my dress. Pulling the skirt up to my waist. My other hand slips beneath my panties, searching. My breath sucks in as my fingertips slip over the seam of my pussy. Playing in the wetness there before slipping over my clit.

I can feel my heartbeat there. My clit is so tender that I feel pressure ache through my sex as I start rubbing it. I haven't masturbated in so long. Not since the last trip Clint took out of town.

When he fucks me, it leaves me dry. The rest of the time, I'm too tired for desire.

But tonight, I'm soaked.

And it's all for a man I barely know.

Downstairs, I hear the men leave the office and go outside. My fingers move faster, my hips thrusting up against my hand hungrily. An orgasm rises and coils closer and closer. Sending heat surging through my lower belly and thighs.

The memory of his hand in my hair flashes through my brain and I come, hips shuddering so hard I almost fall.

Guilt floods me so fast I barely have time to recover. I stumble into the bathroom and wash my hands. My eyes snap up and meet my reflection's glassy stare. My cheeks and nose are pink. My hands shake as I scrub them hard.

For the first time in years, I look alive.

I'm so shaken, I just sit on the bed and wait for Clint. My husband doesn't come up for another hour and I take every minute of that time to compose myself. Guilt still creeps in as he enters our room and closes the door.

He takes his boots off.

"What are you looking at?" He scowls.

I shake my head. "Nothing."

I try to arrange my face to be casual. I know he's pissed from Gerard's comment. I just pray he doesn't take it out on me.

To my relief, he's quiet as he strips for bed and takes his shower. I wash up in the sink, worried I'll set him off if I ask him to leave the shower on for me.

He hates when I wear flannel to bed, he mocks me for giving up when I'm only twenty-one. So I always wear a cream slip even though he rarely fucks me anymore. I have no idea why this matters except I think he gets off on controlling me in meaningless ways.

He comes out of the bathroom in his sweatpants, drying his forearms on a towel.

"What did you think of Sovereign?" he asks.

I freeze. Did he see something?

21

"He seemed fine," I say quickly.

His ash blond brow arcs. "Fine? What does that mean?"

My hands twist under the quilt. "I don't know, it was hard to tell. He didn't speak very much."

He snorts and tosses the towel aside. I watch it land in a heap by the basket, but I don't say a word. My eyes snap back to him and his gaze narrows. Unease curls through my stomach. He's never hit me before, but I've always been afraid of it. He's a big man and he's strong from working the ranch.

"Come here," he says.

My heart thumps.

"Get your ass over here, Keira," he says, his voice hard.

Mouth dry, I crawl on my hands and knees to the edge of the bed and sit back. I can't keep the fear from my face and he scowls as he looks down at it.

"Jesus, I just want to fuck my wife," he growls. "You don't have to look like you're going to cry."

I shake my head. "Sorry, I'm just tired. That's it."

He knows that's not true, but he doesn't care. He takes me by the wrist and pushes me down on his side of the bed. For a second, I think he's going to fuck me missionary, but then he flips me onto my stomach. He rarely looks at my face while we have sex.

I used to wonder why that was because I'm pretty enough, but then I realized that while I might be attractive in real life, I don't look like the girls on his phone. I'm not airbrushed and surrounded by perfect lighting. My body is curvy, I have dimples and stretch marks. And freckles, I have a lot of freckles.

None of the women he looks at look like me. Realistically, none of the woman he looks at look like that either. Not that it matters to him.

He enters me and the pain makes my back arch. His breath heats the back of my neck as he works his hips.

"You're dry as fuck," he grumbles.

I squirm, trying to spread my legs further. "Can I have lube? Please?"

He doesn't like it when I ask for it. It pisses him off, like I'm rubbing it in that he doesn't get me wet. He pulls out roughly and spits in his hand. It's enough I don't see stars when he pushes himself back in, but it dries up quickly. Right away, a friction burn starts and I have to grit my teeth to keep quiet.

I stare at the painted mare on the bedside table.

She's beautiful, lithe like a thoroughbred. When she runs, she steps high. Her bridle glitters like snow under moonlight.

I lie still, even after Clint finishes. He starts snoring a moment later and I shift to my side, still watching the painted mare. She's an angel watching over me. At least that's what I like to hope.

The next day, my husband goes with a dozen other men to Sovereign Mountain. They're rounding up a few thousand cattle and purchasing them before auction. That's what he tells me before he puts his hat on and drives off.

The morning goes like any other morning on Garrison Ranch. I prepare breakfast, serve it, and clean everything up. I have a few spare moments so I steal upstairs and tidy our bedroom. The painted mare is tucked in my bedside table, wrapped in a handkerchief so there's no chance Clint sees it. He thinks it's childish, so during the day I put it away. At night, I ignore his comments because I can't sleep without it watching me.

I expect Clint back around four so I head down to the kitchen and start making dinner at two. The kitchen is hot and my head is stuffy. I didn't sleep well last night after what happened in the kitchen.

After Gerard Sovereign put his hand in my hair, after he told me he could bend me over the desk and fuck me in front of Clint.

A little part of me wishes he had.

It's the part that kept me up, staring at the ceiling until dawn. I have circles under my eyes when I get up and wash my face in cold water and go to make breakfast. I don't know why I feel so guilty, I didn't do anything. I didn't touch or kiss Gerard, I barely spoke with him. Clint might be a cheater, but I'm not. I know he's slept with other women since our wedding, but I won't become him.

But that heavy feeling of guilt stays with me until four rolls around. I have three roast chickens in the oven and a pot of potatoes boiling on the stove when I hear a car pull up the drive. Clint is home.

Pit in my stomach, I creep down the hall and push the screen door ajar. But it's not Clint's truck in the drive, it's Jay's sedan. I freeze, watching as he steps out of the car with a briefcase in his hand. His tall, lined face is tense and there's a grim set to his jaw.

Something's wrong.

I push the door open and step out.

"Where's Clint?" I ask.

He freezes, one hand fussing with the button of his jacket. "Let's go inside, Mrs. Garrison. We should talk."

My heart thumps. "Where's Clint," I repeat forcefully.

He clears his throat, shuffling his feet. "Ma'am—"

"Where is he?" I snap, shocked by my own tone.

"He's dead, there was an accident," Jay blurts out. He's looking anywhere but my face, like he's guilty for telling me.

My pulse slows. Clint always moved fast and recklessly. It doesn't surprise me that it was an accident that took him, but what shocks me is that I feel nothing but surprise that today was the day. A long time ago, I thought I loved him, but months of verbal abuse, neglect, and infidelity killed that. I didn't realize until now just how badly Clint hurt me.

But I know it now because he's dead and I feel nothing.

"Okay," I say, clearing my throat.

His brows draw together. "Can I come inside?"

Numbly, I lead the way into the kitchen. He stands awkwardly in the doorway while I turn off the stove top. The potatoes stop bubbling and float half done in their milky water. I wipe my hands and pull a stool out, indicating he should sit.

"Do you have questions?" he asks hesitantly.

I put the kettle on and take a mug down. "Coffee or tea?"

"Coffee."

He lays his briefcase on the table and waits. The kettle whistles and I pour it out, stirring instant coffee into his cup. Then I make up a mug for myself because I need something to do with my hands.

"How did it happen?" I ask.

"Um...he was rounding up cattle and they spooked. He fell from his horse and into the stampede."

I sink into the stool opposite him. The coffee sears my hand and I let it.

"Where is he?"

"They brought him to the coroner," Jay says. "He was...clearly gone by the time they brought him to the hospital so they just sent the body on."

My lips crack and I lick them. "What time did it happen?"

"Around one."

I nod, sipping the coffee. It's cheap, but it's soothing. "Alright. What happens now?"

He seems relieved to get off the subject of Clint's body. His fingers fumble over the briefcase and then he appears to decide against opening it. I frown, watching something I can't recognize pass over his face.

"Clint left everything to you," he says, eyes averted.

I feel something finally—disbelief. "What?"

He keeps glancing over the room like he's guilty. "Um...Clint left you Garrison Ranch, the portion that belonged to him, and all the money in his account to you."

My jaw is slack. It takes me a full minute to get control of myself and formulate my thoughts.

"Clint hated me," I whisper. "There's no way he left me shit."

I didn't mean for the words to come out so harshly, but right now I have no filter. Jay releases an uncomfortable sigh and leans back, steepling his fingers.

"I can't tell you why, but I can tell you it's true."

My mind whirls and all I can think about is last night when Clint got angry because I didn't obey him fast enough. I glance down, noticing I still have a little mark where he gripped my wrist to push me down onto the bed.

My eyelids are sticky when I blink. Nothing makes sense.

"I can handle all the paperwork for you," he says.

It feels like he's a million miles away. I nod and he's saying something I can barely process. He tells me the Garrison brothers, Avery and Thomas, will likely contest the will. But I shouldn't worry because he'll handle the case. I don't have to do a thing but show up in court when he tells me to. My head keeps nodding and at one point he puts paper down in front of me and I sign it without reading a word.

This has to be a cruel trick from the universe.

There's no way my cheating, abusive husband is gone and I'm conveniently left with his ranch and all his money.

He asks me a few more questions I can't remember and he says he's sorry for my loss. He means it, Jay is a good man, not like Clint. Before he goes, he takes my hand and asks me if I'll be alright if he leaves me alone. My mouth is so dry I can't answer so I just nod hard.

I stand at the foot of the stairs and listen while his car drives off. Then I tiptoe around the house and feel how still it is. Dust sparkles in the evening sun that splits through the blinds. Horses nicker in the field. I can hear the birds trill from the marsh on the other side of the road.

This house is mine.

Clint will never desecrate it with his sharp voice or loud footfalls again.

I stand there frozen for what feels like forever before I remember dinner is still cooking. Anger pours through me and I stride to the kitchen. Wrapping my hand in a towel, I yank the half done chicken out and pile it on the stove. I'm not fucking making dinner for anyone tonight. They can feed themselves.

Everyone can fuck off and leave me alone for one night of peace.

The bottle of whiskey I poured from last night sits on the counter. I grab it and the shot glass beside it. Unwashed. I bring it to my lips and push my tongue inside, cleaning up the half dried bit of whiskey. The guilt from meeting Gerard Sovereign is gone.

Last night I was afraid.

Today I'm free.

No one comes in for dinner because I never ring the bell. Surely they heard the news already. If they haven't, they'll figure out soon enough.

Whiskey in hand, I go upstairs to our bed and take the painted mare from the drawer. She stares at me with dark eyes, perpetually in motion. Forever on the run.

I take a shot. I'm twenty-one years old, I've been married since I was eighteen. It's only been four years, but it feels like I wasted eons. Today I'm going to drink until the emptiness is gone and tomorrow I'll figure this mess out.

I push myself up against the headboard, whiskey between my knees.

What do I do now?

I could try getting laid by someone who cares if I finish or not.

A wry smile twists my lips. My hands shake as I pour another glass and shoot it. It burns like fire again and again until I've had so much I'm worried I won't be able to stand. Half the bottle is gone when I finally roll it onto the empty side of the bed. My head spins as I peel myself from the bed and wobble to the silk slip hanging behind the door.

I strip and pull it on. I'm so drunk I can barely untangle my braid, but I manage to get it free and shake my hair out. My heart thumps at breakneck speed. Gerard buried his hands in my hair, right at the base of my neck, and just that touch made me feel things I've never felt.

Fear, excitement.

Unadulterated lust.

When he held me by the nape, my body came alive. I'd never been touched like that before. Roughly, but without malice—the complete opposite of Clint. My fingers slip down my body and clench so hard my knuckles go white. Crushing the silk in my grip until my nails scrape my skin. Holding me the way he held me.

That's what I need. To be loved so hard it hurts.

CHAPTER FOUR

KEIRA

SEVEN MONTHS LATER

I step out of the courthouse and feel the heaviest weight I've ever carried fall from my shoulders.

I did it.

All of Clint Garrison's ranch is mine, including what he took from me when we married. It's taken me a long time to acknowledge that he annexed my land into his ranch. He had me so convinced it was normal. Just like opening a joint bank account.

It wasn't until I lifted my eighteen-year-old hand from the paper after signing away everything I had left of my family that I realized what I'd done. The Garrison Ranch owned Stowe Farm. I had nothing and my new husband was the legal owner of everything. He even marched me down to the courthouse and made me change my name.

Mrs. Clint Garrison.

Within a week, he erased Keira Stowe from existence.

The courthouse door slams behind me. My brother-in-law, Thomas, strides out. He stops to put his Stetson back on his head and shoot me an evil glare from beneath the brim. My heart thuds, I step back. My back collides with a warm body and I whirl, my fists clenching.

My other brother-in-law, Avery Garrison, stands behind me. Avery has always hated me.

My mouth is dry. I used to wonder if Clint knew the way his brother looked at me. The way he'd walk past me in the barn and accidentally hit me against the wall with his hip. Or that his hand would graze over my torso before I realized what was happening. Maybe he'd wanted me and that was why he hated me so much. Likely he just enjoyed torturing things that couldn't hit back.

Well, today I'd hit back.

"Leave me alone," I say, trying to stand as tall as I can.

It doesn't do much. I'm five-three. The Garrison brothers are well over six feet and pack on more muscle than beef cattle. I'm in my sundress and heels and when I step back, my shoe catches on the courthouse stairs. My entire body hurtles backwards and my arms windmill.

I hear their laughter as I grip the guardrail and fall onto my knees. Pain shocks down my legs. My folder of papers spills out onto the dusty pavement.

My hair falls forward and shields my face. I know my knee is bleeding, but I ignore it. Tears stinging my lashes, I scramble to gather my things. From the corner of my eye, I see Avery's boots draw close. He kneels down and I freeze, pulling back.

"I'm going to call the police," I whisper.

"Go ahead," he says, shrugging. "If they were going to help you, they'd have done it already."

I know he's right. Since Clint died and left everything to me, I've been harassed relentlessly by Avery and Thomas. I find my fences clipped, my cattle bitten by dogs, my barn that I know I left locked wide open in the morning. On one occasion, Avery pinned me against the wall in a bar and poured a beer down the front of my dress. Not one person in that bar did anything to stop him.

The Garrisons are South Platte's darling family. The only ranch bigger and wealthier than theirs is Sovereign Mountain, and Gerard Sovereign doesn't meddle with our affairs. He rarely leaves the mountain save for the occasional city planning meeting or auction.

I've lived here my entire life and I've seen him once.

Avery's jaw tightens and he spits onto the sidewalk. Ever since Clint's death, I've been locked in a nightmare legal battle with the remaining Garrison brothers. They say the will is a fake. My husband's lawyer says it's real as they come. And now the judge declared it so.

But Avery doesn't set much store by what the judge says. I flinch and draw back, trying to control my anger. The law might be on my side, but outside the courtroom, I'm helpless against him. When Clint gave me the ranch, he painted a bright red target on my back.

Avery rises, kicking one of the papers towards me. I stay where I am, eyes on the ground. Glued to the place where his saliva drips into a crack in the sidewalk. My chest simmers, but I know better than to antagonize him.

The sound of their boots die away. Slowly, I take my heels off and gather up the papers. My knee burns as I limp down the cold sidewalk to the corner where I parked Clint's old truck. I shift inside and push the seat back so I can stretch my leg out and inspect the damage.

It's not bleeding as badly as I thought. I lick my finger and dab the blood. The little shock of pain makes my eyes well up with more tears. I'm frustrated, angry enough I want to scream and punch the seat beside me. But sad enough that all I'll actually do is go home and cry into my pillow.

I take a deep breath and brush my hair back. It's a quiet day in the city, but inside I'm churning with a million different emotions. It's been seven months since Clint died on Sovereign Mountain.

Seven months since Jay Reed walked into my house and told me that Garrison Ranch is mine.

31

All of it. The land, the horses, the cattle, the money in Clint's bank account.

Anyone with half a brain would have turned around and sold all of it back to the Garrison brothers. But all I could think about was how much I fucking hated their entire family and I was determined to never let it fall into their hands again.

They took my farm once before. They'd treated me like a servant in my own home.

Never again.

I shift the truck into gear and pull out onto main street. The papers from the judge sit beside me in the seat. They should be the nail in the coffin of the war between myself and the Garrison brothers, but I have a feeling this is just the beginning.

A shudder moves down my spine. It's getting dark and I hate driving alone on the back roads. Clint and I had a short and miserable marriage, but at least he'd kept me safe in this remote wilderness.

It feels like it takes an age to get back to the Garrison Ranch. I pull slowly up the drive and jump out, taking my farm boots from the bed of the truck. The floodlights from the barn illuminate my path as I head to check on the horses.

They're all fast asleep. I breathe in the sweet hay as I move silently down the center of the dark barn. I do a slow loop and lock the barn up, pausing a moment to lift my head and look up at the sky overhead.

I was born under this sky. Under the heavy net of diamond stars with the mountains standing like guardians around me. I'll probably die here.

What happens between now and then is a mystery.

Eyes burning from exhaustion, I trudge across the driveway and climb the front porch steps. My keys slip through my fingers and clatter on the floorboards. I'm grumbling under my breath as I pick them up, but my entire body freezes when I realize there's something taped to my door.

A black envelope with a silver monogram. I glance over my shoulder.

The night is chilly and empty.

Quickly, I yank the envelope down, unlock the door, and burst into the warm kitchen. Thankfully, I left the heat running from the night before. We're still in the time of year when it's balmy during the middle of the day, but the night has a bite to it.

I kick off my boots and pad barefoot to the kitchen table and sink down. The envelope is made of thick, expensive paper. I turn it over and stare at the silver letters on it.

SMR.

SMR?

It hits me all at once and I feel stupid. Sovereign Mountain Ranch. Of course, I've seen those letters before. On that night seven months ago—when Gerard Sovereign sat in my husband's office. My stomach flutters and I'm not sure why.

Maybe because the memory of his bright eyes is burned into my brain. Maybe because he'd looked me dead in the face and said, "Mrs. Garrison, I could bend you over this desk and fuck you with your husband watching and he wouldn't say a goddamn word."

Heat curls in my lower belly. I clear my throat and press the back of my fingers to my cheek. I'm glad to be alone, just as I was when...I've thought about him before. Because, as ashamed as I am, once Clint was gone, and I had time to spend on my back upstairs with my rose vibrator, the image that never failed to get me off was those words falling from his lips.

And the realization that he meant it.

And in my fantasy...I let him.

I rip the envelope open and a card falls out. One side is black with SMR in gunmetal gray and the other is white scrawled with masculine handwriting in black ink.

Miss Garrison,

I'm extending an invitation to talk with you now that you are the owner of Garrison Ranch. Please join me for a business dinner on Wednesday, the 14th of September, at six-thirty.

I will see you then.

Sovereign.

His email address is printed at the bottom along with his phone number. There's something so arrogant about him signing only his surname like that. It's a scrawl, it takes up space, it's big and loud. It eats up my tiny name that isn't even correct. I'm *Mrs.* Garrison, not Miss. It feels like he's trying to make me smaller than him.

I flip the card over and over in my fingers.

Am I afraid of Gerard Sovereign?

Should I be?

When Clint died, he left me the largest plot of Garrison land with the original house on it. And all the land he'd taken from me when we married. It puts me between Avery and Thomas's land on the front and west side.

On the north and east side, I'm right up against Sovereign Mountain. I'm stuck between the three wealthiest men in the state. Like a fly in a spiderweb. They all have the police in their back pockets and no one would help me if I found myself in danger.

It's a wild country...and I've heard what the people of South Platte say about Gerard. He's a necessary evil, so they do business with him, but when he walks into a room, it goes quiet.

After meeting him, I understood that part.

There's no law on Sovereign Mountain but his. It's the reason I barely got any information around Clint's death. I only knew that he'd been thrown from his horse and run over by cattle while purchasing livestock for auction. The police won't go out to these remote places, and the coroner is a close friend of Gerard's.

I get to my feet and double check that the front door is locked. Then I leave the kitchen light on and move through the silent house and up to my bedroom.

I undress and curl up beneath my quilt. My iPad is charging on my bedside table and I swipe it open, typing his name into the search bar. It's slow—the internet is terrible out here—but eventually it brings up a page of photographs of him.

They're all from newspapers. In the first one, he's standing with the mayor of the city at a ribbon cutting event. They've both got black Sovereign Mountain hats on. Below it is a photo of him holding a check beside the city commissioner. A hundred thousand dollars for the emergency worker's fund.

The city might not love him, but they're all happy to take his money. Funny how that works.

He's handsome, I have to give him that. Heat creeps up my throat again. He's got a Hollywood face, chiseled with low brows and a square, stubbled jaw. In the photo, his dark hair is tousled and his ice blue eyes stand out against his black lashes. There's a grim set to his jaw that I see in the men who've worked the land their entire lives.

Like nothing phases him anymore.

Like he's seen it all. Death, taxes, and everything in between.

My eyes shift over the photo of him standing with the mayor. Gerard Sovereign towers over him. He's easily six and a half feet of solid muscle, broad shoulders, and thick forearms. He has thick, heavy body that make me wonder what he feels like naked.

My toes curl. I set the iPad up on the bedside table, propped against my water glass. Then I flip onto my side and pull the quilt to my chin.

The painted mare still sits on my bedside table. She's always there, like a guardian angel, keeping me company, every night since Clint died. Sometimes I take her with me when I leave the house, just so I'm not alone. Tonight, I wrap her in my handkerchief and tuck her into the drawer.

The photo of Gerard swims before my eyes. He's in a pair of work pants and a Henley rolled up to expose his forearms. His clothes are broken in by his body, hugging him in all the right places. Faded by the sun.

Would it be so bad...to just look while my hand slips under the covers? It's not like anyone would ever know. The house is empty, the painted mare is put away. My pulse increases, but it's in the most pleasant way that sends warmth down between my legs.

Fingertips skim over my thighs.

My eyes lock on him, tracing down his thick neck to his broad shoulders. Down his hard stomach to his groin. There's a very faint rise under his zipper, like whatever he's got in there is too big to conceal properly.

If I could have him any way I wanted—my fingers find my wet sex—I would let him take me the way he said he had wanted that night. Bent over in front of him. Skirt pushed up...his big hand in my hair pulling my head back until it hurt. I'd let him show me just how much strength he has in that big body.

My fingers speed up.

My lashes flutter and between them I see flashes of him on the screen before I shut them and give into the fantasy. I never came with Clint, and now that he's gone, I find it's so much easier to finish when I'm not constantly worried about his temper. Pleasure surges after just a few minutes and washes over me, arcing my body.

Then it's gone. I peel my eyes open, flushed and sweaty.

I should feel ashamed, but I don't. Instead, I get up and go to the window, drawing aside the curtain. I can see the hill where my land meets his in the distance.

I wonder if he thinks about me the way I do him.

I wonder if his hand wanders too.

CHAPTER FIVE

GERARD

Westin Quinn, my oldest friend and manager, calls me at night, right as I'm getting undressed for the day. As soon as his name appears on my screen, I know it's bad news. I answer, reaching for my pants and pulling them back on.

"There's a break in the fence," he says. "On the Garrison side."

"Fuck," I say. "Any cattle out?"

"No, but there's one stuck in the fence. They think, anyway."

He hangs up. I shrug into my flannel and push my boots back on. My black hat sits on the desk, the Sovereign Mountain insignia burned into the leather. Settling it on my head, I move downstairs and out the front hallway, grabbing my coat on the way through.

It's fuck-all cold. That's what Westin calls it. Even though it's only September, I can tell we're in for the kind of winter that makes me question my sanity living out in northern Montana. The leaves are golden, the grass is pale brown. I can smell weeks of snow on the horizon.

It'll be a hard winter, but if everything goes according to my plan, I won't spend it alone.

I stride towards the barn. The thought of Keira Garrison in my bed has sat at the edge of my mind since the night we met.

I'd gone to Garrison Ranch expecting to have a brief business transaction. I hadn't expected to walk away on fire.

Now I'm so much closer to making her mine.

One look at that pensive little redhead and I was fucked. I'm not a soft man, most of my emotions are covered with thick calluses. Out here, where the sun burns in the summer and the winter wind can take the tips of a person's fingers off with frostbite, I've learned to love the silence and isolation.

I've learned to become part of it. Then I saw her—my enemy's wife—and I felt something.

A splinter in my steel facade.

I barely remember what we talked about—although I recall drizzling whiskey into her mouth in the kitchen. The clearest memory I have is stepping out of the house when the meeting was done and realizing that I'd never in my life wanted anything as much as I wanted Clint Garrison's wife.

But I'm not a fucking cheater.

I look up, broken from my thoughts as Westin walks Shadow and Rocky, our geldings, out into the yard. They're already tacked up and ready to go. I catch Shadow's bridle and swing up, settling my weight. Westin does the same and we head through the yard and out to the path that leads to the west side of the pastured fields.

Neither of us speak until we locate the break in the fence. This area is too rocky to be accessible by truck, so we have only the electric lantern to work by. There's a shed several yards away where we keep supplies for repair. I walk the fence line while Westin drags wire and cutters out and tosses them to the ground.

"I don't see any cattle caught in the fence," he says.

I lift my head, inhaling. There's no scent of coyotes, but we're downwind. I scan the dark horizon. I don't worry often about wolf kills, but it can happen up here in the mountains. It's possible something got to the bull first and dragged it off before we arrived.

"Could be dogs," Westin says.

"Could be," I agree.

We had an attack earlier in the year. Dogs from the Garrison farms had broken through the gate and taken down one of our calves. I went to Thomas Garrison's farm with the remainder of the animal's carcass and a shotgun.

"I'll shoot anything that comes over that property line again," I told him. "Man or animal."

I don't like the way the western pasture feels tonight. It's the only pasture that borders the Garrison Ranch. It provides direct access to my land as well as a shared source of water that comes down from the mountain.

Westin shrugs and starts unraveling the wire. I join him and we work in silence. Bringing the broken portion of the fence together and pulling it tight. When we're finished, we head back down the mountain, both barely awake.

"What happens if she never replies to you?" he asks.

Westin is the only person who knows everything. When I got home after meeting her, I couldn't sleep. So in the early morning, I went outside and he found me sitting on the porch staring at the silhouette of the mountains. He asked me what was wrong, and I told him that come hell or high water I was going after Clint's wife. He didn't judge me, just like I don't judge him.

"She'll answer me," I say. "And if she doesn't, she will as soon as she realizes she isn't safe."

He clears his throat, brows pensive. "Are you afraid the Garrison brothers will get to her first?"

Yes, the truth is, I am. But I can't force her hand...yet. I have to give her an opportunity to come to me before I take her forcibly. She doesn't know what the Garrisons are capable of, that if she stays on her dead husband's land, she's in danger.

"I'm watching her," I say.

"How? Don't tell me you did something weird like assign a guard to her house?" Through the dim light, I see him roll his eyes.

"No, I installed a security camera outside her barn."

"Jesus," he says, but he doesn't berate me about it. He knows if she didn't really mean something to me, I wouldn't have done this.

He's used to the shades of gray we operate in at Sovereign Mountain. There's no way anyone builds the largest ranch in Montana in two decades without stacking the deck and playing a few dirty hands.

And he knows I won't stop until I have what I want.

We didn't get to sleep until past midnight. I wake so early that my eyes burn as I dress for the day and go into my office to check my emails. My laptop is still open on my desk by the window.

I sink down and her name jumps out.

Keira Garrison.

It took her long enough. I rarely have patience for procrastination. Everything in my life runs efficiently and promptly because I've made it do so.

But for the redheaded Garrison girl, I seem to have all the patience in the world.

I have the biggest ranch in the state and everyone asks for favors eventually. That means that all roads lead to Sovereign Mountain at some point.

I'm confident her road will bring her here as soon as she realizes she's out of options.

I crack my neck and click on the email. That last name bothers me to no end. In my last several months of research, I discovered she was the reason my land now directly bordered the Garrison ranch. Before that, I'd shared a boundary with Stowe Farms. She was the Stowe daughter who had inherited the land and married into the Garrison family. She was the reason that land had been annexed into theirs, putting me squarely against their ranch.

Keira Stowe sounds better, and I wonder why she hasn't gone back to her maiden name. Her husband is gone.

Thoroughly gone.

I watched the accident happen. I stood over his broken body and helped load it into the truck to take to the hospital.

Her email loads on the screen.

Dear Mr. Sovereign,

I've thought it over and will accept your request for a business meeting.

I look forward to speaking with you Wednesday.
Kind regards,
Keira Garrison.

The corner of my mouth tugs up. She's trying to be formal, but she's probably never had to arrange a business meeting before. I wonder if my invitation made her nervous. Or maybe she wanted to make me wait.

I cock my head. Normally I don't like to chase. But for this woman, I'll make an exception.

Every night for seven months, I've fallen asleep to the thought of Keira. The irony that I'm pining after a woman with that surname isn't lost on me. Garrison used to be poison on my tongue.

Now I whisper it while I come.

Keira Garrison.

I snap the laptop shut and rise, leaving the office and going back to the bedroom. In the upper dresser drawer is a folded piece of silk. My rough fingertips catch the fine fabric as I unwrap it to reveal a silver chain with three clamps at each end.

I've been collecting things since that night.

Imagining how they'd look on her body. I take up one of the nipple clamps and into my mind flashes the image of it on her breasts. Pinching her pink nipples while I lower my mouth and trace the exposed tip.

I lay the clamps aside and take up the silver collar. It's simple with a circle that will rest between her collarbones. Marking her as taken, as mine.

Someday soon, she'll wear this and I can pleasure her the way she deserves. With my tongue on her pussy, my cock buried in her mouth...in her cunt. But for today, I do what I do best and practice patience. Sliding the drawer shut, I take up my coat and leave the bedroom, hoping chores will give me some relief from my thoughts.

But she's on my mind every second for the rest of the day.

CHAPTER SIX

KEIRA

On Wednesday night, I put on my best dress. I don't go into the city and it's hard to get delivery this far north, so I don't buy a lot of clothes. But I do have a thin cotton sundress made of pink print. The material clings to my body and the ruched neckline makes my breasts look a lot bigger than they are.

I turn in a circle in front of the mirror. I don't normally wear pink, but this shade isn't bad on me.

It's chilly out so I put on a blue sweater and my boots. Then I leave the house and take the truck out onto the main road.

I've never been to Sovereign Mountain, so I put the address into my phone and follow the directions. It's not more than thirty minutes from the entrance of Garrison Ranch, but it feels like hours. I don't see a single car the entire time.

I hate that he summoned me like this. It makes me feel helpless.

I start sweating with the heat on and I struggle out of my sweater, pushing it aside. My fingers tighten on the steering wheel. Knuckles white.

I'm not helpless. I have money in my bank and a lot of land to my name.

I deserve to be treated as his equal.

The driveway up the mountain is long. I lean forward in my seat and go slow. Never sure when the next curve will creep up on me. When I see the pavement even out and turn into a gravel parking lot, I finally sink back and release a sigh.

Not out of relief because my heart is pounding.

I park the car.

The engine dies as I pull the key out.

I scan the empty yard around the house. It's a typical Montana ranch house. Fairly new and sprawling over the size of three normal houses. It has two stories and a wrap around porch on both levels. The wood siding is smooth and stained a rich, dark brown. Over the front door is a plaque with the SMR emblem burned into it.

I get out. The cold bites my skin, but before I can turn to grab my sweater, the front door bangs open.

A huge black dog bursts out and skids to a halt at the edge of the porch. It has bright blue eyes, thick fur, and a pointed nose. I wonder if there's some wolf in there somewhere because it clocks me at once.

I freeze, my heart in my throat.

Of course he has what looks like an attack dog on his porch. I shrink back against the truck and feel around for the door handle.

The screen door pushes out. I snap my eyes from the dog and my body tingles as he appears in the doorway.

He's just as handsome as when I last saw him—maybe more. His square jaw is set, his mouth pressed in a thin, grim line. His beard is short and his dark brown hair slightly wet. Like he washed his hands and ran them wet through the waves. His dark brows, sitting low over his eyes, are not quite a scowl. More a brooding stare.

His broad, muscled body is covered in a dark Henley, the buttons undone, and a pair of worn work pants and boots.

My eyes keep going to his chest. Heat stirs deep in my belly as I notice ink rising up above the collar of his shirt. He's got tattoos. Of course he does.

Suddenly, I feel naked. I'm a curvy woman and the thin sundress only makes that more apparent. I should have worn something that covered my cleavage. My breasts are fighting against the thin fabric.

It's too late for that. I'm here.

He steps out onto the porch and crosses his arms over the broadest chest I've ever seen. His jaw tightens and I think I see a faint glimmer of something like amusement in his face.

"Does your dog bite?" I ask, my voice hoarse.

He whistles once and the dog sits.

"She won't bite," he says. "Myself...I can't promise anything."

My breath hitches. His voice is deep with a hint of gravel. Just as I remembered it. The corner of his mouth turns up and he steps down from the porch, clicking his fingers for the dog to follow. It sprints up ahead and sits directly before me.

I extend my hand. She licks it and her tail wags in the dust.

"She's pretty," I say, petting her silky head. "What's her name?"

He pauses a few steps away. "Big Dog."

I jerk my head up, but before I can speak, I'm overwhelmed by how close he is to me. I can see all the little details of his body. The scar on his knuckles. The faint lines by his eyes. The droplet of water hanging in the waves. The thick hairs on his chest, between the open buttons of his Henley.

He looks big, warm, and solid.

I shiver and his eyes dart down. His gaze is like the brush of hot fingertips. Lava pools in my veins and pushes blood down to where I feel it the most. For a shameful second, the last time I touched myself fills my brain.

I thought about him. Why? I have no idea. Perhaps because I'm so touch starved.

But I thought about him, I fantasized about him turning me around and bending me over the table.

Flipping my skirt.

Dragging his rough palm up my thigh. Slapping my bare ass hard enough I cry out. Peeling my panties from my wet pussy and pushing them down before his fingers sink—

"You alright?" he asks.

I jump. My body feels oddly sensitive. Heat radiates from my face and I shake my hair back, trying to pretend I was just lost in petting Big Dog's head.

"You should name her something else," I say.

He smiles. It's a polite, short curve, like he doesn't know how to do it properly.

"Really?"

"Big Dog implies a Small Dog," I say.

He jerks his head, holding out his hand to point the way to the house. Heart thumping, I follow him up the path and enter the front hallway. The ceilings are tall and the floor is dark wood. Probably harvested from the ranch. I scan the decor as I follow him down the hall, appreciating how tasteful it is. Either he or an interior designer somewhere has a good eye.

He pauses and I almost crash into him. We're at the edge of a spacious living room with ceilings nearly twenty feet tall. Gerard leans in and whistles. From the couch comes a grunt and a tiny black dog that looks like a fox jumps to the floor. It's graying and stiff, but it manages to make its way to us.

"That's Small Dog," he says. "He's got one foot in the grave."

I kneel and Small Dog lets me scratch his chin. "You could give them real names."

"Do you name all your horses and dogs?"

"I don't have a dog." I look up at him. "But I name my horses. Every single one."

He smiles, that polite smirk. "Why?"

I straighten. "All creatures great and small, you know. They deserve to be noticed."

His eyes narrow, but not angrily. It's more of a contemplative look that swallows me up and drags me to the depths of his eyes. In the dark, they're the color of a waning sky. Blue with a hint of gray.

"Are you hungry, Miss Garrison?" he asks.

"Yes, sir," I say quickly.

"We're having roast," he says. "You can wait in the four season porch while I change."

I consider telling him that my name is *Mrs.* Garrison, but I don't have the courage to be confrontational. I still have no clue why I'm here, and that's fraying at my nerves.

He ushers me across the living room and I'm wide-eyed. Taking in the huge, lofted ceilings, the fireplace so tall I could walk into it, and a row of cow skulls over the mantel. Everything is big, even the couches, but that doesn't surprise me. He's a big, broad man and he's built the world to fit him.

He moves me through a rounded doorway and into a dining room. He described it as a four season porch, but that's a bit of an understatement. Everything is dark, expensive wood and the windows that look out over the lake are thick glass and reach from the floor to the ceiling. An oval table takes up the center of the room.

He pulls out a chair. I sit, taking my purse off and putting it in his open hand. It looks tiny in his palm and I can't help but stare as he sets it aside. What size are those fingers? A thirteen maybe? Bigger? It's hard to say.

"Excuse me," he says. "I'll be right back."

He pours me a glass of wine and leaves, his footsteps rising as he heads upstairs.

Movement stirs in the corner of my eye. I glance over and Big Dog is peering into the dining room, head cocked. I lean down and hold my hand out. She doesn't budge, so I click my fingers. The look she gives me is almost disdainful.

"Here, girl," I say.

Big Dog backs up a step and sits. Small Dog is nowhere to be seen, but I think I can hear faint snores coming from the next room.

Maybe his dogs don't like me after all. I flip my palms. They're damp and I notice my heart is pounding. My dress is sweaty under my arms. I hope my deodorant holds up.

The truth is, it's not just being here.

It's what he said, how he looked at me that night seven months ago. Like he wanted to devour me whole.

Maybe it's because the first and only time we met, I told him something I'd never told anyone before—that I was afraid of Clint.

I'd mulled over my accidental admittance for weeks after that. Hoping it never came up again. Hoping he would fade away as quickly as he'd appeared in my life so I never had to address my confession.

So much for that.

Flustered, I click my fingers again. Big Dog yawns, but keeps her hunches firmly glued to the floor.

"Come here," I say, holding my palm out.

"Dogs aren't allowed in the dining room."

I jump, whirling. He's standing at the far end of the room. He must have come from the back entrance, as quietly as a lion stalking its prey.

"Really?" I say, gathering myself. "They never beg for scraps?"

He clears his throat. "My dogs know better."

"That's no fun," I say.

He crosses the room and pulls out the chair beside mine. I hear it creak as he sits down. My eyes drift to the side and run over his chest and shoulders. God, he looks good. His biceps are the size of my head. His chest is wide enough I could comfortably use it as a pillow.

"It's good manners."

"So I'll take it they don't sleep in the bed with you?" I say, jerking myself back to reality.

"They're working dogs."

I glance back to the couch, where Small Dog is sawing logs.

"Is Small Dog retired?" I ask.

"No," he says. "But he's never won employee of the month."

I laugh and his head snaps up, those pale eyes glittering. Like I did something right. At that moment, a woman in her sixties appears pushing a cart.

She pulls up beside me, and I offer her a smile which she doesn't return. There's suspicion in her eyes as she sets down a plate and lifts the lid to reveal roast beef, vegetables, and whipped potatoes.

47

"I've never had beef from Sovereign Mountain Ranch," I say. "Let's see if it holds up to Garrison cattle."

"It holds up," he says. "And Maddie makes the best roast you'll ever have."

"Thank you," she says, a hint of pride in her voice.

She finishes serving us and leaves. Gerard pours himself a glass of water, ignoring the wine. Then he sits back and spreads his knees. I try not to stare, but it's hard when his body takes over the regular sized chair and makes it look small.

"Let's cut to the chase," he says.

My mouth feels dry and I try to wet it with a sip of wine. "Okay."

"You are underwater in debt, Miss Garrison."

A ripple moves through me, but I'm unsure if it's shock and disbelief.

"No, I'm good," I say slowly.

"I take it your husband never told you that he took a mortgage out on your ranch and I own the bank he did it with," he says.

"No," I squeak.

"And it hasn't been paid in months."

"Okay," I say frantically. "I can pay it. Just get me the paperwork."

His lids flicker. He plants one arm on the side of his chair and I'm temporarily distracted by the bulge of his bicep. It's incredibly hard to focus on my world crashing down while he's wearing a t-shirt that doesn't properly fit him.

"You can't pay this," he says.

He's not mocking me, he's just stating a fact.

"How much?" I lick my dry lips.

"A quarter of a million dollars," he says.

"In total?" My voice cracks.

"No, that's the payments from the last year and a half," he says. "The mortgage is a total of twelve million dollars. Your husband sold off portions adjoining my land, or it would be a lot more."

He'd sold part of the ranch?

My body is cold around the edges. My heart beats so fast it feels like it's trying to jump right out of my ribs.

48

How could Clint have done this? The Garrison Ranch was doing so well, our bills were paid...at least I'd assumed they were. Why had he risked everything and gotten into such a sickening amount of debt?

Was this why I'd been left everything in the will?

Because it was worth nothing?

My hands clench and my vision goes dim at the edges. I turn and Big Dog's face swims in my vision. Gerard leans in and his rough hand cups my elbow, gripping it hard.

"Miss Garrison," he says. "Are you alright?"

I turn on him. "*Mrs.* It's Mrs. Garrison."

The deep furrow between his brow appears and his mouth presses together. I try to sit up, but my head spins. My torso feels like it's sinking beneath water and I can't get my lungs to expand.

"I can't breathe," I gasp.

The last thing I remember is reaching in my pockets for the painted mare.

But she isn't here, I left her on my bedside table. I came here alone.

CHAPTER SEVEN

GERARD

She faints and I catch her, letting her body slump into my chest. For a second, I sit there holding her, but she doesn't wake. I roll her over and check her pulse. She's breathing, but deeply.

She's totally out cold.

Fuck.

I hadn't meant to do that. I gather her soft body in my arms and carry her through the living room where Small Dog lifts his grizzled head and stares through his milky eyes. I send him and Big Dog a look and they both stay where they are, watching me as I carry her upstairs.

The guest rooms are done up, but I don't bring her to any of them. Instead, I keep walking down the hall to the door at the end and push it open with my boot. She's in a flimsy, little sundress. She needs the warmth of my fireplace.

I lay her in the center of my bed and pull the woven blanket up from the end, wrapping it around her lap. Then I turn the gas on and the fireplace showers the room in warmth. I shoot a text to Maddie, asking her to make tea and toast and bring it up to my room.

When I turn, my chest tightens.

I'd left her husband's house seven months ago haunted. Something about this girl has split fractures through my rock solid world.

Whatever it is, I've thought about this moment for a long time. I wanted her here at Sovereign Mountain. In my room, in my bed. Just not under these circumstances.

She stirs and her lids flutter. She's got the prettiest pair of blue eyes and dark gold lashes. Her red hair falls around her shoulders in a cascade. I'd caught a hint of its scent when I'd lifted her. Sweet and smelling faintly of pomegranate shampoo.

"Feeling alright?" I ask.

She looks around. I know my room is probably overwhelming with its tall ceilings, roaring fireplace, the window that showcases the sweeping mountains, and the bull skull above the hearth. I glance back to where her eyes are glued behind my head.

I preserved the skull from the biggest bull we ever had at Sovereign Mountain. It was an anomaly, a Goliath of an animal. I'd kept it for breeding and when it died, I'd sent its head away to be scraped clean.

Now it hangs over my fireplace. A trophy of success.

"Where am I?" she manages.

Her chest heaves and I allow myself the luxury of one look. She's curvy and I know that, despite how big my hands are, her tits would fit in them perfectly.

"My room," I say. "You passed out."

Her eyes widen and she tries to sit up, but I shake my head. To my surprise, she obeys. Sinking back on the pillows.

"That's right," she says weakly. "I owe you a hundred million dollars."

"Twelve million."

"It could be my immortal soul at this point."

What about her body? I cock my head. Her dress is flimsy and I can see her curves straining against it. What size are her tits? It's been such a long time since I fucked anyone, I'm not good at guessing anymore.

"I have a way out for you," I say.

Her eyes dart up. "If it's not total forgiveness or death, I probably can't pay it."

I laugh, shaking my head. "I need to be able to talk to you about this without sugarcoating it."

She nods. "You can. I'm sorry I fainted. I think I'm just hungry."

"Maddie is bringing you food and tea."

She sighs, nestling back and gripping the blanket. She looks good in my bed.

I drag a chair around to the side of the bed, flip it, and sink down backwards. She stares at me and I see her throat bob. Her cheeks go faintly pink and she looks away.

"Your brothers-in-law are going to come after you," I tell her. "I'm breaking confidentiality by telling you this, but they will try to buy you out. And if they can't buy you out, they'll hurt you. They'll frighten you into submission until you cave to them. If you're not dead."

She gasps. "Avery and Thomas aren't like that. They're bullies, but they're not dangerous."

She's so innocent. She hasn't sat across from the Garrison brothers and faced the glitter in their eye as they presented their offer to buy her out. The only thing that kept me from blowing their heads off were the dozen bank officials seated with us.

"She'll sign," Avery said. "One way or the other."

I didn't make it to where I am by putting my head in the sand. I can read men like him like an open book. He would start by financially pressuring her, then he would threaten. Then he would hurt her. I saw his family hurt women like Keira without a second thought.

She doesn't understand the danger she's in.

"Avery and Thomas Garrison are not your friends," I say. "It's my professional opinion that you shouldn't speak or interact with them. You leave that shit up to me."

52

Maddie knocks on the door and I go to take the tray. Her forehead is furrowed and she sends me a curious look, but I just thank her and shut the door. Sliding the lock down so we're not interrupted.

I put the tray of buttered toast, soup, and hot, black tea with cream before her. I expect her to balk, but she starts eating right away. Tearing the toast and sopping it in her soup before pushing it into her mouth. As I sink back into my chair, I can see the glow return to her face.

"I want you to live at Sovereign Mountain," I say.

She goes still for a long moment. She's got butter on the tip of her thumb and she slowly licks it off. Flashing the tip of her tongue.

"Why?" she asks.

"For protection."

Her brow rises slowly. "Are you trying to take my land too?"

I shake my head. "Technically, it's my land until you pay the mortgage. No, I want something else, Miss Garrison."

She keeps eating toast, watching me owlishly. She must have been starving, she barely got a chance to eat downstairs.

"Okay," she whispers. "What do you want?"

"You," I say. "In exchange for my protection and a hold on all repayments until our contract is over."

Her jaw drops and she goes crimson. We sit there in stunned silence for a moment and when she wipes her hands, I see them shake.

"I'm not paying you with sex," she says.

"It's not like that," I say. "I want you as my submissive."

She levels a blank stare on me. Okay, so we're starting from square one.

"Do you know what that means?" I ask gently.

She blinks, jerking her head. "Yes, I know what it means. I've watched movies and read...you know, books."

I smile. "Dirty romances?"

She shrugs. "So what if I did?"

It strikes me as...cute, although I'm not the sort of man who usually finds anything cute. I've been on Sovereign Mountain for so long that most things are just...grim. I haven't seen anything as beautiful, as soft, and, well, cute, as she is up here in a long time.

She shifts her thighs, squeezing them together for half a second. I catch the movement and I know what it means. She's turned on by my proposition.

Now I just have to get her to admit that.

Maybe if I can get her to play once, she'll see how good I can make her feel. That I can offer her so much more than just protection.

"Is that what you like?" she asks hoarsely.

"Do I like being a dominant?" I ask. "Yes, that's why I want you as a submissive. I pick and choose my partners carefully and I've wanted you as mine for a while."

It's not the whole truth, but she doesn't need the exact details. She swallows hard. Her fingers tug at the blanket. Tearing the threads.

"This is really important for you," she says quietly. "I guess I wasn't aware people did this seriously."

"People take BDSM relationships seriously," I say. "Some more so than marriage."

That makes her chew on her lower lip. "It's not legal, is it?"

"No, not at all. It's an honor system."

"You strike me as the sort of man who takes that seriously."

"Deadly."

She stares at me, still making a meal of her lower lip. Then she shakes her head hard enough to make her hair fall over her breasts. That's probably a good thing because now they're out of sight and out of mind.

"How long do I have to stay?" Her brows draw together.

"I think a year would buy you all the former Stowe land," I say. "During which, you won't pay anything on the mortgage, I'll handle that. And you'll be safe here."

"And if I want out?" Her voice is small.

"You can leave, but your payments will resume. And I can't protect you out there."

Her eyes glisten and I know she's fighting back tears. A part of me wants to have mercy on her, she's innocent. But the bigger part knows this is the only way. If I don't get this woman somehow, I'm going to lose my mind. She's all I can think about.

I can't live like this anymore.

"No, no, I can't do that," she says huskily, wiping her eyes.

"Why?"

"You don't know me."

"I probably know you better than you think."

That is an understatement. I get to my feet and cross the room to my workspace. I have a copy of the proposed contract on my desk. Her eyes bore into my back as I flip through it and make sure it's in order.

"Take a look at it," I say, walking over and tossing it into her lap. "I think you'll find it more than fair."

She picks up the folder, but doesn't open it. "So my brothers-in-law get a real meeting, in an office, about the future of my ranch. And I get a meeting in your bed with my body as collateral? Seems fair."

I gaze down at her, admiring her spirit. "It's not fair. I never said it was. And you know why it's different between us."

Her breath hitches, her lips part.

"Why is it different?" she says. "Sir."

I sink to my knees by the bed, just a little shorter than she is, and look up into her face. "Because I want you," I say quietly. "Because you're in danger and you need my protection."

"If you were a good man you'd offer me protection for free," she whispers.

"Who told you I was good?"

She swallows hard enough I see her throat bob and her knuckles go white on the folder. My eyes fall to the rise of her thighs beneath her thin dress. I'm so close...all it would take for me to see what I've fantasized about for months is for me to spread those thighs and pull her panties to the side.

Is she wearing any? She doesn't seem like she'd go without, not in a dress that short.

I'm hard and I stand, not caring if she sees what she does to me. "I'll let you sleep and mull this over," I say. "I'll take the guest room tonight."

She bites her lip, like she's considering something. "You can...sleep here."

I lift my brow, looking down at her, trying to read her face. "You trying to fuck me, Miss Garrison?"

She flushes dark pink and shakes her head hard. "No, but it's a big bed. We won't touch."

I laugh once. "I'll take the guest room."

Her eyes follow me as I gather up my sweatpants and head for the door. I have a lot of patience and self control, but not enough to spend the night beside her and not break. She makes a little noise in her throat and I pause in the doorway. She's curled up against my pillows, arms wrapped around her bare thighs.

Eyes big, like she doesn't want me to go.

"You need anything, I'll be in the room at the far end of the hall," I say.

She nods.

"Um...thank you," she whispers.

"I haven't done anything for you yet," I say. "But give me what I want and you'll have plenty to thank me for."

She shifts, chewing the inside of her mouth. "How do you want me to thank you, Mr. Sovereign?"

Is she baiting me? I narrow my gaze, stepping out into the hall. It's become clear in the last few minutes that she wants me, but she's confused. She doesn't know if she can trust me yet.

Probably because I just asked her to trade her body for protection, a bit of forgiveness, and a plot of land.

"Read that contract," I say. "Goodnight."

I shut the door and stride down the hall. Instead of going to the bedroom, I push open the doors to the game room and shut them behind me. I'm not a smoker, but fuck...every time I go near her, I feel like I need a cigarette. I know there's an old pack in here somewhere and I retrieve it and kick open the balcony doors.

The stars are bright. Up to my left are the distant bumps of the cliffs, barely visible. The night feels just like it did seven months ago, when I pulled off on the side of the highway.

I think that was the moment when I decided to make her mine.

I've been patient. Now I see the fruits of my labor so close I can almost sink my teeth in and feel the juice drip down my neck. I see that she wants me too, even if she doesn't know it yet, and that makes me want to snap and eat her alive.

Instead, I wait. Patience is my only virtue.

There will be no sleeping tonight. I doubt there will be until I'm in my bed with her beside me, so I stay where I am for a long time after my cigarette is done.

Watching the moonrise over Sovereign Mountain.

CHAPTER EIGHT

KEIRA

It's early when I wake. I'm still in his bed and I can smell him on the sheets. It's a masculine scent mixed with something more natural. I bury my face in the pillow and breathe it in. My head spins and I sit up sharply.

What am I doing?

I'm still in my thin sundress, but the room is warm and the gas fireplace is still crackling. I shudder as my eyes shift up to the bull skull staring down at me. It reminds me of him. Big, rough around the edges, and intimidating.

I get up and pad silently over the cool hardwood floors to the huge window. Outside, everything is covered in a light layer of frost. The lake steams and a group of ducks float in tranquil silence by the dock. I can see the corner of the barn and the paddock to my left. There's a handful of horses out, one of them a brown and white paint mare.

A shock goes through me.

She looks just like my painted wooden mare. Down to one white sock, a spot over her back and halfway down her face. The only difference is her mane is white instead of auburn.

Is this a sign?

Heart pattering, I turn and duck out of the bedroom and creep silently through the huge house. From somewhere downstairs, I can smell someone cooking in the kitchens. Everyone else, I'm sure, is out in the barn or the fields already.

I slip on my boots in the hallway. Gerard must have brought them downstairs after I fell asleep. I can't remember much after I had my tea and I wonder if he drugged it. I slept better than I have in years.

Probably since before my father's death.

The cool air bites my bare legs and arms. The yard is empty and my shoes crunch over icy grass and mud. I pick my way to the paddock and the horses ignore me, all except for the paint mare. She lifts her head and stares at me from below her forelock.

As I draw up to the fence, she lets out a heavy breath that clouds the air.

We stare at one another and I think I'm in love.

Gravel crunches behind me. I know who it is without turning around. Warmth like a blast of heat covers my shoulders and back, and a heavy weight settles over me. He puts his jacket on me and it smells like him.

I pull his coat closer, feeling shy as I turn to face him. He leans on the fence, the muscles in his arms apparent beneath his shirt, and narrows his eyes at the paint mare.

"She's not fully broken," he says.

I clear my throat. "Where did you get her?"

"Won her at a game of poker," he says. "Some addict gambled away everything he had, plus his horse. I wasn't going to take her, but I saw the way she shied from him. There's no need for an animal to shy from your hand unless it's not been treated right."

"She was abused?" I whisper.

He nods once. "I work with her a few times a week. Progress is slow."

I stare into the mare's eyes, my stomach turning. How could anyone look at such a beautiful animal and want to hurt it? I sniffle and run my hand over my nose and he glances down at me.

"She's alright now," he says.

59

"What's her name?"

"She doesn't have one."

Why am I not surprised? This is the man who came up with Big Dog and Small Dog. He'd probably call himself Tall Man With Hat if he could.

I feel the corners of my lips tug back in a smile and he looks over and notices. His mouth thins and he turns, but not before I see a glimmer of amusement in his eyes.

"What would you call her?" he asks.

I stare at the paint mare and she stares back. "Angel, maybe. She looks like an angel standing in the frost, with all the steam coming off the lake."

He cocks his head, studying me. "By that logic, should I call you Redbird? I saw you walking across my yard, looking like one of the redbirds at the edge of the woods in winter."

My heart skips and I turn to look at his profile. There's something personal about the word when he says it like that. It feels more intimate than the brush of his hand against my bare skin. My mind spirals, wondering what it would feel like to be in bed with a man like him. Pinned between his hard body and the sheets.

"You don't know me like that," I whisper.

"I could."

I swallow and drag my eyes back to the mare. My pulse thrums and my head feels light. He's an enormous presence just standing beside me in his t-shirt with the misty cloud of his breath hanging before his lips in the chilly air. The implications of his contract are unfathomable. If he can make my body react like this just standing beside him, he could break it if he had a chance to be alone with me.

Door locked. Sheets on his bed pulled back. Big, heavy body between my thighs and hard mouth on my neck.

Beneath my dress, my body curls with heat. It spills through my chest, up my neck, down my thighs. It centers in my core and I feel the urge to let out a little sigh.

I'm rooted to the frozen ground.

Do I want him?

I can't trust my taste in men anymore. After all, I picked Clint. He was quick, talkative, and had a temper like a snake striking. I liked how witty and intense he was. Now, I find I like that Gerard is the exact opposite, not the kind of man I ever saw myself wanting. He's guarded, he moves slowly, as impenetrable as the mountains around us.

He's been hurt. No one builds walls that thick without good reason.

But he doesn't strike me as cruel the way Clint was.

"Maybe you're right," I say, my throat tight. "Maybe I am a redbird."

His brow twitches. "Why is that?"

"I feel...fragile. Like every gust of wind blows me in a different direction."

I hate that I'm being vulnerable with him, but he's listening. And so is Angel. For the first time in fucking years, I'm being heard. It feels extraordinary.

"My wings aren't strong," I whisper.

Clint taught me that. When I lived in the shelter of girlhood, my father told me I was strong, brave, and worth the same as any man. Then came the painful years of growing into a woman and learning that all those words were just a smokescreen to hide a harsh truth.

The world was made for men like Clint, like my father, like Gerard. Not for women like me.

That had become clear to me at age eighteen when I talked back to my husband. He took my hair—the same auburn waves my father had taught me were beautiful and rare—and held me still with a fistful of it. That was the first time he used a part of my body as a weapon to subdue me, but not the last.

"Don't fucking talk to me like that if you can't back it up," he snapped that day.

I wanted to obey him, but the problem was, I wasn't saying anything that wasn't the truth. Usually, I was expressing frustration at my crushing workload. Or simply loitering nearby, hoping for some small scrap of attention from him. But he'd push himself into my space until I felt small. Trying to goad me into hitting first.

"I'm not a man," I begged once. "Stop trying to fight me like one."

He never hit me, but he liked to tell me that a lot. He was a good man for not beating the daylights out of me and I was the bitch who deserved it. That scared me enough to keep my real thoughts to myself.

"You're fucking lucky," he'd hiss. "You're lucky I'm not the kind of man who puts his hands on his wife."

I still don't know what I did to make him hate me with such venom.

I shudder and drag myself out of my memories. This man, standing in his yard with the sun creeping over the mountains, is far more pleasant. I clear my throat and take off his jacket, holding out to him.

"I should go," I say

His eyes fall on my body and I swear I'm on fire. How does he strip me bare with a single glance?

"Let me feed you first," he says.

I shake my head. "I really think I need to go."

He clears his throat. "I'll walk you to the truck."

He holds the coat with one arm and his other drifts to my lower back. Is this normal? Clint usually walked up ahead, his legs much longer than mine.

We stop outside his truck and he opens the door. I turn to say goodbye and he takes a step closer, pinning me between his big body and the front seat.

"Sure I shouldn't take you down the mountain, redbird?"

I stare up at him. My mind is an empty slate. I've never felt such a magnetic attraction to anyone. It doesn't help that one of his hands rests on my hip, and it's making me wonder if he could break me in half.

He has the kind of body I'd like to curl up with on a winter's night. And I'm feeling so cold right now in my thin dress with frost melting on my shoes.

I swallow, lowering my lashes.

"Why do you want this?"

"This?"

"You said you wanted me," I rasp. "As your submissive. Why?"

He's silent and when I look up, he's gazing over the cab of my truck. That's how tall he is. After a moment, he clears his throat and narrows his ice blue eyes.

"It's not complicated," he says. "You're a beautiful woman."

His guard is back up, and I know he's using it to hide the truth. Does he want me because Clint died on his land? Is this some kind of honor code where he feels an obligation to care for me and this is his odd way of doing it?

I don't put much weight on that theory.

With one arm, he lifts me into the driver's seat and spreads my sweater over my lap. Before I can react, he turns the car on and slips something into my passenger side. I glance over and scowl. It's a folded envelope.

That damn contract.

"Just read it, redbird," he says.

He shuts the door, and I watch him head back to the barn. He's in his work pants, boots, and a Henley the color of his eyes. The morning sun glints off his dark hair.

My hands grip the steering wheel until my knuckles go white. I guide the truck down the driveway and around the bend, going slow down the hill in case there are patches of ice.

The road is scraped and salted.

I glance around as I drive, taking in the pastures of clean, healthy cattle and horses. I've spent my life on ranches and I've never seen one so well cared for. He's meticulous and he has a firm grip over Sovereign Mountain and all the surrounding counties.

There's natural dominance and care to the way he does everything.

Is that why he wants a submissive and not a girlfriend? Because that way everything is spelled out for him in a contract? Maybe he really does just want to sleep with me, but he doesn't do the messiness of hookups. That's too bad for him because if he'd been straightforward and never brought up a contract, I'd have fucked him stone cold sober.

It doesn't occur to me until I'm back at Garrison Ranch that despite him not being able to name his horses or dogs, he found a name for me without trouble.

Redbird.

CHAPTER NINE

GERARD

I can't sleep. The night she leaves, I lie in the same spot she slept in my bed. When I turn my head, I swear I can smell the soft pomegranate scent of her hair.

Seven months of waiting, watching, obsessing. Weeks of planning and she walked right into the belly of the beast and spent the night. Like I'm someone she can trust.

And I still can't sleep.

It's past midnight when I get up, put on my clothes and coat, and head to the barn. Shadow stands with his head hanging over the stall door. When I run my hand over his neck, he blows hot breath out in a white cloud. His whiskers prickle my palm as he rests his muzzle in my hand.

"We're both up," I say. "Let's clear our heads."

I tack him, mount up, and hang the electric lantern in front of me in the saddle. Shadow and I have taken late night rides for years. He's a quiet, stoic horse who enjoys the stillness of the mountains while everyone is asleep.

Tonight, I have an itch, and not even the moonlight and frosty air scratches it.

It's an hour later when I see the rise of smoke in the distance from Garrison Ranch. At first, it looks like it could be coming from her chimney. Then I realize there's far too much for that. I squint and click my tongue, sending Shadow forward. He feels my mood shift and his gait goes jumpy, forcing me into a posting trot. We crest the hill over the river and he skids back, rearing up on his back legs for a second.

My center of balance is thrown back. My instincts kick in and my abdominal muscles tighten as Shadow's front feet hit the ground. We can both tell something is wrong, and it's making him want to move. I keep my weight steady, forbidding him from running.

At first all I see at the bottom of the hill is a blur of orange. Then I blink and it comes into focus.

Fuck.

The barn is burning.

Flames spill from the front door, eating at the wood. Casting shadows across the yard.

She's alone in that house, probably asleep oblivious to the danger she's in. Or she's in the barn trying to save her horses. She said she'd named each one, there's no way she'll leave them inside.

I rip my hat off and dig my heels in. My legs tighten and Shadow shoots forward, slipping to a gliding gallop. The path down the hill with the fence to my right is clear and Shadow takes it easily. The wind bites my face and my eyes water.

We careen around the corner. The yard gate is shut, but Shadow doesn't stop. His hoof beats thunder over the dusty ground and he soars over the fence, landing with an earth-shattering impact on the other side.

We skid to a halt by the truck. I dismount before he's at a full stop and throw his reins over the horn in case he needs to run. He'll go home if he spooks, he knows his way around the mountains.

The barn crackles. The heat sears my face as I run up the porch and try the lock. It doesn't budge, so I back up and throw my shoulder against it. The wood groans, but stands firm.

Fuck this. I kick it in, right above the knob, sending wood shards flying.

As I enter, I almost collide with a small, soft body. Keira darts back, her eyes wide, and hits the light switch. She's in her nightclothes, a short white slip, and her hair is a tangled mess of red. Her eyes are frantic. She reminds me of my unbroken mare, Angel, when I first brought her to Sovereign Mountain. Wild with terror, unreachable.

"My horses," she gasps.

"Get into the yard," I order. "Stay with Shadow."

Her feet are bare and she's barely covered, but she obeys. I practically carry her down the steps and when she sees the barn, she starts fighting me. Her chest heaves and her nails come out. Shredding my shirt as she tries to get away. I keep pushing her further from the barn and house, forcing her to where Shadow waits.

"My horses," she screams. "My horses are locked inside."

"I know, I'll get them," I say, pulling her back. "But only if you stay with Shadow."

She twists and I grab her wrists, yanking her against me. Our eyes lock and I send her a look that makes her go still. She's crying and I'm not sure she knows it. Tears stream unchecked down her face.

"Please," she whispers, chin shaking. "Please."

"Stay here," I say, my voice low and urgent. "Do not move. Or I'll have to pick between saving you or the horses. You know which I'll pick."

She nods, running her hand under her nose. I pick her up and put her up on Shadow and she grips the saddle horn. Shadow is a giant at seventeen hands tall and her body looks so small up there. But it's the safest place for a quick getaway, and I know he'll bring her back to Sovereign Mountain.

He gives me a sharp nicker. I move past him and head for the barn.

I hear her quietly sobbing as I circle the building. The side door is still intact. I take off my jacket and wrap it around my hand before touching the metal door. It slides back to reveal crackling flames on the far side by the front door. The horses hit their hooves against the doors, throwing their heads. The whites of their eyes catch the fire like coals.

Ignoring the sweltering heat, I bolt to the far end closest to the flame and rip the bar off the first stall. The chestnut horse inside bursts free and tears into the darkness outside. One after the other, I free each one. Their thundering hooves fill the air as they race into the void.

They'll seek shelter in the mountains and I can go after them later.

The barn is too hot and the smoke is so thick I can barely see. My skin burns like it's been striped raw and my eyes stream. My shirt is soaked in sweat and dusty with ash and I can feel the heat through it.

I need to get out now.

Yanking the last stall door open, I send the final horse out through the back door. I'm right behind it, circling the barn and skidding to a halt. A second set of flames fills my vision, smaller than the first, but just as deadly.

The back of the house is on fire.

How is that possible?

It hits me right then that this wasn't an accident and I have a pretty good idea of who's responsible. This wasn't an electrical fire or a careless cigarette. Someone did this and their target is alone right now. Sitting on my horse in her front yard.

My chest tightens.

Not again.

They took everything from me once. I won't let them do it again.

I break into a full run and see her, climbing down from Shadow. She couldn't be obedient this one time?

She starts running towards the house on her bare feet and I catch her before she gets to the porch. Wrapping my arms around her waist and lifting her from her feet.

She screams, arcing. Her fists pound my back.

"It's all I have," she wails. "Please, Gerard, it's all I have."

It's not.

She has me. Whether she likes it or not.

I carry her ruthlessly back to where Shadow waits and put her down. She wrenches herself back and attempts to dart towards the house, but I grab her wrist and pull her into my chest. Turning her so she can't see the flames eating the back of the house.

"It's just bricks and wood," I tell her. "It's not worth it, redbird."

She sobs, hyperventilating. Her chest heaves in until it's concave and she's barely able to breathe. Her hands shake in my grasp, her eyes wide like a deer in headlights. I brush her tangled, sweaty hair back and cradle her face.

"Breathe for me," I urge.

"It's all I have," she gasps out. "I've never had anything until this. I have no home...I have no one."

I grip her shoulders and pull her against my chest. Her entire body goes still. I wonder if she can hear my heart pound against my ribs as her breathing eases. She's no longer struggling for air the way she was, but I feel her shake like a leaf in the wind.

"I will take care of you," I say into the top of her head. She smells of smoke and pomegranates.

There's a long silence.

The fire crackles on.

"Why?" she whispers, sniffing. "Why will you take care of me?"

I want to have the words. God, I wish I had them. But that part of me is calloused and dead. If I had the ability to speak my emotions, I could say all the foolish things I'd felt since I'd laid eyes on her. That she was the first woman in twenty years who'd made me feel human again. That I was used to loneliness and she was the opposite of that.

But I don't know how.

That's why I need her to sign the damn contract.

Then she'll be mine. Then I can sink with her into the type of intimacy that I understand.

One with structure. Rules to keep her safe.

But without the safety of those rules, that contract, I can't do anything but hold her body against mine.

The barn burns on and fills the dark sky with smoke. Sparks shower like fireworks over the yard. I step back and lift her chin, wiping her sticky face. Her eyes are glassy like she's slowly checking out. I hope she's not going into shock.

"You're cold as ice, redbird," I say hoarsely. "I'm taking you home."

CHAPTER TEN

KEIRA

My cheek presses against his chest and the wind stings cold on my back. My eyes sting so badly I can't open them. The front of my body is warm where he burns through his shirt and my back is numb. He had a coat when he arrived. It must have fallen in the barn.

In my curled hand, pressed against my chest, is the painted mare. She was the only thing I took when I ran down the stairs.

His hand is on the back of my head and his arm is locked over my spine. Keeping me tight to his body. Beneath us, his enormous bay gelding runs like he's never been allowed to. I feel the sleek rhythm of his gallop, four beats like a drum through my body, and it lulls me like the rocking of a cradle.

Inside, I'm empty.

No fear, no sadness.

Just a void that hurts worse than anything.

Sometimes Garrison Ranch felt like a prison, but when I inherited it, it became my home. I know the name of every horse that's now wandering through the darkness. I can ride that property line with my eyes shut.

Now my home is gone after only seven months of being mine. Washed away in my scream of terror and black smoke billowing up to the sky. I doubt there will be anything left when the sun rises.

We don't stop until we're in the barn at Sovereign Mountain. Gerard hits a buzzer just inside the door and a moment later, I see a light flick on in the gatehouse on the other side of the driveway. I lift my head just as he dismounts, taking me with him and setting me on my feet. I sway and his arm slides around my waist.

Am I in shock?

I lean into him, seeking his heat and he curls me into his chest. A dusty blanket is wrapped around my body and I hide the painted mare deep inside. It feels childish to be holding a toy. Footsteps sound. Around the corner comes a tall, fit man with chestnut hair. His belt isn't done and he's fastening a flannel with the buttons lopsided. I can tell by his messy hair and red eyes that he was fast asleep.

"Is that the Garrison girl?" he asks.

Gerard nods. "I need you to cool down Shadow and put him away. He's breathing hard and he's soaked."

"What happened?"

He lifts me in his arms and I flail, grabbing onto his shoulders. "Someone, and I have a pretty good idea who, burned the house and barn. I got her out and released the horses."

"Garrisons?"

"I wouldn't be surprised."

I hear them, but dimly. The idea that my brothers-in-law would try to kill me and my horses sounds far-fetched.

The man doesn't stay for introductions. He takes Shadow's reins and heads to the back of the barn. Gerard carries me across the driveway and around the back entrance of the house. I hear the dwindling clip clop of Shadow's hooves. My eyes flutter shut.

"Who is that?" I whisper.

"Westin Quinn, my property manager," he says.

"Is Shadow hurt?" I murmur.

He shakes his head and gives a short laugh. I can hear the rumble deep in his barrel chest. Warmth blossoms inside and starts to melt the numbness.

"Shadow's gone on harder runs than that," he says. "He'll get cooled down and spend tomorrow resting."

"Are you hurt?"

"No, redbird, I'm not hurt."

He kicks the back door open and enters the hall. His housekeeper, Maddie, appears at the end of the hall, wringing her hands. I know I must look terrible. Dirty, sweaty, in just my night slip. I probably smell terrible too.

"Can you make a tray up like last time?" Gerard asks.

She nods. "Right away."

His boots ring out as he carries me up the stairs and into his bedroom. A sense of safety creeps over me as he sets me down. He walks past me and pushes open a door on the opposite end of the room, revealing a bathroom.

"Let's get you cleaned up," he says.

I hesitate. "May I have privacy?"

He turns on the shower and steps out. I slip into the bathroom, but he pushes his boot in the door when I go to close it.

"Leave it cracked," he says. "I don't want you passing out in the shower alone."

There's no point in arguing. He's one of those belligerent men with a head thicker than wood.

I nod, pushing it until it's just ajar, and duck behind it. I know he could easily see through the opening and catch my reflection in the mirror, but I don't care. I'm cold and shaken and I want to sleep so badly. I want to take two Benadryl and fall into a stupor that lasts hours.

I fold the painted mare into the blanket from the barn and lay it on the chair. Then I strip naked and drape my slip over top, hiding her away.

My head aches as warm water spills down my sore body. When I close my eyes, all I can see is orange fire and the shadows of my horses disappearing into smoke.

Grimly, I wash my hair and body until I don't reek. When I step out, I notice there's a light gray sweatsuit sitting on the floor. I try it on, surprised to find it's my size. The soft fabric is a balm to my shocked body. I lift my hand and turn it, studying the little Sovereign Mountain insignia embroidered on the left cuff.

He's got his name on everything, now he's got it on me.

Shyly, I leave the bathroom. He's on his phone, standing by the fireplace. My stomach flips. His profile is gorgeous. Big arms and hands. A flat stomach and broad chest that rises to a thick neck. Hair slicked back with sweat and short beard shading his jaw until it looks like stone.

He sees me and sets aside the phone.

"Gerard," I whisper.

He clears his throat. "What is it, redbird?"

"What about my horses?" My throat feels raw and my eyes burn.

He moves across the room and touches me and my whole body warms. His rough palms slide up my forearms and cradle my elbows. He's so tall I have to crane my neck back to look up into his face.

"I promise I'll send out my best in the morning," he says. "Horses are smart. They'll be fine until we find them."

There's a knock at the door and he goes to retrieve the tray from Maddie. Like last time, he doesn't let her in. I wonder if he lets anyone but me into his bedroom.

I'm hungry and limp as the shock wears off. Exhaustion makes me bold, and I crawl into his bed, sitting up against the pillows. If he's surprised, he doesn't show it. He just sets the tray in my lap and points to the food.

"Eat," he says. "I'm going to shower."

He shuts the bathroom door and I look around, stunned. Sovereign Mountain feels different than last time. More like a real home. Maybe because before I had a choice to stay or leave, but now I have nothing to go back to. Either I stay here with Gerard

74

Sovereign or I take the little money I have left, beg him to defer my debt, and try to find another place to call home.

A minute ago, I was so tired I couldn't keep my eyes open.

Now I'm buzzed.

I sink down and start eating the buttered toast. My stomach growls, but the hot food goes right to my soul. Soothing my shock. It's gone by the time the bathroom door opens and he appears in a pair of sweats and a t-shirt. His hair is wet and pushed back. A trickle of water moves down past his ear and etches along his neck.

Every ridge of his stomach is visible through the worn, gray t-shirt. It's tight on him. I'm sure most clothes barely fit that broad body. Maybe he has to order them custom.

He notices me staring and tosses the towel in his hand aside.

"You still hungry, redbird?"

I shake my head, wordless.

There's something about the way he said that word that sets me alight and soothes me at the same time. His voice is hushed and hoarse. It's so familiar. Like in another life he said that word to me and it's still echoing through my memory.

"Say it again," I whisper.

His pupils dilate.

"Redbird," he says.

My body wants comfort, and he looks like a sanctuary. It's been such a long time since I've craved sex, perhaps because Clint stopped wanting me and turned elsewhere. Nothing is more humiliating than begging for attention from a man. So I stopped early on and let him come to me when he wanted it. After a while, it was a relief when he didn't reach for me.

I won't beg for Gerard Sovereign either.

If he wants me, he'll take me.

He picks up the tray and sets it aside. Behind him, the bull skull glowers over the fireplace. His body moves close and fills my vision, sitting down on the edge of the bed. My breath hitches and his eyes drop as my breasts heave.

"Do you need to see a doctor?" he asks.

His words feel so out of place in the tense room. I shake my head.

His hand comes up, touching a thick strand of my hair. My eyes flutter closed. He'd called me a redbird, a spark of color against the winter. Has he lived in the cold for so long on Sovereign Mountain that he needs a sign of hope?

That's what a redbird is—hope.

I crack my lids and study his face, tracing the laughter lines with my eyes. I count a few strands of gray hair by his ears. He'd look better with it cut very short. He's got one of those hard, bullet heads I find so attractive and I want to see the shape of it.

I want to run my nails down the back of his scalp, and slip my fingertips over his broad, muscled shoulders. He's so effortlessly powerful and right now, I'm broken.

I'm tired of being strong. I tried for so long and I'm fucking done.

"Fuck me," I breathe.

His eyes snap up. "What?"

Before I can lose my nerve, I pull the sweatshirt over my head and toss it to the ground. I hear his breath hitch and a flush creeps up his neck. His gaze falls and stays glued to my naked breasts.

His hand comes up and I tense, my body tingling. But it moves past me and taps the nightstand. The lights flick off and we're left with nothing but the fireplace. It floods the room in an orange glow that cuts heavy shadows down his face and nose.

He clears his throat. "If that's what you want, redbird, I won't tell you to change your mind."

My body is empty, especially that place between my thighs that hasn't been filled in so long. When I shift my hips, I can tell I'm soaked just from the thought of sex with him. I want him to break through to me like he broke down my front door.

"I won't change my mind," I whisper.

He puts his hand against my back and it's so big and rough it sends heat down my spine that centers in my sex. Our bodies move together like we're connected. His other hand slips up the side of my waist and brings me into his embrace, wrapping me in the weight and warmth I've craved for so long.

I let my head fall back over his forearm and his mouth comes down on mine. His lips part and when I taste him my body comes alive. I'd thought it was wide awake before, but that was nothing compared to the burst of sensation moving through my veins.

I've never been kissed like this. His mouth is hard and soft all at once and he tastes faintly of mint. He probably brushed his teeth after his shower. Or maybe he's just that perfect.

When he slips his tongue into my mouth, I moan around it. My hips work and blood pounds through the emptiness between my thighs.

I need it filled.

He breaks off the kiss and his rough palm cradles my left breast. My eyes roll back as he palms it, running his thumb back and forth over my nipple. Teasing it until it hardens beneath his touch. My hips jerk and his eyes fall, watching the tremble in my thighs.

"I've been tested," he says. "We can fuck without a condom."

"I'm not on birth control," I pant, "But I've been tested too."

He picks me up and flips me onto my back on the bed. My sweatpants are off and he's between my thighs under the blankets. The heavy weight of his body shifts over me and it's so much better than I imagined. All that power between my legs makes my head spin.

He bends and catches my nipple in his mouth. Sucking first one and then the other before pressing a kiss on the base of my neck. Each touch sends a tendril of the most delicious pleasure down my stomach. It centers deep in my pussy and I let my head fall back. Wishing he'd slip those big fingers into me and fuck me with them.

Instead, he reaches down to the tie of his sweatpants.

My hand shoots up, bracing against his chest. His winter-blue eyes flick to mine.

"I don't want to get pregnant," I breathe.

"I won't knock you up, redbird," he murmurs, kissing beneath my ear. "I've been snipped."

That isn't what I expect to hear, but to my horny brain and desperate body, it's the best news in the world. My hips lift and I rub them up against his...oh God...up along the ridge of his hard cock beneath his sweatpants.

Fuck, he feels so big and hot.

His hand pushes between us and my lower back arcs as his fingers slide into me. God, yes, it burns like sweet fire. Two big fingers stretch me, slipping gently against my sensitive inner walls. He's looking for something and when he finds it, I moan as he strokes that spot with precision.

I've found that spot myself, but I've never had it touched by a man's fingers. It's so incredibly intimate, especially with his eyes locked on mine in the dark.

I know he feels the slickness and the slow tightening of muscles around him. My desire can't be a secret because he's knuckle-deep in it. Feeling my body from the inside.

His fingers leave me and I almost cry with how empty I am. Then his hips sink down against mine and I feel him push his sweatpants down. My heart pounds. My breasts heave against his chest. I spread my thighs and wrap my ankles around his hard lower back.

He pauses, reaching into the nightstand drawer. Before I can speak, he's uncapped a bottle and he's gently rubbing lube over the entrance of my pussy.

"Am I not wet enough?" I whisper.

"You're soaked," he assures me. "But I don't want to hurt you."

He sets the bottle aside. My stomach quivers with anticipation and my fingers dig into his shoulders. He breathes out, bracing his elbow beside my head. The outline of his head and shoulders fills my vision completely.

He reaches down and I feel it. The hard head of his cock against my entrance.

The tip is warm and smooth and feral need rips through me. More wild than anything I've ever felt. I lift my hips, rubbing my pussy up against the underside of his cock. Begging him to slide it into me and settle it against my deepest point.

I need the emptiness to be gone.

He braces his knee and pushes. Pain splits through my hips and my muscles tense in response. What the fuck does he have down there? A battering ram?

"You're tight, redbird," he murmurs.

Has it really been so long that I've gotten this tight? I just nod because he's pushing the head of his cock into me, forcing me to stretch to take him. A sharp little burn starts at the intrusion and quickly splinters into pain. Tears spring to my eyes and my head falls back. I gasp and dig my nails into his shoulders.

"You're hurting me," I pant.

Our eyes lock.

"I know, redbird," he says.

He pushes again and I arc back. The pain ebbs once and morphs into something else I've never felt before. My head spins as the most intense kind of pleasure blossoms inside. A heady blend of ecstasy and torment.

"Is it too much?" he asks.

I shake my head.

His mouth grazes mine. Mint and Sovereign.

"Good girl, I knew you could take it."

Can I take it? It's probably better I didn't see his cock beforehand because I'd have balked. Now I can only cling to him and let him break me into a thousand pieces.

I focus on my breathing and my muscles ease. Just enough for him to push the rest of the way in. His hips settle against mine and my weak legs spill open on the bed. Shaking too badly to wrap around his waist. He takes my nipple into his mouth and teases it gently, sucking and circling it with his tongue.

The burn leans into pure pleasure. I'm not a virgin, but this is all new to me. This is all consuming. We're on fire and the heat melds us together. Fusing our bodies where they're joined.

I feel my pussy pulse around his intrusion. Easing just enough I'm not cramping anymore. His hips rock and he strokes gently up against my cervix. I never imagined I would like that feeling, but it's new, it's painful, and so incredibly intimate.

I've never been intimate like this, with anyone before.

Sex was just mechanics.

But this...this is being ripped open and laid bare.

He could have warned me. Clearly he knew because he'd used a lot of lube, so he'd expected to be too big for me. I want to be pissed, but I'm too turned on by his lack of concern. He'd known I could take him. He made the choice for both of us without me.

There was something sexy about that. And a little shameful.

I didn't want to be forced.

But I do want him to force me.

How can that be? Confusion swirls in my head and chest. I'm feeling things I've never experienced before, and I can't identify them. I don't have time because he draws out slowly and my mouth parts in a silent cry as he thrusts back in.

"Please," I pant.

He looks as if he can barely feel my fingernails raking down his back. His big body ripples and he thrusts again, forcing me to take him. Pleasure and pain swirl and the only thing I know for sure is I need release. If I can just come, I'll fall over the edge to total pleasure.

His gaze flicks over my face. Then his hand slides between us and my spine arcs as his fingertips find my clit. I'm slippery with lube and his touch moves over me like silk. Our gazes lock, but I can't read him.

My lips part. My eyes roll back.

Pleasure crashes over me in a torrential wave and my entire body shudders. I can't control the spasms as I buck up against him, fucking myself onto his cock. Not caring that he's hurting me. Waves of cramps ebb into waves of desire under his thrusts.

All I want is to be ruined.

My orgasm slows. He shifts and his hand comes up to grip the headboard. The wood groans. He draws his hips back and I feel the power of them as he begins fucking me in earnest.

I cry out.

The bed hits the wall in a steady, loud beat. Sending a shudder through the room. His hand holds the headboard so hard I wonder if he'll break it. The veins on his forearm stand out beneath his tanned skin. Sweat etches down his chest.

I'm either going to come or die.

I'm not sure which.

I've never taken anyone, or anything, this big. And never like this—so brutal and unrelenting. He has a distinctive signature to the way he fucks and it reminds me of a freight train. A relentless beat that throbs through me like the turning of a steel wheel on railroad tracks.

Bang.

Bang.

Bang.

Somewhere inside is a dull throb that aches with every stroke. It's so sweet and it's spreading through my hips. He's bottoming out, the head of his cock stroking up against my cervix as he fucks.

My lashes flutter open and he's so close, his eyes burning with need.

"You're doing so well," he rasps.

I whimper, incoherent.

He relents, shifting his hips so he can look down and see between us. I wish I could see what he does because I know it must be extraordinary. His lips part and his hot breath kisses my face.

"God...girl, you are a pleasure to fuck," he gasps.

He bends and his mouth brushes over the tears tracking down my cheeks. The hot tip of his tongue tastes them. I feel the stutter of his hips, like he's considering easing up on me. My nails dig harder into his back.

"Don't stop," I beg hoarsely. "Make me feel something."

CHAPTER ELEVEN

GERARD

I give it to her the way she wants. Usually, I don't fuck without a dynamic already established, but there's no world where I'm waiting a single night longer. For the last seven months, I've been patient. I've moved the players and the pieces of this game, edging her ever closer to me.

And now she's here, she's willing, and I can't hold back anymore.

Tonight is the first night of the rest of my life with her. She doesn't know it, but this is a consummation.

My fingers circle her clit. Her freckled face flushes and her eyes flutter shut. Tears stream from beneath her lids.

I taste them and kiss her mouth. Salt and sweetness combined on my tongue.

Her spine rises and her body pushes up against mine. Her fingers curl into the pillows. I feel the tremble of an oncoming storm, I see it quiver down her belly and tighten her thighs. Her eyes fly open and lock to mine.

"Oh, God," she whispers.

"Sovereign," I correct gently. "Say my name while you come on my cock."

The depths of her eyes are hazy, but her lips tremble and I hear my name tumble out on her breath. Sovereign. My hips drive against hers. Her hand flies up and slides up the back of my neck. Tangling in my hair so hard it hurts.

She comes, and it's the most beautiful thing I've ever seen.

My orgasm hits me out of nowhere. She's still going, her hips bucking up against my groin, when I feel it rush down my spine. I fall against her, catching myself just in time, and she gasps as she realizes what's happening. Maybe she feels it, the throb of my desire, the warmth emptying up against her deepest point.

We both go still. Our breathing fills the silent room.

"Are you alright, redbird?" I murmur.

She stirs and nods, her hands going to my chest. Her finger trailing through the hair and down to my stomach. Warm tingles follow her touch as it continues down...down...to where we're still joined together.

Fuck. Me.

I feel her finger and thumb attempt to wrap around my length and I fight not to thrust against it. Her eyes widen and I shift my hips back, the head still inside, and let her stroke over the base of my cock. Her exploratory fingers are gentle—I can't remember the last time I was touched so gently.

"You're not what I expected," she says.

I bend and nuzzle her neck. "Neither are you."

Shifting my body, I pull out slowly. She winces and a tremor moves down her thighs.

"I'm going to be sore," she says. "You could have mentioned you have a monster cock."

I laugh, running a hand over my face and sitting up. Her eyes widen as I grip her thigh and move it apart, giving me my first look at her sex.

My groin tightens again even though I've just finished. She's beautiful. And she's bleeding a little, a single smear of crimson on her inner thigh and another at the entrance of her pussy.

I touch it with the backs of my fingers. She's swollen and when I move my fingertips to her opening, she winces. I spread her gently and her stomach tenses, sending my cum trickling onto the bed.

"I'm messy," she whispers.

I stroke up her thigh. "Let's put you in the shower again."

I lift her to her feet and we get into the shower together. It's big so we have space, but she huddles back against me like she's cold. I slide my arms over her breasts and stomach and pull her against my chest. Her soft ass settles over my cock and I let my face sink into where her shoulder meets her neck.

"Why did you get a vasectomy?" she asks.

"That's a question for another time," I say.

"Okay, sorry I asked," she whispers. "I just thought you seem young for that."

I turn her around, brushing soft strands of auburn hair back. She's tied it up in a bun and the stray bits are curling in the steam. "How old do you think I am, redbird?"

Her eyes flick over me and she bites the inside of her mouth. Her forehead draws together and I have the urge to trace the line with my fingertip.

"I don't know," she admits. "You have lines on your face, but they're the sexy kind. It's hard to tell if they're from age or from working outside."

"I like your honesty."

"You have gray hair, but I only saw two."

"So what do you calculate?"

She cocks her head, staring up at me from beneath her hooded eyes. "Maybe...you know what, just tell me."

"Thirty-eight," I say.

Her lips part. "Oh...that makes sense."

I study her quietly, wondering if the gap between our ages is a good or bad thing in her mind. She notices my silence and a slow smile starts on her lips. She cocks her head and sucks in her lower lip like that will keep that smirk off her face.

"You don't know my age either," she says.

I shake my head.

Of course I do, I know when and where she was born. I've seen her birth certificate. But I play along because if she finds out how much I already know about her, she'd be horrified.

"Guess," she says.

I shake my head again. She rolls her eyes and something bolts down my spine and makes my dick pulse. When I have her name on that contract, every time this little redhead sasses me, I get to punish her and make her come until she cries.

"I'm twenty-one," she says. "Almost twenty-two."

I knew it, but hearing it from her lips is different. I've seen her life laid out in certificates, bills, receipts, court documents. Each one more tragic than the last. She's far too young to have suffered so much.

I study her as she watches my face for a reaction. "You're young."

She shrugs. "I was emancipated at seventeen because my father died and I was so close to eighteen. Clint and I married two days after my birthday. At the courthouse in the city."

"Did...why did you marry him?" I ask.

She shrugs. "I thought I was in love with him."

"And you weren't?"

The sigh that escapes her mouth is heavy. Weighted with years of tension.

"I think it faded when I realized all he wanted was my farm," she says. "He absorbed my family's land. I know it was a lot smaller than your ranch or his, but it was my father's legacy and he left it to me. I was really stupid to fall for Clint and sign it over to him. When it sank in that maybe I'd been played, I kind of hated him."

"The farm belongs to me," I say. "Sign that contract and we'll see what happens."

Her brows arch. "So you get to spank me and I get my farm back in a year. Which belonged to me in the first place."

"It's about a lot more than spanking."

She turns back around like she's pouting, but I'm too distracted by that perfect, heart-shaped ass to care. "I'll read the contract in the morning."

I touch the little bump of spine at the nape of her neck. She shivers and I trace all the way down to her ass. My hand dips and cups the soft curves for a second before pressing between her legs. She's slippery with my cum and her arousal and my finger pushes up into her body easily.

Soft heat envelopes the tip. Her head falls back and she moans.

"You have a lot of spirit, redbird," I say.

"I'm thinking I'll sign your contract," she whispers. "As long as there's nothing extreme in it."

"As in?"

"You know, urine and that stuff."

"No, there isn't. That's in the hard limits section. I'm not interested in it."

"Good."

"But the point of you going over the contract is so you can negotiate it with me."

She sighs. "Alright. Let's go to sleep and we can talk in the morning."

CHAPTER TWELVE

KEIRA

My eyes skim over the paper. In no particular order, sentences leap out at me. I'm holding the desk with one hand and sipping coffee with the other. Trying to pretend I'm unbothered while reading the paper, despite the crimson flush creeping up my neck.

The dynamic will remain in place at all times when the submissive and dominant are alone. Outside of those spaces, both participants will behave in a manner that is respectful to the consent of those not involved.

The submissive will refer to the dominant as sir when alone.

The submissive agrees to a maintenance spanking of medium intensity every week on Sunday night, regardless of behavior.

The dominant will provide aftercare for every session regardless of the dynamic or punishment.

There's an entire section on the back of that page labeled COMMUNICATION. I take a breath, straighten, and flip the page over. I expect something equally as surprising, but I'm intrigued by what I find.

The submissive will keep a journal accessible to the dominant at all times. The submissive agrees to be completely honest in writing down their thoughts and emotions. The dominant agrees to never use this material as a reason for punishment.

The submissive agrees to be completely honest with the dominant. Lying or refusing to communicate is considered a heavy offense and will result in punishment.

The dominant agrees never to use the submissive's honesty against them or as a reason for punishment.

My head spins. Maybe Gerard Sovereign should consider being a relationship therapist. Kinkiness aside, these sound like pretty good communication rules.

I take a sip of coffee and glance up. I'm sitting at his desk in his room, overlooking the lake. I took the painted mare from the bathroom and now she's sitting on the corner of the desk, watching me. There was a light fall of snow last night and Gerard is out breaking the ice on the animal's water. He promised to return for breakfast after handing me a coffee and the contract and ordering me to sit and read it.

I flip the page.

Punishment includes spanking over the dominant's lap with a hand or implement. The submissive may not fight or speak unless a safeword is needed.

My breasts tingle. My mind drifts back to the way his hand feels...so big and rough. I have a feeling being spanked with that palm would hurt like hell in the best way.

Other punishment includes delayed gratification, and other safe, agreed upon methods of implementing pain or humiliation.

The dominant will never publicly humiliate or verbally punish the submissive in front of another person. All punishments are to be strictly private.

I have to take another break to focus my attention back out the window. I hear distant laughter and the steady clank of machinery behind the barn. The ranch is operating with perfect efficiency. Now I realize why that is.

Gerard has an attention to detail that amazes me. He's thought through this contract and written up clauses for everything. As someone that struggles not to be messy and chaotic, I'm impressed.

My eyes return to the contract and shift to the next section. This one is labeled DAILY TASKS, ETC.

The dominant will pick the submissive's bra and panties the night before and they will be worn. Failure to abide by this will result in punishment.

The submissive will offer herself to the dominant each night before bed.

The submissive agrees to free use.

The submissive will take care of herself reasonably by eating well, exercising, bathing, and wearing proper clothes.

I'm not sure how I feel about that last part. I flip the page and there's a section called FINANCIAL before me.

The dominant will provide the submissive as much money as needed or desired.

The submissive will never conflate sex and financial compensation. Nor will the dominant.

The submissive will not pay for anything during their time in the contract. When money is needed, the submissive will request it from the dominant.

Hold up...does that mean I won't have my own money? I narrow my eyes and run them over that last line again. Then I grab a highlighter from his desk and swipe it over those words.

Behind me, the door opens and I hear his heavy boots on the floor. My hand shoots out and pushes the mare out of sight. I turn and he's standing by the door, his pale eyes washed out in the light from the window.

He looks so good it makes my heart patter against my ribs.

I clear my throat.

"Interesting contract," I say. "What's free use?"

He shuts the door and walks over to me. I'm sitting down and he's so tall that I'm eye level with his lower stomach. My eyes drop and I can see the faint rise of his groin. Even soft, I can still make out a hint of the monster in his pants.

His fingers slide under my chin. Tilting it up.

"If I walked up to you right now," he says. "Took my cock out and fucked your mouth until I came and then went down to breakfast...that would be one example."

My jaw drops. He slides his thumb up and between my lips. The taste of soap and the feeling of his rough skin fill my mouth.

My pussy aches. He runs his thumb over my tongue in a slow circle. His eyes are glued to my lips and there's a flush at the base of his throat. I like this feeling of being used as he gently strokes the inside of my mouth. Petting me like I'm nothing but a toy here for his pleasure.

Is this what I could feel like if I sign that contract?

He thrusts with his thumb and I feel saliva slip down my chin. It's humiliating, but I keep perfectly still. I don't even move my eyes from his face to see if he's fully hard.

He pulls it out and licks it clean. I'm speechless, rooted to the spot.

"You hungry, redbird?" he asks.

I nod.

"Let's go eat."

Head spinning, I follow him downstairs with the contract in hand. We enter the four season porch, which is empty except for two covered plates of food at the far end closest to the windows. He guides me to the seat beside the head of the table and I sit down meekly. The folder goes on the chair beside me.

I'll have to discuss it with him and I'm dreading that.

He pours coffee. I grip the hot mug in my hand, shifting my eyes out the window. It's so cold there's ice on the glass and I'm grateful I'm inside and not back at Garrison Ranch. There's surely nothing left of my house at this point.

"Have you found my horses yet?" I ask.

He shakes his head once. "No, not yet. We're looking."

My brows scrunch. I feel distantly guilty that I'm in a warm house, in a soft sweatsuit, with a hot cup of coffee in my hands and my horses are out there roaming in the cold.

"It'll be okay," he says.

I nod and bite my lip.

"Your horses know what they're doing," he says. "I wouldn't be surprised if they bring themselves home."

"I won't be there though," I say.

"I have someone watching the ranch. They'll let me know as soon as they see anything."

He pulls the cover off my plate to reveal eggs, sausage, biscuits, and gravy. My stomach rumbles and I pick up my fork and wait. Watching him to see if he's going to eat too. It's already weird enough for me that I'm not eating in the kitchen and I need him to start so I feel less awkward.

He just sips his coffee. I put down my fork.

"Do you have questions about the contract?" he asks.

I nod. "Yeah, I have a lot."

"Fire away."

I lean back in my chair. "I want to keep my bank account. I don't mind if you want to pretend I don't have it, but I'm not letting you strip what little money I have from me."

His jaw works and he dips his head. "You may keep it, but there's no need to use it. I'll pay any and all expenses you have while you're here."

I blink, surprised it was that easy.

"Why aren't you eating?" he asks. "I can have Maddie make you something different."

91

I shake my head, grabbing my fork. "Sorry, I was waiting for you."

He gazes at me for a long moment, but clearly decides not to pursue his thoughts. Guiltily, I start eating. I'm not sure why it's so embarrassing. Maybe because for the last handful of years, I've eaten standing up at the kitchen sink. Shoving my food in as quickly as possible before the men in the dining room needed service.

All it had taken was for Clint to come looking for me once for me to realize I needed to be available until dinner was finished.

"What did you do at Garrison Ranch?" he asks.

I shrug. "I cooked and cleaned. Clint ran it like a bed and breakfast during parts of the year for conferences and business meetings. I was the housekeeper and the cook and he handled the financial stuff."

"That's a lot of work," he says.

I shrug, taking a sip of coffee. "I got used to it."

"Maddie has a whole kitchen staff to help her with that."

"Garrison Ranch is smaller than Sovereign Mountain."

He cocks his head, one hand rested on the table. "Still, that's a lot of free labor your husband got out of you."

I'd never thought of that before, but yes, he had gotten a lot of free labor out of me. He would have had to pay multiple people a lot of money to do my job. I'd gotten up at five in the morning and worked until eleven at night for free. For the privilege of eating a quick meal over the sink three times a day.

Suddenly, I feel both stupid and incredibly grateful that he'd never tried to get me pregnant.

"I made the best of it," I say shortly.

"You won't do any housework here or cooking. Unless you want to, but I prefer you don't. Maddie rules the kitchen, she's paid well for it."

I consider him. Now that my stomach is full and my coffee has hit my veins, I'm thinking more clearly. Last night, I'd fallen asleep open to signing his contract because I'd lost everything. Shock and grief pushed me right into his bed and made me more than willing.

But now that I've had time to recover, I'm determined not be taken advantage of again.

"I want to go over the contract sentence by sentence," I say.

He dips his head.

I draw myself up. He's three times my size, and he's got me right where he wants me. Holding me up like a puppet by the strings. But I still have my dignity and my resolve.

"How about tonight?" I say.

"Now."

His tone is firm. He reaches across the table and touches my elbow. My entire body tingles and the memory of him inside me comes crashing back. Now, in the light of day, I'm not sure why I let him fuck me. Was it this animal magnetism that glowed from him effortlessly? Or just the high of adrenaline?

Whatever it was, it's hitting me again.

I slept with Gerard Sovereign.

No...I *survived* sleeping with Gerard Sovereign with nothing more than soreness and a bit of blood in my panties.

He starts eating. Nothing seems to bother him. I finish my food and wait for him to set his clean plate aside. He wipes his hands and sits back, knees spread. He probably can't cross them properly with what he's packing.

"Let's see that contract, redbird," he says, holding out his palm.

Obediently, I pass it over and he flips it open on the table. It falls to the page where I've highlighted a section in yellow. My stomach somersaults as I realize which part it is.

His eyes fall and they flick back up to me.

"No oral?"

I want to squirm in my seat, but I have to behave like an adult. We're having a very adult conversation and I can't crack under his steel gaze. His mouth thins and his eyes remain on me, pressing me for an answer.

"I don't mind giving you oral," I say. "But I'm...honestly, I don't really like getting it that much."

His face doesn't change. A bit of wavy hair comes free and falls over his forehead. I can't help but think a haircut would look amazing on him. He needs it short to compliment the brutal cut of his jaw.

"I don't believe you," he says.

My jaw drops. "Excuse me? I think I know what I don't like."

"Did Clint take your virginity?"

This time, I squirm in my chair. "Yes," I admit. "I was eighteen when we married."

His face goes hard and something glitters in his eyes that makes my stomach cold.

"Did he fuck you when you were underage?" he asks.

I shake my head. "We waited."

His jaw works. "So...he fucked you at midnight on your birthday?"

My cheeks heat and I draw myself up. "No. It was later."

"That day?"

Defeated, I nod.

He clears his throat, the sound rumbling in his chest. "So you only ever slept with your husband?"

Without realizing it, I'm chewing the inside of my mouth hard enough to draw blood. It spreads over my tongue and jerks me back to reality. My face is so flushed it's probably glowing.

"Yes," I whisper.

"Most likely your husband was just bad at going down on women," Gerard says. "Before we cross it off, let me eat you out so we can take this off the hard limits list."

My brows rise. "You're confident."

"Yes, I am," he says.

His eyes drop to the second highlighted line and his brow arcs. "Let's add anal to the soft limits list as well. I'm not willing to forgo it."

My stomach swoops like I took a tumble. "If you have anal with me, I might die," I say.

He laughs and his gaze lights up. "You won't die. I can train you to take it."

94

"I don't want to be trained."

He flips the page and sits back again. His gaze falls on me, thoughtful. "That's too bad. You'll have to train to be my submissive. We'll have a month where we work together to figure out our limits, our likes, dislikes. At the end of it, we'll write amendments to the contract. Then I'll collar you."

I feel my eyes widen. How is he saying these things so casually? He must be so deep in this lifestyle it's second nature to him.

"What...do you mean?"

"If you want to be my submissive, redbird, you'll wear a collar. During the day, when others are around, I'll put a discreet collar on you. When we're alone, you'll wear a leather collar with an O-ring. You'll sleep in it, play in it, and when you need to shower, you'll come to me and I'll remove it."

I'm speechless, my mind whirling. What stands out most starkly aren't his words, but the reaction my body has to them. There's a vivid image in my brain of myself kneeling at his feet while he buckles a leather pet collar around my throat.

I swallow and between my thighs, my sore pussy tingles.

"I...I don't know how I feel about that," I whisper.

He leans across, his face intense. His hand slides under the waistband of my sweatpants. Before I can react, he's pushing his fingers between my legs and swiping the tips over the seam of my pussy. When he draws his hand out, I see the glisten of my arousal.

"I think you know how you feel about me," he says.

He licks his fingers, slowly. Like he's savoring the taste of me. Never in my life has a man wanted to taste me and it's a power trip to watch him.

"What do I taste like?" My voice is barely audible.

His eyes snap to mine. The air between us crackles.

"Like pussy."

I was expecting something more eloquent. But my surprise is wiped away as my body reacts to him saying that word. I thought I didn't like it, but hearing it fall from his lips puts a new spin on it.

He's so big, rough, and male. The word slips from his mouth like a piece of silk.

Suddenly, I don't want to fight anymore. I reach across the table and take the contract from him and flip to the next highlighted section.

"Tell me about the diary. What's that for?"

"Aftercare and communication."

That sounds harmless. "Okay...um, there was one other thing," I say. "Why do I need spanked every Sunday?"

His mouth twitches. "Because I don't enjoy brats. A lot of submissives act up trying to get a rise from their Dom when the dynamic isn't enforced often. Some subs want to be spanked every day. I think to keep you respectful, we'll try a spanking every Sunday night after dinner. If you need it twice a week, we can make an amendment."

My lips part and my hips shift. I'm soaked, I can feel it in my sweatpants and I wish I had panties on. If I sit up and there's a wet spot, I'll die of embarrassment.

"Won't I get...used to it?" I whisper. "I thought it was a punishment."

His eyes glimmer, arousal and amusement in their depths. "You'll know the difference between being spanked for maintenance and for punishment."

My mouth feels so dry. "What's the difference?"

"When you're spanked for maintenance, you'll cry and come," he says. "When it's for punishment, you'll just cry."

"I don't want to cry," I say automatically.

He cocks his head. "Why's that, redbird?"

He has this way of saying things when he's this close to me that's more intimate than sex. It isn't helping me that whenever he calls me redbird, it feels like being naked in his arms.

I draw myself up. "I never have the time."

That's a lie. I cry easily and often, but Clint hated it so much I learned to keep it secret.

He leans back. "No time to cry? That's too bad. You look like you could use a good cry."

"I'm not weak," I whisper.

"No, this is about release, not weakness," he says. "Once a week on Sunday nights, I'm going to spank you and let you cry it out until you feel better."

"Do you cry?" I shoot back.

"God's honest truth?" He tilts his head back like he's thinking deeply. "The last time I cried was at my mother's funeral and I was eleven. My father told me he'd hit me if I cried in public again, so I haven't done it since."

My jaw goes slack. It's the first piece of information he's volunteered. My mind latches onto it hungrily, trying to imagine Gerard before he was the hard, closed off man sitting before me.

"Was your father abusive?" I whisper.

He shakes his head. "No, he just drank until he turned into somebody else. Now, sign the contract."

I pause and mentally check in with myself. I don't feel scared, my body isn't tensed up the way it always was with Clint.

He reaches into his pocket and takes out a metal pen with blunt ends.

I look up at him.

And down at the pen.

"What happens if I change my mind?" I whisper.

His head cocks. "Then you're right back where you started."

I hold out my hand and he places the pen firmly in my palm. It's cold and smooth and heavier than expected. It feels like a little Pandora's Box, tempting me to just pull the cap off and sign my name.

What's the worst that could happen?

I study his face. He has me right where he wants me and I'm dismayed that I don't mind. Last night was the best sex of my life and now he's offering me an entire year of that.

Slowly, I realize I've been asking myself the wrong question. I should be asking what's the best that could happen.

97

The best would be good sex, having him listen to me like I'm the only person in the world, letting him call me redbird, falling asleep in his warmth every night.

I want to experience that. Even if it doesn't last beyond this year.

He leans forward in his chair. His two fingers tap the paper.

"Sign it, redbird," he says quietly. "Sign it and let me give you everything."

How does he read my thoughts so easily? Ears burning, I uncap the pen and put it to paper. My hand shakes, my signature is sloppy.

But I manage to scrawl it across that dotted line. And it feels so different than when I did this with Jackson.

For the first time, it feels like opening a door instead of closing it.

CHAPTER THIRTEEN

KEIRA

We go to bed early, but he doesn't fuck me. I slip into bed wearing one of his worn t-shirts and he gets in next to me in just his sweatpants. I wait for him to roll me over and push himself into me, to leave me aching again, but he doesn't.

Instead, I feel his hand slide over my hip. Holding me gently. When I peek over my shoulder, he's asleep.

Curious, I shift onto my back. The blanket is around his waist. I have my half pulled up to my chin because it's freezing outside, but he radiates heat. I reach out and touch his bicep. I didn't get a good look at it before, but he's got a black and white traditional tattoo of a bull skull on his chest. It extends to his upper arms and stops above his elbows.

My fingertips contact his warm skin, tracing the sightless eyes of the skull. The thick muscle under it is relaxed. A slab of skin, muscle, and bone. I shudder. I've always been wary of big men the way I am with big animals.

They're unpredictable and when they go off, the damage is like a bomb blast.

I nestle my head deeper into my pillow and pull the quilt up to my chin. The problem with Gerard is that, despite how he reminds me of a bull, I'm not scared of him.

In fact, he looks warm and inviting.

And I'm cold.

I inch closer. He doesn't move so I shift even closer. He rumbles in his chest and his hand moves out, his palm gripping my hip and flipping me. Like I weigh nothing, like a pancake on a griddle. He pulls me back against him without waking and I'm enveloped in his heat.

It's like sinking into a hot bath.

Oh God, it feels good to be held. The hand that drapes over my waist might suffocate me, but I don't care. I've waited too long for this.

My father loved me and taught me to be strong. To stand on my own. My husband ignored me and I taught myself not to need him.

In Gerard Sovereign's arms, I feel my walls crumble. I haven't felt safe since my father died. But here, at the top of the mountain, in this kingdom he's built, I feel untouchable.

It's early when I wake, the sky is still dark. Gerard moves around the room, already dressed. I can hear the gentle tread of his boots on the ground. It comes closer until he's right in front of me in the firelight.

He crouches and shakes me gently. "Wake up, redbird."

I cough the hoarseness from my voice and lift my head. "What is it? What's wrong?"

"Nothing," he says. "We're going to the blacksmith shop."

He rises and my stomach flutters as I sit up.

"What are you going to do to me?" I whisper.

His mouth turns up. "Nothing, redbird. I won't surprise you with punishment. I'm making something for you and I want you to sit with me while I do."

That explains nothing. I get up, shivering in my t-shirt and he hands me another sweatsuit. Where are they getting these suits in my size? And when can I have my real clothes?

He watches me as I pull on the clothes. Then he pushes me back down on the bed and gets back down on one knee. I'm on high alert, unsure what he's doing. But he just pulls a thick pair of woolen socks over my feet and tucks them in.

He carries me downstairs and out the door. Overhead, the sky is deep blue and the stars twinkle like diamonds. There's light pollution from the barn, but otherwise, we're in total darkness.

I've seen stars like this my whole life, but at the top of Sovereign Mountain, they take my breath away. Every color is brighter, deeper, bolder.

I let my head nestle against his shoulder. He took a checkered green and white blanket from the hall closet and wrapped it around me. Between his heat and the blanket, I'm deliciously warm.

He carries me past the barn to a long building on the opposite side. It's a newer structure, although everything is in perfect repair here, and I can see the light is already on inside. He carries me over the threshold and places me on a table just inside. The door shuts and we're in total silence.

It's warm, a wood stove crackling on the far side. The floor is cement and I follow it with my eyes to the left end of the long structure. There I can make out an anvil and a forge in the darkness. That side is darker and I feel the cold radiating from it.

I tear my eyes back to him. He opens the vents on the wood stove and fire blazes. Pausing before me, he pulls the blanket around my body and takes a thermos from the bag over his shoulder. He shakes it once, flips the lid, and fills it with steaming coffee. I hold out my hand eagerly, but he keeps it back.

"Ask for it, redbird," he says.

I feel a faint heat creep over my cheeks. "May I please have some coffee?"

He shakes his head. "What do you call me?"

I want to squirm. This is so embarrassing.

"May I please have coffee, sir?" I correct.

He dips his head and puts the cup in my hands. "Good girl. You're bright and quick. This month should be easy."

I hope it is for my sake. I snuggle back against the wall, crossing my legs on the wooden table, and cradle the coffee in my hands. He strips down to his Henley and pushes the sleeves up to his forearms.

I have to curb my stare because....goddamn. He has nice arms and every time he takes them out, my brain goes empty.

He goes to the far side of the room where he takes a long, wide strip of leather from a plastic box. There's a set of cubicles on the wall beside me and his eyes skim them. Then he takes out what looks like a scalpel and lays the leather out flat on the table.

"You're pretty handy," I venture.

"How do you mean?" His eyes don't lift as he takes a thin measuring tape out.

"I didn't know you could work with leather," I say. "What are you making?"

"Everything you'll need," he says. "Today we're working on the cuffs for your wrists."

I stare at him, heat creeping down my spine. He glances up and our eyes lock. Electricity crackles in the dim blacksmith shop.

"I thought you'd buy those," I whisper.

He shakes his head. "Custom is better. More comfortable. Hold out your hand, redbird."

"Yes, sir." I'm surprised by how easily the words slip from my lips.

This time, he doesn't praise me, he just takes my hand and wraps the measuring tape around my wrist.

There's something thrilling about him winding it around my wrist. I glance up, but he's unbothered. He takes multiple measurements and scrawls them across a piece of brown paper. His handwriting is neat and he's left handed, so he writes from above. The veins on the back of his hand shift and I squeeze my thighs together.

His gaze flicks over me. "Alright, redbird?"

I nod, biting my lip. His eyes drop and linger on my mouth, and I feel like I'm in a spotlight. Nervous, I take a sip of warm coffee and cough as the acrid taste fills my mouth.

"That's strong," I manage.

His mouth twitches. "I'll let you teach me how you like it next time."

"I like a lot of cream and sugar," I say.

"However you like it is how you'll have it."

He takes up his pencil. I watch him put marks on the leather in silence. Occasionally, he uses a clear plastic tool like a ruler to keep the lines clean. I lean my temple against the wall and sip my thick coffee, trying not to grimace.

"What do you like, redbird?" he asks out of nowhere.

I stare at him, unsure what he means. "Like...to do?"

He nods.

"Well, I didn't have a lot of time for hobbies," I admit. "But when I was a girl, I loved riding. I had a bay mare my father gave me and he used to let me ride the perimeter of the ranch to check it sometimes."

"Your father gave you a lot of freedom?"

I shake my head. "My mother died in a car accident a week after I was born. He was pretty scared for me most of the time."

His head jerks up and his lips part. There's a long awkward silence and then he clears his throat.

"Sorry for your loss," he says gruffly.

Did I upset him? He goes right back to tracing leather like his strange reaction never happened.

"Go on," he says.

"I...um...I went riding a lot. After I got married, my horse died. Just from old age. I asked Clint for another horse, but he said it was a frivolous expense."

His brow raises, but he stays silent.

"I really liked riding," I muse. "I used to take my horse up to the mountain ridges behind Stowe Farms in the morning and come back at night. My father gave me a gun for my tenth birthday to protect myself against cougars. And men, probably. He'd let me go out as long as I came back by five."

His jaw works. "Can't say I'll give you that much freedom. But I'll give you Angel."

I sit up straighter. "Really?"

103

"You want her, she's yours."

I blink, staring at the firm press of his mouth. I wish he'd joke and smile, but he's as hard as the packed earth beneath the field grass in summertime.

"What about a gun?" I say daringly.

He turns his head, glancing at me with those winter-blue eyes. "Now what would you do with a gun, redbird?"

I shrug. "Protect myself."

He goes back to cutting the leather. "You have me. No one will hurt you when you're under my protection."

There's an undercurrent of possessiveness in his voice. I'm not sure if he even realizes it, but I hear it for a second. His shoulders have been tense since I told him how my mother died. I see a glimpse of the man who held me back from running into my burning house.

"What do you like to do?" I ask, trying to change the subject.

"I like riding too," he says slowly. "I like making money. I like fucking you. Palm out."

I obey and he measures a cut out strip of leather around my wrist. He nods and I pull back.

"What do you want your safeword to be?" he asks abruptly.

Off guard, I stare at him, but I can't think of a single word I'd feel comfortable shouting out during sex. I know a little bit about safewords, and I know they have to be something unusual. But I don't want to pick something ridiculous.

"Um...any suggestions?" I ask.

"We can't use red because you're my redbird," he says. "How about crimson?"

I nod. That feels different enough, but not embarrassing. "That's good to me."

"Have you been physically punished before?" he asks. "Do you have any places you don't want me to touch like that?"

I shake my head, blushing. "I don't think so, sir."

"Why were you scared of Clint? Did he hit you?"

The way he changes subjects gives me whiplash. I blink, shaking my head hard.

"No, he didn't. He said I was lucky that he never put his hands on me and I think that was his way of threatening me. Reminding me he could hurt me if he wanted to."

"You still haven't answered my question. Why did he scare you?"

I take a quick breath and set the empty coffee cup aside. "I was worn down. I hated when he'd get angry because he'd shout and get in my space. Sometimes he'd grab my hair. He never hit me, but he made my life hell when I crossed him. I was just tired, and I did wonder sometimes if he would snap."

He's silent, the way he always is when I reveal something less than savory about my late husband. I realize that outside of me, Clint and Gerard were barely civil. Friends, never. Business partners maybe, but there's clearly no love lost between them.

"I'm glad he didn't," he says. "Hold your palm up."

Timidly, I obey. He moves closer and I have to force myself not to clench my fist. His hand comes up and his rough fingertips trace over the lines by my thumb. His touch is light and it sends a shiver down my spine.

"You have calluses," he says. "You shouldn't have to work."

"Why?" I frown.

He cocks his head. "You're too pretty to be anything but a plaything."

It's not the most misogynist thing I've heard from a man out here in the male-dominated hills of Montana, but it still lifts my brows. Then I remember that it's training month, and I can't tell if this is him...or if this is my Dom.

I'm struggling with that part of the contract. When does it start and when does it end? Is this him or is this him in his role?

I swallow and my dry lips part. Truthfully, I don't know how to play these games.

"Thank you," I whisper. "Sir."

He growls, deep in his chest. His hand curls around the back of my neck and he pulls me in. His mouth contacts mine and my entire body lights up. Lava floods my veins and gathers deep in my pussy. Everything tingles, down to the soles of my feet.

He tastes so good that I follow his mouth when he pulls back. Hungry for more.

"That's my girl," he says. "You're learning."

My chest glows at the praise. So I guessed right. We are playing.

He sets the tools aside and pulls me close to the edge of the table. "Lean back on your elbows and spread your thighs."

I hesitate. His head cocks.

"What are you going to do?"

A muscle in his cheek twitches. "Did you or did you not sign that contract?"

Dry mouthed, I nod and obediently lean back. Resting on my elbows and letting my knees fall apart. Without breaking eye contact, he tugs my sweatpants down around my knees.

Cool air washes over my legs and bumps rise on my skin. I'm not sure if they're from the cold or from the way he's looking at me.

He strips my pants off and rolls my socks up to my knees. His firm hands grip my thighs over the cuffs.

My heart hammers. It's been a few years since I've been on the receiving end of oral. And I was telling him the truth when I said I hadn't enjoyed it. Clint was rough and impatient. Trying to come from his tongue had been a uniquely frustrating experience.

Gerard presses my thighs apart. He leans in and his hot breath washes over my sex. My hands clench and my heart flutters.

His other hand slides up, gripping the back of my neck. He's so big he can lift me across his forearm and eat me out at the same time. I sink into his grip. His hot breath scorches me and his tongue skims over my pussy.

Oh.

This isn't in the same universe as what I've experienced before. He licks the outer edge of my sex and heat explodes. I have no anxiety about this the way I did the few times Clint did it. My brain is empty and the only place I can feel anything is between my legs.

My inner muscles clench. Wetness trickles into the cold air.

"Fuck, redbird," he breathes.

All I can do is moan.

The tip of his tongue forces inside me. My hips buck, but he holds me down. Pushing his tongue into my sensitive opening almost an inch. Making my eyes widen and a whimper force its way up.

I want to grip his hair and ride his face. But I have a pretty good idea of our dynamic and we're not there yet. I know what he's doing and I'm determined to pass his test. To show him I can be good for him.

I hold perfectly still. The sight of this big man, musclebound shoulders bent, face buried between my legs is enough to make me come. I hold off, trying to relax and breathe the orgasm back.

He's too good at this. That itch of pleasure that signals my impending orgasm grows unbearable.

"I'm...I need to finish," I whisper, barely audible.

"No," he says.

A spark of annoyance moves through my chest and I squash it down. He spits on his fingers and eases one—the middle—into me. My eyes roll back. It fills me so well and I find my hips working. Riding his hand as his tongue laps over my swollen clit.

Oh God, I'm so close I can barely breathe. My hand flies up, bracing on the wall. My other hand grips his hair before I know what I'm doing.

He pulls back like I've burned him.

"Palms flat on the table," he says.

He's not angry, but I see that he's dropping a boundary. Like a dog raising its hackles. Right away, I plant my hands on the table.

"Yes, sir," I whisper.

"Good," he says. "Tell me when you're right on the edge. Understood?"

I nod hard, desperate for his tongue on my pussy and the rasp of his jaw on the inside of my thigh. He goes back to work and I practically purr.

His fingers stroke that sweet spot inside me. His tongue moves in slow circles. Silence falls except for the wet sound of his fingers and my heavy breaths.

He brings me closer and closer. Working my pussy the way he works his cock. Decisively, with perfect rhythm, like he knows what the fuck he's doing.

Clearly he does because it barely takes any time for pleasure to surge. Helpless, I feel myself riding the wave higher. My fingers tighten on the table, knuckles going white.

"I'm going to come," I gasp.

He pulls away. One second I'm right at the edge of the best orgasm I've ever had, and the next, I'm empty and throbbing with need. He steps back and wipes his fingers on a rag and puts my pants back on.

I stare, shattered.

"What was what?" I whisper.

He lays the leather down, bending to make sure the lines are even. The scalpel-like blade slices through it and leaves a clean cut behind. He holds it up and I can see he's pleased with it.

"When I tell you to do something, do you hesitate?" he asks.

He's so calm. I shake my head quickly. Am I being punished?

His jaw tightens. "No, sir."

I catch on, sitting up. "No, sir. I'm not supposed to hesitate."

"That's correct," he says, glancing at me. Ice blue eyes flicking over me. "I'm not angry, I'm pleased. You're a good girl, but you need training."

I stay quiet because I'm feeling something new and overwhelming. The truth is...I like this dynamic. It feels secure, despite me having no control other than my safewords.

For the first time in years, I feel like a person again. Not just a machine that spits out free labor. And I know the bar is low, but it means a lot to me, what he's doing this morning.

No one has ever given me their undivided attention before.

The only downside is...God, I want to come so badly. I'd get down on my knees and beg for an orgasm, but I know I won't get it. He's laid down a boundary. I'm learning he's not the sort of man who concedes his ground.

"I'm sorry," I say.

"I know," he replies. "I'm almost done here for the day. You'll have breakfast, then spend some time unpacking what I purchased for you upstairs. I'll meet you at noon."

My stomach flutters and he notices my flushed cheeks. The corner of his mouth turns up. He's so sexy, in a gruff, masculine way, and when he smiles, I see his humanity.

Like he wasn't always thirty-eight, scarred, tattooed, and encircled in walls.

"Why? What happens at noon?" I whisper.

"I'm going to edge you again," he says.

I can't bite back the noise of disappointment in my throat.

His eyes flash. "You'll learn how to behave," he says, not unkindly. "Tonight, if you are good for the rest of the day, I'll let you come as many times as you want."

CHAPTER FOURTEEN

GERARD

I leave her at the breakfast table later that morning and meet Westin at the truck. I've known Westin for two decades, he's my right hand, and he's fully aware of everything going on with Keira. We're as close as brothers—his family is my family.

He puts away his horse and joins me in the truck, reaching for my thermos of hot coffee. Steam rises off the top and he leans back, stretching his legs out. I don't need him to evaluate the ranch, but I'd like a witness for our visit to Thomas Garrison's farm.

"Fuck-all cold for September," he says.

We pull out onto the road and head towards Garrison Ranch. My head is cloudy with what I did to Keira in the blacksmith shop. It's been a long time since I went down on a woman, but I know what I felt is different.

My cock twitches in my pants. I shift and clear my throat, glancing up to see the faint trail of smoke still rising over the hills.

"Are you gonna keep missing morning chores?" Westin asks.

"I was with Keira," I say.

"Could have guessed," he laughs.

We don't talk until we're pulling up in front of Garrison Ranch. Westin swings out and his boots hit the gravel as he settles his hat on his head. I circle the truck and follow him up the remainder of the drive.

The barn is gutted. We're both silent as we circle the house and meet by the still intact front porch.

"The house isn't bad," Westin says, resting his hands on his hips. "It looks like the part that burned was probably the original farmhouse. You can see the seam there."

I follow his gaze and nod. It's clear the house was once an older farmhouse with sizable additions built onto the southern and western sides. The burnt portion is the older part. It looks like the fire flickered out, perhaps due to flame resistant materials in the newer side.

Westin loiters around the side and I head up the porch. The front door creaks open as I step into the hallway. Everything smells of smoke and my eyes smart. I take my bandanna and pull it over the bottom half of my face, lowering the rim of my hat.

I move through the charred portion to the untouched upstairs. The first room is clearly made up for guests with a crisp quilt and no sign of dust. I glance over it, impressed. Miss Garrison was quite the homemaker.

I hear Westin downstairs on his phone and I lean over to look out the hall window. He's standing with one foot against the truck tire, a cigarette hanging from his mouth.

Good, I want to be alone right now.

My boots creep along the floor and carry me to the largest room on the second floor. I push the door open and stop short.

It's clearly the room she shared with Clint. But she hasn't changed anything. He's been dead for seven months and his boots are still behind the door. His flannel is hanging over the chair in the corner.

Like that motherfucker was going to walk in here at any moment.

I enter the room and shut the door and flick the lock.

Despite the smoke, there's a faint feminine scent. I run my fingertips over the end of her side of the bed. Up to her pillow and lift it, bringing it to my face. Sweet like pomegranate shampoo. My cock twitches again, and this time I reach down and adjust it.

The bedside table is made of cedar. Over it hangs a painting of bluebells that match the embroidered blue flowers of the bedspread. There's a lamp and a short stack of books on top. I pick one up and flip it over. It's a diary with a strip of leather tying it closed and a pen tucked underneath. I untie it and skim through the pages, but they're empty.

She never wrote anything in it.

I push the diary in my back pocket and pull her bedside drawer open. There's a makeup purse, a bottle of lotion, and a velvet drawstring bag. I open it and my brows lift.

Inside is a pink, rose shaped vibrator.

Arousal surges down my spine. She laid here on her back with her legs spread. Her slender fingers held this toy to her clit and her hips bucked as pleasure tore through them. I pull the blankets down, revealing the fitted sheet.

There's a faint stain, right at hip level.

I'm so hard my eyes swim. This is the bed she shared with her husband, maybe the bed she'd lost her virginity in on her birthday. When she was too young to be used like that.

But it's also the bed she slept in alone for the last several months.

Blood surges. I fucking hate that I wasn't the first man to have her. It should have been my name she cried out all along. I shouldn't care because she's mine now and she'll never walk away, but I do because I'm a jealous motherfucking bastard.

I unzip my pants and take my cock out.

My hands wrap around my erection and my fist grips her vibrator. How many times did she push her pretty, tight cunt against it and come? Was that stain from lubricant or had she squirted hard enough to soak the sheets?

I brace my knee on the bed. I'm primed from eating her out this morning and it takes less than a minute for pleasure to shoot down my spine. Cum explodes from my cock and hits the bed she shared with her husband. Soaking over the stain she left from pleasuring herself.

My head spins. My cock tingles as I push it back into my pants and fasten my belt.

I have good, solid reasons to hate every member of the Garrison family, but I've always hated Clint the most. I hope that whatever part of hell he's burning in, he knows I fucked his wife.

I hope he knows I'm about to go home and edge her until she cries.

There's still water in the pipes so I wash up in the bathroom. Then I toss her vibrator and leave with nothing but her diary in my pocket.

Back in the truck, Westin is having another cigarette. He hangs up the phone as I approach and yanks open the truck door.

"That was the cleaning crew," he says. "They can be out Thursday."

I nod, settling in the front seat and pull back onto the road. We have a few hours left and I need to go see one of my least favorite people.

"Can I ask you a question?" Westin says, rubbing his stubbled jaw.

"Sure," I say, not looking over.

"Is this girl just about revenge?" he says slowly. "Or is this something more?"

I simmer on that for a minute even though I know the answer. My redbird belongs to me. She has since the night we first met in her husband's office, whether she knows it or not.

But I can't deny she's uniquely situated to be part of my revenge as well.

"Why?" I ask.

"Because this could get ugly," he says.

I trust Westin's opinion, but I also recognize that he's not me. He doesn't live with this burning anger in his body. He's never felt the deep sting of injustice the way I have for most of my life. He's never watched the people he hates take everything from him.

And he's not fucked up for the redheaded Garrison girl in my bed.

My knuckles go white on the steering wheel. I take a beat to sort through my thoughts.

"I'll handle this part of my business," I say.

"I get it," Westin says. "Just don't hurt yourself. You've got enough scars as it is, Sovereign."

He never calls me by my first name, most of the men who work for me don't. When we were boys, he called me Gerry. Then, after everything went to hell, he found me in a bar one night trying to drink myself to death, and something changed.

"Come on, Sovereign," he said. "Let's get it together."

I didn't realize it then, but he was giving a new name for a fresh start. He took me to a motel and cleaned me up. The next morning, he bought me breakfast and marched me downtown to the basement of a church in South Platte. I was at rock bottom so I went along with it because it couldn't get any worse.

"My name is Sovereign," I said. "I'm an alcoholic."

Westin stuck by me for the next few months. He cleaned me up and took me back to his mother's house. There I recovered and paid my bills by working on their ranch. After two years of hard labor alongside Westin, his father offered us a plot of land that bordered the Garrison Ranch. Westin was adamant he didn't want to manage a ranch, but I accepted it without question. I didn't have anything to fall back on the way he did, this was my one chance to make something of myself.

I'd never had anyone believe I was anything but trash before that. Westin finally agreed to work alongside me, so long as he didn't have to bear the brunt of management. I leapt at the chance to build something, to finally have a piece of land to call my own. From that small plot, we created Sovereign Mountain Ranch. The wealthiest cattle and quarter horse operation in the state of Montana.

Westin told me to forgive and forget what the Garrison family had done to me, but I couldn't. They'd destroyed my family and one day, I would return the favor. If it took me until I was eighty, I'd wait until the opportune moment to strike back.

Then I met Keira Garrison and suddenly everything felt urgent.

I was at peace with eating my revenge ice cold, but not with leaving her with that man.

My thoughts carry me in a haze down the road. We pull up before Thomas Garrison's ranch and I cut the engine. My pistol is at my hip, where it always is regardless of where I'm going or what I'm doing. I flip the holster strap open—just in case—and get out of the truck.

A sheepdog bursts around the side of the house and yaps at me. The screen door creaks open and Thomas's wife steps out. She's in jeans and a white t-shirt and I see Westin's eyes linger on her curves. Westin used to date her a while back, but then Thomas swooped in and got to her first. She's a pretty thing with curly blonde hair and sharp, brown eyes.

She has a scowl on her face. "What are you doing on my land, Sovereign?" she snaps.

Westin swings out of the truck and lifts his hand to me. "Hold on, I believe this is earth I've plowed. Let me handle this."

Oh, this will be good.

Westin moves up to the bottom of the steps. The sheepdog bounces at his mistress's feet, aching for a chance at him.

"Where's your husband?" Westin drawls.

She jerks her head towards the barn. "He just got in. What do you want?"

"We want to talk with him," he says, tilting his head. "Nothing you should worry about, darling."

Her jaw tightens. "Don't call me darling unless you want to lose your fucking balls, Westin Quinn."

I cock my head, squinting through the sun. Westin plays it straight in most areas, but he's got no respect for the Garrison brothers. He'd just as soon fuck one of their wives for no reason other than to kick the hornet's nest.

Given my current circumstance, I can't say I'm any better.

Through the barn door, I catch sight of the youngest Garrison, Thomas. He's the least guilty in my eyes because he was young when everything went to shit, but he's got their blood in his veins. And now he's put a black mark on his record by burning down my woman's house.

He sees us and his eyes narrow. All the Garrison brothers have tall faces, sandy hair, and gray eyes. Thomas still looks like a teenager even though he's in his twenties, and he already has the glitter of a bully in his gaze.

"What you doing on my fucking land, Sovereign?" he barks.

"Wait in the truck," I say.

Westin puts his hands on his hips. "Don't do anything you regret."

I cross the yard to the barn and a few feet from Thomas. Every time I see one of their faces, it sends my mind back to every dark memory I have. There's always been a Garrison involved, from my first experience with death, to cheating, and back to death again.

My muscles are tight up my spine.

"I've been out to Clint's ranch," I say.

"Yeah? That right?" His eyes narrow. He spits to the side. "That Stowe slut still living out there?"

Anger tears through me like a wildfire, but I keep my face impassive.

"No, Keira is with me," I say.

He freezes and he's not as good as I am at hiding anger. It flashes over his face like a thunderclap. It takes him a moment to get control of it. Then he shrugs.

"Hope you like Clint's leftovers," he says.

I fit my hat back on my head. "If you come around her ranch again, I'll shoot you. She's under my protection on Sovereign Mountain. I own her, just like I own more than half your family's motherfucking land."

He's trying to goad me into talking about her body, but that's between me and her now. The fact she slept with my enemy means nothing to me anymore. Not after the way she cried and came when I fucked her in my bed the first time.

But I won't talk to Thomas Garrison about my woman's body. If I had my way, I'd cut out his tongue to keep her name from his mouth.

I cross the yard and pull open the truck door. "Stay off her land. I've got people watching it."

He flips me off. "Take your slut and her ranch. Fuck off."

He's bad at bluffing. That's why he has an ocean of debt from the casino he's concealing from his older brother. I know how hard the

Garrison brothers fought in court to contest Clint's will and keep Kiera from owning their largest plot of land. I know how much it means to them.

And I know that me fucking Clint's widow is salt in their wound.

I shut the door and turn the truck around, heading back to the main road. Westin sits beside me with his brows raised, waiting for me to talk. I keep silent for a good twenty minutes. It always takes me a while to get a handle on the hatred that flows through me when I speak to a Garrison.

"How'd it go?" Westin goes.

I clear my throat. "You should go after Diane."

"Jesus Christ," Westin mumbles. "You're crazy."

"You could do with taking a page out of my book and going after the things you want."

He glances sideways at me. There's a hint of sadness in his eyes. "I hope your past doesn't fuck up your future, Sovereign."

We're both quiet the rest of the way home.

117

CHAPTER FIFTEEN

KEIRA

Up in the bedroom closet, I find a stack of boxes and bags that weren't there yesterday. My name is written on the side of each one in black marker. I drag everything out into the middle of his room and start unpacking it all.

It's clothes, shoes, outerwear. And for some reason, a box that contains a beautiful leather bridle. My name is engraved into the underside of the browband. I run my fingers over it, hoping this isn't some kink he has because this is definitely a real bridle.

Meant for a horse. Not a person.

I set it aside and go over the clothes. Somehow, he guessed my size exactly. Or maybe he measured my body in my sleep. I shiver as I pull on a Henley and a pair of jeans, turning to admire how they hug my ass. I've always had good curves and they're finally getting appreciated. By both the jeans and Gerard.

I spin, watching my reflection in the bathroom mirror. For the first time in a while, I don't look tired. My eyes glitter and my hair is soft and falls down my back. Loose over my shoulders instead of tied up to keep it from the greasy stove.

I remind myself that this is temporary. The contract will end or one of us will want out.

At least...that's what I assume.

After some of the things he's said and done, I'm starting to question his motives and his intent.

Maybe he didn't mean for me to be just temporary fun.

But if that's the case...then what does he have planned for me?

The thought leaves me cold like the frost that gathers on his bedroom windows. I shudder and collect the bags of the clothes and drag them downstairs to the laundry room off the kitchen. Maddie helps me wash and dry them, but she barely speaks except to ask if there's anything I'd like added to the next grocery order.

I can't tell if she's just shy. Or she doesn't trust me.

I am a Garrison after all.

Upstairs, I mull it over. The empty eyes of the bull skull watch me as I fold my clothes and put them in the empty drawers of his dresser. The coats and shirts, I hang up. The panties and bras, I can't find a place for so I push his boxer briefs to one side and put them in the drawer together. There's something exciting about sharing an underwear drawer with him.

It's almost noon when I'm done. I leave the quiet bedroom and move down the hallway, turning the corner near the doorway of the game room at the far end. I've never been inside, but I know there's a hot tub on the balcony because I've seen it from the yard.

Out of nowhere, a solid wall crashes into me and I yelp. A hand covers my mouth and I'm spun around. Blue eyes meet mine as he backs me against the wall. My chest heaves, my breasts brushing the front of his shirt. Sending tingles to the soles of my feet.

We both stand frozen, then he releases my mouth.

"Gerard," I gasp. "You startled me."

The corner of his mouth twitches. "Where are you going, little girl?"

The way he says those words gets me flustered. Little girl. It falls lazily from his mouth, but there's an edge of softness that makes me want to lean in and beg for a kiss. He always tastes so good when he comes in from outside. Like winter and fresh air.

"Down to lunch." My voice is a whisper.

His hand slides down my outer thigh and up the seam of my jeans. Heat curls in my lower belly.

"Down to lunch, sir," he corrects. "Address me properly when we're alone."

I nod, but I'm so distracted I can't think straight. My zipper hisses as he pulls it down. I'm in the panties he bought for me. Pale blue silk. He pushes his hand into my pants and his fingertips brush my clit through the fabric.

My stomach quivers. The muscles in my thighs tighten.

"What do you say?" He steps closer.

My head falls back against the wall. "Yes, sir."

He lifts his two fingers and taps my lips. I part and his big middle and pointer fingers slip into my mouth. Filling it completely. My stomach tightens and arousal floods my pussy, making the tender folds of my sex ache.

He pulls them free and my eyes shut as he pushes them under my panties. I know I'm soaked, but I'm not prepared for the heavy groan that reverberates in his chest as he slides his touch over the seam of my pussy.

"Do you need relief so badly, redbird?" he murmurs.

I nod. "Please, let me come. I'll be good."

His eyes darken. "I'll let it go this time, but don't try to change your punishments. If I'm edging you, you accept that you won't come until I say. Understood?"

Embarrassed, I nod. He can be so stern about things and I'm not sure if I like it.

"Use your words when I ask you a question." His low voice is firm.

My eyes widen. "I'm sorry, sir."

"Good girl." His tone shifts. It's huskier, lower, and it fills the air between our bodies.

I bite my lip. His fingers stroke my sensitive pussy, drawing all the blood down between my thighs. I fist my hands and let my head fall back.

I should be angry. But I'm too busy wrestling with how much I'm enjoying his denial. This is a completely different world than being

120

ignored by Clint. Gerard is denying me, but he's not withdrawing his closeness. I feel safe that he won't reject or hurt me. It's such a new feeling and it takes my breath away.

He slides his middle finger over my clit again and again. My hips ride up against his hand.

"Oh," I gasp. My stomach goes tight and I feel myself about to fall.

He pulls back and licks his fingers and draws my pants back up. The air between us feels like a brewing storm. Thick and sultry. My God, I'd let him push that enormous cock into me and fuck me however he wants if he'd just give me some relief.

His brows are lowered in thought. He takes something from his back pocket and holds it out.

I take it, realizing with a jolt that it's my diary. The empty one my father gave me, the one I never had anything good enough to fill it with.

"I want you to use this as your diary," he says.

I chew my lip, unsure how I feel about that. "My father gave me this."

He shrugs once. "It's just a book. Paper and empty lines."

I nod, but I'm not entirely sure. I've always been good at putting my feelings into a box and burying them deep inside. This empty book has sat in my bedside table for years. Is now really the time to mark the pristine pages?

The last time I considered writing in it was on my wedding day. Now I'm grateful I didn't taint the pages with my disaster of a marriage. My fingers close on the book and I make up my mind to leave it for now. I have time to decide.

"You went to my house," I say.

He nods. "I needed to assess the damage."

He heads down the hallway and I follow him, my legs still wobbly. I'm soaked between my thighs, but I do my best to ignore it.

"Is it bad?" I ask.

He doesn't answer. We descend the staircase and enter the large dining room accessible via a doorway below the loft stairs. I'm taken aback for a second, looking around at the huge table packed with men. I scan the rows, hoping to see another woman, but it's all testosterone as far as the eye can see.

Clint had the same set up. All the men who worked on his farm ate in the dining room for breakfast, lunch, and dinner. They lived in on-site housing and I was expected to cook and clean for the endless people streaming through the ranch house.

All at once, I realize I'm in the wrong place. I draw back, clutching the book to my chest.

"I'm going to go," I say.

He frowns, pivoting on his heel. "Where?"

"I'll eat in the kitchen with Maddie," I say, frowning.

Is he expecting me to eat with the men?

"Maddie doesn't eat in the kitchen. She sets the food out and then she eats with her husband in their lodging," he says. He's still looking at me with that heavy crease across his forehead.

"Oh," I say, looking around. I notice that a few dozen of the men are staring at me curiously. I back up to the doorway and he follows me, blocking their view.

"I didn't give you permission to leave," he says. "Where did you eat at Garrison Ranch?"

"In the kitchen," I say.

"And before that?"

I'm so uncomfortable I'm squirming. "With my father in the dining room."

"Then you'll do the same here."

He takes my hand and leads me through the room to the table on the far end. I notice the man from the other night who cooled down Shadow.

He glances up and waves. Gerard ushers me to a seat beside him.

The man leans over and extends his hand. "Westin Quinn."

I shake it. He's got calluses like Gerard. They probably all do.

"Mrs. Keira Garrison," I say.

His brows shoot up and he glances at Gerard. He's gathering up our plates and turning to head to the buffet table. I jump to my feet to help and he shoots me a look that's so hard and commanding I sit back down at once.

"How well do you know Sovereign?" Westin asks.

It takes me a second to realize he means Gerard. "Not well. I was surprised he wanted me to come stay here."

He laughs. "All roads lead to Sovereign Mountain."

I'd heard the phrase before. It was never a good thing. It usually implied desperation and unwillingness. I glance over the room and the atmosphere feels relaxed, everyone seems well fed and happy. Maybe the distrust the people in town feel towards Sovereign Mountain is unwarranted.

Gerard returns and places a plate of thick stew poured over mashed potatoes and a slice of bread before me. It smells amazing and the roasted meat is so tender it's falling apart. He hands me a fork and sets a drink down. Then he sits.

"So how bad is the house?" I ask.

"It'll need cleaned and the older portion repaired," says Westin.

"Did you go?" I ask.

He nods. "The house is salvageable. The barn will need rebuilt."

Gerard shoots him a look and he falls silent. I wonder if he said something I wasn't supposed to know, or if Gerard is just territorial. They both eat in silence so I clean my plate because I'm starving. It's been hours since the egg on toast I had at breakfast.

I've always lived with men, watching them like they're zoo animals. Wondering what it would feel like to have been born with the kind of confidence they have to take on the world.

No fear. That sounds like heaven.

Our pocket of Montana is a wild place. My father taught me I was worth the same as a man, but he never shied away from telling me I'd have had an easier life if I'd been born male. He taught me to ride and shoot, to defend myself, but I'm still half the size of most of the men in this room.

If I didn't have Gerard Sovereign for protection, I'd be a deer among starving wolves.

CHAPTER SIXTEEN

GERARD

She's so desperate that night when I flip her onto her back and spread her legs, she gives in without saying a word. Her thighs clench when I dip my head to kiss her lower belly, she shudders and strains up towards my mouth.

I can smell how wet she is.

It's the first time I've gone down on her in bed. There's something luxurious about it. Outside, the wind howls through the trees. Inside, we're warm, and there's nowhere to be on a night like this but in bed together.

She sits up against the pillows and I push my face into her lap. Her pussy is so soft—I'm not used to things as soft and fine as her—and she builds slowly as I lick her clit. Her long fingers with her oval nails play with my hair and trace the tattoos and scars on my shoulders. The taste of her is sweet and I want it on my tongue forever.

Her toes curl and her thighs clench when she comes.

"Oh God," she gasps.

She lays in bed afterwards and watches me undress. Her head is propped up on the heel of her hand and her eyes are distant. I wonder where she goes when she's quiet like this. When I lay down with her, she shifts close and tentatively leans over.

I kiss her and her lower back arcs in. The taste of her mouth and the pomegranate scent of her shampoo fills my senses, reminding me I haven't come. When I pull back, she follows my mouth. Hungry for more.

I fucking love the way she wants it.

Her hand wraps around my cock. Her fingers don't meet as she starts jerking me off. Our eyes lock and I brush back her hair to kiss her again. Pleasure moves down my spine and before I can come on my stomach, I flip her onto her back and push the tip of my cock against the entrance of her pussy. I let out a low groan as I come. Filling her, putting my cum where it belongs.

She's flushed when I pull back. When she moves to get up, I take her wrist and pull her back down.

"No, you leave it inside you," I say quietly.

She's flustered, pink cheeked, but not displeased. Her body curls up against my chest and I pull the blankets up to her chin.

The next morning, Westin and I get up earlier than usual and take the truck to Garrison Ranch. The sun is still cresting the mountains when I swing out of the truck and cross the driveway. Jensen, the head of the local construction crew of South Platte, breaks off from a group of his men and heads over.

"How's it look?" Westin asks, coming up behind me.

Jensen pivots and waves a hand at the barn. "That's all fucked. But the house is mostly fine except for the back section. Are you wanting us to tear that away and build onto it? Or do a restoration project?"

I squint, taking in the scarred exterior of the Garrison house.

"Restoration...right?" Westin glances at me.

I shake my head. "Tear it down."

We circle the house and Jensen kicks at the charred back stoop. "What are you thinking you'll put in its place?"

"I don't mean tear down the damaged part," I say. "I mean, tear the entire building down."

They both reel back and stare at me, but I'm already circling the barn. Taking in the piles of charred wood, ash, and melted equipment.

"Sovereign," Westin says, appearing at my elbow. "You might want to think about this before you do something like that."

I glance up. "I own the mortgage. It's my house."

He steps in front of me, eyes narrowed. "It's Keira Garrison's house. If you do this, she'll have nothing to go back to."

"I know," I say.

His jaw squares. Jensen appears beside him. Neither of them seem surprised by my announcement, but I can tell it's not sitting right.

"Any sign of her horses?" I start walking around the rubble and head to the edge of the yard. The hills behind the house are quiet. The day after the fire, I moved her cattle into my pastures and put her people on my paycheck. All the worker housing sits empty.

"Nope," says Jensen, leaning on the fence. His hat comes down low, shielding his eyes as the sun cuts over the mountain. "Are you sure you want us to tear this place down? It's worth a lot."

"I can eat the cost," I say.

"But...can she?" Westin asks.

I turn, crossing my arms over my chest. "She's in debt over her head. The only way she gets to keep anything is if I let her. She's already fucked."

"So your solution is fuck her too?" Westin says, appearing on my other side.

I push off the fence, adjusting my hat lower to keep the sun from my eyes. "My solution is to keep her alive."

They shut up right away. Both of them know me and they know what I've been through. They also know how evil the Garrison brothers can be. Jensen brings me the paperwork and I spread it out on the hood of the truck. Westin lights a cigarette and I hear them talking as I go over each piece and sign my name.

I'm leaving a paper trail.

It's not like she has anywhere to go if she finds out.

The drive back to Sovereign Mountain is quiet. Westin has a short span of attention and better things to do than try to persuade me my behavior is immoral. He jumps out of the truck when we get back and heads to the barn. I take my hat off and walk around the yard to the pasture where we keep Angel. Hoping for a glimpse of red hair.

She's inside the paddock. Leaning on the fence with her cheek against the top rung. Big Dog is sleeping on the ground and she offers me a glance without raising her head.

I draw up to the other side and Keira jumps. Her expression shifts as I lean in and kiss her forehead. When did she stop looking at me with wariness? Because right now her sky blue gaze feels like warm sunshine.

"How's it going?" I ask.

She nods, smiling. "Really good. We've just been doing laps around the paddock."

Angel nickers, throwing her head. I send her a look to let her know I'm onto her—I've worked with this horse and I know she's a menace. She's more like me than I care to admit.

Keira turns and rests her hands on the fence. The way she's looking up with her fiery hair falling down her back is doing things to me. My palm is itching to slide up her face and brush her waves back.

"Where'd you go today?" she asks brightly.

"Your place. We're working on handling the damage to the house," I say.

"Again?"

I nod. "Last time I stopped by your brother-in-law's place on the way back."

"Which one?" Her face falls. "Why?"

"Thomas. I went to warn him I don't want any Garrisons on your land."

"*Your* land," she says flatly.

"We'll see, redbird. The world changes fast."

Her eyes dart up. "Sometimes I don't understand you."

I slide my hand around the back of her neck, pull her close, and kiss her over the fence. Her breath hitches and she moans in her throat. She likes being kissed, maybe just as much as being fucked. Her entire body melts and I feel her blood pump fast in her veins.

When I break away, she's flushed and her eyes are glassy.

"You don't have to understand me," I say. "Everything, all in good time."

I leave her there and go inside to wash my face up in my bathroom. My shirt is damp with sweat despite the cold and I strip it off. From outside, I can hear Angel nickering and thundering in her paddock. Big Dog lays by the gate, always at her side.

I go to the window, wiping my hands and forearms on a towel. Keira stands at the center and Angel trots in a circle, the lead attached to her halter.

She's making progress.

They both are.

CHAPTER SEVENTEEN

KEIRA

I've saved this diary for years hoping for something significant enough to happen that I can write in it. Yesterday morning, I was sitting in the window watching the smoke rise from the chimneys where Gerard's staff live. It was cold enough that bits of frost covered the edges of the window glass. There was a redbird in the tree. I could hear laughter from the barn.

Maybe what I need isn't a cataclysmic event. I've had enough of those in my life. Maybe I've been waiting for life to slow down so I can see it well enough to put it on this page.

He's going to read this. That makes me uncomfortable, but I promised to be honest. The truth is, I haven't had a moment to slow down since I was a child. Every day was just another notch in the tumbling of seasons around the calendar.

I'm safe here, for however long I stay or he chooses to keep me. So far the sex has been a small price to pay for my protection. He's gentle when he chooses to be and when he doesn't, it's the sweetest storm.

It scares me, but not the way Clint scared me. I've never met a man who lives with the same intensity as Gerard. He's a mountain, a force of nature. And if he's reading this right now, that's not always a good thing—so don't let it get to your head, sir.

I think what surprises me most about this arrangement isn't the sex or the man, it's that I haven't wanted to leave Sovereign Mountain once since I came here.

I've never been safe before. I could get used to this.

I just wish I knew what happens next.

CHAPTER EIGHTEEN

KEIRA

The days inch by at a snail's pace. Maybe time is slow because I'm so used to being busy. Other than working with Angel, my only tasks are to wear the clothes he picks out for me and fuck him at night.

I'm not keeping track of the days as they inch by. My phone sits unused in my dresser drawer. There's hardly any signal at Sovereign Mountain and I have no one to text or call. The internet works almost never. The realization that I just disappeared from the world is sobering. I had friends in school, but after my father died and I dropped out to live with the Garrisons, they'd faded into the distance.

Gerard sleeps next to me, but he hasn't fucked me since he ate me until I came. Sometimes he'll push his fingers into my panties and stroke my pussy absently. At night, I wake and he's got his palm over it. Holding the heat of my sex in his hand.

During the day, he works outside the house. Occasionally he has to do something in his office that's just off the bedroom, but he hasn't invited me in, so I don't ask.

I start to see the patterns of Sovereign Mountain. He runs the whole thing, the sun rises and sets with him. Westin is his right hand and advisor. They always confer in the driveway in the early morning. Both standing in the cold in their flannels and jackets, steam rising from their lips. Billowing out beneath the brims of their hats. Then they part ways and the ranch runs smoothly for another day.

I hold up my end of the bargain. I obey him, I say yes sir and no sir. Shyly, I start offering him sex or oral at the end of the day. He praises me, but he doesn't fuck me as often as I anticipated he would.

What are we waiting for?

Then, all at once, the structures of our dynamic come into focus. I'm in the bedroom, late one night, under the covers with a book I pulled from the shelf downstairs. It's a war memoir. Maybe it's too heavy for before bed, but it pulls me in even though I don't usually read nonfiction. I'm heavy eyed when I finally set it aside and reach for my cup of water.

The door opens and Gerard enters. He locks it, as he always does.

"What is it?" I ask.

"It's Sunday night," he says.

At first, I'm not sure what that means. Then it floods back to me and my cheeks explode with heat. There's no sound but the gas fireplace in the corner. The great bull skull towers over us both. The air between us crackles as we stare at each other across our bed.

His bed. Not mine, I'm still a guest here.

"Okay," I manage. "What would you like me to do...sir?"

He crosses to me and sits on the edge of the bed. His rough fingers graze my chin. "You're such a good girl. But you need this, I think I haven't played with you enough this week."

"Did I do something wrong?" I ask.

"No, I'm just easing you in. My absence is never a punishment. If you need punished, you'll know right away."

I appreciate his honesty. He rises and disappears into the bathroom and I hear the shower run for a while.

He returns in nothing but a pair of sweatpants. My eyes run over his hard stomach and my sex aches at the way the waistband hangs from his hips. He's so lean there I can follow the veins down the trail of hair until it disappears.

He goes to the closet and when he returns, he carries a folded square of leather. I pull myself up against the pillow to watch him unfold it. Revealing a set of implements. They look brand new.

"Tonight, I'll use my hand," he says. "But I want you to look at those and tell me what you're willing to experiment with."

There's something so confusing and humiliating about vetting the items he's going to spank me with. I kneel beside them and pick up what appears to be a paddle and run my fingers over the handle. It's light, but long enough to be laid across my ass. I know in his hand, it'll hurt.

"Did you make these too?" I ask.

He shakes his head. "I have someone who makes them custom. Nothing I use on you has ever touched anyone else."

"What do you prefer?"

He cocks his head, picking up a ruler. It looks small in his hand. "I like the riding crop. It's good for beginners because it sounds worse than it is. The sound of it will get you wet."

I'm bright red. My stomach flutters.

"You can use it if you want," I say.

"I will when it's done. I'm making one for you."

I run my eyes over the ruler, the hairbrush, the paddle, and the thin switch. I'm unsure what to expect with them, but I'm willing to try each one before banning it.

"I'm comfortable with experimenting with any of those," I say.

He nods and rolls the leather up. Then he sets it aside and returns to the bed and sits on the edge. His gaze bores into me and I lower my eyes and realize he's rock hard. I can see his heavy length hanging in his sweatpants.

My mouth goes dry and my pussy does the opposite.

"When I spank you with my hand, it will always be over my lap on the edge of the bed," he says. "You'll remove your clothes and lay over my knees. You won't struggle or fight me. If you're good, after your maintenance spankings, you'll get to finish."

Breathless, I nod. "Yes, sir."

He extends his palm. "Go on."

133

Shakily, I get to my feet. His eyes follow my every move as I tug my sweatshirt off, leaving me in nothing but my panties. My fingers clench as I hesitate. Chewing my lip and waiting for instruction.

"You'll be spanked without padding," he says. "Panties down."

Oh God, I wish I could moan out loud. I push my soaked panties down, hoping he doesn't see the wet spot.

"Fold your clothes and lay them on the bedside table," he orders.

I obey and return to him, standing with my hands at my sides. My nipples ache. I know my cheeks are burning. There's no way he doesn't know how aroused I am.

"Come," he says.

His warm palm slides over my hip and he guides me over his lap. I settle my hips over his thighs, realizing he's too big for me to rest my elbows on the bed. I'm hanging awkwardly a few inches above the quilt. He notices and he pulls a pillow below my chest for support.

My breath comes heavy and fast. My eyes squeeze shut.

His fingers run over my bare ass. His palm rubs gently, massaging the muscles, being careful not to touch my exposed pussy.

"I want you to know that you're a good girl," he says. "This is for when you're tempted to disobey me. Do you understand?"

"I understand," I whisper. "Sir."

He caresses my ass and upper thighs. Taking his time with every inch of naked skin. I'm breathing hard and doing my best not to squirm. He said I was to keep still, so I'll do my best. His hand slides up my nape, up against my scalp, and closes. Holding my head in place by my hair.

He spanks me once. It barely stings, but I feel it in my pussy. I bite my lip.

"Good girl," he murmurs.

My brain goes blank. I can take a lot if it means he'll praise me like that. With a voice as smooth as fine, dark whiskey, edged with rough gravel beneath.

He spanks me harder this time, three times in a row. My eyes widen and I grip the pillow. He waits, like he expects me to react, but

I don't. I suck my breath in as he starts spanking me with little blows, just heavy enough to sting, but not enough to really hurt.

"Do you know your safeword?" he asks.

I nod. "Yes, sir."

His grip tightens in my hair and he spanks me hard where my left cheek meets my upper thigh. I gasp this time and my eyes water. My skin is starting to feel warm where he's striking me. But it has nothing on the heat pulsing between my legs.

He spanks both sides of my ass in rapid succession. More like quick swats, like he's trying to deny me the pleasurable thuds that send vibrations down to my clit. He's making sure it hurts before it feels good. I want to call him a sadist in my head, but if he's a sadist and I'm wet from what he's doing...does that make me a masochist?

I'm not sure I'm ready for that label yet.

My inner muscles clench and I feel my pussy leak. It drips down my sex and I know it's on his thigh. Staining his pants.

My ass is warm and I'm struggling to keep still. He doesn't let up, he just spanks me evenly on both sides again and again. The same way he fucks—without reprieve. I wish he'd given me something to bite down on because my jaw aches from clenching. My fingers grip the pillow and I force myself to focus on my white knuckles.

I can breathe through this.

My lips part and without my consent, a whimper bursts out. He goes still for a beat and I freeze. Was that the wrong thing to do?

"I'm sorry, sir," I breathe.

His palm moves over my burning ass and up my lower back. His other hand doesn't loosen in my hair, it holds my head down so I'm unable to raise my eyes higher than the pillow.

"It's alright, redbird," he says. "You may whimper. Just no backtalk."

He spanks me again, hard enough I cry out. Something thick rises in my throat and I realize it's a sob. Part of me is humiliated that I'm crying. It doesn't even hurt that badly. I've had worse period cramps in the last few months. But there's something so vulnerable about allowing him to hurt me.

It's safe.

It's pain, but not the kind I'm used to. This pain is closer to the intimacy of pleasure. Like a whisper against my throat in the dark. Like the soft thud of his hips meeting mine as he ruts into my body.

My mind latches onto the memory of the bed hitting the wall.

Thud. Thud. Thud.

Every one of his thrusts calculated to hit every inch of my inner walls. I pinch my eyes shut and I realize I'm getting used to his palm on my ass. My hot muscles are relaxing and calm rises up my spine.

Sweet, painful release.

I feel it before I realize what it is. My pussy tightens as his hand cups it, sending heavy vibrations through my lower body. My clit throbs as it contacts the rough fabric of his pants over his hard thigh. Back and forth with each spank.

One tear and then another slip from my eyes. My throat clenches and a sob bursts up. And another until I'm crying into the pillow. But I barely notice because suddenly I'm aware that I'm right on the edge of coming on his thigh. I freeze, realizing I don't know the boundaries around orgasm during punishment.

"Sir," I gasp.

He pauses. "What is it?"

I'm a ball of mortification, but I force the words out because he told me that failure to communicate was one of the worst offenses. If this is being spanked for maintenance, I'm nervous to imagine what real punishment is like.

"I'm going to come...I can't stop it, sir," I whisper.

"Fuck me," he says reverently.

His fingers graze the entrance of my cunt. His fingers feel rough on my raw flesh. He tugs my head back by the hair and slips his middle finger down to my clit. I know I stained his thigh, I can feel it.

He uses my arousal and circles my sensitive bud. Using slow, even pressure until I feel my muscles clench and spasm, releasing a well of pleasure. It's not the most tumultuous orgasm I've had, but it's the clearest.

I feel every ebb and flow of blood, every release of muscle. The blood surging through my body and culminating in my sex throbs, heightening every sensation. Etching out every bit of pleasure until I'm limp across his lap.

"That's my girl," he says.

He lifts me up and sets me on my feet. My knees wobble and I can't meet his eyes.

"Can you walk to the dresser?" he asks.

I nod, inhaling shakily.

"Go and get the bottle in the top drawer out," he orders.

I obey, bringing the small bottle of lotion to him and putting it in his outstretched palm. My arousal stings my inner thighs. The emotion in my chest is gone and all that's left is calm.

"Lay down and flip over," he says.

I do as he says and I feel his weight sink the bed behind me. Then cool lotion spreads over my ass and thighs. The relief is immediate and my eyes flicker shut as he gently rubs it in.

"Tomorrow, I want you to write in your diary," he says. "Tonight, I want you to process."

"I wrote in it already," I whisper. "But not really about sex."

"Good girl," he praises. "Write some more, leave it out for me on the desk when you're done. And write about the sex too."

I'm glad he's giving me time to understand my emotions. It was such an endorphin rush, such a wave of adrenaline. And now I'm drained of all the tightness in my chest, all the anxiety and worry that built up over the last seven months.

I nod and then remember I'm supposed to affirm him aloud.

"Yes, sir."

He shifts up behind me and pulls me back against his warm body. Being comforted by the person who just held me over his lap and spanked me is confusing. He gave me pain and now he's giving me comfort.

It's so vulnerable it makes my chest ache.

My eyes close.

I'm going to have to watch this man. Without me realizing, he's going to have my walls down faster than he got my panties around my ankles.

CHAPTER NINETEEN

GERARD

She's curled up somewhere deep in the blankets the next morning. I drag myself from the bed and get ready for the day. She must have been up during the night because the diary is on my desk. I pick it up and flip it open.

She's settling in.

A small smile tugs at the corner of my mouth.

I lay the diary where I found it. She's doing so well. I'm trying to ease her into this. I can tell she's doing everything she can to follow the rules as she understands them.

I'm proud of her, she's got the fundamental qualities that make a good submissive.

I select a pair of cotton panties and matching bra. They're simple, but they'll be so fucking sexy on her body. And my name is embroidered into the band of both. Marking my property.

She sighs when I tug the sheets down. After I spanked her pretty ass red, she fell asleep against my chest, still naked. The longer she's with me, the more feral my reaction is to seeing her bare.

I roll her onto her stomach. There are small purple and pink marks on the underside of her ass.

She stirs and I sink down onto the bed.

"Let's go, redbird," I say.

She grumbles and rubs her face into the pillow. Her eyes crack open and she stares at me through a haze.

"Are we going to the blacksmith shop?" she whispers.

"No," I say. "We're going for a ride."

That perks her up instantly. She sits up and rubs her eyes, yawning. Seeing her fully naked in my rumpled blankets is doing things to me. I'm going to have to start fucking her daily. She's had enough time to get acclimated.

"Where?"

"I have someone ride the west border and to the upper pasture every morning," I say. "Today it's my turn and I'm taking you with me."

She pauses and I lift my hand and lay it on her waist. She's got beautiful curves. I touch the line of her abdominal muscle and run my fingertip down over her lower belly to her clit. I gather her wetness and use it to stroke her. Until her breasts heave.

"Do you want me?" she whispers.

I nod. "Tonight."

She chews her lip. "I thought you would fuck me more often, sir."

She says those words with a sigh. I can't hold back a short laugh as I withdraw my hand. She's horny, and I can't blame her. I've teased her, I've made her sleep in my bed, but I haven't fucked her for almost four days.

"Did you find the bridle I left you?" I ask.

Her forehead creases. "Yes, what is that for?"

"You wanted to work with Angel so I ordered you a bridle for her," I say. "She's able to wear it, but I wouldn't try riding her yet. Give her a little longer."

"Oh," she says softly. "Thank you, sir."

"Let's go ride," I say.

She pulls on her warm clothes and boots. With the dogs at our heels, I lead the way out to the barn and she sits on a stack of hay bales and watches me tack up Shadow. He's watching her over his shoulder, his big, glassy eyes glued to the way her auburn hair glitters.

This woman has enchanted my animals. Big Dog and Small Dog follow her around the house all day. They couldn't care less when I get in at night. They're in the living room, curled up at her feet or draped over her lap. If I didn't make them sleep in the living room, they'd be trying to crawl into the bed with her. And now Shadow is staring at her like she hung the moon and stars.

Maybe they're just feeding off my energy.

I bring my secondary horse, a chestnut mare with white socks, from the back of the barn. She's big enough to carry me, but smaller than Shadow. Keira's face lights up when I lead her out.

"What's her name?" She slides to her feet and extends her palm.

"I just call her girl," I say.

That frown appears instantly. "You need to hire someone part time just to name your animals for you."

I look down at her with faint amusement. She's running her palm over the mare's neck. The horse nuzzles her head and nips at the strands of red hair over the back of her jacket. They all seem to like how her hair looks in the light of the electric lantern.

"Can I call her something different?" she asks.

Her blue eyes turn on me, wide and begging. Without thinking, I nod. Just to see that smile flash over her lips.

"Bluebell," she says, stroking down the horse's side. "We always had fields of them in the spring."

I don't protest. I watch as she brushes Bluebell down and I help tack her up. The saddle is heavy and she struggles to get it above her head. She doesn't try to get up on her own, she just lets me lift her and watches silently while I mount Shadow.

We ride to the outer yard, leaving the dogs at the barn door. The sun is just kissing the horizon, sending streaks of pale blue across the early morning sky. The air is cold, but with a promise of sunshine later. I don't trust it—I know we'll have a snowstorm before November.

The view of the western side of the ranch is breathtaking. We pause for a moment and she lets out a little sigh. I glance over and I see a new emotion on her face. It looks like freedom, like joy.

I should take her out riding with me more often.

"Have you always lived at Sovereign Mountain?" she asks.

I shift my weight and Shadow begins trekking down the slow hill. She falls into step beside me, riding easily with one hand on her thigh. The faint wind whips her hair back even though she's wearing a knit cap. I should get her a real hat to contain that brilliant hair.

"No," I say. "I'm from the east."

Her brows rise. "Really? Where?"

"Boston," I say gruffly. I don't like talking about the past.

Either she can't read social cues or she just doesn't care. She leans forward curiously, studying my face.

"Why did you come out here?"

"My parents moved out," I say. "I had aspirations to be a fighter. So I stayed."

It was true, I had trained in Colorado, but only for a year in my teens. Then I'd been shot in the thigh during a summer job back in Montana and my aspirations to box died.

She opens her mouth and I clear my throat.

"You tell me about yourself," I say.

"I already have," she says. "I don't have an interesting story."

"Tell me about your relationship to the Garrison family."

Her eyes dart to my face and she works her jaw. I can tell it's not something she wants to delve into. But I don't really care. I need to know her version of her history with the Garrison family.

"Did you know the senior Garrisons well? Abel and Maria?" I press.

She nods. "Abel was very insistent that I marry Clint. I felt that...maybe he would have kicked me out if I didn't."

Wait...what did that mean? I turn and my expression must be sharp because she notices it.

"I lived with them after my father died," she says quickly. "I worked on the ranch and they helped run Stowe Farms. We weren't

142

much of an operation, mostly unused land, by that point. When I married Clint, Garrison Ranch absorbed everything and they tore down the barn and house. It's all pasture now. And...then they died on that trip overseas. I felt really guilty about feeling relieved, but Maria was so difficult to me."

I knew most of that, but I hadn't known she was living with Clint's parents before her marriage. It was no wonder she folded so easily. The thought of it turns my stomach. She was young, not even legal, in a house full of people who wanted her property. I had no doubt Abel and Maria knew exactly what they were doing by pushing their son onto her. Not caring that she wasn't old enough to consent.

At least I had some lines I wouldn't cross. I'm not a good man, but I gave her more of a choice. And she's old enough to give full consent.

We pause as we crest the hill. The horses blow steam into the air and the sun has risen enough to see the field stretched out before us. Far away, barely visible to the eye, is the line that separates my land from the Garrison's.

"That's the border," I say, jerking my head.

Her eyes narrow. "I thought it extended further in."

"It did," I say. "But I bought it off them."

Her brows shoot up. "I can't imagine the Garrisons selling to you."

"They sold to the bank," I say. "I own the bank. And now, in the last year, I've absorbed seven thousand acres of Garrison land."

She gazes at me and her lips part. My eyes wander and I remember how soft they are. How they wrap around my fingers. How they parted in the blacksmith shop as I licked her soft pussy.

Fuck...she's a pretty thing.

My thoughts turn quickly darker. Her skin marks easily. She's delicate, but she's also sturdy from working on the farm. I could lay my belt across her ass until she bruised and she'd probably let me. This little redhead is a slut for pain, that much is obvious.

I got a taste for dominating her the other night, and now I'm hungry again. I want her tied up in my bed, ass flushed red, cum seeping from between her legs. Tears dusting her thick lashes.

"What are you staring at?" she whispers.

I shake my head once. "I'm not friendly with the Garrisons, Keira. We have a dark...bloody history. There's no love lost."

I can tell she wants to pry, but instead she stays quiet.

"Don't speak to any Garrison," I say. "And you don't need to fear them. If anyone goes after you, I'll consider it theft of my property and deal with it accordingly."

She knows we're so far out the law is a loose memory. The penalty in these parts for hustling cattle and horses is a quick shot to the side of the head. And a shallow grave in the mountains. Her eyes widen and her throat bobs.

"What do you say?" I press.

"I understand, sir," she says in a rush.

"Good girl."

The thing that surprises me most about Keira is that, whether she knows it or not, she wants this as badly as I do. Maybe she didn't know it before, but she seems to want the security of obedience from someone she trusts.

If that's the case, I'm doing something right because she's offering her obedience to me.

It's almost ten when we get back to the house. She's cold so I send her inside while I brush down the horses and put them out to the pasture. When I go to drop some things off in the bedroom, I find the bathroom door ajar. The shower is running and thick steam wafts through the crack.

Something catches my boot. I look down to see her clothes on the floor.

I don't like messes. Everything in my house must be neat.

Bending, I pick up her shirt and jeans. Her panties fall out and I catch them before they hit the ground. The pale pink cotton feels like silk in my rough fingers. I turn them over and there's a little wet stain where her pussy sat. I bring it to my nose and inhale.

Sweet...pure pheromones.

Something animal wakes in me. She's not on birth control and I can smell she's ovulating. The scent is a little sweeter and it hits me

144

like a brick wall. It's like an electric shock that blows my pupils and turns my senses all the way up.

I want to wrap my cock in her panties and jerk off into them. To paint my cum on every intimate thing she owns.

The bathroom door creaks open and she's standing there, patting her hair dry. Looking clean and flushed pink from her shower.

"Come here," I say.

She obeys, setting the towel on the bedside table. There's hesitancy in her steps, but I can also see her nipples tighten.

I don't stand on ceremony. She gasps as I spin her around and bend her over the bed. Her fists clench the sheets.

My belt clangs as I undo it and unleash my cock. It's hard, straining to be inside her, and wet at the tip. I see the tremor of muscle in her back as I spit into my hand and rub it over my length and her entrance. She's wet, perhaps from arousal, perhaps from ovulation. It's hard to tell.

I push in. She can take me.

"Fuck—Gerard," she gasps.

My hand comes down on her ass and she yelps as I thrust my cock into her pussy. Not caring that it doesn't fucking fit. I grip her face, forcing her lips open, and push her panties between her lips.

"Don't use my name when I'm inside you," I say. "It's sir or nothing."

Between us, her pussy stretches to take me. I know it hurts her, but instead of crying out, she's moaning. Her face is shoved into the bed and she's pushed back against me. She wants the pain, the fullness. Her needy, tight cunt needs to be used.

I hit resistance. She's tensed up. I slide my fingers between her thighs and stroke her clit. Her pupils dilate and her naked breasts heave. Slowly, her muscles relax enough I can thrust the rest of the way inside.

She wriggles her hips to wrap her legs around my waist, but I take both ankles and flip them over my shoulders. She's folded in half beneath me and there's nothing between us to hold me back. I pump my hips out and thrust hard, getting all the way to the soft resistance of her cervix.

Her spine arcs, her eyes roll back, and she screams around the panties between her teeth.

If I wasn't snipped, this woman would be pregnant. There's no fucking way I'd pull out of her.

Wetness slips down my cock. She's such a sweet, perfect slut for me. She lives for the feeling of being forced, of being filled. I feel her muscles relax all the way and each thrust gets easier as she gets so wet I can hear it.

I keep working her clit until she tenses in my arms. Her spine locks back and her head falls in a cloud against the sheets. She screams around the gag and her eyes roll back as she shakes hard.

Her body goes limp. I flip her easily to her hands and knees and mount her from behind. She's small enough I can slide my hand up between her breasts and wrap it around her throat. Holding her still so I can rut into her pussy.

I've never felt anything like her cunt. Soft like silk, soaking wet, and so tight it grips me and caresses every inch of my length as I fuck it.

The bed frame slams against the wall. She whimpers with every thrust. My orgasm draws closer and I push myself into her again and again, chasing it without a thought in my head.

I feel her tense. My orgasm shoots down my spine and I push in deep and go still. Feeling the pleasure throb through my cock as all my tension releases into her body.

She moans as I pull out and sit up. Her pussy is swollen and my cum seeps out and drips from her clit. Her inner thighs are slick with arousal and I bend, licking it up. Savoring the sweet taste of my submissive's cunt.

She pushes herself to her knees, still facing away from me, and spits the soaked panties out. I gather her wet hair and stroke it. A little purr of satisfaction sounds in her chest.

"Good girl, redbird," I say.

There's a short silence and she sighs.

"What are you doing to me, sir?" she whispers.

I could ask her the same thing. I spend all my free time thinking about her like a lovesick teenager. She's got me so horny I can't keep my cock in my pants. I grip her hair, wrapping it once around my fist. Dragging her head back to make her look at me.

"What do you mean?"

She blinks up at me. "I was never this slutty until I met you."

I laugh. "You hadn't been fucked properly."

She nestles her head back against my chest and I let her feel my warmth. Just long enough I know she's feeling alright. I draw back and turn her around.

"I want you to get down on your knees and thank me for letting you come," I say.

Her eyes widen and she stands. "Sorry, sir. I didn't know."

"No, you don't have to do it every time," I assure her. I tuck my cock in my pants and fasten my belt. "Go on."

Her cheeks flush and she wobbles before sinking down to her knees. She tucks her heels under her ass and uncurls her palms on her lower thighs. Like the perfect girl she is, she drops her head and keeps her eyes to the floor.

"Thank you, sir," she whispers.

"For?"

"Thank you for letting me come," she manages. "Sir."

She's so humiliated she probably needs to come again, but that can wait. I crouch down and lift her chin. Her big blue eyes flick to mine and she studies me, trying to read my face.

"You're doing well," I say. "The cuffs for your wrists are almost done."

She nods. "Thank you, sir."

We have a few weeks left before I collar her and the amended contract begins. Part of me is looking forward to it, but the other part doesn't care because it changes nothing. Maybe we'll end up staying in this dynamic, maybe we won't, but whatever happens, Keira Garrison will sleep in my bed from now on.

147

CHAPTER TWENTY

KEIRA

I go out to the paddock behind the barn early one morning. Big Dog and Small Dog reluctantly follow me out into the cold and sit puffed up on the porch. The sunlight is cool, still shaded behind the mountain. Tiny flakes of snow spiral from the sky. So few I have to look twice to see if they're really there.

Angel is quiet as I put her tack on and lead her out to the paddock. We've been practicing a lot lately. I spend a few hours with her every day and she's learning to trust me now. I'm not sure I'm ready to get on her yet, but that will come with time.

How much time?

How long will I be here?

Angel pauses outside the barn, blinking her dark eyes up at me. I stroke down her velvety nose and she buries it in my glove.

The painted mare sits heavy in my pocket.

Other than the mare, the only thing my mother left behind was a book of Swedish fairy tales. I read it cover to cover, so many times it fell to dust. Right now, I'm reminded of a story about a woman who goes out into the wild to rescue her father and is snatched by a dark mountain spirit. She has to answer a riddle to get by his bridge, but in the end he lets her pass for a single kiss.

I think back to how Gerard looked when I left. Still sleeping, the blanket pooled around his waist. He's taken a lot more than a kiss, but I'm still not allowed to leave his mountain.

It tickles me to think of him as a mountain spirit. Long claws, even taller than he is now, bright white eyes.

Speak of the devil.

I hear his boots on the frozen ground. His presence fills the space like smoke. Angel lifts her head and rests her chin on my shoulder, staring past me at him.

I turn. He's leaning on the fence, one boot on the first rung.

The corner of his mouth turns up. Without breaking his stone visage, he whistles. For a second, I think he's trying to get Angel to come, but then I realize he's wolf-whistling at me. Heat creeps up beneath my coat and scarf. I don't know what he's looking at, every inch of me is covered.

"Come here, redbird," he says.

I release Angel and she stays still as I cross the hard, crunchy ground to the fence. He tilts his head so we don't knock our hats off and I stand on my toes to let him kiss me. He tastes faintly of coffee. His face is smooth—he must have shaved it this morning after I'd left.

"No beard?" I ask.

He shakes his head. "Not today, but it'll be back in a day or two."

I think I feel a crack in his cold so I offer him a smile. "You make me think of a story I read when I was little."

"Really?"

I relate the story to him briefly and his brow rises. There's a faintly amused shadow over his mouth. He looks at me like that a lot. When I fall silent, I start to wonder if he'll be offended by his portrayal as a dark woodland spirit. But he just reaches out and tugs my braid and taps my chin with the side of his curled finger.

"I see how it is," he says.

"How what is?" I frown.

"My price is much higher for passage."

"I know that."

He leans in, his breath a cloud. "Don't lie and say you don't enjoy it."

A shiver moves down my spine and I can't think of anything but the last time he fucked me. When I walked from the bathroom and he pushed me down on the bed. My toes curl in my cold boots.

"Show me what you've been doing with Angel," he says.

"We've been working on lunging," I say. "I'll get on her in the barn and let her sit with that, but we haven't been riding in the pasture."

"Good girl, that's smart," he says. "Gives her space to obey, but not feel restricted."

He takes the lead rope from the gate and hands it to me, following me inside the paddock. I'm a little nervous with him watching me, but I'm confident Angel can at least do this. He stays by the gate, arms crossed over his broad chest. Hat pulled low.

I pause in the center of the paddock. Angel backs up obediently and lines herself up with the fence. She waits, gazing at me through her forelock. I take the loose end of the lead and swing it in slow circles. Right away, she breaks into a clockwise walk around the perimeter of the fence. Pride fills my chest and I want to look at Gerard, but Angel deserves my focus.

I switch hands. Angel pivots and moves counterclockwise.

"Good," Gerard says. "Bring her in to you."

I stop swinging the rope and loop it over my arm. Angel turns and starts walking slowly in my direction. She comes to a halt, drapes her head over my shoulder, and follows me back to where Gerard stands by the gate.

"She's doing really well," he says.

I open my mouth to reply, but out of nowhere there's a sound like a gunshot. Angel throws her head so fast I only have time to fall back against the fence. Her eyes flash white and I see panic set in as she whirls. She takes the paddock at a gallop, kicking up ice and dry grass and heads back at us.

Panic sets into me too and I scramble back, but it's too late. Her chestnut and white body swings around and her hindquarters fill my vision.

At the last minute, I feel his body over mine. I hear his grunt as he takes the weight of Angel's body against his. Big Dog barks from somewhere outside the paddock. And I see Gerard grit his teeth as he's slammed against the fence.

His hat falls off and his eyes flash, but he stays calm. Angel throws her head and Gerard's body ripples as he shoves her back. Pushing half the weight of a horse off him.

Oh my God, that's both terrifying and impressive.

Angel bolts to the far side of the paddock and stops. She's heaving, her skin shivering.

I turn to run to Gerard, but he's already standing, dusting his hands off. He's got a dirty print on his back, but otherwise he's unharmed. My feet are frozen to the ground as he walks back over to me.

"I'm so sorry," I burst out. "It won't happen again. It was my fault."

He glances up, eyes calm. "It's fine, redbird. She's a horse and horses spook."

My clenched hands uncurl. Heat floods my body in an uncontrollable wave. If that had happened with Clint, he'd have berated me for days. He'd have made me feel terrible and taken away my horse as punishment, telling me I didn't deserve to train her anymore.

"It was probably a car backfiring by the employee residences," he says. He takes his coat off, hanging it over the fence. "Let me get Angel."

I stand by the gate, speechless. He's in his Henley and he's rolled the sleeves up just enough to show his wrists. I can see the outline of his undershirt beneath. There's a faint sweat stain around the buttons. I can tell he runs hot, even in the winter.

I watch the muscle move beneath his shirt as he centers himself in the paddock. Angel balks, backing into the fence. He kneels down, making himself smaller, although he still comes up to my shoulder when he's on his knees.

He whistles. Angel stands perfectly still.

"She doesn't like men," he says quietly.

I like that he doesn't fault her for it, he's just stating a fact. He holds out his palm. We wait in silence for several minutes. I'm trying to keep myself under control, but how patient he's being is driving me wild.

Seeing him get thrown against the fence scared me, but seeing him lift half a horse off his body set me on fire.

I want to pull him into the barn and drop to my knees.

Angel moves, slowly. She rounds the paddock and drops her head, coming close. He reaches into his pocket and takes out a handful of grain. Her eyes flicker and she moves in, nibbling it from his palm.

He stands slowly, letting her body drape against his. She rests her neck in the curl of his elbow and he pats her shoulder.

"Good girl," he says.

He gathers her reins and leads her back to the gate. I push it open and we head for the barn without speaking. Together, we strip the tack from her and brush her down, putting her away for the day. She'll be anxious for a while, but later in the evening, I'll put her out to pasture for a few hours.

He picks up her saddle and disappears into the tack room. Heart thumping, I follow, shutting the door as best I can. The frame is uneven, leaving an inch of space.

He turns and I swallow hard.

Our gazes clash and the air burns with electricity. The barn is heated, but it's not as warm as the house. That doesn't bother me as I take my hat and coat off, dropping them to the ground. His brow rises slowly, his pale eyes taking in my every move.

I haven't initiated sex with him since that first time.

It's terrifying.

His face is unreadable. My fingers feel weak as I pull my sweatshirt over my head, leaving me in just my bra and jeans. I'm nervous, but it's overpowered by the wave of desire soaking me. I've never been attracted to power before, I've always been afraid of it. I wonder what the difference between his strength and Clint's is and why I'm not cowed.

He takes a step closer.

"You saved me," I whisper.

It sounds silly when I say it out loud in the quiet of the barn.

"Did you expect me to let you be crushed?"

I lick my dry lips. "I just didn't think you would take the hit yourself."

His jaw works.

"I can take it."

He closes the space between us, backing me up until I hit the wall. My eyes dart down and I see the hard ridge beneath the front of his work pants. My fists clench. God, I want to undo his belt and take him in my grip. Hold his desire in my hand, feel how much he wants me.

His eyes run over my face, light blue as the sky and heavy lidded. He clears his throat.

"I'm not fucking you," he says.

I swallow my disappointment. I know better than to let it show on my face.

"Why, sir?"

He reaches out and forces the door shut and releases it. It swings open.

"Because one other man seeing your body is one man too many."

He steps back and hands me my sweatshirt. Confused, I pull it back on and let him settle my jacket overtop.

"There's no one in the barn, sir," I say.

He cocks his head, leaving the tack room. I follow him to the doorway and he looks up at the sky. Sometimes I wish he would just speak so I didn't have to guess what's going on behind those hard eyes.

"What are we waiting for?" I whisper.

He lifts his hand. There's a beat of silence and the breakfast bell rings out.

"The barn will be full in a moment," he says.

Disappointed, I turn to go, but his arm shoots out and he grabs my wrist. I open my mouth, but before I can speak, he's pulled me against his chest. His hand slides up my cheek and buries in my hair. He takes his hat off and bends, his mouth brushing mine.

My whole body tingles. I love kissing him, he's so good at it.

And I can tell he knows it.

When he pulls back, I'm a panting mess. He presses his mouth to my forehead for a second and I'm so weak I can barely stand.

"Your cuffs are done," he says. "I laid them by the bed."

I stay still, not wanting to leave. He extracts me from his arms and turns me towards the house, giving me a little spank to get me going. I give him a look—which I'm careful to keep respectful—and he smiles. It's tempered, but it's real.

Back in the bedroom, I find the cuffs on the bedside table. Reverently, I lift them and run my fingertips over the embossed, dark brown leather. Over the center is a line of bluebells and above and below it run two rows of intricate braiding. At each end, where they come together, is half of the Sovereign Mountain emblem. I push the edges together to make it whole.

I know what it means.

His.

He's so selfish and jealous—I feel it even though he never cracks and shows it with his face or words. He doesn't have to, my presence here is proof enough.

I change into my slip and sit back on the bed to fasten the cuffs around my wrists. I've never had anything custom made for me before. The amount of care and attention to detail amazes me.

But what do they mean?

Are they just for sex? Just because he likes fucking women in restraints?

I thought things were going to be different after reading and signing the contract. I thought our relationship would be purely transactional. That he'd get what he wanted out of me in the bedroom and I'd be kept safe. That he wouldn't step between me and danger or press kisses to my forehead in the barn doorway.

But here he is, putting cuffs made of bluebells around my wrists.

And he's barely fucked me.

Apparently he's not very good at sticking to the rules of his contract. I'm not either because I don't understand when we're playing and when we're not. Sometimes he says something that jars me and I have to remind myself that he's playing a part.

Or is he?

Whose words does he speak when he fucks me and tells me I belong to him? His or my Dom's?

That night after dinner, he strips my clothes off and cuffs me to the headboard. My heart pounds as he takes a thin switch from the dresser and braces one knee on the edge of the bed.

"Let's test what you can take," he says.

He's still dressed and I'm fully naked. My ankles cross and my toes curl, anticipating pain. I hear the hiss before I see it and pain sears over my nipples. Fuck, that wakes me up. My eyelids fly open and I cry out, my spine arcing.

"Good girl," he says.

He doesn't stop because I don't safeword him. At first, the pain of the switch across my breasts makes me want to scream. But he gives me a strip of leather to bite down on and I keep it in, diving headfirst into being out of control. The pain numbs and leaves behind the sweetest burn I've ever felt.

It travels down my belly to my clit.

My brain disengages. All I can feel is the slow build in my clit, the slippery arousal between my thighs.

And the ceaseless sting of the blows across my breasts.

He stops and sets aside the switch. I'm so close, teetering on the edge of orgasm. My lashes flutter and he hears me whimper.

"What, redbird?" he asks.

"I was so close," I pant.

He makes a sound in his throat that's pure desire. A growl and a groan intermingled. I bite my lip as he flips me onto my knees, my wrists crossing. His zipper hisses and he enters me so hard from behind I see stars. Sometimes the pain is just pain, but tonight it's so much more.

He takes me by the throat and holds me against his chest. His cock is deep inside, but he isn't fucking me. With his other hand, he slaps my right breast. Right at the tip where it hurts the most.

I spill over the edge, my body jerking so hard in his grip he almost drops me. He throbs and I moan, my head falling back as I pulse with him, pleasure shattering through my hips. I'm dimly aware of him pulling the cuffs from the headboard and wrapping the chain around his fist.

Then he throws me on my back, holding me down by the wrists, and fucks me like an animal. I lay there, stunned and exhausted from my orgasm, and let him. I've never had sex like this and every time with him is different. It's deeper, it's harsher, it feels so much more intense.

We're both quiet when he's done. After a while, he picks me up and carries me into the bathroom. I sit weakly on the sink while he rubs lotion into my breasts. His rough fingers taking care with the tender pink stripes across my nipples.

"How do you feel?" he asks.

I clear my throat. "I feel like I have nothing left. I came harder than I have in my entire life."

His fingertips graze my sensitive nipples. His mouth is a firm line and his lids are heavy.

"You astound me," he said finally. "I never expected you to want this as badly as I do."

My breath hitches. "It's a lot...but I've never felt so...raw."

He's quiet for a long time as he rubs my breasts. Despite how hard I came, I feel my sex tingle. And ache.

"It's not the pain," he murmurs. "It's the way it breaks down your walls and lets me in."

He wipes his hands like he didn't just say something vulnerable. He's such an enigma. Musclebound, shrouded in mystery, and so handsome it feels like looking at the sun.

We lay on our sides in bed, our bodies almost touching. There's a vein in his neck that thrums with each heartbeat.

I touch it with my fingertip just to feel how alive he is.

CHAPTER TWENTY-ONE

GERARD

I go into the city later that week. I make the two hour drive once a month and set up meetings all afternoon so I can get everything done as efficiently as possible.

Today, I need to see some bank officials about a certain mortgage. She's kept up her side of the deal, so I need to keep mine.

It's the only time I get dressed up. When I come out of my bedroom in a dark gray, tailored suit with an open collar shirt, I find my redbird curled up in the bed even though it's the middle of the afternoon. She has a book in her hand and her lids are heavy. When she hears my step, she startles and her head lolls.

Her eyes snap open. "Oh my God," she breathes.

Her jaw is slack. She pushes her back against the headboard and the book slips to the floor.

"What?" I turn and glance behind me.

Her mouth parts. Her cheeks are a distinct shade of pink I've come to realize arrives before the soaked spot in her panties.

"Oh," I say, taking a step closer. She tenses and I kneel on the edge of the bed. She shivers as I kiss the side of her throat and down her shoulder.

She moans. "You look good," she whispers. "Sir."

I sink down to a sitting position and she leans in. Her hands graze my chest, touching the triangle of bare skin where my shirt collar parts. Her nimble fingers tug the top button and she strokes my bare chest. I stay still and let her explore me, enjoying how wide her blue gaze is.

She tilts her head, looking up at me through her lashes. In the last two weeks she's been with me, she's gotten comfortable expressing herself. She offers her body to me in the morning and at night. She's always soaked when I slide into her cunt.

The way she moans drives me wild. They're breathy, like a series of little gasps. The sounds get faster as I drive her to orgasm. Her lower belly quivers, her thighs go tight. When she comes, she's so fucking wet it leaves a stain spreading across the sheets every time.

I'm not a sadist without pleasure. And how easily she comes for me is the best high I've ever felt. Her pleasure is like syrup and it flows without stopping some nights. I've never had much of a sweet tooth, but I find myself savoring her every night before I sleep.

The pain balances it out. Like salt in caramel.

***

Last night, I spanked her across the palm and fucked her with my hand until she came all over the hearth. Right below the bull skull with the heat of the fire on her back. Not for punishment, but for training. I have to be able to find her limits before I administer real punishment.

She's a good girl. I send her to the dresser for the leather case of implements and she goes obediently and brings it to me.

"On your knees," I tell her. "Palm up and out to the side."

She obeys, sinking down before the fireplace. The bull skull watches over her, eyes empty. The fireplace glitters against her naked back and her beautiful, full ass. She shifts onto her heels and curled toes.

Her head sinks back and she looks up at me, hesitantly
Eyes so big I'm lost in them.

"May I look up, sir? Or should I look at the ground?" she whispers.

"I want you to watch your palm," I tell her.

I retrieve the ruler and she tenses, but instead of using it on her hand, I kneel before her. "Open that dirty little mouth."

Her full lips part, flashing her pink tongue at me. I slide the ruler between her teeth. Tentatively she bites down. It pushes the corners of her mouth back and I find myself wondering how pretty she'd look with my cock in her throat.

Tears running down her cheeks. Spit dripping from her chin. Trying so hard to be a good girl and take as much as she can.

My cock thickens against my zipper. I take the switch out and she holds perfectly still, but I see a quiver run down her naked stomach.

It strikes her palm, just hard enough she tastes the bite. She gasps around the ruler and her poor palm flushes. I apply it four times to her hand and she doesn't move her arm an inch. When I'm done, I kneel and kiss her palm as I slide my fingers into her soaked pussy.

She moans around the ruler as she comes. When I've soothed her and put her to bed, I go back to the fireplace and kneel to run my fingertips over the little spatter she left where she knelt.

Traces of her.

***

I used to be a stickler for privacy. I fucked, but never brought anyone home to my room. Now I take pride in the way she's made her mark on my private spaces. Her clothes are in my closet, my pillow smells like her hair. Her makeup and bottles are lined up on my sink. The last time I showered, I found one of her red hairs wrapped around my dick.

"Sir."

I jerk my head, tearing myself from the memory. She's leaning in so close I feel her breath on my lips. Her lashes are lowered, dark feathers against freckled skin.

"What is it, redbird?" I say, my voice hoarse.

"Where are you going, looking like that?" she asks.

There's something in her voice I've never heard before. It sounds a bit like a pout. Is she resentful I'm going into the city and not taking her?

"I have business meetings," I say. "Sovereign Mountain has a lot of moving parts and I own other operations."

She tilts her chin up and stares into my eyes. Inches away like she's trying to imprint my image into her brain.

"Are you sure?" she whispers. "Sir."

I stand and she shifts to the edge of the bed, sitting back on her heels.

She's pouting her lips with a hurt look in her eyes. She knows what pulls at my heartstrings.

"Remember the part in the contract about communication?" I ask firmly. "If you don't speak up and tell me what's wrong, I will punish you."

She hesitates and I see the gears turning in her head. Then she shakes it and flops onto the pillows. "I'm just wondering...if I'm the only one."

There's a little crease between her brows. Oh, she's jealous. I dip my head to conceal my smile and she scowls. Maybe I should punish her for that, but I don't care to right now. I click my fingers and hold my hand out and she takes it reluctantly and allows me to lift her to her feet.

I brush her hair back. "You're lucky you were a good girl last night. Otherwise I'd take your panties down and spank you."

Heat creeps over her face. "I'm not trying to be bad. It's just...Clint used to go into the city like this. And sometimes he'd smell like someone else when he got back."

I don't tell her that I already know about Clint Garrison's infidelity—it's part of the reason he was in so much debt. Cheating is an expensive hobby. I saw his bank statements when I pulled some strings to look over his will post death. I noticed she went to the gynecologist's office more than normal. Most likely obsessively getting herself tested.

But I'm not supposed to know any of that. She won't forgive how deeply I've intruded into her personal life in the last year if she finds out.

"Come here," I say.

She obeys, and her eyes are on the floor as she approaches. I lift her chin with the side of my curled finger.

"Eyes on me," I command. Her gaze flicks up. "There is no one but you. When I get home tonight, I expect you to be in bed, naked and waiting."

She pouts, I see the push of her lower lip, and her forehead creases in a scowl. I bite back my displeasure. If I had more time, I'd take my belt off and make her count until she's whimpering an apology. But I'm late as it is, so I just turn and leave her sitting on the bed. Her pretty face scrunched.

I'm still thinking about her words as I leave Sovereign Mountain. I don't like her jealousy—it feels too much like defiance.

And I don't enjoy defiance for defiance's own sake. It's always been a trigger for me. I need the structures of BDSM because, to me, it's a holistic practice of trust. Defiance without consent feels like a violation of that.

I know her submission intimately and I feel that she stepped out of its bounds. Maybe just to test her limits for the first time.

Is that what she wants? To feel my resistance?

My shoulders are tight the entire drive into the city. And I can't get that angry, little scowl out of my head.

CHAPTER TWENTY-TWO

KEIRA

For the first time since meeting him, I'm pissed off.

I understood when I signed the contract that this was an impersonal arrangement. He gets gratification and I get protection and deferment of debt. He doesn't owe me the truth about where he's going or what he's doing.

I get that.

But after everything we've done together, I can't help feeling possessive. So I allow myself the luxury of pouting in bed for a while after he leaves.

The afternoon stretches on. I get bored of sulking and take a nap. When I wake, the house is empty and it's evening.

He'll be home soon.

My stomach flips, but I ignore it. Instead, I climb out of bed and pad naked down the hall to the game room at the far side of the hall. It's always been shut, but I've investigated it once. I know it has a set of double doors that lead out to the balcony where the hot tub sits.

I slip into the chilly space, my toes curling on the thin carpet. There's a gas fireplace on the right side, and I hurry over and flick it on. The fire roars up and I bask in it for a moment. Stomach fluttering.

He told me to be naked and waiting for him in his bed.

But a little part of me is feeling rebellious. I pull open the door and cold air hits my naked body. Taking my breath away. The stars hang overhead, the milky way a glistening trail across the sky. Shivering, I tug the cover off the hot tub and hit the button on the side. It takes less than a minute for it to start churning.

Experimentally, I poke my finger in. It's lukewarm, but heating up rapidly. I climb over the side and sink into the delicious water, letting it cover my shoulders. It smells clean and faintly like chlorine.

This is heaven.

If only I had some wine.

I clamber from the tub and scurry back into the game room. In the kitchenette I find a bottle of chardonnay in the wine rack and a stack of fluffy towels. I gather both and sink back into the tub, leaving the porch door wide open.

The view from over the railing is breathtaking, but I can't think of anything but how he told me to be naked and waiting and I'm disobeying him. He's on his way home...maybe he's already downstairs. I've never seen him angry before—I wonder if this will make his stone exterior crack.

Why do I want it to anyway?

Maybe because he makes me feel everything, but shows me nothing of himself. I've laughed in front of him, I've sobbed in his arms. He's seen me stripped naked, in every vulnerable position I can think of. Yet he's offered me little more than a flash or two of vulnerability in return.

I want to feel what's behind those pensive eyes. He's full of secrets, I can tell. And I want to pry open his walls.

Faintly, I hear his truck pull up the drive. My stomach twists and I freeze. The door slams and it snaps me out of my panic. I might be his submissive, but I'm not a doormat.

He can take a little pushback.

I pull myself from the hot tub and move to the railing. Down below I see him lock the truck. He pauses in the driveway and checks for his keys. My stomach clenches and my eyes eat the sight of him hungrily. He's taken off his suit jacket and his sleeves are rolled to his elbow. His tousled dark hair is brushed back, but a few strands hang over his forehead.

Brashly, I lean over the railing. My two fingers find my mouth and I whistle. Loud enough for him to hear, but not loud enough to wake the horses.

He pivots and his head jerks up.

I know I have to be a sight. I'm completely naked, except my wet hair hanging down my back, and my tits are hard against the cold. His brow jerks, but his face stays the same. Then his mouth thins, he fits his hat back on his head, and strides up onto the porch and out of sight.

A thrill of terror moves down my spine.

My ass tingles at the memory of how much his maintenance spankings hurt. My toes curl against the cold porch. Maybe I made a miscalculation.

I freeze at the railing and then I snap into action and burst through the game room and into the empty hallway.

Naked and soaking wet, I tear down the hall and head for the bedroom. Maybe if I get on my knees, into the submissive position, he'll forgive me.

I round the corner and he's right there. Over two hundred pounds of solid muscle. His eyes are dark and his jaw is set.

Suddenly I remember that my husband died on his land.

And I never really found out how.

A bolt of real fear moves through my body. Maybe he's been shielding me from himself for a reason. He takes a quick step towards me and I gasp, stumbling back against the wall. From the soles of my feet comes the most delicious shudder that moves all the way up my thighs to my core. It's quickly followed by shame.

I'm wet from fear.

And maybe...a little part of me likes the thought that he's that dangerous. The feral, animal part of my brain that hasn't evolved in thousands of years wants him. He's the biggest, baddest motherfucker in our corner of the world. I'm completely ashamed to admit it, but some, unevolved part of me wants to roll over and open my legs at that thought.

Quick, like a snake striking, he pins me to the wall with his hand on my throat. My mouth pops open in shock and he kisses it, hard and long. Filling my senses with the taste of his mouth. My head spins and I can't breathe. His fingertips press harder and harder, trapping blood to my brain.

He's panting slightly. His pupils are blown. Black against ice blue.

"You are a dangerous woman," he says from between his teeth.

I'm dangerous? Has he looked in a mirror?

I gasp, a strangled sound coming from my throat. He eases up and I inhale, coughing.

"I'm sorry," I manage.

He's so close I can feel the heat rising from his fully clothed body. Kissing over my naked, wet breasts and thighs. His mouth parts, flashing his bottom teeth.

"My redbird," he says softly. "Thinks she can disobey me."

His fingers ease, stroking down the side of my throat. Sending tingles down to my breasts and making my nipples harden.

"How should I punish you?" he says.

Fear bursts in my stomach and goes right to my pussy. Tender blood throbs in my clit and confusion swirls. Why do I feel like I'm going to come right here in the hall, without even being touched? Am I sick? Am I fucked up?

"I could do anything I want with you, Miss Stowe," he murmurs. "No one stops me. Sovereign Mountain is mine and you are my woman."

My eyes widen. If he'd said these things to me another day, without deadly calm in his eyes, I would have thought this was just play. But he means his words. This realization is quickly followed by a heavy throb between my thighs and my fingers twitch. I'm aching, I'm right on the edge. So close I wonder if I'm going to come just from his words.

My lashes flutter. I know my face is flushed pink.

"My name is Garrison," I whisper. "Not Stowe."

He leans in. "I will fuck your dead husband's name out of your mouth," he says. "Then I'll decide what I want in its place."

I'm trying to make sense of his words, but his hands tighten on my throat and my thighs squeeze together. Rubbing at that tender place where my pleasure is coiled, pounding like a drum. I throb once and my eyes widen, fixing on his.

His brow arcs and he glances down.

"Don't you dare come," he warns.

My breasts heave, my body twists. I'm going to pass out if he doesn't give me air soon, but I can barely think about that right now. I can't unlock my thighs and the pressure is pushing me higher and higher. The calm in his eyes shatters and wildness replaces it. Like he's gotten a taste of something and he can't control himself.

"Don't you do it, little redbird," he says, his voice low.

My eyes roll back. Pleasure rips through my lower body and a little gasp bursts from my throat. He releases my neck as my orgasm hits me and the combination of oxygen to my brain and pleasure turns my legs to water. I sink to my knees, my palms flat on the floor.

It hits me what I've done as my orgasm ebbs.

He has rules and I broke them. Not just by coming without permission, but by not being in bed, ready to offer myself to him when he returned.

I fucked up.

I look up at him, towering over me. Hat still on his head. I have a feeling that whatever happens tonight, I'm about to see his walls come down for the first time. I thought he showed me flashes of honesty before, but they're nothing on what's simmering in his eyes.

"I'm sorry," I whisper.

Too late. I can tell without him saying a word.

CHAPTER TWENTY-THREE

GERARD

Her full, soft mouth trembles. Her eyes are huge. They follow my every move as I strip my belt off.

"You can safeword me—or hit my leg if you need out," I say. "But it's better if you just take it."

She won't safeword me. She's a filthy little slut and now that she's gotten a taste of what I can give her, she'll go right over the edge with me.

I see how hungry she is to feel alive. To taste fear and pleasure at the same time.

Her potential is limitless.

I crack the belt in my hand once and she flinches, but she doesn't back away.

Her pupils blow as I slip the looped end around her throat and tighten it just enough she feels the burn. She gasps and I take a second to look at what a pretty picture she makes. On her knees, naked and flushed. Her mouth is swollen and I know she's soaked between those soft thighs.

I'm going to get her off until she cries.

One handed, I unzip the front of my pants. The whites of her eyes flash and she pulls her head back.

"Quiet, be a good girl," I tell her, pushing down the front of my pants. "You've taken it in your cunt. You can take it in your mouth too."

Her pink tongue darts out and wets her mouth. I unleash my cock and it hangs heavy right before her lips. I'm so fucking hard and hot, I might blow my load all over her perfect face.

"I don't know if I can," she whispers.

I slide my hand under her chin and tilt it up. "Open up. You're going to do your best for me."

She nods and I tug the belt tighter, bringing her face close. Her tongue flicks over her lips again and she opens her mouth as I push the head of my cock into it. Hot, silky wetness wraps around the tip and my vision blurs. I've thought about her mouth for so long. And it's a hundred times better than in my fantasies.

I keep the belt taut. My other hand slides up her hair and grips it in my fist.

"Breathe on the out," I tell her.

I fuck into her mouth, not giving her more than half my length. Her throat fights me and tears spill from her eyes immediately. I know she can barely get air. But she's not trying to resist me, she's just taking it. Pretty mouth slack so I can fuck it.

My hips pump. Spit gathers on her chin and drips on the steel tips of my boots.

She chokes and I ease up on the belt. Just a trace. Her breasts heave as she gasps for breath around me. I give her a moment, then I fuck her mouth relentlessly. Putting her back in her place with every moan and gag that comes from her throat.

"Is this who you are?" I say from between gritted teeth, "Just a place for me to get off? A pretty little bitch with bruised knees and a belt around your neck?"

Her lashes flutter and her eyes roll back. I push in so deeply her throat convulses before pulling out to let her breathe. My fist grips my cock as I tug her head back.

"Open your mouth and put your tongue out," I order.

She obeys, tentatively. Her face glistens with saliva and tears. A bit of makeup is smudged under her eyes.

She's never looked more beautiful.

Fuck. I would die for this woman.

Cum shoots from the tip of my cock and splashes across her face. Shocked, her eyes snap shut, but she keeps her tongue fully extended. Catching the next pump of cum. Painting her face and dripping down her neck to the belt until I'm empty.

I release her, stepping back and taking my hat off.

She falls onto the heels of her hands, gasping. I sink down on one knee and take her by the chin and turn her face up.

"Open your eyes," I order.

She obeys, fixing them on me. They're glittering like she's feverish. I slide my hand down her neck to her right breast and pinch her tight nipple hard enough she moans.

"Do you need to come again, redbird?" I ask.

She nods eagerly. Cum slips down her chin and I catch it with the side of my finger and feed it back to her. Forcing her lips apart until she gives up and cleans it from my finger with her tongue.

"May I have a break?" she whispers.

I stand, backing up. "No," I tell her. "You'll get a break when you earn it."

My hat hits the floor. She blinks at it and her eyes snap up to me as I back slowly down the hall. I can see she's trying to figure out what I want.

I come to a halt just inside the open doors to the game room. She wanted to play fucking games tonight, so I'll give her what she wants so hard she won't be able to sit tomorrow.

"Put my hat between your teeth, girl," I order. "And crawl to me on your hands and knees."

Her cheeks are bright pink, but she does as I ask. Taking my black hat and putting the brim between her white teeth and full mouth. I can tell it's heavy for her, but she's being such a good girl and holding it steady.

"Now crawl," I say again.

169

Her beautiful face glistens with cum and tears. Her eyelids are heavy with desire and her cheeks are flushed. The brim of my hat pushes back the corner of her lips like it did when I made her hold the ruler. Reminding me of how she looked with her mouth full of cock.

She crawls slowly down the hall on her hands and knees. Her soft ass sways side to side as she makes her way slowly to me. Those big, blue eyes are loud. She doesn't need to speak a single word for me to know she's eating this up—dirty, little redbird.

I sink to a crouch and whistle. A short, stilted sound I use to call my dogs.

She pauses, and I know she understands what I'm doing.

"Did I tell you to stop?" I say.

She shakes her head, managing to keep the hat in her mouth.

"Then crawl," I order, rising.

She keeps moving, her eyes glued to me. Just as she's about to reach where I stand, I back up into the game room. Her brows crease and she follows me as I keep moving back and in a slow circle around the pool table.

How far will her obedience go?

I pause by the bar. "Get up and put my hat on the counter."

She rises and places my hat down. Carefully. Then she turns and tucks her hands behind her back, waiting for my next order. My cum is dried on her face—a work of art—and her knees are pink. I hope they bruise. I want evidence of tonight under her skin.

Fuck, I'm so hard it feels like I didn't just come all over her face.

"Bend over the pool table and put your hands behind your back," I tell her, jerking my head towards the empty table.

She turns and I get the best view of her soft, round ass jiggling as she walks to the table. She bends over it, going up on her toes, and her hands slide behind her lower back. Fingers intertwining.

I consider her for a second. There's an ocean of things I could do to my redbird. I should punish her without pleasure. I should keep to the rules we set down when she first came here. But she's such a good girl and maybe, if she behaves for me, I can find it in myself to forgive what she did tonight.

I cross to the table, hat in hand. She lifts her chin, her breasts pushed against the tabletop.

Fuck. Me.

I lean forward and she tilts her chin up and I fit my hat on her head. Her lips part and she blushes as I step back, cocking my head to enjoy the sight of my redbird. Naked, smeared with cum, wearing my hat.

Clint Garrison is rolling over in his grave.

The corner of my mouth turns up. "You keep still like that."

"Yes, sir," she whispers.

I circle her and she arches her lower spine. Pushing up her ass, begging for my cock in her cunt. I grip her thigh and pull her soft, pink pussy open. It's glistening with arousal, so much it's creamy around her entrance. My cock aches and I fight back the urge to unzip and push it into her slick opening.

She moans as I touch her pussy. Playing with the softness there before dipping my fingertip inside. Her toes curl against the carpet.

"Do you have something to say, redbird?" I ask.

She shakes her head. "No, sir."

"Nothing?" I push my finger to the middle knuckle before withdrawing.

Her inner muscles tighten. "I just...I feel so empty."

I slide my hand up her spine and spread my fingers on her upper back. She tenses and then she moans as I draw back my other hand and slap her across her right ass cheek. It shakes and I grip it hard and spread her open. My thumb brushes over her asshole.

She freezes. We both know anal is on the table. It was written into the contract and she agreed to at least try it.

"Sir," she whimpers.

I lean over her and she spreads her ass and legs, pushing her sex up to me. Her ankles curl around my outer thighs and one foot hits against the gun in my thigh holster. Usually I carry on my hip, but today I had to remove my weapons to get into the bank where I had my meeting. I'd disassembled my holster and reassembled it to fit on my thigh afterwards.

"Why do you always carry that thing in the house?" she whispers.

I slap her across the ass again and flip her to face me. She bites her lip, muffling her yelp. Her pussy clenches, dripping onto the pool table. I know she's dying to come so badly she'd do anything for me. My hand hesitates. Then I flip the holster open and take the handgun out. Her body freezes and she jerks her head, the hat falling to the side.

"Sir," she whispers.

The high I get from sex like this is exploding in my brain like a drug. I drag the flat side of the barrel up her inner thigh and pause right before her delicate sex.

The cold metal lies in sharp contrast to her body. She's all soft curves and pretty angles. Maybe that's why the gun in my hand looks so good against her skin.

Hard against soft.

The unblemished against the scarred.

My mask is slipping. It's fallen and shattered at her feet. Do those blue eyes see me for who I am?

The world slows and I have to make a choice.

Do I stand behind these walls, watching her from the inside? Or do I stop building walls between myself and the world? Do I let her in and show her the man I am?

In this moment, I want to lower my defenses more than anything. I'm tired. I've built so many walls my hands are bloody.

I lift my eyes to hers and I see deep inside them a single flame. Flickering, calling me to fall into her depths. To show her all the ugly rage, the hunger for vengeance, the spite, and my selfish obsession over the woman in my arms.

So I fall, because I'm tired of pretending I'm not broken. And I hope to God that this woman gives me grace—that when she sees me clearly, she won't turn away.

CHAPTER TWENTY-FOUR

KEIRA

He's fucking psychotic.

My head spins. My breathing feels shallow. Maybe it's from all the blood pooled between my legs. I can feel it throb in my clit and I'm so sensitive right where I need him most. I swear the emptiness is going to be the death of me.

Then he took his gun out and put it to my inner thigh.

Right below my sex. Right where I've dripped down my leg.

I should be afraid, but something else overpowers it. My senses are sharp, but my better judgment is dulled by lust. I need Sovereign in a way I've never needed anything before. I'd drop down on my knees and take that gun in the back of my throat if it means getting him inside me.

He withdraws. A cry of disappointment moves up my throat, but he cuts it off by flipping me on my back.

My stomach twists. At some point, he took off his coat, leaving him in just his button up. The front is soaked in sweat and open halfway. Revealing his upper chest, covered in dark hair and tattoos.

His bare forearms are so thick, so corded with muscle from hard labor. I want to drag my nails down them so hard he bleeds. I want to lick his blood and sweat off his skin just to taste what he's made of.

Maybe that's the only way to get close to him.

"This wasn't in the contract," I moan, unsure why I'm even speaking.

He leans in and his fingers wrap around my throat.

"We're not playing anymore," he says. "*Mrs.* Garrison."

Fear thrills up my body and my head spins. He gently lifts me by the throat until I'm a foot from his face. Hanging from one of his enormous hands. I should be shaking, I should be fighting him, but all I can think about is the night we met. The way he looked at me in Clint's office, eye-fucking me in front of my husband.

The question lurking on the back of my mind feels so much more real. Clint went to Sovereign Mountain and never returned. And somehow, despite all the strange coincidences, I've ended up in this man's bed.

His grip tightens. Stars spark and my pussy throbs. I'm leaking and I know he can see it wet the pool table.

"Why did you call me that?" I manage.

The cold barrel of the handgun drags up my outer thigh. Down over the soft flesh of the underside and up again. My lids flutter and heat scorches my cheeks as he pushes it between my legs and up against my clit. Electricity shocks to my deepest point and my eyes fly open all the way. My breathing comes heavy and fast.

"You call yourself that," he says from between his teeth.

My hips twitch, and the sight on the barrel touches the soft entrance of my pussy. It's cold, but it's delicious. Like having an ice cube touched to my sex.

"Are you just a Garrison slut?" he growls.

I feel the venom in his words when he says my surname. The gun presses a little lower and angles. Fear spikes and my survival instincts threaten to take over and make me fight him. But the need to release is far stronger.

I lock my eyes with him and hitch my hips and hump the barrel of the gun.

His jaw twitches.

"Fuck," he breathes.

My head spins and I feel the steel tip of the gun enter my body. Oh God, I'm going to come or die. Just like the first time he put that enormous cock into my body and fucked me until I bled. What kind of man made someone bleed when they weren't even a virgin?

He thrusts the barrel once. "Answer me."

The grip on my throat eases just enough I can speak. Stars pop as air floods my brain, sending even more blood thrumming between my thighs.

"I am a Garrison," I gasp. "Neither of us can change that."

He tilts the gun and I feel it push against my G-spot. The entrance of my sex throbs, so sensitive it aches as my tight muscles grip the weapon.

"It should have been me," he says, jaw tight. "I should have been the one to fuck you first."

I'm rising higher and higher. Pleasure is a hot itch deep in my hips and I can't keep my body still. He thrusts the gun into my pussy and I thrust back onto it.

"You had enough blood," I gasp.

He growls in his chest, his forearm flexing and fingers tightening on my neck again. "He might have fucked you first, but I'm going to ruin you for any other man."

My head rolls from side to side. My eyes are wet and my hips are shaking so badly they're rattling the table.

I can feel his rage. This is bigger than me...and yet here I am right at the center of it.

"Come for me, little redbird," he says, his voice dropping until it rumbles. "This cunt was made to come for me. Give it what it wants."

Pleasure bursts around the barrel of his gun, now warm from being inside me. My eyes snap shut and my spine goes hard as steel. Arcing and locking. He pumps the weapon up into me and I hear how wet I am past the sound of our panting breaths.

The gun is jerked from me and the euphoria of not being dead from it hits my brain. Better than when he released my throat while I was coming in the hall. I hear his zipper and then he's inside me. So hard and fast that the pain splits like a knife through my hips.

Will I ever get used to his size? Or will I always scream like this?

Bang.

Bang.

Bang.

The pool table shakes as he takes me. Relentlessly, the heavy, slow strokes thudding against my hips. It has to be bolted to the floor, otherwise he'd be moving it easily.

My lids flutter and I roll my head. Still coming around his length. His narrowed eyes are fixed on me, a spark of triumph in them. He said he would ruin me and he has. I'm drenched with my wetness and his cum is still dried on my face. I can feel where it stuck to my skin.

He thrusts one last time and I feel him paint the inside of my pussy. I'll feel everything tomorrow. I'll get up in the morning and he'll trickle down my thigh. I'll smell the faint scent of his cum when I go to clean myself. Every time I slip my panties down, I'll remember the high of coming for him.

I hope every time he sees his gun tomorrow, he thinks about my pussy wrapped around the barrel.

Pushing myself up on the heels of my hands, I stare up at him. He looks so good that somewhere in the depths of me, I twitch. There's nothing like the feeling of our bodies joined. And I want it endlessly.

But I'm still jarred by the things he said.

Neither of us know what to say.

He picks me up. I grab his hat and he carries me down the hall. In the shower, he washes my body and gets down on his knees. I rest one leg on his shoulder and let him inspect me.

The tip of his rough fingers are surprisingly gentle on my sex. When he's done, he kisses my clit.

And despite everything that just happened, I melt for him.

CHAPTER TWENTY-FIVE

GERARD

The contract was supposed to protect us both from what happened last night. She wasn't supposed to see that side of me.

I know how to be her Dom, but I don't fucking know how to be her man.

Or at least I thought I did. I've never broken the rules with anyone before. But with her, all the things I've held sacred are changing.

I wake the next morning and she's lying with her eyes wide open. The blankets are pulled to her chin, the top one made of white fur stark against her red waves. I slide my hand up to brush a tendril from her cheek. She watches me. Her lids flutter and her tongue darts out to wet her mouth.

"I want to work with Angel today," she says.

"You can do whatever makes you happy, redbird," I say.

She sits up, moving to the edge of the bed. Quick as a flash, I wrap my arm around her waist and pull her back to me. She yelps as I flip her body around and set her in my lap. We sink back against the headboard. Her nails dig into my shoulders and her breasts heave.

My eyes rove down.

She's got a little mark around her throat where the belt bit her skin. Otherwise, she's flawless. Entranced, I run my palms over the inward curve of her waist and relish the way her hips widen.

"What is it?" she whispers.

I feel my throat bob. "Our contract isn't what I anticipated it would be."

My words hang in the air. She twists, but I keep her still.

"I'm sorry," she says. "Maybe I'm not very obedient."

I touch between her breasts with the tip of my middle finger. She shudders as I trace it down to her navel. The little dip is warm, and I gently push my fingertip in. Exploring each part of her with the slowness it deserves.

"No," I say, not looking into her eyes. "I'm going to rewrite the contract."

I glance up. Her brows arch.

"You want something...different?" she says. There's a trace of unease in her voice.

"I'm going to limit it," I say. "But not take it away."

"Oh," she says. "Why?"

How can I tell her the truth when I can't speak it myself? I needed to be her Dom because I have to protect her from my darkness. Maybe that simple, safe dynamic would work with another woman. But despite having met less than a year ago, there are tangled threads surrounding Keira and I that go back decades. Outside of our contract, we're two people with complicated histories.

Our pasts are shadowed with secrets. With deceit and death.

Last night, the past caught up with me. I looked down at her, and remembered who she was, and the darker side of me came out.

She was the wife of my enemy.

And yet, I have no right to hold that against her. She's a helpless player in this game. I saw her from my place of wealth and privilege and wanted her, so I took her as mine.

A better man would regret that.

But I don't.

One of us won the war. Clint is in the cold ground and I have his warm, naked wife in my lap.

She puts her hand on my chest, right below my collarbone. Her touch sends tendrils of heat through my torso that find their way to my groin. My cock hardens slowly beneath her ass and I know she feels it.

"I don't want to hurt you," I say finally. "We both lost control last night, but you're inexperienced. This is adding a layer of complication you're not ready for."

"You knew I was inexperienced going in," she protests. "You're thirty-eight. I'm twenty-one. What were you expecting?"

"I know, but I think this is for the best."

This part is real. She is inexperienced and I'm wondering if we should have a dynamic outside sex for that reason. I can tell she's second guessing the boundaries, unsure if we're playing or not.

That can't happen if there are feelings involved. And I have some strong feelings about this woman.

"I want to keep some aspects. I love rough sex," I say.

She bites her lip. "I...like it too. I don't want to stop that part."

"I'd never deny you a good fuck. We can still play during sex," I promise. "I'm still your Dom, you will call me sir. You'll continue to journal and be truthful and communicate. Or you'll be punished. Is that fair?"

She chews her lip. I tap her chest.

"You be you for right now," I say. "And I'll just be me. Alright?"

She nods, her hair falling over her shoulder. Brushing her left breast. I push it back and cup the soft roundness of it. Running my finger over her nipple until it hardens. Her hips move in a slow rotation, brushing against my erection.

"You're a needy slut," I murmur.

She lets her head fall back. I spit into my hand and rub it over her already wet sex. It takes a moment to work my cock into her tight pussy, but it's all worth it as she sinks down and her eyes roll back. A husky moan rises from her lips and she humps her hips against me.

"Ride your man, little redbird," I urge.

I'm not sure where that came from, but it feels right. Her mouth tugs back in a quick smile and her hazy eyes lock on mine. "What is it they say? Save a horse, ride a cowboy?"

I can't keep back my smile. My hand cracks across her ass and she clenches around my cock. Tight, hot muscles working me from base to tip. She grips my shoulder and braces herself, grinding those pretty hips hard. Like she's starving.

Something changed last night. She trusts me enough to show me some spine.

Maybe letting down my walls wasn't a complete mistake.

Her submission is beautiful, but her confidence is breathtaking. She's so confident in her soft, curvy beauty and she's hungry enough for pleasure that she's taking it.

No hesitancy, no asking if she can come. Just fucking my cock however it feels good.

I grip her body and fuck her back. The bed shakes against the wall. Outside the window, snow falls gently over the lake and the mountains are barely kissed with the rising sun. I should be outside starting chores right now. No doubt Westin is wondering where I am. But I can't pry myself from bed until I see her come.

I stroke her clit with my thumb. The combination sends her over the edge with a silent cry. Her body shudders and I follow her, pleasure shooting down my spine. When I pull from her, my cum slips out and trickles down her thighs.

She falls back onto the pillows and watches me get ready for the day.

CHAPTER TWENTY-SIX

KEIRA

We broke some rules last night. I can't tell if he regrets it or not.
I feel like I should regret it. But I don't.
I feel like I should hate what he did to me. But I didn't.

All I know for certain is that the further we fall together, and the more I see of him, the more I realize I had no idea who I was getting into a contract with.

Last night, when he got in from chores, he said they found my horses on the other side of the ranch. It's far away, so it'll take two days to round them up. There's a cabin on the other side of the property and he said he'd be gone overnight there.

I begged him to let me go too. He said no. I hate hearing that word from him because he doesn't elaborate. He just says no, and it doesn't even sound unkind, so I can't be mad at him.

But this morning, he shook me awake and said, "You can come with me, redbird." I don't know what made him change his mind, but I'm already packed.

He said he'd be back from chores by noon.

CHAPTER TWENTY-SEVEN

KEIRA

We ride up to the northern side of Sovereign Mountain Ranch later that day. Gerard has two saddlebags and I brought a backpack. He says the cabin is stocked with enough food for a week in case of emergencies. I'm imagining a shack, but he laughs and says, no, it's just a small version of the main house.

He rides Shadow and I take Bluebell. I wanted to take Angel because she's finally allowed me to ride her around the paddock without trouble. She trusts me more every day. But Gerard shakes his head when I ask if I can ride her out. He says no, he doesn't trust Angel not to throw me if she spooks.

So I take the painted mare instead, pushed deep in the pocket of my coat.

"Do you think I'll ever get Angel to the point where I can take her out?" I ask.

I turn in the saddle. We're out beyond the pastures, heading up the gradual tilt of the highest northern point of Sovereign Mountain. He's riding behind me, hat pulled low over his face. In the last few days, he's let his beard get thicker. Last night after we talked, he fell asleep on his back and I ran my fingers over his face and down his chest. Enjoying the way he feels when he's rough like this.

"What's that, redbird?" He lifts his head.

"Do you think Angel's confident enough to be ridden out?"

He considers it, squinting up at the mountain looming closer. "She's unsure of herself, never been allowed out beyond a fence."

It feels like he's not talking about Angel. I chew the inside of my cheek until a bit of blood stains my tongue.

"You're good at being patient," I say.

"Some things are worth being patient for," he says. "If you really want Angel to be your horse, you'll work at her pace. If she feels forced, she'll always be nervous."

My chest feels strange, like there's something sitting on it. My fingers tighten around the reins.

It would be a lie to say he hasn't forced a great deal onto me since we met. I wouldn't be here if he hadn't offered me a contract. Or showed up at my door when my house was burning and rode off with me on Shadow.

So why haven't I shied away from his touch?

Perhaps because I trust him. Like it or not, when I look up and see him coming, I feel safe.

We don't talk for a while. The path leads higher until we reach a flat area that winnows down to a wide path between twin mountain cliffs. My stomach freezes as I realize where we must be. When Clint died, they'd said he'd been trampled when a herd of cattle stampeded through a narrow opening between two mountains. I look up at the solid gray walls on either side and a shudder moves down my spine.

"Did you want to ask something?"

I turn and he's taken off his hat. His dark hair is tousled by the wind. His hat rests in his hand, on his thigh. His winter-blue eyes are washed out until his pupils are two black dots against ice. There's a hardness to his face that scares me, like he's thinking about something that conjures loathing in him.

It hits me right then that I'm alone with him.

Completely isolated.

The wind whistles through the opening. It smells like winter and on it I catch his scent. An odd sensation follows, a feeling like I've known him before this. In another life, a long, long time ago.

The hair on the back of my neck raises.

There are secrets like ghosts on his ranch. I have a feeling Gerard knows where each one is buried, because he put them six feet under.

"How far are we from the cabin?" I ask, my mouth dry.

Shadow moves up beside me and we fall into step together. Gerard's jaw works grimly.

"Not far," he says.

We move silently between the cliffs and the landscape opens up. The further we go from the mountain pass, the better I feel. When it's just a smudge in the distance behind us, I look up and see the cabin at the top of the mountain. It's barely peeking from the trees, but I can see it's simple, but comfortable. There's a small barn beside it with a paddock big enough for several horses.

"We built this ten years ago," he says. "That way if we have to be on the far side of the property, we've got a place to spend the night. And it makes a good hunting cabin."

"Do you hunt a lot?"

He shakes his head. "Maybe once, twice a year. All the meat on the ranch is from the cattle. But a couple times a season we bring in elk and deer. Do you hunt?"

I shake my head. "I've always been too busy on the ranch."

His eyes linger on me as we climb the hill, but he doesn't speak. I know he's thinking of my life before him—I see it in the grim line of his jaw. I know he disapproves of the way Clint treated me and that look in his eyes reminds me of the one I saw at the mountain pass. For the first time, a horrible, dark thought creeps into my mind.

No, Gerard might be intimidating, but he's not a murderer.

A chill moves down my spine and even Bluebell feels it and prances to the side. Gerard leans in and catches her right rein, steadying her. His brows crease in an unspoken question, but I'm speechless. He hated Clint, that's obvious, but...no, I should be ashamed of entertaining such a thought.

And yet...it was so convenient that Clint died the day after Gerard met me.

I shake my head hard. My husband was killed in an accident. That was verified by the coroner.

The coroner who's close friends with Gerard.

Damn it.

We pause outside the cabin and barn. He swings down from Shadow and the sound of his boots hitting frozen ground jerks me back to reality. Gerard isn't evil. He's rough, obsessive, and maybe a little controlling in some areas, but he's not that twisted.

He looks up at me, his dark lashes and brows making his pale eyes stand out like the sky against snow. My mouth goes dry. He moves close to me and lifts me down and I feel his hands on me for a fleeting moment. Strong, warm, safe. The first time I've felt safe since my father died.

My body wouldn't feel safe with a murderer. The wilderness is making my mind go down dark paths. Perhaps it was seeing the place where Clint died that triggered it.

I make the conscious choice to stop these thoughts in their tracks.

He takes both horses by the reins and walks between them to the barn. We brush them down and put them in their stalls with grain and water. Then he leads the way to the cabin and unlocks the door.

It's all one room inside except for the lofted bedroom upstairs. He taps the thermostat and the heat kicks in. Then he crosses the living area and crouches by the fireplace to stack logs and kindling inside.

I peel off my coat and flannel and let them drop to the ground. The clock above the stove shows it's almost six. I know he's probably hungry and for the first time in a while, I actually want to cook something. I pull off my boots and pad into the kitchen in my socks and start going through the cabinets.

"What's this, redbird?"

I turn. He's standing in the hall, looking down at my coat and boots with a faintly amused expression. My stomach flips and I gather my things up. His eyes follow me as I back down the hall and I'm at a loss for what he's thinking.

"Where do I put my things?" I whisper.

He jerks his head towards the loft.

I scamper up the stairs and place my coat on the bed and my boots by the bathroom door. The mattress is covered in a white quilt and a thick fur blanket. The floor has a southern style print rug, and there's a little lamp by the bed. Otherwise, it's bare. I stand on my toes to look out the window. The view is astounding. I think I can see the ranch in the distance. A tiny speck.

When I return, he's taken off his coat. His Henley is rolled up to his elbows and he's kneeling by the fireplace, nursing the flames.

"Are you hungry?" I ask.

He nods. "I could eat."

I go to the kitchen area. There's everything I need in the pantry for biscuits, even dry milk, and I get to work. He leaves the fireplace crackling and comes over to lean on the island counter. His eyes burn like his touch as they watch me cut biscuits and arrange them on a greased tray.

"You're good at that," he says.

"I'm a good cook," I say.

He runs a hand over his jaw, short beard rasping. "I wasn't snubbing your skills, you're just not on my payroll. Take your clothes off."

My head whips up. "What?"

"Remember our contract is in place right now."

My jaw is slack. "You want me to cook naked?"

The corner of his mouth jerks up. "Strip, redbird."

I freeze and he circles the counter until he's right behind me. His heat washes over me and his big, rough hands slip under my sweatshirt and pull it over my head. My pulse quickens. He unfastens my jeans and tugs them off. Leaving me in nothing but my bra and panties.

He slaps my ass, gripping it. "You can keep your bra and panties. For now."

I flush to the roots of my hair. He goes upstairs and I hear his boots in the loft and when he comes back down, he's in just a pair of sweatpants. The bull skull on his chest looks at me first, but I can't look away.

He sinks down in the chair by the fireplace and leans back, spreading his knees.

The oven beeps. I slide the tray inside and wipe my hands. There's maple sausages cooking on the top. I'm making biscuits, gravy, eggs, and pancakes.

I've never met a man who didn't get excited about breakfast for dinner.

"Can I get you a drink?" I ask, looking around.

He cocks his head. "For me?"

"Yeah." I put one hand on my hip. "You want some whiskey or something?"

The corners of his mouth turn up. There's tempered amusement in his eyes. "I'm sober."

He is? I run through our interactions and try to remember if I've ever seen him drink before. I recall having wine with him...but now that I look back, I don't remember ever seeing him pick up a glass and take a drink.

I wonder why I didn't notice until now. I've never lived with a man who didn't at least have a shot of whiskey at night when the work was done.

I wonder what he does to unwind, and then realize that's a stupid question.

Me—he does me to unwind.

I pad barefoot across the room. "I guess I didn't know."

He pats his knee once and my stomach flips as I sink down onto it. His palm rubs a slow circle on my lower back before gripping the swell of my ass. I can feel the heat coming off his body and I have to resist sinking against his bare chest. He's so big and solid and when I'm with him, I don't mind feeling weak.

That part caught me off guard. I never liked showing weakness before. It made me a target for Clint's ire. With Gerard, I feel myself reverting to a state of dependency that would have horrified me weeks ago.

187

It feels natural. He's got a wild mind and a cold heart, but for me he's willing to forgo both. The least I can do is not question his authority in the world he built.

"Yeah, I got the liquor before the liquor got me," he says.

There's so much about him I don't know. Never in a million years would I have imagined Gerard Sovereign had weaknesses. I reach out and skim my fingers over his tattooed chest. Does he have more secrets hidden behind his hard front?

"Can you tell me about it?" I ask.

"There's not much to say. I had some shit happen to me when I was nineteen. I was young and couldn't hold it together, so I started getting fucked up. Then Westin cleaned me up and I lived with his family. Stayed there a while, got sober. Been sober ever since."

My brows rise. "You've been sober since before you could legally drink."

He dips his head. "That's true."

I shift so I'm facing him. He puts his other hand on me, encircling my waist.

"Can I ask...what happened?"

His lids lower. For a moment, I think I've gone too far. But he lets out a slow sigh and I think I feel his walls come down. Just a little bit.

"I was engaged," he says. "About to get married. Then she died."

My stomach drops. I wasn't in love with Clint, so I don't know what he felt. But I did lose a spouse so I know how disorienting it is to be the one left behind. I know what being suddenly untethered feels like, and it's not pleasant.

"I'm so sorry," I whisper.

He looks at the ground. "It was a long time ago, redbird. And I was so young I thought it was the end of the world."

"And it wasn't?"

He shakes his head. He raises his eyes to mine and I can't read them.

"I'm not the same person I was back then."

"But it still hurt you," I whisper.

"It...destroyed me," he says. "But I moved on."

I try to find the right words, but my brain is still trying to wrap my head around the concept of a nineteen-year-old Gerard. Who was he then? Why was he so alone that there was only Westin to save him from his grief? What had happened to his parents?

I know nothing about the man who has total control over me.

I open my mouth to speak, but he pulls me in by the nape of the neck and kisses me. My stomach curls with heat and my brain goes silent.

From the first time his mouth touched mine, I've craved being kissed by him. He's slow, thorough, and deliberate. Like he's got nowhere to be and nothing to do but make sure his taste is burned into my lips.

My lower spine arcs. He pulls back an inch and our breath mingles.

"Put your tongue out, redbird," he says, his voice husky and quiet.

Hesitantly, I obey. He bends in and spits onto it.

"Swallow," he says.

Pussy aching, I swallow for him...because what else am I supposed to do?

He tells me what to do and I do it without thinking. Especially after that night in the game room. When he slipped the barrel of his gun into me and called me a Garrison slut. That night made me understand why everyone on Sovereign Mountain obeys him without question.

Because he might not be evil, but he's not good either.

He's a lot like the wilderness surrounding us tonight. Placid, breathtaking on the surface. Wild and harsh, deadly underneath.

I glance up and our gazes clash.

"Can I ask you something?" I whisper.

"Anything," he says. "But I might not answer."

"The game room...what you did to me there...what would you have done if the gun went off?"

He tilts his head, sinking back. "It didn't go off."

"But what if it had?" I press. "You risked that to...prove a point?"

His grip tightens on my hips until it hurts. "I wasn't proving a point about me, redbird. It was about you."

189

"Okay...what point?"

His other hand goes to my knee, curling around it. Yanking me closer in his lap until my palms are flat on his chest.

"I discovered that my redbird has an appetite," he says. "One that I can satisfy."

He's talking in riddles again. I've grown to realize that's how he hides his secrets. He flips every answer into a question or statement about the inquirer.

"But what if?" I whisper.

"What if, redbird?" he says softly. "You tell me what if?"

I can barely breathe when he's close like this. My eyes flick over his face. Noting the few bits of gray at his temple. It's only a few hairs, but it reminds me with a sharp jolt that I'm only twenty-one.

"What if another man put his gun in my pussy?" I say, knowing my words are explosive.

His eyes narrow. "Do you think I've never killed before?"

My jaw drops and my body tingles. I don't know what I expected, but it wasn't for him to go right for the throat. I stare at him, waiting for his face to crack. For a smile to appear. But his expression is set in stone.

"You...um...have you?" I whisper.

He grips my chin and pulls me in for a rough, open mouthed kiss.

"Better get to that gravy," he says.

The food—I forgot it's still cooking. Dizzy, I scramble out of his lap and head to the kitchen. My face is bright pink, I can feel it burning down my neck, and my legs are unsteady. I pull the biscuits from the oven and take the gravy off the low burner. I know he's looking as I pour leftover grease into a cast iron skillet and start frying eggs. When I turn around, his pale eyes are fixed to me.

"What are you staring at?" I whisper.

I get a hint of a smile.

"Just you," he says.

Why?

Why does he stare at me like he's eating me alive with his eyes?

Why does he hold me like he never wants to let me go?

Why does he care at all?

And did he do something so terrible I can't let the thought form in my head without guilt?

Pushing it aside, I set the table for two and fill our plates. He makes coffee and we sit opposite each other. He tries the gravy and his brow goes up.

"You're quite the cook," he says.

"Thank you," I say. "I know."

The corner of his mouth turns up. We eat in silence, and I manage to sip half a cup of his coffee even though it's so strong it could stand up on its own. When our plates are clean, he puts them in the sink.

"Can I ask you something?" I say.

His gaze flicks up and holds. "Depends."

"What...what did the Garrisons do to you?" I whisper.

The towel he's drying his hands on slips to the table. My heart beats against my ribs like a scared bird. Have I ruined everything?

"Why do you want to know?" he says finally.

I hesitate, chewing on my lip. Once upon a time, when I was young and hadn't tasted how cruel the world was, or how harsh men could be, I was braver.

Now I know life is so much colder and lonelier than I could have imagined. But I hope there's a spark of warmth in Sovereign.

I've felt it. I swear I have.

"I feel like you're a tangle of threads...it all leads back to the Garrisons," I whisper. "Clint was my husband and that means something to you. But I don't understand what."

His eyes flash. "Sir. When we're alone, you call me sir."

His walls are back up, good and hard.

I stand, tired of him being evasive. "Alright. I don't understand what the Garrisons mean to you. *Sir*."

He hears the bite in my tone. His hand comes up and he beckons me with two fingers. I go, but only because I signed my name on a dotted line. His big hands wrap around my waist and he lifts me onto the countertop.

I'm still shorter than him. He brushes back my hair and goosebumps rise down my arm and his fingers skim around my back. He unhooks my bra and slips it from my breasts. Methodically, he lifts my hips and takes my panties down my legs, pushing them into his pocket.

He's going to fuck me because he doesn't want to talk. I'm not doing that tonight.

"I want the contract completely off," I blurt out. "Just so I can talk to you without anything between us. Just for tonight."

His gaze snaps to mine. "No, you don't."

"Yes, sir, I do."

His hand closes around my throat and my hips tighten. The countertop is cool beneath my bare pussy and I know I'm wet.

No, fuck being wet, I'm soaked.

Our eyes lock.

"Did you like being fucked with my gun, redbird?" he says, jaw tight. "Is that who you want me to be with you?"

I swallow past his grip. "I want you to stop being afraid. Stop hiding behind your contract."

His head cocks. Slowly. I'm on the thinnest of ice.

"What are you going to do? Put a gun inside me? Fuck me until I bleed? You've already done both," I breathe.

His jaw tightens. "I've never done anything to you that you haven't begged for with that sweet, perfect mouth and body."

I grip his wrist, just below where his hand is wrapped around my throat. His other hand comes up, heading towards my sex, but I slap it. Battering it away.

My pussy aches deep inside, drenched at the feeling of his hand around my throat.

What does it say about me that I want this side of him most of all?

"Don't fucking deny me," he says.

That's when I realize the contract is off for the night. He's looking at me like he wants to devour me whole, and I know we're off the edge of the map.

Do safewords still count here?

I want him like this...raw and threatening. So I do the stupid thing and lift my gaze to his. Even though I know that when faced with a big, dangerous animal, I should avoid eye contact, drop, and cover myself as best I can.

"Don't fucking touch me," I shoot back. "*Sir*."

His hand moves between my thighs again and I lash out at his forearm with my nails. Blood wells up in two, short stripes from my pointer and middle fingers.

We both go still with shock as it drips once onto the counter.

"Fucking wildcat," he breathes.

I'm horrified, but still angry. He's drawn blood from me before and now we're even. He pulls me closer by the neck and his bleeding arm slides between us. I cry out as two fingers plunge into my pussy. Filling me with a shock of pleasure and pain.

"Fuck you," I hiss, arcing my hips.

His eyes flash like a thunderclap. "This is what you want, isn't it, redbird? You want to make me lose control? Hit me, you dirty little bitch."

My jaw drops. His words sting, but I don't know why. His jaw squares and his fingers flick my G-spot hard to remind me who's really in control. I swear I'm going to come just from being fucked on his hand.

"No, sir," I burst out.

"Fucking hit me," he orders.

"Gerard—"

"Do not use my name when I'm knuckle-deep in your cunt," he hisses. "Fuck me up, redbird. I'm already so fucked up for you there's nothing you can do that'll hurt me."

I backhand him across the face. The sound is like a whip cracking. I gasp and clench my smarting fist. He freezes, his face slapped to the side, a mark blossoming on his jaw. Then he whips his head around like an animal and lifts me by the neck, pulling me so close I can taste his breath.

Mint and Sovereign.

The slap doesn't phase him any more than the blood on his arm. I doubt he felt the sting.

"Did you do it?" I gasp.

I can't believe I let the thought that's been weighing on my mind out of my mouth.

Fuck.

I have to find a way to backtrack so I don't have to explain myself.

"Do what?" he says, eyes on my mouth.

His grip tightens and my vision flashes. Into my mind rushes a torrent of images from the night we met. His eyes burning into me as I confessed that I was frightened of Clint.

"Is your husband a mad dog?" he'd asked.

The cliffs—they're haunted by something. The mountain pass is stained in blood, and I wonder if seven months ago, that blood also stained the hand around my neck. His fingers tighten and my head spins.

"If you're going to accuse me, be a big girl and do it to my face," he says.

"Did you kill my husband?" I whisper.

He withdraws abruptly and I sink back, gasping. His chest, covered in that black and white bull skull, heaves. God, I can't get away from those sightless eyes. Sweat breaks out on his neck and trickles down between his pecs. Catching in the hair.

"You and I, redbird, our interests aligned," he says.

"Don't." I'm raising my voice and I don't mean to, but I can't stop. "Don't talk in riddles. Give me a fucking straight answer. Sir."

He comes back to the counter and his palms slide up my waist. Touching me so gently I want to crumble. He's cradling me and it's a stark contrast to the anger pounding through his eyes. He wants to break something, but he's touching me like I'm made of glass.

"I saw you," he says, his voice low and husky. "I wanted you. And now you're mine."

My stomach goes cold. This time, I understand what he's saying without him spelling it out. He saw me, he wanted me, so he killed Clint to make me his. My stomach turns. This is the dark undercurrent I feel when it's just us. I felt it on the pool table, his gun against my pussy. And I feel it now.

My lips part. My mouth is so dry.

"I don't like your riddles," I whisper. "But this time...I know the answer."

He bends in and kisses the side of my neck. My nipples go hard and my hips tighten, my lower spine arcing towards his body. His hot mouth trails down to my shoulder and he bites it gently. I gasp, letting my head fall back.

The ceiling spins. How can I still want him?

"I will never let you go, redbird," he says.

His words are soft, like a declaration of love, but chilling like the cold wind through the pines.

CHAPTER TWENTY-EIGHT

GERARD

I lift her in my arms and she doesn't struggle. We sink to the kitchen floor and her hair pools around her head. My hand goes down to the tie of my sweatpants and she shakes her head. Her wet lashes flutter.

"Don't," she whispers.

I slide my hand up her inner thigh and my fingers meet warm slickness. Coating her sex and upper thighs. When I part her with my finger and thumb, I can see how flushed and ready to be fucked she is. Her lower back arcs and I graze my touch over her clit. Her mouth parts and she whimpers.

"Please," she begs.

My cock is so hard it aches. Every move I make, I feel the fabric of my sweatpants rub against it. Threatening to set me off before I can get inside her pussy. I push the waistband down and unleash my length, sinking down until our hips meet. Our mouths are inches apart.

"Sovereign. Don't." Her eyes are wide.

If she were locked up, I'd get off her. But she's drenched and her hips ride up, rubbing her wet cunt along the underside of my cock.

From the base all the way to the tip, pelvis tilting like she's trying to get me inside.

"Are you ashamed to be fucked by the man who killed your husband?" I breathe.

Her eyes roll back and her hips stutter. Maybe she hasn't put the feeling into words yet.

"This changes nothing," I tell her. "You've already come on my cock, my face, my hands."

"I didn't know," she whimpers.

I shift my lower body to press hers down against the floor. Pinning her body beneath mine to keep her still.

"And now you know," I say. "And nothing has changed. You're mine, little redbird."

I'm being cruel, I know that. She was innocent—she doesn't know what the Garrison family did to mine or what they took from me. She wasn't there for all the years where the only thing that kept me going was the fantasy of looking in the eyes of each Garrison son before I put a bullet in their heads.

She doesn't know that Clint's murder was just one chapter in the dark story I've shielded her from. All she knows is that she had a shitty husband, but not one that deserved death. And now the man who killed him has her pinned to the kitchen floor, ready to take the spoils of war.

Of course she's fighting me.

I lift her thigh and wrap her leg around my waist. The soaked heat of her pussy touches the head of my cock and feral need erupts in my chest. So strong I have to bit my tongue to keep from devouring her right here. She shakes her head from side to side and her hand pushes against my chest. Her palm is flat and her nails pierce my skin.

The pain makes my eyes roll. Fuck.

"Wait," she begs.

Her hips push up against mine. Seeking the head of my cock.

"You're telling me no, but you're rubbing your pussy on me like a whore," I spit. "Do you even know what you want, redbird?"

"Fuck you," she pants. "Fuck you, Sovereign. Fuck you for everything you've done to me."

"I did you a favor," I say.

Her lids flutter. "You're a murderer."

"You know what to say if you really want me to stop."

"I hate you."

"That doesn't sound like your safeword to me."

She just shakes her head again. I take her hands and gather them in one fist and pin them above her head. Her hips rise and fall like she's begging to be filled. But when I slide up between her thighs, she moans and jerks back.

"I'm not yours," she pants.

"Can you hear yourself moan for me? Your body already knows who it belongs to."

"Fuck you—"

I put my hand over her mouth and push into her pussy. It welcomes me easily, soaked and hot as it pulls me in deep. Her eyes go wide and she cries out as I draw back.

Then I thrust to the hilt and her blue irises roll back as she takes me all at once.

Without warning, she comes so hard her body convulses.

Her stomach shudders beneath me and she wails against my hand. Tears soak her lashes and stream down her face to her temples. Arousal floods my groin, the wet sounds loud as I grind myself against her clit.

It hits me all at once

The dark part of me I was afraid to show her...she gets off on that.

She wants me, as I am.

The realization should throw me off, but it doesn't. I've seen her come from having her breasts whipped. She needs pain and humiliation to feel pleasure. And whatever it is we're doing on the kitchen floor, she's soaked from it.

Her inner muscles tighten around me. I release her mouth and she gasps. She wails aloud and I let her because no one will hear her up here at the top of Sovereign Mountain. She can cry and beg, but there's no mercy at the edge of the world.

Just darkness and monsters like me.

She lashes out and I catch her wrist, flipping her onto her belly. Her ass lifts, begging for me even as she writhes under my hand. I gather her breathtaking hair in my fist, a river of soft red, and pin her to the floor with it.

Then, my other hand braced beside her head, I sink back into her cunt. Filling her until she gives a quiet sob and gives up.

"That's a good girl," I praise.

She's loose now. Her body goes limp and soft beneath mine. Instead of hissing like a cat, she's moaning as I fuck into her sweet pussy. All her fight is gone, and her acceptance drives my desire to new heights.

I slam into her hips and her ass shakes beautifully. Her head falls back and as I thrust in hard, I bend and kiss her forehead. Breathing in the pomegranate scent of her hair. Intoxicated, I rut my hips against her ass and find that sweet place where her throat connects to her shoulder with my mouth.

She gasps as I bite down. Her skin is so fucking soft.

Her nails scrape the floor. Her body shakes under me.

Then she comes again and I feel the wetness against our bodies and the kitchen floor. She gives a harsh sob and starts fighting again. Arching her back and lashing out with her claws. Unperturbed, I grip her wrist and pin it down, subduing her rage.

She doesn't know what she needs. She's just fighting blindly because she's never been safe until now.

My hips stutter and I know I can't hold back for long. The scent of her hair fills my nose, the taste of her skin between my teeth, and the hot pulse of her pussy are too much.

I fall over her, hips bucking as I empty myself. My hand grips her around the throat, forcing her back up against my chest. My hips ride out the final pulses of my orgasm against her cervix. My mouth hovers just over her ear. I can feel her lungs flutter in her chest.

"Is this what you want, you pretty whore?" I whisper through my teeth. "You want to be forced like this? On your knees on the kitchen floor?"

She twists, but I have her firmly in my grip. Holding her down like an animal in a trap.

"Answer me," I press, kissing down the side of her neck.

"Fuck you, Sovereign," she hiccups.

"Why?" I urge.

She sobs, her whole body shaking. "Because...because you are a monster. And I'm...I'm falling for you."

My entire body goes numb. Like I've been hit with a bolt of lightning. I'd dreamed of those words in my unconscious mind. But I've only ever hoped to hear her speak them. I pull from her and flip her onto her back.

She's flushed and her big eyes are stained with tears. She bit her lip and there's a spot of blood.

I bend in and kiss it. Licking the crimson from her skin.

"Fall for me, redbird," I breathe. "I'll catch you."

She shakes her head hard from side to side. High from desire, weak with emotion, and still limp from the aftershocks of her pleasure.

"You are...not a good man," she whispers.

"So what?" I brush a strand of hair from her forehead.

"I thought you were giving me a choice with the contract. You never gave me a choice." Her fingers curl into her open palms. She has my blood under her nails.

I study her, focusing on a little strand of red hair that's stuck to her temple with sweat.

She's right. I never gave her a choice.

I should have, and if my life had gone much differently a long time ago, I would have taken a gentler route. But that's not who I am anymore.

The problem is, I'm struggling with the moments and memories and people that made me the man I am. I haven't done that in years.

Not since I built a fortress at the top of Sovereign Mountain and locked myself in it.

Then she came, my redbird.

My little spark of color in a lifetime of winter.

Does she deserve to know why I'm all fucked up inside? I know the answer already. If I'm going to be her man, if she's going to fall for me, she deserves the truth.

We're so embedded in one another it's only fair I tell her what the Garrisons did to me and the ones I loved most.

CHAPTER TWENTY-NINE

KEIRA

I'm so ashamed I can't move. I'm not sure what he just did to me. The word that bounces around my mind doesn't fit. A part of me knows that if I'd started crying in earnest, if my body had locked up, he would have stopped.

If he didn't force me, then what did we just do?

He's a sadist.

So that makes me his masochist.

Does that mean what we did was play? Because it felt deadly serious.

I don't have time to unravel my feelings because I'm angry that I told him I was falling for him even though he killed Clint. I'm so fucking angry that even though I said no and I meant yes, neither of those words meant anything to him in the end.

And I'm so ashamed because I should hate him, but I don't.

Tears spill down my temples. Catching in my hair. He picks me up and I sag against his naked chest as he carries me up the stairs. We're both a mess. Both sticky with his blood and our cum. He pulled his sweatpants back up, but I see the wet stains seep through the front.

I must have been soaked.

Distantly, the shower runs. Then he lifts me and we're standing on cold tile with steamy water running over our bodies. He tilts my chin up and all the anger is gone from his face.

"Do you want the truth, redbird?" he says hoarsely.

I swallow hard. The last time he told me the truth, it was horrifying. But I have to know, so I nod weakly.

"The woman I was engaged to...Clint Garrison killed her," he says. "She was twenty, I was nineteen. There was an ongoing feud between myself and the Garrisons. Clint ran into her at a bar one night. He offered to drive her home, but instead he crashed his truck outside the lodging house I was staying at with Westin. We heard the noise from the house. I pulled her body from the vehicle, but she was gone."

My jaw is slack. He's staring at the wall, his thumb moving over my chin in a slow circle.

"I'm so sorry, Sovereign," I whisper.

"She was pregnant, about seven weeks," he says. "After that, I got snipped. I thought if I couldn't have her babies, I wouldn't have any. I regret that."

"You can get it reversed," I whisper.

He shrugs. The slow realization of what he said is sinking in hard. Clint did that. My dead husband killed his fiancée.

It was no wonder he'd wanted revenge, or that he had a chip on his shoulder about me being Clint's widow.

"How did Clint survive?" I whisper.

He clears his throat. All I can see is that black and white bull skull swimming in my vision. Dotted with dark hairs and water droplets.

"The police said it was accidental," he says. "But he ran the passenger side of the truck into a wall. The rest of the car was fine, he barely had a scratch."

"Do you think it was an accident?" I manage.

His eyes go dark. "It doesn't matter to me."

I'm still aching from what he did to me on the kitchen floor. But I lift my hands and lay my palms on his hard stomach. He feels like life, like warm flesh and blood. I want to close my eyes and pretend everything leading up to this moment was a dream.

Pretend there was no Clint.

No contract.

No death.

My breath hitches. He pulls me against him and strokes my soaked hair.

"Don't cry, redbird," he rumbles. "No one will hurt you again."

"No one, but you," I whisper.

He doesn't answer, he just washes me and turns off the shower. We lay down in the bed in the loft. His mouth finds my neck and he's so gentle this time when he kisses me.

His tongue soothes the place where his bite mark is imprinted in my skin. I stroke over the scabbed scratches on his arm as his finger and thumb tease at my nipples until they're hard.

He doesn't fuck me even though my sore pussy aches again. His mouth moves down my stomach. Kissing lightly until he gets to my sex. Desire roars back to life, and I find myself spreading my thighs wide to beg for his touch. His tongue slips hot and wet over my clit and I let my head fall back into the pillow and give in.

My hand weaves in his hair.

"I hope you're being honest with me," I whisper.

He kisses the inside of my thigh. "I will always protect you."

I know that means he's still not telling me everything. Maybe because it's too ugly for me to see. My heart thumps and I'm so ashamed.

Am I so starved for love that I'll swoon over my husband's murderer?

A part of me wonders...did Clint kill that poor woman on purpose? Or was it really an accident?

Because to me, the truth would change everything. But to him, it means nothing. He's got a black and white view of justice. He's the sort of man no one wants as their enemy because he won't stop until the scales are balanced.

I look down at him and his hard eyes are soft for the first time. He's looking at me like there's no one else in this world. My throat tightens and tears gather in my eyes. He dips his head and licks slowly over my entrance. Soothing the sore places with his tongue.

"You taste like mine, redbird," he says hoarsely.

My eyes smart.

Maybe I'll tie him to a chair and call the police and make him confess. Maybe I'll slip away and catch a train up north to Ontario and never see him again.

But I know I won't do either of those things. Just as I knew I'd sleep with him without a contract, I know I'll follow him anywhere. We're a swift train heading into darkness and only he knows what's up ahead.

CHAPTER THIRTY

GERARD

I feel so naked I can't sleep. I'm not used to letting anyone see my scars and I feel almost guilty for having shown them. Part of me wishes I could take it all back. It's not her responsibility to bear my burdens.

It's not anyone's but mine.

She sleeps fitfully beside me. In the early morning—or is it just late at night—I pull her body back against mine and trace the full curve of her naked hip and the sharp dip of her waist. I kiss the back of her neck until she stirs and her eyes flutter open.

"I need you," I murmur. "Open your legs."

She arcs her back and her eyes slip shut. "Do what you want to me, Sovereign. I'm going back to sleep."

I push my hand between her thighs and stroke her pussy and listen as her breathing deepens. She doesn't stir again as I wet her sex with saliva and push my cock into her entrance. I'm hard, but my desire to come wanes as I bask in the feeling of being inside her.

She feels like home.

More than Sovereign Mountain ever has. The ranch is my fortress, but she is the warmth, the heart, inside.

I nestle her soft ass up against me and exhaustion finally hits my brain. Outside the wind howls and bits of freezing rain bounce off the windows. Beneath the quilt and fur blanket, I'm so deep in her I can feel her heartbeat around my cock. Her scent has gone from something I notice to something so familiar it's just the air I breathe now.

There's no going back.

No letting go, no giving up now. We were meant to be like this, I feel it in my bones. I'm certain of one thing. This woman and I were made from the same kind of stardust.

CHAPTER THIRTY-ONE

GERARD

It's late when I roll over to find her still sleeping. She's relaxed and her hair covers the pillow in a soft cloud. She has a mark on her throat where I gripped her, a bruise on her knee from the kitchen floor, but otherwise she's unharmed. Bending, I kiss her thigh. Moving up to kiss just above her clit. I can smell my cum on her pussy and it's so fucking satisfying.

I slip from the bed, pull on my clothes, and leave the cabin to check the horses.

It snowed, but not heavily enough to impede our trip back.

Bluebell and Shadow are ready to be out of their stalls and they both do several laps around the fence. Kicking up snow and dried grass. I break the ice on their water and toss a bale of hay into their paddock.

She's awake when I get back inside. Naked and frying eggs on the stove. I linger in the door just to look at her perfect, heart-shaped ass, but she hears me and turns around.

She swallows, her throat bobbing hard. Then she lifts her arms out.

"Hold me," she whispers. "Please."

I shed my coat and gather her in my arms, lifting her onto the counter. She buries her face in the cold front of my shirt. I feel her give a shudder and I run my palms down her spine. Soothing her with gentle strokes.

I kiss the top of her head. "I've got you, baby girl."

She pulls back and kisses my mouth and, fuck, she's sweet. I dart my tongue in between her lips for an extra taste and she moans. Her lids are lowered when I pull back.

She's still hungry.

"I have something for you," I say.

Her brows go up. "What?"

"Stay," I tell her.

She sits still on the counter as I retrieve a small package from my saddlebags. I open it and take the discreet collar out first. It's a fine silver chain with a matching circle at the center.

She lifts her hands, opening her fingers. Then she flicks her gaze up and pulls back, waiting obediently for me to make the first move.

"What is that?"

"Your day collar," I say.

Her tongue darts out and wets her lips. "Is the contract...still what you want?"

"Yes," I say, without hesitating. "I need a place where I can fuck you the way you need fucked without hurting you. If you want to keep it in the bedroom, that's fine. But I want you collared."

Her naked breasts heave and her pink nipples contract. I put the discreet collar around her slender throat and click it into place, rotating the latch. If she wants it off, she'll need a pair of wire cutters. Her fingers come up and touch the little silver ring between her collarbones.

Satisfaction floods my chest. She drops her hand and I touch the chain, playing with it between my finger and thumb.

"How do you feel?" I ask.

I slid my grip loosely over her throat. She looks up at me through her lashes.

"I feel like you are not a good man, Sovereign," she says. "And I shouldn't want you."

My mouth turns up. "But you do."

"I do," she whispers.

That's all I need to hear. I pull out the leather play collar next. Her eyes widen as I unfurl the rows of bluebells engraved and polished into the dark leather. The edges are smoothed and the inside is soft fabric so it doesn't irritate her skin.

I fit it around her throat, over the discreet collar, with the soft inner lining against her skin. She shivers and her eyes widen. It's engraved and sealed so it looks like glossed wood. In the front is the Sovereign Mountain Ranch insignia and at the nape of her neck are my initials in gunmetal gray.

A little tag hangs between her collarbones. I tap it and it jingles.

"What is that?" she asks.

"Name tag."

"What does it say?" Her gaze is wary.

"Sovereign. I want my whore wearing my name."

Heat floods her face and she tugs the metal tag. "Is that how you think of me?"

"When you're on your knees with my cock down your throat, yes."

I'm trying to keep things light. But seeing her in my collars is pushing me to the point she was at when she said she was falling for me.

Feelings aren't my strong suit. I know how I feel for her, but I'm not good at saying those words aloud.

So I swallow past the lump in my throat. And take her own words.

My hands come up, cradling her face. Her eyes are huge.

"Maybe...I'm falling for you," I say.

Her lips part and her breath catches. Her lashes flutter and I know tears simmer right on the edge.

"Really?" she whispers.

I open my mouth to tell her more, but I find I don't have the words to describe what I'm trying to say. She doesn't know everything I've done to get her, and when she finds out, she'll know just how obsessed I am.

But for right now, I just kiss her. So hard I swear I feel her heart beating in my mouth.

When I pull away, she's flustered. She pushes her hair back.

"That's it?" she asks.

"That's it, redbird," I say. "For now."

I put her on her feet and slap her ass hard enough the recoil shivers down her thighs. She gives a little huff, but when I swipe my finger over the seam of her pussy, it's soaked.

She makes eggs, naked except for both my collars. I wash up and sit at the table to soak in the view. She's so fucking beautiful it feels like a physical ache in my chest just looking at her.

Every little dip, every curve, every soft line, every dimple in her thigh—a work of art.

I could spend my lifetime tracing the lines of her body with my tongue and never get tired.

We eat and then we fuck. In the loft, the bed thudding against the wall so hard it leaves a dent in the wood. I wrap my belt around her wrists and bind her to the headboard. Her hips barely touch the bed while I eat her out until she comes over and over. The sheets are soaked after the fifth orgasm.

"Stop," she begs, trying to kick me off her. "Fuck you, Sovereign, I need a break."

I kneel and push the front of my pants down.

"Fuck you too, sweetheart," I tell her, slamming my cock into her soaked pussy. "You can take it just fine."

She cries and comes, then we eat leftovers and have coffee. The horses are somewhere in the mountains, but we both forgot why we're here. Instead of leaving at noon, we go back to bed and she pushes me on my back and sinks down on my cock.

Her lip quivers and she bites it as our bodies join. I know she's in pain, I fucked her raw last night and this morning. But she's insatiable, and she digs her claws into the tattoos on my chest as she grinds her hips. Her eyes roll back in her head.

"You're a fucking wildcat," I pant.

She grins breathlessly, white teeth flashing. It's cold downstairs, but it's hot in the loft and sweat etches between her breasts. I grip the soft swell on either side of her hips and work with the rhythm of her body. Rising and falling, grinding until she shudders and her head falls back.

Her tits heave.

A warm flood soaks my groin. The tag on her collar shakes.

"That's right, redbird," I pant. "You fucking come all over this cock."

She's so weak she can barely sit up, so I flip her over and stroke her clit and fuck her until she comes again. I'm in no hurry to finish. As long as I can stay hard, I'm keeping her on my cock. And I've never had a problem staying hard.

She cries. That's fine, she can safeword me when she's had enough.

CHAPTER THIRTY-TWO

KEIRA

I don't ask him when we're leaving. The afternoon wanes into night. He goes out before dark and takes care of the horses. I stand by the window and watch him whistle for them to come back to their stalls. It's cold out, but he's just in his shirt. The muscles ripple across his back as he pulls the bar over the door.

Cold comes in on his skin as he returns. I shut and lock the door, turning to lean against it.

"Is there any meat for dinner?" I ask.

"There's a freezer in the kitchen pantry," he says. "But it won't be defrosted until tomorrow."

"Are we staying that long?"

He's by the sink, washing his hands. He pauses, wiping down his forearms with a towel, and his eyes snap to mine. That faintly amused expression is back.

"Yes, we'll stay," he says. "I'll ride out tomorrow and locate the horses. We'll leave the morning after."

He spanks my ass lightly as he walks by, gripping it hard through my panties. There's a driving possessiveness to the way he touches me and, my God, it keeps me wet.

I hear him rummaging in the pantry and then he sets a pack of frozen meat in the sink. He watches me, leaning on the kitchen counter, while I cook breakfast again. His stoicism is attractive, but it's also frustrating. After everything we've done together, I assumed he'd be more open.

Maybe there's nothing left to be open about. Maybe it died with the woman he loved first.

I swallow past my dry throat.

"What was her name?" I ask.

His expression doesn't change. "Mariana."

"Was...was she pretty?"

He nods.

"Do you...do you still love her?"

He's somewhere far away. I can see the mist settle over his face. Finally he shakes his head.

"No, I stopped loving her a long time ago. Young love only stays if it has a chance to turn into something more," he says finally.

Bacon spits in the pan, leftover from the morning. I turn, leaning on the counter and grip the edge so hard it bends my nails. My heart picks up.

"When did you start falling for me?" I whisper.

He doesn't look up for a moment. Then he finally lifts his azure gaze to mine and my breath hitches. For the first time there's something there that looks like peace.

His jaw works. "When I saw you in your husband's office."

Deep inside, I knew this already. He upturned our world for no reason. He could have taken revenge on Clint at any point, but he chose the day after I confessed I was scared. He opened the gates of his fortress and let me into his bed despite how deeply he'd been hurt before.

I bite my lip, worrying it hard.

He picks me up and sets me on the counter. It should bother me the way he likes to move me around whenever he likes, but it doesn't.

"Do you love me?" he asks.

I don't know the answer to that yet. "I'm falling for you," I whisper.

His mouth thins. He takes my chin between his finger and thumb. I reluctantly shift my eyes up to meet his piercing gaze.

"You might not love me yet, redbird, but you will."

"Do I have a choice, sir?" I sigh.

"No." He kisses my forehead and I close my eyes.

"What are you going to do about the Garrison brothers?" I ask.

He rumbles, like he's laughing somewhere in his chest, and pulls back. "You let that up to me. I know if their parents were still alive, I'd skin them slowly before I took mercy on them and put a bullet between their eyes."

My jaw goes slack. "What did his parents do to you?"

"That's an ugly story."

"I want to hear it."

"My parents were tenants on their land, back when my family had nothing," he says. He's using the same flat tone he used when he talked about his fiancée's death. "Abel Garrison tried to rape my mother and my father defended her. After that, the Garrisons evicted them. They had nothing. My father started drinking...my mother got cancer and passed away. My father died of hypothermia. Drank too much, it was winter, he fell asleep in a ditch and never woke up."

My entire body tingles with shock. When he said he had a dark and bloody history with the Garrisons, I'd expected a feud over land.

"How old were you when your father passed?" I whisper.

"Sixteen." He lifts his chin. "After that, I went to Colorado to train. During the summer, back in Montana, I thought it would be a good idea to go after Avery Garrison at a bar one night. He shot me in the leg."

"He shot you?" My voice rises.

He releases me and unfastens his belt, pushing his pants down enough to expose his upper thigh. I didn't notice it before, but there's a faint scar there. Round and silvery. He pulls his pants up, but leaves his belt hanging.

"I told you, redbird, you and I, our interests aligned."

I touch his cheek, his short beard coarse under the heel of my palm. His skin is so warm with a little bit of roughness from being tanned in the Montana sun. His lids fall halfway and he leans into my touch. Like he's starved for it.

"Maybe we were destined to be tied together by all of this," I say quietly.

"No," he says firmly. "I chose you and made you mine. Despite you having that son of a bitch for your husband."

"Does it bother you that I slept with him?" I whisper.

Flame flickers in his eyes and he leans in and takes hold of my throat. His fingers encircle it and hold me firmly as he kisses my mouth. When he pulls back, I feel my nipples harden. My chest heaves and he puts his hand between my breasts.

"Do you remember how he felt?" he says softly. "Inside you?"

He's so jealous and it's giving me a tender ache between my thighs.

"Sometimes," I admit.

His lip curls. "So you need fucked harder if I want that memory erased."

"It's not a good one."

He puts me on my feet and strips my panties off. Not taking his eyes off mine, he spits into his hand and pushes it between my thighs.

My head spins as he sinks two fingers into me and finds that sweet spot. I feel more tender than usual, maybe because he's used me so hard the last twelve hours.

His mouth meets mine.

When he pulls back, my lips tingle.

"I shouldn't be jealous of a dead man, but I am," he says hoarsely.

My hips ache, but it's not pleasant this time. I push back and he pulls his fingers from me and I clap my hand over my mouth. His pointer and middle finger are stained red, a little rivulet dripping down his wrist.

He glances down, but his expression doesn't change.

"I'm so sorry," I rasp. "I guess I started my period."

He lifts his bloody hand and studies it. "I've never been with a woman who wasn't on birth control. It's the first time I've had period blood on me."

I wish I could crawl into a hole and live there forever.

"Here, let's wash it off."

He lifts his hand to his mouth and I panic, slapping his wrist away. His brow shoots up.

"What the fuck is wrong with you?" I hiss.

"It's just blood," he says, but he lets me grip his arm and wash his fingers in the sink.

I'm so mortified I can't speak. He's on the brink of laughter—I can feel his chest shaking. I order him out of the kitchen. Face burning, I slip upstairs and grab my panties and tuck a handful of toilet paper inside. I return to find him leaning on the counter with a glint in his eye.

"Go wait in the living room, please," I whisper.

He bends, kissing the side of my neck. "Whatever you like, redbird."

He sits on the couch. I feel his eyes follow me as I finish making dinner. When we're done eating, he carries me upstairs. I stand with my arms wrapped around my body, wondering what he's doing as he disappears into the bathroom. I'm too sore for sex, so I hope he's not expecting it. But he walks out with a towel, which he lays over the sheet. Our eyes meet as he kneels down and slips my panties off and lifts me into the bed.

He pulls me close, stretching his body out against mine. He's like a furnace, wrapped around me. It soothes my aching muscles and I feel myself relax into him. His fingertips move softly through my hair to my scalp, massaging gently over my temples.

I've never been comforted on my cycle. It's strange—I'm used to concealing it and pretending I'm not in agony. But I feel so safe wrapped up in his arms with his hand in my hair.

"Thank you," I whisper. "Sorry, I didn't mean to put a damper on things."

He rumbles in his chest. "Don't apologize for being in pain. Just lay there and rest."

His lips brush my hair. My lashes flutter shut.

I haven't felt this safe in a long time.

CHAPTER THIRTY-THREE

GERARD

I wake early the next morning and she's still sleeping soundly. Rolling to my side, I tuck a strand of hair behind her ear. She doesn't stir, even when I peel back the covers to reveal her bloody thighs. Maybe she needs more rest when she bleeds.

I fill up a hot water bottle, wrap it in flannel, and lay it over her lower belly. She stays still, her breathing even as I part her thighs and tuck a folded towel between them.

Then I write a note and leave the cabin. I know exactly where the horses are, so I tack up Shadow and we take the main trail over the mountains. They've been less than a five minutes ride from the cabin this entire time. I see their backs huddled in the three sided shelter near a round hay bale.

I rope them, one by one, and bring them to the paddock. It's crowded, but we won't be here long and they'll fit in the open barn tonight. When I return to the cabin, she's still upstairs. I climb the stairs to find her standing in the shower, steam clouding thick between us.

"You alright?" I ask.

She turns, her arms wrapped around her body. "Yeah, I just...um, I forgot to bring pads. I didn't think about it."

I lean against the sink and cross my arms. "There's extra flannel sheets, but that's about it. We don't get too many women up here at the cabin so you won't find pads."

"I think I can make flannel work," she says. Her gaze darts over me and fixes on the shower wall. "I'm not feeling great. I don't know how much use I'll be in rounding up the horses."

"Already done," I tell her.

She brightens. "Are they all okay?"

"They're fine, I put them in the barn. And they have enough space to wait until you're ready to leave."

"Maybe I'll go out to see them."

I shake my head. "No, you're getting back in bed."

She's not used to being taken care of. I see her struggle to accept my words, but finally she nods. I linger while she dries off and runs a comb through her hair. It takes her a while, but she finally gets her hair hanging in a wet curtain down her back.

She goes to braid it over her shoulder and I stop her.

"Let me," I say.

She watches me in the mirror, eyes wary. Gently, I gather her hair and braid it down her back, tying it off with the rubber band she hands me. When I'm done, she turns to inspect my handiwork.

"I've never met a man who can braid hair," she says. "Why did you learn how to do that?"

I take the braid in my fist, wrapping it twice around my grip. Immobilizing her head. Her breasts heave and our eyes meet in the mirror.

"Okay, I see," she whispers.

I release her and she lays back down in the bedroom. I feel her curious eyes on me as I rip strips of flannel to fold and put between her legs. When I refill the hot water bottle and place it on her lower belly, her lids flutter and sink down.

"Thank you," she whispers.

I kiss her forehead and leave her resting while I find breakfast. When I return to the bedroom, she's sitting upright with her back against the pillows. I lay the tray of reheated biscuits, jam, and coffee on the end of the bed and sit down at her side. My boot catches on her coat on the floor by the bed and something tumbles from the pocket.

It's the little painted mare she hides from me.

I pick it up and her eyes widen, her hand darting out to snatch it up, but I hold it back.

"Why do you carry this with you?" I ask.

"I don't," she says.

I give her a stern look. "No lying, redbird."

She twists her hands, picking her thumbnail. "My mother was from Sweden. She died right after I was born and that's all I have left."

I turn the wooden horse in my fingers. It's about four inches tall and the craftsmanship is impressive. Every ripple of muscle or knob of bone is visible. The body is painted with chestnut red and white markings. It reminds me a lot of Angel.

"You hide it from me," I say. "Why?"

Her finger digs harder. "It's a child's toy," she says, glancing up. "Clint said it was stupid that I carried it with me."

My brow rises. "Grief isn't stupid, redbird. The way you grieve doesn't have to make sense to anyone else."

She swallows and her eyes are wet again. "Thank you," she whispers.

I take her wrist, flipping her hand, and put the painted mare into her palm. "It looks like it was repainted. Did your father do that?"

She nods, a little smile gracing her lips. "He did it before he died."

"You must have loved him a lot," I say.

She never volunteers information about her past. I don't pry because I know so much about it already. Everyone she's ever trusted was bought for a blank check. Doctors, lawyers, judges—they gave up her secrets easily.

The only ones who didn't spill are dead.

"He was amazing, but he was pretty sick," she says quietly. "That's all I remember...this weight on my mind that he didn't have a lot of time. He got really ill near the end, that's why we sold our cattle and equipment. I wish…I wish I'd focused more on him and less on thinking about how he was going to die. I feel like his life is just…a blur in my memory."

A tear slips down her cheek.

"But you remember him," I say. "And the land he loved, that's still yours."

She blinks hard, wiping her face. "No, it's yours."

"Whatever happens, Stowe Farms will stay in the family," I say. "Break my heart, redbird, and I'll still give you what you're owed."

She sniffs and meets my gaze shyly. "Really?"

"I know what it feels like," I say simply.

She's quiet, turning the painted mare over and over in her fingers. Then she sets it aside and pats the bed.

"Have breakfast with me," she says.

I sit beside her and she tells me about her girlhood. Her words are colorful, filling my head with images of bluebells, sunsets, evenings by the fire while the winter wind tore at the farmhouse. She tells me how her father taught her to ride and shoot and rope cattle. How he always brought her candy or a book from South Platte when he went on errands.

She tells me about the little fragments her mother left behind. The Swedish dessert she baked from an old recipe. The burning wreath her father wove and put on her head for St. Lucy's Day and told her she was the most beautiful girl in the world. The book of fairy tales she read so often it fell apart in her hands.

She's lived her life in the shadow of death.

Maybe we're not so different, my redbird and I.

We sleep for a few hours in the afternoon. I wake before her, disoriented. It's been decades since I took a nap during the day. She's still sleeping soundly when I go to put the venison roast into the oven.

Then I go out to the back porch because I found a cigar that's still good and I want to have a fucking smoke. I never get a chance to unwind, so I'm taking it while I can.

The ground is dusted with snow. The entire world is silent.

I lean on the railing, the earthy tobacco taste on my tongue.

When I first met her, it was an instant attraction. A scorching hot lust that nothing could satisfy but her body. But now, what I feel for her is so much softer and deeper than anything I've felt before. I thought I loved Mariana, but now that I know Keira, I'm not sure I've ever been in love before now.

I'm never coming back from this obsession.

Westin told me once that I'm like a dog trained to fight. Once my jaws are locked in something, I'll never let go. He's right, especially when it comes to my redbird.

I smoke for a while, looking out over my ranch. Around two, the door opens and she steps out. She's in sweats, her bra, and my extra jacket. It's slipping off her shoulder, the light making her freckled skin glow.

"You feeling alright?" I ask.

She leans against my body, pushing her arm around my waist. "The meds kicked in. I didn't know you smoked cigars."

"One of my many vices."

She turns her face up, a little crease between her eyes. "You have no vices."

She's so fucking sweet. I kiss her forehead and she bends into me.

"I'm a hedonist for you," I say.

She smiles. "You are pretty dirty in bed," she admits.

"I've gone easy on you."

Her brows rise and she turns, leaning against the railing to face me. "What else do you want to do to me that you haven't already?'

I release a stream of smoke and lean over her, a hand on the rail on either side of her body.

"Choke your perfect throat. Fuck you until you pass out and fuck you to wake you back up. Find out how much fucking your mouth can take before you tap out. Paint your ass with bruises until you can't sit on it."

Her eyes widen, lids fluttering.

"You're a painslut and I want to know how far I can take that," I say.

Her lips part, her tongue flicking out. Her throat bobs.

"Why are you a sadist?" she whispers.

I consider feeding her some bullshit like I usually do, but I'm starting to think we're past that. I bend in and her breath washes over my face. Our lips brush, our bodies tense, and then our mouths come together.

I kiss her slowly, thoroughly. Until she moans and I break away.

"I need a lot to feel," I admit. "I'm just...numb. I have been for years."

Pain flickers through her eyes. "You can change that."

"Do you want me to?" I ask.

She takes a second to respond, but then she shakes her head.

"I want you as you are," she whispers.

This time, when I kiss her like it's the first and last time our mouths have touched. If I had the words, I'd tell her that she's the only cure I need for all the numbness in my heart. But I'm not good with words. So I let my body do the talking.

And I think she knows.

CHAPTER THIRTY-FOUR

KEIRA

We get back to the house at noon and Gerard disappears into the barn to get the horses settled. I drop my bag in the hall and walk through the quiet house. It's the middle of the day so everyone is out, even the dogs. I slip off my boots and pad up the stairs.

"Miss Garrison."

I turn to find Maddie standing in the living room. She looks almost nervous and that makes me nervous too.

"What's wrong?"

She climbs the bottom few stairs and holds out an envelope. "This is from your late husband's lawyer. I wasn't sure to give it to you or Sovereign."

"I'll take it," I say, pushing back my irritation. Has he been telling his staff that I'm not the point person for my ranch? "Thank you, I appreciate it."

She nods, frowning, and turns to go, but I clear my throat.

"Maddie," I say.

She pivots. "Yes?"

"Did...did I do something wrong to you?"

Her brows shoot up and I can see regret flicker through her face. "No, I'm sorry if I gave you that impression. I'm just...with you being a Garrison, I'm never sure what I can say. You know how Sovereign feels about your family."

I don't fault her for that.

"I'm not really a Garrison," I say in a rush. "I...it's hard being a woman up here. Would you be interested in maybe having lunch together sometime? Gerard said you eat with your husband, but if there's a day he's busy, I'd like to."

Her face softens. "Sure, he'll be gone this weekend."

I can't hold back my smile. "I'll look forward to it."

She smiles, and this time it's genuine. I skip upstairs and I think I hear her hum lightly as she heads back to the kitchen.

I push the bedroom door open and stop short. On Gerard's desk is a cardboard box with a lid, the kind used for storing documents. I push the door shut and pad silently across the carpet. There's black marker scrawled across the top that takes me a minute to work out.

Mrs. Clint Garrison.

I open the envelope so quickly it rips down the side and the paper inside falls open. It's a typed letter with Jay's name printed at the bottom.

Mrs. Garrison,

Enclosed is the remainder of your late husband's personal items left in my possession. If you have any questions regarding these or any other legal matters, I am handing his account off due to the unpaid balance detailed here.

My eyes skim down to the phone number below. And to the second number that's almost the same length.

Fuck. Why did I not realize I had to pay his lawyer?

The door opens behind me and I turn to see Gerard taking his coat off. I've never been good at finances because I never had access to my own money until Clint was gone. The impending doom of unpaid bills scares me. I turn and meet his eyes, panic tearing at my throat.

"What's wrong, redbird?"

Speechless, I hold out the paper. He takes it and there's a short silence before he hands it back.

"Don't worry about it," he says.

Don't worry about it? What the hell is that supposed to mean? I'm on the hook for over a hundred thousand dollars and I'm just supposed to not worry about it?

My hand shakes as I grip the paper. He removes his coat and pulls his shirt off. He goes to unfasten his belt, but he sees the tears spilling down my cheek and stops short.

He's beside me in a moment, pulling me against his bare chest. "I've got it, sweetheart. I'll pay it this afternoon."

"I'm sorry," I manage. "I feel so stupid."

He pulls back and wipes my tears with his thumb. "Stupid for what? They're not your bills."

I laugh weakly. "I don't know why it never occurred to me that I had to pay his lawyer. He did a bunch of work after Clint died and I guess I thought it was prepaid."

He lifts my chin and I sniff, trying to pull myself together. I'm not weak, but I cry as easily as turning on a faucet, and it's embarrassing. Clint hated it at the beginning, and then he liked to goad me until I burst into tears.

Gerard just wipes them from my cheek and kisses my forehead.

"What's in the box?" he says.

I go to the desk and lift the lid. Inside, there are stacks of folders and dozens of papers shoved between them. He leans over my shoulder as I grab a handful and pull them free. The top file falls open to reveal some tax documents from a few years ago.

"I think it's just some paperwork," I sigh.

He nods, but just before he turns to walk away, the files slip from my hand and thud to the ground. Papers fly everywhere and we both kneel down at the same time to catch them. I'm scrabbling on my hands and knees, burning with embarrassment, when I realize Gerard is perfectly still.

I look up.

He's holding a black business card and his eyes are dark. Not the way they are when he's angry with me. No, this is so much more terrifying. He's got an expression that could wither the skin off a person.

227

Cold and sharp like ice breaking over the lake. Dark ink spilling from his pupils.

The card is tiny in his fingers. Yet he's looking at it like he's holding a venomous snake.

"Gerard," I whisper. "What's wrong?"

He turns the card over. There's nothing on the black matte paper except a little silver terrier dog. His eyes narrow and jump to me and back to the card.

"You're scaring me," I whisper. "What's wrong?"

He shakes his head once. Then he rises and pushes the card into his back pocket and reaches for his shirt. I hate being ignored, especially when I'm panicking because he looks like he's going to murder someone with his bare hands. I scramble to my feet and cross the room to him.

I never had the courage to confront him before. But after the last few days, I'm not scared of him. My hands fall to his chest and I realize I'm cold because his bare skin burns my fingertips. He stops, his shirt half buttoned, and studies me.

"Sovereign," I whisper. "Please talk to me."

He shakes his head once.

My hands twist in his shirt, but he ignores them and finishes buttoning it. His hat sits by the bed and I make a grab for it before he can. He goes still, eyes crackling.

"Please," I beg. "I thought we promised to communicate."

His jaw works. I know what I said isn't true—I promised to be honest, he didn't—but I hope he doesn't point that out.

"You shouldn't know everything," he says finally, his voice a low rumble.

That pisses me off. I came here under the impression that my husband's death was an accident. I slept with Gerard, I signed a contract to share his bed, not knowing he had murdered my husband. He kept so much from me and I can tell he has more secrets buried behind those eyes.

He's good at being silent—too good.

"If you don't stop lying to me, I'm not going to be here when you get back," I say, my voice shaking.

His brow raises. "I thought you were falling for me, redbird."

Hot tears spill over. "I am, but you can't do this. You fucking killed my husband. You trapped me here on Sovereign Mountain, and now you look...you look like you're going to kill again. Please, just tell me what's going on. I can't do this, I won't."

His lashes lower. "You're not a coward."

"I am," I say. "I am a coward. And I'm not ashamed of it because not everyone is like you...you sit up here like a god and decide who lives or dies. I'm not like you. I'm not numb."

I regret it as soon as the word leave my mouth—that was his word, the one he used when he opened up to me on the porch of the cabin.

He winces.

"I didn't mean to...say that," I stammer. "I meant...heartless."

"You think I'm heartless," he says quietly. "If I'm heartless, then why does the thought of losing you feel worse than death?"

I reach for words, but come up with nothing. His dangerous eyes have softened. Maybe because he knows that I'm right, even if I never meant to hurt him.

"Redbird," he says. "My scars aren't thick enough to protect me when it comes to you."

I'm not sure how it happens, but somehow I'm up against the door. His warm, broad body is against mine. His mouth moves against my lips, filling me with his familiar taste. I'm molten lava in his arms. Blood pumps through my body in a frantic rush and pools somewhere near my heart. Filling me with the strongest warmth.

He pulls away, his mouth an inch from mine.

"Keira," he breathes. "I've lost everything, but I can't lose you."

My throat is dry. My entire body tingles.

"You're not just falling for me, you love me already," I whisper, tears pouring down my cheeks.

"Always." His gaze is steady.

"Where are you going?"

"I'm going to see a dog about a man," he says.

"I hate your fucking riddles," I manage.

"I know."

His final kiss is so soft it breaks my heart. He pulls back and puts his hat on, tugging it low over his eyes. Then he walks out the door without another word.

It doesn't occur to me until hours later that I didn't tell him I loved him back.

CHAPTER THIRTY-FIVE

KEIRA

*I hate him. I love him. I want to kill him.
I want to be his forever.*

CHAPTER THIRTY-SIX

GERARD

I go to see Jack Russell.

He's a friend and business partner. We both have a mutual understanding that he stays on my retainer for when I need someone taken care of, and I'll stay out of his business.

If our agreement stands, there's no good reason that my personal hitman's calling card should be in a box of Clint Garrison's things.

I take the truck south. Jack lives outside South Platte, that's all I know. But he's got a contact at a bar in West Lancaster, a large town that falls an hour's drive below the city. When I need to speak with him, I know I can find him there.

It's late when I pull up outside the bar. The lights are on and music thrums from the lower level. I make sure my gun is fastened to my belt and get out of the truck, putting my hat on and pulling it low. I don't like being recognized, it gets the rumor mill moving.

I push open the front door to reveal a packed front room. The bar has men lined up all the way down and there's a crowd at the pool table.

My eyes skim over the room until they fall on a platinum blonde head of hair and a heart-shaped face. She turns and I recognize the bright red of her lipstick.

The crowd parts for me, one of the benefits of being tall. I slide into the last empty seat at the end of the bar and rap my knuckles on the table. The woman turns to cuss me out and stops short. Her red mouth falls ajar and her eyes dart over me.

"One second," she says.

I lean back. The room smells faintly of whiskey, but after all this time, I don't find it tempting. I've tasted addiction too thoroughly to go back to it.

The woman returns and leans on the counter, tapping her red fingernails on the shiny wood. She's wearing a cropped shirt that shows the tattoo coiled on her lower belly. A blue snake surrounded by black flowers.

"What the fuck are you doing in my bar, Sovereign?" she says quietly.

"I'm here to see your brother," I say.

She narrows her eyes, cocking her head. "You still single?"

I shake my head. "Locked down."

"Good for you," she says, clearly taken aback. "Lucky woman."

I glance over the room. "Where's your girlfriend, Lisbeth? I thought she worked with you."

She rolls her eyes, shaking back her hair. "We broke up. She quit. It's fine. Want a drink or still sober?"

"Still sober," I say. "Is Jack upstairs?"

She jerks her head to the back of the room. "Go on up, I texted him the minute you walked in."

She goes back to pouring beers and I push through the suffocating crowd to the back stairwell. The roar of voices dulls as I turn the corner to reveal a dark hallway with a cracked door at the end. It's been a while since I met with Jack, but he knows we have an agreement to uphold.

I knock once on the door. He clears his throat from somewhere inside.

"Come in, Sovereign."

I enter, my boots loud on the glossed wood floor, and shut the door behind me. It's a dimly lit room decorated a lot like the main house back at Sovereign Mountain. A bull skull glowers down from above his enormous fireplace. A thick bearskin rug covers the floor beneath the couch. Against the far wall is a bar, a shelf of whiskey, and a stockpile of barrels.

Jack stands by the fire with a whiskey in hand. He's in his late thirties and his glossy black hair doesn't have a speck of gray. It's slicked back over his head, complimenting his clean shaven face. The eyes that fix on me are usually bright green, but in the dark, they're two glittering points.

"What can I do you for?" His voice is low and smooth as silk.

I take the card and cross the room, holding it out between two fingers. His eyes dart down and snap back up.

"I didn't give you that," he says.

"No," I say. "You didn't."

"So where did it come from?"

I take my hat off and smooth back my hair. "You tell me, Russell. I thought I was paying out the nose for a non-compete clause with you. So why was that card in Clint Garrison's possession?"

His brows rise. He flicks the card around and in between his fingers quick as a flash. In another life, Jack would have made an excellent magician.

"Clint is dead," he says. "How did you come by this?"

I sink into the couch and cross one ankle over my knee. He stays by the fire. The tension between us is palpable. There's a short silence and he realizes I'm not going to answer so he sets aside his whiskey and crosses to the other side of the room. There, he rolls the top back on his desk and sets the card down.

"Clint approached me two years ago with a job," he says.

"And you took it?"

"Yes and no."

He turns around, sitting on the edge of the desk. He crosses his arms and the miniature silver terrier around his neck glints between his open collar. My eyes dart down to his wrist. There's a leather band with an O-ring barely visible under his cuff.

He follows my eyes and the corner of his mouth turns up.

"I'm not sharing this one," he says.

"I'm not looking."

I met Jack when I was young, in my mid-twenties, and just discovering that my tastes ranged outside the regular. We started talking at a bar one night and he offered to share his sub with me. Watching him guide her through fucking me without touching her once made me realize I wanted that too. They were my gateway drug to the intricacies of BDSM.

"Are you locked down?" he asks. "Is she your...girlfriend?"

"She's my sub," I say. "But I'm going to marry her, just haven't told her yet. Back to the calling card."

He blinks. "The card...so Clint hired me...sort of."

Anger surges in my chest. "You broke our agreement."

"I was playing both sides. I didn't intend to follow through."

He doesn't look like he's lying, but I've learned enough not to trust anyone. Especially not men like Jack Russell. I sink back on the couch and cross my ankle over my knee. The amount of debt Clint was in is starting to make more sense. Jack Russell's services are expensive, and he would have charged thousands just for a consultation. I've seen his accounts. Most of his debt was bad investments, years where he was in the red, and a fuckload of money on cheating and gambling.

But this explains some of the gaps in his receipts.

"Who did he want you to kill?" I ask grimly.

He sighs. "Well, my confidentiality agreement is over because Clint is dead. It was his wife."

Deep down, I knew the answer to my question and I knew it from the moment I saw the calling card. But that doesn't keep white hot rage from pouring through my chest and making my vision flash. I don't move, but I feel my nails pierce my palms.

"Did he tell you why?"

Jack saunters over and sinks down onto the coffee table a few feet from where I sit. I'm on high alert because he doesn't have my trust anymore. Or maybe it's because when it comes to Keira, I can't be too careful.

"It's pretty obvious."

I stay silent.

"Clint married his wife because her father left her Stowe Farms," he says. "He annexed her farm into his ranch and got what he wanted. Now, all he had to do was get rid of his unwanted wife."

It feels like my heart is beating in absolute silence. Thump, thump, the way it does when it's just me standing at the edge of the frozen lake at the top of the mountain.

In my head is a stark image of Keira, painted in high definition with every detail seared into my mind. She's curled up in bed, the way she was the first night she slept with me. Bright hair spilling over the pillow, eyes closed, body relaxed.

If I hadn't brought her to Sovereign Mountain when I did...what would have happened to my redbird? It's not Jack's way to kill women, but that wouldn't have stopped the Garrisons from doing it themselves.

I clear my throat. "Was anyone else involved?"

He leans in, resting his elbows on his knees.

"That would be breaking confidentiality." he says.

"So the people who hired you are still alive?"

"Very alive."

"Both of them?"

He nods and then his jaw clenches, his narrowed eyes flashing a poisonous green. Now I know there are two more people involved in this plot. And I have a pretty good idea of who they are.

"Would these people happen to go by Garrison as well?" I ask.

He presses his lips together, but I already have my answer. Silence stretches on until he releases a heavy sigh and sits back.

"I shouldn't have gone behind your back," he says.

"Our contract is over." I'm on my feet, reaching for my hat.

"Wait."

I'm halfway to the door when that word rings out. I pivot on my heel, gracious enough to offer him one more opportunity to explain himself. He lifts his palms.

"What we have is a non-compete clause. At that point, you weren't competing with Garrison Ranch."

"I'm their biggest competitor," I say.

"But not their enemy. You were doing business with Clint."

Darkness and rage seep through my veins like ink. Inside, my anger simmers low. Waiting for when I can release it.

"I was, but only because behind the scenes I've been buying up their land," I spit. "Why do you think I own the banks? I've been squeezing the life out of those Garrison fuckers with interest until they had no choice but to start selling. You know these things, Jack, it's your job."

"No one knows anything unless you want them to, Sovereign," he snaps.

"That woman...the one I said I was going to marry," I spit out. "She's Clint's widow. So forgive me for distrusting you."

He pulls back, his brows drawing together. I see the gears turning in his head as he soaks in this information.

This changes everything because that makes Keira my family. And a long time ago, I'd agreed to finance his underground business in order to get Lisbeth away from her ex-husband and out of debt. He owes me for saving the two of them, and the weight of that debt makes his shoulders sink.

"I was never going to see this job through," he says finally. "I don't kill women, but I was curious why he wanted her taken out, so I gave him the card."

He has me there. We both know that's over the line for Jack. It might be a rough, wild country out here, but he still has his decency. Maybe he's telling the truth.

Jack releases a long sigh and rubs his eyes. "Jesus...fuck, Sovereign," he mumbles. "What do you want from me?"

"What I've always wanted from you—a hitman."

He swallows hard, throat bobbing. His hands go to his hips.

"Avery and Thomas?"

I nod.

"That'll be six million for both," he says. "That's a fucking deal too. Friends and family discount."

I hold out my palm and he locks eyes with me. Giving me a piercing stare, like he's trying to split me open and look inside my head.

Then he shakes my hand and I feel the balance of the world shift. I suppose this could be considered signing a death warrant. But I prefer to think of it as doing the Lord's work.

Jack goes to his desk. There's a wooden card box printed with a little silver dog that he slides open and takes two black cards from. I keep still as he walks over and tucks them into my shirt pocket.

"I'll collect them when it's done," he says.

I shake my head. "Pack your shit," I say. "We're doing this together."

He freezes. "I work alone."

The image of Keira in my lap, riding me with her crimson hair falling down her back, bursts into my mind. She's so fucking alive, so warm and real. When we first met, I'd wanted her...perhaps I'd thought I loved her. But the realization I could have lost her before I even got a chance to be hers shakes me to my core.

She looks like forever now.

Like, if I can undo the bindings of the past, the mother of my children.

My eyes shut and against my eyelids I see our entire future laid out. Sons, maybe a daughter, running free on Sovereign Mountain. My name and hers together on the deed to our ranch. Hot summer breeze coming through the open window at night while I fuck her beneath the quilt after the children are asleep.

My throat closes.

A long time ago, the Garrison family took that dream from me. They broke my heart and my pride and as good as killed my parents. At their hand, I tasted grief before I had a chance to become a man.

They tried to break me, to erase my name all because my father did what was right and defended his wife. It's time to close that chapter.

I am the only son of the Sovereign line and their death is my birthright.

I waited long enough.

It's time for retribution.

"Jack," I say, my voice quiet. "This is your expertise, but it's my blood to spill. We do it together."

He knows what they did to me. He knows how long I've waited for justice. There's a short silence and then he gets his hat.

"Let's go kill some Garrisons."

CHAPTER THIRTY-SEVEN

KEIRA

I cry again after Gerard leaves. There's a sense of foreboding in my chest and I tell myself it's just the oncoming snowstorm. In the evening, I creep down the hall and push open the game room balcony. I'm wearing the sweatsuit from my first night at Sovereign Mountain. It smells like him because it was in his dresser drawer, folded with his things.

The sky is black. Snow starts to swirl, but I know the storm won't hit until tomorrow at noon.

The feel of it on the wind reminds me of being a girl. The world was simple then, and I looked forward to storms because I never had to go out into them. I'd wait by the fire for my father to burst through the door, covered in ice and snow. Chilly from putting the horses to bed.

My eyes sting.

I never really had time to grieve for my father. But in the last several weeks, some of that sadness has tugged at the edges of my mind. Maybe because I feel safe now, safe enough to stop masking everything.

My feet are numb by the time I stumble back into the bedroom. All the papers that fell earlier are still in a heap on the ground. I flick on the fireplace and pad over to clean them up, but the memory of his reaction to the card stops me short.

I shiver. There are so many secrets at Sovereign Mountain that sometimes I wonder if I really know anything at all.

But I do know one thing for certain—he said he loves me.

I want to believe him.

He has nothing to gain from me. He already has my ranch in the palm of his hand. I'm drained dry by Clint's debt. I'm powerless against him and that's my saving grace.

Clint used me, but Gerard can't do the same because I have nothing left to take.

After his confession, I know he never intended on it.

My eyes are wet again as I sink down to my knees to clean up the papers. It's just a bunch of shit. Weeks and months I wasted with Clint right here on the floor at my feet. Receipts, faded bills, folders of paperwork. I wish I could stuff it all into the fireplace and watch it go up in a blaze.

I gather it all up and shove it back into the box and go to slam the lid.

There's a plastic folder wedged in the corner. Something about it draws me in, so I pull it free and flip it over.

Last Will & Testament.

My heart picks up. I never saw the will, I just signed everything Clint's lawyer put in front of me because I was too numb to care. I let him fight everything out in the courtroom without ever showing me a document. Now that I'm sitting here, I realize how stupid and naive I was not to oversee everything he did. I'd been groomed to be quiet and let men handle this kind of thing.

I simply hadn't known better.

My hand shakes as I unfasten the folder and let it fall open.

My eyes skim over the contents, but they halt at the date scrawled over the top.

The day Clint died. The time is four-thirty in the afternoon. An hour after the coroner came to take his body to the hospital.

What the fuck?

My eyes dart over the paper. Down to the bottom where Clint's signature is scrawled. Clear as day. Below it are two lines marked for witnesses and on those lines I see two names that make my heart go still.

Gerard Sovereign.

Westin Quinn.

My breathing comes fast and my vision flickers. This is the original will, this is notarized. My fingertips skim over the bumps where it's been stamped. But there's no way this can be real because it has my husband's signature on it, and by four-thirty that day, Clint was dead.

I stumble back to the bed, sinking down.

The will was a fake.

It was always a fake. Avery and Thomas were right to fight it in court.

I was wrong.

The folder spills onto the bed as I scramble for my phone. It has a solitary bar of signal. Shakily, I tear down the hall and burst out onto the cold balcony.

Now I have two bars.

I call Clint's lawyer. Snow falls in soft spirals and lands on my face. Melting on my cheeks. The phone rings three times and cuts out. I dial him again and wait.

"Hello?"

He sounds confused, and he has good reason to be. It's almost ten at night.

"Jay," I whisper. "This is Keira."

"Is this about the unsettled accounts?" he asks. "They've been paid up as of this afternoon."

A sob pushes up my throat.

"No," I whisper. "I have something I want to ask."

"Okay, but there's a consulting fee."

"No," I whisper harshly. "There's not, not for this. If you or the judge in my court case have ever taken money from Gerard

Sovereign, I want you to tell me that you can't answer this question because it pertains to confidential information."

There's a long, long silence. My eyes burn with hot tears threatening to spill down my cold cheeks.

"I'm sorry, Keira," he says finally. "I can't answer that question as it pertains to confidential information."

Everything changes. It feels like the sky shatters, and I close my eyes and let the tears flow. My hands shake as I lift the phone from my ear and hang up. It takes me almost five minutes to jerk myself from my reverie. My face prickles with cold and my feet are totally numb.

He didn't just kill Clint and disappear for seven months. No, he'd orchestrated everything from the beginning.

Nothing that had happened was by accident.

He bought out the bank to get ownership of Clint's mortgage. He'd put pressure on my husband until he started selling off his land to Sovereign Mountain.

He forged a will so everything was left to me, he bought out Clint's lawyer, and South Platte's judge to ensure it passed the court system.

He handed my land back to me knowing it would force me into his arms. Knowing I would have no one to turn to for protection but him.

He set a trap, laid the bait, and I'd walked right into it.

My mind whirls.

I can't make sense of this. The threads are so tangled I can't find my way through.

My eyes fall on the second name signed to the will.

Westin Quinn.

I run my hand over my face to wipe the tears. I cry too much, I always have, but tonight I'm going to find out the truth, even if I'm sobbing the entire time. I have to know if he's being honest about his past and if he means it when he says he loves me. Because nothing else will make me forgive him.

I put Gerard's coat over my sweatsuit, snatch the painted mare from my bedside table, and slip downstairs to find my winter boots.

Then I lock the dogs inside and go out into the yard and head for the gatehouse.

CHAPTER THIRTY-EIGHT

KEIRA

Westin opens the door after a solid minute of knocking. He's disheveled, his belt undone and his shirt unbuttoned. When he sees it's me, he turns and hastily finishes doing up his clothes.

"What are you doing here?" he says, scowling.

"Gerard left," I whisper.

He stares at me, eyes narrowing. "Okay?"

"Something's wrong," I say, unable to hide the tremor in my voice. "I was going through a box of my husband's things and there was a black card with a silver dog on it. He got really quiet when he saw it and left."

Westin freezes. His eyes dart behind me and he reaches out, grabbing my elbow and pulling me inside. He shuts the door and locks it, glancing around the room before pointing at the kitchen table. I sink down, looking around at the open concept interior. It's masculine, but clean, with dark wood and leather furniture and blue plaid accents.

He puts his hands on his hips. "You want something?"

"Whiskey," I say.

He pours two glasses and sinks down opposite me. Westin and I don't talk often, but he's close with Gerard. If anyone can answer my questions, it's Westin.

"What did that card mean?"

He swirls his whiskey, watching me critically. "That's Jack Russell's calling card. Everyone knows that."

"I didn't. Who's Jack Russell?"

"He's a hitman."

"Like...an assassin?"

He nods once, swirling the whiskey some more. "Yep, just like that."

My stomach sinks. Clint had that card locked in his safe at his attorney's office. Which meant, my husband had done business with a hitman.

But...why?

Westin sets aside his glass and steeples his fingers. "When you hire Jack to take someone out, he gives you a calling card. When the job is done, he brings you a receipt. Maybe it's a finger, or a tooth. And he takes the calling card back. Leaves no trace."

Sickness passes over me in a wave and leaves me weak.

"So if my husband...he paid Jack Russell to kill someone?"

"You don't get a calling card unless Jack gives it to you," Westin says. "So yeah, he had a deal...that looks like it didn't pan out. Stroke of good luck for the bastard he paid to kill that he happened to die."

I stare at him, anger flickering.

"I'm not dumb, Westin," I say coolly. "I know Gerard killed my husband and forged the will."

Westin's brows shoot to his hairline. He gives an uncomfortable cough.

"Oops," he says.

"And I saw your name was on it. I think Gerard meant for me to find out eventually, it wasn't hidden."

He swallows and lets out a heavy sigh. "Everything Gerard did was justified. Did he tell you about Mariana? About his parents? Your husband had that coming to him. It's not murder, Miss Garrison, it's fucking justice."

"I know he was engaged," I whisper. "And she was pregnant."

Westin shakes his head, downing his whiskey in a single gulp. I take a large sip of mine and shudder as it slides down my throat and burns in my stomach. My nerves buzz, but they're less fragile.

"That wasn't his baby," Westin says.

My jaw goes slack. "What?"

He runs a hand over his face, scrubbing his eye. "Mariana was cheating on him. I showed him evidence. But he just shoved his head up his ass because he treated her like she was a saint. She stopped wanting to fuck him and he chalked that up to her being scared off by his...interests. But she was fucking Clint and the baby was his. Sovereign admitted he hadn't slept with her in months when she told him she was pregnant. She kept going on about how she was further along than the doctor said. Bullshit."

My stomach turns for the most selfish reason.

If Clint took Gerard's fiancée...does that mean I'm just compensation? An eye for an eye?

My throat hitches. Tears start in my eyes and burn down my face.

"Fuck, Keira, don't cry," Westin mumbles.

I scrub my face with my sleeve. "Does Sovereign even love me?" I whisper.

His face softens. He reaches out and awkwardly pats my elbow.

"He's fucked," he says quietly.

My head spins with whiskey. If Gerard turns out to be a liar using me to get revenge, I know my heart will die in my chest. He told me once I was too young to be so hurt. And he was right.

"I hate this," I whisper. "I just want him to love me. That's all."

Westin sighs and leans back. I watch him refill our glasses and my hand shakes as I lift it to my lips.

"He does love you," he says.

"Then where the fuck is he?" I sob.

"Sovereign is a proud man," he says. "If he doesn't see justice through to the end, it'll break him. He watched his mother die, his father drink himself to death. He pulled his fiancée from a ditch. The Garrisons did that to him. This isn't about land or money or hurt feelings. It's justice for his family, his future children."

I'm too drunk to tell him Gerard can't have children without a reversal. I shouldn't have had so much whiskey, my body isn't used to it. I cover my face with my hands and let my body sink down over the table.

It feels like Westin and I are on a seesaw, rising and falling, both washed by the tides. By the powerful force of one man who isn't even at this table.

"This isn't about pettiness," Westin says quietly.

I lift my head and wipe my eyes. "He won't be at peace until he balances the scales," I whisper. "I get it, but I don't understand it. I wasn't raised with principles like that...I was raised to survive. Sometimes that means doing humiliating things like signing my body away in a contract with a man I don't know."

Westin looks at me and his brows furrow. He has a habit of scowling hard when he's thinking. There are faint lines left around his eyes from it.

"I don't know everything about your situation," he says. "But, I think Sovereign gave you back your dignity."

I open my mouth to argue that he'd made me sell myself for a mortgage, but then I remember his involvement goes further back. When I met Sovereign, I had no future. I was living in the house of a man who hated me. I'd told him I was afraid of Clint, that I was powerless, and he'd delivered me from evil.

Something that feels like hope flutters in my chest.

Maybe...maybe trusting him isn't the same as when I trusted Clint.

Westin sits across from me with his hands loosely folded. He's got scars on his knuckles the way Sovereign does. I study them, wondering if they're from bar fights or barbed wire. For men like them, either is likely.

"You've known Sovereign for a long time," I whisper. "Do you trust him?'

"With my life," he says. No hesitation.

"How...how do I know he's not just using me?" I'm struggling to get the words out. They feel like a betrayal after everything that's happened between us.

His eyes soften. "You're the only woman who's slept in his bed. He's not using you, Keira."

My eyes shut and tears seep down my face. I want to just give in. God, I want to surrender myself to Gerard Sovereign. And I would if I just knew what lay on the other side of all his darkness and need for vengeance.

Who will he be when this feud is over?

Does he know how to live without pain?

We hear a faint slam in the distance. Westin's gaze snaps to the door and we listen to the faint rumble of tires come up the drive. The engine of Gerard's truck dies away and I hear boots hit the gravel. Low voices rumble and a pang shoots through my chest as I recognize one as his. The other I can't place.

"He's back," Westin says.

I nod, wordless.

He looks to the side and in the corner of his eyes, I think I see something. Fear...maybe? Or is it hunger? Does he want this vengeance just as much as Sovereign?

I shiver, wrapping my arms around my body.

He stands. "Trust Sovereign and you'll be safe. Understood?"

The wind whistles through the trees. He pushes open the door and I see the shape of two men coming in from the yard. Walking side by side, their hats pushed low on their heads. Pistols on their hips. Heading for the gatehouse.

"Do you want to go out the back?" Westin asks.

I shake my head. "I want to talk to him."

249

CHAPTER THIRTY-NINE

GERARD

Jack and I step into the gatehouse and our conversation dies. Keira sits at the table, engulfed in sweats and her oversized coat. Her hair is tied up and her face is blotchy from tears. That doesn't alarm me because she cries often, but what I don't like is the half empty whiskey bottle before her. Other than the few drinks she's had at dinner, I've never seen her reach for a bottle before.

She drags her sleeve under her nose.

Our eyes meet.

And right then, I know that she knows.

Everything.

"What are you doing here, redbird?" I ask.

Her chin quivers. "I came to talk to Westin."

I know why, but I don't want to air out our dirty laundry in front of Jack and Westin. I jerk my head at Westin and we step to the far side of the room, out of earshot.

"You let her drink?"

"She was fucked up already. She knows everything."

I nod. My eyes wander back to her hunched shoulders. It hurts to know that I did this to her, regardless of my intention. I never wanted to cause her pain. If I had it my way, I'd build a castle at the top of the mountain and keep her safe behind a barricade.

"I need to talk to her alone," I say.

His mouth thins and he crosses his arms over his chest. "It's not my business...she's hurting. I hope you don't contribute to that, Sovereign."

I shake my head. He gives me a hard stare as he heads over to pour a drink for Jack and I beckon Keira. She gets up slowly and takes my hand, letting me lead her to the guestroom at the top of the stairs. The door shuts with a loud click.

"Where did you go?" she whispers.

"To see Jack Russell," I say.

"Westin told me what the card means. Who...who did Clint want to kill? You?"

I wish more than anything to protect her from all the ugly things in the world. But she deserves to know.

"You," I say.

The color drains from her face. Her throat bobs. She steps backwards and sinks down onto the bed.

"He...was going to kill me," she whispers.

I sit down beside her and she doesn't resist when I pull her into my lap. That's a good sign. She's not shutting me out after finding out everything I did to make her mine. The soft scent of pomegranate fills my senses as I bury my face in her hair. Her body shakes.

Fuck, I hate when she cries like this. I love her tears when they're from pleasure. But when they're from pain, it fills me with rage like I've never felt.

I want to gut the Garrisons. One by one. I want to burn everything they own to the ground, to wipe any memory of them from the earth.

"Redbird," I say. "No one will ever hurt you again."

Her body shivers in my arms.

"I swear it."

She wriggles back so she can look up at me. I brush her wet hair from her cheek and tuck it behind her ear.

"Is all that you want? Revenge?" she whispers.

I try to follow her train of thought and give up. "I've been waiting to take out the Garrisons for a long time," I say. "But what they were planning on doing to you...makes me realize it needs to be done. Now."

Her lip trembles. "You mean kill them," she says flatly.

My God, seeing her in pain hurts so badly, worse than anything that was done to me. My fingers grip her upper arms, pulling her back in as her face crumples. I rub her back and stroke my fingers through her hair while she shudders with sobs.

"I got fucking groomed," she bursts out. "They took my farm and they were going to kill me."

What I've known for a while is just now hitting her. Her body shivers and the whites of her eyes flash. I can tell she's right on the edge of panicking.

"Let me put you to bed and give you some sleeping pills," I urge. "You've been through a lot."

She wrenches from my grip and jumps to her feet. Her blue eyes, that are always so mild and beautiful, burn. I know that look—I've seen it in the mirror for years. She's starting to realize for the first time that she's a victim and she has been for years.

"No," she says sharply. "I'm not drugging myself so I don't have to feel this. I told Westin I didn't understand why you wanted revenge, but I'm starting to get it now. They don't deserve to live after everything they've done."

Her eyes are so wide her irises look small and her pupils are blown. She's frantic, trapped. I get up and she goes still as I rest my palm against her cheek.

"What do you want me to do to them?" I ask.

I let her take as long as she needs with the question. Her eyes are hazy and she's gazing up at me like she's never seen me before.

Maybe it's because until now, she never really has. Now she sees all my faults, my failures, my desire for justice and vengeance. She sees the lengths I went to make her mine and she has to know I'll do anything to keep her.

She pushes her face into my palm, her lashes fluttering shut.

"Tell me what you want," I murmur.

"I want you to love me," she whispers.

"Redbird," I say. "There's never been a question of that."

She pulls back from me, and for a second, I think she's angry. But then she turns and presses herself against the wall. Palms flat on the sanded wood. Her spine arcs like a cat and she pushes her ass out, just enough I know she's asking for my cock inside her.

Fuck. It's not the right time for that.

"Keira," I say, my voice hoarse. "Say it back."

Her eyes squeeze shut tight. "Let me feel you."

I close the space between us, mindful our steps can be heard downstairs. Her breath hitches and her soft ass pushes back against the front of my pants. Our breathing quickens in tandem. I yank her pants and underwear down to the floor.

"Please," she whispers.

I gather her hair with my other hand, dragging her head to the side. Then I take my cock out, pushing my pants down just low enough, and spit into my hand. Rubbing it over my length and her soaked entrance. When I enter her, she lets her head fall back against me and a little moan escapes her lips.

She feels the burn as I slide in. Her muscles fight, trying to adjust.

"Good girl," I breathe. "All the way for me now."

She whimpers as I bottom out. Her tight inner muscles clamp down around me. I drag out halfway and thrust slowly back in. I push my face into her neck, bracing my foot back to accommodate the difference in our height, and fuck her gently against the wall.

"Tell me," I pant.

She moans, her voice muffled. "I would have slept with you that first night. You didn't need the contract, I would have fucked you."

My hips move, pumping.

"Fucking isn't enough, I want to love you."

I don't say the rest—*let me love you, let me be your man, let me make you the mother of my children. Take my name and the land that I love.* She's not ready for me to say all those things to her yet.

But, God, they're right on the tip of my tongue.

"You could have just asked," she pants.

"Would you have said yes?"

She doesn't answer, but we both know. She wouldn't have accepted my terms if she hadn't been forced into it. We both know that whatever we have is born from desperation. Maybe that makes it taste all the better.

Like salt in caramel.

Pleasure from our pain.

She moans and I don't care that she's loud. I pull out and flip her, lifting her up and sinking my cock to the hilt in her soft pussy. She wraps her arms around my neck and her legs around my waist. She digs her nails into the base of my neck so hard pain sparks down my back. It sharpens my senses, giving me clarity.

"Tell me the truth," I order. "You swore to be honest."

Our bodies thump against the wall. I push her sweatshirt up and pull her bra down, baring her right breast. It marks pink when I tug her nipple hard enough to make her hips buck.

"If I kill the Garrisons, you can never leave me, redbird," I say. "We'll be tied together by that secret forever. So tell me you love me."

CHAPTER FORTY

KEIRA

He demands my love.

So I give it to him the way I've given him everything else.

My mouth is so close to his I can taste him. I wish he'd offer me more than just the grim set of his square jaw and the depths of his winter-blue eyes. He blinks slowly and his lids stay heavy, dark lashes stark.

"I love you," I whisper.

"You're mine," he says, his voice like gravel in his chest.

"I'm yours."

He kisses me and catches that word on his tongue.

CHAPTER FORTY-ONE

KEIRA

Maddie and I stand in the open front door. The barn light sheds a blue glow over the driveway. The men went into the barn and I can hear them talking in low tones.

My senses are sharp, the blur of whiskey gone from my brain after Sovereign fucked me. In the gatehouse, he put a blanket around my shoulders before he kissed me, using the edges to draw me near.

I pull the blanket close.

Hoofbeats sound and Shadow breaks from the barn and pulls to a halt, gravel spraying. Gerard is a silhouette on his back, his black cowboy hat stark against the clouded sky. Westin and Jack, both astride their horses, are at his heels. They loiter, talking in low tones.

I shudder.

"I don't like this," I whisper. "I feel like something bad is going to happen."

Maddie comes up behind me and pats my shoulder. It's the first affection she's shown me, and it feels awkward.

"It is," she says. "But Sovereign will come back. Hopefully before noon because there's a storm coming tomorrow."

They're all so confident in Gerard that it makes me want to turn my brain off and do the same. But I don't know him the way they do.

I'm a newcomer here in comparison with the years that Maddie and Westin have been by his side. They have a reason to trust him.

In the dark, he turns Shadow to look back. His eyes glint below the rim of his hat. For a second, I entertain what might happen if he doesn't come back and the pain that rips through my chest is almost unbearable. The blanket falls from my shoulders and I close the space between us, reaching up for his hand.

He's wearing gloves, but I feel the hard grip of his fingers around mine.

"I'll be back," he says hoarsely.

I can't speak. He looks like a giant sitting astride his enormous horse, so tall I have to stand on my toes just to hold his hand.

Feeling silly, I kiss my palm and hold my hand up to him. The corners of his mouth turn up and he cradles my hand, letting my invisible kiss fall into his grip.

"Fuck," he says hoarsely. "You're so sweet."

"I do love you," I say quietly. "I really do. Please come back."

"Just give me time, just tonight. And I swear, when it's done, I'm all yours," he says.

I nod, tears streaming down my cheeks and neck.

He pushes his hat low. "I love you, redbird."

I pull back as their horses move past me and—damn it, I'm crying again. Big Dog and Small Dog circle my ankles, pacing. I feel Maddie's arms slide around me and lay the blanket back over my shoulders. Through my wet lashes, I watch their shadows disappear into the dark yard. Hoofbeats fade into the distance. I know it'll be the last night the Garrison brothers ever live through.

That doesn't bother me the way it would have before tonight.

If I love him, I have to love every part of him.

And that includes his darkness and desire for justice no matter how bloody the consequences. If I want to love this complicated, scarred man and everything that came with him, I have to be able to accept his past.

Maddie pulls me into the house, the dogs at our heels, and locks the door. The wind shrieks over the mountain and I feel the sides of the house shudder. I hate that they're out in the cold dark and I'm in here, safe and warm.

"Let's get you something to eat," she says.

She ushers me down the back hallway to the kitchen. The dogs are pasted to me, as if they sense my raging emotions. I wait in the doorway as she turns the lights on and starts taking things out of the cupboard. My head feels stuffy, and my eyes burn, so I lean my forehead against the cool wall. Maddie turns and her gaze narrows.

"You don't look very good," she says.

I shake my head. "I drank and now it's wearing off."

She takes my elbow and tugs me to a chair in the corner, pushing me down and wrapping the blanket around my shoulders. I'm having trouble telling how much time is passing. It feels like half a second later when she puts a cup of warm peppermint tea in my hand and sets a plate of strudel on the table beside me.

"Eat that, it's apple and cinnamon so it'll help settle your stomach," she orders.

Obediently, I push the fork into the flaky pastry and put a bite in my mouth. Warm butter and sweet apples melt on my tongue and my sickness ebbs as I eat until there's just a smear of cinnamon on the white porcelain. When I look up, Maddie is watching me with a hint of sadness in her eyes.

"Let's get you to bed," she says.

I stand to put my plate in the sink. "Are you okay?"

She nods. "I worry about Sovereign."

"Really?"

A slight smile crosses her lips. "Of course, I've worked with him since the beginning. When Sovereign Mountain was just a farmhouse and a stable."

"What...was he like then?"

"He was the same," she says, her tone soft. "He's always been stubborn. His head is as hard as a brick. And getting on his bad side was always ill advised. But he'd die for the people in his circle."

I swallow, brushing back my hair. "Was he always so...grim?"

Her eyes mist over. "No, but he's always been the type to look life straight in the eyes and get on with it. Nothing stops him, or scares him. He doesn't want much, but when he does...well, that's how you got here."

My neck is warm. I gather my hair, twisting it into a knot.

"I know it's not my business, but did he bring other women here?"

Her brow crooks. "No. He hasn't shared a room with anyone as long as I've known him. Now, I don't think he was celibate, but he never had anyone the way he has you."

Relief moves over me. I hate the thought of him with anyone else.

Hard head or not, he's mine.

I realize Maddie is looking at me and there's a faraway expression on her face. She notices me staring and she jerks her head, wiping her hands on the kitchen towel.

"You're good for him," she says. "I know I'm only fifteen years older than him, but he feels like a son. And I hope you choose him because he's one of the good ones."

"He's done a lot of bad things," I whisper.

She nods. "That's true. But what's that they say about casting the first stone? He who is without sin, and all that."

It hits me right then that I could cast a stone at him. I look down at my hands, twisted together. They're clean.

But they're untested.

I've spent my life being washed on the tides. Bouncing from one caretaker to the next, bending to their will. I had the luxury of keeping my head down, but Gerard didn't.

His hands are bloody so mine can be clean.

And that's enough for me to choose him.

And I do—I do choose Sovereign. Despite everything he's done, despite his cold mind, his scarred heart, and his calloused hands. I have a soft enough heart and plenty of tears for us both.

Which means, if he's not back in the morning, I'm going after him.

CHAPTER FORTY-TWO

GERARD

It's fuck-all cold at the top of the hill overlooking Thomas Garrison's house. We stand in a silent row, like grim reapers on our horses. At the bottom of the hill, with the road in the far background, sits the final third of the farmland that's been a specter at the corner of my mind for so long.

Tonight I'm laying that ghost to rest.

There's a light on in the kitchen. I glance at Westin because I know he's staring at it, painfully aware Diane is inside.

"She'll be free after tonight," I say quietly.

He snorts. "Like she'd fuck me after I kill her husband."

He realizes what he says as it comes from his mouth and Jack laughs. It's funny, but my chest tightens at the memory of Keira's tearstained face in the guest bedroom. She was so broken, and I hate that in order to extract her from her situation, I had to hurt her even more. I hope when the Garrisons are in the ground, the dust will settle and we can focus on healing.

I want to lick her wounds for her, to kiss her forehead, tell her she never has to hurt again.

I wonder if she feels the same.

Does love mean the same for her as it does for me?

Part of me doesn't care. So what if I love her most? I've always been cold until I find something that forces me to feel. And then I'm on fire, so intense I feel it course like blood through my veins.

When I saw the bare plot of land that would be Sovereign Mountain, I felt the future. I'll stand on this plot of earth until I die and am buried in it.

When I saw Keira, I knew she was the woman I'd sleep beside forever.

I don't know how to live in shades of gray.

"What's the plan?" Westin says.

"I'm going in after Thomas with Jack. I want you to go after Diane and make sure she doesn't get caught in the crossfire. We're here for the Garrison men only."

"And do what with her?" Westin frowns, barely visible in the dark.

"Whatever you want," I say. "I don't care where she goes, but she can't stay here."

The clouds part for a brief moment. The heavy wind blows them across the sky quickly, each one thicker and darker than the next. Through the opening, the moon is a pale silver disk.

It's the same moon that bore witness to what the Garrisons did to my parents. I look up and all at once I'm back there.

In that fucking room.

***

I'm laying on my back staring at the nearly full moon through the window. The cold air creeps in through the cracks of our employee housing. I'm a child, wrapped in the frayed quilt my grandmother gave me before we left Boston.

My mother is crying in the kitchen. Heavy, wet sobs like she'll never stop. My father's voice is a deep rumble. I hear his chair scrape back and her footsteps patter. I know he's holding her, probably stroking her hair. He always does that when she's upset.

Earlier in the day, I came back from school to find the house empty. The kitchen chair was overturned. There was something red on the floor, like dark red paint was dripped across the dusty boards.

I followed the drips to the back of the house and found my mother sitting by the laundry sink.

Ice cold fear gripped me. Her eyes were puffy and her nose dripped blood down her chin. My father knelt at her feet with a wet rag in his fist. Dabbing at her mouth and nose, trying to stem the flow.

"Dad," I whispered.

I didn't know what to ask. Is she alright? Who did this? Surely my father didn't do that. He's never even said an unkind word to my mother in my entire life.

My mother made a muffled sound and covered her mouth with her hand. Her eyes were so sad, so swollen with tears.

"Baby, go to your room," she said, putting on that fake happy tone that means she's trying to protect me.

I swallow hard because my throat is bunched up. My father nodded, jerking his head towards the doorway. I fled to my room and here I am, wrapped up in a quilt. Still in my school clothes and shoes. My lids are heavy despite my pounding heart.

I lie there with a sickening sense of dread in my small chest. Listening to them talk and cry until finally the moon winks out and I fall asleep.

For almost a year, I don't know what happened. I'm sure my father hit her, but I'm confused why she still kisses him and lets him hold her against his chest. And I don't know why we have to move into a cheap motel and my father has to go to work before dawn and return drenched in mud from the oil fields.

On my ninth birthday, I decide I'm a man now and I confront my father about it one night on the back porch.

How could he have hurt mom? Why is she so scared now? Why did she go from being soft and pleasant to rail thin and haunted?

He starts crying and I sit there, heart in my mouth, and wait for him to stop.

He tells me that Abel Garrison tried to rape my mother. He held her down and beat her face when she resisted. If my father hadn't walked in the door with a shotgun, he'd have gotten away with it.

He chased him down the road, shooting at him once and missing.

My father doesn't cry. He doesn't believe in it, but for my mother, he makes an exception.

The cold northern mountains make for hard men. My father only showed softness to my mother. He hit me at the end, after her death destroyed him. But I never hated him for it because I remembered, when things got dark, that he wept for her that day.

My first introduction to the concept of sex is through an explanation of rape. I'm innocent so he gives me The Talk with tears streaming down his face before he explains the rest. It's not lost on me that this isn't the way these things should happen.

He keeps his gaze on the ground.

Worn hands tangled together, eyes fixed on his boots.

He tells me why we had to leave Garrison Ranch. That while I was at school, the Garrisons evicted my parents at gunpoint. Driving them out with nothing but a few belongings in the back of their truck.

I'll never fucking forget that.

Not if I live a thousand years.

***

The wind picks up, cutting across my face, snapping me back to the present.

The memory of what happened all those years ago feels dim tonight. Learning that Avery and Thomas planned on killing my woman lights a different kind of fire in me. One that burns under my ribs, right where I hope I have a heart left.

At the very least, I can still protect my redbird before it's too late.

The waiting is over.

I shift my weight and Shadow begins moving down the hill. Jack and Westin fall into step behind me. We've never hunted together like this, but we all know what to do.

We'll work quickly, we'll get in and get out. We'll do the Lord's work and do it well.

263

CHAPTER FORTY-THREE

GERARD

Jack wants to be diplomatic. Westin is just here for a good time so he doesn't care how we do this. I open the door and walk right in.

No one locks their doors this far out.

Diane Garrison is in the hall in a slip and a terrycloth robe. She stumbles back, her mouth moving as she tries to scream. Westin skirts around me and snatches her around the waist. His hand goes over her mouth and he hauls her back against his body.

Her eyes widen, terror making her pupils blow.

"Hush, darling," he says. "We're not here for you."

Her hips buck and her bare foot kicks back into his shin so hard he lets out a soft, "Fuck!" under his breath.

"Where is your husband?" I ask, keeping my voice low.

Her eyes dart down the hall before she can stop herself. I lean in and I can see the shape of two men on the back porch. The cherry tips of twin cigarettes burns in the dark.

"Take her to the kitchen," I say.

He picks her up, hand still clamped over her mouth, and carries her into the kitchen to our left.

My eyes meet Jack's and he nods. He has his revolver at the level of his eyes, his hat pulled low. His face is covered in a dark bandanna. I took off my hat and my face is bare.

I want them to see—to know it's me—when I kill them.

Jack follows at my heels as I make my way down the hall. If we were going after anyone but the Garrison brothers, I would have used Diane to pull them out. But Thomas doesn't care if I put a gun to his wife's head. I've already witnessed how they treat their women.

Silently, I pull the glass door open.

Then I train my gun on the back of Avery's head.

"Keep still," I say.

They both whirl and Jack's gun whips up and points at Thomas. It takes a moment for their eyes to adjust, but then the color drains from their faces.

"Guns out of your belts and on the ground," I order.

They hesitate and Jack cocks his revolver. The sound spurs Thomas into action. He's always been the weak Garrison. He takes the pistol from the small of his back and drops it to the porch, kicking it behind him. Avery holds out a moment longer, but then he flicks his cigarette and throws his gun away.

"Walk inside," I say.

Jack keeps the door wide open. I back down the hall, my gun glued to them. The door falls shut and Jack takes the rear, his gun a foot from Thomas's head. The youngest Garrison is shivering.

Avery is stone cold. But he was always the meanest son of a bitch out of all of them. Even more of a motherfucker than Clint. I'm surprised he wasn't picked as the brother to marry and torment Keira until it was time to kill her off.

My stomach knots. The rest of me is numb.

We enter the kitchen. Diane is tied to the chair at the head of the table. There must have been a struggle because she's gagged and the terrycloth robe is on the floor, leaving her in just her slip. Westin stands in the open kitchen door, having a cigarette. When he turns, I see a bright red scratch across his jaw.

"Sit," I say.

Diane's eyes are wet, tears spilling down her cheeks. She looks to Thomas for reassurance, but he doesn't meet her pleading gaze. He just kicks a chair out and sinks down. Avery pauses by the table, narrowing his steel gray eyes at me.

"If you're going to act your little revenge fantasy, go ahead," he snaps. "I'm not letting you play with us."

"Sit the fuck down," I tell him quietly.

He sits.

I jerk my head and Jack ties their hands behind their backs. This isn't a fair fight, but it's never been a fair fight between the Garrisons and I.

They weren't going to have mercy on my redbird.

They were going to kill her, perhaps slit her throat while she slept. The thought of blood on her perfect skin, of her blue eyes open and lifeless, turns my stomach.

I sit down opposite Avery and spread my knees, gun still pointed at him.

"I found your calling card," I say.

His brow raises. He's got an angular face with tall features. He'd be handsome if he wasn't such an evil cunt. It seeps out in his narrowed gaze, in the harsh line of his mouth.

"What card?" Thomas asks.

"Mine," Jack says.

He flicks his wrist and a card appears between his two fingers. Black with a silver terrier. It flashes as he flips it between his fingers and then it disappears into thin air. He gets a lot of women with that trick.

"Who did you pay Jack to kill?" I ask.

Avery's face tightens. He darts a cold stare at his brother and Thomas shrinks back. I stand and flip my chair, sinking down and resting my arm across the top. This way I'm focusing on Thomas and he's squirming.

"Don't look at your fucking brother," I say. "Look at my face. Who did you pay Jack to kill?"

He's chewing on his lip so hard it's bleeding. Red trickles down his chin.

"Ask him," Avery snaps, jerking his head up at Jack.

Jack shakes his head. "I have confidentiality agreements. I can't squeal the way you can, Garrison."

Avery swings his head back to me and his lips curls. "I always thought you were smart, Sovereign. But after you picked that stupid bitch as your woman, I realized you're not as smart as you want people to think."

My jaw twitches. I've called Keira a bitch before, but not like that. When I use that word, it means I love her enough to degrade her and she still feels safe in my arms. The way Avery uses that word gets my blood moving.

"Who said anything about my woman?" I ask.

Thomas swallows hard. He's having trouble staying quiet. I can see the sweat etching down his temple.

"How does it feel having our brother's fucking leftovers?" Avery snaps.

He just can't help himself.

"Pretty good," I say. "Especially because I was the one who put him six feet under."

Thomas's jaw drops and Avery jerks at his bindings. I guess they're a lot slower than I thought, because I'd assumed all this time they put two and two together. But apparently they didn't because Avery is twisting, pulling at his ropes.

"You cunt," he barks. "I'm going to fucking kill you."

I sit back. "Let him out, Jack. Let's make this a fair fight."

Jack sends me a look and I can tell he disapproves by how his mouth thins. But he doesn't have to make a choice because Thomas clears his throat and the room falls silent. He lifts his eyes up to mine and hatred simmers, somewhere beyond the fear.

"This is because Clint fucked Mariana, isn't it?" he says.

I tilt my head. He's not going to get to me.

"That was your fucking fault," Thomas says, his restraint breaking. "Maybe you should've satisfied her and she wouldn't have opened her legs in someone else's bed."

I stand and push in my chair slowly. Two pairs of steel gray eyes, burning with anger, follow me as I circle the table to where Diane is tied. She's almost naked and her cheeks run with tears and makeup.

She trembles as I kneel beside her, resting my gun on the table.

"Diane," I say, keeping my voice soft. "Have you ever fucked another man while married to Thomas?"

I reach up and pull the wet gag from her lips. She gasps, her chest heaving.

"Come on, Diane," I urge. "You can tell Thomas all the dirty things you did. He won't live long enough for it to matter."

Behind me, Westin is frozen to the ground. He doesn't know that I know he still fucks Diane. It's never been my business up until now.

Was it a betrayal of trust for him to be sleeping with my enemy's wife? Maybe, but not a malicious one. So I let him think it was a secret, occasionally making remarks as if I didn't know what he was doing.

She sobs once, trying to twist her head to look at Westin. I reach up and grip her chin and turn her back around to face her husband. Thomas is shaking, his jaw set. If he wasn't tied down, he'd have his hands around his wife's throat.

She lowers her eyes.

"No, you look at Thomas and you tell him that Westin fucks you so hard I can hear you scream all the way from the gatehouse," I say.

I hope my relationship with Westin recovers after tonight. I'm going to need to give him a substantial raise and an apology tomorrow morning.

I glance over my shoulder and Westin has his arms crossed, but to his credit, he's not breaking eye contact with the Garrison brothers. Jack stares straight ahead with his brows up by his hairline.

"Shut up," Thomas roars. "Just shut the fuck up."

I tilt my head. "I thought you were interested in the topic of infidelity."

He spits on the floor.

"Now, tell me who you paid Jack to kill," I say.

The room is quiet for a second and Diane gives a short sob.

"Just tell him," she whispers.

"Shut the fuck up, you bitch," Avery snarls.

I stand up and shoot him in the foot. The sound is deafening in such a small space. Diane loses her shit, screaming and twisting her ropes. Thomas starts writhing so hard his bonds strain and I can see them loosening. Avery jerks forward and goes white. His body locks up and his eyes glaze over.

I cross the room, kneeling. My gun goes to his temple.

"Who. Did. You. Pay. Jack. To. Kill?" I breathe.

He shudders, his chest heaving.

"Keira," he breathes. "We wanted Keira dead."

I just needed to hear him say it—now I can close this chapter. I squeeze the trigger and the bullet blows a hole in his temple. He jerks to the side and his head flops. Thick blood drips from the hole and his body twitches. Convulsing as the life drains from him.

Diane screams, the sound ripping through the night. Westin has his hands on her thighs, on his knees at her feet. He's trying to calm her down, but she's going into shock. I can see the glaze over her streaming eyes.

Thomas's chair hits the ground and I realize he's not in it.

A knife falls to the kitchen floorboards.

Boots clatter down the hall.

The back door slams.

"Fuck," I snap, rising.

That motherfucker had a knife in his hand. He was playing the role of the cowardly little brother and the entire time he was just biding his time before he could make a run for it.

Jack swears under his breath. "I'll go after him," he says.

"No." I put my hat on and holster my gun beneath my belt. "Westin, take Diane out of here and get her somewhere safe. Jack, you're with me."

CHAPTER FORTY-FOUR

KEIRA

I almost fall asleep at the kitchen table, but Maddie shakes me awake around midnight and helps me upstairs. I crawl into bed on Gerard's side and pull his blanket up to my nose. It smells like him, and I can feel the faint indent in the bed where he lies. Big Dog curls up by the fire and Small Dog sneaks into the bed with me. I don't scold him, I just pull him close. Grateful for his warmth.

It's almost six-thirty when I wake abruptly and rush to the window to see if I can spot anyone in the yard. Everything is frozen over and snow falls lightly, not yet covering the grass. The world feels strange, like we're all stuck in a snow globe waiting for someone to shake it.

I know he's not back. If he'd returned, he'd be in our bed with his arms around me.

Which means...I'm going after him.

The Garrisons took my pride, they took my farm.

But I'll be damned if they take my Sovereign.

I dress quickly in my warmest clothes, stealing his warm wool socks and gloves from the closet. He has an extra black cowboy hat in there that's adjustable. I snatch that up too.

My boots sit under the window and on the sill sits the painted mare. Light glinting from the curves of her body, the reins thrown over neck glittering like starlight. My throat feels tight as I snatch her up and push her deep in my pocket.

There's only one more thing to take. The pistol Gerard hides beneath the bed. He thinks I don't know it's there, but I saw the free end of the strap of the holster poking out, one night when he had me facedown, ass up in bed.

I kneel down and feel for it, unhooking the fastening and pulling it free. It's loaded, the safety is on. I push it into my belt and tug my flannel down over the top to hide it.

I'm at the door when Small Dog lifts his head from the blankets. Big Dog lays on her belly by the fireplace, eyes glittering. They're waiting for instruction.

"Wait here," I whisper. "I have to go find Sovereign, but I'll be back."

Big Dog whines, but she stays put.

Downstairs, everything is quiet. It's late for the crew that does the first round of chores. They're already out in the pastures. Maddie is probably cleaning up breakfast.

I put on my boots in the hallway and slip out. It always smells fresh like pine at Sovereign Mountain, in the morning before the scent of horses and cattle creep in to overtake it. The lake is placid, the edges glittering with thin ice.

The whole world feels like it's taken a breath and held it.

Maybe it has. This ranch loves Sovereign back.

In the barn, I check each stall for a horse, but they're all taken or out in the secondary barn and pasture. When I get to the end, I hear a rustle and a soft nicker. Angel pushes her head over the edge and nuzzles me with her velvet nose. My stomach flips as I press my head against her neck. I haven't taken her out of the paddock yet. Doing that today seems like a colossally bad idea.

And yet...I take the painted mare from my pocket.

She's beautiful and delicate like Angel. I flip her upside down and lift her to the light. The words my mother put there so long ago, when the horse belonged to her, are barely visible.

Angel Stowe.

If anyone can bring me to Sovereign, it's them.

I lead Angel out and brush her down. Inside, my heart hammers like a war drum, but I keep my breathing even so Angel doesn't catch onto my emotions. We can't be at odds today. We have to work together as seamlessly as Sovereign and Shadow. He doesn't even use his reins or the heels of his boots to control Shadow, he just shifts his weight or clicks his tongue.

She stands perfectly still as I tack her up and lead her around the back of the barn. She's small enough I can put my foot in the stirrup and swing up without a mounting block. When my weight hits her, she shies and prances. I breathe and let my center of balance shift with her. Riding out her nerves until she falls quiet.

"Good girl," I whisper, patting her shoulder.

She tosses her head, throwing that mane of bright red. Now that I'm ready to leave, I realize I'm not sure where I'm going. The world around Sovereign Mountain is vast. I could ride for hours and get nowhere.

I set my jaw, the painted mare still balled into my fist.

The only place to start is Garrison Ranch.

I pull my scarf over my chin and push my hat down, cinching the strap. It's bitterly cold, but deep in my layers, I barely feel it.

It takes me a half hour of hard riding to get to Thomas Garrison's ranch. I see the spiral of smoke before I even see the house. Angel throws her head and starts prancing as we crest the hill. Something is making her nervous. It occurs to me that perhaps Thomas was the abuser Sovereign rescued Angel from. From the flashing whites in her eyes, it seems like she knows this place.

That makes me fucking angry. On top of everything, he probably beat my horse.

The house is halfway burnt and still smoking. A spiral of dark gray creeping into the white sky. The dusting of snow is thicker here and I see a mess of footprints in the yard. Man and horse. Tire tracks etch their way down the drive to the main road.

I guide Angel along the crest of the hill. The hoof prints of two horses make a trail up over the ridge and behind me. Heading north, towards the cabin on the other side of the ranch.

Frowning, I turn Angel.

My stomach starts tightening the further along we get. We're heading north from a different route than the one Sovereign took me before. It's taking me through a flat, open grove of Ponderosa pines.

There's something about not being able to see all around me that's unnerving. Anything could jump out of the woods, or down from the trees. I glance up and scan for cougars every few yards.

I've never been afraid of bears, wolves, or elk, but I've always had a fear of cougars after seeing the wounds of a man mauled by one when I was a child. They're better left to themselves in the remote mountain peaks.

Angel prances and I breathe in, hold, and breathe out.

I can't let her throw me and leave me out here.

When we break from the pines, I feel a weight sink from my shoulders.

We're in an open grove with the mountains rising to the left and the hill curving up to my right. I can barely make out the cabin in the distance, right at the top. There's something in the field to the far left. I freeze, squinting hard. It's a black shape and it's moving fast towards Angel and I.

My heart thumps. Angel shifts and throws her head.

Fuck, what is that?

I glance over my surroundings. I can try to disappear back into the pines and hope they cover me. That's my only option other than stand and wait. The shape is between me and the cabin, so I can't go there.

It's getting closer. I turn Angel around and squeeze my thighs, sending her bolting into the forest.

She wants to run, she loves it. I feel her muscles loosen and elongate. She's quick and she darts around trees, keeping to the loose trail up ahead. I barely notice that we're not going back the way we came until suddenly we're screeching to a halt. Faced with a wide, shallow river etching through the trees.

Where am I?

I cock my head and my whole body tingles.

A twig cracks and Angel rears back. I grip the saddle horn as she comes down. My teeth clash and my vision flashes as her hooves hit the ground. She whirls despite me trying to keep her restrained. Her ears prick forward and we both hear it this time.

Hoofbeats. Pounding the earth.

I stare into the empty pines as the sound grows closer. There's nothing I can do now except face whoever pursues me. My pounding heart begins to slow and my breathing evens. Angels stops prancing and falls quiet, ears pricked and eyes round.

I inch my hand closer to the pistol at my hip. I'm a good shot, my father made sure of that. But I've never had to aim at a moving target and I know it's not the same thing.

Thomas Garrison bursts into view, astride a deep bay horse. He sees me and veers to the left without missing a beat and he's gone.

Water sprays from behind me, but before I can turn, Angel rears hard. I don't have time to grip the saddlehorn. My feet come free of the stirrups and I'm falling through space. My teeth clack together and my head hits the ground hard enough to make stars pop overhead. My limbs are a tangle on the forest floor.

From the corner of my vision, I see Angel disappear through the trees.

I don't blame her. She wasn't ready.

Before I have a chance to recover, I'm grabbed by the collar of my coat and yanked upwards into a warm wall. My legs automatically wrap around his waist and my head lolls back. Sovereign is holding me with one arm, trying to shift to sit behind him.

"Get behind me, redbird," he says, his jaw clenched.

I wriggle to get into position and lock my limbs around his body. Euphoria bursts through my brain as the scent of leather fills my nose. He's here, he's warm, he's real. He didn't die last night.

"Sovereign," I pant, sliding my arms around his waist.

"Hold on," he says. "I've got one more thing to do and then we'll go home."

CHAPTER FORTY-FIVE

GERARD

Her arms wrap around my body so hard I can barely breathe. When all this is over, I'm going to bring her back and let her recover. Then she's getting punished. Not for fun. She's going to feel her disobedience across her beautiful ass and thighs.

Avery Garrison is dead. Thomas is the only one left. He ran out the back door, leaving his wife sobbing as Westin dragged her out to the truck. Leaving his brother's dead body slumped over the kitchen table.

I dropped a match in the living room and went after him with Jack.

It's been hours and I finally tracked Thomas to the north cabin. He crossed the border into my land, which pisses me off even more, but fair is fair. I entered his ranch last night and killed his brother and let Westin take his wife. I'll let him fight on my ranch if that makes him feel better about dying.

He's only loosely familiar with this part of the ranch. He'll move through the pines and try to get back down the ridge to the house. Probably in search of the main road. I have to head him off before he gets to the ridge.

I shift my weight and Shadow moves seamlessly from a trot to a canter. His big body winds easily through the trees.

My muscles ache. I've been hunting Thomas since after midnight. I thought this would go faster, I had lower expectations for him. But he's angry and he's fighting back.

I shift my weight and Shadow picks up speed as we break from the woods. We leave from the northeast side where the mountain flattens out to reveal the river winding through the center of a grove of pines.

Up ahead, I catch sight of the hind end of Thomas's horse. Spraying water as he fords the river.

Shadow senses my mood shift and he lengthens his stride. Rocks and dirt kick up from his hooves as we ride down the bank. Icy water drenches my boots and I hear Keira yelp softly as it hits her legs.

Shadow is tiring. The disadvantage we both have is that we're big, and carrying a lot of muscle tires us easily. And he's carrying us both. Thomas is lighter and so is his horse. They can go for much longer than we can.

We burst from the other side of the river. For a second, I think we're alone.

Then a bullet whizzes by, striking the ground behind us. Shadow shies back, and Keira's arm clamps around my torso like iron. I pull my gun free and spin Shadow in a quick circle, scanning the area.

I can't fucking see where he's coming from.

The underbrush is too thick at the edge of the pines. I need to get to them or he's going to take us out easily. If it were just me, I would have called on him to come out and fight fair. But I have Keira and the soft press of her body reminds me I have something to live for now.

My heart slows. I feel the bitter wind on my face.

There's a rustle from deep within the pines and it hits me that he can't get a clear shot. My senses sharpen and I pivot Shadow hard and urge him up the bank to the opposite pine grove. We're almost there when a huge crash turns our attention to the other side of the river.

Thomas erupts from the woods on his horse. He darts through the river so quickly I only have time to spin Shadow to make a shield of my body so Keira is safe.

His revolver glints. I see the faint puff of smoke. The sound cracks like a whip and a flurry of birds surge from the trees and take to the sky.

My body jolts. There's no pain, just spreading warmth in the side of my head. Something sticky seeps down the side of my neck.

Smells like blood.

Shadow spirals hard, spooked by the sound. The world spins in a circle and the ground rises up to hit my body hard. Forcing all the breath from my lungs.

I'm on my back on the rocky ground.

Up above, I see her take the reins. She's wearing one of my black cowboy hats and her brilliant hair whips around her face. Fear grips me and I try to force myself up, but my body won't respond.

My head lolls to the side. Thomas is riding hard at her, revolver up.

Her hand moves faster than I can follow. She flips the holster at her thigh, raises a black pistol, and unloads it. Jaw set and eyes narrowed.

Bang.

Bang.

Bang.

Fuck me, I didn't know my redbird could shoot like that.

For a second, I think she missed. But then a riderless horse surges past me and skids to a halt by the edge of the pines. It stands there, eyes wide and ribs heaving. Foam flecking down its neck.

My body tingles as I force myself up onto my elbows. The side of my head feels raw, like it got skinned, but I can't feel any pain.

I'm bleeding, I can tell because my shirt collar is soaked and rapidly freezing to my neck.

Over the brush, I can make out a dark pile of limbs on the ground.

My body gives out and I sink back against the dirt.

It's done. It's over.

A weight lifts from my chest for the first time since I was a child. They're gone, all of them. Keira is safe and my heart is free to love her without this dark weight on it.

No one ever has to put up with their abuse again.

No Garrison will ever rape, murder, or prey on anyone ever again.

The sky is gray overhead. Thick clouds crowd each other and snow begins to fall harder. The flakes are thick and they melt on my skin.

My revenge cost me everything. I'll never be the man I could have been.

The sky fills with the most beautiful woman I've ever seen. I must be high from blood loss because it takes me a moment to realize who she is. A pale freckled face, frightened eyes, and a river of crimson hair. It falls over my face and kisses my mouth.

No, it didn't cost me everything.

I can live without a heart or soul because I have her, and she's got enough for us both.

Her cold fingers brush my hair back and turn my head to the side. Her lips press together grimly and she takes off her hat and unwinds her scarf. She rips it in half and begins wrapping the thinner end around my head. Pain twinges as she ties it, pulling it tight.

"I got shot," I whisper.

Her eyes are full of tears. They're dripping from her lashes and the tip of her nose. One falls onto my lips and I taste salt.

"Don't die," she whispers.

I feel the corner of my mouth turn up. "I won't leave you, redbird. It's just a scratch."

She swallows hard. "You're going to pass out from blood loss in a minute. You have to stand up and get on Shadow *now*."

The urgency in her voice wakes something in me. I know what she's afraid of. If I pass out, she won't be able to lift me. I'll freeze to death while she's riding back to the house to get help.

My lids flicker.

I see her hand flash and pain explodes across my jaw. Suddenly I'm sitting upright with my eyes wide open. Blood seeps over my tongue and my heart hammers as adrenaline surges back through my veins.

"Fuck...you hit me," I spit.

"Don't pretend you don't like it," she whispers. "Now get on Shadow. We're going to the cabin."

CHAPTER FORTY-SIX

KEIRA

I killed Thomas Garrison and I'm not sorry.

That's the part that shocks me. I've always been sensitive and shooting a man three times should make me crumble.

But I didn't.

He had it coming.

Yes, I'm terrified. My hand shook so badly I had to shove the gun back into the holster to keep from dropping it.

All I know is he would have shot Gerard, and I was not letting a Garrison take from me again.

Still, I want to vomit or faint, but I can't. We have to get back to the cabin. My heart pounds as I scramble up to sit in front of Gerard on Shadow. He managed to pull himself into the saddle after I hit him, but he's pale, and sweat beads on his neck. The entire side of his head is drenched in crimson.

I hope it's just a flesh wound. I remember once my father told me even minor head wounds bleed the most.

He pulls me back against his chest, his broad arm locking over me. I shift my weight the way I've seen him do and Shadow breaks into a smooth walk. He seems to understand he has to be careful. I dig my hands into his mane and narrow my eyes, trying to see through the thickening snow.

It's almost noon. The snow is falling faster.

I can smell the chill moving in.

It feels like it takes forever, but somehow we get to the cabin. I halt Shadow by the door and I'm about to slide off when I hear hoofbeats. Gerard doesn't turn to look. I glance over my shoulder and his head has fallen back and his eyes are shut. He's breathing, but he just keeps getting paler.

I spin around and reach for my gun, but it's Westin and Jack who appear about the other side of the cabin. Relief washes over me.

"He's shot," I manage.

My voice squeaks. I don't realize until now, but I'm shaking like a leaf in high wind. Jack and Westin both jump from their horses and run to Shadow's side. Just in time because Gerard sways and slides to the left and right into their arms.

"Fuck, he's heavy," Jack grunts.

Gerard mumbles something incoherent. I hate seeing him like this, he's only ever been strong and in control around me. My stomach twists as I hurry ahead and tap the code into the door, pushing it aside. Westin and Jack haul him inside and lift him onto the countertop. He's so tall the lower half of his legs hang off the edge.

"What do we do?" I ask.

Tears stream down my face. Jack waves his hand, clearing us back.

"I've done this shit before," he says. "Get me wet and dry cloths. We need to get the blood flow stopped. Westin, get me all the first aid equipment you can find."

I run up the stairs and wrench open the cabinet door in the bathroom. The ripped flannel from when I had my period is washed and folded beneath the sink. I gather an armful of it and run back downstairs. Jack has his head propped on a rolled blanket and he's using a wad of paper towels to apply pressure above his ear.

"Get some of those wet," he says.

Westin veers around the corner with a large first aid bag in his hand. Jack empties it on the counter, sorting through. His jaw is set and he's totally focused. I wonder if he's been through something like this before.

"Fuck...here we go," he mumbles.

He pulls out a bundle of gauze, tape, and sticky bandages. I finish soaking the rags and he takes one and starts dabbing the flowing blood.

"Shouldn't you apply pressure?" Westin asks.

"I don't think it's that bad," Jack says, not looking up. "But I need to get a look at it."

We gather around. He gently wipes the blood back, revealing a long wound about a half inch tall and five inches long. There's no sign of his skull showing through. Jack releases a low whistle and folds a strip of gauze, applying it to the area.

My throat clenches.

"We just need to get the bleeding stopped. That could be a problem," Jack says. "Westin, check the time."

"It's twelve-thirty," he says.

"Okay, fifteen on, fifteen off," he mumbles.

He puts one hand on the other side of Gerard's head and keeps gentle pressure on the wound. I sink over the counter, reaching for Gerard's hand. It's limp, but still warm and familiar. I turn it over and stroke up his palm, tracing a faint scar that runs to his knuckle.

My Sovereign.

I shot a man for him. I saw Thomas raise his gun and I knew he would kill Gerard without hesitating. Something hard and detached filled my chest. Muscle memory took over and I barely remember my hand going up or flipping the safety off.

I remember the sound. Thunk. The look on Thomas's face as the bullet hit him in the shoulder. He jerked and swayed. I emptied the next two chunks of metal into his chest and upper thigh. His lips parted and blood covered his teeth.

I slid off Shadow and hit the ground. Something snapped under me.

My heart sinks. I reach in my pocket and pull out the painted mare. In my open palm sits two broken front legs.

I lose my shit.

Tears erupt and my chest heaves so hard I feel like I'm being crushed. My nails dig into Gerard's palm. He twitches and turns his head, eyes cracking.

"Keira," he murmurs.

Jack stares at me, frozen. He can deal with a head wound, but not a hysterically crying woman. Westin springs into action, circling the table and prying my grip from Gerard. He ushers me out of the kitchen and into the living room, pointing me towards the couch.

"I'm sorry, I'm fine," I gasp.

"What happened, Keira?" he says, forcing me down on the couch.

My hands are shaking so badly I can barely hold onto the painted mare. "I went after Gerard and found him...he was in the pine grove. Then we were at the river and Thomas shot him and he went down."

"So Thomas is still out there?" he says, his jaw set.

"No, no, I shot him," I whisper, that sick feeling returning. "I shot him and blood came out of his mouth and he fell on the ground. He's dead, up by the river."

His brows go up and a slow smile moves over his face.

"Look at you, Mrs. Garrison," he says.

"Miss Stowe," I manage, wiping my face hard. I unfurl my hand and hold out the pieces of the painted mare. "I fell after I shot him and smashed my horse."

Westin stares down at the broken wood and I can tell this is above his paygrade. My fingers close around the piece and I hold them to my chest.

I'm not crying over the horse.

Everything changes, but this little piece of wood has been constant. It's my earliest memory. I held it when my father told me how my mother passed. It lay beside me the first night I slept at the Garrison house after my father was gone. I've been alone with nothing but wood and paint to keep me company for as long as I can remember.

And that's just so fucking sad I can't go back to it.

"Is he going to make it?" I whisper.

Jack looks up. His hands are bloody.

"He'll be fine," he says. "He's not in danger, the bleeding has slowed. The wound was surface level, but it was enough to put him into shock."

A wave of relief passes over me and the urge to vomit wanes. I'm cried out, and there's nothing left to do but be strong. Westin gets up and holds out his hand and I take it, letting him help me up. I go to Gerard and slip my hand into his, watching Jack apply a bandage to his head.

"He's fine," he says. "He just had a sudden loss of blood."

I nod, wiping my nose.

Westin blows out a sharp breath and goes to the door. He kicks it open and lights a cigarette. "He'd better live so I can kick his ass. Motherfucker didn't have to call me out like that."

Jack glances up. "He didn't say anything that wasn't true. You were fucking Thomas Garrison's wife."

Westin jerks his chin, blowing smoke from his nose. "Fair, but he was an asshole about it."

My tired brain can't comprehend what they're talking about. Nothing but the man sleeping on the table is important anymore. I lay my head on his shoulder and watch his chest rise and fall. He's going to live.

And the scales are balanced.

CHAPTER FORTY-SEVEN

GERARD

My head aches, my body is stiff. My lashes feel stuck closed and when I turn, natural light burns my lids. It takes me a moment to remember what happened and I roll onto my side, abruptly sending a shot of pain through my head that makes sickness roll through my body.

I open my eyes.

The outline of her face is blurry. I blink rapidly and she comes into focus. Beautiful face at rest, eyes shut. Pale lashes rested against her freckled cheeks. Relief floods me that she's safe, here in my bed where she belongs.

I push myself up on my elbows, using my fingertips to inch back against the headboard until I'm sitting upright. I'm in the loft in the cabin, which means Westin and Jack must be around because she couldn't have carried me up the stairs.

It's the middle of the day, I can see the pale sun glittering over the hills. I can't have been in the cabin long because the storm still hasn't fully hit. Thick, pale clouds gather on the edge of the sky, just above mountains touched with falling snow.

I can hear someone walking in the kitchen. Working carefully so I don't wake her, I slide from the bed. My head spins, but I manage to make my way across the loft and climb down the stairs. I'm shirtless and there's still dried blood on my chest, but someone put sweatpants and socks on my lower body.

Westin stands in the kitchen, holding a cup of coffee. Our eyes meet and it hits me right then what we did last night and today. For almost two decades, we've worked and lived together under the shadow of vengeance. And now it's suddenly gone.

We're free.

I wonder what he'll do with that freedom. I know what I'll do with mine.

"It's good you're up," he says, jaw working. "Storm is holding off, but we need to get back."

"Where are the horses?" I ask, leaning on the counter.

"In the barn."

"And Jack?"

He shrugs, leaning back to squint through the window at the mountains below. "He's gone. I expect he'll be back to collect what you owe him and take his calling cards. But he doesn't stick around."

"Jack's always been whatever the opposite of a fair weather friend is," I say. "When the storm's over, he's gone."

We sit in silence for a long moment.

"Where's Diane?" I ask.

His mouth thins. "I left her with Maddie. She was understandably upset."

"She was never in love with Thomas, that marriage was bullshit," I say, clearing my throat. "But I'm sorry for airing your shit."

I don't apologize unless I mean it and he knows that. He takes a second, I see his jaw work again like he's trying to wring out his annoyance. Then he takes a sip of coffee and shakes his head.

"It's all water under the bridge," he says gruffly. "But I want a raise."

"You'll get one," I say. "Are you staying?"

He frowns. "Staying? On the ranch? Where would I go?"

"I didn't know if you wanted to try things with Diane. Maybe move out of the gatehouse and get a real place."

He shakes his head, emptying his mug and setting it in the sink. "No, we're a long way from reconciliation."

"I think you can get there," I say.

He nods once, and I'm not sure if he believes me, but I do. Keira and I have been through just as much and now I know she loves me enough to kill for me. Westin puts his coat on and pauses in the doorway.

"I'm getting the horses ready to go. You should wake Keira."

He leaves and I climb the stairs slowly to find her up. She's still in her jeans and sweatshirt and she's braiding her red waves over her shoulder. She hears my steps and turns, relief evident on her face.

"How do you feel?" she asks, padding over in her socks.

"Like I got shot in the head," I say.

I pull her in and kiss her and she melds to me. Her fingers dig into my bare chest for a second before they slide around my torso and clench behind my back. I brush the stray bits of hair from her face, cradling it.

"You were so brave," I tell her. "Are you alright? You shouldn't have had to kill him."

"I wasn't going to let him take you from me," she says firmly. "I feel sick...when I think about killing him, but...I don't regret it. Does that mean I'm a bad person?"

"No, redbird. You defended us both."

Her lips quivers and I press my forehead to hers.

"Your father taught you to shoot like that," I say.

She nods, pulling back, eyes glittering. "I felt him there, telling me how to aim and when to shoot."

"You're never alone, redbird."

Her chin quivers and I kiss her mouth again to keep her tears at bay. When I pull back, she's smiling. It's a weak, brave smile and I know it's taking everything she has not to shatter. I kiss her forehead and go to put on my coat and shirt. She pulls on her boots and holds out her hand.

I take it.

"It's done, Sovereign," she whispers. "Let's go home."

CHAPTER FORTY-EIGHT

KEIRA

Westin, Gerard, and I managed to get back to the house upstairs. Westin went to the gatehouse, saying something about trying to fix all this bullshit. I helped Gerard upstairs and he took some painkillers and fell asleep.

He's in our bed.

Our bed.

That sounds like forever.

I'm sitting next to him, watching him sleep. The bull skull on his chest rises and falls. The sickness I felt at shooting Thomas is lessening.

Gerard is right. I defended us both.

The Garrisons are gone. After everything they did to us, it's over just like that. It feels like the tie that binds us together. We killed for each other and that feels more permanent than saying vows.

He never hesitated when it came to protecting me. I'm glad I didn't either.

I want to love him the way he loves me.

Without hesitation. Without fear.

That Evening.

I talked to Westin at dinner and he told me that Gerard demolished my house so I had to live with him. I'm back to watching him sleep, but right now I want to slap him across the face. Too bad it'll just turn him on.

God, he's such a dick. And I still love him so fucking much.

CHAPTER FORTY-NINE

GERARD

I don't want to lose my stride so I force myself to stick to my usual schedule. The wound on my head scabs over quickly. The pain resides. The only thing leftover a few days later is a lingering fatigue.

Then that's gone after a long afternoon nap. She wakes me three days after that morning on the mountain by shaking my leg. Her face fills my vision, like an angel. I clear my throat and sit up slowly. Now that I'm not bleeding, my clarity has returned.

I reach out and put my hand on her thigh.

She scowls.

"You demolished my house," she whispers wrathfully.

She's in just a slip. It's black silk and the top fights to keep her tits under control. Her brow arcs, but all I can see is how fucking pretty she looks sitting cross-legged in my bed. Slip hitched to the top of her thighs, and the outline of her nipples apparent.

"Come here," I say.

She shakes her head. "My house. You tore it down."

I shrug. "What do you need a house for, redbird? You live with me."

A dark cloud moves over her face and she scrambles down from the bed and stalks to the bathroom. The door slams so hard the bedside table wobbles.

I wait, listening. The lock doesn't click.

She wants me to come after her.

Slowly, I rise and I'm surprised to discover the world doesn't spin anymore. I pull on a pair of sweats and follow her, pushing open the door. She's standing in the shower with her back to me and her heart-shaped ass on display. I lean in before she can turn around and crack my palm across it.

She jumps, spinning.

"How could you demolish my house without asking me?" she snaps.

I strip and step into the shower with her, taking care not to get the bandage above my ear wet. She backs against the wall and her fists ball. I know she's trying to get me to take her seriously, but all I can think about it how much I fucking love this woman.

"You're an asshole," she grumbles.

"Hmm," I muse. "Tell me that again."

"Asshole," she hisses.

My hand shoots out and pins her by the neck to the shower wall. Her eyes widen and her freckled breasts heave. The pink of her nipples darkens as they tighten. She's on her toes, trying to keep her airway open as her claws dig into my forearm.

"You are still wearing my collar," I remind her.

I ease my grip enough she can speak. She's struggling with what to say, biting at her bottom lip until it's red. I bend and kiss it gently. Then harder, giving her a taste of my tongue.

Her body sags as I kiss her thoroughly, inhaling her breath, soaking in her taste. When I pull back, her mouth glistens and I lick it clean.

Her eyes are hazy. She fucking loves being kissed.

I slide my hand down over her stomach and delve between her thighs. Our eyes lock through the steam.

"If you talk back to me like that again, I'll wash your fucking mouth out with soap," I say quietly. "You're still my submissive. That's my collar locked on your neck. What happened on the mountain changes nothing."

"Get off me," she whispers.

I lean in and kiss her again, pushing my middle finger deep into her warm, wet cunt. It clenches and her lashes flutter shut as I pull back. Her tongue darts out to lick her lips and I catch it with my tongue. Biting her just hard enough to sting.

She moans, hips riding my hand.

"You ass—"

"Think carefully before you keep talking."

She glares at me even as she whimpers. I'm knuckle-deep in her beautiful pussy. My cock is so hard it aches and I can tell I'm leaking precum. It feels like it's been years since I was inside her. I'm not going to be able to hold back to argue the attitude out of her.

"You got that safeword, sweetheart?" I breathe.

She nods, a flicker of fear moving through her wide eyes. I turn the shower off and pull her by the wrist to the sink. We're both soaked and breathing hard. Her ass keeps brushing against my thighs and my cock rides up on her lower back.

"Bend over," I order.

She drops down. I take my belt from the chair in the corner and she turns, her lips parting.

"Keep your eyes on the mirror," I say, gripping her hair and turning her head back around. "I don't give a fuck what you want. You keep those pretty eyes open and watch."

Her hips buck against mine as she realizes what I'm about to do. She shakes her head frantically, but I tighten my grip to keep her still. Her body tenses, and I know she's getting ready to fight me again. Just like she did on the kitchen floor.

But she doesn't safeword me.

That's all the permission I need. One hand on her nape, I gather her wrists and bind them to the faucet. Drawing the leather tight and fastening it. It cuts into her freckled skin and locks her wrists into place.

She's not fucking going anywhere.

293

I step back and cock my head, ignoring the faint ache down my neck. Now that I'm feeling better, the deep, unquenchable need I have for her roars back to life.

I need to mark her body, to lash my signature across the back of her thighs, to leave my bite marks on her soft, round ass.

But she needs to be prepped if I'm going to punish her first.

I go to the cabinet and pull a black case down from the top shelf. It still has the plastic wrap on it and she hears me peel it free and cranes her neck to look over her shoulder. Her eyes fall on the slender white syringe and they widen.

"Fuck, no," she breathes.

I return to the sink. My palm strokes from beneath her arm to her hip. She's breathing hard enough to make her breasts shake.

Fuck, she's got good curves. Her body is thick, full, and so soft all I want to do is mark every inch.

I don't know what the fuck Clint Garrison was thinking sleeping with other women when his wife had an ass like this.

Satisfaction wells in my chest. She's mine now, my redbird. My pretty, perfect whore. I strike her hard across her right ass cheek and she yelps and bites her lip.

"Do you like humiliation?" I ask softly.

Her mouth trembles. Her eyes are wet.

"Use your words," I order.

Our eyes lock in the reflection. Her cheeks burn pink.

"Yes, sir," she whispers.

My palm runs over the hot mark where I just slapped her. My fingers trail down to her inner thigh and...there it is. A wet line of arousal dripping from her pussy. I scoop it up with my pointer finger and lean over her body.

"Open those pretty lips," I say into her ear.

She hesitates. My other hand comes down on her ass and her pupils blow. I grip her hair and draw her head back and she moans aloud. Her hips start working and her eyes roll back.

"Watch," I order.

She obeys even though she's burning with shame. Slowly, so she has to see every second of it, I put my wet finger to her lips.

"Lick it off, sweetheart."

Her tongue flashes pink and I feel it curl wet and hot around my finger. My cock throbs against her ass and I can't keep myself from riding her. Feeling the soft curve of her ass push back where I'm most sensitive.

I push my finger deep in her mouth. Tears spring to her eyes and she gags, but I don't relent. She's taken my whole cock before, I know she can do it. I pull my finger out and wipe her tears and make her eat those too.

"Stay still," I tell her, unfastening the belt and releasing her. "Palms flat on the counter."

She obeys, but she watches my every move as I prep the syringe. I've done this before, but it feels special this time. Maybe because she's so obviously dying of shame and I get off on her humiliation the same way she does.

Her fingers curl as my touch grazes her skin.

"Hands flat," I warn. "Unless you want me to spank your palms."

Her hands go flat right away. Satisfied, I gently spread her ass. Her pussy is soaked and swollen, so inviting I have to sink down and lick it clean. She tastes sweet and I want more so I push my tongue inside her.

She moans, biting her lip.

I kiss up the entrance of her pussy. Her hips tense, but I keep going. I know she wants it, despite how nervous she is because when I spread her wider and my breath hits her skin, she starts panting. She writhes as my tongue runs over her asshole. Her spine ripples and I hear the sweetest moan escape her lips. Fuck, she's trembling.

I lick her asshole slowly, circling around and around with my tongue. Until she's sagging over the sink. All her muscles relaxed and her eyes rolled back in her head.

I stand and slip the syringe into her and release it slowly. Her head jerks up and her lips part.

"Oh," she whispers.

Our gazes lock in the mirror. I pull the syringe free and toss it. Her lashes flutter and I know she feels the warm water inside. It's turning her on and I need to feel that too. I slide my fingers into her mouth to wet them, leaving a trail of saliva on her chin, and push them into her cunt.

It's tighter, if that's even possible.

"Gerard," she gasps. "Please."

I run my hand up her spine and grip her hair, dragging her head back. "You came after me when I told you to stay put," I say.

Confusion flickers over her face.

"I saved you," she whispers.

"I wouldn't have needed saving if I hadn't run into you in the pine grove. I had him in my sights. You put yourself in danger, redbird. You haven't apologized for it."

She swallows hard. "I'm sorry."

I shake my head and pick up my belt. Her thighs tremble and her hands shake as she tries to keep them flat. I don't draw this part out because it's not for pleasure. I just keep her still with my hand in her hair and bring my folded belt down across her ass.

I told her she was going to regret not trusting me.

The belt cracks.

She screams, a sob surging from her lips.

But she doesn't safeword me, even though I know she's in agony.

My cock aches, and I bring the belt down on her upper thighs. Hard enough to leave a pink and red mark on her freckled skin. Sobs spill from her throat as I lash her once, twice, three more times. Until I see creamy arousal on her inner thighs.

I drop the belt and pull her into my arms. She's warm, trembling. She cries quietly for a moment, rubbing her face into my chest. I wipe her tears with my thumb and kiss her forehead.

"You need to use the toilet," I say gently. "I'll leave you alone. But come out as soon as you're done."

She hiccups, wiping her face with her palm. Her eyes are glassy and her shoulders sag. When I run my palm down her spine I can tell her muscles have relaxed. It makes me realize how tense she is most of the time.

She's still stuck in fight or flight.

My mouth brushes her hair. "Is this what you want? For me to brutalize you, redbird?"

She gasps, pushing her face into my chest. "Yes."

"Beg for it then."

I turn her face up and she's deep in a submissive state. Her eyes are dreamy and swollen. She's breathing in little pants.

"Please," she whispers. "Please, Sovereign. Hurt me."

I stroke through her soft waves. She's so beautiful, so good. Too good for me, but I've always known that and it never mattered. If I'd listened to that voice in my head that said she was too sweet for a man like me, I wouldn't be here right now, holding her tight.

"I'll hurt you, but only if I can put you back together," I say.

CHAPTER FIFTY

KEIRA

My face burns as I shower and my hands shake as I scrub my skin until it's silky smooth. Of course, he's not embarrassed. Nothing seems to embarrass him. He got down on my knees behind me and licked the most intimate part of my body and he was rock hard.

Not even Clint touched me there. I'd always counted myself lucky he didn't want anal.

Maybe that's why I'm so nervous for this. When it comes to that part of my body, I'm a total virgin. I've never had a man touch me there until tonight.

I slam the shower door and scrub myself dry. I'm still wearing his discreet collar, but when I look down at the sink, I realize he left the leather one there for me.

My heart picks up. I wipe the steam from the mirror and fasten it around my neck. The little tag swings, glinting.

Sovereign.

There's no fighting that I'm his anymore. He never asked, never bothered to give me a choice. He just walked into my life and took what he wanted.

No apologies. No regrets.

I wish I could be truly mad at him for what he did. But for the first time since I was a child, I feel peace. I felt it the first time I set foot on Sovereign Mountain. And I didn't realize it then, but I felt it the first time his mouth touched mine.

I come out of the bedroom in nothing but the collar. The lights are out, and the fireplace sheds an orange glow over the room. He dragged a chair to the middle of the hearth, right below the bull skull. And he's sitting in it, shirtless, his knees spread. I can make out the hard length of his cock beneath his black sweatpants.

He lifts his head. His eyes glint.

"Come here, redbird," he says.

I feel small with him sitting there like that. My bare feet pad across the floor until I'm standing between his knees. He leans in and his touch burns as it drags down my waist to my hips.

He's got something wrapped around his fist. A silver chain.

"What is that, sir?" I whisper.

He doesn't answer, but I didn't expect him to. He's gotten so used to concealing himself that he'll always talk in riddles. He can talk around a question like an elite lawyer. Or just ignore it altogether.

"I want your full submission, redbird," he says. "No speaking unless I ask you a question or you need to use your safeword. Tell me you understand."

I nod, licking my dry lips. "I understand. Sir."

His hand circles to my lower back and he grips my left ass cheek. Squeezing it hard enough to hurt. Pleasure bolts down and tingles warm in my hips and thighs.

"You have the prettiest ass," he says, softly. Like he's just thinking aloud. "Turn around."

My heart flutters, but I obey. His fingertips brush over my ass, exploring the curves. He bends, and I feel his hot breath wash over me as he presses kisses to my bare skin. His tongue flicks here and there. My fist clench and I bite my tongue to keep from moaning.

He turns me back around. Then he leans in and unwinds the silver chain from his hand. It's got three long strands with a little clip that looks like a hairpin at each end. He cups my right breast, and before

I know it, he's sliding one of the clips over my nipple and pulling it tight.

It aches, and pleasure starts in my clit.

My eyes widen. I want to moan, but I promised to be good.

He moves to my left nipple, flicking it first to get it fully hard. I jolt and squeeze my thighs together.

He glances at me, amusement in his eyes.

He loves torturing me.

When he fits the other clip onto my left nipple, I have to bite my lip to stay silent. Then he lifts me onto his lap and spreads my legs. I keep perfectly still even though I can feel his cock against my thigh. Hard, blood pulsing. My core clenches, begging to feel him inside me.

He licks his fingers and reaches between my thighs. I just finished my period and I shaved this morning. My hormones are at an all-time high, and my pussy is silky smooth. I've never felt so sexy, so desirable in my life.

He pinches my clit. My hips jolt.

"Fuck, your cunt is so perfect, sweetheart," he murmurs. His middle finger teases my entrance. "Soft, tight, wet. I'm going to fucking ruin it tonight."

Cold metal slides over my clit. My thighs tense. He adjusts it tighter and leans back to admire his work. There's a delicate silver chain connecting the clips on my nipples to the one on my clit. In the center is a little silver bell. He taps it with his fingertip.

"Are you going to be my pet?" he asks.

I nod, mouth dry.

"Use your words when I ask you a question," he reminds me. "Are you going to be my dirty, little pet and let me ruin your cunt tonight?"

"Yes, sir." My breath hitches. "You've already ruined me, sir."

His jaw tightens and he leans in. "Not the way you've ruined me for any other woman. I'll give you everything, redbird. You deserve to have the world at your feet."

I didn't expect him to get vulnerable, but it doesn't last long. He bends in and flicks the bell with his tongue Then he takes it in his teeth and tugs it viciously, sending little shocks of pain and pleasure through me. I moan, my hips riding his lap.

He slaps my ass. "Don't forget, this is punishment too. Now, are you going to be a dirty whore for me?"

"Yes, sir." The words are a gasp.

He stands and pulls the chair aside, revealing a padded kneeler before the fire. He points and I circle him and sink down. The fire is warm on my back, which is a relief because the night is cold. Wind and snow lash at the window.

He stands over me, running his hand through my hair. Gripping it to pull my head back. My eyes drift up his broad, muscled body. Up over the hard cock in his pants. The trail of hair going up to his naval, the ridges of his stomach. His pecs covered in ink and hair, his broad, scarred shoulders.

To his face.

My chest warms. I've grown used to the stern expression in his eyes.

"Stay there," he says.

I nod and watch him go to the bedside table. I didn't notice until now, but there's a number of implements laid out. I can't see what he's doing, but when he returns, I can tell he's got a plug in one hand. My cuffs hang from the other.

My thighs tighten.

"Put your hands behind your back," he orders.

I obey and he kneels down. I feel the cuffs slip around my wrists. He applies pressure to my upper back until I understand he wants me to lean over. He guides my chest over his knee and gathers my hair at the nape of my neck.

"Try to relax your body, redbird," he says.

I'm trying, but it's hard when I have so much tension between my legs. He slips his fingers over my pussy, dipping the tip of his middle finger inside me for a brief second. Then he drags it up to my poor clit, pinched in the clip.

My eyes roll back. Arousal shoots through me like electricity.

I bite my lip hard, but I can't keep from whimpering aloud.

He doesn't correct me. He just keeps stroking the strangled tip of my clit, teasing it in circles. An orgasm starts and he doesn't stop it. He lets it wash over me until it's throbbing hard and I'm moaning through my teeth.

"Good fucking girl," he praises. "That'll loosen that pretty asshole."

Cold lube splashes down my hip and I know he's putting it on his fingers. His touch slides over my ass and finds my most sensitive point. He rubs in a circle before slipping his middle finger in. All the way to the middle knuckle.

Pain sears. My breath hitches.

Fuck, he's got big fingers.

He starts moving it, just a half inch in and out. The pain ebbs and pleasure replaces it. My face burns, my nipples and clit ache. But nothing is more acute than the perfect humiliation of being bent over, tied up, and at his mercy.

"That's my girl," he growls quietly, the sound vibrating in his chest. "Now let's get the plug in and you can come again. How does that sound?"

I just nod, my head blank.

His finger slips out and I feel cool metal at my entrance. It works slowly, but I can't keep my muscles from clenching.

"Bear down, baby," he murmurs, stroking my back. "You can do it for me. You're such a good girl, you've done so well already."

I want to please him so badly. Eyes shut, I bear down and pain bolts through my hips as the plug settles inside me. To my surprise, it feels amazing. Like it's touching all the right places at once.

He shifts me back so I'm on my knees and leaves me sitting there. I watch his broad body disappear into the bathroom, I hear him wash his hands. Then when he returns he has something in his hand that I don't recognize.

He crouches in front of me.

"Open your mouth," he says.

I hesitate. His eyes narrow.

"It won't hurt you," he says, holding it up.

I inspect it. It's a rectangular tab of leather with a metal ring as a handle. There's a little silver tag hanging off it. He flips it and I can make out the word etched in it.

Painslut.

Oh God, that makes me shudder.

The corner of his mouth jerks up. "You like that, redbird?"

I nod hard.

"Then open that pretty mouth," he orders.

I part my lips and he slides the leather into my mouth. It's about two inches long and an inch wide, big enough to cover the surface of my tongue and pin it down. Right away I can tell it isn't just leather.

"Bite it with your front teeth," he says. "Hold it steady."

I obey. It tastes a bit like sour candy, but a lot more intense. Right away my mouth goes into overdrive, saliva pooling under my tongue.

"Swallow," he orders.

Automatically, I try to swallow, but the leather tab keeps my tongue down. I gag, barely keeping my teeth together. The sweet and sour taste is making me drool so badly it slips from my lips. His eyes follow it down my neck, spilling over my tits.

He's so turned on, I can see the vein pulsing in his neck.

"Fuck," he murmurs, touching my chin. "You're such a good slut."

My body trembles. Humiliation has me so wet it's slipping down my inner thigh. I wonder if it's soaking the kneeler or if that's just the saliva dripping down my chin and neck.

He circles me and I hear him crouch behind me. His breath grazes my neck. "You want out, drop your head all the way back. Understood?"

My heart pounds as I nod. Gently, he gathers up my hair and starts braiding it down my back.

Oh God, what is he going to do?

His mouth brushes kisses down my shoulder and upper arm. Then his fingers slide between my legs and my vision flashes as he slips a slender vibrator up into my pussy. My inner muscles clench, pushing it deep inside. So it moves against my G-spot.

I whimper around the leather. My eyes start running.

303

He stands and unfastens the ties of his pants. "Close your eyes, painslut."

I snap them shut. I hear him spit into his hand and start jerking himself off. I doubt it will take long. He's panting and I wish I could see him. I know he's beautiful, aroused, rock hard. Sweat etching down his carved abs.

He groans. Warmth hits my breasts and chin.

My eyes snap open and he's just as I imagined. So fucking sexy, standing over me with the firelight glinting off his tattooed chest. His hard cock in hand, still coming on my tits.

I shudder, unable to help myself. The pressure of the clip on my clit and vibrator inside me is too much.

An orgasm washes over me and I sink back onto my heels to keep from falling over. He tugs the leather from my mouth and pulls me back up, pushing his wet cock between my lips. His other hand draws me back by the braid. Forcing me to look up into his eyes as he feeds his length, inch by inch, into my mouth.

My throat convulses, saliva spilling down my chin. My nose runs and my eyes sting. His hand clenches against the back of my head and he pushes slowly. Forcing himself deeper until I have no air. Until we're way past worrying about my gag reflex.

I might pass out. My fingers clench in the cuffs. My head spins as a rush of arousal washes over my body. So strong it feels like that desperate moment before orgasm. Where the only thing that matters is pleasure.

My vision blurs and darkens. He's in my throat now because he reaches down and cups it. Squeezing it just hard enough I can tell he feels the bulge of his cock.

Then he pulls back and I suck in air, coughing around his cock. I have one moment of relief before he's back in. Pushing all the way until my face is against his groin.

I'm back to drowning. Falling through dizzying space where there's nothing but his ravaging touch.

Then he's out just enough I can inhale.

And back in.

He reaches down and tugs the chain connecting my nipples and clit. Arousal sears like fire, and I moan as he pulls back at the same time he releases the tension on the chain. It takes me moment, but I start to feel a pattern.

Air in my lungs.

Sweet release of the pressure on my clit.

Suffocation.

Tension that burns like fire.

He's building me back up, using my breath and the clip on my clit. An orgasm surges quickly and hits my hips hard. Making my toes curl and my legs stiffen until I rise an inch off my heels. As I come, he pulls his cock back and releases his hold on the chain.

I shake, arousal dripping down my thighs and calves.

He pushes back in one last time and comes with low groan. Dragging his cock out as he does so the first pulses go down my throat and the last spatter my chin.

"Fuck," he says hoarsely. "Pretty whore, mouth full of cock, covered in cum."

I'm so overstimulated I can't tell if I'm still orgasming or not.

"Tongue out," he orders.

Weakly, I obey, spilling saliva and cum out onto my chin. It slips warm down my breasts and stomach and the corner of his mouth turns up.

Euphoria bursts in my brain. He's pleased—I pleased him.

He studies my eyes, which I know are glassy, and his hand comes up to stroke my face. I push my chin into his cupped palm, not caring I'm filthy. I've never wanted anything more than to hear him tell me I'm a good girl. That I did exactly what he wanted.

His grip returns to the back of my head. His other hand fists the base of his cock.

"Clean me up, little whore," he says.

Eagerly, I run my tongue up the underside of his cock. Licking up all the wetness. When I get to the head, I swirl my tongue all the way around. Getting every bit. His grip tightens, sliding down towards my mouth. A drop of white appears at the tip.

"Get it all," he orders.

I push the head into my mouth and suck. His jaw twitches and his chest rumbles with satisfaction. When I pull out, I unfurl my tongue. Showing him without being asked. Begging for his approval.

His head cocks slightly and the corner of his mouth twitches.

"Good girl," he says softly.

CHAPTER FIFTY-ONE

GERARD

I saw the moment where she slipped into total submission. Her eyes went from bright to soft and dreamy. All the tenseness eases from her body. Leaving her soft and pliable to my desire.

It's so fucking sweet.

She swallows the last bit of my cum and her full mouth closes. I bend and gather her wet, sticky body up in my arms. She gasps as I lift her and carry her to the bed, ripping the blankets back.

This is going to get messy.

She's still got the cuffs on, her arms behind her back. The clips are still on her pink nipples and her swollen, overstimulated clit. I'll keep everything on her until I'm done.

"Stay on your knees," I order.

She nods, sinking back onto her heels. I know she's so overstimulated she couldn't speak if she wanted to. I lean past her and flip the headboard. There's a mirror on the other side positioned so she can look herself in the eye while I fuck her ass. I've been saving it back for a night like this.

Her jaw drops. Her eyes rake over her reflection.

I kneel behind her, pulling her soft ass against my groin. My hand slides up to her breasts, gathering my cum and rubbing it into her pinched nipples. She whimpers, but she's too weak to move.

I kiss where her shoulder meets her neck.

"Dirty fucktoy," I whisper. "I'm going to bend you over and fuck your ass and you're going to watch."

Her tits heave. Her eyes are so big. She's soaked as I push my two fingers inside her, finding her G-spot and tapping it hard. Her eyes rolls back, she clenches.

"Please," she yelps.

"Please...what?"

"Sir," she whimpers. "Please, sir, I can't take it."

Her inner muscles tense. She's going to come again, this time all over my hand.

"You can take this," I say through gritted teeth. "And then you'll take every inch of my dick up your ass too and you'll fucking thank me for it."

Her eyes roll back, she arches, and she shatters. Her eyes fly open and connect with mine. Lashes fluttering and mouth moving soundlessly until her blue irises roll back and she goes limp.

Fuck, that's a beautiful sight.

Wetness dripping down my wrist, I pull my fingers free of her cunt as her orgasm wanes. She slumps against my chest and I lift my hand to her lips, working her jaw open. Her lashes flutter and she cranes her neck to look up at me, but I grip her hair and jerk her head back to the mirror.

"No. I want you to watch yourself eat your cum off my hand," I growl. "Keep those pretty eyes straight ahead" —my hand comes down on her ass so hard she screams— "and lick it clean."

Her tongue pushes out and curls around my fingers sticky with her arousal. Twin tears overflow her eyes and make tracks in her messy, perfect face. When my fingers are clean, I slide my hand under her chin and grip it so I can feel those tears against my skin.

"Good girl," I praise.

I release her hair and she whines, clearly disappointed. She's turned her mind off, she's nothing but a blank canvas.

And she's doing it because she loves it, because she's a pretty, perfect painslut.

She trembles. My gaze flicks lower. I've waited for this moment, patiently. Giving her time to get used to being fucked rough before I take it a step further. But I'm not waiting anymore.

Taking a pillow, I lay it before her knees and lower her over it. She turns her head and her cum and tear stained cheek rests on the sheet. Her blue eyes follow my every move as I go to the bedside table and retrieve the lube. We're going to need a lot of it.

Her breathe hitches as I kneel behind her. My pants are pushed down to expose my already rock hard cock. I know she can't take me for long in her ass, so I'll fuck her pussy first, until I'm close to coming.

She'd let me do anything to her right now. But I don't want to hurt my redbird.

Her breath hitches as I dip my finger in her cunt and pull the vibrator out. It's slippery and smells like her lust. I grip her hair and drag her head back, pushing it into her mouth.

"Clean it," I order.

She gags as it fills her mouth. Holding it by the string, I pull it out enough she can get a breath. Her tongue works, cleaning up her mess.

That's my good girl.

I toss it aside and release her hair. Lining my cock up with her cunt, I brace the heel of my hand beside her head. And thrust into her slippery pussy.

Fuck, with the plug in her ass there's barely room for me to get my cock halfway in her cunt.

Her mouth parts. Her pupils blow.

"You can be loud, sweetheart," I pant, fucking the first few inches into her. "I want to hear you cry and beg."

Her lips part and a soft whine escapes. A little sob that makes those tears spill over and her eyes roll back in her head.

It doesn't take long for another orgasm to start in my hips. I pull out and work the plug from her ass. She's loosened enough I can drizzle lube into her and slip my middle finger past her opening. Her lips part in a silent cry as I fingerfuck her ass. I reach under her stomach and tug the chain gently.

Her hips shudder. She rubs her face into the sheet, leaving smears behind.

Wetness drips from her cunt as she comes again. I work my fingers harder and release the chain.

She's loose, she's ready.

I grip my cock at the middle and guide the head to her asshole. I've been fucking with a big dick for a while, and I know this should actually be easier for us both than the first time I fucked her pussy. There's more room, I won't hit resistance the way I do when I'm fucking up against her cervix.

Her fingers clench in the cuffs.

"Bear down," I tell her.

She whimpers, but I feel her obey. The head of my cock slides into her ass and she gasps, her eyes rolling back.

"Does it hurt?" I press.

"No—no, sir," she manages. "Yes...maybe."

She doesn't know what she feels yet. That's normal. I stroke my hand down her naked back and let her adjust.

She's being such a good girl and I want this to be a reward, not a punishment. Her hips tremble and I adjust the pillow, making sure she has support.

She needs it. She came so many times her muscles are limp.

I brace myself and push again. This time she opens for me beautifully and I slide in. All the way to the hilt in my redbird.

"Sovereign," she gasps.

I gather her red braid in my hand and wrap it around my fist. Pinning her to the bed, her cheek sticking to the sheet.

"I know, sweetheart," I murmur. "You're such a fucking good girl."

I don't make her come again, she's past that point. I'm not even sure we can tell if she's stopped coming from the last time. Instead, I focus on dragging myself out an inch and thrusting back in. Moving my cock just enough to get the friction I need, but not enough to hurt her.

She moans, twitching. Her face rubs into the bed. She mouths something, but I can't hear her.

"Speak up," I urge.

I lift her head with her braid and her lips tremble.

"You feel good," she manages, her voice breaking. "You feel so good, sir."

My cock throbs and she feels it, writhing those pretty, soft hips beneath me. My hips thrust faster and she moans like the sweet whore she is.

She loves this, she loves the pain, the humiliation.

Heat shocks down my spine. We're so perfect together, my redbird and I.

Cum spills from me and I push in and shudder. My groin pressed into her ass, my fingers in her hair.

"Take it," I grit out. "Take all of me."

She does, she lays there until I'm done. I bend, still inside her, and kiss the side of her head. Right on her temple.

"That's my girl," I tell her.

Her lashes flutter. "Did I do what you wanted, sir?" she whispers.

"Everything," I assure her. "You're so good, such a good girl. I'm going to pull out and clean up now."

She nods, wincing as I disengage my hips. My cock leaves her warmth and her chest constricts and releases.

A deep, deep sigh.

I take everything off until she's naked. She clings to me as I fill the bathtub and let her sink into the steamy water. When I return from cleaning up the mess on the hearth and in the bed, her eyes are heavy.

She reaches for me weakly.

"Hold me," she whispers.

I sink into the water and pull her into my arms, facing me. Her legs wrap around my body and her arms drape around my neck. She burrows her face into my chest. I kiss the top of her pomegranate scented hair.

There's no place in this world I'd rather be than in her arms.

CHAPTER FIFTY-TWO

KEIRA

It takes a week for the snow to stop.

Everything between Sovereign and I is put on hold because he's gone so much. Winter on a ranch is hard, and it's even harder up on Sovereign Mountain. He leaves early and comes back late. Frosted with snow and smelling of the outdoors.

I spend a lot of time sleeping, exhausted from everything that happened. When I'm not out cold, I'm occupied with Angel in the barn or helping Maddie in the kitchen. She's a lot warmer to me now, she even told me she was impressed with what I did by the river.

We start decorating the ranch for the holidays early even though Sovereign narrows his eyes. He doesn't say anything, but he does leave a pile of cut fir branches outside the front door early one morning.

It's Sunday night when I finally get him to myself. The men finish the chores early and the main house clears out. The clock chimes. I'm laying in bed with my eyes fixed on the snow covered mountains through the window.

The painted mare lays on the bedside table. She doesn't stand upright any longer. I tied her broken legs together with a ribbon so they don't get lost.

Sovereign doesn't come in when he usually does around eight. I slip from bed, the goosebumps rising on my skin, and pad out into the hallway. I'm in my silk slip, the one I wore the night my barn burned. I scrubbed away the smoke stains and now it's back to its original white.

I don't wear it because I have to anymore. Just because I want to. Because Sovereign's eyes light up when he sees me in it.

I pad down the stairs. Maddie hung the fir branches over the fireplace and wound them with little white lights. The gas fireplace burns. Otherwise, the big main room is quiet.

Sovereign sits on the couch facing the fireplace, knees apart. He's got a glass in one hand.

My stomach tightens.

Is he...drinking?

Small Dog and Big Dog are sprawled out at his feet. Both flipped on their backs, paws in the air, snores rising from their slack jaws.

I creep down the curved staircase, my bare feet silent on the wood. He doesn't see or hear me until I circle the couch and sink down on the floor at his feet. Small Dog sneezes loudly and flips to his side. He cracks an eye.

"What is that?" I ask, taking the glass and lifting it to my nose.

It's water. My shoulders sag with relief.

The corner of his mouth turns up. He touches the side of my face, his rough palm cradling my cheek. I burrow my face into it. He feels so strong, so safe.

"It's Sunday night," he says.

"I know," I whisper.

His mouth thins, his eyes flick over me and rest on the fire. "I still want a contract with you, but I want it to be simple."

"That's alright with me," I whisper. "Contract or not, I still love you."

He bends down and kisses my forehead. My entire body goes still and my lids flutter shut. No one ever touched me this gently before he came along. My heart is tender and wide open like a flower

314

reaching up to the sun. I feel his touch on my chin, tilting it, and I open my eyes.

"It took me a long time to settle my scores," he says. "I wanted the Garrison bloodline gone and now it is. It's time to close the book. I'm glad you were here for the last chapter."

My stomach flutters. His words sound so grim.

"What happens next?" I whisper.

He takes my hand. "Come here," he says hoarsely, lifting me to my feet and guiding me into his lap. I climb up and straddle him. We're eye level and I can make out the pale blue of his iris and the dark icy outer ring surrounding it.

"You're very young," he says. "I forget how young you are because...you've been through so much already."

I swallow, feeling awkward. I'm not even in my mid-twenties and I feel like I've lived half a lifetime already. But he's almost forty, even though he doesn't look it. There's over a decade of life between us, and I feel the weight of it tonight.

"I don't mind," I whisper.

He smooths back my hair, playing with a strand. "Tell me what you want for the future?"

The future has never been easy for me to imagine. I'd given up hoping when I realized I'd married a man who hated me and stole my family's farm. The future had always looked bleak and short.

But with Sovereign...I feel like I'm just waking up.

"I don't know," I admit. "But I'd like whatever it is to be with you."

His jaw works and his hand leaves my hair and trails down to my stomach. My body goes still as his fingertips skate across the curve of my lower belly. His lashes are lowered. His face is unreadable.

"Sovereign," I whisper.

He clears his throat. "I scheduled an appointment for a reversal."

My heart picks up. His eyes flick up. The air between us feels thick with tension.

"You...what are you saying?" I whisper.

"The reversal success rates are very high for what I had done," he says.

"You need to slow down," I blurt out.

He goes quiet and he can't hide the devastation in his eyes. I slide off his lap, unsure what to say. The fire crackles, the dogs snore. I back up to the bottom of the stairs.

"I...my painted mare is broken," I whisper. "I was hoping you'd fix it."

He stands and his face is strained. I know I hurt him, but I'm not sure how to get myself out of this situation without causing more pain. I grip the railing and back up onto the landing.

"Of course," he says.

I swallow past my dry throat. "Thank you. I'm going to bed."

Up in our bathroom, I splash my face with cold water. My hands shake as I dry them and tears push up past my lashes. I spread my left hand and lift it, studying the bare spot on my ring finger.

Is he expecting to get me pregnant without even talking about marriage?

I want to be married and I want it right this time. I want the ring and the wedding and the promises. And a husband who doesn't hate me. I take a shuddering breath and it hits me that I'm having a panic attack. My hands shake and my heart pounds. There's a sick sensation in my chest and my head spins.

I realize now that Clint fucked me up more than I care to admit.

I don't hear him knocking at the door until it's too late and it's being forced open. He crouches down and scoops me up, carrying me out to the bed. Dimly I'm aware that he's holding me and we're both propped on the pillows. And his boots are on the bed, propped on the folded fur blanket at the end.

I frown, rubbing my wet face against his shirt.

"Boots are on the bed," I whisper.

He laughs. "Hush, it's fine. We have a washing machine."

My lids feel sticky and I don't care what he thinks about me anymore. He's seen me in every compromising position. With my hair messy, my eyes swollen, gagging, begging. He's seen my rage, my wrath, my vengeance. And I've seen his, laid out in all its ugliness.

I've only loved him for a short time.

But I know him. I stood witness to his vengeance.

"Why don't you marry me, sir?" I ask softly.

He turns abruptly, flipping me onto my back. He leans over me and slides his hand up my forearm to weave his fingers through mine. Pressing my hand back against the pillow.

"I don't know what will happen in this next chapter, but I know who I am in it," he says. "I am your husband, redbird. I thought that went without saying."

Tears leak from the corners of my eyes. I wish I didn't cry so easily, it's so fucking embarrassing.

"Really?" I whisper.

His jaw works. "I killed Clint because he was sleeping in my bed with my wife."

My breath hitches. Deep down, I know I should be horrified. But instead, I feel the slow burn of arousal kindle between my thighs.

"What does that mean?" I whisper.

"It means, of course I'm going to marry you."

There's something about the intensity of his voice that's setting me off. That growl at the end of his words has me burning. I writhe slightly and his grip tightens, holding me to the bed.

"You are the mother of my children," he says. "My wife."

My eyes are wide. My lashes are wet.

How does he always get me like this? Aroused and in tears seems to be my default mode when I'm in bed with him. But I don't have time to think about it because he bends and kisses my mouth and my body sets on fire.

His kisses are always so slow and thorough. He takes his time to explore my lips with his. I distantly feel his arousal growing against my leg and it stokes the flames of mine. He breaks our kiss and uses his hard head to push mine aside and kiss the side of my neck.

He bites it gently and returns to my mouth.

"Give me your tongue, redbird," he murmurs.

My hips rise, rubbing against his body. I part my lips as his distracted eyes find my mouth. He dips down and captures the tip between his teeth. I feel his saliva slip into my mouth and I swallow without thinking. Our mouths draw apart and our eyes connect.

He's fucked up for me, just like Westin said he was.

"Do you want to be Keira Stowe or Sovereign?" he asks.

My breathe comes out in a slow shudder. He doesn't know how much it means to me that he's letting me choose. Clint just forced my hand down on the paper, his grip firm on my lower back. He took my name before I had a chance to realize what he'd done.

I never wanted to be a Garrison. But I do want to belong to Gerard Sovereign.

My dry lips part.

"Get me a ring and I'll be Keira Sovereign forever," I whisper.

He rumbles, moving to lay halfway atop me. His body is so heavy and it presses me down into the mattress. His knee shifts and I let out a little gasp as it lifts enough I can breathe. His hips move, gently humping against mine. He's got a satisfied, drunk expression in his heavy eyes.

"I can't you pregnant tonight, redbird, but let's practice."

CHAPTER FIFTY-THREE

GERARD

The world gets smaller in the dead of winter.

We can't bring the trucks out until the snow has been cleared from the road. We spent all summer preparing for this though, so it doesn't matter. The freezers and cupboards are packed with food. We have enough gas and fuel to last till spring. Everyone on Sovereign Mountain hunkers down and slips into the slow wait until the first scent of spring touches the air.

Keira loves comfort and she thrives in winter. I find her curled up in the bedroom window wrapped in blankets. Hot coffee and a stack of books nearby.

She naps every afternoon in our bed because I keep her up late at night. She stays up till past midnight, usually cuffed in leather, on her knees. Letting me fuck her and force orgasms from her body until she collapses with exhaustion.

She's had a hard life, and I can give her comfort and pleasure.

So I do. More than she could ask for.

At the end of the month, I manage to get to South Platte to pick up an order I've had waiting for me since October. It sits silently in the passenger side of my truck all the way home. A flat cardboard box with her initials in silver across the top.

KS.

Except this time, the S isn't for Stowe.

She's out in the barn with Angel and Westin when I get back. I asked Westin to distract her and he dropped the bomb on me that he has something he's been waiting to tell Keira for a few weeks. Apparently Angel is pregnant, expecting in the spring. I slip past the barn door and head into the house, knowing Keira is completely distracted in the barn. Probably clinging to Angel's neck with tears running down her face.

Westin won't know how the fuck to deal with that.

The corner of my mouth turns up as I ascend the stairs. I love that she's soft and her tears flow easily. All the cruelty she endured didn't scar her the way it did me. She still feels everything to the fullest.

In the bedroom, I lay the package down and flip the lid. Inside is a little wooden box with the SMR logo burned into the top. It's tiny in my hands as I flip the lid open and reveal the ring I ordered back in October.

It's a diamond, the shade of the ferns that grow in the mountains, by the edge of the lake. The tall stone is surrounded by little diamonds that glitter like the stars on the bridle of the painted horse.

I knew it was the one for her the minute I laid eyes on it. The shade of green is beautiful against her auburn hair. I'm not sure how to explain myself, but it just looks like the ring of a beautiful woman.

And my redbird is the most beautiful woman I've ever seen.

I snap the lid shut and slip it in my pocket. Beneath it in the box sits a set of fern green lingerie wrapped in black paper and tied with a silver ribbon.

I know she's used to living in rough country, but she deserves to feel beautiful and spoiled now and then.

She never asks for anything.

I hear her steps, rushing up the stairs. I move fast, snapping the box shut and setting it in the dresser. The door bursts open and she's there, still in her coat and boots. Eyes glassy and lashes wet.

"Angel is having a baby," she bursts out.

She runs to me and I lift her in my arms. Her legs wrap around my waist and her arms encircle my neck. It's the first time she's done this and my heart is pounding. But I have to play it cool, I don't want her getting self-conscious.

"How do you feel about being a grandmother?" I ask.

She laughs, her head falling back.

Fuck, she's pretty and I'm getting hard at the wrong time.

She sobers, sliding from my arms and stripping her boots and coat off. I watch her shed the rest of her clothes, leaving them in a trail on the floor. This time I just gather them up and drop them into the chair without saying anything.

She climbs naked into the bed and pulls the blankets up to her chin.

"I'm so cold. Do you want to go out and see Angel after dinner?" she asks.

I shake my head. "No, I have an appointment tonight."

Her face falls and I lift my brow.

"Don't pout," I tell her.

She rearranges her face, but I can tell she's crestfallen. "Okay, that's fine. I'll probably eat with Maddie in the kitchen then."

"Maddie actually asked me if you would go down and help her out with dinner tonight," I say, trying to keep my voice casual. "She's finally admitted you make the best biscuits."

She smiles, although I can tell she's disappointed. But she's a good girl and she'd never complain about it. I cross the room and bend to kiss her waiting mouth and she grips the front of my shirt.

"Do you want a quickie?" she asks, a flush creeping up her face.

That's tempting.

I cup her right breast, rubbing her nipple until it's hard beneath my thumb. I should wait until tonight, after she's got my ring on her finger. But, fuck it, I can go as many round as she needs tonight.

She yelps as I flip her over the edge of the bed. Her spine arches and I can tell she's wet. She wanted to be fucked all along, that's why she stripped and got into bed. Holding her by the hair with one hand,

I take my cock out with the other and push it mercilessly into her pussy.

She yelps.

"You wanted it," I tell her, slapping her thigh.

I fuck her until I come, but I don't get her off. I want her needy and dripping so she has to think of my cock in her every time she feels her wet panties against her clit. She's panting, still bent over the bed, when I tuck my cock into my pants and kiss the nape of her neck.

"Good girl," I praise. "See you tonight."

I leave her there, naked except for my collar.

CHAPTER FIFTY-FOUR

KEIRA

Everyone is being unusually nice to me. Maddie never wants help in the kitchen, but tonight she has me cutting out sheets of biscuits. She has an ancient record player in the corner of the kitchen and we work to the muffled sound of classical music.

"Angel is having a foal," I say.

She glances up. "That's what Westin says."

"It's so exciting," I muse. "It'll give me something to look forward to. Spring seems far away."

"I'm sure there's lots to look forward to," Maddie says, banging the oven door shut as she sets the last sheet inside. She can't seem to look me in the eye.

"Are you alright?" I ask.

She nods, ducking into the pantry. When she returns, she has a picnic basket in her hand. She sets it down before me and I stare up at her, confused.

"This is your dinner," she says. "Yours and Sovereign's."

"Um...thank you," I say carefully. "Sovereign has an appointment tonight though."

She looks at me pointedly. "You are his appointment, Keira."

It hits me right then why everyone is acting strange. Why Westin took the time out of his day to stand in the barn with me for two hours. Why I've been cutting biscuits in the kitchen since four in the afternoon. My lips part and my heart starts hammering at the base of my neck.

Her brow arcs, she jerks her head towards the door.

"Better get upstairs, missy," she says. "And take your basket with you."

My eyes are already wet, but I blink hard. I can't think of words so I just grab the basket handle and make a dash up the hallway. Up the stairs and to our bedroom.

It's empty.

The fire is burning. There's a black box laying on the carefully made bed. But it isn't that that draws my attention.

My painted mare is back, sitting on the bedside table. And beside her is a dark brown, varnished wood stallion with a bridle made of painted stars. Between them is a little wooden box with the lid popped open.

And inside is a ring.

My entire body feels like it's made of air. I place the basket on the bed and float to the bedside table. My painted mare is whole again, her front legs seamlessly attached and painted over. My eyes fall back on the ring. I'm almost afraid to look at it. What if it's just my imagination?

Except for the sterling silver band Clint gave me, I've never had a piece of jewelry before meeting Sovereign. It always felt sad to buy my own, so I just pretended I didn't want any. He gave me the silver collar and that felt like a luxury.

But this ring is different. This is a delicate work of art. Like something I've seen on the fingers of rich women in movies.

I should savor this moment. The only useless pretty thing I've ever had is the painted mare.

And that had an element of sadness attached to it.

But this ring is the beginning of a new chapter.

"You like it, redbird?"

I whirl and he's standing in the doorway. He's in good clothes, a dress shirt and pants. His sleeves are rolled up, exposing his thick arms. He looks so good I can't think of a single word.

He crosses to me, tilting my chin up.

"I don't know if that ring is pretty enough to be on your finger," he says. "But I gave it my best shot."

I just nod hard. His mouth turns up as he takes my hand and leads me to the bed. I don't know what I expected, but it's not for Sovereign to sink down on one knee at my feet. We're still almost eye to eye, but I don't care. Nothing about my life has been conventional. I missed everything—I've been just an accessory until now.

He's giving me this because he knows it means something to me.

He takes my hand. I'm shaking so hard I can't speak. He picks up the ring and a laugh catches in my throat because it looks so small in his fingers. Our eyes meet.

"Marry me," he says.

He doesn't ask, but he's not the type. Those pale blue eyes demand the answer he knows he's going to get. Because he gets everything he fucking wants.

So I give it.

"Yes," I whisper.

He slips the ring on my finger. I lift my hand and turn it slowly to catch the firelight. It's stunning.

He gets to his feet, taking my face in his hands. When he kisses me, my heart beats so fast it feels like it's going to lift from my chest. He's so good at it and I'm fucked. Fucked for the slow, thorough way he kisses. Like I'm the most important thing in the world.

When he pulls back, I'm so choked up I can't speak.

"My redbird," he murmurs, running his fingers through my hair. "I have something else for you."

He releases me and flips the lid on the box on the bed. Inside is a delicate, moss green set of lingerie. I've never had real lingerie before, but I've always wanted at least one nice set. I bite my lip and glance up at him, suddenly shy.

"You want me to wear that?" I whisper.

"You will wear it," he says.

He strips me slowly and I'm glad I just took a shower and shaved everything.

The panties slip up my legs and the soft lace settles over my hips. They fit me perfectly, made for the curves of my body. I wonder if it's a custom set. There's no tags. He lifts the bra and it looks so strange in his big, rough hands.

"You're my wife and my submissive," he says firmly, eyes locking on mine. "You sit at my feet because you choose to. Do you understand?"

I nod shakily.

Somehow we both know what's on his mind. That first night we met, when Clint made me stand and wait in case he needed something.

He circles me and clasps the bra over my breasts. "Good girl."

He tugs my hair free, letting it fall down my back. His fingers skate over my throat and down between my breasts. His hand flattens, pulling my body back against his. He turns me and I find my gaze in the mirror on our headboard.

"I'll be your husband and your dominant," he says. "And the father of your children. Is that what you want?"

The light glints off my collar. My breasts heave as I take a quick breath.

"Yes, sir," I whisper.

"Good girl," he says again. "I want you to sign something for me."

Before I can speak, he releases me and goes to his office. He rarely unlocks it, so I haven't been inside, but he beckons me through the door. It's a small, plain room with a window that looks out over the lake. There's an office chair at the oak desk and a closed laptop. Gerard has never been one for frills.

"Is it an updated contract?" I ask.

He pulls the desk drawer open and takes out a black folder. "No, but we do need to rewrite and update our contract before the wedding."

I hover at his elbow. "So what is it?"

He flips open the folder and sinks into the chair. His hands are on my waist and he lifts me into his lap so I'm facing the desk. I'd be distracted by the feeling of his thigh between my legs, but my eyes are on the paperwork.

It's a surveyor's map.

My heart sinks. It's showing all the Garrison land and Sovereign Mountain Ranch as the same piece. Did he...did he annex all my land into his?

I feel like I'm sinking in cold water.

How could he do this after what Clint did?

"Sovereign," I whisper.

"Turn the page, redbird," he rumbles.

Hand shaking and eyes blurred, I obey. The second paper is a deed of some kind. I have to read it three times before it makes any sense at all. What does it mean? Is he giving me the Garrison land?

"Sovereign, what is this?" I ask, my voice trembling.

He leans in, his chest warm against my back. His finger taps the empty line at the bottom below where he signed his name.

"Dual ownership," he says. "Just sign your name."

I shift, turning so I'm sideways on his knee. He's watching me intently, clearly waiting for me to say something.

"So...we would have dual ownership of the Garrison Ranch?" I manage.

He taps the paper. "Read it again, redbird."

He flips the map so the paper is side by side and it hits me like a brick wall. The land is consolidated into one piece. There are two dotted lines on the deed. My entire body tingles and I whip back around, my hands going to his chest. At the base of his neck, where the vein pulses when he wants me.

"You can't do that," I manage.

"We absorbed the Garrison land, I paid for it," he says. "It's all Sovereign Mountain Ranch now. And when you sign there, redbird, you'll own it all with me. Is that what you want?"

He's giving me equal ownership of Sovereign Mountain and all the land that goes with it. Including the Stowe and Garrison farms. If I sign my name, I'll own it all alongside him.

My hand goes over my mouth.

"How's it feel to be a billionaire, sweetheart?" he asks.

"You can't do this."

Sovereign Mountain is everything to him, he can't just give me legal ownership of it. It's what lifted him up and kept him safe all those years. It gave him back his dignity when that was stripped from him by the Garrisons. It's a fortress in the mountains where he's king.

Where he kept me safe.

"I can do whatever I want," he says. "Now sign that paper so I can fuck my fiancée."

He turns me around and pushes a pen into my hand.

So I sign it.

Not because I know what I'm doing, or what this means for our future. But because it hits me right then that he's going to be my husband. His ring is on my finger. He's going to get his vasectomy reversed and make me the mother of his children. I'm going to wake up every day for the rest of my life with Gerard Sovereign's arms around my body.

With my head nestled against the bull skull on his chest.

And that's all I really want.

He flips me around and pulls me close. Our mouths meet, just for a second.

"You look like an angel," he says.

I cradle his face between my hands. His jaw is scratchy beneath my palms.

"Do you love me?" I whisper, just wanting to hear it in his words.

His lids are heavy. "I love you, redbird."

We kiss, our breath clashing. When I pull back, I hear him groan.

"Now fuck me like you hate me," I beg.

EPILOGUE

PART 1

KEIRA

EIGHT MONTHS LATER

I climb the stairs and turn the corner. My hand wraps around the doorknob, but I don't turn it. Instead, I take a deep breath and close my eyes, smiling.

This summer has been perfect. Beyond anything I could have imagined.

He married me in the springtime on the front porch with Westin as the officiate. The whole ranch was there and Maddie cried loudly into her handkerchief the entire time. The dining hall was decorated in bluebells and silk ribbons. Everyone ate there and we cut the cake in a white tent in the lawn under the pine trees. Music was still thumping and everyone was thoroughly drunk by the time Gerard and I stole upstairs.

After that, we sat down together and negotiated a contract.

A few nights out of the week, we set aside time to be completely immersed in our dynamic. Outside of that, I still call him sir and he still calls me his redbird, but the lines are clearer now.

It's the perfect balance.

I blink, jerking from my reverie. The clock downstairs strikes seven and I slip into the bedroom. In the upper dress drawer, he laid out a black silk set of lingerie. I put it on and pad into his office to make him a cup of black coffee. The curtain is still open and I can see him walk through the barn doors with Shadow at his heels.

My heart flutters.

The coffee machine beeps. I carry the mug out to the chair in the corner I ordered for him as a surprise on his birthday. It's dark leather, plush, and big enough he can sit in it and have me over his lap.

We've gotten a lot of use out of it. Especially on Sunday nights.

I set the coffee on the table beside it and fold a clean pair of sweatpants over the back of the chair. Faintly, I can hear him talking in the yard. My pussy tingles as I hurry into the bathroom and turn the shower on for him.

On the sink sits my collar, the leash attached.

I lift my eyes to my reflection and braid my hair so it's out of the way. It took me a while to get used to the feeling of voluntary submission. At first, it had always been initiated by him. It's a different feeling to act it out as part of our daily routine.

The collar slides over my throat. The feeling is so familiar now that my body reacts to it. Heat sparks deep inside and aches as I leave the bathroom and circle the bed. At the foot, in the wooden board, he attached a metal anchor. I sink to my knees and clip the free end to it.

And wait.

I hear his heavy footsteps on the stairs. The door creaks open, but I keep my gaze lowered. From the corner of my eye, I can see him take off his boots and deposit them into the hallway.

He walks by me and into the bathroom.

The faint scent of his soap fills my lungs. It reminds me of giving him oral because he's always clean and smells like soap. Now the scent triggers a Pavlovian response and heat pours through my body and makes my toes curl.

I squirm, noticing I'm already soaked.

The door opens. I hear him put on the sweatpants I laid out for him. Then he's beside me, and his fingers are under my chin. Lifting my face up, giving me permission to drown in his pale blue gaze.

My heart thumps.

"Good girl," he says.

He has a soft, firm way of saying it that makes me feel so safe. I keep still as he sinks to a crouch and unhooks the leash from my collar. Then he takes my hand and leads me to his chair. I wait until he's settled, my hands interlaced over my lower stomach.

I thrive in this environment.

It's so exciting, and yet completely predictable. I never wonder what he'll do next, if he'll be angry, if I have to walk on eggshells. He's got an even temper, a short store of words, and endless affection.

We had a rocky start. There's no denying that.

But we made it through, and he's so at peace. I was worried that without the need for vengeance that drove him for years, he would start drifting. But it's the total opposite. He's so calm, so grounded. I still taste his darkness and the brutality that he's capable of, but only when I want to, only when he fucks me rough, makes me cry, and then puts me back together again.

He pats his knee once, and I sink down, wrapping one arm around his neck. We sit in silence for a moment while he drinks his coffee.

"How was today?" I ask.

"Good, we're ready for auction next week," he says.

He's been out for days doing inventory. Taking stock of losses, estimating what we need to make a profit this year. In the spring, we had a huge crop of Quarter Horse foals and Gerard confided in me that if we sold all of them, we'd be set for the first two quarters.

He had.

I never doubted him. It's such a good feeling to trust my husband.

He sets aside the empty cup and turns me to face him. His hands rest on my waist. I smooth back his dark hair and bend, kissing him slowly. When I pull back, his eyes are heavy with desire.

"I want your opinion on something," he says.

I nod, a little unsure. After he gave me dual ownership of the ranch, he started roping me into big decisions. I was hesitant to do more than offer advice, and when I told him that, he respected my choice. As much as I appreciated that he was gifting me autonomy, I was not ready to help run the biggest ranch in the state.

"The strip of land on the southern side of the old Garrison ranch just went up for sale," he says. "I was thinking of purchasing it."

I know what he's talking about. It's a rocky strip of earth where the river bottoms out and turns southeast. The land isn't suited for pasture or farming, but it's got a solid water supply.

"Why?"

He shrugs. "The earth needs restoration. In a few decades, we could have it back to pasture. Maybe plant some pines."

"Do you have the extra money for that? It sounds like a project rather than an investment," I say.

"It is. But I can afford it," he says, nodding. "But it's worth it if the land recovers. Nobody's worked it in a long time."

I know how deeply he cares, and I care too, so I nod. "I think you should buy it then."

He leans in and kisses me again. Slowly, thoroughly. His tongue grazes mine, tasting faintly of coffee. My body warms and I lean into him, winding my arms around his neck. When we break apart, we're both flushed.

"Get up on the bed, redbird," he says hoarsely.

His hands roam over my body, his fingers digging into my thighs. The roughness of his palms drags over my skin and catches at my silk panties and garter. He kisses my mouth again, and the side of my neck, and between my breasts.

"Fuck, redbird, get up on that bed." he says, setting me to my feet.

I turn and he slaps my ass so hard it sends a rush of heat between my legs. He's behind me as I climb up on the bed and sink to my back. Spreading my thighs for him.

His eyes roam my body and I can see the heavy ridge of his erection in his pants. My pussy throbs, aching for the warmth of him inside me.

"Please, fuck me," I beg.

He shakes his head, eyes glittering. "Get on your knees and hold onto the headboard. I want your pretty, wet cunt on my face."

Oh my God. My stomach flutters as I scramble to my knees and turn. He slides up behind me, slapping my thigh and gripping my ass so hard I whimper. He kisses the back of my neck, gathering both wrists and putting my hands up on the headboard.

His breath spills hot over the nape of my neck.

"I'm going to eat your pussy until you come all over my face, redbird," he breathes. "I want to taste you, until you're begging me to stop. Can you be a good girl for me and come until you can't come anymore?"

My throat is so dry I have to clear it.

"Yes, sir," I whisper.

He slaps my ass again and my head falls back. My nails dig into the headboard.

"That's a good girl," he says.

His warmth disappears and I close my eyes, knowing he's laying down between my thighs. His fingers grip my hips and he pulls me down onto his face. The moan that sounds in his throat makes my toes curl.

His tongue drags from my pussy to my clit.

And I give into him.

My Sovereign.

EPILOGUE

PART 2

GERARD

I get in early from chores one night in late summer. It's warm and dry, so we keep the cattle in the lower pastures. They spend their days sleeping at the edges of the woods or standing in the river and pond to keep cool. Most of the time, I feel like doing the same.

Keira's not at the house when I get in, and Maddie tells me she took Angel out to the top of the hill that overlooks the old Garrison Ranch. I mount Shadow bareback and go after her. The late afternoon shadows lengthen. The sun spills its light like molten gold over Sovereign Mountain.

She's in the grass, laying on her back. Angel grazes a few dozen yards away. Silently, I slide down from Shadow and give him a light slap on the shoulder to send him walking to Angel.

Keira hears my footfalls and she rolls to her side, lifting her head. I sink down on my hands and knees over her, bending and kissing her temple.

"What are you doing up here, redbird?" I ask.

She smiles, her nose scrunching. Her freckles multiply in the summer and her hair bleaches until there are strands of gold intertwined with red.

"I was hoping you'd come after me," she sighs.

I sink down until we're laying side by side. She touches my temple and her soft mouth twists, like she's trying not to smile. I let her stroke through my hair and down my neck to my shoulder. She doesn't hesitate when she touches me anymore.

She's so confident now.

She's not afraid.

And she never will be again.

Her fingers skim down my jaw and she presses them to my lips for a kiss. Our eyes lock and I have to pull her in and press my mouth to hers, letting her taste fill my senses. When I release her, she reaches down and takes my hand, stroking my palm with her thumb.

"Gerard," she whispers.

I lean in closer, our bodies almost touching.

"What is it, redbird?"

Her throat bobs. Her eyes are glassy with tears as her fingers tighten on my hand. Then she moves it down and presses the heel of my palm to her lower belly.

Fuck.

My entire body freezes and my brain goes quiet. I got the reversal in March, but I kept my expectations low on purpose. I want children with her so badly, but I kept myself open to the possibility that might not happen.

That didn't stop me from carving a little wooden foal one night in the barn. I painted it deep red and sealed it so it was shiny and smooth. It's in a sitting position so the delicate legs don't break and written on the underside is our names.

I've carried that foal in my pocket for months.

Hoping.

Now, I clear my throat and realize my hand is shaking. When I look back at her, she's smiling past the tears sliding down her face and falling into the dry grass. I've imagined this moment before, but now that it's here, I'm frozen in place.

"Well...say something," she whispers.

"Are you...pregnant?" I manage.

Her mouth shakes as she laughs, reaching up to wipe her face. She nods hard and the strangest sensation fills my chest. Like something broke and now it's bleeding inside me, flooding me with warmth.

I'm not crying, but it's the closest I've come in decades.

"How far along?"

I can't keep my voice steady and she's so sweet she pretends she doesn't notice.

"I've missed two periods," she says, sniffing. "I wasn't sure the first time, but then I missed another so I had Maddie get me some tests and they were very positive."

"So eight weeks," I say. "We need to get you a doctor's appointment."

"Maddie has me set up for next week," she says.

She rolls onto her back and her fingertips skim over her lower stomach. She's wearing a plain cotton sundress with a slit up the middle so she can pull it aside to ride Angel. I stretch out on my side and slide my hand through the opening to grip her thigh.

Her eyes flicker up and lock to mine. I bend and kiss her the way she deserves. Slowly, enjoying her taste, her scent, the feel of her mouth. I pull away and use my head to push hers aside and kiss her neck.

"Thank you," I say.

"For what?" she murmurs.

"For being my wife, for having my baby. Thank you for seeing me for the man I am and loving me anyway."

"I love you," she whispers. "And Sovereign Mountain."

"And the children we have here."

She's trying not to cry again. I push my hand in my pocket and take the little wooden foal out. Her eyes widen as I gently place it on her lower belly, on the little rise between her hipbones. The tears break through and trickle down her temples into her brilliant hair.

"I made that in the spring," I say. "I wanted to hope."

She turns it over and over in her fingers. "It's perfect."

I kiss her forehead. When I lift my eyes, I see the sun is setting over Sovereign Mountain. In the distance, I can make out the cliffs where Clint died. I know beyond it runs the river where she shot Thomas and his body bled out into the dirt.

I'm not haunted by what could be anymore.

Or what has been.

Soon the snow will come and cover Sovereign Mountain. Then it'll melt and flow into rivers that make green grass cover the pastures. And bluebells will grow over earth that was once stained in blood.

There will be a new Sovereign—perhaps a little boy with my eyes or a girl with her brilliant hair.

Sovereign Mountain will be new again.

And I owe it all to this woman I call my own.

THE END

If you enjoyed Gerard and Keira's story please consider leaving a review or rating.

OTHER BOOKS BY RAYA MORRIS EDWARDS

The Welsh Kings Trilogy
Paradise Descent
Prince of Ink & Scars (May 2024)

The King of Ice & Steel Trilogy
Captured Light - Lucien & Olivia
Devil I Need: The Sequel to Captured Light
Ice & Steel: The Conclusion to Captured Light & Devil I Need
Lucien & Olivia: A Christmas Short

Captured Standalones
Captured Desire - Iris & Duran
Captured Light - Lucien & Olivia
Captured Solace - Viktor & Sienna
Captured Ecstasy - Peregrine & Rosalia

Acknowledgments

Thank you to my husband. This was the hardest book I've ever written that hit the closest to home in my heart. Your support during late nights, early mornings, and everything in between got me through to the last word.

A special thank you to Corinne who read this book before anyone else. Your insight into this story and wonderful advice was truly invaluable!

Thank you to my editor, Lexie, for your hard work on this story. Thank you to my cover designer for another amazing cover. Thank you to my MIL (who is never allowed to read this book) for her extensive, firsthand knowledge of horse and cattle ranching in Montana.

And thank you to everyone I spoke to in my research who provided their insights, opinions, very thorough contract examples, and thoughts regarding BDSM dynamics and relationships.

A huge thank you and shout out to my beta and ARC readers, you are amazing! Thank you to everyone on Booktok and Bookstagram who is so supportive and wonderful. I will always be grateful for your support in my author journey.

Made in the USA
Middletown, DE
06 March 2024

50949819R00208